UNITED STATES ARMY IN WORLD WAR II

The Technical Services

THE CHEMICAL WARFARE SERVICE: CHEMICALS IN COMBAT

by

Brooks E. Kleber

and

Dale Birdsell

MILITARY INSTRVCTION

OFFICE OF THE CHIEF OF MILITARY HISTORY

UNITED STATES ARMY

WASHINGTON, D.C., 1966

This volume, one of the series UNITED STATES ARMY IN WORLD WAR II, is the third to be published in the group of three Chemical Corps volumes in the sub-series THE TECHNICAL SERVICES. The volumes in the over-all series will be closely related and will present a comprehensive account of the activities of the Military Establishment during World War II. A list of subseries is appended at the end of this volume.

Library of Congress Catalog Card Number: 66–60001

FIRST PRINTING

For sale by the Superintendent of Documents, U.S. Government Printing Office
Washington, D.C., 20402 – Price $5.25

UNITED STATES ARMY IN WORLD WAR II

Stetson Conn, General Editor

Advisory Committee

(As of 15 March 1965)

Fred C. Cole
Washington and Lee University

Lt. Gen. August Schomburg
Industrial College of the Armed Forces

James A. Field, Jr.
Swarthmore College

Maj. Gen. David W. Gray
U.S. Continental Army Command

Ernest R. May
Harvard University

Brig. Gen. Ward S. Ryan
U.S. Army War College

Earl Pomeroy
University of Oregon

Brig. Gen. Elias C. Townsend
U.S. Army Command and
General Staff College

Charles P. Roland
Tulane University

Lt. Col. Thomas E. Griess
United States Military Academy

Theodore Ropp
Duke University

Office of the Chief of Military History
Brig. Gen. Hal C. Pattison, Chief of Military History

Chief Historian
Chief, Histories Division
Chief, Editorial and Graphics Division
Editor in Chief

Stetson Conn
Col. Albert W. Jones
Col. Joseph S. Coulter
Joseph R. Friedman

History of

THE CHEMICAL WARFARE SERVICE

Organizing for War

From Laboratory to Field

Chemicals in Combat

. . . to Those Who Served

Foreword

This is the third and final volume of the Chemical Warfare Service subseries of *The Technical Services* in the series UNITED STATES ARMY IN WORLD WAR II. Concluding the chemical warfare story that was begun in *Organizing for War* and was continued in *From Laboratory to Field*, *Chemicals in Combat* records in meaningful detail the ultimate and most rigorous test of all things military: performance in battle.

Entry of the United States into World War II found the nation's Armed Forces, like those of its principal allies and enemies, mindful of the possibility of gas warfare. The gas attacks of World War I did not recur, but the Chemical Warfare Service was in the position of being ready for a type of war that did not happen. Thus the CWS, the only technical service having combat troops armed with weapons it had specifically provided for itself, was forced to show its flexibility. The Service sought to fulfill its supporting role with smoke, flame, and incendiaries; with 4.2-inch mortars and flame throwers; and, having no gas to contend with, its decontamination companies provided front-line troops with the means for simple physical cleanliness. *Chemicals in Combat* recounts the administrative, logistical, and tactical problems arising from the Service's dual responsibility, and highlights the flexibility and ingenuity demanded of chemical troops in World War II. These are, of course, qualities that military men have and will always find essential.

Washington, D.C.
15 March 1965

HAL C. PATTISON
Brigadier General, USA
Chief of Military History

The Authors

Dr. Brooks E. Kleber received a Ph.B. degree from Dickinson College and M.A. and Ph.D. degrees in history from the University of Pennsylvania. From 1950 to 1963 he served as historian with the U.S. Army Chemical Corps Historical Office. In January 1963 Dr. Kleber was appointed Chief Historian, United States Continental Army Command.

Dr. Dale Birdsell holds an A.B. degree from Reed College, an M.A. from Brown University, and a Ph.D. from the University of Pennsylvania. He served as historian with the U.S. Army Chemical Corps Historical Office from 1952 to 1963 and is now Chief, Historical Division, U.S. Army Munitions Command.

Preface

Chemicals in Combat is the last of three volumes concerned with the activities of the Chemical Warfare Service in World War II. It is devoted to the overseas story—administration, logistics, and combat. In World War II the CWS faced a unique situation, in that it found itself in the unenviable position of preparing for an unconventional kind of warfare that never came to pass. Yet, even as it served as insurance in the event of the introduction of gas by the enemy (United States policy permitted the use of gas only in retaliation), it also had to be useful in a gasless war.

The CWS was useful in World War II. Its contributions included the missions of smoke, flame, and incendiary weapons, which, less heralded at first, eventually eclipsed the gas mission. How the CWS carried out these various missions in the theaters of operation is the main theme of this volume.

"Chemical Warfare" is a term meant to include the employment of artificial smoke, flame, and incendiary munitions as well as gas offensive and defensive munitions. While the practice at the time of this writing is to refer to the "employment of chemical weapons" rather than to "chemical warfare," the latter term is appropriate to a World War II setting, and the term "chemicals" retains its inclusive World War II meaning.

In planning a volume devoted to the overseas activities of the CWS, the authors found the logic of either of two alternative organizational methods was appealing: (1) trace each CWS activity, such as preparedness, administration, and logistics, and each of the combat functions, from war area to war area in a unified account by subject; or (2) treat all CWS activities for each overseas area in a unified account under an area heading. The first alternative tended to obscure the administrative and logistic individuality of the CWS overseas branches. It also tended to minimize the impact of area physical characteristics, of area organizational policy, and of area tactics. Even two theaters so intimately connected and in many ways so parallel as the European and North African were decidedly different entities from the CWS point of view. The theater chief chemical officers operated from different echelons of command, and these individuals did not hold the same conception of operating control. The possibility of gas warfare was great in Europe but usually remote in North Africa. The CWS supply system was highly centralized in Europe; it was in part decentralized in the Mediterranean area. But neither did the second alternative solve all the problems. The development of mortar and smoke tactics and techniques in the Mediterranean area was much more closely related to the employment of those tactics and techniques in the European theater situation than it was to the evolution of the Mediterranean theater supply systems. Further, in the Pacific the development of flame weapons and tactics would not observe area boundaries, and Pacific incendiary bomb experience was only a grand enlargement of European experience.

The authors fully realize that the war was carried on in more than the four major areas usually considered herein. They have no desire to detract from the considerable contributions of the CWS branches in the other major areas and in those outposts which could not be designated major. But the authors believe that most CWS problems can be illustrated from activities in the European and North African/Mediterranean theaters and the Southwest and Central Pacific Areas with some reference to the South Pacific Area. The China, Burma-India, North Pacific, and Middle East areas are thus excluded.

The CWS in the United States is treated in two complementary volumes which have preceded the publication of *Chemicals in Combat*. The first of these, *Organizing for War*, traces matters of organization, administration, and training from World War I CWS origins through the end of World War II. The second, *From Laboratory to Field*, deals with CWS research, development, and supply.

The present volume was begun by and under the direction of the late Dr. Paul W. Pritchard, then Chief, U.S. Army Chemical Corps Historical Office. While Dr. Pritchard's work appears only in portions of the chapters on smoke, the authors greatly benefited from his guidance and advice and from his unflagging interest in overseas military operations. He was one of those historians who could become personally involved in and enthusiastic about his subject without impairment of objectivity. Dr. Pritchard's successor, Dr. Leo P. Brophy, continued to provide valuable guidance and advice. Dr. Brooks E. Kleber wrote Chapters VIII through XVII. Dr. Dale Birdsell wrote Chapters II through VI. These authors collaborated on Chapters I and XVIII. Mr. Sherman L. Davis wrote Chapter VII. Dr. Kleber co-ordinated the work on the volume.

The authors are greatly indebted to Dr. Stetson Conn, Chief Historian, and to Dr. John Miller, jr., Deputy Chief Historian, Office, Chief of Military History, Department of the Army, for guidance and suggestions. Many members and former members of the staff of the U.S. Army Chemical Corps Historical Office also contributed knowledge, preliminary research, or early drafts of portions of this volume. Individuals who were especially helpful and their areas of interest are: Mr. H. Gilman Wing, flame throwers and administration; Lt. Col. Leonard J. McKinney, flame throwers; Dr. Ben R. Baldwin, mortars and readiness; Dr. Alfred J. Bingham, mortars, readiness, administration; and Mr. Innis Brown, chemical troop units. The following U.S. Army Chemical Corps Historical Office enlisted research assistants were especially helpful: Thomas J. Morgan, Nelson Ledsky, Richard Breault, William Piez, Harvey Fergusson, John J. Keeley, Victor H. Walton, and Arthur Macqueen. Mrs. Alice E. Moss supervised the preparation of the manuscript, did yeoman service in checking source locations, and diligently performed preliminary editorial tasks. Mrs. Doris M. Jacobson displayed extraordinary skill in preparing the final typescripts.

Research for this volume was greatly facilitated by personnel of the World War II Records Division, National Archives, especially Mrs. Lois Aldridge, Mrs. Hazel Ward, and Mrs. Caroline Moore. Mr. Howard Bauté, Mrs. Mary K. Stuart, and Mrs. M. Virginia Nester of the Federal Records Center in Alexandria were most helpful in locating CWS records, and personnel of the Federal Records Center, Kansas City, the Archives Division, The Air University, and the Marine Corps Archives provided many collections of overseas records. Mr. Israel Wice and Miss Hannah Zeidlik of the Office, Chief of Military History, steered the authors to many records sources they might otherwise have overlooked. Miss Ethel M. Owens, Office of the Chief Chemical Officer, provided valuable information on the careers of CWS officers.

The veterans of the Chemical Warfare Service have been remarkably frank in supplying materials which do not appear in the official records, and many have given unstintingly of their time. The authors are grateful to all these officers whose interviews or comments have been cited as well as to others who provided more general background information. They are especially grateful to Maj. Gen. Alden H. Waitt, Brig. Gen. Hugh W. Rowan, and Col. Maurice H. Barker, all of whom followed the project throughout the entire span and contributed much to the authors' understanding of the World War II experience of the CWS. The following officers were always ready with good counsel: Cols. William A. Copthorne, Alexander Batlin, Frank M. Arthur, and Nelson McKaig, Jr., Lt. Col. Levin B. Cottingham, Maj. Gen. William N. Porter, Cols. Siegfried P. Coblentz, James H. Batte, and Robert W. Breaks, Brig. Gen. Charles S. Shadle, Cols. Alfred J. P. Wilson, Alexander Leggin, John C. MacArthur, Thomas H. Magness, Jr., Claude J. Merrill, Carl V. Burke, Irving R. Mollen, John C. Morgan, Harold Riegelman, and Patrick F. Powers.

Thanks are also due to several other members of the Office of the Chief of Military History: Mr. David Jaffé, editor, Mrs. Marion P. Grimes, assistant editor; Miss Ruth A. Phillips, who selected the photographs; and Mr. Elliot Dunay, who prepared the maps.

For errors in the facts presented and in the conclusions drawn, the authors assume sole responsibility.

Washington, D.C.   BROOKS E. KLEBER
15 March 1965   DALE BIRDSELL

Contents

Charts

Maps

Illustrations

All illustrations are from the files of the Department of Defense except for the cartoons by Bill Mauldin on page 176 and page 341 and the photograph supplied by Col. Thomas H. Magness, Jr., on page 607.

771-608 O-66—2

THE CHEMICAL WARFARE SERVICE:
CHEMICALS IN COMBAT

CHAPTER I

Origins of the Chemical Warfare Service

The great paradox of America's wartime gas experience is that in World War I, when the nation was unprepared for it, gas was used, and in World War II, when the nation was prepared, gas was not used. The gas warfare experience of World War I is important not only as the sole example of large-scale use of toxic chemicals in battle, but also because this experience in large measure dictated the chemical mission, organization, weapons, tactics, and techniques with which the belligerents entered World War II. The Allies and the Central Powers used no fewer than twenty-eight gases and sixteen mixtures of gases during World War I. Although the United States retained or developed nearly a dozen gases, only four, mustard, phosgene, lewisite, and chloracetophenone, in order of importance, were considered as basic at the beginning of World War II. The first two were accorded this priority as the result of actual World War I combat experience; lewisite owed its prominence to its likeness to mustard, while chloracetophenone was similar to, although less expensive and less corrosive than, the World War I tear gases.[1] The ground weapons available for gas at the beginning of World War II had for the most part likewise been developed and battle-tested in World War I. These included artillery with toxic shell, the Livens projector, chemical cylinders, and toxic candles. The Chemical Warfare Service (CWS) in the United States had modi-

---

[1] (1) Brig. Gen. Amos A. Fries and Maj. Clarence J. West, *Chemical Warfare* (New York: McGraw-Hill, 1921), pp. 24–27. (2) WD TM 3–215, 1 Oct 40. (3) Leo P. Brophy, Wyndham D. Miles, and Rexmond C. Cochrane, *The Chemical Warfare Service: From Laboratory to Field*, UNITED STATES ARMY IN WORLD WAR II (Washington, 1959), pp. 49–74.

fied the 4-inch Stokes mortar into the longer range, more accurate
4.2-inch chemical mortar, again on the basis of World War I experience.[2] The aerial chemical bomb was a development of the period between the wars, but even this new weapon did not significantly alter
gas warfare tactics. The concept of the massive gas attack adopted by
most of the major World War I combatants dominated tactical doctrine in the period following the war. Retained too was the practice of
using mustard in defensive operations. In offensive chemical operations
nonpersistent agents were to be used in terrain over which friendly
troops would advance, whereas the persistent mustard would be placed
on areas to be neutralized and bypassed.[3] In general, the troops who
successfully stood up in the face of such gas attacks were those who had
training and gas mask discipline.

Two comments about the American use of gas in World War I are
in order. First, troops in the American Expeditionary Forces (AEF)
used a disproportionately large amount of Allied matériel. In time, the
United States did send bulk toxics to Europe where they were poured
into British and French shells. And although four million American-
made masks were eventually shipped to Europe, soldiers of the AEF
initially used almost a million British and French masks. The second
point concerns the place of gas warfare in the thinking of American
battle leaders. These officers had to be won over to the usefulness of gas
warfare and this task was not always easy. Brig. Gen. Amos A. Fries tells
of the case of the operations officer of an American corps demanding
written assurance that gas used in support of an attack in the Argonne
would not cause a single friendly casualty. Fries also brings out another
point, supported by contemporary documents, which involves the reluctance of American commanders to use gas because of the possibility
of retaliatory fire. They held this attitude despite the fact that the
Germans had made good use of the chemical weapon regardless of
enemy reaction.[4]

    [2] (1) Brophy, Miles, and Cochrane, *From Laboratory to Field*, pp. 123–38. (2) The gas cylinder and
the Livens projector were dropped early in World War II because the range of both and the accuracy of
the Livens projector suited them only to trench warfare conditions.
    [3] (1) Maj. Gen. C. H. Foulkes, *"Gas!" The Story of the Special Brigade* (Edinburgh and London: W.
Blackwood & Sons, 1934) (hereafter cited as Foulkes, *Gas!*) p. 267. (2) Brig. Gen. Alden H. Waitt,
Gas Warfare (New York: Duell, Sloan and Pearce, 1942), pp. 137–54.
    [4] Amos A. Fries, MS, History of Chemical Warfare in France, 1919, pp. 52–53.

World War I

The First Gas Attack

Late in the afternoon of 22 April 1915 three flares glowed from a German balloon hoisted in the salient near Ypres, Belgium. At this signal plumes of greenish-gray smoke began to pour from the earth in front of the German trenches. The plumes suffused into a yellowish cloud rolling downwind toward the Allied trenches at the juncture of the French and British lines. The first notable gas attack in military history was in progress. The chlorine gas cloud enveloped a French colonial regiment. Some soldiers emerged from the cloud blinded, choking, and coughing, but other soldiers, incapacitated, dying, or dead from the effects of the gas were left in the trenches. German gas breached the Allied lines for four miles, and German soldiers captured fifty French guns.[5]

The French did not announce their casualties from this first attack, but the Germans estimated them at 15,000, including 5,000 deaths in the attack of 22 April and in that of 24 April in the same sector.[6] Although the German estimate may have been high, the casualties were nonetheless extensive. These losses, along with the shock and panic resulting from the surprise introduction of a new weapon, could have been a serious blow to the Allies had the Germans followed up their initial success. They failed to advance more than a few hundred yards, however, and before they could gain ground significantly, the Allies had plugged the hole in their line.[7] The failure of the Germans to exploit their initial success and Allied lack of preparation for the introduction of gas can best be understood in the light of the strategic concepts and views of the military art held by the belligerents before World War I.

[5] (1) Foulkes, *Gas!*, pp. 18–19. (2) Fries and West, *Chemical Warfare*, pp. 10–13 (eyewitness accounts cited). (3) Victor Lefebure, *The Riddle of the Rhine* (New York: The Chemical Foundation, 1923), pp. 31–32 (statement of Sir John French, British Commander-in-Chief in the field, cited). (4) Waitt, *Gas Warfare*, pp. 16–19. (5) Capt. Basil H. Liddell Hart, *The Real War, 1914–1918* (Boston: Little, Brown and Co., 1931), pp. 130, 175–81. (6) Rudolph Hanslian *et al.*, *Der Chemische Krieg* (3d ed., Berlin: Mittler, 1937), I, 16–17. All references to this work are to the third edition unless otherwise noted.

[6] (1) Foulkes in *Gas!*, page 306, cites these figures, which appear in Hanslian *et al.*, *Der Chemische Krieg* (2d ed., 1927), page 12, but believes they are exaggerated. In the 24 April attack 122 soldiers of the Canadian forces holding a section of the British line were hospitalized and eleven died. (2) Waitt, *Gas Warfare*, page 18, indicates 5,000 casualties. (3) A French authority, Henri le Wita, *Autour de la Guerre Chimique* (Paris: Tallandier, 1928) page 34, accepts the German estimate without question.

[7] Liddell Hart, *The Real War*, p. 176.

Background of Gas Warfare

While the nineteenth century industrial and technological revolutions produced a new arsenal of weapons that radically altered the character of warfare, the new technology produced no toxic war gases. Such were envisaged, however, and several suggestions for the use of toxic chemicals in war had been made.[8] The prospect of the union of the science of chemistry with the art of war was sufficiently real by the end of the nineteenth century to cause the nations deliberating at The Hague during the International Peace Conference to attempt to ban the use of "projectiles, the sole object of which is the diffusion of asphyxiating or deleterious gases."[9]

The attempted ban did not run counter to any area of military opinion. Military leaders, theorists, and innovators were engrossed, and in the early years of the twentieth century became even more engrossed, in the concepts of mass armies, grand strategic offensives, and the undreamed-of firepower of modern weapons.[10] The nations of Europe entered World War I dominated by the grand strategic conception of mass offensive through which one set of belligerents or the other would claim victory—probably in as short a time as six weeks.[11] No nation envisioned the need for large-scale industrial preparation; the initial stockpile of weapons and ammunition would serve for the brief duration of the war.[12] Since gas was expected only to hamper the progress of assaulting forces in mass offensive, each nation reviewed its potential for producing toxics in but cursory fashion.

Only Germany, with the world's largest and most varied chemical industry, appeared to have the potential for war gas production. Germany set Professor Fritz Haber, director of Berlin's Kaiser Wilhelm Institute, and a small group of chemists to work on war gases in Haber's own institute in the first month of the war.[13] At first there must have

---

[8] See Brophy, Miles, and Cochrane, *From Laboratory to Field*, pp. 1–2.

[9] Carnegie Endowment for International Peace, Division of International Law, Pamphlet 8, *The Hague Declaration (IV, 2) of 1899 Concerning Asphyxiating Gases* (Washington: The Endowment, 1915).

[10] For pre-World War I military theory, see (1) Theodore Ropp, *War in the Modern World* (Durham, N.C.: Duke University Press, 1959), pp. 143–212; (2) Lynn Montross, *War Through The Ages* (New York: Harper and Brothers, 1960), pp. 590–698.

[11] Ropp, *War in the Modern World*, pp. 177–217.

[12] Liddell Hart, *The Real War*, pp. 44–45, 127–29.

[13] (1) Lefebure, *Riddle of the Rhine*, p. 35. (2) Foulkes, *Gas!*, p. 25. (3) Hanslian *et al.*, *Der Chemische Krieg*, pages 9–10, denies that the Germans were working on war gases prior to October 1914 and he cites Professor Haber to refute Lefebure. It is noteworthy that the quotation from Haber is given in the second edition, pages 6–7n., as: "*Wahrend der ersten drei Monate des Krieges hat in Deutschland*

seemed little likelihood that any product of Haber's laboratory would be used. The German strategy of mass offensive was overwhelmingly successful until the Allies decisively halted the German advance in the famed September 1914 battle of the Marne.[14] In October and November 1914 the first battle of Ypres taught the Germans that they could not resume their offensive in the west, at least for the time being. The Germans reacted promptly by digging in. Deadlock, static trench warfare, soon characterized the Western Front while the Germans prepared to press the offensive on the Eastern Front and to undertake large-scale, long-term economic and industrial war mobilization within the homeland. In these preparations Germany began to look for "keys to the deadlock."[15] War gas could be such a key.

A Period of Improvisation

German forces experimented with an eye and nose irritant powder on the Western Front in October but it was so ineffective that little or no notice was taken of it. Gas was then used on the Eastern Front, possibly as early as December 1914, but certainly in January and February 1915.[16] British and French disregarded other more definite warnings of the impending German employment of gas. In March 1915 a German officer captured in a raid told a British noncommissioned officer that gas cylinders were in place, ready to use, on the Western Front. On 30 March the French 10th Army bulletin contained a prisoner of war report that indicated where gas cylinders were emplaced, how they were to be used, and what protection German troops had against gas. The 10th Army information was confirmed by another war prisoner on 15 April and again confirmed shortly there-

niemand an Gas gedacht. Wir Lasen in der "Pall Mall Gazette" von 17 September 1914 zum erstenmal von Gasvorbereitungen des Feindes. Erst drei Monate nach Beginn des Kreiges begannen wir mit Gasarbeiten." In the third edition, page 10n., the quotation is given: "We had actually first to read in the French, Italian and English Press—as for instance in the 'Pall Mall Gazette' of Sept. 17, 1914—of the terribly [sic] things that were in preparation for us before we began to make similar preparations in view of the commencement of the war of position." Foulkes, in Gas!, page 24, points out that the Pall Mall Gazette reference was not to gas but to a new French explosive, "Turpinite."

[14] Hanslian et al., Der Chemische Krieg, I, 15.

[15] (1) Ropp, War in the Modern World, pp. 222–25. (2) Liddell Hart, The Real War, pp. 67–70, 80–102, 115–16, 127–35. The phrase quoted above is Liddell Hart's.

[16] (1) Foulkes, Gas!, pp. 30, 31. (2) Hanslian, Der Chemische Krieg, I, 12, 15. Foulkes, page 30, cites a report that gas was used on the eastern front in December 1914 but indicates that the first confirmed attack was in January 1915. Hanslian, volume I, page 15, indicates that a tear gas was employed on the Eastern Front in January 1915.

after by a captured German document and a Belgian General Staff report on German offensive and defensive measures. The Belgians further advised their allies that the Germans were manufacturing gas respirators in Ghent. Again, British and Canadian air and ground troops actually saw and even counted gas cylinders and shell. And, perhaps as a final indication of intent, the Germans were accusing the Allies of employing gas.[17]

All warnings went unheeded. The German gas attack on 22 April took the Allied forces by complete surprise, and, what is more astonishing, its success was a surprise to the Germans. The German high command initially had looked upon the scheme with tolerant acquiescence, not bothering to provide the reserves to exploit a possible breakthrough.[18] Consequently, instead of achieving a major victory, the Germans had to settle for merely straightening their line. But major victory or no, after Ypres toxic chemical warfare clearly became a force to reckon with.[19] The French, the British, and the Germans all began to concentrate on the offensive and defensive aspects of gas warfare.

Within a few days after the Ypres attack, on the appeal of Lord Kitchener, Secretary of State for War, British women had equipped the entire British Expeditionary Forces with gauze pads which could be used as a crude mask to protect against toxics.[20] The French provided similar pads, and, like both the British and Germans, furnished chemicals to wet the pads in order to increase their filtering potential.[21] The development of an offensive capability in gas warfare naturally took longer. The British designated elements of the War Office to initiate

---

[17] (1) Foulkes, *Gas!*, pp. 28-35. (2) Hanslian repeats charges that the French were using gas, but he doubts the authenticity of reports detailing the lethality of so-called Turpinite. The French had used a riot control agent (tear gas) in grenades, but it had not been effective. It is unlikely that the French would have used lethal gas offensively without being prepared defensively, and there is no indication that the French took any protective measures until after the Ypres attacks. *Der Chemische Krieg*, I, 11-15, and 2d ed., pp. 7-10.

[18] One German authority states that German commanders lacked faith in the weapon and only allowed the attack as an experiment. (Ulrich Mueller-Kiel, *Die Chemische Waffe Im WeltKrieg Und—Jetzt* (Berlin: Verlag Chemie, 1932; unpublished U.S. Army translation, 1932), p. 17) Maj. Gen. William N. Porter, USA (Ret.), World War II Chief of the Chemical Warfare Service, speculated that German commanders and staff officers who were nearly all professional soldiers disapproved of a weapon developed and managed by reserve officers and civilians. Professor Haber personally supervised the Ypres attack. Interv, Hist Off with Gen Porter, 24 Aug 61.

[19] Liddell Hart, *The Real War*. pp. 129-30.

[20] Foulkes, *Gas!*, pp. 36-37.

[21] (1) Fries and West, *Chemical Warfare*, pp. 195-96. (2) Hanslian *et al.*, *Der Chemische Krieg*, pp. 190-93.

and supervise work on both protection and weapons and organized a chemical laboratory in France. Sir John French, commander-in-chief in the field, made Lt. Col. Charles H. Foulkes (later promoted to brigadier) his adviser on gas and gave him the responsibility for gas offensive operations in the field.[22]

The availability of weapons dictated the tactics of gas warfare. The Germans used chlorine cylinders because chlorine was readily available and because the cylinders provided the best method of placing large quantities of an agent on a nearby enemy. Toxic fillings in artillery shells were not immediately effective because of problems of containing a liquid, corrosive toxic under pressure and because use of liquid fillings required ballistic re-engineering. Moreover, an artillery shell contained a relatively small amount of agent. Most of the early German and British attacks thus took the form of the chlorine cloud of Ypres.[23]

The first British cloud attack took place at Loos, Belgium, on 25 and 27 September 1915 and involved 6,400 chlorine cylinders on a twenty-five mile front.[24] Since it was impossible to cover so large a front with the available cylinders, an innovation was introduced—more than 12,000 newly developed smoke candles were deployed to supplement and simulate the gas cloud and to conceal troops moving forward. While natural smoke had been used for battlefield concealment for centuries, this was probably the first use of artificial smoke on a battlefield of a modern war. The tactical employment of artificial smoke gave the new chemical warfare and gas services another mission.[25]

The use of cylinders to disperse gas had inherent disadvantages. These munitions were difficult to transport, hard to emplace, and quick to expend their filling—they took three to five minutes to empty. Moreover, the success of a cylinder attack depended on the wind direction. The fact that the prevailing winds in France were westerlies might cast

[22] Foulkes, Gas!, pp. 16–17, 36–41.

[23] (1) Foulkes, Gas!, pp. 36–48. (2) Wyndham Miles, "Fritz Haber, Father of Chemical Warfare," Armed Forces Chemical Journal, XIV (January–February, 1960), 28–30.

[24] British tactical organization provided a section headed by an officer to handle the cylinders for 250 yards of trench. Ten sections made a company, four of which were authorized by the time of this first attack. Foulkes, Gas!, p. 57.

[25] (1) Foulkes, Gas!, pp. 54–66. (2) Hanslian et al., Der Chemische Krieg (second edition pages 322–24) credits the first use of smoke to the Germans, but he names neither date nor place, and he indicates that British smoke apparatus were being delivered to the front as early as July 1915. In his third edition, volume I, pages 619–20, Hanslian credits the English claim, citing Foulkes.

some doubt on the wisdom of the Germans in introducing the cylinder method of gas warfare.[26]

In December 1915, again near Ypres, the Germans introduced a new war gas, phosgene, a highly toxic commercial gas used in the dye industry. As a matter of fact, the Germans, British, and French had discovered the military effectiveness of phosgene almost simultaneously during the summer of 1915, but the Germans used it first because they were in a much better position to produce it in large quantities.[27] While Germany was first to use gas in cloud attacks, the French retaliated with phosgene-filled artillery shells in February 1916. The first employment of a nonexplosive artillery shell for gas represented a decided technological breakthrough. The use of explosive shell had resulted in too great a dispersion of gas, but a shell with only enough explosive to rupture the container allowed the toxic contents to form a small cloud at the point of impact. A tremendous bombardment was required to create a large cloud, and the French possessed the means for firing such a bombardment in their astonishingly effective 75-mm. gun. French artillery fire, both the phosgene-filled shells and later Vincennite, a hydrocyanic gas mixture, was significantly more effective than German artillery gas fire at the time. A measure of this greater effectiveness was the statement of a German commander: "In order to reply to the dangerous gas shells of the French I have only shells which are filled with 'eau de Cologne'." [28]

Allied intelligence had predicted the German introduction of phosgene, and the British developed the small box respirator to cope with this new agent. Air was taken into this mask through a canister filled with charcoal and soda lime. The wearer inhaled and exhaled through a rubber tube held in the mouth. The tube was connected to the canister for fresh air and to a "flutter valve" for exhalation. Nose clips were an integral part of the rubberized fabric facepiece as were eye lenses. The mask was uncomfortable and become more so with long wearing, and the heat of the face on the lenses caused condensation which greatly

---

[26] (1) Foulkes, Gas!, pp. 43–44, 48, 64–65, 86–88, 122–26, 176–78, 182–83, 186, 206–09.   (2) Fries and West, Chemical Warfare, pp. 390–91.

[27] Foulkes, Gas!, pp. 52–53.

[28] Hanslian et al., Der Chemische Krieg, I, 20–23. The quotation, page 21, is from General von Deimling: "Zur Beantwortung den gefarblichen Gasgeschosse der Franzosen habe ich legidlich Granaten, die mit 'Eau de Cologne' gefullt sind."

interfered with vision.[29] The British mask was the best protection available despite its defects. It had replaced gas helmets—porous fabric hoods impregnated with chemicals to filter gases—which were much less effective. The French M2 mask which was standard until nearly the end of the war was a modification of the gas hood wherein a facepiece was attached to the head with straps.[30]

Full-Scale Gas Warfare

The British gas offensive at Loos, the German introduction of phosgene, and the French employment of phosgene-filled artillery shell ended the first phase of gas warfare in World War I. The British at Loos successfully challenged German domination of gas warfare and the French improved upon the German introduction of phosgene. The era of emergency improvisations of weapons and protective equipment and of dependence upon the only readily available commercial toxic, chlorine, was over. The chlorine cloud attack had been effective when used with surprise against unprotected troops, but protection against chlorine had not been difficult to provide and surprise could not be counted upon since an enemy could be on guard when wind conditions favored an attack. The remainder of the war was to be characterized by a fairly equal race between Germans and Allies to discover and employ new methods of protection, new gases, and new methods of conducting attacks. Gas warfare became a series of technical and scientific battles, with sometimes one set of belligerents ahead and sometimes the other. Gas warfare, along with the tank and military aircraft, became part of the World War I revolution in the art of war.

In 1916 the British introduced a new means of projecting gas, the 4-inch Stokes mortar, developed from the 3-inch version of this weapon, which had been the standard mortar in the British Army. Because of their inability to manufacture gas shells, the British first used the mortar to fire improvised smokes and incendiaries. The Stokes gas shell, or bomb, as the British called it, contained six pounds of agent as compared to three pounds for the British 4.5-inch heavy howitzer shell.

[29] (1) *Ibid.*, pp. 198–200, 214–18. (2) A number of interviews with World War I veterans confirm the discomfort and poor vision experienced by wearers of the British mask. Interv files in CMLHO.

[30] (1) Hanslian *et al.*, *Der Chemische Krieg*, volume I, pages 195–207, maintains that the German leather mask, with a filtering canister attached directly to the facepiece, was the best mask of World War I, but Foulkes, in *Gas!*, page 119, challenges that claim. (2) Foulkes, *Gas!*, pages 53, 182, 306, comments on the gas helmets. (3) Fries and West, *Chemical Warfare*, pages 201–02, described the French M2 mask.

Its 1,000-yard range was adequate for situations in which opposing trenches were not far apart, and its accuracy, while not pinpoint, was good. Crews were capable, under combat conditions, of firing fifteen rounds per minute, a rate of fire more rapid than that of the howitzer.[31] Still, the Stokes mortar had its limitations.

The British and French had adopted a tactic of gas warfare dependent on overwhelming the enemy with vast quantities of toxics.[32] The massive cylinder attacks of the British and the artillery barrages of the French met this requirement. The Stokes mortar also could have met such requirements for targets less than 1,000 yards distant, but the number of mortars, shells, and crews necessary was beyond the capacity of the Allies at this time. The need was for a simple inexpensive projector with a longer range and a larger capacity shell. Such a projector was invented almost by accident.

Capt. William H. Livens, commander of the British Special Brigade flame projector company, sought to extend both the range over which incendiary materials could be dispersed and the quantities of materials which could be employed. He found that a large steel drum buried in the ground almost up to the open end made a makeshift mortar from which could be fired a smaller drum filled with oil and cotton waste. He used black powder as a propellant and guncotton to ignite the oil. The improvised weapon was capricious and dangerous to its crew, but it was effective. What was more pleasing to the British was that it turned out to be equally effective for the projection of toxics. Livens, accordingly, set about making a more reliable version, one which used a boxed propellant charge detonated electrically and which fired a cylindrical bomb equipped with a light bursting charge. This Livens projector could shoot a thin-cased bomb nearly 8 inches in diameter and 20 inches long and filled with 30 pounds of toxic for a distance of nearly a mile. Range could be varied by increasing or decreasing the propellant charges; direction was determined by careful placement at the time the weapon was buried. The weapon was not accurate but it did not have to be:

---

[31] (1) Foulkes, Gas!, pp. 182–83.   (2) Fries and West, Chemical Warfare, p. 20.

[32] (1) Foulkes, Gas!, pp. 197–98. It is evident throughout Foulkes' work that the massive attack tactic was adopted early (see Chapter VIII) and was increasingly dominant as the war progressed (see especially Chapter XVI). (2) Hanslian et al., Der Chemische Krieg, I, 23–27. The implication in Hanslian's work is that the Allied tactical concept placed more emphasis on massive gas attack than did the Germans, at least until the use of projectors became common, but it is difficult to see any great difference between the tactical concepts of the Allies and those of the Germans.

the simultaneous firing of a 25-projector battery, each projector firing a 61-pound drum, was ideal for a large area gas barrage.

Emplacing the Livens projector entailed a good deal of work. A trench had to be dug for each battery, the weapons emplaced, and then the trenches filled. Once this task was done the projectors could not be re-aimed. Even considering the amount of work involved, emplacement of the Livens projectors had certain advantages over the emplacement of cylinders. While the Livens projectors could usually be dug in some distance behind the front lines in daylight, cylinder emplacements were usually made at night because there was no practical means of denying enemy observation of the forward trenches. Although enemy observation was denied by nighttime emplacement of cylinders, the sound of digging in positions close to the front provided noisy clues as to the imminence of a gas attack.

An advantage of the Livens projector, as well as of any means of projecting gas, was that the warning period was reduced to the few seconds between the time the projectiles struck and the gas clouds formed. By way of contrast, the cylinder-bred clouds which billowed across no-man's-land gave much greater forewarning, although this might not prove an unqualified disadvantage to the attacker because the more widespread the alarm the more the enemy might be hampered by protective devices. Use of cylinders continued but the projector proved to be a formidable weapon and became a major means of launching gas attacks.

The first combat use of the Livens projector took place on 4 April 1917, the beginning of the battle of Arras. Three thousand projectors fired nearly 50 tons of phosgene on 31 targets. At the same time 48 Stokes mortars alternately fired phosgene and a new gas, chloropicrin. Chloropicrin, which was also used by the French and the Germans, is a lethal gas and a strong lachrymator, but because of its lightness and instability it was first used primarily as a means for penetrating the German protective mask. The battle of Arras also saw the first employment of a substantial amount of British toxic artillery shell.[33] The Arras experience evidently convinced the Germans of the usefulness of the projector for it prompted them to rush into production their own version of the weapon which was to be first used on the Italian front during the following October.[34]

[33] Foulkes, Gas!, pp. 165–72, 191–92, 202–03, 206–09, 211–13.
[34] Hanslian et al., Der Chemische Krieg, I, 24–25, 164–71, 177–82.

But the immediate German counter to this successful Allied use of gas was the introduction of two new agents, diphenylchloroarsine [35] and dichloroethyl sulfide. The latter, better known as mustard,[36] is a liquid in its natural state, not a gas, although it readily vaporizes. It is a vesicant, that is, it inflames and burns those parts of the body with which it comes in contact. This characteristic means that a mask alone is insufficient protection against the agent. Mustard, persistent in its staying power, clings to clothing and equipment, covers vegetation, lies in pools in low places.[37] The agent is thus particularly effective in defensive situations or in keeping areas clear of the enemy. Such a saturation as required for interdiction demanded heavy bombardment—the Germans used more than a million shells containing about 2,500 tons of gas in the ten days following the introduction of mustard.[38]

The implication of Germany's use of mustard was not lost on the Allies. The American expert, General Fries, termed its introduction "probably the greatest single development of gas warfare." [39] Brigadier Foulkes declared that with it the enemy had achieved "undoubted success in the gas war." [40] While most mustard victims were incapacitated, not killed, the casualty rate was high and most of these victims had to be evacuated for treatment. Evacuation of so many soldiers greatly weakened the Allied line. The Allies immediately wanted to retaliate in kind, but it was more than a year before the gas could be manufactured in sufficient quantity. Mustard had been known before

[35] Diphenylchloroarsine was not a gas but a solid, dispersed from artillery shells in a particulate cloud. The Germans first used it in Flanders in July 1917. Because contemporary masks could filter most vapors but not solid particles, this agent was often used with lethal phosgene in order to "break" the masks.

[36] To the French this agent was known as yperite, after the place of its introduction. The Germans called it Lost, combining the first two letters of the names of the two chemists who devised its manufacturing process. It was also known as Gelb Kreuz and yellow cross after the marking on German munitions in which it was contained.

[37] (1) Hanslian et al., Der Chemische Krieg, I, 26–29; 2d ed, pp. 18–20, 48–55, 56–58. Hanslian indicates (second edition, page 52) that mustard is effective from twenty-four hours in hot dry weather to one month or more in cold weather in a location protected from wind. In enclosed areas such as dugouts and cellars, it is effective for a year or more. (2) Mustard, after heavily soaking into porous concrete protected from weathering, has been known to cause burns after more than twenty years. (3) Fries and West, Chemical Warfare, pp. 150–51, 168–76.

[38] Hanslian et al., Der Chemische Krieg, I, 28–29.

[39] Fries and West, Chemical Warfare, p. 150.

[40] Foulkes, Gas!, p. 323.

the German attack, but the Allies had not adopted it because its manufacture presented so many difficulties.[41]

Gas warfare required not only agents and weapons but also military organizations to handle the myriad technical and tactical problems of its employment. The appointment of Colonel Foulkes as gas adviser for the British Expeditionary Forces and as responsible officer for offensive gas operations, mentioned earlier, initiated attempts to set up an efficient organization in the British Army. Foulkes' organization, designated the Special Brigade early in 1916, grew from four to twenty-one companies. Sixteen of the companies were organized in four battalions, each battalion having four companies assigned to handle gas cloud attacks; four special companies fired the 4-inch Stokes mortar; and a separate company operated flame projectors.[42]

The employment of flame projectors as tactical weapons was a concept that appealed to the Western Front belligerents, perhaps not as a key to the deadlock but as a nonetheless valuable device. The Germans had first used a portable apparatus for projecting flaming oil in June 1915. The French soon developed a similar apparatus, and shortly thereafter Germans, French, and British each developed small portable, as well as large, semifixed, projectors. The value of flame at the time was principally psychological—the fiery spurt of burning oil, the roar of the flame, and billowing clouds of black smoke had a terrifying effect on troops in the trenches. But the portable equipment was cumbersome, resupply was difficult, the field of fire was small, and the range rarely exceeded 30 yards. Furthermore, the operator of the portable apparatus was easily distinguished and highly vulnerable to small arms fire. The various semifixed projectors soon developed, with a range of from 40 to 50 yards and a protected position for the operator in a trench, were a little better, but the field of fire was still small and the equipment difficult to install, maintain, and resupply. The flame projector, with all its faults, became a responsibility of the chemical warfare services.[43]

With the addition of the flame mission, the British chemical warfare elements had their full quota of missions for World War I—gas, smoke, and incendiary. The British still had no central organization to handle

[41] (1) Foulkes, Gas!, pp. 263–66, 323–26. (2) Hanslian et al., Der Chemische Krieg, I, 29–30. (3) Fries and West, Chemical Warfare, pp. 151–52. (4) Liddell Hart, The Real War. p. 340.

[42] Foulkes, Gas!, pp. 94–96.

[43] (1) Foulkes, Gas!, pp. 49–50, 111–12, 162–65. (2) Fries and West, Chemical Warfare, pp. 347–52.

chemical warfare research and development, training, supply, and field employment and remained without one until mid-1916, when they formed a new combined organization of offensive and defensive chemical elements in the field and appointed a director of gas services, Brig. Gen. Henry Thuillier. Although this reorganization made little significant change in the status of Foulkes's Special Brigade, it did create a co-ordinated chemical arm in the field.[44] The French, meanwhile, had established a centralized organization, the *Service Chimique de Guerre,* in September 1915. But the French industrial potential was insufficient to provide the logistic capability for any significant gas warfare offensive until 1916 and the introduction of toxic artillery shells.[45]

The Gas Service, AEF

The discussion of Allied chemical organizations, particularly that of the British, is of special interest from the American point of view since the overseas chemical warfare contingent of the United States patterned its organization after the British who trained the contingent.

Maj. Gen. John J. Pershing and the advance elements of the AEF landed in France in June 1917. The United States was unprepared for waging chemical warfare even though it had been waged in Europe for over two years. Research on toxics had begun in the United States only a few months earlier. The nation had no gas weapons, no toxics, no military gas organization, and no protective supplies. It did have some information on gas warfare gathered by War Department observers with the Allies, notably by Dr. George A. Hulett of Princeton University. Although the War Department had not viewed gas warfare seriously, Pershing's staff saw an immediate need for action, even before the first mustard attack, and appointed a board to make recommendations concerning gas warfare.[46]

The AEF board, which met on 18 June 1917, recommended assigning an officer to "create and handle" an AEF gas organization and providing him with assistants, funds, and authority.[47] A week later Head-

[44] Foulkes, *Gas!,* p. 97.

[45] (1) Lefebure, *Riddle of the Rhine,* pp. 91–110. (2) Hanslian *et al., Der Chemische Krieg,* I, 20–21.

[46] Leo P. Brophy and George J. B. Fisher, *The Chemical Warfare Service: Organizing for War,* UNITED STATES ARMY IN WORLD WAR II (Washington, 1959), pp. 1–5.

[47] Memo, Lt Col John McA. Palmer, Chief Opns Sec Hq AEF, for CofS AEF, 30 Jul 17, sub: Gas and Flame Serv, Offensive and Defensive. A copy of this memo appears as General History, Appendix 2, in History of Chemical Warfare Service, American Expeditionary Forces (unpublished official history).

quarters, AEF, asked the War Department for such an officer and soon thereafter temporarily assigned gas offensive responsibilities to the AEF chief engineer and gas defensive responsibilities to the AEF chief surgeon. Despite advice from the War Department in July that gas responsibilities in the United States were apportioned among the Ordnance and Medical Departments and the Corps of Engineers, Lt. Col. John McA. Palmer and Lt. Col. James R. Church of the AEF staff, in consultation with Dr. Hulett and Capt. Walter M. Boothby, advanced a strong case for the organization of gas services in the United States and France. Church declared that the gas service in the United States should be subordinate to that in France in matters of policy and equipment. Both officers emphasized the necessity of immediate action, especially for protection. The commander of the 1st Division, comprising the first Army troops in France, had called for gas masks—his organization had none at all.[48] The timing of the comments by Church and Palmer suggests that the recent employment of mustard could have fostered their sense of urgency.

By the middle of August 1917 the AEF had received from the United States 20,000 gas masks and the news that a gas and flame regiment had been authorized. No other supplies, officers, or advice were received. About the same time Lt. Col. Amos A. Fries, Corps of Engineers, arrived in France and was about to be named director of roads when his orders were changed to make him engineer in charge of gas as well as Chief of the Gas Service, AEF. Headquarters, AEF, dispatched a cable to the War Department indicating that, since no further delay was possible, the appointment had been made. The AEF staff requested that Fries be designated to command the authorized gas and flame regiment.[49]

Colonel Fries took up his new duties on 22 August 1917 and left Paris on the same day to make his own appraisal of the British gas service in the field and to determine American requirements for gas organization, protection, and weapons. He learned from the British that the American masks recently received had failed to afford adequate protection in British tests, and on 23 August 1917 he accordingly recommended the adoption of the British small box respirator as the standard American mask. American troops were also to carry the

---

[48] (1) *Ibid.* (2) AEF GO 8, 5 Jul 17. (3) Maj James R. Church, MC, "A Suggested Organization of the Gas Service of the American Army," 26 Jul 17, apps. 3 and 5 of General History, in History of CWS AEF.

[49] (1) Memo, H. Taylor, Hq AEF, for CofS AEF, 17 Aug 17, sub: Gas and Flame Service, app. 8, General History, History of CWS AEF. (2) Fries and West, *Chemical Warfare*, pp. 72–75.

French M2 mask for emergency use in event the British mask was lost or became no longer wearable.[50]

Fries returned to Paris on 28 August and completed the draft organization for the AEF gas service. He also drafted the order formally establishing the AEF Gas Service.[51] The AEF order, issued on 3 September 1917, charged the Chief of the Gas Service "with the organization of personnel, the supply of material, and the conduct of the entire Gas Service both Offensive and Defensive, including instruction." [52] At the same time Fries became colonel and titular commander of the 30th Engineers, Gas and Flame, later the 1st Gas Regiment, then being organized in the United States under the actual command of Maj. Earle J. Atkinson.[53] Fries's initial problems were many: he needed officers and men; he needed supplies; he needed to train American troops; and, in order to help discharge the offensive portion of his mission, he needed to persuade American commanders that gas was a useful offensive weapon.

In meeting all these needs except that for officers and men he had to rely on Allied, especially British, help and experience. His own service he organized into an Offensive Branch and a Defensive Branch. Colonel Church became chief of the Defensive Branch, and Fries himself assumed the duties of the Offensive Branch. These branches were intended to operate in the field through gas officers assigned to army, corps, divisions, and regiments, as in the British organizational pattern. Both branches were to join in the operation of gas schools, the first two of which Fries and Boothby opened in the Army school at Langres on 10 October 1917 and within the I Corps Center of Instruction at Gondrecourt on 15 October 1917. The Offensive Branch was to direct the operations of gas and flame troops according to the British brigade pattern. There were then no troops to direct. The first companies of the 30th Engineers did not arrive in France until February 1918, and it was not until the summer of 1918 that officers began arriving in sufficient numbers to staff the gas service.[54]

[50] Fries and West, *Chemical Warfare*, pp. 75–77.

[51] *Ibid.*, p. 76.

[52] AEF GO 31, 3 Sep 17.

[53] (1) Interv, Hist Off with Maj Gen Amos A. Fries, USA (Ret.), 4 Aug 55. (2) Historical Division, Department of the Army, UNITED STATES IN THE WORLD WAR: 1917–1919, vol. 15, *Reports of Commander-in-Chief, A. E. F. Staff Sections and Services* (Washington, 1948), p. 291 (hereafter cited as Reports of Commander-in-Chief, A. E. F., Staff Sections and Services).

[54] (1) General History, History of CWS AEF, pp. 6–12 and apps. 12–15, 18. (2) Fries and West, *Chemical Warfare*, pp. 78–79, 93–95.

As indicated above, supply, both offensive and defensive, came mainly from the British and French. At first, Fries attempted to handle supply personally through liaison offices established in London and Paris and through the supply services of the AEF. Maj. Robert W. Crawford, as Chief of Gas Service supply, soon relieved Fries of supply operating functions. Crawford found that the Gas Service was automatically assigned lowest priority by the established supply services who had their own problems. He accordingly secured direct purchase authority for the Gas Service and arranged for the Gas Service to handle its own supply system all the way from requisition or purchase to actual supply to troops in the field.[55]

Fries felt that his most difficult problems were to persuade American commanders to employ gas and to educate troops to take adequate protection against gas. It was necessary for Gas Service officers to "go out and sell gas to the Army." [56] A service which intended to sell its method of warfare, train the Army in the field, operate its own supply system, conduct offensive operations with its own troops, and advise on the conduct of both offensive and defensive operations by other combat troops clearly required more than a handful of officers and a more comprehensive organization than the one originally envisioned.

The Gas Service was enlarged to meet the demands of its many responsibilities whenever men and equipment became available. For example, a completely staffed and equipped laboratory arrived in France early in 1918 and an officers' training camp was organized in France later in the year.[57] The provision of a laboratory had been one of the projects of the Office of Gas Service since the time of its organization in the United States in October 1917.[58] The increasing demands on the service resulted in the reorganization of Fries's immediate office in March 1918 to combine offense and defense into a Military Division and to establish a Technical and a Production and Supply Division. In May the Military Division was again separated into Offense and Defense Divisions. Finally, in June, the Gas Service in the United States was converted into the Chemical Warfare Service, National Army. The Gas Service, AEF, became the CWS AEF, officially the

---

[55] (1) General History, History of CWS AEF, pp. 12–14. (2) Fries and West, *Chemical Warfare*, pp. 76–79.

[56] Fries and West, *Chemical Warfare*, p. 90.

[57] (1) General History, History of CWS AEF, pp. 18–19. (2) Fries and West, *Chemical Warfare*, p. 88.

[58] Brophy and Fisher, *Organizing for War*, pp. 9–13.

CHART 1—ORGANIZATION, CHEMICAL WARFARE SERVICE, AMERICAN EXPEDITIONARY FORCES, 13 JULY 1918

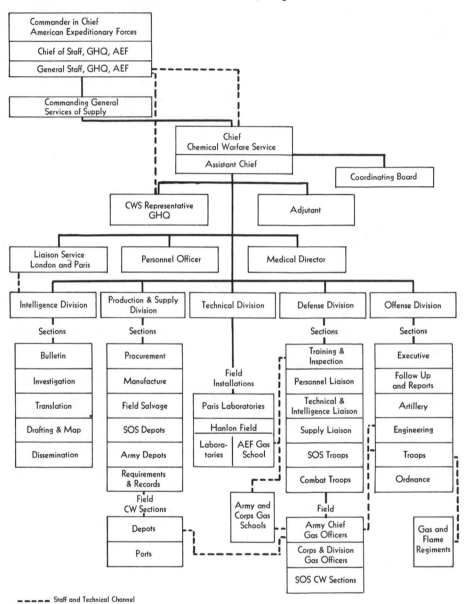

- - - - - Staff and Technical Channel

NOTE: Chief, Chemical Warfare Service, a member of the staff of the Commander in Chief, reported to the Commanding General, SOS, in matters of procurement, supply, transportation, and construction. GHQ AEF GO 31, 16 Feb 18.

Source: Adapted from: Plate VII, General History, History, CWS, AEF.

Overseas Division, CWS, and Fries, now chief of CWS AEF, was promoted to brigadier general.[59] The final CWS AEF organization which was prepared at that time included six divisions, and the duties of these divisions are evidence of the scope of gas warfare activities in the final year of the war. (*Chart 1*)

The Offense and Defense Divisions within the Office of the Chief, CWS AEF, exercised staff supervision over tactical gas warfare activities, evaluated combat experience, planned the employment of gas and flame units, and suggested changes in gas warfare tactics and techniques for all combat elements through army, corps, and division gas officers. These "military" divisions co-operated with the Technical Division in supervising the AEF Gas School and the army and corps gas schools. The Defense Division was also charged with the issue of defensive equipment and therefore supervised the CWS Services of Supply (SOS) troops immediately involved in combat supply support and training.[60] The Technical Division, in addition to controlling the AEF Gas School, directly operated chemical and medical laboratories and a gas research experimental station. The Office of the Medical Director, with divisional status, translated Technical Division findings into procedures for the care of gas casualties and co-operated with the Medical Corps in the development of treatment equipment and the application of care procedures. The Intelligence Division collected chemical warfare intelligence material for the use of the operating divisions and served as a clearinghouse for all CWS reports and requests for information. While the "military" divisions and the other divisions supporting them were mainly oriented toward combat operations, the remaining division, Production and Supply, was the element charged with those functions most clearly associated with the basic, logistics-oriented SOS mission. The organizational relationship of the CWS AEF to the SOS therefore largely depended upon the functions of the Production and Supply Division. Branches of this division computed chemical matériel requirements, procured munitions and equipment, supervised manufacturing plants in England and France, directed field salvage of chemical materials, and controlled four CWS SOS depots, chemical sections in six

---

[59] (1) General History, History of CWS AEF, pp. 25, 29–32. (2) WD GO 62, 28 Jun 18.

[60] General Pershing, in February 1918, had organized the Services of Supply under Maj. Gen. James G. Harbord, formerly his chief of staff, as a major AEF command charged with co-ordinating all the supply services and all AEF supply functions.

ports of debarkation, and chemical sections of several field army depots.[61]

Fries's own office, after the establishment of the SOS command, was located in SOS headquarters at Tours, but Fries continued to report to General Pershing's General Headquarters (GHQ), AEF. Most CWS administrative matters, except those directly relating to SOS, were handled through GHQ with the assistance of a CWS representative stationed at that headquarters. Fries handled detailed administrative work, including the assignment of CWS officers throughout the AEF, through his own administrative staff which included an adjutant, a personnel officer, and representatives in the AEF Liaison Service in London and Paris. Fries, by the time of the armistice, immediately supervised more than 150 officers. More than half of these officers were assigned to CWS staff and liaison duties while the remainder carried on laboratory and training work. Approximately another 30 officers directly supervised CWS SOS field operations. While Fries deferred to field commanders in their supervision of tactical chemical operations, he could exert considerable pressure on tactical planning officers because of his direct control of 168 field army, corps, and division gas officers. These gas officers reported to and advised their organization commanders according to the accepted staff pattern. The Chief, CWS AEF, was empowered to and did require detailed reports of offensive and defensive chemical operations. His "military" divisions presented their summaries and analyses of these reports in a weekly bulletin to organization gas officers. The bulletins contained criticisms of past chemical operations and suggestions for improvement. Gas officers on regimental and battalion staffs, as well as noncommissioned officers, were not members of the CWS; they were chosen by unit commanders from the unit complement. Yet, Fries could exercise some measure of control over these officers inasmuch as AEF orders specified that they be trained at CWS schools and that they be given gas warfare work as their principal duty.[62]

Another change which took place with the formation of the Chemical Warfare Service in the National Army was the redesignation of the

---

[61] General History, History of CWS AEF, pp. 29–33, 38–41, 53–58.

[62] (1) General History, History of CWS AEF, pp. 24–25, 55–56. (2) AEF GO 79, 27 May 18, and GO 107, 2 Jul 18. Apps. 47 and 48 to General History of CWS AEF. (3) Commissioned Pers of the CWS AEF, November 11, 1918, in History of CWS AEF. (4) Comments on draft of this volume, Brig Gen Hugh W. Rowan, USA (Ret.), 16 Dec 60.

30th Engineers, Gas and Flame, as the 1st Gas Regiment, CWS. This organization had been gradually growing as the war progressed, and by the time of the armistice it comprised 4 battalions with a total of 6 American companies and 4 attached British companies. Three platoons of each company fired projectors, and the fourth fired Stokes mortars. The authorized goal of one gas regiment for each field army was not achieved by the time the war ended.[63]

The extent of Fries's control over CWS activities in World War I is important since some CWS officers subsequently viewed Fries's authority as setting a precedent for the authority of principal CWS officers in World War II. The nature of Fries's position is also important because it was one of the factors in determining general and special staff relationships and duties. The U.S. Army had not employed the general and special staff concepts in war before World War I. AEF experience played a part in molding these concepts as they emerged in the period between the wars. General Pershing kept a tight rein on all elements of the AEF organization, and he apparently expected all his staff officers, including his Chief, CWS, to act as extensions of his own person throughout his organization.[64] Thus, Fries dealt with gas warfare matters while cloaked with his commander's rank and authority. The extent of his control is illustrated by the fact that Fries on one occasion relieved a division chemical officer.[65] Fries clearly believed in the necessity for maintaining a field chemical warfare organization broad enough to link research in chemical weapons and protection by "the closest possible ties to the firing line." He felt that he had established a strong, well co-ordinated service in the AEF which encompassed research, development, manufacturing and supply, tactical employment of chemicals, and employment of chemical weapons by chemical troops in the field. "The success of the CWS in the field and at home," he wrote, "was due to this complete organization." [66]

The organizational maturity achieved in the AEF quite early in the war unhappily was not paralleled within the military structure in the

---

[63] (1) James T. Addison, *The Story of the First Gas Regiment* (Boston: Houghton Mifflin Co., 1919), pp. 256–58. (2) Three regiments and a total of fifty-four companies had been authorized in September 1918, but most of these had not been activated. Fries and West, *Chemical Warfare*, p. 94.

[64] Maj. Gen. Otto L. Nelson, Jr., *National Security and the General Staff* (Washington: Infantry Journal Press, 1946), pp. 245–300.

[65] (1) Interv, Hist Off with Rowan, 26 Sep 58. General Rowan was an assistant division gas officer and later division gas officer under Fries. (2) Interv, Hist Off with Maj Gen Alden H. Waitt, USA (Ret.), 13 May 61.

[66] Fries and West, *Chemical Warfare*, p. 73.

United States. Unprepared for gas warfare when the United States entered the war in April 1917, the War Department divided responsibility for this new form of warfare among five different agencies, one of which was a civilian bureau.[67]

It is not strange that the people responsible for the battlefield employment of chemical warfare were stanch and vocal pleaders for a more rational chemical organization in the War Department. Fries's dealings with the Hydra-headed, un-co-ordinated chemical warfare complex in Washington led to repeated requests for organizational improvements which would ease his labors. In making these requests, Fries had the full support of General Pershing.

As indicated earlier, the War Department set up a co-ordinating agency known as the Office of Gas Service in October 1917. This clearinghouse for chemical matters consisted of a director and representatives from the Ordnance and Medical Departments and from the Chemical Service Section of the National Army—a section established at the same time as the Gas Service with a principal mission of providing the AEF with a chemical laboratory. In February 1918 the Chemical Warfare Service and the Gas Division were joined in a move that failed to provide the administrative centralization and the prestige that could only come from the formation of an independent gas corps. This final step was taken on 28 June 1918 with the creation of the Chemical Warfare Service, National Army, with Maj. Gen. William L. Sibert as director.

The CWS Between the Wars

Defining the Role and Responsibilities

When General Fries returned from France after World War I he applied all of his considerable vigor to the establishment of the Chemical Warfare Service as a permanent part of the Regular Army. In July 1919 Congress had given the CWS a year's reprieve, and, in 1920, after debate in which the Secretary of War, Newton D. Baker, the Chief of Staff, General Peyton C. March, and General Pershing registered

---

[67] The organizations and their responsibilities were: (1) Bureau of Mines: research on chemical agents; (2) Medical Department: the provision of defensive equipment; (3) Ordnance Department: manufacture and filling of gas shells; (4) Corps of Engineers: the formation and training of gas and flame units; and (5) Signal Corps: the provision of gas alarms. The organizational difficulties are fully discussed in the first chapter of Brophy and Fisher, *Organizing for War*.

dissent, the Congress of the United States amended the National Defense Act of 1916 so as to make the CWS a permanent part of the Military Establishment. The new service received the functions of development, procurement, and supply of all toxic, smoke, incendiary, and gas defensive materials, the training of the Army in chemical warfare, and the "organization, equipment, training and operation of special gas troops." [68]

The dissent of people as influential as Baker, Pershing, and March should have augured ill for the newly formed Chemical Warfare Service. The fact is that the period of the 1920's and 1930's was a difficult one for the Army establishment in general and the Chemical Warfare Service in particular. Reasons for this are not hard to find. This period between the world wars was one of disillusionment, disarmament, and depression. A nation, indeed a world, appalled by the costs of the recent conflict, looked for ways to prevent such a holocaust from recurring. The Washington conference of 1921 tried to limit the types of armament civilized nations might use in warfare, and four years later the Geneva conference on the regulation of arms traffic looked toward the same end. Both conferences drew up conventions outlawing gas warfare. The Washington treaty failed by one to achieve the required unanimous agreement of the five participating powers. [69] The Geneva Gas Protocol of 1925 did receive the support of over forty nations and thus became the most influential statement regarding gas warfare in the body of international law. The United States and Japan were the two major powers that did not ratify this protocol.

Nonetheless, the War Department General Staff took a defensive position toward gas warfare throughout most of this period—defensive both in the attitude with which it approached the subject and in the type of warfare upon which it concentrated. In 1922 it suspended work on toxic agents and restricted other CWS efforts to defensive measures. Although this restrained approach was frequently reaffirmed in the 1920's and 1930's, modifications in the War Department prohibition of research on toxic gases allowed some work in this field—one had to know the offensive potential of an agent in order to defend against it.

[68] (1) Public Law 242, 66th Congress, sec. 12a. Reproduced in WD Bulletin 25, 9 June 1920, the source of the above quotation. (2) See Brophy and Fisher, *Organizing for War*, pp. 11–17.

[69] The dissenter was France, which objected to the antisubmarine provision in the convention, not to the one against gas.

In addition to these handicaps, the new service faced another rather unpleasant situation. It would seem that the large majority of the people who had faith in gas as a viable system, capable of contributing to success in battle, was centered in the Chemical Warfare Service. There was little support for it within the combat arms. AEF commanders did not properly utilize chemical warfare in World War I, and it is quite probable they later looked upon it with skepticism. Many felt it would be an encumbrance added to the battlefield, not merely in the increased logistical support it would entail but in the burdens it would place on the infantryman and in the difficulties of decontamination it would involve. If it were successfully used by both combatants it would be something akin to two fighters, each with one arm tied behind his back. And why fight under such handicaps?

The Chemical Warfare Service set about accomplishing its rather restricted mission with meager resources of men and money. These restrictions lasted throughout the depression, but by 1939 the war in Europe and subsequent reaction in the United States brought about a definite change. The annual Congressional appropriation for the CWS from 1927 to 1935 came to about one and a quarter million dollars. In 1939 it was almost 3 million dollars, in 1941 it was 60 million, and in 1942 it was over a billion. Manpower was a similar story. In 1933 the CWS had an actual strength of 77 officers and 413 enlisted men; in 1940 the numbers were 93 and 1,035; in 1941, 833 and 5,059; and the peak in 1943, 8,103 and 61,688. Civilian employees ranged from 742 in 1931 to a peak of 29,000 in 1943.[70]

The uneasy situation in Europe also helped modify the restrictions imposed upon the CWS. Two years before the outbreak of war the service began work on a mustard gas shell filling plant at Edgewood Arsenal, Md.

In the process of CWS expansion gray areas of mission responsibility were clearly defined, much of this work done under the direction of Maj. Gen. William N. Porter who became Chief, Chemical Warfare Service, in May 1941. This effort to define responsibilities resulted in expanded duties for the CWS, for example, development of a high explosive shell for the 4.2-inch mortar and the acquisition of complete responsibility for the incendiary bomb program. In 1941 the War Department gave the CWS the mission of biological warfare research.

[70] For complete statistics, see Brophy and Fisher, *Organizing for War*, pp. 25–27.

GENERAL PORTER

Many of the 93 Regular Army officers in the CWS in 1940 had served under and been tutored by Maj. Gen. Amos A. Fries. Many of them believed as strongly as he did in the military efficacy of gas, and they looked upon themselves as custodians of one of the most awesome weapons to come out of World War I. They considered the CWS unique among the services because it had a legal operational function such as only the combat arms had. True, the Corps of Engineers and the Signal Corps had combat roles, but neither had its own weapons which its own troops would employ in combat. There were also dissenters in the ranks of the CWS who felt that Porter and some of their fellow officers overemphasized the uniqueness of the CWS and the extent of its probable contribution to the next war. In countering these dissenters, and they were probably in the minority, the advocates of gas warfare could point out that gas appeared to be the ideal weapon for

aerial bombardment. General Porter, as chemical instructor at the
Army Air Corps Tactical School 1933–37, had in co-operation with Air
Corps tacticians successfully evolved a tactical system for aerial bombardment which was well received by many Air Corps officers.[71] Some
CWS officers felt that a prediction made in 1920 was about to come
true: "gas and military aeronautics will play the principal parts in the
next war, which will be literally finished in the chemical laboratory." [72]

While military aviation became important soon after the 1939 outbreak of World War II in Europe, gas warfare, to the surprise of many
observers, was not initiated. Great Britain, on 3 September 1939, the
day of her declaration of war, sought assurances from the belligerents
that they would observe the 1925 Geneva Protocol prohibiting the use
of gases and bacteriological methods of warfare. Germany, Italy, Bul-
garia, Rumania, Finland, and Japan replied that the protocol would be
observed.[73] Gas was therefore not used, and Japan, in accordance with
her assurance to Great Britain that the Geneva Protocol would be observed, did not use gas in the Pearl Harbor attack which brought the
United States into the war. Six months later, on 5 June 1942, the
President of the United States threatened the initiation of gas warfare,
but only in retaliation against Japan in the event that that nation used
gas upon China. [74] Since the President's statement was accepted as
national policy, it began to appear that gas warfare might not be employed unless Germany or Japan initiated it. The possibility of enemy
initiation demanded that the United States take protective measures
and that it prepare for offensive retaliation, but the preparedness
mandate lacked force and precision.[75] While these events determining
the role of chemical warfare in international policy were taking place,
the War Department was shaping the role the services were to play in
possible future overseas operations. War Department planners built
their concepts of mobilization organization around a combined field
and theater of operations headquarters designated, as the AEF headquarters had been, General Headquarters. Under the GHQ plan, when

[71] (1) Porter Interv, 24 Aug 61. (2) Waitt Interv, 13 May 61. Waitt was Porter's successor as
instructor at the Air Corps Tactical School. (3) Interv, Hist Off with Col John C. MacArthur, USA
(Ret.), 19 Sep 61. (4) Interv, Hist Off with Col Augustin M. Prentiss, Jr., USAF (Ret.), 25 Oct 61.
[72] Edward S. Farrow, Gas Warfare (New York: Dutton, 1920), p. vii.
[73] Dale Birdsell, The Department of State and the Gas Warfare Question (unpublished Monograph
in CMLHO), p. 1.
[74] For additional information on the President's statement, see Brophy and Fisher, Organizing for
War, pp. 63–64.
[75] Brophy and Fisher, Organizing for War, pp. 59–67.

CHART 2—SUGGESTED ORGANIZATION OF OFFICES OF CHEMICAL OFFICERS
THEATER OF OPERATIONS

OFFICE OF CHEMICAL OFFICER, THEATER OF OPERATIONS

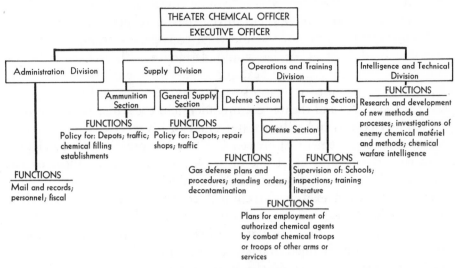

OFFICE OF CHEMICAL OFFICER, COMMUNICATIONS ZONE

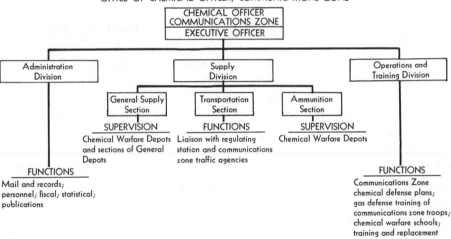

OFFICE OF CHEMICAL OFFICER, FIELD ARMY

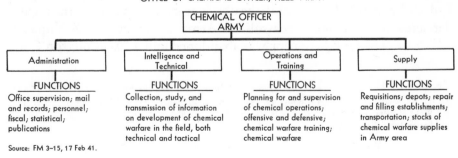

Source: FM 3–15, 17 Feb 41.

war came the Chief of Staff or the ranking War Department officer
designated by the President was to assume command of GHQ, assemble
and train troops, and move them into a theater of operations for combat. The GHQ commander would then convert his headquarters into
a theater headquarters, or he would designate a theater commander
who would organize a theater headquarters. Representatives of the War
Department administrative and supply services were to form a special
staff for the GHQ and theater commander, and the senior representative
of each service was to be the theater chief of his service.[76]

The War Department-approved CWS field operations manual provided that the theater chief chemical officer, "a general officer of the
Chemical Warfare Service," would organize and administer his own
service and would exercise "technical control" over CWS activities
through subordinate service and combat chemical officers. (*Chart 2*)
So far these provisions recapitulated World War I experience, but thereafter the emphasis changed to stress the role of the theater chief chemical
officer as a representative of the War Department Chief, CWS. The
manual indicated that the CWS organization in the United States would
plan theater matériel requirements, set initial stockages and issues, determine the extent of theater matériel procurement, prescribe the movement, supply, and training of officers and troops, specify utilization of
civilian labor, approve interservice agreements, and fund theater finan-
cial transactions.[77] The GHQ CWS was to be much more closely tied to
the War Department CWS than the CWS AEF had been. This closer tie
was a direct outgrowth of Fries's idea of a broad-scope, co-ordinated
service which he had helped make possible by having a clause inserted
in the National Defense Act of 1920 assigning the responsibility for the
supervision and operation of chemical troops to the Chief, CWS.[78]

The Administrative System

When the United States entered World War II, the prewar plans
had to be adapted to a multitheater war and previously unexpected
demands for a strongly centralized Army command in Washington.
(*Map 1*) The GHQ concept was abandoned and a "Washington Com-

---

[76] (1) Mark Skinner Watson, *Chief of Staff: Prewar Plans and Preparations*, UNITED STATES
ARMY IN WORLD WAR II (Washington, 1950), pp. 2, 295–96.   (2) WD FM 100–10, 9 Dec 40.
[77] WD FM 3–15, 17 Feb 41.
[78] Porter Interv, 24 Aug 61.

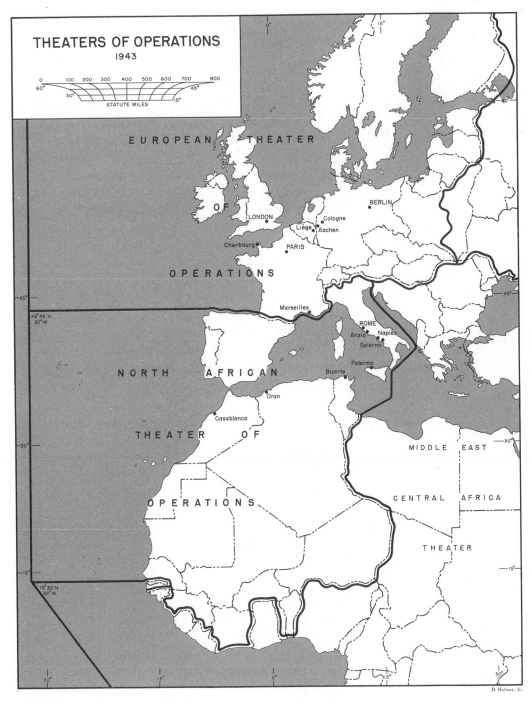

THEATERS OF OPERATIONS
1943

0 100 200 300 400 500 600 700 800
STATUTE MILES

EUROPEAN THEATER

OF

OPERATIONS

BERLIN

Cologne
Liège
Aachen

Cherbourg
PARIS

LONDON

Marseilles

ROME
Anzio
Salerno
Naples

Palermo

Bizerte

NORTH AFRICAN

Oran

Casablanca

THEATER OF

MIDDLE EAST

OPERATIONS

CENTRAL AFRICA

THEATER

D. Holmes, Jr.

MAP 1

771-608 O-66-4

mand Post" was created within the General Staff, and through this post General George C. Marshall, Chief of Staff, exercised command of the worldwide activities of the Army. At the same time, in March 1942, the President and General Marshall delegated the zone of interior (ZI) operating functions of the War Department to three major commands, one each for ground, air, and service.[79] Lt. Gen. Brehon B. Somervell, the service commander, brought the reluctant technical services, including the CWS, under the jurisdiction of his Services of Supply (SOS), later Army Service Forces (ASF). Somervell interposed his headquarters organization between the CWS and other operating elements. Thus, while chemical sections were created in the ground and air forces commands, the formal route of communication for the Chief, CWS, was through Somervell's organization. The question almost immediately arose of forming theater organizations.[80]

There was little chance, in view of the subordination of the services to ASF and considering the command and staff doctrines which had reached formal statement in the period between the wars, that the Chief, CWS, would have any control within overseas organizations.[81] But there were still those Fries-trained officers who were unaware of or prepared to disavow the extent of ASF control. These officers also believed that should command and staff doctrines be so interpreted as to subordinate the CWS in overseas organizations, those overseas organizations would be forced to accommodate themselves to the unique character of the CWS by delegating extraordinary controls and channels to their service.[82] These officers felt that, as an absolute minimum, the Chemical Warfare Service would control gas warfare planning and chemical supply at all echelons from development in the United States to expenditure on the overseas firing line. The new War Department reorganization and the new doctrines were to lead to the establishment of procedures that were not in accord with CWS convictions.

---

[79] Ray S. Cline, *Washington Command Post: The Operations Division*, UNITED STATES ARMY IN WORLD WAR II (Washington, 1951), chs. VI, VII.

[80] John D. Millett, *The Organization and Role of the Army Service Forces*, UNITED STATES ARMY IN WORLD WAR II (Washington, 1954), chs. II and XII.

[81] Porter Interv, 24 Aug 61.

[82] Waitt Interv, 13 May 61. General Waitt, postwar Chief, U.S. Army Chemical Corps, successor to the CWS, counts himself among the Fries-trained officers who strongly believed in the necessity for a unitary CWS organization.

The Logistics System

The global logistics system of the United States was oriented to an "impetus from the rear" pattern.[83] Global warfare and the role of the United States as the principal arsenal of the United Nations made it impractical from a War Department point of view for the World War II logistic impetus to come from the theater commander as it had often come from the theater commander in World War I. Accordingly, the Chief of Staff, or, more specifically, his right arm, Operations Division (OPD), War Department General Staff (WDGS), was the principal logistics authority, the allocator of resources, of the World War II Army. OPD served as the Army logistics policy arbiter whose duties included approving requirements, priorities, and plans, acting as intermediary between the theaters and the forces in the United States, and setting up the formulas and objectives of logistics operations. The Services of Supply supervised all phases of the logistics operations in the United States and served as the principal troubleshooter on theater logistics problems. OPD and other WDGS elements often referred such problems to ASF. The continental technical services, each in its own field, were responsible for the basic computation of requirements and for the provision of matériel. In the Chemical Warfare Service, troubleshooting, both formal and informal, on overseas problems was the province of Brig. Gen. Alden H. Waitt, Assistant Chief, CWS, for Field Operations.[84]

The operational focus of overseas supply was the port of embarkation. Each major port was responsible for a theater or theaters of operations, processing theater requisitions, or its automatic supply, requesting matériel from the technical services, and actually shipping approved allowances. The responsibilities of the continental technical services ended at the port; the port of embarkation was in charge until cargo cleared the harbor. Technically, the theater became accountable for shipments at sea, but the physical responsibilities of the theater organi-

---

[83] The following comments on the nature of the logistics system and theory of supply are derived from: (1) Richard M. Leighton and Robert W. Coakley, *Global Logistics and Strategy, 1940–45*, UNITED STATES ARMY IN WORLD WAR II (Washington, 1955), chs. IX, XIII; (2) Cline, *Washington Command Post*, chs. I, VII, XIV; (3) Logistical History of NATOUSA–MTOUSA, 30 November 1945, compiled under the direction of Cresswell G. Blakeney, Assistant Chief of Staff, G–4, ch. II.

[84] (1) For discussion of requirements computation, see Brophy, Miles, and Cochrane, *From Laboratory to Field*, ch. XII. (2) For organization and functions of the Office of the Assistant Chief, CWS, for Operations, see Brophy and Fisher, *Organizing for War*, ch. V.

zation began at the port of debarkation.[85] The War Department governed supply activities of the ports of embarkation and, theoretically at least, those of the theaters of operations through a War Department provision which specified procedures for computing requirements, requisitioning, and effecting supply.[86] The War Department system thus ordained clearly precluded any unitary control by any technical service, but even had the system permitted such control, the CWS would have been poorly prepared to take advantage of the opportunity.

CWS resources available at the outbreak of war for the evolving global logistics system were slim indeed. Actual CWS supplies in potential overseas bases in the month of Pearl Harbor included 12 major items for gas warfare protection and decontamination and 5 major offensive munitions. In all, the overseas departments stocked 28 items from an active supply list of 34 in limited normal maintenance stocks or war reserves. The most important single item of antigas protective equipment, the service gas mask, in late 1941 was stocked overseas in quantities totaling 281,207.[87] For offensive use in the event of necessity, the CWS and the Ordnance Department in 1941 in the overseas departments stored 242 tons of bulk persistent gases, 259 tons of nonpersistent gases, a small quantity of toxic-filled artillery shell, and a small quantity of toxic-filled 4.2-inch chemical mortar shell. Even in an emergency, combat delivery of toxics on the enemy would have been only by air or artillery. The CWS lacked standard weapons to project toxics except for the 4.2-inch chemical mortar which was stocked in sufficient quantity to equip a battalion in Hawaii, a platoon in Panama, and a company in the United States.[88] Consequently, despite phenomenally accelerated CWS matériel production in the United States, the first large-scale wartime CWS logistics experience overseas,

---

[85] For a discussion of CWS continental distribution, see Brophy, Miles, and Cochrane, *From Laboratory to Field*, ch. XVI.

[86] WD Memo W–700–8–42, 10 Oct 42, sub: Sup of Overseas Depts, Theatres, and Separate Bases.

[87] Stockages in the United States were likewise extremely limited. For example, the total mask stockage, including that in the continental United States, in late 1941, was 2,855,500, an amount almost a million less than the war-end stockage of the lightweight service mask in the European Theater of Operations alone.

[88] (1) Weekly Rpt for CofS, CWS Munitions on Hand as of 12 Dec 41, dated 20 Dec 41. CWS 319.1/2249. (2) CWS Matériel Status Rpt for Overseas Theaters, Mar 45, cited in Ben Baldwin, Alfred J. Bingham, and Paul W. Pritchard, Readiness for Gas Warfare in Theaters of Operations, CMLHO draft MS. (3) Memo, Lt Col Charles C. Herrick, WPD, to Chief Opns Gp WPD, 10 Feb 42, sub: Use of Toxic Gases. WPD 165–23, in OPD 165–10 through 165–24.

in North Africa, involved at the outset no offensive materials and only one new piece of equipment, the mechanical smoke generator.

The administrative arrangements of the CWS and the War Department were to be tested earlier than the logistic procedures. Before United States entry into World War II, the CWS had staff officers and units in the Philippine and Hawaiian Departments, and a CWS officer was on duty as assistant military attaché in London. These overseas CWS elements played a role in the military events following the Pearl Harbor attack, and a CWS section was established in Australia when the first American troops reached that continent. But the first War Department effort to establish a theater [89] headquarters in its own image took place in England. This theater, which was to become the European Theater of Operations (ETO), represented the largest overseas undertaking of the Army in terms of men and materials during World War II. In the European theater, perhaps more extensively than in other theaters, those CWS officers who believed in a unique and unitary service first tried and then modified their administrative concepts.

---

[89] The term *theater* is used in this volume to indicate any overseas area of operations of the United States Army. It is also used to mean the principal United States headquarters in the area under consideration.

CHAPTER II

The CWS in the European Theater

Planning and Organization: 1940–43

Erecting the Framework for an Overseas Command

CWS officers in the United States followed the initiation of World War II in Europe with keen interest as a chance to test predictions that gas would become a major weapon of the war. There was no indication that gas was used in Hitler's attack on Poland, but the British Government had begun issuing gas masks to military and civilians alike even before the declaration of war. Lt. Col. Charles E. Loucks, CWS, in June 1940 arrived in France to fill the position of assistant military attaché in the American Embassy and to serve as CWS observer. With the fall of France shortly thereafter, Loucks was transferred to England in the same capacity. The most interesting development early in the European war from the CWS point of view was the German incendiary bombing of England. Loucks reported extensively on bomb types and effects of bombing.[1]

Loucks did not become a member of the American Special Observer Group (SPOBS), which was organized in England prior to the United States entry into the war, but in February 1942 his successor as military attaché, Col. Carl L. Marriott, was also designated Chemical Officer, United States Army Forces in the British Isles (USAFBI), the first official American command in Europe, in fact a redesignation of SPOBS.[2] Marriott thus assumed the duties of reporting, still principally

---

[1] CMLHO Biographical Sketches: Maj Gen Charles E. Loucks.

[2] (1) CMLHO Biographical Sketches: Col Carl L. Marriott. (2) [Henry G. Elliott] MS, The Predecessor Commands, SPOBS and USAFBI, pt. I of The Administrative and Logistical History of the ETO, Hist Div USFET, 1946, p. 239, OCMH.

reporting on incendiary bombings, and he began to oversee the chemical warfare protection and training of American troops. Lt. Col. Lewis F. Acker established a chemical section in the headquarters of U.S. Army V Corps, the first U.S. ground forces organization to arrive in the British Isles.[3]

On 2 May 1942 Colonel Marriott was forced by ill health to return to the United States, and Col. Charles S. Shadle assumed the dual role. By the time of Shadle's appointment, the duties of Chemical Officer, USAFBI, were demanding full time: there was not only the necessity of seeing to the equipment and training of increasing numbers of American troops but also the requirement for participating in and initiating administrative, supply, and operational planning for what was clearly to become a major overseas command. At that time, a little more than a month before the President's first pronouncement on gas warfare, neither national nor international policy on gas warfare was clear. CWS officers always assumed, in absence of definite information to the contrary, that their first duty was to make as many defensive and offensive gas warfare preparations as possible. In June Col. J. Enrique Zanetti, CWS incendiary expert and World War I liaison officer on Fries's staff, arrived to relieve Shadle of the attaché position.[4] Also in June Col. Crawford M. Kellogg, six officers, and nine enlisted men of the Chemical Section, Eighth Air Force, arrived in England. The Eighth Air Force Chemical Section had been activated along with the Eighth Air Force headquarters at Bolling Field in April.[5]

While the chemical sections in the British Isles were organizing and embarking on their planning and supply duties, other organizational developments were taking place in the United States. The President and his military advisers in consultation with the British had decided to establish a theater of operations headquarters in England. A manual describing theater headquarters organization existed, but the manual had been written before the War Department reorganization into three commands with the attendant revision of organizational policy. Furthermore, United Nations strategists had not yet decided upon launching a ground offensive, so that the first mission of the American

---

[3] Interv, Hist Off with Col Lewis F. Acker, USAR (Ret.), 9 Jun 61.

[4] (1) CMLHO Biographical Sketches: Brig Gen Charles S. Shadle. (2) MS, CWS History, Hq SOS ETO (hereafter cited as CWS SOS History), n.d. (3) Waitt Interv, 13 May 61.

[5] History of the Cml Sec Eighth AF VIII AFSC for the Period 21 Apr 42 to 31 Dec 42 (hereafter cited as History, Cml Sec Eighth AF). CWS 314.7 Eighth AF.

theater headquarters would be co-operation with the British and supervision of a matériel build-up in anticipation of a combined assault upon the European continent at some future date. The second mission would be the support of Eighth Air Force operations and the support of ground and service troop training and equipment. Emphasis upon logistics organization was clearly indicated. The War Department tricommand organization was not prescribed for a theater in the regulations which antedated this organization, but neither was it proscribed. General Marshall set about organizing a tripartite theater command, and, since the air element in the form of Eighth Air Force already existed and the ground element would not be important for the time being, he concentrated on that service element. Generals Marshall and Somervell picked Maj. Gen. John C. H. Lee to be the European theater SOS commander. They oversaw the organization of Lee's headquarters in the United States, and they instructed Lee on Marshall's desires concerning theater organization.[6]

Marshall's, Somervell's, and Lee's organization and organizational concepts proved important to the CWS. The manual provided that a theater chief chemical officer would restrict himself and his immediate staff to the formulation of broad policy. He would operate his service through technical control of subordinates. Subordinates for combat matters, as in the CWS AEF, were to be army, corps, and division chemical officers. Subordinates for service and supply matters were to be on the staffs of the communications zone, regulating station, and advance, intermediate, and base section commanders.[7] (*Chart 3*) With such decentralization of operations, the immediate office of the theater chief chemical officer was to have only one operating division for research, development, and intelligence and a small staff. General Fries, working under a highly centralized policy, had needed a large staff and six operating divisions. The problem in the case of the European theater organization was that neither the World War I type of organization nor the manual organization seemed to apply.

General Somervell's ASF instructed the chiefs of the services in the United States to provide top-quality officers to join Lee's staff before it

[6] Roland G. Ruppenthal, *Logistical Support of the Armies, Volume I,* UNITED STATES ARMY IN WORLD WAR II (Washington, 1953), pp. 31–38.

[7] (1) WD FM 3–15, 17 Feb 41. (2) WD FM 100–10, 9 Dec 40. (3) WD FM 3–5, 20 Jul 42. Previously published in draft, 1 June 1942, and in an unnumbered WD series as Chemical Warfare Service Field Manual, Volume I, Tactics and Technique, 1 August 1938.

CHART 3—PLANNED DISTRIBUTION OF STAFF AND SERVICE AGENCIES, CHEMICAL
WARFARE SERVICE, THEATER OF OPERATIONS

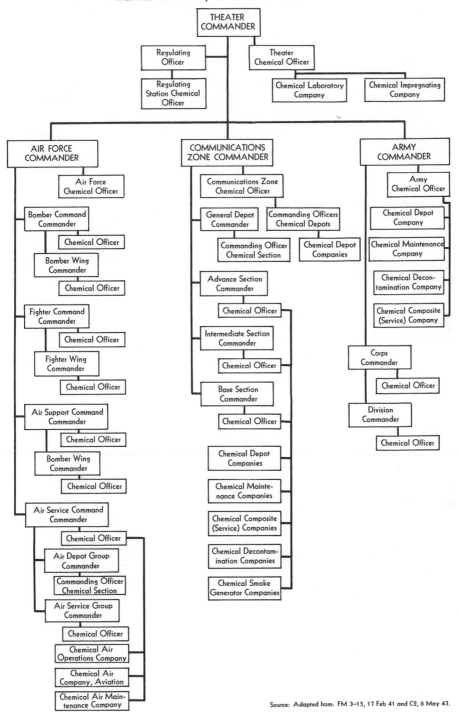

Source: Adapted from: FM 3–15, 17 Feb 41 and C2, 6 May 43.

left to go overseas. General Porter, under the assumption that he was appointing a theater chief chemical officer, chose Col. Edward Montgomery, one of the four Regular Army colonels in the appropriate age group within the CWS, to head the group. Montgomery's deputy, Col. Lowell A. Elliott, and three of his division chiefs, Cols. Hugh W. Rowan, John C. MacArthur, and Edwin C. Maling, were top-ranking Regular Army lieutenant colonels then recently promoted to temporary colonel. These officers, several junior officers, and a number of enlisted men joined Lee's headquarters at Indiantown Gap Military Reservation to await transportation to England.[8]

General Lee and a small advance echelon of his headquarters arrived in London on 24 May 1942 and immediately set to work activating the SOS USAFBI. Lee just as immediately ran into a storm. The USAFBI staff was adamantly opposed to Lee's planned subordination of the theater service chiefs to the SOS commander since that subordination implied exactly what the War Department intended—SOS control of theater service and supply policy. After much discussion and reviewing of directives, the first of many compromises on theater organization was reached in June closely following the redesignation of USAFBI as the European Theater of Operations, United States Army (ETOUSA). In this compromise the chemical warfare and ten other theater special staff sections were given over to the control of Lee's SOS while retaining their titles as theater special staff sections. Colonel Montgomery, who arrived in June, was designated chief chemical warfare officer and a member of the theater special staff. The SOS headquarters and the offices of the theater service chiefs were moved from London ninety miles to Cheltenham. The theater headquarters, now commanded by Lt. Gen. Dwight D. Eisenhower, remained in London. Shadle was named CWS representative at Headquarters, ETOUSA, and given two officer assistants. Shadle's position, reminiscent of the position of CWS AEF representative at GHQ, was established in accordance with the basic theater organizational directive which provided for a service representative when the theater chief of service was not located at theater headquarters.[9]

Still, from the CWS point of view, the situation was not a happy one. If Montgomery was to be represented in, rather than resident in, theater

---

[8] (1) Porter Interv, 24 Aug 61.   (2) CWS SOS History.
[9] (1) Ruppenthal, *Logistical Support*, I, 37–39.   (2) CWS SOS History.

headquarters, the CWS preparedness and advisory mission could only be properly performed if he had a large, strong operational staff such as Fries had had at Tours. The prospects of getting such a staff at Cheltenham were dim since Cheltenham was intended to be a service and supply headquarters only. Montgomery consequently spent much of his time in the London echelon of SOS while Elliott proceeded to Cheltenham in the dual role of deputy and temporary chief of the Supply Division. In Cheltenham, Capt. Warren S. LeRoy, Acting Chief, Storage and Issue Section, Supply Division, at once resumed work on storage and issue procedures for chemical supplies which he and the OCCWS (Office of the Chief, Chemical Warfare Service) staff had begun in the United States. Maj. Maurice H. Wright activated the Procurement Section, Supply Division, while Maj. John J. Hayes set up a Requirements Division. Rowan and MacArthur reported to Cheltenham early in July. Rowan set up the Technical Division while MacArthur established the Operations and Training Division, but for several weeks both officers were confined to planning and background work since their activities were inappropriate to the work of the Cheltenham command and since they had no assistants and very little equipment.[10]

By the end of July Montgomery was able to bring about some improvement in the maladjusted organizational distribution. He secured the transfer of Rowan's Technical Division and Wright's Procurement Section to the London echelon of SOS. The Technical Division was charged with liaison concerning all technical matters both with the British and with headquarters other than the SOS, and Wright was given the additional duty of liaison with the British on lend-lease matters. In both cases, location in Cheltenham would have greatly complicated communications and the discharge of normal functions.[11] Rowan set up his London office at the end of the first week in August with two officer assistants. Wright was allotted one assistant. Approximately two weeks later Shadle was designated Chief Chemical Officer, Allied Force Headquarters (AFHQ), a position at least in theory superior to that of theater chemical officer. AFHQ, a combined supreme headquarters, was preparing for the North African invasion.

---

[10] (1) CWS SOS History. (2) Personal Ltr, Col Rowan to Col William C. Kabrich, Chief, Tech Serv OCCWS, 8 Sep 42. CWS 314.7 Pers Files, ETO. Unless otherwise noted, all personal letters relating to the European theater cited hereafter are from this file (see Bibliographical Note). (3) Comments on draft of this volume, Col Lowell A. Elliott, USA (Ret.), 16 Jan 61.

[11] Personal Ltr cited in n. 10 (2), above.

MacArthur moved in as his replacement and took over supervision of the chemical warfare exercises for which planning, in co-ordination with British chemical warfare authorities, was virtually complete. Since MacArthur was Montgomery's planning officer and his training policy chief, MacArthur's move to London completed the physical transfer of all chemical warfare policy, technical, advisory, and liaison functions to theater headquarters while organizationally all but Mac-Arthur remained in the SOS.[12]

Also in August 1942 the operating elements of the CWS began to sort themselves out. Col. Leonard M. Johnson arrived in Cheltenham to become Chief, Supply Division. Although few CWS supplies were arriving in England, the Supply Division was already working on storage and distribution measures. At about the same time, Colonel Maling, his four officers and five enlisted men, began the establishment of the CWS training operations within the newly authorized American School Center at Shrivenham. The CWS had hoped and planned to establish its own school but had been obliged to participate in the centralization of theater training activities. Centralization did offer advantages of better facilities and equipment and better handling of admissions than a single service could manage.[13] Kellogg, meanwhile, had distributed his ten Eighth Air Force chemical officers among three chemical sections— one, to control supply and training branches in the Eighth Air Force headquarters, another, to direct supply operations in the VIII Air Force Service Command (AFSC), and a third, to supervise ground service and training in the VIII Bomber Command. While these sections were in the process of organization, Kellogg and his staff worked on a revision of the war gas supply plan which had been formulated by his section in the United States. Since, even in this early period, both the War Department and the forces in the theater had accepted the policy that any gas warfare retaliatory or offensive effort would be the operating responsibility of the air forces, the Eighth Air Force toxic supply plan was crucial to the gas warfare potential of the CWS ETO.[14] It then appeared that the CWS ETO pattern was set, and the pattern followed neither the World War I precedent nor the prescriptions of regulations. Whether the CWS ETO could accomplish its

---

[12] CWS SOS History.
[13] *Ibid.*
[14] History, Cml Sec Eighth AF.

mission through the use of this pattern remained to be seen. The first test soon came when England became a base for the North African invasion (TORCH operation) for which the European theater provided logistical support. Largely as a result of providing officers and men for TORCH, CWS ETO experienced sweeping staff changes.

Colonel Montgomery was recalled to the United States for special duty in September 1942. Elliott was appointed to establish a chemical section for the forming Twelfth Air Force headquarters, destined for North Africa, and Maling was attached to the AFHQ planning staff in a nonchemical capacity. One lieutenant colonel, six majors, and three captains from the London and Cheltenham CWS elements soon joined the North African forces. Kellogg was the senior CWS officer remaining with European theater forces, but Rowan, senior CWS officer in the SOS, succeeded Montgomery in acting capacity.[15] Elliott's duties as deputy were divided between Johnson in Cheltenham and Mac-Arthur in London. Maling's post at Shrivenham went to a succession of junior officers.[16]

By mid-September TORCH was not only creating a constant drain on manpower, but it was also demanding matériel, support for operational planning, and readiness inspection. At the same time, the base sections, local supply and service organizations, were organizing in the United Kingdom, and supply and service installations were being activated as rapidly as possible. Furthermore, although the matériel and troop build-up in England had been brought virtually to a standstill in deference to the North African venture, operational and informational demands in the theater were growing apace. Theater officers regarded the strategic hiatus with respect to ETOUSA as only temporary, and they continued to believe that the prime task in the United Kingdom was to prepare for eventual assault on the Continent. To meet an important CWS need for intelligence information, the CWS arranged for Colonel Zanetti, assistant military attaché, to become in effect chief of an intelligence division. Capt. Philip R. Tarr and two other officers were transferred from Cheltenham to London on 19 September 1942 to assist Zanetti. One of Maling's successors at the American School

---

[15] While the manual provided that the senior CWS officer in the theater would be chief of service (see above, p. 30) and while Montgomery's seniority had been a factor in his appointment, the seniority principle did not consistently apply during World War II. Still, Kellogg could probably have secured the appointment had he desired it. Waitt Interv, 13 May 61.

[16] CWS SOS History.

Center and a Supply Division section chief moved out to establish chemical sections in two newly activated base sections. Maj. Frederick E. Powell, another section chief, and seven company-grade officers went from Supply Division to establish chemical sections in general depots and chemical branch depots. Since three other Supply Division section chiefs had gone to the TORCH forces, newly arrived lieutenants filled most supply division staff positions.[17]

First Reorganization

On 9 November 1942 the War Department notified the theater headquarters that Colonel Montgomery, who had been appointed chemical officer in the War Department Air Forces Headquarters, would not be returning to the European theater. The theater commander appointed Colonel Rowan chief chemical warfare officer and assigned him to theater headquarters in London. Thus, Rowan officially became resident at theater headquarters and the position of CWS representative was automatically abolished. Rowan appointed MacArthur his deputy and executive officer.[18] While General Porter had not had a hand in Rowan's appointment, he was well satisfied with it.[19] Rowan's qualifications were good. At 48, he was a year younger than the average age of the ETO technical services chiefs. He held the same permanent rank, lieutenant colonel, as all but one of his peers. At the time of his appointment he held the same temporary rank as three of the service chiefs—the four others having attained general officer rank. Like most other senior CWS officers, Rowan had World War I experience, as assistant gas officer and gas officer of the division in which General Lee had been chief of staff. He was a chemist, a graduate of Yale University, the Chemical Warfare School, and the Army Industrial College. Early in his Army career, Rowan had been marked as an expert on industrial mobilization in the chemical field, and he had served several tours, including one in the Office of the Assistant Secretary of War, in positions relating to that specialty. He had also had assignments in war planning, in chemical technical work, and in troop training, and

---

[17] (1) *Ibid.* (2) History, Sup Div CWS Hq SOS ETOUSA (hereafter cited as History, Sup Div, 42–43). ETO Admin 545A Cml Warfare.
[18] CWS SOS History.
[19] Porter Interv, 24 Aug 61.

he had served a 4-year tour as assistant military attaché in Berlin at the beginning of the Nazi period.[20]

A week after Rowan's appointment ETOUSA clarified and regularized the status of the theater CWS. ETOUSA assigned specific duties and functions to the CWS office at Cheltenham under the control of SOS. These included supervision of all CWS supply activities across the board from requirements, purchasing, and manufacture through storage and issue and maintenance and repair to transportation and shipping as well as supervision of CW training for SOS troops, and CWS administration within SOS.[21] The specification of duties at Cheltenham and the additional provision that he could transfer personnel needed in his theater headquarters office to provide planning, policy, training, technical, and intelligence services from Cheltenham or the London SOS offices, left Rowan free to organize his office as the situated dictated. On 18 November he submitted his proposals to G–3, ETOUSA, and on 23 November published the approved pattern in Office of the Chief Chemical Warfare Officer, ETOUSA, Office Order No. 1. MacArthur officially resumed the post of Chief, Operations and Training Division, which in fact he had never left, in addition to his duties as executive officer and deputy. Lt. Col. Walter M. Scott's position as Chief, Technical Division, was affirmed, and he was given supervision of a liaison officer who had been stationed at the British chemical warfare experimental center at Porton. Rowan named Maj. Roy LeCraw to head a new Administrative Division. Captain Tarr, 1 officer, and 2 civilian clerks were to form an Intelligence Section, primarily an office of record since Colonel Zanetti continued to handle intelligence, within the Administrative Division. The total complement of Rowan's theater headquarters office, besides himself, was 12 officers, 5 enlisted men, and 5 civilians.[22]

The November 1942 reorganization of the CWS ETOUSA produced an organization similar to the one suggested in the manual for the office of a theater chemical officer. The situation of the CWS and the theater itself was not a "book" situation. The theater was active logistically but its strategic destination was more in doubt than it had

[20] (1) CMLHO Biographical Sketches: Brig Gen Hugh W. Rowan. (2) Ruppenthal, *Logistical Support,* I, 1–10.
[21] ETOUSA GO 59, 16 Nov 42.
[22] (1) OCCWO ETO Off Order 1, 23 Nov 42. ETO Admin 544 Cml Warfare. (2) CWS SOS History.

been before the North African invasion. The lines of the theater commands were not clear and no chief of service could be positive about the precise character and scope of his service's mission. In Rowan's case, one element of his office, his Supply Division, was located ninety miles away from him under the jurisdiction of a command which might be considered an SOS field organization. A "book" solution to these problems of communications, relationships, and supervision within the CWS ETO would have been to designate the Supply Division as a communications zone chemical section, but when the SOS command at Cheltenham decided upon this action it served only to further confuse the issue of mission and supervision. Neither Rowan's London office nor the Cheltenham branch was prepared to operate as a separate entity under the prevailing theater pattern.

On 18 October 1942 when Supply Division absorbed Requirements Division, Colonel Johnson supervised eleven CWS officers and twenty-two enlisted men in Cheltenham. He also supervised the procurement and reverse lend-lease activities of Major Wright and his assistant in London. Support of the North African operation and activation of a logistics system in the United Kingdom kept this staff fully occupied.[23] After the reorganization of Rowan's London office and just before Johnson's transfer to the North African forces, the Cheltenham SOS headquarters designated Johnson as Montgomery's successor as Chief Chemical Warfare Officer, SOS, and renamed the CWS Supply Division as the SOS Chemical Warfare Section.[24] Johnson took the position that the SOS order was meaningless. Rowan was clearly Montgomery's successor, and he considered himself as Rowan's assistant. He furthermore lacked the staff and the authority in the field to establish a communications zone (SOS) chemical section. While his office had the operating functions of determining matériel requirements, preparing requisitions on the United States, and directing distribution of chemical supplies within the theater, its functions were more nearly those of a supply policy division in the office of a theater chief chemical officer than they were the functions of a theater supply and distribution command chemical section. Also, if Johnson had attempted to establish a communications zone chemical section, he would have deprived Rowan of the direct control of chemical supply

[23] History, Sup Div, 42–43.
[24] SOS ETO GO 80, 10 Dec 42.

since Rowan had no supply policy element in his London office.[25]
The only outcome of the SOS order was the establishment of the
largely inactive Cheltenham element of the CWS Operations and
Training Division as the Training Branch, Supply Division. A lieutenant was assigned to head the Training Branch and he was allotted
one part-time adviser and one part-time assistant. The branch was
assigned the function of supervising chemical training within SOS
ETOUSA.[26]

Major LeRoy, who succeeded to the position of SOS chemical warfare officer when Johnson was designated Chemical Officer, Mediterranean Base Section, North African Theater of Operations (NATO),
in December, made no change in policy. Indeed, LeRoy experienced
enough difficulty in staffing Supply Division without trying to extend
the scope of his activities. He was the only field-grade CWS officer
left in Cheltenham, and he had no captains on his immediate staff of
fourteen officers. His executive officer, Lt. Arthur T. Hingle, also
served as Chief, Statistical Section. Lt. Ingalls S. Bradley headed both
the Operations and Service Sections while another lieutenant was
Chief, Processing Section, and assistant in the Service Section. LeRoy
did not staff prescribed subsections for salvage, maintenance, impregnating, and filling plants in order to concentrate manpower in the
requirements, control, transportation, and issue areas.[27] Such concentration of effort was demanded in order to meet the needs of the North
African forces, but late in 1942 and early in 1943 when chemical
supply requirements for North Africa were increasingly met by direct
shipment from the United States, the need for concentration in the
same areas did not lessen because now the task of top priority was
preparing the European theater for gas warfare. The first question
raised in connection with theater gas warfare preparedness was that
of the requirement for chemical offensive and defensive materials and
service troops. Once requirements had been estimated, it was necessary
to plan storage and distribution within the theater.

---

[25] Interv, Hist Off with Col Leonard M. Johnson, USA (Ret.), 18 Aug 59.

[26] History of the Tng Div CWS Hq SOS ETOUSA, 27 Jul 42–31 Dec 43 (hereafter cited as History, Tng Div SOS). ETO Admin 545A Cml Warfare.

[27] (1) History, Sup Div, 42–43. (2) CWS SOS ETO Memo 19, 20 Dec 42, sub: Assignment of Pers. SOSCW 200.3 (19 Sep 42)SD, in ETO Admin 545A Cml Warfare.

Gas Warfare Planning

Rowan's staff had completed most of the basic work on a comprehensive gas warfare plan for the European theater before the War Department letter requiring such a plan was received.[28] Kellogg and his staff had prepared air force supply and storage estimates for the offensive portion of the plan. Late in 1942 LeRoy took a draft of the ETO plan to Washington where he discussed it in detail with General Porter's staff and exchanged information on theater and stateside preparations. Later OCCWS referred the draft plan to the chemical liaison officer on the OPD staff.[29] But since the ETO plan was predicated on the vast expansion of the theater for a continental invasion, as yet uncertain, it could only be brought to an indefinite conclusion.

Policy and strategy were in the making. The Allied leaders decided at the January Casablanca Conference to revive the build-up in the United Kingdom and took a number of actions during 1943 to flesh out that decision.[30] In November 1942 the Combined Chiefs of Staff had briefly turned their attention to gas warfare and now an Allied as well as a United States policy was emerging. This policy required: (1) a co-operative American and British effort aimed at arranging the defensive preparedness of all United Nations troops; and (2) the accumulation of sufficient toxic munitions to make immediate retaliation possible should the enemy initiate gas warfare anywhere in the world.[31]

The Second Reorganization

In connection with the determination of Allied policy on chemical warfare and in order to evaluate the status of chemical warfare preparedness among American troops, General Porter and Brig. Gen. Charles E. Loucks of his staff journeyed to England in March of 1943, and from there went on to North Africa. Loucks, writing his own

---

[28] Ltr, TAG to CG ETOUSA et al., 19 Dec 42, sub: Theater Plans for Cml Warfare. AG 381 (12-18-42) OB-S-E-M.

[29] Draft Plan, Hq ETO, Jan 43, sub: Theater Plans for Cml Warfare (noted: "by hand from Major LeRoy"), with cover Memo, CCWS to Maj F. G. Schmitt, WDGS, 5 May 43, sub: Tentative ETO Plan. CWS SPCVO 381, ETO.

[30] Ruppenthal, Logistical Support, I, ch. III.

[31] See Brophy and Fisher, Organizing for War, ch. IV.

GENERAL PORTER AND TOP-RANKING CHEMICAL OFFICERS IN LONDON, 1943. *(Left to right) General Porter, General Loucks, Colonel Kellogg, Colonel Rowan, Colonel MacArthur, and Colonel Zanetti.*

and Porter's impressions, advised OCCWS on several European theater problems and developments. The two officers found that the ETO had enough supplies for the force then in the theater, but they considered some of the items from the United States poor in quality.[32] The theater organization situation, they believed, was unsatisfactory. It appeared to them that "the Commanding General, Army Service Forces in Great Britain [sic] is entirely independent of the Commanding General, European Theater of Operations. The latter is dependent on the former for the supply but does not function as his superior."[33] Officially, the theater commander, now Lt. Gen. Frank M. Andrews, certainly functioned as General Lee's superior, but Loucks's words were probably intended to describe the *de facto* rather than the *de jure*

[32] *Ibid.*, pp. 100–101.
[33] Ltr, Gen Loucks to All Concerned [OCCWS], 23 Apr 43, sub: Inspection of Cml Warfare Activities in Great Britain. CWS SPCWS 319.1 (Cml Warfare Activities in Great Britain).

situation with respect to the CWS. The import of these remarks was that Rowan, despite his official status as theater chief chemical warfare officer, could in fact work only through Lee under whose jurisdiction his office fell. Consequently, he had no direct channel of communication and authority through which he might, in the words of the manual, exercise "general technical supervision over his service as a whole." [34] Such supervision was vital. Although the European theater was active at the time only in the air war, the greatest threat of gas warfare initiation was posed by the known German industrial chemical potential. The heavy concentration of American and British strength in the United Kingdom and the proposed build-up of men and materials there presented to the Germans excellent targets for vesicant gases. Germany was unlikely to launch a gas attack on the United Kingdom since she had not done so in the great blitz bombings of 1940–41 and since she would fear retaliation. But no chances should be taken, from the CWS point of view, by failing to build up a retaliatory potential. Developing such a potential, laying the defensive and offensive plans, and co-ordinating CWS operations in the theater demanded that Rowan have some direct channel through which to operate.

Porter's solution for the organizational impasse was to suggest that "the officer occupying the position of chemical officer for the theater commander" take the initiative in securing the co-operation and co-ordination of all the principal chemical officers in the theater. In other words, he proposed using the informal channels of personal and technical correspondence and communication among officers of the same service, known as technical channels, in place of formal command channels. Porter further suggested that he would personally elicit such co-operation. It is interesting to note that Loucks did not refer to the theater chief chemical warfare officer nor to the chief of service. In a listing of personnel, he cited Rowan as "Chemical Officer, Army Service Forces" and "for the present . . . also the staff chemical officer for the European Theater of Operations." [35]

Clearly, while Porter and Loucks accepted Rowan as theater chief chemical officer, they were not prepared to acknowledge that there was a theater chief of the CWS. Rowan was, as he had been from the previous November, Chief Chemical Warfare Officer, ETOUSA. In

---

[34] FM 100–10, 9 Dec 40.
[35] Ltr, Loucks to [OCCWS], 23 Apr 43.

the same month of Porter's visit, the theater commander ordered SOS headquarters back from Cheltenham. He relocated the service chiefs in SOS.[36] The fiction of a separate chemical section in Cheltenham was thereby dropped, and Rowan officially became Chemical Officer, SOS ETOUSA. Neither of these positions fitted the manual definition of the chief of service nor did they compare to the positions which Fries had held. Rowan, accepting Porter's advice, decided to make his position as theater chief chemical officer equivalent to that of chief salesman for such services and supplies as the CWS could contribute to the war effort in the theater. He found it necessary to employ his own prestige and ability to persuade commanders that it was in their best interest to be prepared against gas warfare, and to use smoke, flame, and chemical mortars. Porter was right in his observation that Rowan did not have the usual channels of a theater staff officer; Rowan could seldom speak with the authority of the theater commander as Fries had done.[37] Indeed, he could sometimes not speak with the authority of his other and more immediate commander, General Lee. Lee, for example did not authorize his chiefs of service to operate within his field commands, the base sections, chiefly because base section commanders complained that the service chiefs interfered in their command procedures.[38] The service chiefs did most of their volume business, supply, through the base sections and were therefore required to control a part of the operation. Rowan solved this problem by using technical channels to base section chemical officers and by frequently meeting with these officers to resolve CWS difficulties.[39]

The looseness of control within the theater organization and within the SOS which created so many problems for the technical services and particularly for the CWS was by no means peculiar to the European theater. Under the principle of "unity of command" General Marshall advocated placing theater and supreme commanders in a position of controlling all forces in their area. Probably as an extension of this principle he gave the theater and supreme commanders broad

---

[36] Ruppenthal, *Logistical Support*, I, 160–63.

[37] Rowan Interv, 28 Sep 58.

[38] Ruppenthal, *Logistical Support*, I, 168–71.

[39] Ltr, Col Ferris U. Foster, USAR, to Hist Off, 13 Oct 59. Colonel Foster was Chemical Officer, Southern Base Section, in the United Kingdom.

discretionary powers.[40] Perhaps as an extension of the delegation concept or perhaps as simply a reaffirmation of the normal staff and command doctrine propounded in the period between the wars, theater and subordinate commanders tended to de-emphasize the operating and co-ordinating functions that members of their special staffs could perform for their own services. Dual exercise of staff and command functions, as permitted by regulations,[41] became virtually unknown, at least in the CWS. As logical and necessary as was the emphasis on command authority and control, it did not make any easier the operation and control of a service which fitted neither into staff nor command lines. Fries had found it necessary to be a salesman in 1918, but, since he controlled CWS staff officers down to the division level, he had a better means than Rowan, two decades later, of conducting his sales campaign.[42] Rowan perforce substituted liaison between his office and the chemical and command elements of the various theater commands for control of his chemical subordinates as a means of selling chemical warfare munitions and services.[43]

Rowan's problems were many in molding his staff to constant liaison with the British, with the ground and air forces, and with the zone of interior. In addition he possessed SOS supply and liaison duties which would normally have devolved upon a communications zone chemical officer. He still lacked officers in sufficient numbers and with sufficient rank to handle all liaison and operating duties.

The April Reorganization

When General Porter left the theater, Rowan asked him to carry back to Washington a list of proposals for less hurried consideration.

---

[40] (1) Forrest C. Pogue, *The Supreme Command*, UNITED STATES ARMY IN WORLD WAR II (Washington, 1954), pp. 41–42. (2) Maurice Matloff and Edwin M. Snell, *Strategic Planning for Coalition Warfare, 1941–1942*, UNITED STATES ARMY IN WORLD WAR II (Washington, 1953), pp. 123–24, 196–97, 262–63. (3) Maurice Matloff, *Strategic Planning for Coalition Warfare, 1943–1944*, UNITED STATES ARMY IN WORLD WAR II (Washington, 1959), pp. 102–05. (4) Cline, *Operations Division*, pp. 21–22, 161–62, 184, 293–94.

[41] WD FM 101–5, 19 Aug 40.

[42] See above, ch. I.

[43] Some CWS officers objected to the point of view that declared "selling" necessary and objected to the use of the term *selling*. These officers believed that the relationship of each CWS special staff officer to his commander was the only important relationship so far as the CWS was concerned. It was the duty of each special staff officer to suggest the employment of CWS munitions and units to his commander when appropriate. No control within the CWS was required, from their point of view, as long as technical information could be disseminated through technical channels. (Col MacArthur, Comments on draft of this volume, 10 Apr 61.)

These proposals related to Rowan's desire to increase the strength and prestige of his immediate office in order better to perform both liaison and operating functions. Foremost on this list was a request for the return of Colonel Johnson from the North African theater or the dispatch of a well-qualified lieutenant colonel to head his Supply Division. Rowan also asked for four or five majors, high-ranking captains, or low-ranking lieutenant colonels with staff experience and training. He further asked that Col. James H. Defandorf and an officer assistant, who had recently been assigned to his office to work on medical liaison and the new, and then secret, work on defense against biological warfare, not be charged against his allotment since their work was on a special project basis and since he desperately needed the spaces.[44] The request for Johnson or a substitute was not intended to disparage Major LeRoy whom Rowan later called "my very best supply officer," but it was intended to point up the fact that LeRoy was still the only field-grade supply officer available and that the important supply operation needed more rank and prestige.[45] The request for majors, captains, or lieutenant colonels was necessary because the CWS needed field-grade officers for staff positions, but the space allotment was such that Rowan could not risk taking a full colonel or a lieutenant colonel about to be promoted.[46]

Porter's reply to Rowan's requests demonstrates that Rowan did not yet realize how weak the ties between the theater CWS and its parent service had become with the growing strength of ASF, OPD, and the theater organizations. Porter pointed out that the matter of Johnson's transfer from the North African to the European theater was out of his hands: it could only be handled officially by intertheater request. Porter could and did attempt to smooth this process by asking a chemical officer in North Africa to intercede in favor of the transfer, but nothing came of this attempt. On the matter of Colonel Defandorf's status and on that of securing additional staff officers for Rowan, Porter's hands were equally tied since the status of officers within the theater as well as requests for additional personnel were considered to be within the province of the theater commander. Porter agreed to evaluate qualifications of officers to be sent upon receipt of the official

[44] Memo [Rowan for Porter], n.d., sub: Things for General Porter's Attention Upon His Return to the U.S. CWS 314.7 Personal Ltr Files.

[45] Personal Ltr, Rowan to Gen Waitt, ACCWS for Field Opns, 22 Jul 43.

[46] Personal Ltr, Rowan to Gen Porter, CCWS, 22 Jul 43.

request, but even in this there was a strictly limiting factor—officers
with staff experience were hard to find in 1943.[47] It began to appear
that the solutions for staffing and prestige problems must be found in
the European theater.

In April 1943 Rowan reorganized his own office to reflect the
expanding responsibilities of the CWS ETO and for better liaison. He
took the Intelligence Section from the Administration Division and
made it a division with Maj. Philip R. Tarr, recently promoted, as
chief. The creation of a new division was no duplication of Colonel
Zanetti's efforts. Zanetti specialized in strategic intelligence and intelligence liaison with the British and with the continental United
States while Tarr assumed the growing burden of chemical tactical
intelligence, which also involved liaison with the British but at a
different level. The Intelligence Division continued to process attaché
reports for Colonel Zanetti.[48] Lt. Col. Maurice H. Wright, also recently
promoted, headed a new Supply Liaison Division whose chief function
was to effect co-ordination between London, where broad supply policy
was determined in the Operations and Training Division, and Cheltenham, where direction of all requirements and supply operations
remained. Wright's procurement and reciprocal-aid duties were delegated to an assistant with the title of branch chief. The Administration
Division, now headed by Lt. Col. Chester O. Blackburn, included three
office service branches and one branch to handle personnel for the
CWS as a whole. The Technical Division, with its important liaison
functions, was assigned more higher ranking officers than the other
divisions: Colonel Scott remained as chief; Colonel Defandorf headed
the Special Projects Branch; Lt. Col. Melville F. Perkins handled liaison
with Porton, the British chemical research establishment, and the CWS
Laboratory, for which a chemical laboratory company had not yet
been received; Lt. Col. Thomas H. Magness, Jr., was in charge of
Offensive Munitions Branch while a captain headed the Defensive
Munitions Branch. In Operations and Training Branch, Colonel
MacArthur had a Training Branch headed by a lieutenant colonel,
who was also his executive officer, an Equipment Branch, and a Plans
Branch.[49]

[47] Personal Ltr, Porter to Rowan, 3 Jun 43.
[48] (1) History, CWS SOS. (2) Ltr, Col J. Enrique Zanetti, CmlC, USAR (Ret.), to Hist Off,
26 Jun 60.
[49] (1) OCCWO ETO Off Order 5, 22 Apr 43. (2) OCCWO ETO Off Order 7, 12 May 43.
Both in ETO Admin 544 Cml Warfare.

LeRoy, now a lieutenant colonel, had 20 officers in his Supply Division, but he still lacked field-grade assistants. His Executive Officer and Chief, Statistical (requirements and control) Branch, and his Operations Branch chief had been promoted to captain along with the Transportation and Issue Section chief. The Processing (formerly Impregnating) and Training Branches were still one-man branches while the Service Branch had a chief and an assistant. One-man branches were common in the London office where five branches were wholly unstaffed. The London office was assigned 22 officers, three of whom were on duty with the Administrative Branch of the Administration Division at Cheltenham. In all, Rowan had 41 officers, 28 enlisted men, and 16 civilians.[50] While 14 officers had been added since the previous fall and while section prestige had increased, mostly through promotions, both members and prestige were still low in relation to the tremendous expansion in theater activities contemplated in the year before the D-day target, which was established in May. Rowan had a personal prestige problem in that the other technical service chiefs had all been advanced to general officer grade.

The First Gas Warfare Plan

An example of the contemplated expansion of theater activities was the issuance, also in April 1943, of the first theater gas warfare plan. Enough strategic information had become available by that time to complete the draft plan of the previous December. The final plan, personally signed by General Andrews, called for an eight months' supply of aircraft gas munitions and a four months' supply of ground gas munitions. The theater requested, in the event of gas warfare, at least 2 chemical combat battalions per corps, 40 air chemical service and supply units, 30 ground chemical service and supply units plus 5 smoke generator companies for ground service, and 23 SOS service and supply units plus 5 smoke generator companies for the communications zone. It also requested 3 base section staffs totaling 9 officers and 30 enlisted men, 75 officers and 150 enlisted men for depot administration, and an SOS headquarters staff of 93 officers and 339 enlisted men. Pointed out in the plan was the fact that the theater was then

---

[50] OCCWO ETO Off Order 5, 22 Apr 43. ETO Admin 544 Cml Warfare.

capable only of passive defense and individual protection against gas warfare.[51]

The theater and air forces chemical sections modified the plan's supply and troop build-up schedule to make it accord with the current theater build-up level and the nongas warfare situation. They then submitted requisitions against the modified schedule, but while cargo flow began to increase, needed supplies, especially toxic munitions, were not forthcoming. A month after the submission of the theater plan, Maj. Gen. Ira C. Eaker, Commanding General, Eighth Air Force, forwarded a strong plea for an interim toxic munitions supply plan.[52] By the end of July, General Eaker's plan had been approved for munitions shipment. But long before the approval was received—in fact, before the original Eighth Air Force interim plan had been dispatched—Rowan had become concerned about War Department slowness in handling theater requests and particularly about the burden placed upon the theater by the necessity of planning and replanning. Rowan expounded the theater point of view to General Waitt, Assistant Chief, CWS, for Field Operations, early in May 1943. He considered it to be the function of the War Department "to assist overseas Commands, and not to attempt to sit in judgment upon their actions and requisitions." He further indicated that he believed the policy of requiring theater commanders to disclose detailed plans of contemplated operations in justification for requisitions of an unusual nature to be an unsound one.[53] Waitt replied that he, personally, agreed completely, and he gave assurance that his own office would not attempt to "sit in judgment on theater requests or actions." He asked only that the theater keep his office well enough informed so that the War Department CWS might "go to bat for you." He pointed out that the War Department higher echelons had to know enough about plans of contemplated operations to act intelligently on requests.[54]

The higher echelons which Waitt defended were not always as reasonable as he was in considering theater requests. Porter, Waitt,

[51] Ltr, CG ETO to TAG, 17 Apr 43, sub: Gas Warfare Plans, ETO. ETO AG 381; also in OPD 385 CWP.

[52] (1) Ltr, CG Eighth AF to CG ETO, 20 May 43, sub: Eighth AF Preparedness for Offensive Cml Warfare, with 1st Ind, CG ETO to TAG, 9 Jun 43. Eighth AF 353, ETO AG 381 x 475.9 MDGS. (2) 2d Ind, TAG to CG ETO, 30 Jul 43. AG 381 (20 May 43) OB–S–E.

[53] Personal Ltr, Rowan to Waitt, 5 May 43. CWS ETO CWO–400/32–Sec.

[54] Personal Ltr, Waitt to Rowan, 21 Jun 43. CWS SPCVO 016 APO 887.

and Rowan were satisfied that the CWS in the United States was doing everything in its power to assist the theater CWS in meeting its obligations as to organization, planning, and supply.[55] Waitt placed the blame for delays and for modification of theater plans on ASF.[56] While approximately ten weeks was not an extraordinary amount of time for War Department action on the Eighth Air Force request, this request was only one of a stream of Eighth Air Force schedules and plans which had followed from the original plan made in April 1942 when Kellogg's section was still in the United States. In many other cases, such as the projects for continental operations begun in mid-1943, the processing delays seemed longer than final results warranted. The theater CWS found itself in a frustrating position: the theater staff was to plan in detail within the framework of the basic plans laid down in Washington because the War Department would not invade the theater prerogative by doing detailed planning; but the War Department apparently felt no compunctions about redoing the theater's detailed planning. A like difficulty existed in organization. The prewar theory of theater organization, under which the theater commander channeled authority through his technical services chiefs as well as his tactical commanders, had been discarded in the ETO under War Department pressure so that the planned channels of authority no longer remained, yet the War Department did not consider the provision of a new authority channel as being within its province.

The June Organization Plan

In June the ETO SOS chief of administration asked Rowan to submit his plans for handling the theater build-up load. Rowan's plan reflected his desire to meet both problems. If he could have direct control of the theater CWS organization, he wanted enough officers of sufficient rank to control it by persuasion. If he must do the planning which, according to the manual, should have been done in the United States, and if he must perform the operation normally the responsibility of the communications zone, he wanted the staff to handle planning and operating functions. Rowan replied by submitting a comprehensive organizational and functional justification for a staff of 100 officers.

[55] (1) Porter Interv, 24 Aug 61. (2) Waitt Interv, 13 May 61. (3) Rowan Interv, 28 Sep 58.
[56] (1) Waitt Interv, 13 May 61. (2) Waitt Comments on draft of this volume, 5 Jan 61.

He asked for a deputy and two assistant chiefs but suggested that the position of deputy and one of the assistant chief positions could be held by one officer. While MacArthur had in fact been deputy since August of 1942, he had in title been Executive Officer and Chief, Operations and Training Division. Rowan proposed that he should officially be deputy and assistant chief for plans and training. As mentioned above, Rowan had become "outside man" for his organization, so that he needed a deputy who could function in his absence. He also needed an additional executive officer who would be "inside man" and function in his or his deputy's stead when both were absent. The second assistant chief was to be the operating supervisor of supply and service functions. Since half of Rowan's staff was to be occupied with these functions and since this portion of the staff was located at Cheltenham, he felt that the position warranted the assignment of a general officer. Considering the growth of the technical services within the theater and considering that the CWS ETO was destined to become fourth ranking among the seven technical services in the operation of general storage space and second ranking in the operation of ammunition storage and shop space, and further considering that the Cheltenham echelon was charged with the chemical warfare training of about 375,000 SOS troops, the establishment of an assistant chief position in the general-officer grade was not unreasonable.[57]

Since Rowan planned for his deputy to hold the position of assistant chief for plans and training, there seems to have been little reason for establishment of the second position of assistant chief except the psychological factor of acknowledging the unique position of the CWS chief as tactical adviser in chemical warfare to the theater commander and to all theater forces. A subsidiary reason for establishing the second position could have been to parallel the OCCWS organization which had recently been revised to provide assistant chiefs for matériel and for field operations.[58] In effect, the two assistant chiefs in the ETO would perform comparable functions to the two in OCCWS. Only one officer, a lieutenant colonel, to act in an executive capacity, was to be assigned directly to the assistant chief for plans and training.[59]

[57] (1) Study, Rowan [to Chief, Admin SOS], Functions and Duties of the OCCWO, 13 and 17 Jun 43. ETO Admin 545A Cml Warfare. (2) Ruppenthal, Logistical Support, I, p. 128.
[58] Brophy and Fisher, Organizing for War, pp. 101–04.
[59] Functions and Duties of the OCCWO.

Six of the nine divisions proposed were to be organized on the pattern
already established in the Technical Division—colonels and lieutenant
colonels would primarily perform liaison and inspection functions
outside the Office of the Chief Chemical Warfare Officer. These
divisions were: Technical; Plans and Training; Intelligence; Medical
Liaison; Supply Liaison and CWS Representative to AC of S, G–5,
ETOUSA; and SOS Training (at Cheltenham). The liaison divisions were to contain branches or sections staffed by lower ranking
officers and enlisted men to perform planning, supervisory, and reporting duties. Colonel Wright had already been appointed CWS representative to ACofS, G–5, ETOUSA, in addition to his duties as Chief,
Supply Liaison Division. His duty as representative consisted of liaison
with the Allied forces planning command (Chief of Staff to the Supreme Allied Commander [Designate] COSSAC). The SOS CWS
Training Division, to be headed by a major, was to operate under the
assistant chief for supply.[60] The SOS CWS Training Division was not
to duplicate the training policy role of the training element in London,
but was to provide staff supervision for chemical training within SOS.

Rowan meant for two of the remaining three divisions to handle
internal administrative functions, but both of these divisions, Administration in London and Supply Administration in Cheltenham, were
also to have advisory roles with respect to the assignment of CWS
personnel in the theater and in SOS, respectively. Rowan and LeRoy
redesigned Supply Division to re-emphasize the position that this
division had always held as an independent CWS supply and service
agency which LeRoy operated, on a small scale, under Somervell's and
Lee's principle of centralized control and decentralized operation.
Supply liaison at levels co-ordinate with and above SOS was to remain
in Wright's hands in both of his capacities. Liaison at SOS level was
to be accomplished by the division itself. To supplement the division
liaison at subordinate levels, Rowan and LeRoy wished to create an
Inspection Branch headed by a lieutenant colonel who would be a
troubleshooter for field problems and carry on technical inspection
of field installations. The pattern of liaison, and indeed the organizational plan of the whole division, demonstrated how free a hand the
CWS had in determining its own supply concepts and procedures.
The division was to have, and in most cases already had, branches or

[60] *Ibid.*   (2) OCCWO ETO Off Order 8, 20 May 43. ETO Admin 544 Cml Warfare.

sections to determine requirements, to control matériel, to ordain storage, issue, and transportation procedures, and to regulate mainte- nance and services such as processing.[61] In sharp contrast to the prac- tice in the Pacific areas, policy could originate within the division or with the chief chemical warfare officer; higher level direction was minimal.

As far as his own office was concerned, Rowan had already imple- mented a part of the organization of the June plan, since that plan did not differ greatly in pattern from the reorganization of April. Some features of the new plan, such as the official designation of Colonel MacArthur as deputy and the appointment of an executive officer, were implemented piecemeal. The post of assistant chief chemi- cal warfare officer for supply was established, but Rowan could find no one to fill it. Several colonels arrived in the theater during 1943, but they were either already assigned to the staffs of field organizations or were needed in the rapidly proliferating field headquarters. Rowan was forced to use captains, majors, and some lieutenant colonels in positions he had intended to fill with lieutenant colonels and colonels. For liaison and inspection he sometimes sought the assistance of field chemical officers. He was still short of manpower. At the end of 1943 his officer allotment totaled forty-six. In Cheltenham he lost Colonel LeRoy who was returned to the United States under a policy of rotating officers with field experience. Major Powell, who had filled assignments both in Cheltenham and in the SOS depot system, became LeRoy's replacement.[62]

The importance of the June plan does not lie in its implementation, although it was implemented at about half strength and became the basic pattern for the remainder of the war. Its importance lies in the fact that its concept and scope demonstrate the changed character of the overseas CWS in World War II. It represents the anomaly of World War II: the technician and the specialist were taking a back seat in the war which was being touted as the technicians' and specialists' war. The technician, the specialist, and the logistician, had achieved positions of great importance in the warfare of World War I. In the period between the wars most CWS technicians, specialists, and logis-

---

[61] Functions and Duties of the OCCWO.

[62] (1) History, Sup Div, 42–43. (2) Ltrs, Rowan to Porter and Waitt, 22 Jul 43. (3) Ltr, Waitt (in ETO) to Col Herrold E. Brooks, Chief, Pers Div OCCWS, 13 Sep 43. CWS 314.7 Pers Files, ETO. (4) Ltr, Col Ernest Greene, USAR, to Hist Off, 22 Jan 60.

ticians had been led to believe that they would work with bureaulike unity. Strategy, plans, matériel, and personnel would emanate from OCCWS to be translated into the theater commander's policy by the theater chief chemical officer who would supervise execution at subordinate levels. More than a year's experience in the theater proved that the interposition of theater headquarters, OPD, and ASF between the theater CWS and OCCWS prevented OCCWS from accomplishing its planned direction. Theater emphasis on the discretion of the individual commander, plus the organizational setup, in effect demoted the special staff officer to the role of supply administrator whose control even in the supply field depended on his ability to institute and maintain decentralizing procedures. In the supply role Rowan and his staff fared very well despite the failure to acquire the personnel specified in the June plan. In the liaison role the failure to acquire the staff and rank indicated in the June plan threw the entire burden on Rowan and a few members of his staff. The Technical Division very successfully maintained liaison with the British in the research and development areas.[63] CWS officials also found the British very helpful in arranging reverse lend-lease for service and supply, areas in which Rowan and many members of his staff performed liaison.[64] In matters of policy, liaison with the British was excellent since Rowan was Porter's representative to the British policy group, the Inter-Service Chemical Warfare Committee.[65] It was in liaison with the American ground forces that difficulties arose. So small a staff with such varied duties could not maintain a regular ground forces liaison program. The partial solution for this problem was to emerge later during operations on the Continent.

Planning and Organization: 1944–45

By the end of 1943 the build-up in the ETO had reached a furious pace. All the CWS ETO supply installations and sections in the United Kingdom were firmly established and supplies, even the long-awaited toxic munitions, were coming in. In the SOS the base sections, the ports of debarkation, and selected general depots had working-strength chemical sections, and scarce chemical service units or detachments

---

[63] Interv, Hist Off with Col Thomas H. Magness, Jr., 5 May 59.
[64] Ltr, Gen Rowan to Hist Off, 8 Jul 60.
[65] Rowan Interv, 26 Sep 58.

were attached where necessary for operation. Arriving ground force organizations usually brought their own chemical sections.

Staff and Organization Changes

Many staff changes were made—some the result of organization and unit activations and some arising from a desire to have officers with theater experience in the United States. As noted above, Colonel LeRoy had for the latter reason returned to the United States in the fall of 1943. Colonel Kellogg had returned to the United States in July 1943 and his position as Chemical Officer, Eighth Air Force, had been assumed by Col. Harold J. Baum who subsequently became Chemical Officer, United States Strategic Air Forces in Europe (USSTAF).[66] One lieutenant colonel from Rowan's London staff also returned to the United States, while Colonel Blackburn left the Administration Division to become Chemical Officer, Ground Forces Replacement Command, in the theater.[67] Three field-grade officers arrived from the United States for duty in the London office.[68]

With the organization of several ground commands late in 1943, the build-up reached the point where defensive gas warfare planning for specific forces had to be undertaken with a probable cross-Channel mission in mind. The requirements portion of such specific planning depended upon the ground forces elements themselves, but Rowan's staff would be called on to co-ordinate planning and, more importantly, to translate plans and estimates into actual supply. The fact that supply lead time was running at about 180 days impressed Rowan's staff with the necessity of anticipating the requirements of ground forces planners as far ahead as possible. Just before leaving for an extensive briefing and conference tour in the United States late in December 1943, Rowan designated a transitional Planning Group within the Operations and Training Division to work under the direct supervision of the deputy chief chemical warfare officer, Colonel MacArthur. This group was, in addition to its planning duties, to absorb the functions of the Supply Liaison Division.[69] A few days later, MacArthur, acting chief chemical warfare officer, brought about

---

[66] History, Cml Sec Eighth AF.

[67] Interv, Hist Off with Lt Col Chester O. Blackburn, CmlC, USAR (Ret.), 21 Sep 59.

[68] Interv, Hist Off with Col Alexander Leggin, USAR, 13 Oct 61. Leggin served as Rowan's executive officer during this period.

[69] OCCWO ETO Off Order 21, 28 Dec 43. ETO Admin 544 Cml Warfare.

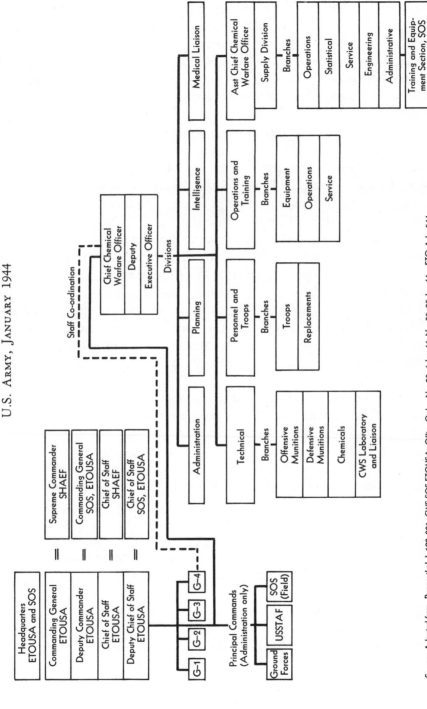

CHART 4—ORGANIZATION OF CHEMICAL WARFARE SERVICE SECTION, HEADQUARTERS. EUROPEAN THEATER OF OPERATIONS U.S. ARMY, JANUARY 1944

Source: Adapted from: Ruppenthal, I, 198–201; CWS SOS ETOUSA, Office Orders No. 23, 4 Jan 44, No. 25, 25 Jan 44. ETO Adm 544.

a realignment of the theater office. (*Chart 4*) The Planning Group became the Planning Division under Lt. Col. Albert C. Bilicke, with Maj. Arthur T. Hingle, who was moved up from Cheltenham, and another field-grade officer as his principal assistants. This division was given the task of determining broad troop and supply requirements for future operations. The parent Operations and Training Division had like responsibilities for current operations as well as for training supervision.[70]

The other divisions remained as indicated in the modified plan of June 1943, but a sign of the times was the appointment of Maj. Alexander Leggin, Executive Officer, OCCWO, ETO, to the added role of liaison officer to First United States Army Group (FUSAG). Leggin's verbal instructions were to initiate the formation of a chemical section and to start chemical planning for FUSAG, then organizing in the United Kingdom as the principal American ground forces headquarters.[71] Also, Maj. William Foley came from the American School Center to Cheltenham to head an SOS Training and Equipment Section, an upgrading of the Training Branch, Supply Division.[72] By the end of January it had become apparent that the Operations and Training Division could not handle all the detailed transactions concerning troops. A new Personnel Division was therefore established, and to it were assigned the personnel records functions of Administration Division.[73]

The Personnel Division had a number of individual changes to record. Col. Marshall Stubbs in January had moved from Ninth Air Force to establish the chemical section for and become the deputy assistant chief of staff, G–4, of Advance Section, Communications Zone (ADSEC), the mobile base section scheduled to operate directly behind the combat forces. ADSEC, as an important distribution agency and link between combat and SOS forces, was of considerable interest to the CWS ETO. The ability to discover ground forces chemical supply requirements and to meet them could well depend on the successful operation of the ADSEC Chemical Section. Maj. Ingalls S. Bradley of Supply Division soon joined Stubbs as his

---

[70] OCCWO ETO Off Order 23, 4 Jan 44. ETO Admin 544 Cml Warfare.

[71] (1) OCCWO ETO Off Order 22, 4 Jan 44. ETO Admin 544 Cml Warfare. (2) Leggin Interv, 13 Oct 61.

[72] OCCWO ETO Off Order 23, 4 Jan 44. ETO Admin 544 Cml Warfare.

[73] OCCWO ETO Off Orders 25 and 26, 25 Jan 44. ETO Admin 544 Cml Warfare.

assistant.[74] Leggin left his executive officer post in February formally to activate the FUSAG Chemical Section.[75] In March, after Rowan's return from the United States, MacArthur became FUSAG chemical officer with Leggin serving as his deputy. Col. Alfred C. Day, a Reserve officer and veteran of World War I's 1st Gas Regiment, who had been on temporary duty as chemical officer of the assault and amphibious training center in England, became Rowan's deputy.[76] Col. Roy C. Charron, another Reserve officer with World War I experience, arrived from the United States to assume, after briefly filling the long-vacant position of assistant chief at Cheltenham, the post of Chemical Officer, Forward Echelon, Communications Zone (FECOMZ). The Forward Echelon was essentially a planning headquarters, a smaller version of SOS itself, which was to plan for and provide logistical support to the combat forces on the Continent from D-day plus 41 to D plus 90 when the main headquarters of SOS, renamed Communications Zone (COMZ), was expected to be in operation on the Continent.[77] The CWS SOS–COMZ complement was filled in May by the arrival of Col. Hubert B. Bramlet, a Regular Army officer who had been commissioned in the CWS during World War I, to fill the position of assistant chief at Cheltenham.[78] (Chart 5)

The change in staff assignments and the addition of the ADSEC and FECOMZ Chemical Sections enabled the CWS ETO to operate more effectively within the theater. Officers entirely familiar with the theater CWS system, such as MacArthur, were now in key positions while the new chemical sections were created in new organizations designed within the theater to serve theater purposes. These organizations therefore had channels of communication, authority, and operations specially suited to theater needs. Thus FECOMZ was a planning headquarters with "built-in" liaison to the parent SOS.[79] ADSEC was

---

[74] Biographical Sketch, CMLHO: Maj Gen Marshall Stubbs. Thirty-seven years old at the time of his appointment, Stubbs was a Regular Army officer and a Military Academy graduate. Of the prominent chemical officers in the European theater, he was the first who was too young to have had World War I experience. (2) Opns History of ADSEC COMZ ETOUSA, Oct 43–10 Jul 45 (hereafter cited as History, ADSEC).

[75] OCCWO ETO Off Order 28, 16 Feb 44. ETO Admin 544 Cml Warfare.

[76] OCCWO ETO Off Order 33, 23 Mar 44. ETO Admin 544 Cml Warfare.

[77] (1) History, FECOMZ ETOUSA, From Inception to Termination (9 Feb to 7 Aug 44) (hereafter cited as History, FECOMZ). ETO Admin 136. (2) Personal Ltrs, Col Charron to Waitt, 2 Feb, 19 Mar 44. CWS 314.7 Pers Files, ETO, Feb 44–Dec 44.

[78] OCCWO ETO Off Order 42, 30 May 44. ETO Admin 544 Cml Warfare.

[79] History, FECOMZ.

CHART 5—ACTUAL DISTRIBUTION OF SERVICE AGENCIES AND COMBAT UNITS
CHEMICAL WARFARE SERVICE, EUROPEAN THEATER OF OPERATIONS, 1944–1945

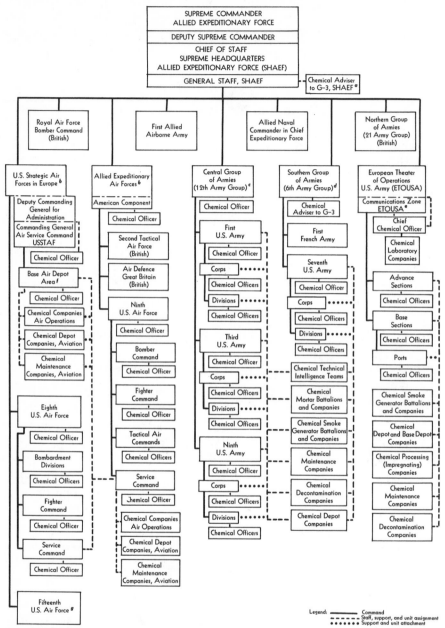

Legend:
——— Command
- - - - Staff, support, and unit assignment
• • • • • Support and unit attachment

a. Position abolished, October 1944.
b. January 1944 reorganization. Allied Expeditionary Air Forces abolished 15 Oct 44.
c. First and Ninth Armies attached to the Northern Group for periods in 1944–1945. Fifteenth Army added to 12th Army Group in 1945. Chemical Officer, 12th Army Group, conducted liaison with chemical officer (British), 21 Army Group.
d. As of December 1944.
e. Theater and Communications Zone (then Services of Supply) Headquarters combined, January 1944.
f. Base Air Depot Area supported Eighth and Ninth Air Force Service Commands in some functional areas.
g. Fifteenth Air Force under USSTAF operational control. Under administrative control Mediterranean Allied Air Forces.

Source: Pogue, Supreme Command, pp. 159, 262, 379, 428, 455; Ruppenthal, Logistical Support of the Armies, Vol. I, p. 199; Craven and Cate, Europe—TORCH to POINTBLANK, pp. 745, 753, 839; Craven and Cate, Europe—ARGUMENT to V–E Day, pp. 111, 398, 576.

a planning headquarters with "built-in" liaison to First Army (FUSA) and Third Army (TUSA), whose basic logistics planning it was handling and extending, as well as to SOS–COMZ, of which it was an organizational subordinate echelon.[80] The ground forces-CWS ties were therefore good.

First Army, whose chemical section was headed by Col. Joseph D. Coughlan, was to direct all American operations on the Continent in the beachhead period. FUSAG co-ordinated all ground planning, and a successor army group headquarters, as yet unannounced, was to take over control of First Army and Third Army when the "secret" Third became operational. Third Army chemical officer was Col. Edward C. Wallington.[81]

Air Forces liaison was more tenuous. Air Forces officers, probably as part of their bidding for a status independent of the Army, took the position that the theater and SOS headquarters had a ground forces jurisdiction only, even in logistics matters. Since Rowan and his staff were firmly identified with theater and SOS headquarters, they were doubly handicapped in approaching the Air Forces. The CWS situation in the Air Forces became worse when USSTAF combined its Ordnance and Chemical Sections under the ordnance officer, but Colonel Baum in USSTAF, Col. Joseph Triner, chemical officer in the Ninth Air Force, and Maj. Leonard C. Miller of Allied Expeditionary Air Forces (AEAF) managed to keep Rowan informed of their more important plans through their personal channels to the chief chemical warfare officer and his assistants.[82] After January 1944 the planning channel for the Air Forces was through the Supreme Headquarters, Allied Expeditionary Forces (SHAEF), rather than through theater headquarters. In January theater and SOS headquarters were combined with the staff serving in a dual capacity. While General Lee became deputy theater commander, the staff carefully defined their theater functions which they performed in General Eisenhower's name and their SOS functions which they carried out in General Lee's. Despite the careful definition, the activation of other operational and planning commands restricted the combined headquarters to administrative and

[80] History, ADSEC.

[81] Biographical Sketches, CMLHO. Coughlan and Wallington were senior Regular Army CWS officers. Both were graduates of the U.S. Military Academy, Class of 1915.

[82] (1) Interv, Hist Off with Col Leonard C. Miller, 2 Feb 60. (2) Rowan Interv, 26 Sep 58. (3) Rowan Comments 16 Dec 60.

supply matters and ultimately resulted in the predominance of logistic function.[83]

In March Col. Adrian St. John arrived in the theater and became the chemical representative on the SHAEF staff. Although Colonel Wright, as liaison officer to COSSAC, the SHAEF predecessor, had been on Rowan's staff, Colonel St. John did not report to Rowan. The air forces chemical officers co-ordinated their gas warfare planning with St. John. Organizational confusion resulted.[84] Even General Porter believed that Rowan was no longer the principal chemical officer in the theater. He was under the impression that St. John, who was at the time senior to Rowan, had been appointed "Chief Chemical Officer, SHAEF," and he asked Brig. Gen. Augustin M. Prentiss, who was on an observer mission to the theater, to indicate proper communications channels.[85] Prentiss replied that the confusion in the United States was understandable since many individuals in the theater were also confused, but he affirmed Rowan's position as theater chief of service, and St. John's as chemical adviser to G–3, SHAEF, and indicated that communications should be channeled through Rowan.[86] Rowan's status became more clearly defined upon his advancement to brigadier general on 25 May 1944.

During the three months of his European duty before the continental invasion, St. John assumed some of the gas warfare readiness planning responsibilities as appropriate to his assignment to the highest planning headquarters. He approved and staffed air forces operational readiness plans which included stocking toxics available for immediate retaliatory missions at operational airfields. He also secured the issuance of a SHAEF directive which required all commanders to make both offensive and defensive plans. Again, Porter was apparently under the impression that this directive had greater significance than it actually did.[87] The SHAEF directive was in fact only a slightly stronger restatement of a number of theater directives which had preceded it,

---

[83] Ruppenthal, *Logistical Support*, I, 195–201.

[84] SHAEF had special staff divisions in only three technical services areas, Signal, Engineer, and Medical. These were all combined staff branches whose roles outside their own headquarters were like those of inspectors general; they did not perform the functions of theater sections or services (Pogue, *Supreme Command, pages* 91–93). St. John was not in a special staff position. He was originally assigned as chemical adviser to G–4, SHAEF, and was shortly thereafter transferred to G–3 with the same title since little of his work had to do with logistics. (Personal Ltr, St. John to Porter, 28 Mar 44).

[85] Personal Ltr, Porter to Prentiss, 22 Mar 44.

[86] Personal Ltr, Prentiss to Porter, 14 Apr 44.

[87] Ltr, Porter to Prentiss, 22 Mar 44.

and the real key to readiness lay in the supply planning which was being handled by Rowan's office, the air forces chemical sections, and the chemical sections in FECOMZ, ADSEC, FUSAG, FUSA, and TUSA.

The liaison method of planning and the organizational confusion in the theater made chemical planning difficult at times and occasionally resulted in personal differences which normally occur in any organization, but both Rowan and St. John could informally handle problems as they arose. One problem was that Coughlan was reluctant to submit to direction and co-ordination by the FUSAG Chemical Section or by Rowan's staff. St. John managed to bring this matter to the attention of the FUSAG commander and planning co-ordination thereupon became effective. On the whole, both planning and actual preparations in the field proceeded apace.[88]

When Porter indicated to Prentiss that, according to the reports, unspecified, which he had received, something was amiss in ETO chemical activities Prentiss replied that he could find nothing wrong. Plans were complete, the staff was competent, the supply situation, at least for immediate needs, was good, and the chemical officers seemed to enjoy the confidence of higher authority.[89] In fact, Rowan felt that he had done precisely as Porter had recommended—he had "sold" his services to the theater forces.

General Porter got the same impression that Prentiss did when he arrived in the European theater shortly before the cross-Channel attack. He inspected gas warfare readiness in both ground and service commands. He found no reluctance to acknowledge Rowan as the theater chief chemical officer and he found theater forces well prepared, from a CWS point of view, for the operation they were about to undertake.[90]

On the Continent

American commanders and staff officers knew that the assault on the Normandy beaches provided the enemy with an ideal opportunity to inaugurate gas warfare. General Omar N. Bradley, then First Army commander and principal United States ground commander for the assault, later wrote that "even a light sprinkling of persistent gas on

[88] (1) Leggin Interv, 13 Oct 61. (2) MacArthur Interv, 19 Sep 61. (3) Interv, Hist Off with Col Maurice H. Wright, USAR (Ret.), 10 Jul 61.
[89] Prentiss to Porter, 14 Apr 44.
[90] Porter Interv, 24 Aug 61.

Omaha Beach could have cost us our footing there." [91] American intelligence experts believed that the German forces had the logistic capability to launch a gas attack although it was a comfort to know that their lack of aerial superiority made it unlikely that such an attack could be launched by aircraft. All assault forces wore antigas protective clothing and carried gas masks and other protective articles. While the adequacy of such protection was assured against known gases in a situation in which warning could be given, the danger of a high casualty rate was great in the event of surprise attack or the introduction of an unknown gas. Further, the adequacy of the warning, service, and retaliatory offensive systems could only be estimated.

First Army requested 3 chemical mortar battalions for retaliation and 4 chemical service companies to meet possible gas warfare. The 3 battalions, 1 chemical depot company, 1 chemical maintenance company, 1 smoke generator battalion headquarters and 4 companies, and 1 small detachment from a chemical laboratory company were assigned or attached to FUSA and scheduled for the assault echelons. The laboratory detachment and 3 chemical decontamination companies assigned to engineer special brigades joined the earliest assault waves with the mission of determining if gas was being used. These units were to identify the gas and take immediate protective measures. [92]

The first chemical staff sections ashore in Normandy were those in the headquarters of the engineer special brigades, the V and VII Corps, and the 1st, 29th, 4th, and 30th Divisions. Three officers of FUSA Chemical Section landed on 9 June, three days after D-day. They found the chemical supply situation adequate and the 30th Chemical Decontamination Company ready to provide artificial smoke protection if needed. The fear of enemy gas attack was still lively as demonstrated by several "gas scares," reports that the enemy had employed war gases. All such reports proved false. [93]

Since First Army was responsible for all logistics arrangements on the Continent in the early period, the first job was to establish dumps, especially dumps at which the chemical mortar battalions could draw ammunition. The initial supply of several chemical items, including

---

[91] General Omar N. Bradley, *A Soldier's Story* (New York: Henry Holt and Company, Inc., 1951), p. 279.

[92] (1) FUSA Rpt of Opns, 20 Oct 43–1 Aug 44, an. 17, Cml Warfare Sec. (2) Ian F. Fraser, Clifford L. Jones, and Hugh Williamson, Opn Rpt NEPTUNE, 30 Sep 44, pp. 38–39, 126. In CMLHO.

[93] FUSA Rpt of Opns, 20 Oct 43–1 Aug 44, an. 17.

ammunition, was being expended faster than anticipated. The FUSA Chemical Section and the assigned chemical service units handled these problems. Officers of the ADSEC Chemical Section, who had arrived a day after Coughlan and his assistants, assisted the FUSA section in these tasks.[94]

The ADSEC Chemical Section gradually assumed direction of the distribution functions in the areas nearest the beaches. The FUSA Chemical Section retained its direct interest in all chemical supply since FUSA did not relinquish supply control to ADSEC.[95] During July the FECOMZ, TUSA, and 12th Army Group Chemical Sections were established on the Continent as the headquarters of which they were part became established. FECOMZ never assumed operating responsibility and the members of its chemical section, like those of Third Army and 12th Army Group, acted as observers and reporters on the combat, supply, and service situations until early August when the main COMZ (formerly SOS) headquarters began to arrive and absorb FECOMZ. Members of the chemical section then assumed their planned operating roles. Third Army and 12th Army Group became operational on 1 August 1944 and MacArthur's chemical section became the senior chemical policy organization on the Continent pending the arrival of the remainder of Rowan's office.[96]

Rowan, Day, and St. John visited on the Continent during the beachhead and breakout period (June–August 1944), as did General Porter.[97] They found little evidence of any enemy intention to initiate gas warfare, but, as insurance the CWS sections and units ashore were striving to increase and improve the level of gas warfare protection by collecting and refurbishing discarded gas masks, by distributing decontaminating equipment and supplies, and by setting up antigas clothing processing plants. The chemical mortar battalions were fully occupied and highly prized in their nongas warfare role, an intended one, of firing high explosive and smoke missions in direct combat support of the infantry. Artificial smoke, other than that produced

---

[94] Informal Comments of CWS Officer [Maj Hingle to Col Charron, CmlO FECOMZ], 20 Jun 44. CWS 314.7 Pers Files, ETO.

[95] (1) FUSA Rpt of Opns, 20 Oct 43–1 Aug 44, an. 17. (2) Ruppenthal, *Logistical Support*, I, 433–36.

[96] (1) Ruppenthal, *Logistical Support*, I, 436–37. (2) MacArthur Interv, 19 Sep 61. (3) TUSA AAR, 1 Aug 44–9 May 45, vol. II, CWS Sec. (4) 12th Army Group Rpt of Opns, vol. XI, Cml Warfare Sec, pp. 104–33.

[97] OCCWO COMZ ETO, Daily Journal, Jul and Aug 44. ETO Admin 467.

by white phosphorus shell, had not been used in expected quantities, and expensive fog oil, the smoke agent used in mechanical smoke generators, was being used to oil emergency aircraft landing strips. The smoke generator units were used as service units. The chemical supply situation was satisfactory at the moment, but Rowan and St. John predicted growing supply problems as the mortar battalions became more extensively used and the distribution area for smoke, flame, and gas warfare supplies became larger. From Rowan's point of view the most immediate problem was the supply and allotment of CWS officers and enlisted men, particularly those for the chemical mortar battalions.[98]

While Rowan had organized a Personnel Division and expanded it into a Personnel and Troops Division, he did not control the assignment of CWS-trained men. All assignments in the European theater were made under the supervision of the ETO SOS assistant chief of staff, G–1, by the theater adjutant general or a command adjutant general or by the Ground Forces Reinforcement System. The assigning agency commonly considered all CWS officers and men as service troops and indiscriminately assigned individuals to any CWS vacancy. While such indiscriminate assignment produced some problems in service units, such as the assignment of decontamination specialists to maintenance units, the real difficulty arose in connection with CWS combat assignment. Mortar battalion commanders found they were receiving service specialists or clerks while CWS-trained combat soldiers were assigned to service units. Chemical mortar battalion commanders consequently requested infantry- or artillery-trained men in preference to those trained by the CWS. It was easier to retrain men who could be counted upon to have received basic combat training than it was to retrain CWS men who had no combat training at all.[99]

Rowan immediately began to tackle this problem both from the field end and from the theater staff end until he persuaded the theater adjutant general to consult the CWS in the allotment of both men and units. While it was still necessary to work through the theater

[98] (1) St. John to Porter, Rpt for CCWS, 28 Jun 44. CWS 314.7 Pers Ltr Files, ETO. (2) Personal Ltr, Rowan to Waitt, 2 Sep 44, inclosing Memo, Rowan, no addressee, 26 Aug 44, sub: Notes on Trip to Far Shore. (3) MacArthur Interv, 19 Sep 61. (4) Leggin Interv, 13 Oct 61. (5) Wright Interv, 12 Jul 61.

[99] (1) History of Pers and Troops Div OCCWO COMZ ETO, D Day to V–E Day (hereafter cited as History, Pers and Troops Div). ETO Admin 545A. (2) Rowan Interv, 28 Sep 58. (3) Waitt Comments, 5 Jan 61.

system, and while the preference of individual commanders could still outweigh OCCWO planning, this concession gave Rowan a much larger hand in the solution. Rowan and his subordinates were thereafter able to correct many inequities in chemical assignments.[100]

On moving to the Continent in September, Rowan began consolidating his offices. FECOMZ, its operational period having been curtailed on the one end by the extension of First Army's control and on the other by the early arrival on the Continent of the main echelon, was absorbed into the COMZ headquarters. Little change was made in the theater chemical section organization when the section was established in Paris. The Supply Division carried on its day and night job much as it had in Cheltenham. The Technical Division remained in the United Kingdom with a liaison section in Paris. Colonel Bramlet remained in England to become Chemical Officer, United Kingdom Base Section, which was in fact a rear echelon of COMZ. The one significant change was the recombination, just after the arrival in Paris, of the Planning and the Operations and Training Divisions into a Planning and Training Division. Since there were no gas warfare operations, the concept of an Operations and Training Division as a successor to General Fries' "military" offensive and defensive divisions faded completely, and toward the end of the war the division devoted itself to demobilization and redeployment planning.[101] Since Colonel St. John had also primarily been employed in planning, his position was abolished in the fall of 1944. He, too, turned to demobilization work, mostly outside the CWS sphere.[102]

Rowan gave much of his personal attention to the problems of operating in a nongas warfare situation. The chemical mortar battalions were in considerable demand for close infantry support from the time of their debut on the Continent, but since their extensive use in a nonchemical role had not been envisioned before the war, there was no well-established body of doctrine relating to their employment. In the resultant controversy over infantry or artillery fire

---

[100] (1) History, Pers and Troops Div. (2) Personal Ltr, Rowan to Waitt, 1 Sep 44. (3) Personal Ltr, St. John to Waitt, 1 Sep 44.
[101] (1) CWS History, 1 Jan 44 to "D Day." (2) History of the Administrative Div OCCWO, D Day to V–E Day, Hq COMZ ETOUSA. Both in ETO Admin 545A. (3) History of Sup Div OCCWO Hq ETOUSA, D Day to V–E Day (hereafter cited as History, Sup Div, II.) ETO Admin 544. (4) History of CWS Plans and Tng Div in the ETO, 6 Jun 44 to 9 May 45. (5) History of the Tech Div CWS Hq ETOUSA, 6 Jun 44–9 May 45. Both in ETO Admin 545B.
[102] Personal Ltr, St. John to Col Elliott, DCCWS, 22 Nov 44.

direction, Rowan aligned himself firmly with the proponents of infantry control.[103] Lacking the means to establish doctrine as a representative of the theater commander, Rowan chose to visit combat commanders to persuade them to use attached chemical mortar battalion elements under infantry control. Though he was sometimes frustrated in this attempt, Rowan usually found personal persuasion effective.[104]

The theater chief chemical officer also used personal persuasion in an attempt to secure the proper employment of smoke generator units. Since many commanders were unaware of the new techniques in use of smoke which had been developed in the Mediterranean theater, they were unprepared and unwilling to initiate the employment of smoke. As a result, many smoke generator troops made their way across France engaged in such miscellaneous activities as service and transportation troops. General Rowan tried to persuade field commanders to maintain the integrity of these units, to keep up their equipment and to employ them on their primary mission wherever possible. Smoke came into great demand for concealment in Germany when the river-crossing operations began. At that time many smoke units were recalled to their primary mission, but re-equipping and re-training was no easy task. Some units and their equipment had been so dispersed that they were never called back to their primary mission.[105]

Rowan's activities on the Continent, such as those in connection with the mortar battalions and the smoke generator units, raise the question of the proper role, in the absence of gas warfare, of the Chemical Warfare Service and of the various staff chemical officers. Neither Porter nor Rowan felt that the absence of gas warfare significantly altered the basic mission of the CWS or of CWS staff officers. Both believed that Fries's concept of a service in which "research was linked with the closest possible ties to the firing line" still applied.[106] Although toxics had not been used and although the likelihood of their use became more remote with each succeeding month of the war, there was always the possibility that the Germans might use gas to cap the offensive which had created the "bulge" in the Ardennes, or to prevent the crossing of the Rhine, or in last-ditch defense of the

---

[103] See below, ch. XII.

[104] Rowan Interv, 28 Sep 58. (2) Rowan Comments, 16 Dec 60.

[105] (1) Rowan Interv, 28 Sep 58. (2) Rowan Comments, 16 Dec 60.

[106] Fries and West, *Chemical Warfare*, p. 73.

homeland.[107] These possibilities were sufficiently real so that European theater forces had to be at least prepared to wage gas warfare. Preparedness meant that gas masks and protective clothing must be available for all troops in potential danger zones, that decontamination equipment and supplies must be available, that gas alarms and detection devices must be in the hands of line units or ready for issue and that gas defensive training for all troops must not be neglected. Furthermore, preparedness meant that chemical intelligence information must be gathered and interpreted, that chemical advisers and service and combat troops must be ready to begin offensive or defensive operations or both with very short notice. And there was yet another threat—the threat of biological warfare. The gas warfare defensive system would serve for defense against biological warfare, but CWS officers had to be acquainted with the latest developments so that should such warfare be initiated, they could recognize it, furnish needed advice, and take proper defensive measures. Retaliation in this field was out of the question since the CWS had no biological munitions.[108] Preparedness was no small task. But preparedness was only the first of the CWS tasks. There were also the tasks connected with the nongas warfare operations of the chemical mortar battalions, with the supply and field employment of artificial smoke, and with the supply and training for incendiary and flame weapons employment.

Rowan had to reconsider, once the pattern of operations on the Continent was apparent, how to accomplish the CWS tasks. Since his own office operated a CWS supply system, he only had to see that his Supply Division was operating and secure the co-operation of the base sections in distribution and of the combat elements in stating requirements. The contacts with the base sections were maintained, as in England, through the base section chemical officers who kept in informal touch with his office.[109] The base section chemical officers also

---

[107] (1) Rowan Interv, 28 Sep 58. (2) Porter Interv, 24 Aug 61. (3) Waitt Interv, 13 May 61. (4) Interv, Hist Off with Col Kenneth A. Cunin, 5 Dec 45.

[108] See Brophy, Miles, and Cochrane, *From Laboratory to Field*, pp. 101–22.

[109] Information on the base sections is drawn from: (1) Wright Interv, 16 Jul 61 (Colonel Wright was Chemical Officer, Loire Base Section); (2) Intervs, Hist Off with Col Christian O. Christensen, USAR (Ret.), 13, 23 Oct 61 (Colonel Christensen was Chemical Officer, Oise Base Section); (3) Ltr, Col Greene to Hist Off, 22 Jan 60 (Colonel Greene was Chemical Officer, Brittany Base Section and Seine Base Section); (4) Ltr, Col Hubert B. Bramlet, USA (Ret.), to Hist Off, 6 Oct 59 (Colonel Bramlet was Chemical Officer, United Kingdom Base Section); (5) Ltr, Col Ferris U. Foster, AUS (Ret.), to Hist Off, 13 Oct 59 (Colonel Foster was Chemical Officer, Southern Base Section in England and subsequently assigned to United Kingdom Base Section).

maintained informal liaison with each other and with combat organization chemical officers. Base section chemical officers operated under their own command, but most of them asserted some independence in chemical supply matters. They were usually able to arrange transportation as they saw fit, and they supervised the activities of chemical service units in their areas. Problems were handled directly with Rowan's office—usually by telephone.

The supply and service aspects of preparedness thus taken care of, Rowan could devote most of his time to his duties as "roving ambassador." He or Day frequently talked to MacArthur and his successor, Col. Patrick F. Powers, or their deputy, Leggin, in the 12th Army Group Chemical Section.[110] These officers regularly, both officially and informally, saw and corresponded with the chemical officers of First, Third, and Ninth Armies, and they occasionally heard from Col. Benjamin F. Mattingly, chemical adviser to G-3, 6th Army Group, and from the chemical officer of Seventh Army. The 12th Army Group Chemical Section also maintained liaison with the British 21 Army Group Chemical Section as long as General Sir Bernard L. Montgomery, 21 Army Group commander, was also Allied land commander. In September 1944, 12th Army Group was transferred to the direct control of SHAEF, and the chemical officers continued, as they had throughout the planning and early continental period, to correspond with St. John.[111] Preparedness occupied much of the time of the 12th Army Group Chemical Section. MacArthur's first problem on arriving on the Continent was to determine what might be done to relieve the combat troops of the need to carry the gas mask. Soldiers individually discarded burdensome masks whenever they felt that there was no further danger of gas or whenever they had what they regarded as a more important item to carry. Even when retained masks suffered abuse because carriers were used as catch-alls. Instruction and training were useless in persuading soldiers to care for their masks. MacArthur met with members of the army group staff on this problem, and General Bradley himself suggested at the conference that division commanders be given the option of withdrawing masks

---

[110] Information on the 12th Army Group Chemical Section is from: (1) MacArthur Interv, 19 Sep 61; (2) Leggin Intervs, 13 Oct 61, 22 Nov 45; (3) Interv, Hist Off with Col Powers, USA (Ret.), 24 Sep 59; (4) 12th Army Group, Rpt of Opns, vol. XI, Cml Warfare Sec.

[111] MacArthur (comments on draft of this volume) minimizes St. John's role since it was only that of an adviser with SHAEF headquarters.

from individuals if transport could be found which would carry the masks with advancing troop units, making them readily available for reissue. Since no combat element either below or above division had an organizational baggage train, the only feasible solution from the army group point of view was to suggest that divisions allot the necessary space for masks in their division trains and this soon became SHAEF approved policy.

The 12th Army Group Chemical Section was to perform its more routine duties through an organization which consisted of four branches: Administrative, Supply and Logistics, Operations, and Technical and Intelligence. Five officers and 7 enlisted men were allotted to the organization, and on 13 October 1944 this allotment was reduced to 3 officers and 3 enlisted men. The duties of stating requirements for supplies and dividing scarce supplies, such as chemical mortar ammunition, among the three armies proved to be time consuming. Formulating chemical annexes for army group tactical plans was also time consuming. Liaison, inspection, and intelligence duties and the constant and thorny problems posed by the necessity of advising on the allotment of chemical mortar units took the remaining time. Powers greatly regretted that no time remained to co-ordinate the direct gas warfare training being carried on by division chemical officers. He was not satisfied with the state of gas warfare preparedness although he felt that Rowan and his staff were doing an excellent job, considering the personal effort required for communication among the various elements in the theater. Powers managed to reverse the earlier policy and secure the reissue of the gas mask to individual soldiers. He felt that even a gas scare would have caused panic at the time of the Battle of the Bulge when troops had no individual protection.[112] He was never able to achieve the movement of more than a token stock of toxic ground ammunition to the Continent, and no aerial toxic munitions were ever moved from England. On the point of the adequacy of aerial retaliation, Powers disagreed with both Porter and Waitt. He shared the view of the Chief and Assistant Chief of the CWS that strategic aerial retaliation in kind against the initiation of gas warfare was possible, but he maintained that essential tactical retaliation, which would have taken a ground effort, had been overlooked. Because ground retaliatory preparation was only token, Powers, like many of

[112] For discussion of supply problems caused by this decision, see below, Chapter IV.

his colleagues, believed the Allied forces fortunate in that the Germans never took advantage of their opportunities to initiate gas warfare.

Lt. Col. Kenneth A. Cunin, who succeeded Coughlan as First Army chemical officer on 24 July 1944, also believed the American forces inadequately prepared for gas warfare because of the shortage of ground toxic ammunition.[113] Cunin considered the protective supply adequate, but his section agreed with 12th Army Group policy in reissuing individual protection at the time of the December threat. The First Army Chemical Section could do little to improve the preparedness situation from the standpoint of toxic supply or gas warfare training. Although the section allotment was 6 officers and 16 enlisted men, 3 officers and 13 enlisted men more than the 12th Army Group Chemical Section, First Army chemical officers found themselves fully occupied with the problems of the mortar battalions and those of nongas chemical supply and gas warfare intelligence.[114]

Colonel Wallington, Chemical Officer, Third U.S. Army, throughout the European campaigns, was less concerned about gas warfare preparedness than Powers and Cunin. He believed in preparedness, but he considered the gas warfare retaliatory potential in the European theater adequate in view of the absence of gas warfare. In Wallington's opinion the theater command and combat commanders in Europe justifiably took the risk of being less than fully prepared for gas warfare. He believed the risk was justifiable because there were so many other pressing demands on commanders' resources, because United States national policy forbade the initiation of gas warfare, and because intelligence was expected to provide warning if a policy change was required.[115]

While Wallington believed that the state of gas warfare training among U.S. forces in Europe was such that the initiation of gas warfare would have resulted in panic, he conceived his job as being primarily that of supporting nongas warfare activities of the corps and divisions under Third Army. At the same time, he gave all the support he could to protective preparedness and intelligence activities.[116] This conception of duties meant that the TUSA Chemical Section, like the

---

[113] Cunin Interv, 5 Dec 45. Cunin was succeeded as First Army chemical officer by Col. Frederick W. Gerhard in April 1945.

[114] FUSA Rpt of Opns, 1 Aug 44–22 Feb 45, vol. 4, an. 13, Cml Warfare Sec Rpt, pp. 253–67.

[115] Interv, Hist Off with Brig Gen Edward C. Wallington, USA (Ret.), 1 Dec 59.

[116] Ibid.

FUSA Chemical Section, devoted maximum attention to supply and to the needs of the chemical mortar battalions. It also meant the provision of supply support and tactical advice for the smoke generator units which were heavily employed by TUSA, especially in its river crossings. As a result of experience in these tasks, the TUSA Chemical Section found that the one chemical depot company attached could not handle all supply requirements. It recommended that two such companies be assigned, and more important still, that CWS should have far more transportation for the depot company, the smoke generator, and the mortar units. The CWS could not operate its own supply system, which it did with very little help from other supply services, and at the same time shift men and equipment in a fast-moving war without greatly increased transportation. The chemical section suggested addition of a truck company to the Army for CWS use.[117]

To accomplish the intelligence mission, which Wallington deemed so important since warning of necessary policy change was to come from intelligence information, two technical intelligence teams were attached to Third Army. Several of these CWS technical intelligence teams were organized and trained by the CWS in the United States and several more were organized and trained by Rowan's office. These teams were attached to Army chemical sections. They reported to the section to which they were attached and to Colonel Tarr's Intelligence Division in Rowan's office and to the CWS in the United States.[118] The work of all such teams is revealed in an account of the activities of CWS Enemy Equipment Intelligence Service Team (EEIST) Number One, under Capt. James F. Munn.[119]

EEIST Number One, consisting of Captain Munn and three enlisted men (a driver, a photographer, and an interpreter) was organized and trained in the United States and shipped to Europe in time to arrive in France on 18 July 1944. It was first attached to FUSA and was later under orders of the 12th Army Group Chemical Section until attached to the TUSA Chemical Section in September. During the campaign across France, the team investigated several French laboratories and chemical factories used by the Germans, and analyzed, photo-

---

[117] TUSA AAR, 1 Aug 44–9 May 45, vol. II, CWS Sec.

[118] CWS COMZ ETO History of Intell Div, From D Day Through V-E Day. ETO Admin 545B.

[119] The following account is derived from: (1) Rcds of CWS EEIST No. 1, Apr 44–Aug 45, CWS 314.7 EEIST No. 1; (2) Information furnished by Lt Col James F. Munn, USAR (Ret.).

graphed, and inventoried laboratory, manufacturing, and protective equipment. Although several rumors of German toxic stores were reported, the team found no German toxics and no equipment for manufacturing them.[120] Interviews with Frenchmen who had been pressed into German employment revealed only that the Germans were interested in and had continued French toxic and munitions development. As the campaign moved into Germany, the team was called upon for numerous similar analyses and descriptions, and it became increasingly involved in the interrogation of prisoners of war who might have chemical information. Such interrogations were carried on in co-operation with Army prisoner of war and intelligence authorities. This team and others operating on the battlefront gradually accumulated a fairly good store of information concerning German individual and collective protection, doctrine, and instructions for civilians as well as military forces. The teams also collected adequate, although not abundant, information on German weapons and agents and chemical investigative processes. On 20 April 1945 the Chemical Officer, Seventh Army, informed EEIST Number One that the forward elements of the 14th Armored Division had discovered a German war gas factory in Velden, Germany. The XV Corps Chemical Section moved in to investigate.[121] A few days later, on 24 April 1945, XII Corps discovered a German toxic depot, whereupon the team set out, in co-operation with Colonel Wallington and Col. Ragnar E. Johnson, XII Corps chemical officer, to investigate and inventory this depot. The chemical analysis of captured munitions was beyond the capacity of this small team, but they were able to sort out munitions which could be sent to Rowan's Intelligence and Technical Divisions for further analysis. The findings of EEIST Number One proved beyond a doubt that the Germans were well and elaborately prepared for gas warfare and that they possessed toxic munitions unknown to the Allied forces.

The Ninth Army Chemical Section under Col. Harold Walmsley and the Seventh Army Chemical Section under Lt. Col. Bruce T. Humphreville operated in much the same way as the First and Third Army Chemical Sections. Again the principal interest was in nongas warfare and defensive gas warfare supply. The Ninth Army Chemical

---

[120] A small store of French toxics was found. Ltr, Chief EEIST No. 1 to CmlO TUSA, 3 Oct 44, sub: Ammunition Dump at Fameck, France. CWS–EEIST–ETO–R13 in CWS 314.7 CWS EEIST.

[121] Journal Memo, CmlO Seventh Army, 20 Apr 45. CWS 314.7 EEIST.

Section additionally performed extensive liaison functions since that Army was for a time attached to the British 21 Army Group.[122]

Rowan was satisfied that chemical matters were well handled at the army group and army level. His greatest concern was that corps and division do their job well.[123] This job was a demanding one. The division chemical officer was actually in charge of field training and intelligence. He was adviser to his commander on gas warfare preparedness and on the employment of mortar battalions and was also adviser to his commander and to engineer and infantry teams on the employment of the flame thrower. His section either actually handled or kept close track of the handling of chemical supply and it was called upon to mix flame thrower fuel and fill flame throwers whenever they were used. The ability of the division chemical officer to handle this job depended upon his own energy and inventiveness since he was handling weapons and materials not familiar to most line soldiers and since his job concerned gas warfare preparedness, which was not popular with many commanders and most troops. His ability to do his job also depended upon the encouragement and support he got from the division commander and his staff and from higher echelon chemical officers. It was the duty of the corps chemical officer to oversee all these activities for the several division chemical officers under his corps except that he had no specific duties in supply. Since the corps head-

---

[122] (1) Ninth U.S. Army G–4 Per Rpts, 3–16 Sep 44; AAR's 1–31 Oct 44, Dec 44–Jun 45. Files L196–Envelope 10 Cml Sec and L216–Envelope 1; (2) Seventh U.S. Army CWS Staff Sec Rpts, 1 Jan–31 Oct 44, and Dec 44. File L–1139 7th Army Staff Sec "43."

[123] The following account of the corps and division chemical officer's activities is derived from: (1) Rowan Interv, 28 Sep 58; (2) Rowan Comments, 16 Dec 60; (3) Col Ragnar E. Johnson, CWS, Study, Functions and Orgn, Cml Warfare–Liaison Sec Hq XII Corps, n.d.; (4) Interv, Hist Off with Col William C. Hammond, 26 Nov 56 (Colonel Hammond was Chemical Officer, VI Corps); (5) Ltr, Col John B. Cobb, USAR (Ret.), to Hist Off, 17 May 60 (Colonel Cobb was Chemical Officer, 35th Infantry Division and XIX Corps); (6) Interv, Hist Off with Col Edward J. Barta, USAR (Ret.), 23 Sep 59 (Colonel Barta was Chemical Officer, XVIII Corps); (7) Cunin Interv, 5 Dec 45 (Colonel Cunin was Chemical Officer, 1st Inf Div, before becoming Chemical Officer, FUSA); (8) Interv Hist Off with Lt Col Levin B. Cottingham, 9 Oct 45 (Colonel Cottingham was Chemical Officer, 5th Infantry Division); (9) Intervs, Hist Off with Col William Foley, 16 Oct 46, 19 Dec 57 (Colonel Foley was Chemical Officer, 1st Infantry Division, succeeding Colonel Cunin); (10) Intervs, Hist Off with Col John L. Miles, 12 Apr 56, 9 Mar 61 (Colonel Miles was Chemical Officer, 26th Infantry Division); (11) Interv, Hist Off with Col Russell W. Dodds and Lt Col Samuel J. Boyles, 8 May 56 (Colonel Dodds was Chemical Officer, 65th Infantry Division, and Colonel Boyles was Chemical Officer, 91st Infantry Division); (12) Interv, Hist Off with Lt Col Thomas B. Crawford, USAR, 18 Apr 56 (Colonel Crawford was Chemical Officer, 80th Infantry Division); (13) Interv, Hist Off with Lt Col Herbert B. Livesey, Jr., USAR (Ret.), 8 Jun 56 (Colonel Livesey was Chemical Officer, 106th Infantry Division); (14) Interv, Hist Off with Col Alfred G. Karger, USAR, Jun 56 (Colonel Karger was Chemical Officer, 8th Infantry Division); (15) Daily Log, Cml Warfare Sec, 29th Inf Div, 6 Jun 44–30 Dec 44.

quarters was primarily a tactical element, the corps chemical officer naturally centered his attention on tactical employment of chemical weapons and equipment.

Rowan was of course concerned about the energy and resourcefulness of division and corps chemical officers since he, like Fries, believed that CWS services should be sold to combat commanders, but even after his arrangement on manpower with the ETO adjutant general, he could seldom control the assignment of division chemical officers since most such officers arrived with their divisions from the United States. Even in the few instances when replacements were made in the theater, the nearest ranking CWS officer was usually chosen by the organization commander without reference to theater manpower channels. Rowan was most anxious that the organization give the chemical officer a chance to do his job. Many commanders felt that in the absence of gas warfare, the corps or division chemical officer had nothing to do and was therefore available for any assignment in which there might be a vacancy. Rowan and the organization chemical officers expected that organization chemical officers would receive the normal quota of additional assignments to military courts, investigating and inspection teams, and the like, but Rowan urged all chemical officers to resist assignments to nonchemical duties which would occupy most or part of their time. Whenever Rowan had an opportunity in his tours he asked corps and division commanders or their chiefs of staff to permit chemical officers to devote most of their time to what were, in his opinion, the crucial duties of chemical training and intelligence. He also felt that chemical officers should be active in the staff supervision and tactical control of chemical mortar and smoke units which operated under the organization commander. Despite Rowan's pleas, most chemical officers received additional assignments which consumed most of their time. The usual assignment was the operation of the organization liaison section which handled liaison with other organizations and higher echelons, received and briefed visitors, and maintained a tactical and/or intelligence information center. One energetic chemical officer so assigned maintains that he spent precisely one and a half hours exclusively on chemical work while his division was in combat, but he believes he was a better division chemical officer because of his additional assignments.

Those organization chemical officers not assigned the liaison task had many other regular or part-time assignments such as reconnaissance for the division commander, acting as headquarters commandant, and even serving as divisional mess officer. Many organization chemical officers disagreed with Rowan and welcomed these nonchemical assignments since they were usually with the forward or command echelon of the division where the chemical officer could not expect to be in a nongas warfare situation, and since the work usually kept them in better touch with the tactical situation than most staff officers. As one chemical officer phrased it, the CWS officer was an orphan, away from any CWS command echelon—he increased his own prestige and that of his service if he could make himself useful in a combat organization. Frequently his ability to sell CWS services varied in direct proportion to his usefulness in a nonchemical capacity. Lt. Col. William Foley, Chemical Officer, 1st Infantry Division, was assigned as assistant to the division assistant chief of staff, G–3. He felt that this assignment to the operations and plans element was ideal since in the event of gas warfare he would have been acquainted with the tactical situation and able to render his advice as a member of the staff section charged with applying the tactical plan. Most organization chemical officers with other assignments, like Foley, believed that they were not neglecting their chemical job. The assistant division chemical officer, a captain, and some or all of the four enlisted men in the section could handle supply and administrative functions from the division rear echelon. The assistant chemical officer could and usually did refer really knotty problems involving liaison with higher echelons or special requests for authority or supplies to the organization chemical officer in forward echelon.

Many assistant division chemical officers and their enlisted assistants became proficient at handling chemical training, to which the whole section had usually devoted most of its efforts in the United States.[124] Because of severe manpower restrictions on the CWS, every combat organization, just as in World War I, usually maintained unit gas officers (UGO's) in all elements at regiment and battalion levels. Unlike the World War I precedent, these officers were usually given this duty as an additional assignment, and they did not report to the organization chemical officer except for training. The division chemical officer was also responsible for training unit gas noncommissioned offi-

---

[124] See Brophy and Fisher, *Organizing for War*, pp. 382–93.

cers (UGNCO's) for every company-sized unit. This, too, was an additional duty and UGNCO's usually reported for this duty to UGO's. Most chemical officers attempted to keep the roster of UGO's and UGNCO's current by offering courses and demonstrations, even conducting them in forward areas, whenever commanders and operations officers would allot the time. The more ambitious chemical officers also trained decontamination squads from combat units, gave flame thrower training, and demonstrated the use of incendiary and smoke grenades. Corps and army chemical officers frequently co-operated, or at least provided moral support when the physical assistance they could give was limited.

Division and corps chemical officers, like their seniors in army and army group, emphasized intelligence activities. Protecting captured munitions from souvenir hunters was one of the problems in this field as was securing transportation to take samples back for analysis. Corps chemical officers usually called upon the army chemical officer for EEIST assistance in such cases.

A few corps and division chemical officers found it possible to participate actively in tactical plans and preparations, especially for smoke operation.

Nearly every activity of the division and corps chemical officers presented problems. They were perpetually short of transportation and of service personnel. Supply of wanted items, such as incendiary or smoke grenades and mortar ammunition, was often short and communication to the rear to remedy these shortages was difficult. But despite these drawbacks, most corps and division chemical officers felt that they accomplished their mission and that their organizations were reasonably well prepared for gas warfare and had made effective nongas warfare use of mortars and smoke. The few who had biological warfare defensive training also felt that they were ready to cope with this kind of warfare should it come. Very few organization chemical officers seriously considered offensive gas warfare since, aside from the mortar battalions, they had no contact with any of the units scheduled to wage it and did not handle offensive supplies.

Summary

There is no simple way of measuring the work of the CWS in the theaters of operations. There is no accounting comparable to that of tactical objectives taken, bridges built, and miles of communication wire laid. The 2,097 CWS officers and 26,909 CWS enlisted men in the European theater in March and April of 1945 were there, first, to provide the insurance that the American forces could continue to fight and retaliate in kind if the enemy initiated gas warfare.[125] Second, these "chemicals" as some denominated themselves, were there to provide CWS gas protective services, fire CWS nongas weapons, provide supply of CWS items, and support the combat forces in any way which they or the theater commanders could devise. There was no question in Porter's, or Waitt's, or Rowan's mind that they provided gas warfare insurance and that they performed extraordinarily well at their nongas warfare tasks.[126]

Theater commanders, with a few exceptions, willingly supported the preparedness effort since they valued the insurance. They increasingly welcomed the CWS nongas warfare activities as the war progressed. They had no heavy mortar other than the chemical mortar, which proved tremendously effective, and they had no means for sustained provision of artificial smoke other than the smoke generator units and CWS-furnished smoke pots and ammunition.

There were many problems in accomplishing the CWS tasks ranging from lack of staff and service manpower to a general lack of understanding of what the CWS might do in a nongas warfare situation. As in the Fries and Porter ideal, the ties between research and the battle lines, although tenuous, did exist, and Porter's conception of the CWS as a unique service, which participated and aided in almost every phase of military activity, was most nearly realized in the European theater. Rowan came closer than any other theater chief chemical officer to Porter's goal of operating a unified service although the unity in many cases completely depended on the personal obligation which most chemical officers felt toward their service and its senior representatives in the theater.

---

[125] Strength figures compiled from STM–30, Strength of the Army, prepared by The Adjutant General's Machine Records Branch monthly. The 31 March 1945 figure of 26,909 enlisted men is the peak CWS strength for the European theater as is the 30 April 1945 strength of 2,097 officers. (Brophy and Fisher, *Organizing for War*, app. B.)

[126] (1) Porter Interv, 24 Aug 61. (2) Waitt Interv, 13 May 61. (3) Rowan Interv, 28 Sep 58.

CHAPTER III

CWS Administration and Supply: Mediterranean

The Chemical Warfare Service, like the rest of the Army, matriculated in the logistics school of the North African campaigns. The Army had directly participated in the global supply effort for eight months before the planning for North Africa got under way, but this was the first Army participation in an Allied logistics operation of great magnitude. Supply of any considerable force at any time during the war was far from a simple matter, but probably no other logistics operation of the war was surrounded by so many complicating circumstances as this initial venture. Planning got under way late. Allied forces strategy for a landing originally projected for October 1942 and finally for November did not assume a clear pattern until 5 September 1942. The Allied commander-designate, General Eisenhower, set up his planning headquarters, AFHQ, in England, though the source of the bulk of materials was the United States, and a major combat force under Maj. Gen. George S. Patton, Jr., was to sail directly from the United States for the assault. The Navy had determined that an acute shortage of cargo ships, the grave threat of submarine warfare, and the shortage of escorts made small, fast-moving, infrequent convoys a necessity; thus, the quantities of materials and the numbers of men to be shipped were severely limited and the intervals between deliveries were lengthened. Few troops had received enough training to be considered ready for operations, and elsewhere in the Army, as in the CWS, few production lines were furnishing equipment, especially new equipment, in desired amounts. Furthermore, the administrative mechanisms were not yet working properly. Jurisdictional boundaries between the Army Service Forces and the two other major War Department commands, Army Ground Forces and Army Air Forces, had not been clearly delineated. Strategic or tactical alterations time and again upset logistical plans. Details of port operation and organization still had to be fixed, and co-ordination among the ports, the technical services, and the Services of Supply headquarters was to be developed through the North African experience. General Eisenhower later wrote that the operation was ". . . in conflict with all operational and logistical methods laid down in textbooks. . . ."[1]

General Eisenhower called in Colonel Shadle one day in the middle of August 1942 and told him that he was appointed Chemical Warfare Officer, AFHQ.[2] This appointment to a supreme allied headquarters placed Shadle in a position that no CWS officer had ever been in before; the headquarters of Marshall Ferdinand Foch, the only pertinent World War I example, had no special staff. General Eisenhower created AFHQ from a number of military concepts both current and new to comply with his basic directive. AFHQ was, first, an instrument for co-ordinating Allied strategic plans and operations and a combined command for ground, sea, and air forces. It was next a theater headquarters or at least it was designed to contain the nucleus of a theater headquarters in that it had a full general and special staff oriented to the direction of American Army activities in a theater of operations. It was, third, a tactical and operational headquarters approximating that of a field army with initial supervision of three corps. It was, fourth and least, the parent organization for a communications zone headquarters whose operating elements, the base section headquarters, were being formed as adjuncts of the corps headquarters.[3]

Shadle and an officer assistant immediately set about making general chemical plans for the scheduled invasion, known as Operation TORCH. On 15 September 1942, Shadle's section was officially organized as the Chemical Warfare Section, AFHQ. Lt. Col. Ian A. Marriott, British Army, was appointed deputy and one of the two American officers assigned became executive officer. One British major, three American enlisted men, and two British enlisted men completed the staff. While

---

[1] (1) George F. Howe, *Northwest Africa: Seizing the Initiative in the West,* UNITED STATES ARMY IN WORLD WAR II (Washington, 1957), ch. II. (2) Leighton and Coakley, ch. XVI. The quotation from General Eisenhower is cited on page 455. (3) Ruppenthal, *Logistical Support,* I, 87–90.

[2] Interv, Hist Off with Gen Shadle, 16 May 61.

[3] History of AFHQ, pt. I, Aug–Dec 42, pp. 1–26. (2) Pogue, *Supreme Command,* pp. 56–58. (3) Howe, *Northwest Africa,* pp. 32–59.

the section was intended to serve both AFHQ and the planned American theater Headquarters, North African Theater of Operations, United States Army (NATOUSA), the manpower allotment, as authorized by the AFHQ chief of staff, was sufficient only to form two divisions, one Administration, the other Technical and Intelligence. Despite the lack of a supply or logistics division, the AFHQ Chemical Section, in its NATOUSA role, was assigned staff responsibility for chemical matériel through the entire overseas span from requirements to salvage.[4]

Since at this time national policy and the toxic supply capability of the Army forbade the employment, even in retaliation, of war gases, Shadle and his staff made no gas warfare offensive plan.[5] They were also unable to make any nongas warfare offensive plans involving the use of chemical mortar units or the new portable flame throwers as neither units nor weapons were yet ready. Brig. Gen. Lyman L. Lemnitzer, AFHQ assistant chief of staff, G–3, suggested to Shadle that artificial smoke protection would be valuable in view of German air superiority over the Mediterranean and North Africa. Shadle accordingly requested smoke pots both from the United States and from the British and drew up tactical smoke plans. The CWS in the United States could furnish only the prewar training allowance of one pot per twenty soldiers, a ratio which Shadle viewed as entirely inadequate. A part of the smoke deficit was made up by the supply of British pots and another part by the inclusion of some new mechanical smoke generators and a smoke generator unit in the forces to arrive from the United States. Still, Shadle considered preparedness for smoke operations to be below the desirable standard.[6]

In the absence of gas warfare supplies, and with inadequate nongas warfare supply, the principal responsibility of the AFHQ and NATOUSA Chemical Sections was to provide for gas warfare protection, and the prime corollary task was the computation of protective matériel and service requirements for all forces expected to be in North Africa. Time was too short and the AFHQ staff section too small to accomplish this prime task without aid. Consequently, all

[4] (1) History of AFHQ, pt. I, pp. 35–37, 59–61. (2) Personal Ltr, Shadle, Chief Cml Sec AFHQ, to Porter, CCWS, 11 Feb 43. CWS 201—Shadle, Charles S. (O) in CWS 314.7 Pers Files, NATO, Feb 43–Feb 44.

[5] For national policy and toxic supply potential in 1942, see Brophy and Fisher, *Organizing for War*, Chapters III and IV, and above, Chapter I.

[6] Shadle Interv, 16 May 61.

the existing and forming chemical sections in the European theater, the Office of the Chief, CWS, in the United States, and the Chemical Section of General Patton's newly organized Western Task Force (WTF) headquarters in the United States pitched into the job, not only of estimating requirements, but also of actually supplying staff sections, materials, and troops. The OCCWS participated in these activities through liaison provided by ASF and OPD with the overseas staffs and with the WTF headquarters which was at first divided between Washington's Munitions Building and Indiantown Gap Military Reservation and was later consolidated at Fort George G. Meade, Md.[7] All echelons began planning before the character of the TORCH operation had definitely been determined.

In the United Kingdom, Maj. Gen. Mark W. Clark's II Corps Headquarters, in which Col. Walter P. Burn was chemical officer, assumed most of the planning burden for what was to become Center Task Force (CTF), an American force scheduled to make an assault on and in the vicinity of Oran, Algeria. The Office of the Chief Chemical Warfare Officer, European theater, transferred one officer and four enlisted men into II Corps headquarters in September 1942. During September, October, and November, the remainder of the planning period, a number of CWS ETO officers and men were transferred into or detailed for service with the forming Mediterranean Base Section (MBS) and Twelfth Air Force headquarters in which supply matters were being co-ordinated with II Corps.[8] Maj. Herbert F. Croen, Jr., scheduled to be acting chief of the MBS Chemical Section, remained for some time with the CWS ETO to assist in the task of apportioning available chemical resources in England for TORCH. Although SOS ETO had been advised that all TORCH troops arriving from the United States to assemble in the United Kingdom would be fully equipped, the CWS ETO discovered that units and organizations inspected on

[7] (1) Memos, ACofS G–2 WDGS for CG's AGF, AAF, SOS, and A Task Force, 11, 20 Aug 42, sub: Security Control, A Special Opn. (2) Memo, Col Norman E. Fiske, WD Security Officer for All WD Security Officers, 18 Aug 42, sub: Rules Governing Security in the War Dept for A Special Opn. (3) Ltr, TAG to ACofS Opns SOS et al., 26 Aug 42, sub: Security Control, A Special Opn. SPX 312.11 (8–25–42) MS–SPEX–M All in CWS 314.7, A Special Opn, TORCH.

[8] (1) History of CWS Per Activities, in History, Sup Div CWS ETO (ca. Jan 1944). ETO Admin 545A. (2) Narrative History of Mediterranean Base Section, NATOUSA–MTOUSA, Sep 42 to May 44 (hereafter cited as History of MBS), no paging. OCMH. (3) Ltr, Maling, CmlO XII AFSC, to Porter, CCWS, 3 Apr 43, sub: Orgnl History of Cml Warfare Sec, Twelfth AF. CWS 314.7 Twelfth AF.

disembarkation reported critical shortages of chemical equipment, especially protective equipment.[9]

The European theater BOLERO build-up was brought to a sudden halt.[10] The CWS ETO diverted chemical equipment and supplies from BOLERO reserves and from ordinary issues to fill shortages for TORCH organizations and units. These organizations and units made requisition directly upon the CWS ETO for chemical supply, and the CWS in turn extracted requisitions to depots. Shortage of time, shortage of materials, and the fact that establishment of the depots had just begun did not permit the operation of the normal supply pattern under which a designated depot would receive requisitions from and make issues to all units in its geographical area. Since the impromptu supply arrangements were unlikely to cover all cases of critical shortage, the CWS ETO also undertook a program of inspecting the chemical readiness of units about to be shipped to North Africa in order to remedy needs which had been overlooked.[11]

In the United States, OCCWS and the Chemical Section, WTF, computed requirements and determined shortages, as did the CWS ETO, by checking tables of basic allowances (TBA's) and tables of organization and equipment (TOE's) against unit and organization requisitions and against inventories of materials in the hands of troops. While the supply of troops scheduled for the assault was being completed, OCCWS and the various chemical sections of organizations scheduled for TORCH also computed the reserves necessary to maintain supply when forces were operating in the combat zone. The level of supply reserves in terms of days of supply was set by agreement among War Department agencies, AFHQ, and ETO headquarters, and OCCWS arrived at estimated expenditure rates in order to translate day of supply into actual quantities of materials.[12] Since no conclusive expenditure data were available, these estimates were at best educated guesses, but problems arising from lack of experience did not become apparent in the planning and early operational period. The CWS was able to supply gas warfare protective items, which made up the largest

[9] Interv, Hist Off with Col Herbert F. Croen, Jr., USAR, 21 Sep 59.

[10] BOLERO was the code name for the build-up of supplies in the British Isles for a projected Allied attack on continental Europe. Ruppenthal, *Logistical Support*, I, pp. 87–99.

[11] History of CWS Sup System, CWS ETO (27 Jul 42–1 Jan 44) (hereafter cited as History, Sup System). ETO Admin 545A Cml Warfare.

[12] A "day of supply" was the amount of any item, group of items, or entire category of supply calculated to support a given number of men (force or theater strength) in one day's operation.

portion of the requirements list, in sufficient quantities to meet demands.[13] Problems arose in providing commanders' special requirements, in providing service troops, and in limiting both troops and supplies to available shipping space.

In connection with commanders' special requirements, Col. Maurice E. Barker, WTF chemical officer, declared that General Patton would have "included a regiment of wizards" if such an inclusion would have given promise of help on the far shore.[14] Regiments of wizards were in short supply, but each

COLONEL BARKER

service conducted a search for any special equipment or special allowances of ordinary supplies which might be valuable in the operation. One OCCWS contribution was the recently developed mechanical smoke generator which was not available in time for shipment to the forces assembling in England but was included in WTF.[15] WTF also requested and received special allowances of incendiary hand grenades so that six grenades could be placed in every vehicle of the force and be used for destroying the vehicle in event of capture.[16] Army Service Forces made a special allotment of chemical land mines for Maj. Gen. Ernest N. Harmon's Subtask Force BLACK-

[13] (1) Requisitions and statements of shortages checked by OCCWS appear in CWS 320.2 files. (2) Memo, Brig Gen LeRoy Lutes, ACofS Opns SOS, for Chief of Sup Servs; Dir of Distr Div SOS; and Dir of Mil Pers Div SOS, 14 Sep 42, sub: Distr of Equip. SPOPP 475 in file CWS 314.7 A Special Opn, TORCH. (3) Interv, Hist Off with Lt Col Lyman C. Duncan, 3 Jun 55. (Colonel Duncan was a member and chief of the OCCWS requirements staff during most of the war period.) (4) Howe, *Northwest Africa*, pp. 65–67. (5) Interv, Hist Off with Lt Col Matthew A. Capone, USAR, 24 Apr 58. (Colonel Capone worked at requirements computation in CWS ETO in the fall of 1942.)

[14] Personal Ltr, Col Maurice E. Barker, USA (Ret.), to Hist Off, 12 Jul 49.

[15] (1) For development of the mechanical smoke generator, see Brophy, Miles, and Cochrane, *From Laboratory to Field*, Chapter IX. (2) For smoke generator operations in North Africa, see below, Chapter VIII.

[16] (1) Ltr, AG Task Force A [WTF] to ACofS OPD WDGS, 10 Oct 42, sub: Request for Grenades, Incendiary, M14. (2) DF, ACofS OPD to CG SOS, 11 Oct 42, sub: Request for Grenades, Incendiary, M14. OPD 400 TF (10-10-42). Both in Class V Sup File, Theaters Br Plans Div SOS.

STONE, an element of WTF, and in answer to Shadle's request, ordered 16,000 smoke pots and 11,300 incendiary grenades shipped to England for early delivery to CTF.[17] While the number of smoke pots was inadequate from Shadle's point of view, the shipment at least denoted the firm intention of providing smoke cover for the debarkation ports. This port concealment operation was one the CWS had not previously attempted.

Port defenses required the provision of chemical troops not only for smoke generator operation and for manning pot lines but also for supply, service, and maintenance of smoke units and their equipment. Very early in North African planning, before the operation had even acquired a code name, and before even chemical officers realized how large the smoke mission might be, the OCCWS decided that no chemical troops would be required in the initial phase of the operation and recommended that two chemical composite companies and three decontamination companies be landed only after beachheads were firmly established. The OCCWS also suggested that four impregnating companies should be considered as later additions to the force then contemplated while requirements for depot units and smoke generator units should be determined by the field commander on the basis of the tactical and logistical situation.[18]

These OCCWS troop recommendations and suggestions established the minimum chemical service requirement according to doctrine then current, and reflected the idea that gas warfare protection would be needed until forces started moving inland. Even this minimum service could not be provided until long after the beachheads were established. Lack of shipping space and lack of troops who could complete training and be prepared for overseas shipment in a short time caused a drastic alteration of plans. Commanders of the troops mounting in England, assuming that reserve stocks of chemical supplies would not arrive in the combat zone before service troops could be made available to handle them, and agreeing with the view that gas warfare would not start early, accepted a schedule under which chemical service troops were not provided in the initial phases of the operation. The possibility

[17] (1) Memo, CG SOS for CCWS, 23 Oct 42, sub: Mines, Land, for Mvmt 9999–Q–CWS–V. SPDDO 476 Mines. (2) Memo, CG SOS for Dir Distr Div SOS and CofT, 3 Oct 42. SPOPP. (3) Memo, CG SOS for CCWS, 2 Nov 42, sub: Ammunition for 9999–R. SPDDO 471.6 Grenades. All in Class V Sup File, Theaters Br Plans Div SOS.

[18] Ltr, Chief Field Serv OCCWS to Lt Col George H. Decker, Opns Div SOS, 28 Jul 42, sub: Cml Troops for BOLERO. CWS 320.2/314 (7–28–42). CWS 314.7, A Special Opn, TORCH.

of enemy initiation of gas warfare before arrival of chemical service troops was accepted as a calculated risk. Even had commanders requested such troops, few were available; the 6th Chemical Depot Company was the only chemical service unit available in England. The planners scheduled this company to arrive in the CTF area about one month after the initial landings. CTF planners also requested that a smoke generator company be scheduled to arrive as soon as possible from the United States. General Patton and his chief of staff, Col. Hobart R. Gay, wanted both service and smoke generator troops in the initial phase. WTF plans provided, because of superior resources in the United States and because General Patton deemed it a logistic necessity, for building up both reserve and operating stockages, including chemical, to a 90-day level as soon as troops and supplies could be landed. Colonel Barker decided to take along in the earliest echelon one platoon of a decontamination company, since such a unit could provide decontamination services in event of gas warfare, could initially handle chemical supply, and could use its decontaminating equipment to clean and disinfect buildings to be occupied by WTF headquarters and troops. He also obtained a smoke generator company to embark on the initial resupply convoy in order that smoke cover might be provided in port areas as soon as supplies began to be landed in quantity. Colonel Barker devised a plan under which the smoke generator company could provide convoy smoke cover using deck-mounted generators from its own organizational equipment.[19]

Planning completed, or at least terminated, the assault and assault support convoys, late in October and early in November, sailed from Hampton Roads, Va., and England's Mersey ports. The first convoy from England entered the Strait of Gibraltar on 5 November 1942.

---

[19] (1) For data on units, see Brophy and Fisher, *Organizing for War*, Appendix F. Units involved were the 6th Chemical Depot Company and the 69th Chemical Smoke Generator Company for CTF, and one platoon of the 21st Chemical Decontamination Company and the 78th Chemical Smoke Generator Company for WTF. No chemical units were originally scheduled for Eastern Task Force, a predominantly British force scheduled to land near Algiers. (2) Memo, ACofS OPD for CG SOS, 6 Oct 42, sub: Preparation of the 78th Cml Co, Smoke Generator, for Overseas Mvmt. OPD 370.5/CT (10-6-42). (3) Memo, ACofS OPD for CG SOS, 6 Oct 42, sub: Assignment of the 69th Cml Smoke Generator Co. OPD 320.2 (10-6-42). (4) Memo, with Incl, ACofS G-3 Hq II Corps CTF for CG II Corps, 9 Oct 42, sub: Over-all Troop Rqmts. (5) Ltr, CG Task Force A to ACofS OPD, 7 Oct 42, sub: Request for Cml Co, Smoke Generator. (6) DF, ACofS OPD to CG SOS, 11 Oct 42, sub: Request for Cml Smoke Generator. OPD 320.2 TF (10-7-42). Last three in 7B Troop Unit File, Theaters Br Plans Div SOS. (7) Personal Ltr, Barker to Hist Off, 12 Jul 49. (8) Ltr, Burn, CmlO Hq II Corps CTF, to CCWS, 5 Dec 42, sub: CWS Opn in the Field. MTO CWS 370, Employment, Opn and Mvmt of Troops. (9) Barker, Comments on draft of this volume, Feb 61.

The WTF convoy moved into assault position off the Moroccan coast a day later. On 8 November the three task forces struck and war in the Atlantic area began for the United States ground forces.[20] The token chemical sections and units still at sea on the support convoys probably had but little comprehension of the magnitude of the logistics operation in which they were about to participate.

Chemical Supply—The Beachhead Phase

Chemical supply experience in the North African and Mediterranean Theaters of Operations passed through several phases, each illustrative of a development in both the theater supply system and the chemical supply system. The terms *theater supply system* and *chemical supply system* are employed advisedly, because the theater system and each technical service system tended to develop independently although both were dependent to a considerable degree upon the War Department system. But that War Department system was only eight months old at the time of the landings in North Africa, and, as it was never able completely to overcome the traditional autonomy of the technical services in the United States, so was it even less able to exert its influence on the theater technical services through the intermediary of the theater organization.

The theaters themselves had developed no consistent policy of supply organization. It was, for example, more than two years after the initial landings before the North African theater corrected a "serious flaw in the structure of organization," the assignment of base sections to NATOUSA rather than SOS NATOUSA headquarters.[21] War Department and theater attempts at supply system evaluation and co-ordination were consequently sporadic. With an almost overwhelming amount of logistical work to be done in an unfamiliar and difficult set of circumstances and in the apparent absence of specific and consistent guidance from the major commands, each supply officer in the theater, whether of high or low echelon, pitched in to do the job as he saw it, creating his own policy in the process. Such *ad hoc* procedures inevitably resulted in the establishment of several systems, and, as the Mediterranean theater assistant chief of staff, G–4, later pointed out

---

[20] Howe, *Northwest Africa*, pp. 84–96. The third force was Eastern Task Force, a British controlled element.

[21] Logistical History of NATOUSA–MTOUSA, p. 30.

with some asperity, each theater chief of technical service developed his own supply system.[22]

The period of the landings and the two months thereafter represent the initial phase in the establishment of the theater CWS supply system. During this phase the confusion and frustration of the lower echelon chemical supply officers led to measures for co-ordination at theater technical service level.

Western Task Force

Maj. Bruce T. Humphreville, Colonel Barker's assistant, who had won a coin toss with his chief for the honor, and four of the chemical section's enlisted men went in with the first wave of the WTF landing at Fedala and in the process lost all their personal equipment except the clothing they were wearing and their weapons. Colonel Barker, Capt. James J. Heffner, and the remainder of the WTF CWS contingent arrived in the D+5 (11–13 November 1942) support convoy outside the wreckage-strewn harbor of Casablanca, French Morocco, but the lack of facilities ashore kept them from landing. A few hours before debarkation at Casablanca on 19 November 1942, Colonel Barker informed the men of the decontamination platoon through their commanding officer, 1st Lt. Robert D. Myers, that they were to operate the task force chemical depot while the 78th Chemical Smoke Generator Company, which was to arrive with the D+20 convoy, worked with the Navy and the antiaircraft regiment on port air defense. Depot operation proved to be more of a job than the sixty days of chemical supply carried on the D+5 convoy and the thirty days from the assault convoy would seem to indicate. The principal difficulty was the lack of operating equipment and vehicles. The first platoon unit equipment was never unloaded from the transport, at least not at Casablanca, since the support convoy turned back after discharging only half its load. Unit transportation was scheduled to arrive on a later convoy. Most of the equipment and transportation of the task force chemical section had been lost when three transport ships were torpedoed and burned off the Moroccan port of Fedala. Chemical supplies were widely scattered throughout the Casablanca-Fedala area, even as far away as Safi (120 miles from Casablanca),

---

[22] *Ibid.*, p. 76.

in an all-services, all-classes [23] jumble which became only the more confused with each incoming shipload.[24]

Barker and Humphreville had fortunately been furnished money belts well stuffed with worn French francs, mostly in large notes. They bought a Ford truck and a Renault sedan, rented a tile factory for a depot, and hired some local labor. In Barker's opinion the money was the most valuable commodity they took ashore. The first platoon moved into a part of the tile factory, borrowed some quartermaster trucks, and proceeded to collect, transport, sort, stack, and inventory chemical supplies, most of which were located by a bicycle-mounted squad that regularly patrolled the docks. Barker's own WTF Chemical Section, except for two men, worked with them. The bulk of the supply, Class II protective items, was stored in the factory warehouses. Class V items, mostly incendiary and smoke grenades and fog oil, were stored in an open courtyard adjacent to the factory. On 21 December Colonel Barker reported the local supply position stabilized with about 3,000 tons of all supplies in storage. The chemical supply plan was entirely of chemical section creation. WTF headquarters, while it had not interposed objections, had offered no help and no direction to the chemical procedures. Each of the other technical services represented had likewise set up its own procedures and was operating according to its own policy.[25]

Center Task Force

Chemical officers with CTF—Colonel Burn, task force (II Corps) chemical officer, Major Croen, acting chemical officer of Mediterranean Base Section, and Colonel Elliott, chemical officer of Twelfth Air Force and XII Air Force Service Command—landed near Oran from the assault and assault support convoys (11–21 November 1942) to find

---

[23] *Classes* refers to classes of supply, designated as follows: Class I, food; Class II, unit and organization allowances of clothing, weapons, vehicles, and tools; Class III, fuels and lubricants; Class IV, unit and organization special equipment not subject to prescribed allowances but allotted according to operational needs; Class V, ammunition, pyrotechnics, mines, and chemical warfare agents.

[24] (1) Personal Ltr, Barker, CmlO WTF, to Porter, 20 Nov 42, no sub. CWS SPCW 314.1/188 in file CWS 314.7 Barker Corresp, NATO, 1942–43. (2) 21st Cml Decontamination Co History, Sep 42 to Sep 44. (3) Leighton and Coakley, *Global Logistics, 1940–45*, pp. 449–51. (4) Ltr, Barker to Hist Off, 11 Aug 59.

[25] (1) 21st Cml Decontamination Co History, Sep 42 to Sep 44. (2) Personal Ltr, Barker to Porter, 21 Dec 42. CWS SPCW 319.1/188 in file CWS 314.7, Barker Corresp, NATO. (3) Barker to Hist Off, 11 Aug 59.

a supply situation as bad as the one first experienced at Casablanca.[26] Although the lack of service units and materials had enabled the planners to schedule only twenty-seven tons of Classes II and IV and only nineteen tons of ammunition for these convoys, the landing organizations had strewn poorly marked supplies of all shapes and sizes throughout the beachhead area. The chemical officers found that to distinguish between maintenance supplies and the 60-day reserve, which organizations and units were scheduled to retain as their property, was virtually impossible. Even when the organization property was identified, the combat commanders understandably asked to be relieved of the burden of caring for it.[27]

Colonel Burn, his 3 officers and 7 men, established a chemical depot in a slaughterhouse on the outskirts of Oran, Algeria, in which they handled more than 70 tons of Classes II and IV in less than a month with the help of local labor and a detail of engineer troops. Burn vigorously stated his need for chemical service troops and suggested that service troops be assigned to the leading elements of any future operation.[28] Croen and his section, which eventually numbered 8 officers and 17 men, established themselves in Oran where Mediterranean Base Section became operative under the supervision of II Corps on 11 November 1942, the day on which the first echelon landed. The MBS Chemical Section concentrated on setting up chemical storage and supply operations. The base section group took over the slaughterhouse depot and began gathering such chemical supplies as Burn and his men had been unable to locate or unable to move. Knowing that British smoke pots were subject to spontaneous combustion when wet, Croen made an extra effort to collect them with the idea of establishing several small ammunition dumps at some distance from the city. The sites had been prepared and most of the pots collected in the slaughterhouse courtyard awaiting the availability of transportation, when one of the pots ignited. The courtyard, which had been the only storage point, became an inferno minutes after the first pot flared. Most of the other supplies were saved, and the slaughterhouse was sufficiently isolated so that no other damage was done, but the new AFHQ head-

---

[26] Colonel Maling, who was at the time assigned to staff duty with the advance echelon of AFHQ, reached the landing area from a ship which was torpedoed and sunk just offshore.

[27] (1) Burn Ltr, 5 Dec 42. (2) Capone Interv, 24 Apr 58. (Major Capone was a member of the Twelfth Air Force Chemical Section.) (3) History of MBS. (4) Maling Ltr, 3 Apr 43.

[28] Burn Ltr, 5 Dec 42.

quarters in Algiers had to await resupply before effective smoke concealment could be provided. The lesson of this unfortunate accident was that specialist service troops and transportation are needed early in any operation. After the arrival of the 6th Chemical Depot Company with the base section third echelon on 6 December to take over the job of establishing chemical depots and depot sections, the service problem was considerably eased.[29]

Since there was no transportation available, members of Elliott's section hiked several miles to their designated area near La Sénia, Algeria, on the day of their landing. They bivouacked in a sea of mud and returned the next day to the port area to begin collecting supplies. Whenever any form of transportation could be begged or borrowed or whenever space could be obtained on any truck going in the right direction, they shipped supplies to La Sénia. Since they had no materials-handling equipment, no shelter and no depot setup, the only virtue in sending the material to La Sénia was that it could be sorted, identified, and piled in some sort of order. They hired local workers whenever possible, sometimes paying them from personal funds or by bartering personal possessions. Arrangements had been made in planning for the Twelfth Air Force to draw chemical supply from II Corps stocks while that organization controlled supply and subsequently from the base section. II Corps was unable to meet the air force's demands, and when the responsibility passed to the base section, that headquarters was forced to restrict the air force share to 25 percent of available supplies. MBS early became the focal point of supply for the Tunisia Campaign, and, in view of the fact that its original maintenance level was half that of WTF, a quota issue policy was the only answer to an increasingly perilous stock situation. Air force's chemical officers approved the quota imposition because they understood that their requisitions would otherwise have exhausted base section supplies. Under these conditions, the Chemical Section, XII AFSC, was six months in building up to a 30-day balanced supply.[30]

Shadle, his 2 British colleagues, 1 other American officer, and 2 American enlisted men arrived in the theater in early December. As

---

[29] (1) History of MBS. The base section became independent of II Corps on 6 December. (2) Logistical History of NATOUSA–MTOUSA, pp. 20–22. (3) 6th Chemical Depot Co History (12 Jul 42 to 8 Aug 43), 1944. (4) Croen Interv, 21 Sep 59.

[30] (1) Capone Interv, 24 Apr 58. (2) Maling to Porter, 3 Apr 43. (3) Elliott Comments 16 Jan 61.

Shadle indicated to the Chief, CWS, 2 officers could not thoroughly perform the multifarious duties demanded of the American (NATOUSA) complement of the Allied Force Headquarters, but they devoted as much time as possible to "one of the biggest jobs" they had, the supply of troops. Shadle examined operations in MBS and noted that, despite great obstacles, Croen was doing "a 'bang-up' job." Then, accompanied by Elliott, he visited WTF, which had not yet received the designated base section complement from the United States, and discussed chemical matters with Barker. Shadle found the whole theater force prepared to provide individual protection against gas warfare, and he found the CWS capable of meeting its supply responsibilities of the moment, but offensive preparedness was only in the early planning stage while almost the entire theater chemical supply organization and process remained to be developed.[31]

Chemical Supply—Theater Organization Phase

Colonel Shadle's first task in the second phase of North African logistics development, after the task force service groups were absorbed in and supplanted by Atlantic Base Section (WTF) and Mediterranean Base Section (CTF) under AFHQ on 30 December 1942, was to decide upon an issue policy and to make corresponding storage and handling arrangements.[32] In theory, the base section chemical sections would simply have ordered their depots to fill table of equipment or table of allowance shortages for any organization or unit according to unit or organization requisition, but continental theory failed to cover the rough facts of life on the far shore. Many tables of allowances and tables of organization and equipment were incomplete, and the chemical sections were unacquainted with many others which had recently been revised or introduced. Even had information concerning new tables been provided in the theater, it would have been of no help. The North African logistics arrangements had been made with the old tables in mind and implemented with matériel available; therefore, chemical section depots lacked the quantity and variety of equipment demanded. Furthermore, many units arrived without basic equipment or with unusual demands for equipment to suit special operational

[31] (1) Personal Ltr, Shadle, Chief Cml Sec AFHQ, to Porter, CCWS, 11 Feb 43. CWS 201—Shadle, Charles S. (O) in file CWS 314.7 Pers Files, NATO, Feb–Dec 43. (2) Barker to Porter, 21 Dec 42.

[32] Base sections were organized by AFHQ General Orders, 38, 30 December 1942, cited in History of AFHQ, Part II, Section 1, pages 169–75.

needs. Shortages developed, but the chemical supply officers' immediate concern was the determination of the extent of these shortages and the forecasting of future demands on the issue system. Colonel Shadle; Col. Siegfried P. Coblentz, Chemical Officer, Atlantic Base Section, who had arrived with part of his section in Casablanca on Christmas Eve, 1942; Colonel Johnson, who arrived in February 1943 to become Chemical Officer, MBS; and Colonel Barker, who became Chemical Officer, Fifth United States Army, when it was activated at Oujda, Morocco, on 5 January 1943—all found that the principal obstacle to the determination of an issue policy was lack of information on current and forecast demand and on supply allowances.[33]

As an interim measure pending the establishment of an issue policy, Shadle adopted a compilation of chemical logistics data prepared by Colonel Barker on the basis of his experience.[34] This compilation was intended to serve as a guide in estimating issue, storage, and handling requirements, but the chemical officers were aware of the fact that it was far from definitive. They exhorted their colleagues in the United States to supply them with such information as the number of troops scheduled for the theater, the current descriptions of items and packaging in shipments, and the new development of material and techniques. Barker particularly requested a compact compilation of logistics data for field use which would be so handy and so valuable that it could compete for space in personal baggage with such essential items as candy bars and toilet paper. General Waitt, Assistant Chief, CWS, for Field Operations, promised that a pocket-size supply and issue catalog would be forthcoming, but no War Department approval for such a publication was ever secured.[35]

OCCWS found it difficult to provide information to the theater chemical officers. Both Porter and Waitt tried to include all information possible in personal letters. The personal letter method was un-

---

[33] (1) Shadle to Porter, 11 Feb 43. (2) Personal Ltr, Coblentz, CmlO ABS, to Waitt, Chief Opns Div OCCWS, 25 Feb 43. CWS SPVCO (4–3–43) in file CWS 314.7 Pers Files, NATO, Feb–Dec 43. (3) Ltr, Johnson, CmlO MBS, to CCWS, 12 Apr 43, sub: Résumé of CWS Problems. CWS 314.7 Corresp, NATO, Apr–Jun 43. (4) Ltr, Barker, CmlO Fifth Army, to CCWS, attn: Waitt, 9 Jan 43, no sub. CWS 314.7 Barker Corresp, NATO, 1942–43.

[34] (1) Coblentz to Waitt, 25 Feb 43. (2) Hq Fifth Army Cml Warfare Memo 1, 4 Feb 43, sub: Data on Cml Warfare Sups [Col Barker's logistics data compilation]. CWS MTO 050 Logistical Data.

[35] (1) Ltr, Waitt, Chief Opns Div OCCWS to CmlO Fifth Army, 5 Mar 43, sub: Development of CWS Items. CWS SPCVO (3–5–43) in file CWS 314.7 Barker Corresp, NATO, 1942–43. (2) Ltr, Waitt, ACCWS Fld Opns, to CCmlO [sic] MBS, thru CCmlO AFHQ, 30 Jun 43, sub: Résumé of CWS Problems. CWS SPCVO (30 Jun 43) in file CWS 314.7 Corresp, NATO, Apr–Jun 43.

orthodox, but it was effective for some kinds of information particularly since the small number of regular CWS officers were so well acquainted with one another that there was little chance that personal letters would be misunderstood. When Porter and Loucks came to North Africa in April 1943 after their sojourn in the European theater, Porter appraised the information problem as being the most serious matter facing the chemical officers overseas. He accordingly directed the establishment of a liaison officer position for each theater in his own office.[36] These liaison officers were assembled in a theaters division operating under Waitt. Waitt inaugurated a special series of "Theater of Operations Letters" in May to let all principal overseas chemical officers know what was going on in the United States and in other theaters. Waitt almost immediately ran into a stumbling block. ASF wished to clear all information sent to the theaters and even wanted to control the content of technical channels communications. The CWS and the other technical services were forbidden to reproduce or even make extracts from official publications. Waitt deemed it necessary to continue technical channels communications which, as he later expressed it, "short-circuited ASF." [37] The use of theater of operations letters continued, but they were carefully oriented to technical, mostly research and development and intelligence, matters. Waitt's listing of official publications must have been frustrating to North African chemical officers since assembling a set of such publications was not possible at the time.[38] Indeed, Waitt and his liaison officers in the United States were frustrated at being unable to furnish all the information required in any form the chemical officers overseas might want it. Waitt felt that most of the information desired was eventually supplied, even if by means almost clandestine.[39] But the problem of the moment early in 1943 was information on which to base an issue policy and that need was not met at the time. During the second phase of NATOUSA CWS development, for approximately the first six months of 1943, each of the base section chemical officers decided what allow-

[36] Ltr, Loucks to All Concerned [OCCWS], 23 Apr 43. CWS SPCWS 319.1 (CW Activities in Great Britain).

[37] Ltr, Waitt to Hist Off, 14 Sep 59.

[38] (1) Barker to Porter, 9 Jan 43. (2) Johnson to Porter, 12 Apr 43. (3) Croen Interv, 21 Sep 59.

[39] (1) Waitt Comments, 5 Jan 61. (2) Waitt Interv, 13 May 61.

ances of matériel to make as each instance of demand on the chemical supply system arose.[40]

Theater Chemical Section Organization

The fact that base section chemical officers had to make their own interim policy decisions demonstrates that Shadle had a communications problem of his own. During the first two months ashore, no communications system was operating well enough across the 1,500-mile range of the North African campaign to permit a comprehensive assessment of the situation. Personal visits provided the only feasible solution to this problem. Shadle visited the field elements, as he had done soon after arriving in North Africa, whenever he could, and field officers, in turn, visited him and each other. As a means of control these visits were too infrequent and too brief to be effective, but they at least kept chemical officers informed on the activities of their colleagues. In February 1943 the War Department drew new boundaries and created the North African Theater of Operations. While Americans in AFHQ had long assumed that this theater was to be activated, there was officially no theater organization in North Africa. The theater organization in charge was the ETO in recognition of General Eisenhower's dual role as AFHQ and European theater commander. Upon the official creation of a new theater, Eisenhower designated the American element of AFHQ as the NATOUSA headquarters without physically separating the Allied and American elements. Shadle then added to his own office two American-staffed divisions, one for operations and training, the other for supply and requirements.[41]

Neither of these new divisions had any operating function comparable to that of Supply Division in the European theater. Again, distance prevented direct control. Barker was handling training in the Fifth Army headquarters, and supply operations were still handled by the base section and combat organization chemical officers. A supply co-ordinating and operating agency was in the process of activation. The Services of Supply, NATOUSA, had been organized, and Maj. Arthur C. Rogers, assisted by one enlisted man, opened the chemical section on 25 February 1943.[42] Col. Lewis F. Acker served as Chemical

---

[40] (1) Col Siegfried P. Coblentz, USAR (Ret.), Comments on draft of this volume, 9 Jan 61.   (2) Croen Interv, 21 Sep 59.

[41] History of AFHQ, pt. II, sec. 4, pp. 510–11.

[42] History, COMZ NATOUSA–MTOUSA, Nov 42–44, pt. I.

Officer, SOS NATOUSA, during the month of March, but he could accomplish little beyond arranging section organization since supply supervision channels were not yet in operation. In any case, early SOS lines of authority were not clear, manpower was not allotted in sufficient numbers for the task at hand, and existing regulations failed to cover the functions or the procedures of the organization. During April, with a section enlarged to three officers and twelve enlisted men, Maj. Alfred J. P. Wilson, acting chemical officer, began to assume the responsibilities of requirements computation and supervision of supply status reporting. Shadle pointed out to Wilson and to Col. Alfred L. Rockwood, who became SOS NATOUSA chemical officer in May, that chemical supply policy was the province of the theater chief of service. Shadle exercised his policy control through his Supply and Requirements Division which was assigned the additional duty of compiling and reporting statistical data on supply levels and on handling of chemical warfare supplies in the theater. In practice, the function of Shadle's office became more one of review than of control since nearly every operational act involved policy decisions, and the SOS headquarters at Oran was too far removed from AFHQ and NATOUSA organizations in Algiers to permit concomitant review.[43] The control-review situation was, however, not the only complication. The base sections continued to report to NATOUSA rather than to SOS, and base section chemical officers sometimes looked to Shadle's office for co-ordination of activities. Further, as in the European theater, many chemical problems continued to be handled through informal, personal contact outside the established channels of authority. Maj. Gen. Thomas B. Larkin, SOS NATOUSA commander, once asked Shadle to handle a chemical staffing problem in SOS. When Shadle pointed out that the SOS, a separate command, was outside his area, Larkin disagreed and reasserted that Shadle as theater chief chemical officer should deal with the matter.[44] Shadle did provide a solution to this problem and in so doing set his own precedent for an authority crossing a command line. Subsequently,

---

[43] (1) History of COMZ NATOUSA–MTOUSA, pt. IV, Introduction, and History of Cml Warfare Sec SOS NATOUSA. (2) History of AFHQ, pt. II, sec. 4, pp. 510–13. (3) Personal Ltr, Shadle to Waitt, 26 May 43. CWS 314.7 Pers Files, NATO, Feb 43–Feb 44. (4) Interv, Hist Off with Col Alfred J. P. Wilson, USAR, 16 Oct 58.

[44] Shadle Interv, 16 May 61.

Shadle, or members of his immediate staff, did informally handle a number of other problems outside the theater headquarters.

While problems of control did arise and while the CWS of AFHQ and NATOUSA was tending to be a separate service as in the European theater, Shadle did not view his control problem as being as serious as Rowan's. Shadle was in a better prestige position than Rowan since his position on the AFHQ and NATOUSA staffs was not complicated by an SOS jurisdiction over the technical services. Also, while Rowan from the end of 1942 to the end of 1943 was left largely without the support of ranking, experienced chemical officers, Shadle had experienced, aggressive, ranking chemical officers in almost every field position.[45] He could count on the field officers to perform their own liaison with field elements and to direct field CWS activities. Shadle did have a matter of some personal embarrassment in this connection—both Rockwood and Barker were his seniors in rank and the seniority rule for appointment to top positions had been almost inflexible in the Army prior to World War II. Shadle did not view seniority as being of great importance in his own case; only on one occasion did a senior officer point out his junior status.[46] On the whole, the autonomy of the field chemical sections and the rank represented there worked in the favor of the NATOUSA CWS and its chief.

Shadle concentrated on the staff relationships within his own headquarters and he consulted with or worked with the AFHQ and NATOUSA assistant chiefs of staff whenever chemical warfare matters were under consideration. He informed Waitt that his advice was sought and accepted by these officers.[47] This is not to say that there were no stresses and strains in CWS administration in North Africa. At the time of the organization of NATOUSA, Shadle praised the work of his American and British subordinates, but privately complained to Porter that Rowan and Montgomery had prevented his acquisition of more experienced officers. How the European theater officers could have blocked him he did not make clear since his own headquarters allotment prevented an increase in his immediate staff and

---

[45] Rowan highly valued the Reserve and AUS officers serving on his staff and in the field in the European theater. Both he and General Porter indicate that the contribution of such officers to the success of CWS operations in Europe can hardly be overstated, but the fact remained that prior to the cross-Channel attack Rowan suffered from a lack of sufficient rank and experience among ETO CWS officers. (1) Rowan Comments, 16 Dec 60. (2) Porter Interv, 24 Aug 61.

[46] (1) Personal Ltr, Shadle to Waitt, 26 May 43. (2) Shadle Interv, 16 May 61.

[47] (1) Shadle to Waitt, 26 May 43. (2) Shadle Interv, 16 May 61.

since most of the senior ETO CWS officers had moved into North African field commands.[48] By the time of Porter's and Louck's visit to North Africa in April, the CWS NATOUSA had apparently adjusted to the staffing situation since the visiting officers did not mention it in their letters reporting North African troubles. The pressing problem at the moment was that the chemical supply situation as a whole in North Africa had deteriorated to a "dangerously low position." [49]

Chemical Supply Situation: Spring 1943

The serious threat to the North African theater's chemical warfare potential in April was the result of failure to obtain sufficient material from the zone of interior to raise the theater stock level and to balance it. As in the case of issue, the acquisition and balancing of theater stocks was, in theory, a simple matter. Theater levels were determined by the War Department on the advice of the theater commander. The ports of embarkation then automatically furnished food, fuel, and spare parts according to theater strength and number of vehicles in use. The theater requisitioned shipments in supply Classes II and IV to bring stocks up to desired levels. Ammunition was to be furnished according to War Department allotment.[50] But again, as task force experience demonstrated, theory rode high in the clouds while fact plodded the Tunisian sands. In the first place, the War Department instructions were issued at the time that planning for the North African operation was at its peak; even if the official publication was immediately and widely circulated, it is doubtful that supply officers would have had the time to give it much consideration. In the second place, the War Department for some time in effect suspended its own procedures, supplying Class II and IV supplies automatically rather than on requisitions based on actual consumption rates in the theater. The New York Port of Embarkation (NYPE) could not adjust quantities or kinds of supply until there was a considerable easing of the problems of shipping space and supply documentation.[51] The

[48] Shadle to Porter, 11 Feb 43.

[49] Rpt, Cml Warfare Statistical Summary, Text Summary (hereafter cited as Statistical Summary), 30 Apr 43. MTO CWS 400.19 Statistical Summary.

[50] WD Memo 700-8-42, 10 Oct 42.

[51] (1) Leighton and Coakley, Global Logistics, 1940–1943, p. 321 and ch. XVI. (2) Logistical History of NATOUSA-MTOUSA, pp. 51–54.

theater staff found over-all supply documentation virtually impossible: there was no common reporting form, and, if there had been, the situation was too fluid and communication too poor for assembling data, particularly from the combat units.

The base section chemical officers assumed the burden of evaluating chemical supply status on the receiving end because no one else possessed as much chemical information. They then submitted requisitions for shortages to the United States (NYPE), but some of these were edited or rejected by the port of embarkation because of noncompliance with the WD overseas supply procedures memorandum. Even in cases when the material was shipped, the port required a 90-day processing and shipping period. The base section chemical officers pleaded with the OCCWS to expedite supply, particularly items such as FS smoke, colored smoke, white phosphorus and thermite grenades, stocks of which were entirely depleted. General Waitt replied that he was unable to influence the requisitioning and shipping situation which was entirely governed by ASF and higher headquarters.[52]

The North African chemical officers could do little but wait and hope that shipments would be forthcoming from the United States. Their hopes were met, quantitatively at least, during the next month. Shipments received during May increased stocks so that 80 percent of major ground forces items were stocked in levels above the authorized forty-five days. The air force's chemical supply position also improved although not as much as the ground force supply. The Chemical Section, Eastern Base Section, established by Capt. Carl E. Grant in February, was authorized to allot 50 percent of its stocks to the XII Air Force Service Command. Balancing stocks among the base sections continued to be a problem until at least the fall of 1943, since congested ports and inadequate railroad facilities rendered inter-depot transfers extremely difficult.[53]

Qualitatively, the supply picture was not so bright. Most of the items reported stocked at or exceeding authorized levels were protective items. The level of individual gas protection had been high and had

---

[52] (1) Personal Ltr, Barker to Porter, 21 Feb 43. CWS 412.3 APO 464 (Sabotage Device) in CWS 314.7 Barker Corresp NATO, 1942–43. (2) Personal Ltr, Coblentz to Waitt, 3 Mar 43. CWS 314.7 Pers Files, NATO, Feb–Oct 43. (3) Personal Ltr, Coblentz to Waitt, 22 Apr 43. ABSCW in same file. (4) Personal Ltr, Waitt to Coblentz, 3 Apr 43. CWS SPCVO (4–3–43) in CWS 314.7 Pers Files, NATO, Feb–Oct 43. (5) Waitt to CmlO MBS, 30 Jun 43. (6) Johnson to Porter, 12 Apr 43.
[53] (1) Statistical Summary, 30 Apr, 31 May 43. (2) Maling Ltr, 3 Apr 43. (3) Logistical History of NATOUSA–MTOUSA, p. 23.

remained so although the quantity of individual protective items in the resupply system was low in April. The collective protection potential,[54] on the other hand, was lower than that for individual protection: the SOS Chemical Section reported shortages of the common decontaminating agent, bleach (chloride of lime), of the power-driven decontaminating apparatus, and of the collective protector.[55] These shortages of protective supplies were important given the assumption that gas warfare could be initiated at any time, but the supply of gas warfare items to be used offensively should gas warfare retaliation be necessary was even more important. Supply of the nongas warfare chemical munitions such as incendiary bombs and high explosive mortar shell was highly important also.

At the end of May, Shadle expressed his satisfaction with the chemical offensive potential and ammunition status in the North African theater. His view seems to have been overly optimistic since smoke pots, tear gas, and HC smoke grenades were the only ammunition items available in sufficient supply. All the chemical supply officers reported urgent requests for unavailable white phosphorus grenades. The Twelfth Air Force reported limited quantities of ANM50A1 4-pound incendiary bombs, a few M52 500-pound incendiary bomb clusters, and a considerable number of M54 100-pound incendiary bomb clusters. There was no other chemical ammunition in the theater although the New York port had promised that 120 days' supply of high explosive and smoke shell was en route for the three chemical mortar battalions which had recently arrived in the theater. Aside from a small amount of artillery shell stored by Ordnance, no toxics were available in the theater and none was scheduled to arrive until the fall of 1943. The March theater plan for gas warfare, the first such plan, was based on meeting possible enemy gas attack with this plainly inadequate supply of artillery shell. The new War Department policy for retaliation in event of enemy initiation of gas warfare called for the use of aerial munitions as the principal gas weapons. Shadle's satisfaction with the toxic supply status can be explained by the fact that he did not con-

[54] Collective protection is that provided to units or groups of men. For example, units and organizations were provided with area and equipment decontaminating agents and the means to apply them should vesicant gases be used. The collective protector, a machine for filtering and circulating air, was to be provided for command posts and other crucial command and service installations which could not readily be moved in the event of gas attack. Brophy, Miles and Cochrane, *From Laboratory to Field*, ch. IV.

[55] (1) Statistical Summary, 30 Apr, 31 May 43. (2) Shadle to Waitt, 26 May 43.

sider the lack of aerial munitions to be a critical problem. He believed that the Axis Powers were in no position to initiate gas warfare in North Africa, a correct estimate, as it happens, for subsequent investigation proved that there were no German toxic munitions in North Africa. Still, in terms of War Department policy and authorized theater levels, the North African theater was critically short of offensive chemical munitions.[56]

Field conditions produced a further complication in the supply problem which was not unanticipated among chemical officers but which was not provided for by the War Department. Troops in the field are ingenious at adapting supplies to their own purposes. While the use of the gas mask carrier as a carry-all was frowned upon because it meant loss of the mask, chemical officers overlooked or unofficially encouraged secondary use of other gas warfare supplies in a nongas warfare situation. An acetate eyeshield had been developed by the British to provide readily available individual protection against liquid vesicant droplets in the absence of the gas mask. The United States forces in North Africa had been supplied with these eyeshields before the War Department declared them obsolete. North African troops used eyeshields in lieu of sunglasses and as protection against swirling dust and sand. Constant demand nearly exhausted the supply and, since there was no resupply channel for obsolete items, created a problem for which chemical officers saw only one solution. The War Department had to be convinced that gas warfare items such as the eyeshield could be used in a nongas warfare situation so that a resupply channel such as existed for other items could be provided. Antigas shoe impregnite could be used as "canned heat," as could the chemical fire starter, and, when applied to tents, shoe impregnite proved an excellent waterproofing substance and served as a base for sand camouflage. Antigas covers could also be used as a waterproof covering for shelter tents, and antigas curtains, when obtainable, served as ground sheets, tarpaulins, and foxhole covers. The decontaminating appa-

---

[56] (1) Statistical Summary, 30 Apr, 31 May 43. (2) Shadle Ltr, 26 May 43. (3) Maling Ltr, 3 Apr 43. (4) Col Gerhard to CCWS, 13 May 43, Notes on Visit by Col Frederick W. Gerhard, CWS, to Theaters of Operations in England and Northern Africa. CWS 314.7 Observer Rpts. (5) Memo, Actg ACofS OPD WDGS for CG ASF, 11 Aug 43, sub: Implementation of Theater Plans for Gas Warfare NATO. OPD 385 CWP (11 Aug 43). (6) Ltr, CinC AFHQ to TAG, 19 Mar 43, sub: Cml Warfare Plan for NATO. AFHQ AG 322.095/378 CWS–M in file OPD 385 CWS sec. 11B.

ratuses could be used for insecticide spraying, carrying water, fighting fires, and giving showers. CWS nongas warfare supply turned out to be a considerably more active business than had been intended, particularly since CWS officers could not allow the secondary uses of chemical items to lower the gas protective potential.[57]

As the second phase of the chemical supply operation in the North African theater drew to a close in June, the weapons and ammunition status took a turn for the worse. Supplies earmarked for the Sicilian operation were withdrawn without the prospect of immediate replacement. The process of chemical supply planning for the assault on Sicily had begun in March when Major Humphreville, newly designated Chemical Officer, Seventh Army, sent the supply unit of his section to Oran to plan with the Chemical Section, SOS NATOUSA.[58] Since logistic data were not available, the Chemical Section, MBS, supplied estimated data which the SOS and Seventh Army sections used to compute requirements. The SOS Chemical Section submitted requisitions to the zone of interior for assault matériel requirements and for maintenance stocks which were to be built up to a 30-day level as soon as depot operations in Sicily were practicable. The SOS section computed requirements on a regular table of allowance and maintenance factor basis, relying on estimates in cases when information was lacking.[59] This system presented no problems in Class II supply except for spare parts for which maintenance factors were unavailable. Any determination of spare parts usage rate was purely guesswork, and, even had estimates been accurate, spare parts stocks both in the theater and the ZI were wholly inadequate to meet the demand. The SOS supply officers found that the great drain on theater reserves came in the Class IV and special equipment categories. Major Humphreville requested special allotments of grenades and flame throwers and, in view of the constant need for smoke concealment in

[57] (1) Statistical Summary, 30 Apr, 31 May 43. (2) Barker Comments, Feb 61. (3) Coblentz Comments, 9 Jan 61. (4) For more information on eyeshields, see Brophy, Miles, and Cochrane, *From Laboratory to Field*, Chapter IV.

[58] Seventh Army was not officially activated until 10 July 1943. The predecessor headquarters was I Armored Corps.

[59] A maintenance factor was the estimated resupply quantity per month, stated as a percentage of the total theater stock, or of any item, necessary to maintain stock level, both in depots and in the hands of troops, while losses because of wearing out, capture, abandonment, pilferage, and the like were occurring. This designation was, in November 1943, changed to "replacement factor" to avoid confusion between repair and resupply. WD Cir 297, 13 Nov 43.

the North African ports, 100,000 smoke pots for emergency use in the Sicilian ports.[60]

Major Wilson, then acting chief of the SOS Chemical Section, protested this smoke pot allotment to the SOS commander, General Larkin, for two reasons: (1) regardless of requirements, a lack of shipping dictated a space allotment plan for Sicilian cargo, and most of the CWS space would be filled with smoke pots; (2) filling the Seventh Army demand for smoke pots would exhaust theater stocks and would require special shipments from the United States. General Larkin agreed to revise the Seventh Army requisition to a smaller amount, but General Patton, now Seventh Army commander designate, appealed directly to General Eisenhower. Reasoning from the point of view which thereafter governed supply policy for both the North African and European theaters—that the combat commander should have anything he wanted—General Eisenhower insisted on the supply of the original smoke pot requisition.[61]

In this particular instance Major Wilson was probably right. But, in retrospect, this incident and the supply operations which it represents assume more significance than the immediate problems imply, for this operation marks the bifurcation of the chemical supply system. Henceforth, one element of the chemical supply system was oriented, despite doctrine to the contrary, to an impetus from the front.[62] This element of the system was primarily devoted to meeting the demands and special requirements of the combat forces, especially for new equipment, such as the lightweight mechanical smoke generator, or equipment used in new missions, such as the 4.2-inch chemical mortar.[63]

---

[60] (1) Maj Humphreville, CmlO Seventh Army [to CG Seventh Army] (copy to CCWS), 15 Sep 43, Rpt of Cml Warfare Opns, Sicilian Campaign, reproduced as sec. H, pt. II, of Rpt of Opn of the U.S. Seventh Army in the Sicilian Campaign, 10 Jul–17 Aug 43, Sep 43. (2) History of Cml Warfare Sec SOS NATOUSA, in History of COMZ NATOUSA–MTOUSA. (3) Wilson Interv, 16 Oct 58. (4) IOM, A.L.R. [Col Alfred L Rockwood, CmlO SOS NATOUSA] to CofS [SOS NATOUSA], 20 Jul 43, no sub. CWS MTO 400.19 Statistical Summary. (5) MBS reported no spare parts, except for a wholly inadequate supply of some mortar parts, on hand as of 28 June 1943. CWS MBS [to Cml Sec SOS NATOUSA], Stock Status and Matériel Issue Rpt, 28 Jun 43. CWS MTO 142.1 Inventory (Corresp).

[61] (1) Wilson Interv, 16 Oct 58. (2) Memo for Rcd, Rpt of Material on Hand in Depots and ASP's in Sicily as of 20 Aug 43, dated 29 Aug 43, Cml Sec AFHQ and NATOUSA. In CWS MTO 142.1 Inventory (Corresp). (3) Min of Staff Conf, Hq SOS NATOUSA, 4 May 43. CWS MTO 337 Confs.

[62] Colonel Coblentz maintains (Comments, 9 January 1961) that the impetus from the front orientation started earlier when base section chemical officers began deciding their own issue policy.

[63] For use of new equipment and smoke technique development, see below, Chapter VIII, and for mortar operations, see Chapter XI.

Impetus from the front meant that line organizations determined their own requirements for materials, determined how those materials should be used, and what the procedures of the supply system which provided them should be. It must be noted that under the impetus from the rear theory the line organizations had also always determined their own requirements, but the point of difference is that they selected their requirements from a list provided by and with procedures ordained by supply organizations, whereas under impetus from the front they drew up their own lists and established their own procedures. The other element, which retained the impetus from the rear orientation, was concentrated on the development of gas warfare offensive and defensive potential. Although the two elements of the chemical supply system overlapped and although they were both handled by the whole CWS organization in the theater, base and field chemical sections became increasingly concerned with the immediate nongas warfare support of combat forces and their routine preparedness for gas warfare defense. The impetus from the front pattern imposed great strains on the supply system. War Department long-range supply planning and even the planning of the SOS in the theater was frequently scrapped or greatly amended when combat forces demanded a 6-month supply of an item for a 30-day operation or when a standard item of supply was rejected. This pattern also called for many improvisations. Many front-line organization chemical officers gave reality and immediacy to Fries's concept of the closest possible connection between research and the fighting line by carrying on a certain amount of research and even manufacture in the combat zone. Initially, the CWS in the theater used the same supply channels and procedures for both elements of the system, but as the Joint and Combined Chiefs of Staff and their subsidiary committees assumed more direct control of gas warfare policy,[64] the impetus of supply for the preparedness mission moved even farther to the rear than formerly.

Chemical Supply and Administration—Development of the Theater Chemical System

The accommodation of the existing system of impetus from the rear to the new demands of the unofficial system of impetus from the

---

[64] See Brophy and Fisher, *Organizing for War*, ch. IV.

front characterized the third phase of chemical supply in North Africa. This phase in the theater CWS supply and administrative system, in contrast to the second phase, was marked by the availability of an increasing amount of supply information to chemical supply officers. This development had its inception in the establishment, mentioned above, of a statistical reporting function in Shadle's office. It gathered momentum from the activities of each supply officer in the field and from the operation of the SOS Chemical Section and from the improved communications throughout the theater. In April, for example, Major Wilson invited the chemical supply officers to a conference in which they arrived at a common understanding of procedures and where they received the latest information available to SOS NATOUSA.[65] At the end of May the theater "went on" the matériel status report, which was a War Department prescribed report prepared in the ports of embarkation to show the zone of interior, in-transit, and theater status of certain controlled and critical items. Since only about one-quarter of the 200 stock chemical items in North Africa was included, the immediate impact on theater chemical supply was not great, but the matériel status report and its supporting perpetual inventory in the ports of embarkation required more exact reporting of theater on-hand and expenditure data—data which became part of a more extensive accounting and reporting system.[66]

The base sections had begun to report stock status to the theater and SOS chemical sections in April under the increased reporting requirement. However, their reports were little more comprehensive than the earlier informal reports until June, when comprehensive reports from ABS and MBS and a partial report from Eastern Base Section permitted the theater and SOS chemical sections to compile the first full-scale stock status report. Even then, quantity in the hands of troops was known for only one item, the eyeshield, which had been reported 500,000 short. The theater chemical section assumed

[65] Min of Sup Officers Mtg, Hq SOS NATOUSA, 24 Apr 43.   CWS SOS NATOUSA 337/4 in CWS MTO 337 Confs.

[66] (1) Logistical History of NATOUSA-MTOUSA, pp. 59–60.   (2) History of COMZ NATOUSA, pt. I.   (3) Rqmts and Stock Contl Div ASF, Rpt, Survey of the Opn of the Matériel Status Rpt, Aug 44. Files of Rqmts and Stock Contl Div ASF.

that supply of all other items in the hands of troops equaled authorization since no other complaints had been received.[67]

The SOS Chemical Section requested, in July, that the Commanding General, NATOUSA, require troop units and organizations to submit full reports of chemical materials in their hands.[68] These reports began to arrive in August, and the chemical supply officers thereafter calculated the status of theater supply much more realistically. The improvement in calculating supply status again raised the question of the adequacy of requirements and logistical data computations. While the CWS supply catalogs, which contained detailed information on requirements, allowances, spare parts, and item nomenclature, were not available until January 1944, chemical supply officers assembled such data from other sources in 1943.[69]

The Army Service Forces manual, Logistical Planning and Reference Data, arrived in the theater in May 1943. Although the ASF manual primarily dealt with transportation of supplies, it did present some helpful examples of requirements computations.[70] Such information as the ASF manual provided was useful, both in the headquarters and to the supply officers in the field, but it met only part of the need. To satisfy the whole need, Colonel Coblentz, Chemical Officer, ABS, made his own compilation of logistical data.[71] In July he obtained OCCWS Circular No. 1, issued on 20 June 1943 as a predecessor to CWS supply catalogs. Although the OCCWS circular contained the latest War Department information, Colonel Coblentz' experience in the theater led him to reproduce a table of maintenance factors prepared by the CWS ETO. The European theater was not engaged in

[67] (1) Ltr Rpt, AG EBS to CG SOS NATOUSA, 3 Jul 43, sub: Stock Status and Material Issue Rpt. EBS CWS 400.11 in CWS MTO 142.1 Inventory, Base Sec, vol. I. (2) AG ABS to CG SOS NATOUSA, 4 Jul 43, Stock Status and Material Issue Rpt. ABS AG 319.1 in CWS MTO 142.1 Inventory, Base Sec, vol. I. (3) CWS MBS [to CG SOS NATOUSA], Stock Status and Material Issue Rpt as of 28 Jun 43, 2400 H [29 Jun 43]. CWS MTO 142.1 Inventory (Corresp). (4) [Chief Cml Sec AFHQ and NATOUSA to CG NYPE thru CG NATOUSA], ca. 15 Jul 43, Rpt, Theater Status, Chemical Warfare, Selected Class II Items—30 Jun 1943, and Chemical Warfare, Selected Class V Items—In Depots 30 Jun 1943. CWS MTO 050 Logistical Data.

[68] Ltr, AG SOS NATOUSA to CG NATOUSA, 10 Jul 43, sub: Inventory of Cml Warfare Matériel in Hands of Troops. SOS AG 142.1 in CWS MTO 142.1 Inventory (Corresp).

[69] 1st Ind, Lt Col Lloyd E. Fellenz, ExO CW Sec Hqs NATOUSA, to CmlO Seventh Army, 15 Jan 44, on Ltr, CmlO Seventh Army to CmlO NATOUSA, 8 Jan 44, sub: Request for Logistical Data. Seventh Army 400-CW in CWS MTO 050 Logistical Data.

[70] Unnumbered manual, Hqs SOS, Feb 43, Logistical Planning and Reference Data. Stamped "May 1943" in Cml Sec AFHQ and NATOUSA. CWS MTO 050 Logistical Data.

[71] Memo, Off of CmlO ABS, no addressee, 4 Jul 43, sub: Logistical Data—CWS Supplies. CWS MTO 300.6 Memo Book I.

ground combat, but, from the point of view of the chemical supply officer, the data compiled by the CWS ETO was the best and most realistic then available. Accordingly, the NATO Chemical Section relayed through the OCCWS a request for a complete set of the CWS logistical tables prepared by CWS ETO. In August CWS ETO forwarded to NATO a complete set of its tables plus a description of the computing processes and a listing of pertinent authorities. But, shortly after this material was received the situation in NATO changed. A 26 October note on the ETO letter of transmittal indicated that Colonel Shadle consigned the ETO material to the dead file "as ETOUSA logistics [are] not necessarily applicable here." [72]

It seems probable that Colonel Shadle meant that the ETO data had been useful only until the North African theater had revised and adapted the information to its own use. Theater officers quickly learned a lesson which the War Department seemed to have great difficulty in understanding—that the procedures of one theater were not necessarily applicable to the conditions of another. The theater and SOS chemical sections, having learned this lesson, were consequently in the process of adapting and revising all logistical data to fit the experience of the Tunisian, Sicilian, and early Italian campaigns. Many theater supply officers continued to believe that the War Department supply authorities were unresponsive to their needs, but their logistics analyses led them to request adjustments in the War Department governing directives. For example, the theater CWS suggested, as early as July, a revision in some War Department maintenance factors. As such suggestions demonstrated, chemical supply officers were becoming more sophisticated in the handling of their system, and, as a consequence, the system was becoming more standardized internally; yet, at the same time, it was becoming more individual since its logistical data, the basis for its operation, was compiled and controlled within the system. [73]

By the end of August, Colonel Coblentz, then chemical officer desig-

[72] (1) Ltr with Incls, Col LeRoy, Chief Sup Div CWS ETOUSA, to CmlO NATOUSA, 24 Aug 43, sub: Transmittal of Logistic Tables. CWS ETO SOS CW 050/77 (10 Aug 43) SD in CWS MTO 050 Logistical Data. (2) For more information on the CWS ETO system, see below, Chapter IV.

[73] (1) Wilson Interv, 16 Oct 58. (2) Statistical Summary, 31 Jul 43. (3) Ltr, Harold L. Field to Hist Off, 1 Feb 59. Mr. Field, as lieutenant and captain, was a supply officer in the Chemical Section, SOS NATOUSA. (4) Lt Col Joseph F. Padlon and Maj Howard P. McCormick, War Plans Br OACCWS Field Opns, to CCWS, Rpt on Visit to NATOUSA (hereafter cited as Padlon-McCormick Rpt), 24 Feb 44. CWS 314.7 Observer Rpts.

nate of Peninsular Base Section, which was organizing within Atlantic Base Section for supply operation in Italy, had assembled enough information to compile a detailed set of chemical supply instructions covering definitions, organization methods, reporting forms, distribution, and storage operating data.[74] This compilation is evidence of a significant improvement in procedures, and it is noteworthy that these procedures and the reports which controlled them were largely of theater CWS origin.

At the same time individual performance was improving as the chemical supply officers gained confidence in themselves and their system. Colonel Shadle had advised General Porter in May that ". . . everything pertaining to supply knowledge is deficient. Our officers are simply not trained in supply work and staff procedure." Major Wilson agreed.[75] But in November Colonel Shadle wrote to General Porter, "All of the officers over here . . . are doing a splendid job." [76] The change had been wrought by extensive on-the-job supply training afforded by actual supply experience and by such compilations, both official and unofficial, as Colonel Coblentz had prepared. As Colonel Shadle also declared, ". . . we now know what we are talking about and what is needed. . . ." [77] In other words, the field elements of the chemical supply system, with the exception of that portion applying to the Army Air Forces, were well established during the fall of 1943. In October Colonel Maling's Twelfth Air Force Chemical Section still lacked a basis for requirements computation both for incendiary bombs and toxics. Such information by War Department decision could emanate only from Army Air Forces headquarters in Washington.[78]

At the same time that the supply level was improving during 1943, the supply handling situation was also improving. The SOS Chemical Section increased its operating responsibilities with the addition of such duties as those assigned in June of editing, consolidating, and

---

[74] CWS Sup Cir Ltr No. 1, 1 Sep 43. CWS MTO 300.6 Memo Book I. This copy, apparently a draft, is headed, "Chemical Section, Base Headquarters." There is no signature and no indication that the draft was submitted for staff comment or that the circular was ever issued, either by Peninsular Base Section or by Headquarters, NATOUSA.

[75] (1) Personal Ltr, Shadle to Porter, 4 May 43. CWS 320.2/20 in file CWS 314.7 Pers Files, NATO, Feb–Dec 43. (2) Wilson Interv, 16 Oct 58.

[76] Personal Ltr, Shadle to Porter, 23 Nov 43. CWS 314.7 Pers Files, NATO, Feb–Dec 43.

[77] Personal Ltr, Shadle to Waitt, 2 Dec 43. CWS 314.7 Pers Files, NATO, Feb–Dec 43.

[78] (1) Padlon-McCormick Rpt, 24 Feb 44. (2) Notes on visit to North African theater made by Brig Gen Alden H. Waitt and Lt Col Jacob K. Javits, OCCWS, 17–26 Oct 43. CWS 314.7 Observer Rpts.

forwarding to the zone of interior base section chemical requisitions. Rockwood's section increased to seven officers, a warrant officer, and thirteen enlisted men and women organized into Administration, Supply, Control, and Technical Divisions.[79] These divisions supervised base section requisitioning, inventorying, and reporting activities on what SOS termed "a sort of individual project" basis. The lines of supervision were by no means direct or consistent since SOS still did not have command control of base sections.[80]

The base section chemical officers and those in the air forces continued to develop their own systems of operation. Each chemical officer received a different type of assistance from his own command organization. In Coblentz' opinion, base section headquarters' attempts to help created "nothing more than a bottleneck," because the base section staff knew no more than the chemical officers about supply procedures, and because the staff officers lacked such chemical information as the chemical officers compiled for themselves or got from their colleagues in the United States and in the theater.[81] The base sections did designate storage locations and did provide some co-ordination among the services. Chemical sections improved storage and handling at these locations with the help of a number of service units.[82] By the end of February 1943, the Twelfth Air Force had received its complement of four chemical air service companies.[83]

CWS Staff and Functions, AFHQ and NATOUSA

During 1943 Shadle's office acquired several new functions, in addition to those authorized when the AFHQ Chemical Section was first established. (*Chart 6*) An analysis of actual performance of these functions demonstrates what role the CWS NATO had come to play.[84]

---

[79] History of Cml Warfare Sec SOS NATOUSA, in pt. IV, History of COMZ NATOUSA–MTOUSA.

[80] *Ibid.*

[81] (1) Coblentz to Waitt, 25 Feb 43. (2) Croen Interv, 21 Sep 59. (3) Capone Interv, 24 Apr 58.

[82] In addition to the early units mentioned above, the 11th Chemical Maintenance Company arrived in January 1943; the 63d Chemical Depot Company and the 12th Chemical Maintenance Company in March; the 41st Chemical Laboratory Company, the 92d Chemical Composite Company, the remainder of the 21st Chemical Decontamination Company, and the 52d and 53d Chemical Processing Companies in May; and the 24th and 25th Chemical Decontamination Companies in June 1943. See Brophy and Fisher, *Organizing for War*, app. H, and see below, ch. VII.

[83] The 751st and 758th Chemical Depot Companies, Aviation, arrived in December 1942; the 753d Chemical Depot Company, Aviation, and the 875th Chemical Company, Air Operations, reached the theater in February 1943.

[84] Functions are stated in History of AFHQ, Part I, pages 59, 60, Part II, Section 4, page 511. This analysis, unless otherwise noted, is derived from a survey of the collected files of CWS MTO.

CHART 6—ORGANIZATION OF CHEMICAL WARFARE SECTION, ALLIED FORCE HEADQUARTERS, AND HEADQUARTERS, NORTH AFRICAN THEATER OF OPERATIONS, U.S. ARMY, NOVEMBER 1943

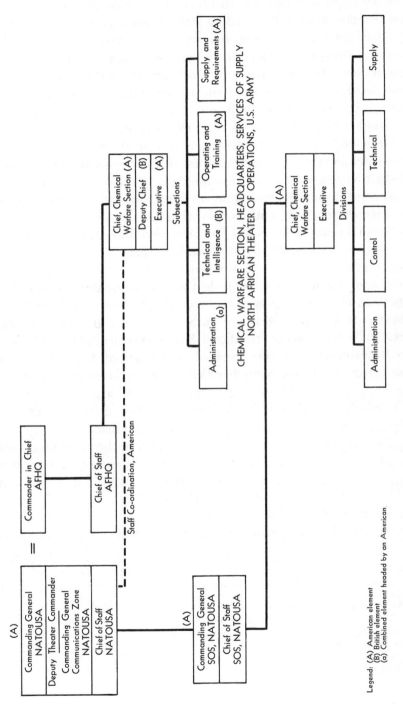

Legend: (A) American element
(B) British element
(a) Combined element headed by an American.

Source: Adapted from: History of AFHQ, pt. II, pp. 203, 223–24, 241, 512; History of COMZ, NATOUSA–MTOUSA, pts. III and IV.

The principal function was to advise the commander in chief (AFHQ and theater commander) and his staff on chemical matters. This was a standard special staff function which involved, for the CWS, gas warfare planning and any other matters which might require theater supervision. In the absence of gas warfare, performance under this function became a routine matter of concurring or advising on theater personnel, operation, and supply.

Another function was to plan the use and allotment of chemical troop units, and in 1943 the scope of this planning was extended to the procurement and supervision of all CWS personnel in the theater. Performance under these functions was advisory since Shadle had no command responsibilities. The advisory capacity was severely limited by theater quotas on both personnel and units, and by the requests of individual field commanders for personnel and units—requests which usually overrode staff advice. Shadle's Chemical Section managed to get enough service units even when training in the United States could not keep pace with worldwide demand. Combat units were eventually obtained on about the same basis on which they were furnished other theaters, three battalions per authorized army during peak combat activity.[85] With respect to officers, Shadle experienced difficulties similar to Rowan's—the theater received a number of CWS casual officers who frequently were badly handled by the replacement system. It was practically impossible to find vacancies for all arriving officers, and it was absolutely impossible to determine their qualifications so as to channel officers to duties for which they were fitted.[86]

The principal mission of the theater CWS in the event of gas warfare was to supervise "chemical operations, gas-proofing, decontaminations, and filling of chemical munitions in the Theater," [87] as well as chemical training. This mission resulted in the establishment of review activities rather than of supervisory controls since, in a nongas warfare situation and under the organization of the theater, actual supervision devolved upon the base section and field army chemical officers and their subordinates. The theater chemical section usually learned of chemical operations after their accomplishment. Shadle did use field reports of experience to supplement War Department directives with theater

---

[85] See Brophy and Fisher, *Organizing for War*, app. H–1.

[86] (1) Interv, Hist Off with Wilson, 16 Oct 58. (2) Waitt Comments, 5 Jan 61. Waitt's comment on the replacement system is "scandalous."

[87] History of AFHQ, pt. I, p. 60.

directives on operation, and he did make his office serve as a clearing-house for operational information, but these activities were too remote to be classed as supervision. In unusual cases either the theater or the SOS Chemical Section followed up on compliance with directives or solutions to problems, but the staff was not large enough to make this an invariable practice.[88] Functions added in the operational sphere during 1943 were planning and advising on the smoke protection of port areas and distributing technical information on area smoke screens. While the theater chemical section became more directly involved in the direction and appraisal of smoke operations, these functions, too, were usually performed by working with field chemical officers who had prime supervisory responsibilities.

Two functions, intelligence and co-operation with the theater surgeon, were primarily liaison and reporting functions. Intelligence was initially handled by the British complement of the AFHQ Chemical Section, and the British continued to play a large part in this activity after it became a joint enterprise. One officer, Lt. Col. Henry I. Stubblefield, was added to the section for medical liaison and to plan protection against the possibility of biological warfare.

Three of the remaining original functions covered the supervision of supply from requirements to distribution. Since the theater section was not staffed to handle supply supervision, since the theater chemical section had no opportunity to inaugurate a basic supply plan like that used in the ETO, and since theater organization in effect decentralized supply operations to such a degree that field chemical officers in fact instituted their own supply plans, the 1943 assignment of functions provided that the theater chemical section should "merely" procure "logistical and statistical data on chemical warfare supplies in the theater."[89] Shadle spent most of his own time dealing with supply matters. He was proud of his accomplishments, and he was commended by British as well as American authorities for performance in this area.[90] From Shadle's own point of view, he and his AFHQ section performed exactly those functions which should have been theirs in the light of tradition and of theater conditions. He saw no need, as chief chemical officers in other theaters did, for enlarging his planning

---

[88] Interv, Hist Off with Julius F. Klaswick, 6 Mar 59. (Mr. Klaswick, as lieutenant and captain, served with the SOS and theater chemical sections.)

[89] History of AFHQ, pt. II, sec. 4, p. 511.

[90] Ltr, Shadle to Hist Off, 18 Aug 59.

COLONEL SHADLE AND STAFF IN ALGIERS, FALL OF 1943

responsibilities, or for attempting to influence combat operations, or for striving to exercise control of the theater CWS through technical channels. He felt that he appropriately operated most of the time through command channels. He later pointed out that his position as a staff officer in a supreme headquarters, AFHQ, made it possible for him to operate differently from Rowan, who did not occupy such a position.[91]

By the end of 1943, Shadle's AFHQ section was authorized 5 American officers, 3 more than authorized at the time of the invasion, and 3 British officers, one more than in the previous year. Enlisted strength had grown from 2 to 4 Americans, but the number of British soldiers had remained at 2.[92] Lt. Col. Lloyd E. Fellenz, a Regular Army officer and a smoke expert, had arrived to become executive officer.[93] Lt. Col. Ian A. Marriott had returned to London to be replaced by Lt. Col. G. des C. Chamier as British deputy.

[91] Shadle Interv, 16 May 61.
[92] History of AFHQ, pt. II, sec. 4, p. 513.
[93] Shadle to Porter, 4 May 43.

Theater and CWS Reorganizations

When, early in 1944, General Eisenhower left the North African theater to take command in Europe, the character of the North African organization was changed slightly to accommodate to a British supreme commander and to new responsibilities. The theater at last corrected what from a staff point of view had been a serious error in the original organization.[94] The Communications Zone, which had been inseparable from the theater organization except in the person of its commander, Maj. Gen. Everett S. Hughes, also deputy theater commander, was combined with the theater SOS, and the new command was given those theater functions which pertained to the COMZ. At the same time, the remaining American responsibilities were restricted to administration—all control of combat operations passing to AFHQ or the combat organizations. The result was essentially the creation of a tricommand organization like that of the War Department.[95]

Shadle's office maintained its staff and its AFHQ-theater position, but the functions of control of COMZ personnel and units, COMZ training and gas warfare defense, and all allocation and issue of supply passed to the SOS Chemical Section. Colonel Maling moved from Twelfth Air Force to assume Rockwood's position as chief of this section which was augmented by the addition of one colonel, three majors, and a captain.[96]

The COMZ Chemical Section then assumed control of the "impetus from the rear" supply system and took over some of the administrative functions which had been the province of AFHQ, and of NATOUSA, then renamed Mediterranean Theater of Operations (MTOUSA). Shadle, who became a brigadier general on the same day that Rowan received his promotion, maintained his section as a clearinghouse for chemical information and did a considerable amount of troubleshooting in the field of both CWS supply systems. But the work of the theater headquarters chemical section was declining while that in the European theater section was as great or greater than it had been.[97] One reason for this was the growing emphasis in MTOUSA on combat organization and function rather than theater organization. Another reason

---

[94] Logistical History of NATOUSA–MTOUSA, p. 30.

[95] (1) *Ibid.* (2) History of AFHQ, pt. III, sec. I.

[96] (1) History, Cml Warfare Sec SOS NATOUSA. (2) History of AFHQ, pt. III, sec. 4, pp. 979–80.

[97] Interv, Hist Off with Col Johnson, 18 Aug 59. (Johnson at the time was Shadle's American deputy.)

was Shadle's view of his own function. Since he emphasized the staff
role and since, ideally, staff work declines when administrative systems
are functioning smoothly, it was appropriate that the work of his own
section would decline. The administrative systems were, for the most
part functioning smoothly by the middle of 1944, or, at least, the
problems which had beset the systems had become less important.

If gas warfare had ever been a threat in the Mediterranean area, it
would have been at the time of the assault landings. Shadle had been
proved right in his estimate that there was little threat in the North
African landings. In the Sicilian landings small stores of enemy toxics
were found, but their placement and manner of storage indicated
that there was no intention of using them.[98] For the landings on the
Italian mainland, Allied intelligence officers feared that toxics would
be employed by the enemy, and as a result retaliatory stocks were
brought in too soon. A tragic gassing of Allied forces in the harbor of
Bari, Italy, occurred when enemy action breached a ship carrying
Allied gas.[99] No clear signs of German intent were found when troops
broke through into the Italian mainland. The prolonged struggle along
the Rapido and the Winter Line would have given the Germans an
excellent tactical opportunity to use gas, but again no evidence turned
up that they had considered the employment of toxics.[100] The principal
CWS mission, preparedness for gas warfare, therefore lost weight in
the Mediterranean theater, and the part of the COMZ Chemical
Section mission which related to gas warfare supply became of little
importance. The whole of the COMZ organization declined in importance late in 1944, possibly because the impetus from the front
system had its own *de facto* communications zone. In the opinion of
the chemical officer, Peninsular Base Section—which supported Fifth
Army—was a communications zone itself.[101] His opinion was confirmed by an organizational change in November 1944 under which
COMZ was discontinued and its functions delegated to Peninsular Base
Section.[102]

[98] Hammond Interv, 26 Nov 56.
[99] (1) Shadle Comments on draft of this volume, 24 Jan 61. (2) Interv, Hist Off with Col Francis
Browne, USAFR (Ret.), 23 Oct 61. (3) Capone Interv, 24 Apr 58.
[100] Porter Interv, 24 Aug 61.
[101] Memo, Coblentz to Rowan [ca. 1946], sub: Comments on Theater CWS Orgn. CWS 314.7.
[102] Logistical History of NATOUSA–MTOUSA, pp. 37–38.

Still another reason for the decline of the theater headquarters CWS sections was that the intelligence activity, largely managed by the British, had never assumed much importance in the American group. Furthermore, since facilities were lacking for a technical activity and since liaison with the British on technical matters was carried on by the European theater CWS, there was no need for a large technical organization in NATOUSA–MTOUSA. The theater chemical laboratory company did not experience, as did chemical laboratory companies in most other theaters, frequent calls for development work.

A recurrent theme of the CWS effort in the Mediterranean area was that the service's most important experience here was supply experience. The CWS MTO supply system entered its fourth phase in the winter of 1943–44. During this phase, which eventually included most of the period prior to victory in Europe, the bifurcation of the supply system was most marked. Ground chemical supply officers brought nearly all of their attention to bear on item troubleshooting which had been a part, but only a subsidiary part, of their concern since the initial landings. As they became more and more concerned with the immediate needs of the combat forces it became more apparent that to wait for instructions and supplies to filter down through the complicated system from the zone of interior was not always possible. The local arrangement, the informal agreement, and the field expedient became the order of the day. The officers in the field evolved new techniques and used supplies and equipment where and when they were needed, regardless of the original intention or function. Whenever it was possible they manufactured supplies or adapted equipment to their immediate needs. They tended to suspect the motives of every rear area organization, even that of their own theater. One base section chemical officer bitterly remarked, perhaps with some exaggeration, that it was easier to manufacture spare parts than it was to "argue SOS [NATOUSA] out of them." [103]

The basic problem was that the War Department's impetus from the rear supply system was not sufficiently responsive to the immediate needs generated by changing conditions in the field. Yet even the suggestion that an impetus from the front policy was being employed

---

[103] Memo, Lt Col Henry C. Hall for Col Rockwood [CmlO SOS NATOUSA], 21 Mar 44, no sub. CWS MTO 333 Inspections and Investigations.

was enough to call forth official investigators.[104] Despite this official disapproval, CWS and other ground supply officers in MTO accomplished their supply tasks.

For example, Lt. Gen. Mark W. Clark's Fifth Army set up its own system. Ammunition supply points (ASP's) were set up close to the front for each corps plus one ASP for troops not attached to corps. Each supply point contained a chemical, an ordnance, and an engineer section manned by service troops of the appropriate branch but commanded by the Ordnance Department representative. Combat troops drew what they needed from the ASP after certifying that the amount drawn plus that on hand would not exceed the basic authorized load for their organization. Supply points for other classes of supply were so located that each combat organization could form one convoy to bring up all its supplies. Late every afternoon, Colonel Barker's assistants visited each supply point and reported back to him an estimate of stock status. Barker consulted operational plans furnished him by the Army staff and calculated necessary levels in each ASP. He then telephoned Coblentz in base section headquarters at Naples to tell him what supplies were needed at what points and depots. CWS officers and men waiting in trucks loaded with supplies, which usually had been sorted, cleaned, reboxed, and marked in the base section depots, received Coblentz' instructions and departed to replenish all Army ASP's and depots before daylight. As the Army moved forward, the base section took over and expanded forward area depots established by Fifth Army so that there would be no change in the distance through which immediate supply action need take place.[105]

Coblentz and his section, plagued by continual shortages of manpower and equipment, by what he considered to be a lack of understanding of combat needs on the part of all echelons to the rear, and by the continual necessity of refurbishing or even making wanted items, found themselves hard put to keep up with Fifth Army needs.[106]

---

[104] IOM, ACofS G–4 MTO to CofS MTO, 13 Dec 44, sub: Rpts of Inspection Made by War Dept Inspectors. CWS MTO 333 Inspection and Investigations.

[105] (1) Barker to Hist Off, 11 Aug 59. (2) Ltr, Coblentz to Hist Off, 17 Aug 59.

[106] Coblentz to Hist Off, 17 Aug 59.

Theater Chemical Supply Problems

The first of the troubleshooting problems the CWS dealt with in the Mediterranean area was that of item overages and shortages. The second was the fact that the condition of some material on reaching the theater was such that extensive repair, renovation, or adaptation was required—this was the maintenance problem. There were many other troubleshooting problems, but, examples of the overages and shortages and of maintenance problems not only demonstrate solutions but also show how the practice of impetus from the front operated.

Overages and Shortages

The problem of item overages and shortages resulted from several causes. Overages were brought about by oversupply from the United States or by failure to deplete stocks as anticipated. Shortages were caused by breakdown of faulty or damaged materials, by failure to unload ships because of lack of facilities, by failure to estimate needs, or by enemy destruction of ships or depots. One major cause of overages was automatic supply. The New York Port of Embarkation continued automatic supply or materiel status report supply, which was virtually automatic, on many items. Consequently, by the end of July 1943, the stocks of three items, noncorrosive decontaminating agent, protective ointment, and shoe impregnite ranged from 125 percent to 143 percent of authorization. Before the end of the year the overages on some of these items reached nearly 200 percent of authorization. Although the SOS Chemical Section cabled the port of embarkation canceling requisitions and requesting discontinuance of automatic supply on the grounds that the storage and transportation expenditures exceeded the value of stocks, stock continued to accumulate. In desperation, theater chemical officers appealed to General Somervell during one of his trips to the theater, but it was 1944 before shipments began to decline. The first three items remained in excess stockage until disposal procedures were instituted late in 1944. Shadle, claiming that the Arabs sometimes pilfered shoe impregnite for use as a butter substitute, suggested that one solution for the problem of excesses was to encourage this practice.[107]

[107] (1) Statistical Summary, 31 Jul 43, 31 Aug 43, 30 Sep 43, 25 Oct 43, 31 Oct 43, 25 Nov 43, 30 Nov 43, 25 Dec 43, 31 Jan 44. (2) Wilson Interv, 16 Oct 58. (3) Ltr, Shadle to Hist Off, 18 Aug 59. (4) "Sup Status of CWS Protective Materiel in MTO," table compiled from theater matériel status reports, reproduced in Baldwin, Bingham, and Pritchard, Readiness for Gas Warfare in Theaters of Operations, app. B.

Other overages in the stocks of canisters for collective protectors, diaphragm gas masks, and dust respirators resulted from changes in the basis of issue. In the absence of gas warfare, replacement stocks of collective protector canisters were not sent forward, and, since there was no expenditure, excess stocks accumulated in depots. The diaphragm gas mask, equipped for voice transmission, proved to be cumbersome and not much more efficient for voice transmission than the service mask with M8 outlet valve. The basis of issue was therefore eventually changed from 30 percent of issue requirements for gas masks of all kinds to issue to artillery and Signal Corps units only. But meanwhile shipments of diaphragm masks continued to arrive at the rate set by estimate, resulting in excess stocks. Although the troop demand for dust respirators in North Africa was heavy, individuals in the field found that they were principally used by drivers of vehicles and that other soldiers were so weighted down with equipment that the respirator could not conveniently be carried. Respirators were therefore issued in substantially reduced numbers on a per-vehicle rather than per-person basis. The new issue policy led to overages in depots. Excess stocks of the diaphragm mask were returned to the United States after issue of the new lightweight service mask, which began late in 1943, was complete. Excess stocks of the collective protector canister and dust respirator were held in the theater until late in the war since it was considered possible that the theater commander might again have to change the basis of issue if events took a different turn.[108]

While theater chemical supply officers found the problems presented by overages annoying, as the overages tended to create inefficiency in the supply system, the problem of shortages threatened, on several occasions, to destroy part of the CWS effectiveness in the theater. The first serious shortages after the stabilization of the supply system were holdovers from the prestabilization period. The CWS in the United States was unable to initiate production of the M15 white phosphorus grenades until July 1943 and was unable to supply the theaters during that year.[109] The M8 HC smoke grenade was substituted in the North

[108] (1) Statistical summary cited in n. 107 (1) above. (2) Sup Status of CWS Protective Materiel in MTO cited in n. 107 (4), above.

[109] (1) CWS Consolidated Rpt of Procurement, 1 Jan 40–31 Aug 45. (2) 2d Ind, ACCWS Field Opns to CCmlO NATOUSA, 15 Dec 43, on basic Ltr, CmlO Seventh Army to CCWS, thru CCmlO AFHQ and NATOUSA, 24 Sep 43, sub: Cml Warfare Opns Sicilian Campaign. CWS SPCVO 319.1.

African theater, but Seventh Army chemical officers reported that the M8 grenade was not effective in the Sicily Campaign because it produced an insufficient volume of smoke and because it lacked the antipersonnel effect of the white phosphorus grenade. The M8 grenade was nevertheless again substituted for the white phosphorus grenade early in the Italian campaign as there was still no theater stock of the M15. The theater CWS acquired some white phosphorus grenades in the fall of 1943, and a sufficient stock was built up by December 1943. Although a total of 269,639 white phosphorus grenades was used in combat in the theater by the end of the war, this munition would probably have been more extensively employed had combat soldiers become acquainted with it during the initial campaigns.[110]

Another, and even more critical item was the 4.2-inch chemical mortar, with spare parts and ammunition. After twenty days of fighting in Sicily, where the chemical mortar battalions saw their first extensive action and where they proved themselves invaluable and practically indispensable in a close support role, the theater had only one complete mortar and about a dozen barrels and base plates in depot stock.[111] Since the mortar was already being used considerably more than had been intended, barrels wore out rapidly—so rapidly in fact that a dozen replacement barrels did not begin to satisfy the demand. The really critical need, however, was not for the barrel, nor even for the base plate, which broke at the excessive ranges demanded of the weapon, but for elevating screws and recoil springs, which were not even listed among spare parts available. In August CWS supply officers listed no mortars or mortar parts whatever. In September they received stocks although still insufficient to meet demands, and the SOS Chemical Section noted that Shadle had requested 120 days' reserve of mortars, comparable to the reserve for ammunition rather than that for other Class II weapons. The need for parts was so great that mortars received in working condition were broken down for this purpose.[112]

In October the North African CWS again had no mortars. In

---

[110] (1) Statistical Summary as cited in n. 107 (1), above. (2) Ammunition Sup Rpt, 31 Oct 43, 31 Dec 43, 31 Jul 45. This report was a feeder report prepared in OCCWS for the ASF monthly progress report. Ltr, CG ASF to CofOrd and CCWS, 3 Nov 43, sub: Instructions for Preparation of Ammunition Supply of MPR. ASF SPX 319.1 (30 Oct 43) OB–P–SPDDL–MB–A. (3) Rpt of Cml Warfare Opns Sicilian Campaign. (4) Padlon-McCormick Rpt, 24 Feb. 44.

[111] Statistical Summary, 31 Jul 43.

[112] (1) Statistical Summary, 31 Aug 43, 30 Sep 43. (2) Padlon-McCormick Rpt, 24 Feb 44. (3) Wilson Interv, 16 Oct 58.

November the War Department increased the maintenance factor from 7 percent to 12½ percent, but experience in Italy outmoded the new factor before it was received.[113] By the end of 1943 General Porter had personally intervened to secure air shipment of 12 mortars and a few critical mortar parts to the theater. In all, late in 1943 and early in 1944, 172 mortars were scheduled to arrive by air or by convoy to relieve the situation in which depot stocks were nil and there was an actual shortage of 16 mortars in the operating battalions. Also in November 1943, the first serious theaterwide shortage of 4.2-inch mortar ammunition was reported. Despite the mortar shipments and the 40,000 rounds of HE mortar shell en route to the theater, supply proved to be insufficient.[114]

In February 1944 Rockwood diagnosed the difficulty as a lack of systematization in mortar supply and repair and the failure of the CWS in the United States to observe existing directives with respect to spare parts and replacement.[115] His analysis undoubtedly covered at least part of the problem, but the CWS in the zone of interior could not supply the parts it did not have. The CWS inaugurated its first comprehensive procurement plan for spare parts in 1944, and it was not until late 1944 and early 1945 that the products of this plan became available in quantity through an integrated spare parts operation.[116] The CWS also made herculean efforts to supply ammunition, and, while theater problems of maintenance and distribution, as will be indicated below, and occasional lags in delivery to the theater caused critical local situations and ammunition rationing, the over-all supply met the demand in 1944 and 1945.[117] Rationing of ammunition also became necessary at Anzio in January of 1944 because of the large

[113] Coblentz Comments, 9 Jan 61.

[114] (1) Statistical Summary, 31 Oct 43, 25 Nov 43, 25 Dec 43. (2) Ammunition Sup Rpt, 31 Dec 43. (3) Wilson Interv, 16 Oct 58. (4) Msg, CM–IN–14914, CG NATOUSA to WD, 24 Nov 43. (5) Ltr, CCWS to CCmlO AFHQ and NATOUSA, 11 Dec 43. (6) ASF, Cml Warfare Serv Monthly Maint Factors, 4 Nov 43; ASF, Cml Warfare Monthly Replacement Factors, 13 Jan 44. CWS MTO 400.6 Replacement and Maint Factors. (7) Ltr, CG SOS NATOUSA to CG NATOUSA, 3 Feb 44, sub: Replacement of 4.2-inch Cml Mortar Parts. SOS NATOUSA 472.4 in CWS MTO 400.6 Replacement Factors.

[115] Col Rockwood, CmlO SOS NATOUSA to CG NATOUSA (attn: CmlO), 1 Feb 44, sub: Sup Procedure of 4.2-inch Cml Mortar. SOS CWS 319.1/48 in CWS MTO 400 Supply of Base Secs, Units, etc.

[116] For discussion of the spare parts situation in the zone of interior, see Brophy, Miles, and Cochrane, *From Laboratory to Field*, Chapter XIII.

[117] (1) Ammunition Sup Rpt, Monthly, 1944–45. (2) IOM, Col Walter A. Guild, CCmlO NATOUSA for ACofS G–4 MTOUSA, 29 Oct 45, sub: CWS Sup Methods. CWS MTO 400 Supplies, Servs and Equip.

number of ammunition dumps destroyed by enemy action. Fifth Army chemical officers improvised ammunition protection by bulldozing earth over stacked ammunition boxes.[118] The parts situation on the other hand became so critical that Barker, acting in the spirit of General Clark's instruction to give the combat commanders what they wanted even if it was necessary to manufacture the material, in December 1943 joined the Fifth Army ordnance officer in re-establishing operations at the Italian Capua arsenal.

At Capua a composite Fifth Army chemical group and nearly 1,000 Italian workmen under the direction of 1st Lt. Anthony Notorangelo cast and machined mortar and smoke generator parts. The "Capua" mortar slide, cast from Italian navy bronze taken from the Naples harbor, was considered superior to the stateside product, as was the "Capua" integrally cast barrel cap and firing pin. For some time in 1944 more than half of the mortar and smoke generator maintenance supplies used were made in Italy at Capua and in chemical service unit shops at Florence and Leghorn. After Fifth Army moved on, Peninsular Base Section assumed the job of operating the CWS half of Capua arsenal with Lieutenant Notorangelo remaining in charge.[119]

In August of 1944, the Army Service Forces promised an adequate stock of spare parts within the next six months.[120] Also in August the theater formulated, and in September put into practice, an individual CWS NATOUSA spare parts policy, concentrating supply and control of spare parts in Peninsular and Delta Base Sections.[121] But, as the investigations of a CWS spare parts team from December 1944 to February 1945 demonstrated, the Mediterranean theater CWS never reached the goal of adequate parts stockage.[122]

Despite these handicaps, the chemical mortar battalions in the North African–Mediterranean theater reported only one instance when mortar fire was actually curtailed because of the shortage of weapons, parts, or ammunition.[123] That there was only one such instance, in this case

---

[118] Barker Comments, 15 Dec 60.

[119] (1) Col. Maurice E. Barker, USA (Ret.) "War Is Not All Fighting," *Armed Forces Chemical Journal,* VII (October, 1953), 16–19, 27. (2) Barker to Hist Off, 11 Aug 59. (3) Coblentz to Hist Off, 17 Aug 59.

[120] Ltr, Actg Dir Plans and Opns ASF to CG SOS NATOUSA, 25 Aug 44, sub: Theaters Plans for Cml Warfare. ASF SPOPP 381 in file CWS MTO 381 Theater Plans for CW.

[121] SOS NATOUSA, Cir 109, 26 Sep 44.

[122] OCCWS, Final Rpt, CWS Spare Parts Team in MTO and ETO, 19 Jun 45. (2) See below, Chapter IV. (3) Statistical Summary, 30 Jun, 31 Aug 44.

[123] History of 3d Cml Mortar Bn, Nov 43, Journal of Co D, 29–30 Nov 43.

an ammunition shortage, is a testimonial to the ingenuity and energy of theater chemical officers who manufactured parts, as at Capua, and arranged for welding teams to repair broken weapons right in the front-line mortar positions.[124] Thus the most serious supply threat to CWS operations in the theater was met.

There were shortages besides those of weapons and ammunition, but none so critical. An example of such shortages was the power-driven decontaminating apparatus, which was diverted from its gas warfare role to water carrying, fire fighting, and providing showers.[125] It was this type of apparatus that was used to provide all the water for the city of Naples during the first ten days after Allied forces took the city because the Germans had cut off the water supply and the Army engineers were unable to re-establish service immediately. The high-pressure pump on the apparatus was also used to open sewage drains which had dried up and become clogged because of the lack of water. The apparatus, using a chloride of lime mixture spray, was also used to disinfect and delouse buildings subsequently used as hospitals and barracks. [126]

The Twelfth Air Force considered the provision of showers for combat pilots returning from missions essential to morale and efficiency, but only in rare cases was it able to acquire engineer or quartermaster shower facilities. Consequently, the power-driven decontaminating apparatus became the most jealously guarded item of chemical equipment allotted to the air force. Stocks of the truck-mounted M3A1 apparatus were low when supply status was first reported in May 1943, and by the end of July the air forces were forty short. Accounting for these had been transferred to the matériel status report, indicating that supply was automatic. Despite automatic supply, the total theater stockage in November was only about 80 percent of authorization and demand had increased so much in the Twelfth Air Force that the AFSC chemical officer maintained a waiting list for issues. At one time the Commanding General, XII AFSC, personally assumed responsibility for distribution within his command. The AFSC chemical

---

[124] Wilson Interv, 16 Oct 58.

[125] (1) Postscript on Ltr, Barker to Porter, 27 Feb 43. CWS 314.7 Barker Corresp, NATO, 1942–43. (2) Barker, "War Is Not All Fighting," *Armed Forces Chemical Journal*, VII (October, 1953), 16–19, 27.

[126] Coblentz Comments, 9 Jan 61.

DECONTAMINATION UNIT FUNCTIONING AS A SHOWER

officer secured copies of ship manifests from SOS and base section chemical officers so that he could have someone on hand to claim the air force allotment as soon as the ship carrying the cargo docked. Since the apparatus was also one of the items which presented almost insuperable maintenance problems, supply was frequently complicated by a large number of apparatus deadlined for repairs. In the month before V–E Day the theater at last reached its quota of apparatus.[127]

Maintenance Problems

Chemical maintenance officers, like many others, got their first real experience and learned their first logistics lessons in the Mediterranean area. For one thing, the Mediterranean campaigns were among the earliest of World War II, and in many instances the latest refinements in equipment and matériel did not arrive there until after the peak of combat activity. Then, too, adverse conditions, such as the damp climate and rough terrain in Italy, made faults and defects far more serious than they would have been elsewhere. Maintenance problems

[127] (1) Statistical Summary, 31 May, 31 Jul 43, 25 Nov 43. (2) Sup Status of CWS Protective Matériel in MTO. (3) Capone Interv, 24 Apr 58.

had their greatest impact in the forward areas where weapons, equipment, and ammunition saw the heaviest use and where, by the time they reached these positions, they had been heavily exposed to weather and rough handling. Again chemical officers were forced to reorient their thinking—repair, renovation, and rebuilding of matériel and equipment had to take place wherever feasible and wherever needed rather than, as planned, in some rear area shop. Again, improvisation was the order of the day.

Theater chemical officers found maintenance and repair of the power-driven decontaminating apparatus only one of their extremely difficult maintenance problems. In the case of the apparatus the prime difficulty was caused by the fact that four different manufacturers produced the equipment, essentially a truck-mounted orchard sprayer.[128] Each manufacturer produced an item according to his own specifications with the result that four stocks of spare parts had to be maintained and that operating instructions varied according to the product used. This situation was further complicated by the fact that another apparatus mounted on skids rather than on a truck was also supplied to the theater. The skid-mounted apparatus early proved unsatisfactory because shortage of trucks made it immobile and mobility was of great importance either for primary or secondary missions. Depending on the local situation, maintenance and repair of the apparatus was performed by using units or by chemical and ordnance maintenance companies. Although the spare parts problem was largely solved by the end of 1944, theater distribution of parts remained difficult. The SOS (COMZ) Chemical Section sometimes found itself in the peculiar situation of dealing with an overage of spare parts, especially small items such as nuts and bolts, interchangeable among apparatus, while field units failed in attempts to acquire an adequate supply of the more critical parts which were not interchangeable.[129]

---

[128] For an account of development and procurement, see Brophy, Miles, and Cochrane, *From Laboratory to Field,* ch. XIV.

[129] (1) Capone Interv, 24 Apr 58. (2) Padlon-McCormick Rpt, 24 Feb 44. (3) Brig Gen William C. Kabrich, Chief Tech Div OCCWS, and Maj Francis B. Stewart [to CCWS], n.d., Rpt of Inspection Trip to NATO, 22 Feb–3 Apr 44. CWS 314.7 Observer Rpts. (4) Ltr, AG Delta Base Sec to CG COMZ MTOUSA, 19 Nov 44, sub: Study To Determine Necessary Replacement of CWS Major Items of Equip. DBS AG 400.61 (DBSCW) in CWS MTO 400.6 Reclamations and Replacements. (5) Ltr, AG MBS to CG MTOUSA, 19 Nov 44, sub: Study To Determine Necessary Replacement of CWS Major Items of Equipment. MBS AG 47 (BMCML) in same file as (4), above. (6) Ltr, Shadle, CCmlO MTO, to CCWS, 22 Dec 44, sub: Rpt of Study To Determine Necessary Replacement of CWS Major Items of Equip. CWS MTO 400.6 CWS. (7) Klaswick Interv, 6 Mar 59.

While the problem of maintaining the decontaminating apparatus was tied in with the problem of shortages, maintenance of 4.2-inch mortar shell and its propellant charges—in many ways the most critical theater maintenance problem—was complicated by problems of ammunition shortages, provision of service troops, packing and packaging, and poor condition of supplies and equipment. Experience in the maintenance of mortar shell is illustrative of similar experience with M1 and M4 smoke pots, grenades, bombs and clusters, and gas masks. From the outset of the Sicily Campaign, the Seventh Army Chemical Section discovered chemical mortar shells in need of reconditioning. The shells were corroded as a result of becoming wet while poorly packaged. The 12th Chemical Maintenance Company, which was attached to Seventh Army for the campaign, was assigned the responsibility of renovating and repacking shells in addition to its supply and mortar repair duties.[130] In the campaign on the Italian mainland the situation was worse. Shell cartridges and fuzes proved to be defective, shells needed cleaning, and, as Barker reported, "the powder came in wet and got wetter." [131] Barker set up a drying operation for propellant charges at the army supply point, and Coblentz started another at the base section. Both used blowers from collective protectors to force air through a heater fabricated from a 55-gallon drum. The charges were hung on wooden rods in a box through which the hot air passed. After the charges were thoroughly dry, the maintenance crews replaced them in their original "ice cream" cartons and then packed the cartons in German shell containers which were sealed to be opened only at the mortar position. German containers were so prized that Fifth Army Chemical Section made it a regular practice to scavenge the battlefield for these items on the heels of the retreating enemy.[132] The drying operation was carried on at Naples in a series of caves which the Germans had used for ammunition storage. A serious fire, later attributed to an unknown store of German ammunition, broke out in the caves and the fire and the explosions which followed destroyed so many rounds of mortar shell, so many smoke pots, incendiary grenades, gas masks, and other chemical supplies that Fifth Army was short until resupply could be effected. Coblentz resumed propel-

---

[130] Humphreville, Rpt of Cml Warfare Opns, Sicilian Campaign.
[131] Personal Ltr, Barker to Shadle, 20 Dec 43. CWS 314.7 Pers files, NATO.
[132] (1) *Ibid.* (2) Barker to Hist Off, 11 Aug 59.

lant drying operations on the new supply with an improved steam coil dryer.[133]

The number of bad fuzes which caused premature shell explosions plagued both CWS and Ordnance throughout the war. During the winter of 1943–44, Barker was forced to set up a line near San Pietro, Italy, to disassemble all chemical mortar shell fuzes and check and clean the components. Coblentz later established a similar line at Naples.[134]

Meanwhile, the OCCWS made strenuous efforts to improve the ammunition and the packing and packaging.[135] A new cartridge was provided. On 1 August 1943 ASF adopted a new method of packing in which two unassembled rounds coated with cosmoline or a corrosion preventative and with noses covered by vinylite sacks were packed in a stained wooden box.[136] Propellant charges and cartridges were packed in sealed waterproof tin cans. A final packing method was developed for all shipments after 1 February 1944 whereby the assembled round was sealed in a laminated fiber cylinder before being packed in the box.[137] These packing methods lessened theater problems with respect to newly received shell except when shipping damage resulted in leaking containers or when shell was reclaimed or repacked in the theater.[138]

The 76 officers and 575 enlisted men of the CWS in North Africa by the end of December 1942 knew their mission—to prepare for the eventuality of gas warfare, to provide artificial smoke concealment, and to support combat troops with chemical weapons and equipment—but few of these men could have had much conception of what the mission involved or how they were to accomplish it.[139] They had no toxics and no means to use them. The mechanical smoke generator was a new

---

[133] (1) Barker Comments, 15 Dec 60. (2) Coblentz Comments, 9 Jan 61.

[134] Barker Comments, 15 Dec 60.

[135] For general packaging improvement, see Brophy, Miles, and Cochrane, *From Laboratory to Field*, ch. XVI.

[136] Fifth Army Peninsular Base Section earlier sprayed white pine ammunition boxes with a tar mixture so that they could more readily be camouflaged in forward positions (Coblentz Comments, 9 Jan 61).

[137] (1) Personal Ltr, Porter to Shadle, 5 Feb 44. CWS 314.7 Pers Files, NATO. (2) IOM, Col B. L. Neis, Chief Conservation Br ASF, for Dir of Materiel ASF, 9 Feb 44, sub: Extracts from History of 2d Cml Bn in Sicilian and Part of Italian Campaigns, 1 May to 9 Sep 43, Commenting Upon Packaging 4.2-inch Cml Mortar Ammunition. ASF SPUPC 4051, in files Off Dir of Materiel ASF.

[138] Such difficulties are illustrated in Proceedings, Board of Investigation, Lt Col Lawrence M. Hoover, President, Hq Fwd Echelon PBS, 2 Oct 44. CWS MTO Folder 100 Accidental Explosion of 4.2-inch HE Shell in MTO.

[139] For strength figures, see Brophy and Fisher, *Organizing for War*, app. A.

item unfamiliar to most men of the CWS. The 4.2-inch chemical mortar had not yet been officially recognized as a weapon which could fire high explosives, and, in any case, there were neither mortar units nor mortars in North Africa at the time. Some of the officers who had come from England and a few from the United States were acquainted with incendiary bombs, but not even all of these few had seen such bombs or knew of the existence of the portable flame thrower. Organizationally, the man who was soon to be theater chief chemical officer then occupied a supreme headquarters position, as AFHQ chemical officer, which was unlike any position ever held by or planned for any chemical officer. No field army chemical section had been organized overseas since World War I. Supply procedures, still in the process of formulation late in 1942, were known but vaguely if at all.

In this situation it is not strange that not only did an autonomous CWS develop in the Mediterranean area but also that each element of it developed its own independence. Such independence was encouraged by Shadle who believed in the importance of his staff function and preferred to give strong field elements their head. The organizational situation was, in turn, excellent seed ground for the development of two chemical supply systems, one oriented toward impetus from the front and the other toward impetus from the rear.

In the final analysis, the CWS in the North African–Mediterranean theater accomplished its tasks and that accomplishment was largely the product of great independence of spirit and a great willingness of chemical officers and men at all levels to improvise and innovate—to adapt the procedures and the equipment and the organization as each new situation demanded.

CHAPTER IV

Theater Supply: Europe

Evolving the Theater CWS Supply System

European Theater—The Strategic and Logistical Pattern

The theater environment in which the Chemical Warfare Service, European Theater of Operations, performed its supply tasks was unusual in that the theater, after remaining uninvolved in ground combat for nearly a year, directed the largest combat effort of the war. While the Army Air Forces was on the offensive in several overseas areas and the Navy was strategically and tactically involved in the Pacific early in the war, the ETO ground forces in 1944 were still striving to build up launching places for assaults. In the Pacific the ground assaults began in August of 1942 and continued in November in North Africa. At the end of June 1943 General MacArthur launched his broad-scale offensive in the Southwest Pacific, and by early winter the ground forces were fighting in the middle Pacific atolls. The European theater, activated in June 1942, had theoretically been responsible for early operations in North Africa, but the whole theater organization had been primarily devoted, from the U.S. Army point of view, to the conversion of the British Isles into a vast supply base for the greatest ground offensive of the war. Two years, lacking a few days, elapsed between activation of the theater and the initiation of that offensive. During those two years the theater, and the Chemical Warfare Service within the theater, built up the most comprehensive overseas supply operation of the war. Under such circumstances it would seem axiomatic that theater control of the technical services would be more encompassing than in any other theater. The fact of the matter is that the CWS ETO was the most independent of all overseas CWS organizations. The CWS ETO developed a supply system unlike any other in the European theater and unlike that of any other CWS organization in any theater, although some supply problems and their solutions were markedly similar to those of the CWS MTO.

The CWS ETO was the largest overseas organization of the service. The extent of CWS activity is shown by the fact that, at peak strength, the number of CWS officers and men in the theater was nearly twice as great as in any other theater or overseas area.[1] The service supplied every individual in this, the theater with the greatest total strength, with complete gas warfare protection. And, although chemical mortars were in action almost a year longer in the North African–Mediterranean theater, the sixteen mortar battalions in the ETO expended nearly twice as much ammunition as did those in the Mediterranean.[2] CWS ETO officers forecast the demands of this supply job in terms of procedures which must be developed almost immediately after establishment of a theater headquarters.

Supply Role of the Chief, CWS ETO

Soon after the activation of the theater and its special staff agencies, Captain LeRoy, acting chief of the Storage and Issue Section of the Supply Division, Office of the Chief, CWS ETO, laid the groundwork for the CWS ETO supply system. Introducing the medium which remained throughout the war as the principal means of disseminating supply instructions, CWS ETO supply circular letters, LeRoy, by authority of Colonel Montgomery, then Chief, CWS ETO, briefed chemical supply officers on their duties and responsibilities and on the theater chemical supply procedures. This initial supply circular letter indicated that the Chief, CWS ETO, would: (1) exercise technical control over CWS depots and chemical sections of general depots; (2) set chemical stock levels for the theater; (3) allocate credits to major theater commands;[3] (4) distribute stocks arriving from the

[1] For a comparison of CWS theater strengths, see Brophy and Fisher, *Organizing for War*, Appendix A.

[2] (1) Ammunition Sup Rpt, 31 Jul 45. This was a feeder report prepared in OCCWS for the ASF monthly progress report. (2) Ltr, CG ASF to CofOrd and CCWS, 3 Nov 43, sub: Instructions for Preparation of Ammunition Sup of MPR. ASF SPX 319.1 (30 Oct 43) OB–P–SPDDL–MB–A.

[3] "A credit consists of a notification to a Headquarters that specific items are available in definite quantities in a specified depot subject to requisition [draft] by the Headquarters for whom the credit is established. Materials which have been credited to a Headquarters may be withdrawn at the discretion of the using Headquarters without reference to Tables of Basic Allowances or Tables of Allowances." In CWS ETO Sup Circ Ltr 1, 30 Jul 42. CWS ETO 300.4/1 (26–7–42) SD. In ETO Admin 545A.

ports of debarkation among the depots; (5) order interdepot transfers; (6) determine stock reporting and recording procedures; (7) receive requests for supplies and services required for depot operations when not available locally; and (8) provide policy for and control over chemical service operations. The depot commanders or chemical supply officers were charged with operating the depots, supervising service operations, securing transportation not otherwise provided, and reporting to the Chief, CWS ETO.[4]

The chemical supply officers of the chemical supply sections which had been established on 11 July 1942 in general depots at Ashchurch and Bristol in Gloucestershire, at Thatcham in Berkshire, and at Taunton in Somersetshire, and the commanding officers of chemical depots which had been activated on 15 July at Savernake Forest in Wiltshire and at Marston Magna in Somersetshire received these instructions, but lacked the means to comply. It was late in August before the 6th Chemical Depot Company and the 51st Chemical Impregnating Company, the only chemical service units in the theater, could provide sufficient men to carry out the operating instructions.[5]

Supply Status, July–December 1942

There was in any case not a large quantity of supply with which to operate. By the end of July, the total accumulation of all supplies in the theater amounted to only 181,979 long tons, and, judging from the CWS portion of total supply arriving in the theater during the first year, CWS stockages could hardly have exceeded 2,000 tons.[6] The 10 August 1942 ETO matériel status report indicates the CWS had received a smaller proportion—69 percent—of its authorized supplies than any other service in the theater. Detailed listings in the same report reveal that fewer than half the number of service gas masks authorized was available.[7]

By the end of September, the CWS ETO reported the supply prospects as encouraging, but the actual status of stocks had not improved. The average number of days of combat maintenance of all items was

---

[4] (1) History, Sup Div, 42–43. (2) CWS ETO Sup Circ Ltr 1, 30 Jul 42. CWS ETO 300.4/1 (26-7-42)SD. (3) History, Sup System.

[5] (1) History of CWS Depot Installation in the ETO, CWS ETO (May 42–Dec 43). ETO Admin 545A. (2) History, 6th Cml Depot. (3) History of the 51st Cml Processing Co.

[6] (1) Ruppenthal, *Logistical Support*, I, 103. (2) Transportation Service ETO, Rpt, U.S. Army Cargo Arrivals—UK: Percentage Composition by Serv, 10 Jan 44. ETO Admin 424.

[7] Msg, S724, CG SOS ETO (G–4) to AGWAR, 10 Aug 42. ETO Admin 311A.

24, but in view of the imbalance of stocks, ranging from 873 days for the gas alarm to zero days for vesicant detector crayon, the average was not significant. The significant fact was that even based on a troop strength of 217,123 then reported in the United Kingdom, there was a serious shortage of both individual and collective protection items, such as the gas mask and the portable decontaminating apparatus. This strength was slightly more than half the strength, 427,000, for which ETO planners set requirements in the same month. The real CWS supply level was estimated at 12 days for Class II (general supplies issued against established allowances) items and practically nil for all other classes. This real level was not more than one-sixth of the lowest authorized theater supply level computed on the 427,000 strength figure for 60 days of supply. The figure for the number of days of supply fluctuated from 60 to 90 days in the several versions of the theater plan formulated in the fall of 1942.[8] The quantity of supply immediately available was critically low. Yet, the ETO was then primarily a planning theater, and CWS ETO officers took the long-range view that the immediate problem of supply shortages was important only insofar as the shortages reflected the need for planning to meet the ultimate goal—supplying the theater at full strength.

Major Hayes, Chief, Requirements Division, CWS ETO, stated in the October supply report to the War Department that the immediate supply shortage resulted from the necessity for filling initial shortages for all units and organizations in and arriving in the United Kingdom. Filling initial shortages depleted stocks much more rapidly than replacing normal consumption, and Major Hayes was anxious to know if plans should provide for the greater issue rate. If so, he pointed out, the CWS ETO planners would have to know the approximate extent of shortages among arriving troops. The CWS ETO was in a poor position to forecast issue requirements even if only normal replacement supply would be required. Planners did not know the theater priority for supply, nor did they know how much shipping tonnage would be allocated to CWS supply and how much of that allocation might be lost because of extensive enemy submarine warfare. Further, they had not been informed whether CWS ETO requisitions would be honored in the United States, and they had received no information on

---

[8] (1) Actg CCWS Hq SOS ETOUSA to ACofS G–4 WDGS, thru channels, Initial G–4 Per Rpt, From Arrival in Theater to 30 Sep 42, 2400 Hours, 1 Oct 42 (hereafter cited as G–4 Rept, 1 Oct 42). CWS 319.1/3040 1942. (2) Ruppenthal, *Logistical Support*, I, 103–05.

the War Department ammunition supply policy. Apparently the
failure to provide information extended even to their own theater
headquarters. At the end of September, the CWS ETO was still planning on a 180-day level of supply for Class II instead of on the 90- to
60-day level mentioned above.[9] Hayes urged the War Department to
provide requirements information at once since, despite the lack of
supplies, supply officers were convinced that the BOLERO and ROUNDUP
build-ups would result in the theater having to handle vast quantities
of materials within a few months.[10]

The CWS Credit System

Anticipating a greatly increased workload, CWS supply officers bent
their efforts to turning out a comprehensive supply plan. The completed plan made the Chief, CWS ETO, as stated above, directly
responsible for stating requirements and preparing theater requisitions
on the United States and for supervising the receipt and storage of
goods. In handling the third element of the supply system, distribution, LeRoy realized that the small number of men and the lack of
available facilities meant that distribution would have to be decentralized for efficient operation. He accordingly based the distribution
system on the allocation of supply credits. The allocation of supply
credits to using units and organizations was an established War Department procedure which the CWS in the United States had incor-
porated into its supply manual.[11] Credit allocations were made sporadically throughout the Army's distribution system and in many
cases, as in corps area distribution in the United States, these allocations
were used early in the war to establish quota distributions for short
supply items of lesser importance than controlled items.[12]

The CWS ETO anticipated a credit-employment trend in the
United States by using the credit system to govern the issue of con-

---

[9] G-4 Rpt, 1 Oct 42.

[10] ROUNDUP was an Allied plan for a cross-Channel attack in 1943. BOLERO was a more encompassing
plan for building up Allied strength in the British Isles for continental invasion and follow-through.
The two plans were complementary until TORCH (the North African plan) outmoded ROUNDUP.
BOLERO continued, through many modifications, as the build-up plan. Ruppenthal, *Logistical Support*,
I, ch. II.

[11] (1) FM 100-10, 9 Dec 40. Revised 15 Nov 43. (2) FM 3-15, CWS, 17 Feb 41.

[12] Controlled items were scarce and important items whose issue was controlled by the War Department (OPD and/or ASF) on a priority or urgency basis. Leighton and Coakley, *Global Logistics and
Strategy*, *1940-43*, p. 304.

trolled as well as less important items when, as early as 31 July 1942, they made all Class II noncontrolled items and the majority of Class II controlled items subject to credit allocations. Theater requirements for Class IV (special supplies outside regular allowances) items were not firm enough to warrant credit allocations, but procedures were adopted to place ammunition (Class V) on credit in accordance with authorized training allowances whenever a sufficient supply became available.[13] Total stocks of air chemical Class V were credited to the Eighth Air Force from the inception of the system.[14] The CWS ETO thus inaugurated the only comprehensive credit distribution system to be used in the theater.

Although administrative arrangements for the CWS ETO issue system were complete by the end of July 1942, operating difficulties prevented more than token allotment of credits during the remainder of the year. The first of these difficulties arose because there was too small a staff at all levels of theater organization to manage the system. The great advantage in the credit issue system was that only one action, the allocation of credits, had to be performed at theater or SOS headquarters level; the responsibility for requesting allocations and for receiving issues from depots lay with major commands subordinate to the theater commander. Issuing allocations to minor commands would have involved theater headquarters in so much detail that the purpose of decentralizing supply operations would have been defeated. Throughout 1942, there were insufficient numbers of chemical supply management officers at the subordinate major command levels to handle the workload for their commands. The planned use of the new base section organizations for area distribution of chemical supplies to SOS units was likewise thwarted by the lack of chemical manpower.[15] The expected major ground forces command comparable to Army Ground Forces in the United States was never organized in the theater, and no acceptable alternative co-ordinating command was available until the activation of an army group headquarters late in 1943. Although the Eighth Air Force became operational in August 1942 and although a bulk Class V credit was issued, the air force head-

---

[13] (1) *Ibid.*, pp. 303–04.   (2) History, Sup System.   (3) CWS ETO Sup Circ Ltr 4, 31 Jul 42. CWS ETO 400-35 (28-7-42)SD.   (4) G-4 Rpt, 1 Oct 42.

[14] For more information on air chemical ammunition, see below, pp. 149–63.

[15] The Eastern, Western, Southern, and Northern Ireland Base Sections were organized by SOS ETO on 20 July 1942, but only with skeleton staffing. Ruppenthal, *Logistical Support*, I, 84–85.

quarters, which served as the theater air command, was not well enough organized for the next several months to handle the issue accounting problems which would result from crediting other supplies.[16]

The burden placed on the supply system by the requirements for TORCH and the virtual suspension of the BOLERO build-up resulted in a diversion of the supply effort from the long-range goal. Shipments earmarked for TORCH began to replace BOLERO shipments in August. In the ensuing three months almost the entire theater supply effort was directed toward equipping units alerted for the TORCH operation and, for two months thereafter, to setting up maintenance shipments for North Africa. The seriousness of the supply situation was greatly aggravated. The CWS ETO participated in the TORCH effort by assuming the burden of detailed supply operations which included receiving unit requisitions from alerted units, extracting requisition items to the depots where stock was known to exist, and conducting unit "show down" inspections to determine if requisitions had been placed for basic equipment and if supplies had been received. To speed up and to simplify the actual details of requesting and handling materials, Captain LeRoy's section devised a multicarbon single control form which could be used as a requisition, tally sheet, packing slip, bill of lading, and notice of receipt. A Control Division, SOS, officer visiting in the ETO saw the CWS forms in Supply Division, CWS ETO, and took a number of them to Washington with him. About six months later ASF published a "War Department Shipping Document" which was similar to the CWS ETO form.[17]

Some conception of the magnitude of the TORCH supply tasks can be derived from the fact that 10,020 U.S. troops sailed as part of Eastern Task Force and 70,800 as part of Center Task Force in convoys originating in the United Kingdom. Many of these troops had to be equipped in part and almost all had to be inspected in the United Kingdom. Also, the War Department directed the European theater to set up twenty-two maintenance shipments of CWS supplies totaling 3,133 deadweight tons to be sent in twelve North African resupply

[16] (1) History, Sup System.   (2) Ruppenthal, *Logistical Support*, I, 84–85, 202–03.   (3) Wesley F. Craven and James L. Cate, eds., "The Army Air Forces in World War II," vol. II, *Europe: TORCH to POINTBLANK, August 1942 to December 1943* (Chicago: University of Chicago Press, 1949), pp. 210–11, 216.   (4) History, Cml Sec Eighth AF.
[17] (1) History, Sup System.   (2) Interv, Hist Off with Col LeRoy, 17 Apr 52.   (3) WD SM 38–401, Jul 43.

convoys between November 1942 and February 1943.[18] Despite the amount of this work, or perhaps because of it, the headquarters supply officers were unaware of the inroads TORCH was making into BOLERO. The CWS ETO supply policy consequently remained unchanged and, indeed, supply officers found it possible to issue twenty credits for local supply during the second half of calendar year 1942.[19]

Logistical Data

While theater stocks were virtually exhausted when the ETO was finally relieved of responsibility for North Africa in February 1943, it was probably fortunate that there had been no change in CWS ETO supply policy. The Allied leaders agreed at the Casablanca Conference in January 1943 to reinstate BOLERO and, at the TRIDENT Conference in Washington in May, they set targets for an approximately 1.5-million troop strength to be ready for a cross-Channel operation about 1 May 1944. The CWS system, which had been predicated on such a build-up, was therefore ready to go into more extensive operation when, about the middle of 1943, BOLERO moved from crawl to sprint. But, in the meantime, from November 1942 to May 1943, the theater staff, including the CWS, had not been idle. The theater and SOS general staffs drew up detailed plans of troop requirements to be used when the order to proceed with the build-up was received, and they decided how to allot forces for the air and supply effort and the eventual ground effort. The G–4, SOS, compiled basic logistical planning factors, such as required storage space per 1,000 men per 30 days' maintenance and tonnage per day required to support given strengths. Colonel LeRoy, now chief of the Supply Division, CWS ETO, realized that these computations prepared at higher echelons would have little meaning for the CWS as long as they lacked basic logistical data for CWS items.[20] The information which Hayes had urgently requested from the United States in October had not yet been received since it was not

---

[18] (1) History, Sup System. (2) History of CWS ETO Statistical Summaries. ETO Admin 545A. (3) Leighton and Coakley, *Global Logistics and Strategy, 1940–43*, p. 437. (4) Howe, *Northwest Africa*. (5) Rowan Comments, 16 Dec 60.

[19] (1) History, Sup System. (2) Ruppenthal, *Logistical Support*, I, 87–113.

[20] LeRoy was acting chief of the Storage and Issue Section, Supply Division, from 27 July to 19 September 1942 and executive officer from that time until 5 December; he was acting chief of the Supply Division from December 1942 to 17 February 1943, then on temporary duty in the United States until 4 April 1943 when, now a lieutenant colonel, he returned to the theater as chief of the Supply Division; on 26 October 1943 he was reassigned and sent to the United States.

then available in the United States. Preparations for the TORCH operation had made CWS ETO planners understand how essential such logistical data were for adequate supply planning. LeRoy accordingly embarked on an extensive project for the assembly of CWS logistical data.[21]

The job done by Colonel LeRoy and the members of the Supply Division on CWS logistical data was monumental. The work was begun in December 1942, and distribution of the initial portions took place in February and March 1943. In June 1943 the CWS ETO sent out a complete set of compiled tables for the guidance of all supply officers and of chemical officers at all echelons of command. The compilation was divided into four sections. The first section provided basic data, a list of all items for which the CWS had procurement, storage, and issue responsibilities together with correct nomenclatures, types of packaging, unit and package weights and cubages, storage and shipping factors, and a list of all British and American cargo vehicles and railway cars which showed weight and load limit and cargo measurement for each type. The second section set forth the basis for computing requirements, giving consolidated chemical supply listings from tables of basic allowances, tables of allowances, tables of organization and equipment, and lists of chemical expendable supplies. This section also listed the basis for issue of ammunition and gave established units of fire, days of supply, and replacement factors on specific items. In the third section the logistic requirements of each type of organization in the Army were analyzed in terms of initial issue of chemical matériel, and the weight and cubage of each item authorized were given together with total weights and cubages converted into total tonnage and shipping space needed. Such special logistic problems as the supply of impregnating materials and the proper calculation of payloads per aircraft for chemical or incendiary aerial bombardment were set forth in detail in the fourth section. The compilation closed with a detailed account of the use of these data in planning operations. This invaluable compilation was amended many times as required by changes in equipment and organization, and an extensive revision was issued, section by section, in 1944. It was the foundation of all CWS

---

[21] (1) Ruppenthal, *Logistical Support*, I, 113–23. (2) History of CWS Logistics in the ETO (hereafter cited as History, Logistics). (3) For logistical data problems in North Africa, see above, Chapter III.

ETO logistical planning throughout the war, even after the issuance of the CWS supply catalogs which covered some of the same area.[22]

The CWS ETO logistical data compilation served, on the one hand, as the basis for computing total theater chemical matériel requirements according to present or expected strengths, and on the other hand, as a source of shipment, storage, and distribution information, including a rapid means of calculating credit allocations once the matériel arrived in the theater. In March 1943 the decentralization of the supply distribution process was encouraged by extending the credit allocation plan to cover all classes of supply.[23] While the basic credit system procedures were thus set, the CWS ETO was well aware of the fact that the system would be workable only when field elements were prepared for storage, issue, and accounting.

Storage and Issue

Storage and issue was one of the original CWS ETO problems. Supply authorities, as mentioned above, had a difficult time staffing the depots and depot sections. This problem was somewhat alleviated, at least in the management sphere, when supply officers arrived in September 1942 to replace the troop officers who had been managing the depots and depot sections. This benefit was almost immediately canceled out, however, by the transfer of some of these officers and most of the enlisted men to the North African forces then being assembled. The 6th Chemical Depot Company, the only such unit in the theater, also embarked for North Africa. The 51st Chemical Impregnating Company became the sole theater chemical service unit. The staff reduction was so drastic that the chemical section of the general depot at Taunton was left with one officer and no enlisted men, and the chemical section of the general depot at Thatcham with two officers and no enlisted men. The chemical section of the Ashchurch general depot had one officer and eleven enlisted men while the chemical section

[22] (1) History, Logistics. (2) Sup Div CWS SOS ETO, Cml Warfare Logistics, various portions dated from 1 Feb 43 to Jun 43. ETO Admin 545A. (3) Sup Div OCCWO Hq SOS ETO and Hq COMZ ETO, CWS Logistics, various portions dated from 15 Jan 44 to 10 Aug 44. ETO Admin 544. (4) Sup Circ Ltr 31, CWS SOS ETO, 18 Mar 43, sub: Computation of Rqmts. SOSCW 471.6/51 (15 Mar 43)SD. ETO Admin 545A. (5) ASF Cml Warfare Sup Catalog, prepared by Field Rqmts Div OCCWS, 1 Apr 44. (This catalog is an assembly of various catalogs and lists on which publication began 23 September 1943.)

[23] Sup Circ Ltr 31, CWS SOS ETO, 18 Mar 43.

in the Bristol general depot had two officers and six enlisted men.[24] The heavy demands of the TORCH preparations could not have been met but for the help of British pioneer troops and civilians. The British could not provide manpower on a permanent basis since their own manpower shortages were severe and since they operated on a strict priority system. The labor problem was further complicated by a lack of facilities. Storage buildings provided were not well lighted, floors were rough and uneven, and in one of the designated locations the maximum safe floor load was so low as to preclude efficient storage operation. In another depot the chemical section was assigned space on the fifth floor of a building with only one small elevator. Only one depot possessed car-level loading platforms, and the lack of mechanized equipment and even roller conveyors meant that all lifting, loading, sorting, and stacking had to be performed manually. This bad situation was made worse by a lack of adequate communications between the SOS headquarters, the ports, and the depots and, until January 1943, the absence of maintenance facilities. The one chemical maintenance company in the theater was being used in depot operation, and the second company did not arrive until November 1943.[25]

The CWS ETO storage manpower situation reached a low in December of 1942. From the supply handling point of view it was fortunate that theater stocks were virtually exhausted and that few shipments were arriving. The 7th Chemical Depot Company arrived in the theater in December and by early January had been parceled out into detachments to operate the two chemical depots and four chemical sections of general depots which had been established six months earlier, and one general depot chemical section which had been established at Sudbury Egginton, Derby, Staffordshire, in December. At the time these detachments were sent out, a new chemical depot, soon to be converted into a chemical section of an ordnance depot, was activated at Cinderford, Gloucestershire. Another general

---

[24] History of CWS Installations in the ETO, CWS ETO, Jul 42–Dec 44 (hereafter cited as History, Depot Installations). ETO Admin 545A.

[25] (1) History, Depot Installations. (2) Personal Ltr, Rowan to Waitt, 5 May 43. CWO–400/32 Sec in CWS 314.7 Pers Files, ETO, Oct 42–Jan 44. (3) G–4 Rpt, 1 Oct 42. (4) For maintenance companies in the theater, see Brophy and Fisher, *Organizing for War*, Appendix H–9. As indicated in Appendix H–7, one chemical maintenance company (aviation) arrived in the theater in August 1943.

depot chemical section was activated at Moneymore, Northern Ireland, before the end of January.[26]

While the Allied leaders had agreed in January to renew the BOLERO build-up, tonnage arrivals remained light for the first three months of 1943, the March incoming CWS shipments amounting to only 25 long tons. The April figure suddenly shot up to 826 long tons of CWS supplies, and, after the official rescheduling of BOLERO targets in May, the June figure reached 4,004 long tons.[27] Such a cargo inflow was certainly more than one depot company could handle, particularly since work had been increased by the establishment of another chemical depot in Sudbury, Suffolk, on 1 June 1943. On 1 July 1943, the handling situation was relieved by the arrival of the 60th Chemical Depot Company. The two companies were then able to operate with a maximum of five detachments each. Incoming tonnage rates soared, plummeting occasionally, but reaching more than 9,000 tons in September, more than 12,000 in December, and a peak of 34,604 tons in June 1944. The handling situation would have grown rapidly worse again but for the arrival of new units and a comprehensive depot installation plan which had been laid down in May 1943.[28]

The unit complement for the build-up period in the British Isles was rounded out during the last six months of 1943. One chemical depot company (aviation) arrived in July and two in August. The 65th Chemical Depot Company disembarked in England about 6 October, and the 761st Chemical Depot Company (Aviation) followed a few days later. Three chemical depot companies, the 9th, the 61st, and the 64th, completed the list in November. Meanwhile, the SOS depot plan brought about the establishment of chemical sections in general depots at Barry, Glamorganshire, in July, and at Hilsea, Hampshire, at Westbury, Wiltshire, and at Histon, Cambridgeshire, in November. Chemical ammunition depots were activated at Shepton Mallet, Somersetshire, and at Loton Deer Park, Alderbury, Shropshire, in November. From December 1943 until after the invasion of the Continent six months later, the CWS ETO, in 9 of the theater's 18 general depots and in 6 of its 54 branch and ammunition depots, managed more than 700,000 square feet of closed storage space, more

[26] History, Depot Installations.

[27] Summary of Army Cargo Arrivals by Port Area and Serv, Statistical Summary prepared by Program Div SOS ETO, n.d. ETO Admin 416.

[28] (1) Ibid.   (2) History, Depot Installations.

CHEMICAL WARFARE DEPOT, LOTON DEER PARK, ENGLAND

than one million square feet of open storage space, more than 50,000 square feet of shop space, and space for 68,400 long tons of ammunition.[29] The CWS ETO stood fourth, approximately equal with the Engineers, among the technical services in operation of both closed and open space. The only service other than Ordnance and Engineers operating shop space and the only service other than Ordnance oper-

[29] (1) History, Depot Installations. Exact totals of storage space given are as follows:

	Closed space sq. ft.	Open space sq. ft.	Shop space sq. ft.	Tons of ammunition
Total	732,006	1,034,975	56,250	68,400
General depots	439,006	924,975	56,250	—
Branch and ammunition depots .	293,000	110,000	—	68,400

(2) ICAF SR 46–8, Rpt of Committee on Production, Jan–Jun 1946 course, sub: Transportation, Storage, Packaging, cites report (of travel) of Col. A. B. Drake to the United Kingdom, 1943, which gives the following total figures for the CWS ETO:

Closed space . . . . sq. ft.	812,016
Open space . . . . sq. ft.	1,265,050
Shop space . . . . sq. ft.	42,600
Ammunition dumps . . . . tons capacity . .	62,000

(3) Ruppenthal, *Logistical Support*, I, 158.

ating ammunition storage space, the CWS ETO was a poor second in these two categories.[30]

Air Chemical Supply

After eighteen months of operations in the theater, the CWS ETO was at last in a position to handle supply adequately. Admirable procedures had been established; facilities and installations were satisfactory if not ideal; and sufficient manpower was available to implement the procedures and to staff the installations. Problems for the remaining six months of the build-up period, as well as for the major part of the subsequent operational period on the Continent, centered about the provision of specific items of supply and the operation of specific supply plans. The CWS ETO was not without experience in these problem areas. While most of the activities of the theater had been directed toward build-up, the CWS ETO had received its logistics baptism of fire in the preparations for the North African campaigns, and the steadily increasing combat activities of the Army Air Forces kept the theater in operational status throughout the build-up period. The CWS ETO was heavily involved in the Army Air Forces efforts for two reasons: (1) the CWS provided the incendiary and fire bombs which became major weapons for both bomber and fighter elements of the air arm; and (2) the greater part of the gas warfare retaliatory effort was to be concentrated in the air forces should the enemy initiate gas warfare.[31]

Founding the Air Chemical Supply System, ETO

CWS computations of air chemical munitions requirements for the European theater were begun in the United States before the activation of the theater organization. Colonel Kellogg initiated the requirements work immediately upon his assignment as Eighth Air Force chemical

---

[30] The Drake report, cited above, lists:

	Closed space sq. ft.	Open space sq. ft.	Shop space sq. ft.	Ammunition (tons capacity)
Quartermaster	6,766,373	4,998,694	—	—
Ordnance	2,716,844	1,444,000	1,002,400	395,000
Engineers	831,000	12,236,000	34,968	—
Medical	1,184,417	85,000	—	—

[31] For description of incendiary and fire bombs, see below, Chapter XVII.

officer and the organization of his chemical section in April 1942. Colonel Kellogg's section, proceeding on inadequate data as to aircraft strength and capacity, submitted its requirements estimate for the second half of 1942 on 16 May, a few days before the Eighth Air Force headquarters moved to an overseas staging area. On reaching England in June, Colonel Kellogg realized that the probable inaccuracy of the May submission was not significant since there was little hope of acquiring any substantial stockage of munitions during 1942.[32] He at once inaugurated a threefold program in the supply field. His objectives were: first, to secure matériel, such as gas defensive equipment, aerial incendiaries, toxics, and smoke munitions, from the United States, or, as an interim measure, from the British; second, to acquire or construct storage space for toxics and incendiaries; and third, to provide a firm basis for supply planning and requirements computations.[33] While the air forces in the theater, like the Army Air Forces headquarters in the United States, were tending to become independent in matters of supply, the whole CWS organization in the theater was vitally involved in all the elements of the Eighth Air Force program because the theater CWS was charged with co-ordination of all theater chemical warfare policy, including liaison with the British. Also, the SOS section of the CWS ETO was already providing storage for air chemical supplies and had begun, as noted above, to work on air chemical logistical data.

The accomplishment of all phases of the Eighth Air Force chemical supply program was fraught with difficulties. The only incendiary bombs in production in the United States in this early period were the small 4-pound magnesium and steel case bombs. Most of the magnesium bombs were going to the British under lend-lease, and all production was slowed by the scarcity of magnesium. The steel case bomb was not an effective incendiary for use on many targets, and it was consequently rarely issued to the theaters of operations. The

[32] (1) History, Cml Sec Eighth AF.. (2) History, Hq Eighth AF, vol. II, pt. 2, 17 Aug 42 to 1 May 43. Eighth AF 520.01-3B, 17 Aug 42-1 May 43. (3) For CWS organization in the ETO Army Air Forces, see above, Chapter II.

[33] (1) History, Cml Sec Eighth AF. (2) Capt John F. Crowther, Cml Sec Eighth AF, to Col Kellogg, CmlO Eighth AF, Staff Study, Study of Tactical Rqmts for New Types of Cml Bombs, 27 Jul 42. Eighth AF 471.6 in app. C, History, Cml Sec Eighth AF. (3) Memo, CmlO Eighth AF for ACofS G-3 Eighth AF, 11 Aug 42, sub: Summary of Requests for Cml Warfare Servs Munitions. App. C, History, Cml Sec Eighth AF. (4) Memo, CmlO Eighth AF for CofS, ACsofS G-3, G-4 Eighth AF, 28 Jul 42, sub: Conf With Principal RAF Officers of 42 Group, Reading, England. Eighth AF 519.225, 4 Jul 42-May 45.

M47 100-pound bomb with an incendiary filling was satisfactory, but it was late in 1942 before a successful filling could be produced in quantity.[34] Quantity production of toxics was just beginning, and not even token shipments to the European theater were authorized until January 1943.[35] Defensive equipment and service supplies were no more available to the air forces than they were to the ground and service forces, and all stockages in and destined for the European theater were subject to the demands of the North African campaigns. Existing demands on the British supply system had reached monumental proportions, but the British were in a position to be of some assistance to the chemical preparedness of the United States forces.

Air Toxic Supply

The United Kingdom had the capacity to produce toxics, but production had almost come to a standstill for lack of containers in which to store the finished product. The small British supply of corrosion-resistant steel, the ideal container material, was diverted to other high-priority purposes. While the chances of obtaining such steel were slightly better in the United States, rigorous shipping priorities forbade the shipment of empty containers.[36] As to munitions for the delivery of toxics on the enemy, the United States had the M47 100-pound bomb which was considered to be satisfactory and which was available in limited quantities. The British had a 65-pound and a 30-pound bomb, but the Eighth Air Force was skeptical about their usefulness; furthermore, the bombs did not lend themselves to economical operational loading in American aircraft. Neither the United States nor Great Britain had a bomb cluster for toxics, but the British 250-pound bomb was considered acceptable pending the availability of larger bombs or clusters of smaller bombs. The British 500-pound bomb for filling with nonpersistent agents was considered so highly effective that air chemical officers requested a comparable American munition. Smoke tanks adaptable to aerial vesicant spray missions were the American 500-pound, available in small quantities but virtually obsolete because of the scarcity of aircraft on which it could be carried, the American

---

[34] See Brophy, Miles, and Cochrane, *From Laboratory to Field*, chs. VIII and XV.

[35] Personal Ltr, Waitt to Kellogg, 11 Jan 43.

[36] (1) Waitt to Kellogg, 11 Jan 43. (2) Rpt of Visit of Col W. Hepburn Chamberlain and Capt John L. Armitage to ETO, 18 Mar 44 (hereafter cited as Chamberlain-Armitage Rpt). CWS 314.7 Observer Rpts.

2,000 pound, which was not expected to be available in quantity for some time, and the British 400-pound Flying Cow, a bomb which sprayed smoke or toxics when released from an airplane. The British were able to manufacture the Flying Cow for the American Air Forces, and it was consequently scheduled to be the mainstay of the potential for spraying toxics from aircraft until a better munition should become available.[37]

In addition to supplying the Flying Cow and a small reserve of toxics, the British agreed to provide their 30-pound bomb with an incendiary fill, their 250-pound bomb with an oil incendiary fill, and about 6,500 of the 500-pound phosgene-filled bombs. Also, since the Eighth Air Force was occupying air stations established by the Royal Air Force (RAF), Colonel Montgomery was able to get the RAF to leave their protective equipment and decontaminating facilities intact when vacating the stations. The British further agreed to manufacture some protective, warning, and detection supplies for the United States Army forces, including the air forces.[38]

While the total quantity of British chemical warfare materials furnished the United States Forces was small, and while only token deliveries were made in 1942, awareness of British capability and British reserves was nearly the only reassuring gleam in the dark chemical supply picture from July 1942 to July 1943. The entire gas warfare retaliatory potential depended on British resources for most of that period. CWS ETO officers measured the British contribution as much or more in terms of their willingness to co-operate and their readiness to provide technical and operating experience data as they did in their provision of supplies under reverse lend-lease.[39]

Through the provision of such technical advice as well as actual labor and materials, the British helped to solve the dilemma with respect to toxic storage. Late in 1941 and early in 1942, the British experimented with the storage of toxics in concrete tanks only to reject that method in the spring of 1942 because the toxics seeped through the concrete.

[37] (1) Crowther Staff Study, 27 Jul 42. (2) Memo, CmlO Eighth AF for ACofS G-3 Eighth AF, 11 Aug 42, sub: Summary of Requests for Cml Warfare Servs Munitions. (3) Memo, CmlO Eighth AF for CmlO's Eighth AF, 11 Dec 42, sub: Cml Warfare Munitions on Order for 1943. In app. C, History, Cml Sec Eighth AF.

[38] (1) Memo for File, CmlO Eighth AF, 24 Jun 42, sub: Conf, 22 Jun 42. (2) Ltr, Chief Sup Div CWS ETO to General Purchasing Agent SOS ETO, 2 Sep 43, sub: Rpt of Material Procured by U.S. Forces in the U.K. SOSCW 400.12/121-Sec (2 Sep 43)SD. (3) History, Cml Sec Eighth AF.

[39] (1) Rowan Interv, 26 Sep 58. (2) Magness Interv, 5 May 59.

Almost immediately after the rejection, however, scientists of the Imperial Chemical Industries working for the Ministry of Supply and the Ministry of Aircraft Production hit upon a simple method of lead-lining the concrete tanks to provide a seepage-proof seal. The British quickly constructed a number of lead-lined tanks at three installations to store some of their own reserves, and they offered to build similar facilities for the U.S. Eighth Air Force. Working with the RAF, the Ministry of Supply, and the Imperial Chemical Industries under reverse lend-lease authorizations, Kellogg and Lt. Col. Albert H. Hooker, Chemical Officer, VIII Air Force Service Command, selected sites for advance chemical parks at Barnham, Suffolk, and at Melchbourne Park, near Kettering, Northamptonshire, and the Imperial Chemical Industries agreed to construct three 500-ton tanks at each location. Hardstandings and Romney huts were also built at each site for the storage of 4,000 tons of chemical ammunition and 6,000 tons of incendiaries. The VIII AFSC later installed American toxic and incendiary filling apparatus at both locations. The tanks at the Barnham site were completed and filled by the end of 1943 and, while the Melchbourne Park facility was not completed until the spring of 1944, 1,215 tons of toxics were in storage there in December 1943.[40]

Although the construction of the advance chemical parks represented a major achievement, Army Air Forces chemical officers never assumed, even at the outset, that these parks would solve the problems of storage space for air chemical supplies. For example, against the air park capacity of 3,000 tons of bulk toxics and 8,000 tons of chemical ammunition, the initial estimate of requirements for bulk persistent toxics alone was 34,000 tons.[41] Furthermore, the air chemical officers were concerned not only with storage of reserve and normal station issue supplies but also with the daily munitions requirements of aerial operations. Combat operations requirements, principally of incendiary

[40] (1) History, Cml Sec Eighth AF. (2) Ltr [CG USSTAF] to CG AAF (Attn: Air CmlO) [1 Aug 44], sub: Status of Cml Cos, Air Opns and Cml Depot Cos, Aviation Assigned to Orgns of USSTAF in Europe. Eighth AF 225 Cmls. (3) Memo, CmlO Eighth AF for CofS, ACsofS G–3 and G–4 Eighth AF, 28 Jul 42, sub: Conf With Principal RAF Officers of 42 Group, Reading, England. (4) History of VIII AFSC (Eighth Strategic Air Depot Area), vol. I, Narrative. Eighth AF 528.01, 17 Feb 42–1 Mar 44. (5) Memo, no signature for Col Kellogg et al., 3 Nov 42, sub: Notes on a Mtg to Discuss FFD, 1 and 2 held at Special Products Dept on 30th Oct 1942. Eighth AF 226.9(8) Cml Warfare Confs. (6) Memo for File, CmlO Eighth AF, 11 Mar 43, sub: Conf on Advanced Cml Parks. Eighth AF 400.24 in Eighth AF 226.9(8) Cml Warfare Confs.

[41] Memo, CmlO Eighth AF for CmlO's Eighth AF, 11 Dec 42, sub: Cml Warfare Munitions on Order for 1943.

bombs, had to be immediately available at each operational base from August 1942, when the Eighth Air Force initiated its famous raids on the Continent, until the end of the war in Europe. In the first month, 6.1 tons of incendiary bombs were expended.[42] Despite the fact that Ordnance was officially charged with storage of toxic munitions and usually with the storage of incendiaries, air chemical officers found it almost as difficult, for the whole of the combat period, to find and maintain adequate storage space as it was to obtain munitions.

As supplies began rolling in, in the second half of 1943, air force storage facilities were soon filled. For example, while 18,875 mustard-filled 100-pound bombs were brought into SOS depots and 12,000 into air force depots between April and July 1943, 205,485 toxic-filled M47 bombs were in theater storage by the end of December.[43] Despite the fact that all ammunition storage was an Ordnance function, SOS CWS and even RAF chemical ammunition depots initially assumed most of the load of air force chemical storage. Eventually so much of the air force storage backlog was in SOS depots that the chemical section of the ordnance ammunition depot at Cinderford became in fact, if not in name, a Ninth Air Force depot operated by air chemical service units.[44] The largest SOS CWS ammunition storage facility, that at Loton Deer Park, was designed primarily for incendiary storage, secondarily for toxic storage, mostly of air force munitions, and only incidentally for the storage of ground forces ammunition.[45]

A comparison of ground and air forces toxic stockages in the theater is illuminating, both because it indicates the scope of the storage problems and because it states retaliatory capability in terms of munitions available. The level of ground forces toxic artillery ammunition, all of which was stored by Ordnance, increased only slightly from December 1943, at approximately 301,000 rounds, until March 1945

[42] (1) History of the Cml Warfare Sec 1st Bombardment Div, Aug 42–Feb 44. Eighth AF 525. (2) Statistical Summary of Eighth AF Opns, European Theater, 17 Aug 42–8 May 45. Eighth AF 520.308A, Archives of AF Hist Off Maxwell Air Force Base, Ala.

[43] (1) Baldwin, Bingham, and Pritchard, Readiness for Gas Warfare in Theaters of Operations, app. B. (2) Draft, History of Eighth AF—History of Special Staff Sec, May to Dec 43. Eighth AF 520.01–4B. (3) History, VIII AFSC (Eighth Strategic Air Depot Area), vol. I, pt. I, Narrative.

[44] (1) IOM, Col Hooker, CmlO VIII AFSC, for Col Stuart, Plans Sec, 3 Feb 43, sub: Supplies for Advanced Air Depots. (2) Ltr, Chief Admin IX AFSC to CG ASC USSTAF, 17 Mar 44, sub: Use of Savernake Forest as an Advanced Cml Warfare Class V Depot for Ninth AF Stations. (3) IOM, Col Baum, CmlO USSTAF, for Dir of Pers, Dir of Sups, Dir of Admin Serv USSTAF, 21 Aug 44, sub: Transfer of Cml Depot Cos (Colored). All in Eighth AF 519.225–4 Jul 42–May 45.

[45] History of CWS Storage Depot C–900 at Loton Deer Park, Alderbury, Shropshire. ETO Admin 545A.

when the number of rounds stored nearly doubled. The February 1945 stockage of 308,352 rounds contained approximately 895.45 long tons of toxic filling while the March stockage of 568,225 rounds contained about 1,500 long tons. Nearly a million rounds in storage at the end of the war in Europe contained only about 650 long tons more filling than the March stockage because the type of shell acquired after March included a small payload. The stock of 4.2-inch chemical mortar toxic shell, also stored by Ordnance but of more direct concern to the CWS, was built up from approximately 26,000 rounds in December 1943 to more than 60,000 rounds in March 1944 and then, suddenly, to 137,732 rounds in February 1945. This peak stock, less than half of the 345,000-round peak authorization level, contained approximately 375 tons of toxics. Bulk persistent toxics which, except for the amount stored in the air chemical park tanks, were stored in ton containers and 55-gallon drums, rose from about 6,600 to 8,200 long tons from December 1943 to April 1945. In April 1945 aerial munitions stocks amounted to 306,963 100-pound bombs, 13,081 500-pound bombs, and 35,898 1,000-pound bombs with a total of approximately 16,785 long tons of toxic filling.[46]

The problem of toxic storage in England was finding, improving, and managing storage space. The difficulties encountered in other theaters, such as corroding and leaking munitions, were not experienced to any significant extent. General Waitt and chemical officers in the theater examined toxic munitions stocks in the theater at the end of the war in Europe. They found a small number of M47 bombs, about one percent, that were leaking persistent gas. A small percentage of the remainder were seriously corroded, and a large percentage slightly corroded. The leaking and seriously corroded bombs were destroyed while the rest were cleaned and painted and prepared for shipment out of the theater. A few of the 55-gallon drums were leaking and others needed cleaning and painting. The cleaning and painting process had been continuous during storage in the theater. No serious defects were found in other toxic munitions.[47]

Despite the problem of finding space for the storage of aerial toxic munitions, the level of supply mentioned above was by no means over-

[46] Baldwin, Bingham, and Pritchard, Readiness for Gas Warfare in Theaters of Opns, app. B.
[47] (1) Ltr, Maj J. T. Herndon, Tech Div CWS ETO to Gen Waitt, 4 Jun 45, sub: Shipment of U.K. Base Stored CWS Toxic Munitions to the Pacific Theater. CWS ETO CWOTD 471/8 in CWS 314.7 Observer Rpts. (2) Chamberlain-Armitage Rpt.

generous. Though ground toxic munitions were available, they were considered only supplementary to the basic retaliation potential. The CWS ETO based its gas warfare retaliatory potential on the bomb stockage plus a large portion of the bulk gas intended to fill aerial munitions, and chemical planners reckoned this aerial supply as capable of supporting only 14 operational days of retaliatory gas warfare.[48] Had the Germans resorted to gas warfare, the possible 2- or even 4-week duration of the initial operation would have been a short time in which to move additional supplies from the United States. Indeed, in May 1944 air planners estimated that 45 days would be required to move a stock of the principal toxic weapon, persistent-gas-filled M47 bombs, into the theater. At that time, less than a month before D-day, the theater command considered the threat of German initiation of gas warfare serious enough to order combat-ready toxic bomb loadings sent to operating air stations so that a retaliatory strike could be launched in a maximum of 24 hours.[49] When the continental invasion produced no indications of the initiation of gas warfare, no new preparations for retaliation were made in the fall of 1944. On two subsequent occasions, in December 1944 and near the end of the war, theater planners feared that Germany might turn to gas warfare as a last-ditch defense of the homeland although Rowan believed there was little danger. Aside from the increase in toxic munitions stocks in the early months of 1945, no further aerial bombardment retaliatory preparations were made in response to the last-ditch threat.[50]

Incendiary Bombs

The CWS ETO was unable for most of 1942 to supply incendiary bombs.[51] The British 30- and 250-pound incendiaries were therefore

[48] (1) Interv, Hist Off with Col Baum, formerly CmlO USSTAF, 5 Dec 45. (2) Estimates of aerial gas warfare capabilities varied. Chemical Section, 12th Army Group, believed the theater air forces capable of supporting 21 operational days. Leggin Interv, 22 Nov 45.

[49] (1) Memo for Rcd, Baum, 18 May 44, sub: Notes on the State of Preparedness of USAAF in the U.K. for Retaliatory and Sustained Effort in the Event Gas Warfare Is Initiated by the Enemy. Eighth AF 519.253, 1944. (2) Baum Interv, 5 Dec 45. (3) Miller Interv, 2 Feb 60. Air Chief Marshal Sir Trafford Leigh-Mallory, AEAF commander, was designated Air Commander-in-Chief for the initial phase of the continental operation. Wesley Frank Craven and James Lea Cate, eds., "The Army Air Forces in World War II," vol. III, *Europe: ARGUMENT to V-E Day* (Chicago: University of Chicago Press, 1951), pp. 80–82.

[50] Notes by Col M. T. Hankins on Conf of CmlO's at Dillingen, Germany, 29 Apr 45. CWS 314.7 Observer Rpts.

[51] For a discussion of European theater development and employment of incendiary bombs see below, Chapter XVII.

adopted for American use, but the British were little more prepared than the Americans to provide supply in the quantities soon demanded. Kellogg obtained 10,000 American thin cased, 100-pound (M47) bomb bodies late in 1942 and had them filled with an incendiary mixture by air chemical service units in England. Just about the time this field improvisation was completed, a substantial supply of American 100-pound clusters of 4-pound magnesium bombs began to arrive. Just as the incendiary supply situation was beginning to look good, air chemical officers discovered that the 100-pound clusters were defective. They were forced to withdraw the clusters from issue.[52]

Beginning with successful incendiary raids on German industrial targets in occupied France during the summer of 1943, incendiary bomb expenditures, especially of the M47 bomb, then available from the United States, reached large proportions in the fall of 1943 and by December accounted for 40 percent of the total American bomb load.[53] The Chemical Section, VIII AFSC, took extraordinary measures to meet operational demands. They routed incendiary shipments from the United States directly from the port of debarkation to the operational air stations. Short supply M126 fuzes for the M47 were airlifted from the United States. Still there were shortages and some of the tonnage expended included the alternative British oil-perspex-filled 250-pound bomb. At the end of December 1943, M47 stocks were double the tonnage expended in that month, and 1,424 tons of the new 500-pound aimable cluster, M17, had been received. Nearly 16,000 of the 100-pound clusters of 4-pound bombs, now capable of modification by a special fuze to permit cluster opening at an altitude safe to carrying aircraft, were on hand. Seven other clusters of small bombs and the British 250-pound bomb were also stocked in small quantities, in one case as low as six tons. By January 1944 the M17 cluster, which contained 110 4-pound magnesium bombs, had reached VIII Bomber Command stations, and within a week, on 11 January 1944, three groups of the 1st Bombardment Division dropped M17's on Wilhelmshaven. Although bombardiers had to learn its aiming

---

[52] (1) History, Cml Sec Eighth AF. (2) History, Cml Warfare Sec 1st Bombardment Div. (3) Interv, Hist Off with Lt Col John A. Martin, formerly OpnsO Cml Sec Eighth AF, 28 Aug 51.
[53] Statistical Summary of Eighth AF Opns, European Theater.

characteristics, the new cluster proved to be an accurate weapon of great power.[54]

The long awaited M76 500-pound bomb filled with incendiary gel arrived in the theater early in 1944, but operational results of this weapon, dubbed the Block Burner, were disappointing. While the M76 was used with moderate success against Berlin on 6 March 1944, subsequent operations proved that target opportunities for so large a bomb, which contained a low percentage of incendiary fuel with respect to total weight, were few in number. By September the Eighth Air Force had no plans for use of this munition, and a large portion of the stock was turned over to the Ninth Air Force whose tactical targets were more suitable.[55]

The 1944 and 1945 expenditures of incendiary bombs were spotty—the highest month of Eighth Air Force expenditure was October 1944 at 11,337.1 tons while the next month was the lowest at 566.4 tons. The monthly average expenditure for 1944 was nearly 5,200 tons and for 1945 nearly 6,400 tons, approximately one-seventh the monthly average of all Eighth Air Force bombs on target. The M17 cluster comprised about 70 percent of the expenditure, and most of the remainder was the M47. Although on one occasion air chemical officers had to request that M17 shipments be rushed, supply was normally excellent. The curtailed usage of M76 and M47 bombs resulted in stockages beyond the authorized theater 75-day level, and supply officers recommended, in the fall of 1944, that further shipments from the United States be halted. They did not propose that the theater overage be returned since variation in operations or types of targets available might again have meant a large demand.[56]

[54] (1) History, Cml Sec Eighth AF. (2) Cml Sec VIII AFSC, Rpt, Incendiaries, Eighth AF, 1943, Jun–Dec, prepared by Statistical Contl Eighth AF, 7 Jan 44. Eighth AF 519.225-1. (3) Hist, Cml Warfare Sec 1st Bombardment Div.

[55] (1) History, Cml Sec Eighth AF. (2) CG USSTAF to CG AAF, Rpt, Monthly Ammunition Rpt, 6 Oct 44. Eighth AF 519.225-1. (3) Ltr, CG USSTAF to CG AAF [5 Aug 44], sub: Level of Sup of Incendiary Bombs. Eighth AF 519.225-1.

[56] (1) Ltr, CG Base Air Depot Area ASC USSTAF to CG ASC USSTAF, 16 Sep 44, sub: Level of Sup of Incendiary Bombs. (2) IOM, Baum, CmlO USSTAF, for Dir of Sup, Dir of Opns, OrdO, and AG USSTAF, 4 Sep 44, sub: Rqmts for M76 500-lb. Incendiary Bombs. (3) Msg, Doolittle [CG Eighth AF] to AWW, 3 Sep 44. (4) IOM, Baum for Dir of Sup USSTAF, 3 Oct 44. (5) Ltr, CmlO USSTAF to Chief, Sup Div CWS COMZ ETO, 14 Oct 44, sub: USSTAF Incendiary Bomb Rqmts. (6) Msg, CG USSTAF to CG Eighth AF [20 Jun 44]. (7) IOM, Baum for Dir of Sup and AG USSTAF, 1 Nov 44, sub: Shipments of M17 Incendiary Bomb Clusters. (8) Msg, MF-03482, CG USSTAF to CG Eighth AF [30 Dec 44]. (9) IOM, Lt Col Clarance H. Breedlove, Asst OrdO and CmlO, Eighth AF for Opn/Research Sec, 5 Jan 45, sub: MF-03482. Eighth AF 471.18. (10) Msg, D-65036, CG Eighth AF to CG USSTAF, 8 Jan 45. All in Eighth AF 519.225-1. (11) Statistical Summary of Eighth AF Opns European Theater.

Fire Bombs

During the second half of 1944 the most pressing air chemical supply problem concerned the provision of another field expedient, the fire bomb. This bomb was a field improvised incendiary bomb fabricated from expendable, auxiliary, aircraft gasoline tanks. Air service units filled the tank with a mixture of gasoline and a thickener (usually napalm) and wired on an incendiary grenade or part of a magnesium bomb as an igniter. The fire bomb was an excellent tactical weapon to use against supply dumps, troop concentrations, convoys, and vehicles. Air chemical officers in the United Kingdom anticipated post-D-day use of fire bombs by the VIII and IX Fighter Commands. The Air Service Command, USSTAF, accordingly increased amounts and priorities on their orders for thickeners and other fire bomb components from the United States. By June of 1944 it was apparent that shipments would not be received in time to meet the demand, and air chemical officers conducted a theaterwide survey of thickener supply. They concluded that interim needs could be met, but with difficulty.[57] Intensive fire bomb missions were inaugurated in July, and supplies proved adequate, particularly since the Ninth Air Force was using the M76 500-pound bomb on the same kind of mission.[58] At the same time, USSTAF requested that SOS transfer 50,000 gallons of the ground forces flame thrower fuel, which was not being used in anticipated quantities, to the air forces.

By the first week in August, SOS had delivered 20,000 gallons of fuel to the air forces and had agreed to lend enough packaged dry napalm from SOS depots for mixing the remaining 30,000 gallons. Air Service Command delivered the entire loan of napalm to the Ninth Air Force and directed the Commanding General, Base Air Depot Area, to complete arrangements, already informally approved, to have the British mix some or most of this fuel. The IX Air Force

[57] (1) IOM, Baum for Dir of Sup, Dir of Opns, and AG USSTAF, 17 Jun 44, sub: Thickened Fuel for Use in Jettisonable Gasoline Tanks. (2) Ltr, CG USSTAF to CG's Eighth and Ninth AF's and ASC, n.d., sub: Nomenclature and Rcds for the Blaze Bomb. Both in Eighth AF 519.225-1.
[58] Ltr, CmlO USSTAF to Air CmlO AAF WD, 5 Aug 44, sub: Eighth and Ninth AF's Expenditure of Incendiaries, Jul 44. Eighth AF 519.225-1.

Service Command was to mix, using a borrowed Canadian mixing apparatus, any fuel that the British could not handle.[59]

Despite the SOS loan and the successful completion of arrangements for British mixing, the anticipated shortage became critical. USSTAF, during August 1944, reminded SOS that the 59 tons of napalm scheduled to arrive from the United States must be available by 25 August and that 64 additional tons already on order must be received by 16 September. Two more pleas for expedited delivery were sent before the first shipment arrived in two parts late in August and about the middle of September.[60]

About 70 percent of the first two shipments—the second had arrived early in October—was dispatched directly to a plant of the National Oil Refining Company, subsidiary of the Anglo-Iranian Oil Company, in Swansea, Wales, which had been ready for processing since 21 August. The rest of those shipments were sent for field mixing by the air force service commands. The British plant mixed more than 375,000 gallons of fuel before the end of October and contracted to continue this job. In addition, a factory in the north of England contracted to supplement the American supply by providing 185,500 gallons of perspex mix fuel from September through November.[61] The fuel supply in the mixing process plus the assured prospect of continuing deliveries from the United States should have removed the fire bomb supply problem from the critical list by the end of September, but plans were knocked awry during the month by startling statements of new requirements and by a distribution problem.

Eighth Air Force in September 1944 decided to drop fire bombs from heavy bombers on targets so well fortified as to have withstood high explosive bombardment. The air force initially requested 600,000 gallons of mixed fuel and in November increased that request to 1,000,000 gallons to be expended at the rate of 130,000 gallons per month. As an alternative to the availability of mixed fuel, the air force

[59] (1) Ltr, CG USSTAF to CG ETOUSA (Attn: CCWO), 21 Jul 44, sub: Flame Thrower Thickened Fuel, with 1st Ind, CG ETOUSA to CG USSTAF, 3 Aug 44, and 2d Ind, CG USSTAF to CG BADA ASC, n.d. (2) Msg, Brig Gen Hugh J. Knerr [CG ASC] to CG BADA ASC, 7 Aug 44, no sub. Both in Eighth AF 519.225-1.

[60] (1) IOM, Baum for AG USSTAF, 16 Aug 44, no sub. (2) Msg, CG ASC USSTAF to CG ETOUSA, 26 Aug 44, no sub. (3) Ltr, CG ASC USSTAF to CG ETOUSA, 28 Aug 44, sub: Rqmts of Napalm and M15 Grenades for Blaze Bomb Fuel. All in Eighth AF 519.225-1.

[61] (1) Ltr, CG BADA ASC to CG ASC USSTAF, 19 Aug 44, sub: Thickened Incendiary Fuel. (2) Personal Ltr, Baum to Brig Gen Edward Montgomery, Air CmlO AAF WD, 16 Oct 44. Both in Eighth AF 519.225.

requested 75 tons of dry napalm and a sufficient number of mixing units to handle it. USSTAF chemical officers reshuffled their planned distribution schedule and notified Eighth Air Force in tones of justifiable pique that, while its original request was out of the question, 60,000 gallons could be furnished at the end of September, an additional 30,000 gallons during October, and that attempts would be made to meet the 130,000-gallon requirement in November and December. At this point the air chemical officer in War Department Headquarters, Army Air Forces, cabled to ask if his headquarters could be of assistance in improving the fire bomb supply situation. USSTAF answered that the greatest possible assistance would be in insuring the delivery of 100 tons of dry napalm per month by setting up fast ship and air transportation in addition to that already allotted to USSTAF. This plea was renewed after Eighth Air Force increased its requests. Meanwhile, air chemical officers even canvassed the Twelfth Air Force in the Mediterranean area in the hope of securing thickener, but the Twelfth Air Force was itself then attempting to borrow thickened fuels from the Ninth. In December 1944 and in 1945 the problem was solved by the arrival of a sufficient supply of thickeners from the United States. About the same time, American mixing and transfer kits became available in quantity. AAF enlarged the table of equipment for chemical air operations companies to provide eight of these mixing and transfer kits for each unit, and USSTAF secured special kit allowances for the Eighth Air Force. Thus, field units could mix enough fuel to greatly augment the British capacity.[62]

The use of mixing and transfer units also helped to solve the distribution problem arising from the supply of fire bomb fuel. The nature of this problem was that the Ninth Air Force was already operating from the Continent by the time mixed fuels began to come off the processing lines in the United Kingdom, sometime in September.

[62] (1) Msg MF–00742, Lt Gen Carl Spaatz to CG Eighth AF, 21 Sep 44, no sub. (2) IOM, Baum for Dir of Opns USSTAF, 30 Sep 44, Sup of Thickened Fuel for Eighth Air Force. (3) IOM, Baum for Dir of Sup and Dir of Opns USSTAF, 2 Oct 44, sub: Cable From Gen Henry H. Arnold re Fire Bombs. (4) IOM, Baum for Dir of Sup and AG ASC USSTAF, 4 Oct 44, no sub. (5) Msg MF–01268, Spaatz for CG Eighth AF, 11 Oct 44, no sub, with 1st Ind, CG Eighth AF to CG USSTAF, n.d., and 2d Ind, CG USSTAF to CG Eighth AF, n.d. (6) IOM, Baum for Dir of Sup, Dir of Opns, and AG USSTAF, 13 Oct 44, no sub. (7) Baum to Montgomery, 16 Oct 44. (8) IOM, Baum for Dir of Opns, Dir of Sup, and AG USSTAF, 1 Nov 44, sub: Supply of Napalm for Fire Bomb Fuel. (9) IOM, Baum for Dir of Sup and AG ASC USSTAF, 4 Nov 44, sub: Eighth Air Force Fire Bomb Fuel Rqmts. (10) IOM, Baum for AG USSTAF, 10 Nov 44, sub: Mixing and Transfer Units. (11) Msg, Spaatz to CG Ninth AF, 19 Nov 44, no sub. All in Eighth AF 519.225.

Routing these fuels, packed for the most part in still scarce 55-gallon drums, through normal supply channels resulted in insupportable delays. The USSTAF Chemical Section accordingly arranged with COMZ ETO to transfer fuel distribution from the normal channels to Army Air Forces priority supply channels from the beachheads and ports forward. The change in channels resulted in special and rapid handling of fuel. Colonel Baum stationed "expediters," chemical officers or air chemical units, at crucial points along the supply line to see that the fuel kept moving. The mixing and transfer kits also permitted the air chemical units attached directly to the operation groups to fill fire bombs on the spot, thus eliminating drum shortage complaints and relieving the overtaxed distribution system.[63]

By the beginning of 1945 air chemical supply was proceeding smoothly, and more than a month before the end of the war in Europe air chemical officers turned their attention to the disposition of supplies on hand. For the air forces as for all forces in the theater, D-day had been a momentous event, and the character of air forces operations had changed substantially because of the nature of D-day preparations and post-D-day requirements, but D-day was not a turning point in air chemical supply as it was in ground chemical supply. The turning points in air chemical supply were two: the first at the beginning of 1944 when the minimum required supply for toxic retaliation was at last reached and when incendiary supply was at last equal to operational demands, and the second at the beginning of 1945 when the availability of fire bomb material could be counted on to meet operational demands. Despite this difference in culmination of air and ground efforts, the problems of air and ground chemical supply were essentially alike. The foremost question was always how to compute requirements for toxics, a weapon which might not be used, or for incendiaries and fire bombs, weapons which had not previously been used. But the question which required greater expenditure of energy and ingenuity was how to meet the requirements once computed or presented by operational usage. The air chemical supply system answered both of these questions but neither answer was quick and easy. To consider ground chemical supply it is therefore necessary to return to the end

---

[63] (1) Baum to Montgomery, 16 Oct 44. (2) Mgs, Gen Spaatz to Maj Gen Hoyt S. Vandenberg [CG Ninth AF], cited in IOM, Baum for Dir of Sup, Dir of Opns, and AG USSTAF, 5 Oct 44, no sub. Both in Eighth AF 519.225.

of 1943 when ground preparations for the scheduled spring continental operation became the dominating theater activity.

Ground Chemical Supply

The CWS ETO and all its sister services in the theater had been involved in preparations for D-day ever since the establishment of the theater headquarters in June 1942, for a build-up supporting the cross-Channel operation was the aim of the BOLERO plan under which they functioned. But, until the end of 1943, the problems of the build-up and of supply shortages were so grave as to obscure the main objective. In the fall of 1943 chemical supply was arriving in a sufficient quantity, as noted above, to make the assault on the Continent seem more feasible. Furthermore, in November and December 1943 the Allied Staffs were beginning to consider the precise nature and scope of OVERLORD, the forthcoming operation.[64] The basic question facing the ground planners was tactical: how can a Normandy beachhead large enough to serve as a point of departure for continental operations be secured? This basic question quickly resolved itself into two logistical questions: (1) how many men could the Allied forces get across the Channel and on the beachhead; (2) how much build-up of matériel would be required to support them?

Plans and Planning Agencies

The answer to the basic tactical question from the American point of view was to mount an overwhelmingly superior force, which would mean using all the men in every combat-ready unit which could be assembled in the United Kingdom and which could be provided with transport to the Continent. The technical services in turn would have to accumulate sufficient matériel to support such a force. The CWS ETO portion of the matériel project involved three basic categories of supply: (1) individual and collective gas warfare protective and decontaminating items for the entire force; (2) weapons and ammunition for chemical mortar units plus flame and smoke weapons and equipment for all combat forces; (3) and special operational requirements such as smoke protection for the beachhead. The first job was

---

[64] Ruppenthal, *Logistical Support*, I, 175–89.

to secure statements of chemical requirements in each category from each of the responsible planning headquarters.

Activation of the planning headquarters had begun late in 1943. First United States Army was to be responsible for all supply operations until two weeks after D-day. Advance Section, Communications Zone, a mobile base section headquarters, was to take over for the next twenty-seven days. Forward Echelon, Communications Zone, was to assume control of supply operations in the remaining forty-nine days of the first three months on the far shore. It was assumed that Communications Zone, the redesignated SOS ETO, would be in operation on the Continent at the end of the third month. Major Hingle moved over from Supply Division, CWS ETO, in January to establish a supply division in the FECOMZ Chemical Section. Chemical sections of all these closely co-ordinated agencies immediately set to work on their requirements planning. Since initial issue of all regular supplies had already been made or materials credited to all units and organizations in or arriving in the United Kingdom, the requirements plans were for cross-Channel resupply.[65]

On 15 April FUSA began submitting requisitions for the materials in its chemical supply plan which had been the last of the major plans to be formulated.[66] CWS Supply Division issued 375 shipping orders releasing 8,364 ship tons of Classes II and IV supplies and 12,072 ship tons of Class V supplies for movement over the beaches in the first 2-week phase. Three weeks later Third United States Army, the organization to which ADSEC was scheduled to render most of its support, submitted requisitions for chemical resupply in the ADSEC control phase. Materials requisitioned totaled 4,026 ship tons of Classes II and IV and 7,815 tons of ammunition. The CWS ETO discovered some shortages in filling these requisitions, but none were serious, and acceptable substitute items were available. FECOMZ phase requisitions required 400 shipping orders for 9,053 ship tons of protective items, weapons, and equipment, and 9,084 ship tons of ammunition. Again, some substitutions which FECOMZ considered satisfactory were made.[67]

[65] (1) History, Sup Div, II. (2) Hq 12th Army Group Final AAR, 31 Jul 45. (3) History, ADSEC. (4) History, FECOMZ. (5) Ruppenthal, *Logistical Support*, I, 219–26.
[66] Personal Ltr, Prentiss to Porter, CCWS, 12 Apr 44. CWS 314.7 Pers Files, ETO.
[67] History, Sup Div, II.

While normal resupply was being set up, theater headquarters, anticipating unpredictable and unusual demands once the operation started, set up two procedures for rapid filling of spot needs. The "Red Ball Express" [68] provided for a daily coaster service shipment of 100 long tons of urgently needed general cargo unobtainable from normal resupply. "Red Ball Express" shipments were to be called for and allocated by the senior commander ashore. The CWS ETO was called upon to provide a total of 90 ship tons during the 3-month operation of this measure. The "Green Light Supply" plan was evolved just a few days before D-day to meet extraordinary ammunition requirements, unavailable from normal resupply, at an estimated rate of 600 long tons per day in the critical period from D plus 14 to D plus 41. CWS shipped 400 ship tons of ammunition through "Green Light." [69] Chemical resupply was thus expeditiously handled with minimum difficulty from the wholesale issue point of view, but the acquisition of some of the items and of services which went into the CWS resupply effort and the initial issue effort had not been easy.

Protective and Decontaminating Equipment

Since the service gas mask had been proved too bulky and too heavy during the North African campaigns, chemical officers in the ETO hoped that the CWS in the United States would be able to provide a promised lighter weight mask before their own campaigns began. Late in 1943 the new lightweight mask began to arrive and the CWS ETO embarked on the not inconsiderable task of exchanging the old masks in the hands of each individual in the theater for the new. Unit and organization and depot mask reserves were also exchanged. Chemical officers and gas officers at all echelons then examined the fit and adjustment of every mask in the possession of every individual and conducted gas chamber and wearing exercises and tests, even in the Supreme Headquarters. The tests and exercises sometimes turned up masks that did not fit and could not be adjusted to fit. Fortunately, the number of nonadjustable masks, a defect which OCCWS blamed on the molds used by one manufacturer in early production, was not great. These masks were called in and facepieces from the old masks were assembled to render them serviceable. Issue of the new masks

---

[68] Not to be confused with the later and better-known motor transport operation of the same name.

[69] History, Sup Div, II.

was completed in March 1944, and chemical maintenance companies examined, cleaned, and repaired salvageable old masks turned in to provide a secondary reserve and to build up an inventory of repair parts. Not long after the invasion, Colonel St. John, chemical adviser to G–3, SHAEF, wrote, "There are sufficient gas masks in the UK to cover the faces of all Europe and Asia." [70]

The gas mask was the most important of the protective items, but, since chemical officers assumed that vesicant gases would be employed in far greater quantities than nonpersistent gases, protective clothing was also very important. Storage and issue of protective clothing was a responsibility of the Quartermaster Corps, but the CWS was charged with impregnating permeable clothing with gas-resistant chemicals. The CWS provided chemical processing companies to perform this service in the theaters. As noted above, the 51st Chemical Processing Company was one of the first two chemical service units in the European theater. Late in 1942 this company began to set up a large capacity impregnating facility, in fact a modified commercial dry-cleaning plant, in the factory of the Blythe Colour Works at Cresswell, Staffordshire. This "zone of the interior impregnating plant," which crated weighed nearly 215 long tons and occupied more than 43,000 cubic feet, was intended to be the first of nearly a dozen such plants to be erected in the United Kingdom; but, when it was discovered that sites were unavailable and that requirements for water, waste disposal facilities, and power were more than the overburdened British economy could bear, the CWS ETO requested that the schedule be changed to provide the smaller "theater of operations" plant. [71]

By the end of 1943, ten more chemical processing companies had arrived in the United Kingdom, had been equipped with two theater of operations impregnating plants each, and had been installed, usually within or adjacent to quartermaster clothing depots. A number of

[70] (1) *Ibid.* (2) Ltr, TAG to CG's AGF, AAF, ASF, POE's *et al.*, 28 Oct 43, sub: Instr on Issuing New Type Gas Masks. AG 470.72 (26 Oct 43) OB–S–E–SPMOT–M, in Rqmts and Stock Contl Div, ASF 470.72 Gas Masks. (3) Ltr, CCWO ETO to CmlO USSTAF, 22 Aug, sub: Special Fitting of Gas Masks. CWO 470.72/499 in Eighth AF 225.5 Protective Equip. (4) 8th Ind (Basic Ltr not available), CmlO USSTAF to Air CmlO AAF WD, 1 Sep 44, no sub. AAF 470.72 (25 Apr 44) in Eighth AF 225.5 Protective Equip. (5) Personal Ltr, Porter to Prentiss, 22 Mar 44. CWS 314.7 Pers Files, ETO. (6) Rpt for CCWS, St. John, 28 Jun 1944. CWS 314.7 Pers Files, ETO. (7) Personal Ltr, Porter to St. John, 2 Aug 44. CWS 314.7 Pers Files, ETO. (General Porter pointed out that ETO mask stockage was 2,246,000, with 213,000 in the hands of troops. This quantity, even considering the 719,000 old-style masks still in reserve, was not a significant overage.)

[71] History, Impregnation in ETO, 1 Jul 42–1 Jan 44, CWS ETO. ETO Admin 545A.

the plants utilized the new water emulsion impregnating process. The Quartermaster Corps had been able to obtain impregnated clothing from the United States to satisfy most of the theater's planned needs, so that there was little initial impregnating work to do. By agreement between the theater quartermaster and the CWS, all but one of the processing companies were given laundry work. Most of the companies "kept a hand in" by doing reimpregnation on clothing which had been turned in and by doing initial impregnation of Navy uniforms. In January 1944 the theater commander assigned to the CWS ETO the responsibility of inspecting clothing in storage to determine how impregnation was holding up. Rowan delegated the inspection function to teams picked from the processing companies. The inspection operation further improved the technical proficiency of the companies and also served to identify lots of clothing needing reimpregnation.[72]

The theater quartermaster called in and reissued protective clothing for every individual in the theater at the same time that the distribution of the lightweight mask was in progress. The European theater was authorized an initial issue of double layer protection, that is, antigas impregnated underwear and socks, hood, combat uniform, gloves, and leggings, for every individual. In April 1944 the War Department authorized in addition to this initial issue a theater reserve (in the absence of gas warfare) of double layer protection for 35 percent of the theater force and one and one half layer, that is, antigas socks, drawers, and outer uniform plus hood, gloves, and leggings, for the remainder of the theater force.[73] Thus, every soldier in the theater had available two complete sets of protective clothing except that 65 percent of the force would lack a second protective undershirt. The invasion plan called for every soldier to wear protective outer garments for the landing, to carry the gas mask, and to carry two cellophane protective covers, four eyeshields, one tube of eye ointment, one can of shoe impregnite, and one package of protective ointment. Most soldiers were also equipped with sleeve detectors (a brassard of gas detector paper) which the CWS had procured from the British.[74]

While most items of chemical protective, gas warning, and decontaminating equipment existed in ample supply by January 1944,

---

[72] History, Sup Div, II.

[73] Ltr, TAG to CinC SWPA et al., 24 Apr 44, sub: Cml Warfare Protective Clothing Accessories and Equip. AG 420 23 May 42 (2) sec. 2.

[74] History, Sup Div, II.

there were several shortages. One acute shortage was for gas alarms, and the CWS ETO through reverse lend-lease procured the British trench rattle as a substitute. Another more acute shortage was for the power-driven decontaminating apparatus. As in North Africa and Italy, the decontaminating apparatus was cherished by the Army Air Forces in the United Kingdom for its secondary uses, such as giving showers, hauling water, serving as fire-fighting equipment, and washing aircraft. The Army Air Forces found the skid-mounted M4 power-driven apparatus completely unsatisfactory for their needs, and the ground and service forces took an equally dim view of this immobile equipment. Consequently, the CWS ETO set its maintenance companies to work truck-mounting the M4 apparatus. The job was completed in the spring of 1944, and, while the M4 apparatus failed to meet Air Forces requirements even when mounted, the ground forces and service forces were willing to accept it. As of June 1944 the authorized theater level for the M3 and M4 apparatus was 1,336 while the supply was 1,298. In the absence of gas warfare, this shortage was not a serious matter, but it did present chemical officers with the problem of giving air forces and ground forces elements reasons for not supplying them with all the apparatus they wanted for secondary uses.[75]

Weapons, Ammunition, and Smoke Equipment

The availability of and requirement for chemical mortar battalions remained in doubt during the entire preparation period, and consequently no firm basis existed on which to compute weapons and ammunition requirements. Weapons supply and ammunition supply, in Colonel St. John's opinion, were adequate, and he believed that the only serious preinvasion chemical shortage was in repair parts for the mortar. ETO chemical officers, aware of the spare parts problems in the Mediterranean area, attempted to improve their own situation by requesting supply from the United States. The CWS at home had not yet remedied the repair parts situation. The task was doubly difficult because ASF was attempting to standardize all repair parts requirements computations, and, owing to the uncertain weapons

[75] (1) Ibid. (2) History, Cml Sec Eighth AF. (3) Msg D–1441, Maj Gen Ira C. Eaker [CG Eighth AF] to Arnold [CG AAF], 30 Jun 43. Eighth AF 519.253 1944. (4) Baldwin, Bingham, and Pritchard, Readiness for Gas Warfare in Theaters of Opns, app. B.

requirement situation and the lack of expenditure experience in the ETO, CWS could furnish ASF with recommendations based only on roughly estimated data. But even had requirements recommendations been firm, it is doubtful that the supply system could have operated rapidly enough to furnish the ETO with stocks in the few months before the cross-Channel attack. Experience was to prove the limited supply of repair parts grossly inadequate.[76]

Other weapons and ammunition furnished by the CWS ETO to the combat forces included the flame thrower, smoke pots, and smoke grenades. The CWS ETO had acquired a sufficient supply of the portable flame throwers, and chemical units had mixed a substantial quantity of thickened fuel. No American tank-mounted flame thrower was available, but fuel had been mixed for use in British models on loan in limited numbers to the United States forces. Soon after the invasion, St. John reported critical shortages of both portable and mechanized flame throwers and of fuels as well as of mortars and mortar parts, but subsequent experience did not warrant the critical designation since flame throwers were not popular in Europe.[77]

Not enough smoke pots or grenades were available to meet antici-pated requirements. British No. 24 smoke generators, similar to the American smoke pots, were procured as substitutes, and the British No. 79 grenade was procured as a substitute for the American M8 smoke grenade. The American mechanical smoke generator should also be included in this category although it was not technically classed as a weapon. The bulky semimobile M1 generator was available in sufficient quantity, but a supply of the newly produced, highly mobile M2 was considered essential for combat operations. The CWS in the United States sent new generators, some by airlift, just in time to be used in the invasion. Generator fuel was provided by the British.[78]

Special Requirements

ETO chemical officers, anticipating the need for concealing mount-ing areas in England and assault beaches in France, had long expected that the need for smoke materials would far exceed the normal demands

[76] (1) History, Sup Div, II.   (2) Personal Ltr, St. John to Waitt, 17 May 44. CWS 314.7 Pers Files, ETO.   (3) Rowan Interv, 26 Sep 58.
[77] (1) For additional information on flame thrower experience in Europe, see below, Chapter XVI. (2) History, Sup Div, II.   (3) St. John to Porter, 28 Jun 44.
[78] History, Sup Div, II.

CONFERRING SOMEWHERE IN ENGLAND JUST BEFORE D-DAY. *(Left to right)*
Colonel Cunin, General Porter, Lt. Col. Thomas H. James, and Colonel St. John.

of combat operations. They also anticipated a number of special demands for other CWS materials for use on the Continent. The fact
that the Germans were to lose their air superiority by the time of the
invasion, negating the need for smoke during the mounting and assault
phases, could not have been counted on or, indeed, foreseen by these
planners.

To take care of such special demands, the War Department set up
a project system known as PROCO (projects for continental operation) soon after the 1943 reinstatement of BOLERO. PROCO was to
be set up by the technical services in the theater. Each technical service
was to state specific requirements for each project together with
shipping weights and cubages and an extensive justification for the
use of materials beyond regular authorizations. The justifications were
to be reviewed by higher authority in the theater and by ASF and OPD
in the United States. CWS ETO PROCO 1 requested 1,164,508 M1
smoke pots and 20,000 M4 smoke pots. The first project was submitted

on 20 July 1943, and on that and the following day nine other projects
for decontaminating, impregnating, and gasproofing materials and
supply handling and maintenance equipment were dispatched.[79]

The first ten CWS projects initially called for 179,283 long tons,
or 590,059 ship tons, of matériel, delivery for which was to be phased
over a period of nearly a year. In view of the fact that this gross ship
tonnage was more than ten times the CWS cubage eventually shipped
to the Continent in the first ninety days, it is apparent that PROCO
was no insignificant matter in the eyes of ETO chemical supply officers;
indeed, PROCO must have been manna to the CWS officers who
believed ETO supply inadequate for chemical warfare. PROCO as
interpreted in the theater presented the first and last opportunity for
the CWS in any theater of operations to prepare for gas, smoke, and
flame warfare on a scale considered by many chemical officers as wise.
CWS ETO in September 1941 accordingly submitted three more
projects, one for flame thrower accessories and two for smoke materials,
before any word had been received from the War Department on the
fate of the first ten. On 22 October 1943 ASF directed shipment of
those items which CWS ETO had scheduled for early theater delivery
in projects one through ten, and theater officers assumed that the
whole schedule would be followed. But, before this first shipment
could be made theater hopes were shattered. On 3 November 1943
ASF withdrew all projects for review by the United States Chemical
Warfare Committee (USCWC).[80]

ASF restored CWS PROCO after review by the USCWC and after
much correspondence with the theater and the intercession of General
Waitt, Assistant Chief Chemical Officer for Field Operations, but they
restored only 40 percent of the original quantities. Project 12 for

---

[79] (1) Ruppenthal, *Logistical Support*, I, 260–61. (2) Ltrs, CCWO ETO to TAG through CG SOS
ETO, 20 Jul 43, sub: Proj 1, SOSCW 470.72/134–C1–Sec (20 Jul 43)SD; 21 Jul 43, sub: CWS Proj
2, SOSCW 470.72/311–Sec (21 Jul 43)SD; 21 Jul 43, sub: CWS Proj 3, same file; 20 Jul 43, sub:
CWS Proj 4, SOSCW 470.72/309–Sec (20 Jul 43)SD; 20 Jul 43, sub: CWS Proj 5, SOSCW 470.72/
310–Sec (20 Jul 43)SD; 20 Jul 43, sub: CWS Proj 6, SOSCW 470.72/134–C1–Sec (20 Jul 43)SD;
21 Jul 43, sub: CWS Proj 7, SOSCW 470.72/311 Sec (21 Jul 43)SD; 21 Jul 43, sub: CWS Project 8,
same file; 20 Jul 43, sub: CWS Proj 9, same file; 20 Jul 43, sub: CWS Proj 10, SOSCW 470.72/134–
C1–Sec (20 Jul 43)SD. All in Planning Div ASF Proj for Continental Opn PROCO.
[80] (1) Ltrs, CCWO ETO to TAG through CG SOS ETO, 22 Sep 43, sub: CWS Project 11; CWS
Project 12; CWS Project 13. All SOSCW 381–Pro Sec (22 Sep 43) SD in Planning Div ASF, Proj for
Continental Opn PROCO. (2) Memo, Col Carter B. Magruder, Chief Planning Div ASF, for Deputy
Dir for Plans and Opns ASF, 28 Apr 44, sub: History of Opnl Projects for ETO. ASF SPOPP 400
(ETO) in Off of CG ASF 400.

smoke grenades was disapproved on the theory that increases in normal allowances would take care of the requirement. Projects 11 and 13 were approved after a 60-percent slash. ASF again directed shipment of the materials specified in these modified projects and six additional projects in February, March, and April of 1944. The CWS ETO had submitted Project 14 for smoke (WP) bombs in November 1943, and Project 16 for smoke grenades, Project 18 for gas mask parts, and Project 19 for flame thrower parts and accessories in February 1944. In March it submitted Project 23 for flame throwers and Project 20 for flame thrower pressure cylinders. ASF disapproved Project 17 for grenades and smoke pots to be used by the air forces, indicating that regular theater stocks would cover the requirement. It disapproved Project 15 for equipment to convert decontamination companies to smoke generator companies, and Project 22 for a combat reserve of smoke generators, on the ground that these materials also could be provided from theater stocks. Project 21 seems to have vanished from the record.[81] The significant feature of the 1944 projects as opposed to the 1943 projects was that the 1944 projects were so limited in scope as to seem almost niggardly. Gone were the implications of vast and all-out preparations for gas, smoke, and flame warfare.

While the curtailed PROCO shipments did help out in the operational period, PROCO did not live up to theater expectations. The CWS ETO undoubtedly expected too much, and it is apparent in retrospect that theater chemical officers got along despite shortages. Materials which CWS ETO requested under the original PROCO would certainly have added to the theater gas warfare defensive potential since they would have provided for more collective protection and more decontamination. ETO combat forces would probably not have used smoke and flame in any greater quantities had more materials been available. That ASF after postwar analysis found it had guessed right with respect to requirements does not alter the fact that ASF

[81] (1) Magruder for Dep Dir for Plans and Opns ASF, 28 Apr 44. (2) Ltrs, CCWO ETO to TAG through CG SOS ETO, 27 Nov 43, sub: CWS Proj 14, SOSCW 381–Pro Sec (27 Nov 43)SD; 15 Jan 44, sub: CWS Proj 15, SOSCW 381–Pro Sec (15 Jan 44)SD; 11 Feb 44, sub: CWS Proj 18, SOSCW 381–Pro Sec (11 Feb 44)SD; 12 Feb 44, sub: CWS Proj 19, SOSCW 381–Pro Sec (12 Feb 44)SD; 3 Apr 44, sub: CWS Proj 20, SOSCW 381–Pro Sec (3 Apr 44)SD; 17 Mar 44, sub: CWS Proj 22, SOSCW 381–Pro Sec (17 Mar 44)SD; 31 Mar 44, sub: CWS Project 23, SOSCW 381–Pro Sec (31 Mar 44) SD. (3) Msg WL–470, Lee (CG SOS ETO) for War, 21 Jan 44 (Project 16). (4) Msg W–11067, Lee for War, 12 Feb 44 (Project 17).

handling of PROCO violated the principle of theater requirements determination.

PROCO's importance from a chemical point of view is that the history of the system demonstrated the lack of understanding and lack of adequate communication between the theater and War Department headquarters, and perhaps even between ASF and its technical services at home. Maj. Gen. LeRoy Lutes, Director for Planning and Operations, ASF, complained in May 1944 that theater officers had misunderstood and misapplied the concept of PROCO. He charged that the theater had failed to plan adequately in advance.[82] General Lutes undoubtedly had grounds for complaint as far as theater strategic and tactical decisions were concerned, but the CWS ETO could hardly have begun requirements planning any earlier since CWS officers did begin planning in the month of theater activation, and CWS ETO could hardly have had less help in such planning from ASF. Specifically with respect to PROCO, the War Department allowed the theater to labor under a misapprehension of the PROCO concept from June until November 1943, and apparently the War Department concept was not understood by the CWS ETO until the reinstatement of the revised projects in February 1944. Almost a year elapsed between the system authorization and General Lutes' statement of his complaints. It is not strange, therefore, that at the time of the Normandy assault the CWS ETO was a vigorously individualistic organization many of whose officers and enlisted men felt that they must meet their own needs without much help from the official logistics organization. The experience of these officers and enlisted men on the Continent was to confirm this belief.

On the Continent

The Landings

The 1st Platoon, 30th Chemical Decontamination Company, under the command of 1st Lt. Bernard Miller, landed on OMAHA Beach at H plus sixteen minutes. The platoon fought its way ashore with the first wave, providing grenade smoke screens to conceal infantry landings. Lieutenant Miller and six enlisted men were wounded or missing

---

[82] Memo, Lutes for ACofS OPD, 25 May 44, sub: Opnl Projects for ETO. Plng Div ASF 400 History of Projects. (Also cited in Ruppenthal, *Logistical Support, I,* 260).

in action. Sgt. John J. Cunningham assumed command of the platoon, which then pushed on, probing for land mines, giving aid to the wounded, fighting as infantrymen, and providing what smoke concealment it could. At 1300 the 3d Platoon under 1st Lt. James W. Cassidy joined the 1st Platoon, and together they salvaged and put into working order a few of the M2 smoke generators which had been sunk on an incoming Dukw. On D plus one Capt. Milton M. Moore, company commander, arrived with the remainder of the company, and the entire unit launched more extensively into its special mission activity, gas reconnaissance. First Army, then commanding all American forces on the Continent, made few calls on the company's secondary mission, provision of smoke concealment, but the company got smoke pots ashore and set up smoke lines in the vicinity of Colleville sur Mer. By the time a company overstrength had been landed, 14 June, the 30th Chemical Decontamination Company was in the supply and service business, setting up and working in supply dumps, furnishing showers, settling road dust, and fighting fires with power-driven decontaminating apparatus.[83]

The 2d Platoon, 33d Chemical Decontamination Company, went ashore on UTAH Beach at approximately H plus 3 (0930). Since resistance at first was light on UTAH, the 2d Platoon at once established the first CWS beach dump of the invasion. By D plus 2 detachments of the company which had landed with elements of the 531st Engineer Shore Regiment were ordered to assemble under the command of Lt. Carroll W. Wright. The assembled 33d Company expanded the original CWS dump into a CWS maintenance and supply dump which the unit operated until D plus 21. It handled about 5,000 tons of CWS Class II and IV supplies during this period. Like their colleagues on OMAHA Beach, the men of the 33d also performed gas reconnaissance, provided showers, and fought fires.[84]

Headquarters Detachment, 60th Chemical Depot Company, Capt. George W. Brown, commanding, debarked on OMAHA on D plus 4 (10 June) and on the following day set up operations of a FUSA CWS dump at Mosles. The advance party of another detachment joined the 33d Company on UTAH on the next day. The whole company was

[83] History, 30th Cml Decontamination Co.

[84] (1) History, 33d Cml Decontamination Co. (2) Gordon A. Harrison, *Cross-Channel Attack,* UNITED STATES ARMY IN WORLD WAR II (Washington, 1951), pp. 302–05.

at work operating FUSA dumps by 28 June.[85] Meanwhile, Major Hingle, FECOMZ chemical supply chief, arrived on D plus 13 (19 June) in ADSEC headquarters, which had become operational three days earlier, to begin preparations for the FECOMZ assumption of supply control. He found Colonel Stubbs's ADSEC Chemical Section, staffed by Major Bradley and six other officers, without enlisted men or the scheduled stock control team. Since the invasion had not been going as rapidly as planned, FUSA had not transferred supply control to ADSEC, and the ADSEC staff members on the Continent were assisting FUSA while preparing for their own operational role. Hingle also visited Colonel Coughlan, Chemical Officer, FUSA, and learned from his assistant for supply, Capt. J. R. Yankhauer, that chemical supply, unlike that of other services, had run into no very serious problems. The expenditure of chemical mortar shell was running greater than had been expected, and a greater proportion than expected, about 35 percent, was white phosphorus shell. Both combat and service troops made extensive use of dust respirators and eyeshields against dust, and Captain Yankhauer called upon the CWS in the United Kingdom for increased resupply of these items. He also requested that the quota be cut on smoke materials which were piling up.[86]

Hingle decided that principal CWS supply efforts on the Continent in the immediate future would need to be directed toward storage, maintenance, salvage, and service. While chemical supplies were arriving in good shape, except for a few inevitable instances of excessively rough handling, he did not believe that all stocks would stand up well under the expected ninety days' open storage. Some chemical weapons and equipment, such as the chemical mortar and the power-driven decontaminating apparatus, were being employed at or beyond rated capacity. Flame throwers and gas masks were discarded by advancing troops. A number of men had their masks hit because the mask bulge in silhouette offered a sniper target. Some troops had ceased to wear gas protective clothing, and, while salvage was a quarter-master problem, the CWS was likely to be called upon for laundering garments as well as for reimpregnation. All these factors meant extensive repair and materials rehabilitation work, particularly since the

---

[85] History, 60th Cml Depot Co.
[86] Informal Comments of CWSO [Hingle to Charron, CmlO FECOMZ], 20 Jun 44. CWS 314.7 Pers files, ETO.

"I see Comp'ny E got th' new style gas masks, Joe."

demand for mortars was increasing and that for flame throwers was expected to increase.[87] FUSA also insisted that the gas warfare protection level be maintained. While several gas warfare scares had all proved false, the Germans still might initiate gas warfare. Capt. John J. O'Brien, Acting Chemical Officer, 29th Infantry Division, who had been captured and had escaped, reported that the Germans would use any weapons in their possession, including gas, to stop the Allied advance. Since Allied progress at the time was halting and uncertain, enemy initiation of gas warfare would have been catastrophic. Hingle, accordingly, in order to accelerate rehabilitation of protective equipment which ADSEC was gathering up, asked FUSA to lend its chemical maintenance company to ADSEC, and accompanied Major Bradley in a search for shop space. He recommended to his chief, Colonel Charron, that chemical supply and service officers and men be sent to the Continent as soon as possible and that service troop build-up plans be closely followed up.[88]

Establishing the CWS Supply Base

Since FECOMZ never assumed control of supply operations on the Continent,[89] Colonel Charron, in his FECOMZ capacity, did not have the opportunity to put Major Hingle's recommendations into effect, but FECOMZ officers did assist ADSEC in its efforts and later opened the COMZ headquarters CWS section on the Continent. ADSEC gradually assumed responsibility for various supply installations after FUSA, while still retaining supply control, on 20 June designated an ADSEC area of operations. ADSEC retained the three FUSA supply dumps. The dump at Mosles it converted into a Class II and IV depot while the the dump at Longueville behind OMAHA became a Class V depot and that at Audouville-la-Hubert behind UTAH became an all-classes depot. Audouville materials were soon transferred to a permanent installation at Montebourg, and both Audouville and Longueville were closed out by COMZ in October. The American lodgment on the Continent failed to grow as planned, but manpower increased almost on schedule, as Hingle had hoped, and tonnages, despite port and beachhead discharge difficulties, accumu-

---

[87] The flame thrower demand did not materialize, but the CWS could not afford to be unprepared in event demand should arise.

[88] [Hingle to Charron], 20 Jun, 21 Jun, 22 Jun 44. CWS 314.7 Pers Files, ETO.

[89] Ruppenthal, *Logistical Support, I,* 436.

lated at a rate in excess of the June-August needs. The ADSEC Chemical Section accordingly established an all-classes depot at Cherbourg, a II and IV depot at Villedieu, a II and IV depot and an ammunition depot at Le Mans, and at Rennes an all-classes depot, which COMZ split into a II and IV and an ammunition depot. The 65th and 7th Chemical Depot Companies and the 66th and 9th Chemical Base Depot Companies operated these installations while the 711th Chemical Maintenance Company set up a shop at Valognes, the site of the first continental COMZ headquarters.[90]

On D plus 20 St. John analyzed the chemical supply situation on the Continent. He noted critical shortages of mortars and mortar parts and expressed the belief that flame thrower supply would not meet demand. On the other hand, he took the view that some protection and decontamination materials were excess to all future needs while smoke materials, for which he expected demand to increase, were adequate for the time being.[91] In reply to these observations, General Porter indicated that while the theater had reached or slightly exceeded supply authorizations in all categories mentioned except mortar spare parts, he could not concede that any of these excesses were significant. Porter believed that the parts need could be met by supplying an overage of complete mortars. The CWS had no outstanding unfilled orders from the theater, and General Porter was powerless to increase any allotment without a specific theater request approved through War Department channels.[92] As in the case of NATO–MTO CWS supply, here was the rub. A supply crisis was coming in the ETO which would affect the CWS, although not as extensively as the other services, but the individuals most concerned could do little to forestall its arrival. Although the theater had top supply priority over all other theaters and although the theater commander was firmly committed to the policy of giving combat commanders everything they desired, the exigencies of transportation and War Department-controlled supply authorization procedures tended to block timely measures for preventing a crisis. Just how much of the ensuing supply crisis might be attributable to physical limitations in obtaining and moving supplies and how much to the complications of supply management in the

[90](1) Ruppenthal, *Logistical Support*, I, 434–44.   (2) History, FECOMZ.   (3) History, ADSEC. (4) History, Sup Div, II.
[91] St. John to Porter, 28 Jun 44.
[92] Porter to St. John, 2 Aug 44.

theater and in the United States is, from the CWS point of view, impossible to say.

The Supply Crisis

General Rowan, on D plus 44, pointed out even more vigorously than Colonel St. John the critical nature of mortar parts and ammunition supply. He suggested to General Waitt that the CWS plan to double its production quotas for those items. The last CWS ETO ammunition requisition, he wrote, had been cut in half, presumably by NYPE, and he had been unable to determine on what basis the cut was made.[93] The CWS in the United States could not raise its production quotas until theater recommendations for increases in War Department allowances had been approved. Three weeks later Rowan paid a flying visit to his new office, which Charron had established in the Valognes COMZ headquarters. Rowan joined St. John for a tour of mortar units, field headquarters, and forward areas. He found the CWS supply situation still satisfactory on the whole, but he noted not only that the shortage of mortars, mortar parts, and ammunition was critical but also that some of the mortar battalion equipment needed replacement.[94]

As the combat forces broke out of the beachhead in July 1944 and headed toward Germany, all chemical sections in the combat organization became increasingly involved in supply.[95] The chemical sections in the base sections became active, as ADSEC had already been, in the support of combat organizations. The 12th Army Group Chemical Section allotted supplies to the armies and kept Rowan's office and sometimes the base section chemical officers informed as to long-range requirements and immediate needs.[96] The 12th Army Group Chemical Section considered protective supply adequate throughout the European campaigns except for a brief period late in 1944 when "cold set" destroyed the usefulness of the synthetic rubber facepiece of the light-weight mask.[97] The First and Third Army chemical officers likewise

[93] Personal Ltr, Rowan to Waitt, 20 Jul 44. CWS 314.7 Pers Files, ETO.

[94] Memo, Rowan, no addressee, sub: Notes on Trip to Far Shore, 26 Aug 44, in Ltr, Rowan to Waitt, 2 Sep 44. CWS 314.7 Pers Files, ETO.

[95] See above, ch. II.

[96] (1) MacArthur Interv, 19 Sep 61. (2) Leggin Intervs, 13 Oct 61, 22 Nov 45. (3) Powers Interv, 24 Sep 59.

[97] 12th Army Group, Rpt of Opns, vol. XI, Cml Warfare Sec.

considered protection adequate except in isolated circumstances.[98] Dissent on the adequacy of protection came from base section chemical officers who felt that, in the early period on the Continent, the CWS distribution plan looked better on paper than it did in practice. The problem was that since supplies were so scattered about in dumps and since so much equipment, especially masks, had been abandoned by troops moving forward, it would have been a tremendous and perhaps impossible task to assemble, rehabilitate, and reissue protective equipment in event of need.[99] Fortunately, no large-scale call for protective equipment was made until the following December by which time chemical service units had collected and refurbished protective equipment. Also, by December the distribution system was working well with the aid of a considerable amount of troubleshooting from most chemical officers in both COMZ and combat organizations.[100]

The CWS supply problems began to multiply with the September 1944 supply crisis. Most of these problems arose not because of the malfunctioning of the distribution system but because of a general shortage of supplies, equipment, and transportation. The CWS problem was increased by the flaws in certain chemical items, notably chemical mortar shell, spare parts, and protective materials.

Chemical Mortar Shell

The armies were moving rapidly forward in September when Rowan and the United Kingdom section of his office moved into the new COMZ headquarters in Paris. Supply of fast-moving items was by then on a hand-to-mouth basis. General Rowan personally visited the ports to expedite the distribution of chemical mortar shell which was finally arriving from the United States. Shortage of docking facilities frequently made it difficult to unload ships. But, when he could get shells ashore, he got the theater chief of ordnance to allot railway ammunition cars for his use and he had these cars included in priority supply trains. Usually no more than one day's reserve of shell was available in forward areas.[101]

In November two barrel bursts of high explosive shell in chemical

[98] (1) Cunin Interv, 5 Dec 45. (2) Wallington Interv, 1 Dec 59.
[99] (1) Wright Interv, 16 Jul 61. (2) Christensen Intervs, 13, 23 Oct 61.
[100] (1) Christensen Intervs, 13, 23 Oct 61.
[101] Rowan Interv, 26 Sep 58.

mortars led to the assumption that some shell was defective.[102] This assumption complicated the supply situation since no one knew how much of the available stocks was serviceable. But in the same month, when a shell shortage in southern France imperiled operations supplied by Southern Line of Communications (SOLOC), the CWS ETO released 50,000 shells to SOLOC in return for a December shipment scheduled for that area.[103] Chemical mortar units in northern France had enough shells at the time to continue operations although rationing was frequently necessary. But rationing had been necessary from time to time since early in the Normandy campaign, and, while mortar men could have used more shell, the 20 rounds per weapon per day usually allotted against the official 25 to 30 rounds per day of supply was enough to keep them going. In December, 12th Army Group Chemical Section, the agency charged with shell allocation, requested 40 rounds per weapon per day for the next six months.[104] Using the 40-round base for all the 10 battalions then in the theater and assuming 36 operational mortars per battalion as allotted under the tables of organization and equipment then going into effect, the 12th Army Group recommendation would have meant immediate supply of almost 15,000 shells per day. Computed on the basis of 15 battalions in the line in 1945 nearly 22,000 rounds per day would have been required.[105] The 12th Army Group ammunition supply goal was never reached.

In January 1945, barrel and muzzle bursts reached epidemic proportions. During theater and OCCWS investigations of the problem, CWS ETO impounded lot after lot of shell until nearly the whole theater supply was impounded. Allotment per weapon sometimes fell from twenty to ten rounds per day. When spring weather came, faulty shell ceased to be a problem. Shell supply improved, but supply never equaled demand during the period of combat.[106]

---

[102] Personal Ltr, Powers, CmlO 12th Army Group, to Porter, 21 Nov 44. CWS 314.7 Pers Files, ETO.

[103] History, Sup Div, II.

[104] Leggin Interv, 22 Nov 45.

[105] See Brophy and Fisher, *Organizing for War*, Appendix H-1, for information on battalions in the theater. Sixteen battalions had entered action by V-E Day, but the sixteenth saw only a few days of combat.

[106] (1) Rowan Interv, 26 Sep 58. (2) Leggin Interv, 22 Nov 45. (3) For more details on the faulty shell problem, see below, Chapter XII.

Spare Parts

The parts situation also failed to improve during continental operations. According to Rowan the "lack of spare parts was the outstanding failure of the American Army supply system, and the CWS was just as bad as the rest of the technical services." [107] In early October, CWS ETO found it necessary to embargo all CWS spare parts issues except "Red Ball Express" shipments which were directed to chemical maintenance companies operating with the armies. Issue for levels of maintenance less than major overhaul was banned. Some items in need of repair, such as masks, dust respirators, and hand decontaminating apparatus, were exchanged for serviceable items in lieu of repair.[108] Chemical maintenance companies repaired chemical mortars, flame throwers, and power-driven decontaminating apparatus on a "parts available" basis and exchange items were supplied, with the specific approval of the Supply Division, CWS ETO, when parts were not available but alternative end items were. The maintenance companies also fabricated parts whenever possible and some parts which would normally have been considered beyond repair were rebuilt. Late in 1944 orders were given to French firms for the manufacture of parts for mortars, smoke generators, then being heavily employed to produce tactical smoke concealment, and flame throwers. In January 1945, the CWS ETO engaged firms in Belgium and Luxembourg to manufacture mortar base plates, reinforcing plates, shock absorber slides, cup forks, tube caps, and base caps. As in the case of manufacture in Italy, many chemical officers preferred the parts manufactured in Europe to those shipped from the United States. In Europe greater skill and better equipment were available for small parts manufacture than in the war-burdened United States industry.[109]

The CWS spare parts team which surveyed the theater situation in 1945 found parts supply still inadequate, and General Waitt confirmed this finding in his visit to the theater at the end of the war.[110]

---

[107] Rowan Comments, 16 Dec 60.

[108] The mask parts situation was one of the few not critical. The principal problem here was the great volume of maintenance work caused by abuse of the mask. Rowan Comments, 16 Dec 60.

[109] (1) History, Sup Div, II. (2) Histories, 211th (71th), 12th, 13th, and 14th Cml Maintenance Cos. (3) Magness Interv, 5 May 59. (4) Rowan Comments, 16 Dec 60.

[110] (1) OCCWS, Final Rpt, CWS Spare Parts Team in MTO and ETO, Dec 44–Feb 45, prepared by OCCWS, 19 Jun 45. (2) IOM, Lt Col J. C. Morgan, Chief War Planning Br OCCWS, for Chief War Plans and Theaters Div OCCWS, 13 Apr 45, sub: Topics for Discussion in ETO and MTO. CWS 314.7 Observer Rpts.

Protective Material

Although FUSA and FUSAG insisted on having each individual maintain his gas mask during the beachhead period, the breakthrough and rapid advance after the end of July brought a change in attitude. Many commanders and some chemical officers assumed there would be no further risk of gas warfare. Indeed, SHAEF itself seemed to assume that the risk of gas warfare was past and St. John, whose position in SHAEF was abolished in the fall, did not express disagreement.[111] MacArthur and other members of the FUSAG/12th Army Group staff were concerned lest mistreatment and abandonment of the mask by individual soldiers drastically reduce the gas warfare defensive preparedness on the Continent. They consequently decided to act upon General Bradley's suggestion that masks be withdrawn from individual soldiers on the organization commander's option. One of St. John's final acts in his SHAEF position was to make the army group decision SHAEF policy.

Rowan conceded, in September, that reduction in the theater protective clothing level was not inconsistent with the calculated risk policy. He further advised reducing the protective clothing reserve to two-layer protection for 50 percent rather than 100 percent of theater strength as he had earlier recommended.[112] Commanders in most cases authorized the withdrawal of protective clothing and masks from individuals. The masks were theoretically available in unit supply trains. A number of chemical officers felt that calling masks back to regimental and even divisional trains was a hazardous policy, particularly since it was reasonable to expect the likelihood of gas warfare to increase as the German homeland was approached. In October when he succeeded MacArthur, who had been requested for a position in the United States, Colonel Powers strongly expressed his disapproval of the mask policy.[113]

Powers paid a call on the Supreme Commander, General Eisenhower, a prewar fellow staff officer. He expressed his misgivings concerning protective policy to General Eisenhower and General Bradley, who happened to be visiting the supreme commander. General Eisenhower

---

[111] Personal Ltrs, St. John to Waitt, 1 Sep 44; to Col Lowell A. Elliott, Deputy CCWS, 23 Oct 44; to Elliott, 8 Nov 44.

[112] Personal Ltrs, Rowan to Waitt, 17 Sep 44. (2) See above, p. 167. The actual reserve authorization at the time of the Normandy operation had been 35 percent double-layer protection.

[113] Powers Interv, 24 Sep 59.

indicated that he thought German initiation of gas warfare most unlikely, but he displayed some interest in the defensive situation.[114] Although not immediately successful in his campaign to increase the availability of individual protection, Colonel Powers found he had strong support among the Army chemical officers. He recommended to the Chief of Staff, 12th Army Group, that the theater be requested to reverse the policy decision so that each individual soldier could again carry a mask.[115]

The 12th Army Group did request a change which was approved by SHAEF in December. Shortly thereafter the German counterattack in the Ardennes threatened the American advance and many commanders were given added incentive to insure individual gas protection since it appeared conceivable that the German forces might try to consolidate their initial success in the Battle of the Bulge by using gas. The reissue of masks caused a flurry throughout the CWS supply system. Some organizations could find no trace of their masks. Others discovered that many masks had become unserviceable because of frequent moves and poor storage conditions. One corps chemical officer finally managed to scrape up enough transportation to send several truckloads of masks forward, only to hear that both trucks and masks were destroyed or captured in the German advance. Spot issues to replace such losses caused temporary shortages, but fortunately the reserve was large enough so that demands could be met and reserves restocked from the United States on an emergency basis.[116] St. John's assertion that there were enough masks in the theater to cover all the faces of Europe and Asia proved to be even more overdrawn than he had intended.[117] Some of Powers' colleagues were critical of his action, contending that his lack of experience in the theater made him overzealous. The possibility exists, however, that the reissue of masks, which could hardly have been unknown to German intelligence, deterred the Germans from exploiting what would have been an excellent opportunity to turn the Bulge into a World War II Ypres.[118]

The maintenance load imposed by mask rehabilitation, particularly in view of occasional parts shortages, was very heavy. When "cold set"

---

[114] *Ibid.*

[115] Personal Ltrs, Powers to Elliott, 7 Nov 44, and to Porter, 21 Nov 44.

[116] (1) Rowan Interv, 26 Sep 58.   (2) Powers Interv, 24 Sep 59.   (3) Barta Interv, 23 Sep 59.

[117] See above, p. 166.

[118] Leggin Interv, 13 Oct 61.

(cold weather hardening) was discovered in reclaimed and synthetic rubber mask facepieces during the winter, the CWS ETO maintenance burden became greater than the maintenance units could handle.[119] Since the facepieces hardened by "cold set" could not be properly fitted, CWS ETO contracted with eight French firms for the exchange of 400,000 faulty facepieces for the natural rubber facepiece from the old-style mask. At the same time another French firm initiated remanufacture of old-style gas mask carriers into 133,000 lightweight mask carriers.[120] After considerable effort, the CWS ETO successfully met the challenge of bringing protective supply up to a highly effective level for the remainder of the war.

The CWS ETO Supply System—Final Form

Considering the many unexpected problems it ran into, the CWS ETO supply system changed amazingly little during the period of continental operation. The credit system continued to operate effectively although during the fall supply crisis it became necessary to delegate credit allocation for ammunition and certain critical supplies to 12th Army Group. Supply Division, CWS ETO, headed during the entire period on the Continent by Col. Frederick E. Powell, continued to allocate credits for normal Class II and IV supply. The supply pattern brought materials into CWS branch depots from the ports and beaches.[121] CWS ETO established forty such depots under COMZ control in the advance across France and Germany. Supply Division or 12th Army Group allocated materials in depots to using organizations on credits or assigned them to reserve stocks. Credit allocation notices were forwarded to ADSEC or to Continental Advance Section (CONAD), to the regulating stations which distributed materials to combat echelons, to the depot commanders, and to the credited organizations. The using combat organizations in northern France and northern Germany then called forward from the depots through the regulating stations and ADSEC, or in southern France and Germany, through CONAD, such materials from their credited

---

[119] (1) For a discussion of "cold set," see Brophy, Miles, and Cochrane, *From Laboratory to Field*, pp 323–24. (2) Leggin telephoned the development authorities in the United States when "cold set" was discovered to ask advice. The only recommendation offered was that the CWS ETO provide warm storage for masks! (Leggin Interv, 13 Oct 61.)

[120] History, Sup Div, II.

[121] No general depots were established on the Continent.

stocks as they desired. The using organization, the regulating stations, and the advance section could always easily calculate the quantities of any item to be transported and the quantities remaining to the credit of any organization in the depots.[122]

[122] History, Sup Div, II.

CHAPTER V

CWS Administration: Pacific

The CWS in the West and Southwest Pacific, 1941–42

Defending the Philippines

After the Japanese attacked Clark Field on 8 December 1941 and brought World War II to the Philippines, Col. Stuart A. Hamilton, Chemical Officer, Philippine Department, the 14 officers, 275 enlisted men, and 12 Philippine Scouts assigned to the CWS in the Philippines immediately stepped up efforts to prepare for gas warfare.[1] Intensive preparations for gas warfare in the department had begun the preceding spring with the dedication of a new impregnating plant in the Manila port area for the production of gas resistant clothing. By the day of the attack the department's defense preparations were in many respects satisfactory, but chemical officers were disturbed that training rather than service masks had been the authorized issue to individual soldiers and that the protective clothing supply was completely inadequate even with the new plant in operation.

Both the U.S. forces and the enemy greatly feared that the other's next move would be a gas attack. On 8 December the Japanese assault commanders on Formosa issued masks to their troops.[2] In Manila, requests for masks poured in to the departmental chemical office. On 10 December General MacArthur's Headquarters, United States Army

---

[1] This section is based on: (1) Log Book and Journal—CWS, Hq Philippine Dept USAFFE and USFIP, 8 Dec 41–17 Apr 42. (Mailed to CCWS in one of the last mails leaving the Philippine Islands before the surrender.) CWS 319.1/2275. (2) Hamilton to CCWS, 6 Apr 1946, Rpt, Personal Experiences During World War II. (3) Hamilton to CG USFIP (Gen Jonathan M. Wainwright), 22 Nov 46, Rpt Activities, CWS, Philippine Islands, World War II. (4) Louis Morton, *The Fall of the Philippines*, UNITED STATES ARMY IN WORLD WAR II (Washington, 1953). (5) Lt Col Charles A. Morgan, Jr., Comments on draft of this volume, 16 Jan 61.

[2] Morton, *Fall of the Philippines*, p. 80.

Forces, Far East (USAFFE), ordered training masks exchanged for service masks. On the same day the CWS began issuing service masks to Philippine Army units. Some training and service masks were later provided for civilian employees of the Army. Chemical troops under Ist Lt. Charles A. Morgan, Jr., operated the new impregnating plant on a 24-hour basis until 23 December, when the power plant was bombed. The clothing was to provide individual protection against expected gas attacks and to equip unit gas warfare decontamination details. About a week later Colonel Hamilton supervised the destruction of the plant, along with supplies and records, to prevent capture. After the loss of the plant, the CWS contingent on Bataan continued clothing impregnation by hand in order to finish equipping the decontamination squads. A day after the plant was destroyed Hamilton moved his office into an improvised chemical laboratory in the Malinta Tunnel, Fort Mills, Corregidor. The CWS hastily completed part of a large gasproofing project so that the ventilating blowers could be used to make the Malinta Tunnel usable for a hospital, offices, and quarters.

The few CWS officers and men not continuously used as infantry labored mightily to adapt existing materials to emergency needs. Hamilton's men improvised field plants to produce liquid bleach (chloride of lime) for sanitation purposes both on Bataan and Corregidor. These plants used lime and liquid chlorine originally intended for decontamination of vesicant gases. Bleach was also used as an insecticide by the hospitals, around latrines, and on the battlefields. The field plant on Corregidor continued to operate even after the Japanese occupation. The CWS laboratory assayed and packaged another vesicant decontaminant, high-test hypochlorite, for water purification. The Philippine Chemical Depot staff, operating on Bataan, prepared tiki-tiki extract from rice bran for the prevention and treatment of beriberi and polyneuritis, but an effort to develop a substitute for quinine sulphate was only partially successful. The CWS also converted FS smoke fillings from Livens projectors and 4.2-inch chemical mortar shells into sulphuric acid to keep in operation the storage batteries in electric generator units, radio sets, and vehicles. After an enemy bomb destroyed the first field acid plant and killed four of its five operators, another plant was set up where production continued until the week of the Corregidor surrender. To aid the fighting units, Lt. Frank L. Schaf, Jr., CWS, assisted by a U.S. Navy detachment, improvised a flame thrower from two 3-gallon decontaminating apparatus. The chemical depot group also contributed to the fighting units thousands of Molotov cocktails hastily improvised from beer bottles and other scrap materials.

When not busy with emergency improvisations, the CWS laboratory analyzed and described captured Japanese materials, such as gas masks and canisters, explosive charges, and flame throwers, brought in by men of the Philippine Chemical Depot. These analyses and descriptions were radioed to OCCWS, and samples of captured equipment were shipped to the United States. When surrender seemed inevitable, the CWS destroyed all remaining chemical materials. Colonel Hamilton and his surviving men were taken prisoner after the surrender of Corregidor on 6 May 1942 and remained in Japanese prison camps for the rest of the war.

Establishment in Australia

On 7 December 1941 the 3d Chemical Field Laboratory Company was aboard a Pacific convoy carrying units and individual officers and men destined to augment the American forces in the Philippines. On 12 December Brig. Gen. Julian F. Barnes, the senior officer aboard, organized the Army forces in the convoy into Task Force, South Pacific, and appointed a general and special staff. The War Department next day ordered General Barnes's convoy and task force to proceed to Australia where Barnes would assume command of United States troops. The convoy docked at Brisbane on 22 December, and General Barnes spent the following month straightening out the confused command situation, organizing the United States Army Forces in Australia (USAFIA) at Melbourne, and making desperate and unsuccessful attempts to send troops, aircraft, and supplies to the Philippines. On 28 January 1942 Capt. John C. Morgan, an officer of the 3d Chemical Field Laboratory Company, set about establishing a chemical section in USAFIA. Col. William A. Copthorne arrived on 2 February with a number of experienced officers and enlisted men. Known as the Remember Pearl Harbor Group, these men were being rushed to the Pacific to serve wherever senior command and staff officers and specialists were needed. Copthorne became chemical officer and was assigned to the USAFIA chief of staff's special mission for co-ordinating relief shipments to Corregidor.[3]

The CWS, U.S. Army Forces in Australia

Colonel Copthorne and Maj. John C. Morgan, now assigned as Copthorne's executive officer, tackled the job of setting up a CWS for USAFIA. First, they had to set up and staff the territorial organization in Australia and allocate personnel and units among other organizations, both those already in the area and those being activated. Then there was the task of providing chemical supplies for American forces. The third undertaking was the establishment of CWS planning and training functions. And the fourth act was to expand and supervise CWS technical and technical intelligence functions established by the laboratory company.

Six numerically designated base sections with headquarters at Darwin, Townsville, Brisbane, Melbourne, Adelaide, and Perth were set up on 3 March 1942. The seventh base section was established at Sydney in the following month. Sixteen CWS officers arrived in April, and Copthorne managed to assign one or two officers and one or two enlisted men to the chemical section of each base section, after a brief period of training and orientation in his own office. Chemical officers, like other base section special staff officers, were directly responsible to their chief of service in matters of plans, policies, and supply, but they served the additional function of advisers to base section commanders under whose administrative control they worked. Since the original intention of the Australian establishment was to support Lt. Gen. George H. Brett's Far East Air Force, Copthorne and Morgan, who held a second position as chemical officer in the Air Section, USAFIA, also sought to provide chemical manpower and service for the air forces.[4] His ability to accomplish such work was severely

---

[3] (1) MS, Mil History of USASOS in the Southwest Pacific, vol. I (hereafter cited as History, USASOS). OCMH. (2) Elizabeth Bingham and Richard Leighton, MS, Development of the U.S. Supply Base in Australia, pp. 1–10. OCMH. (3) Interv, Hist Off with Lt Col John C. Morgan, 1 Oct 45. (4) Col William A. Copthorne, USA (Ret.), Comments on draft of this volume, 13 Jan 61. (5) Col John C. Morgan, USAR (Ret.), Comments on draft of this volume, 9 Feb 61.

[4] The United States establishment in Australia had been set up to provide air and logistical support for the Philippines and for the forces operating in the Netherlands East Indies. After Japanese seizure of the Netherlands East Indies and after it proved to be impossible to support the Philippines, Fast East Air Force was inactivated and the conception of the American command in Australia as predominantly an air command was abandoned. The air command, subsequently designated Fifth Air Force, became an important element of the Allied land, naval, and air forces. History, USASOS, vol. I.

limited by lack of officers and men and by a lack of information as to air forces chemical organization and duties. The information finally arrived from OCCWS in July, and two months later the theater acquired enough personnel to activate four chemical air operations companies, using detachments and a platoon of the 3d Chemical Service Company (Aviation), already in the theater, as nuclei.[5]

Organizing the Chemical Section, U.S. Army Services of Supply

In March 1942 Allied leaders designated the Pacific as one of the three main theaters for prosecuting the war against the Axis. The Joint Chiefs of Staff in turn subdivided the Pacific into areas: the Southwest Pacific Area (SWPA) from Australia to the Philippines, and the Pacific Ocean Areas (POA) to the east of the Philippines, the Netherlands East Indies, and Australia. (Map 2) POA was again subdivided into North Pacific Area, Central Pacific Area (CENPAC) (including the Hawaiian, Gilbert, Marshall, Mariana, Bonin, and Ryukyu Islands), and South Pacific Area (SOPAC) (including New Zealand and New Caledonia). POA came under the command of Admiral Chester W. Nimitz who designated a deputy to head the South Pacific Area. In April MacArthur, now in Australia, organized GHQ, SWPA, an Allied and supreme command over all air, land, and sea forces in the area.[6] The Southwest Pacific Area was not technically a theater but GHQ, SWPA in mission and responsibility was an Allied headquarters as well as the senior American strategic and tactical headquarters in the area. After the creation of GHQ, USAFIA became a supply and service headquarters,[7] redesignated United States Army Services of Supply (USASOS) in July. Copthorne retained his position in USAFIA and its successor. Although he was regarded as chief chemical officer for the U.S. forces, he had no direct role in GHQ. By 1 July Copthorne and Morgan had their section in operation. The

---

[5] (1) History, USASOS. (2) Interv, Hist Off with Col Burton D. Willis and Col Robert N. Gay, 12 Jun 50. Colonel Willis' first assignments were chemical officer of the base sections at Brisbane and later at Townsville. (3) Personal Ltr, Copthorne, CCmlO USAFIA, to Brig Gen Alexander Wilson, Chief Field Serv OCCWS, 13 Jul 42. CWS 319.1 1942. (4) Personal Ltr, Copthorne to Porter, 17 Aug 42. CWS 314.7 Pers Files, SWPA. (All personal letters hereafter cited, unless otherwise noted, are from this file.)

[6] Matloff and Snell, *Strategic Planning for Coalition Warfare, 1941–42*, pp. 164–73.

[7] The term *theater* will hereafter be used to indicate each of the Pacific areas and the senior U.S. Army headquarters therein. The North Pacific and the South Pacific Areas will not be considered here since the major features of the Chemical Warfare Service experience are apparent in the SWPA and POA accounts.

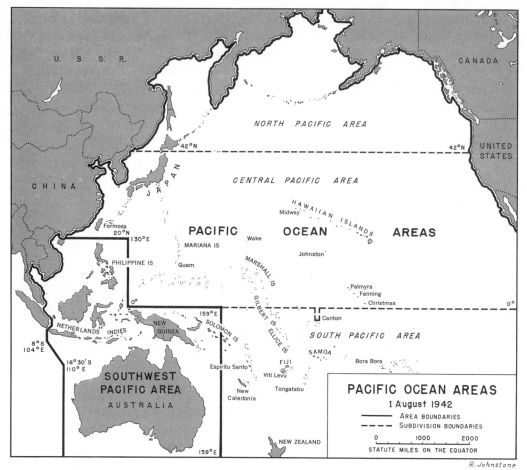

MAP 2

technical function, involving liaison with Australian chemical warfare authorities, and the supervision of the chemical laboratory, recently redesignated the 42d Chemical Laboratory Company, Copthorne exercised through his technical and intelligence officer, Maj. Walter W. F. Enz. Capt. Arthur H. Williams, Jr., handled fiscal and administrative matters, including supply, and was purchasing and contracting officer for the CWS. Capt. Carl V. Burke was operations and training officer. One other officer and three enlisted men completed the section.[8]

[8] (1) History, USASOS. (2) History, Cml Sec Hq USASOS, SWPA Orgn Files, AFWESPAC, Folder USASOS History of Cml Warfare School, APO 923, Jul 42–May 44. (3) Ltr, Copthorne to Hist Off, 16 Feb 51. (4) Copthorne Comments, 13 Jan 61. (5) Morgan Comments, 9 Feb 61.

Copthorne was the only CWS Regular Army officer in SWPA, not only at the time of organization but also for another year. A Military Academy graduate, he was 52 years of age at the time and had seen service in World War I but not overseas. He had a variety of chemical experience, including a tour as Philippine Department chemical officer, a tour as a corps area chemical officer in the United States, and had most recently been an instructor at the Army's Command and General Staff School.[9]

Supply was a very difficult matter to handle. Since there had been no preplanning for a theater headquarters based in Australia, all supplies obtained in the early period were destined for arriving organizations. There was no theater reserve. American forces supplies and services of all kinds were obtained from the Australians when possible through a necessarily complicated series of procedures which prevented a fatal drain on the Australian economy and which precluded competition among American and Allied forces for available goods and services. Captain Williams had little to work with; Copthorne wrote to OCCWS that he could determine neither theater strength nor the availability of supplies in the hands of troops.[10]

The Theater CWS School

The training job was more readily, although not easily, handled. Copthorne urged all base section chemical officers to give the troops as much chemical training as possible. Many of them were too short-handed to accomplish much training outside their immediate headquarters, but Maj. Burton D. Willis, Chemical Officer, Base Section 3 in Brisbane, had a larger staff, and he could call upon the 42nd Chemical Laboratory Company (formerly the 3d Chemical Field Laboratory). He gave several courses in chemical warfare defense, using a classroom in the University of Queensland. Although base section training was on a part-time basis, such training was a good foundation on which to build, and Copthorne dispatched Captain Burke to open a theater school. On 12 July 1942 Burke reported to the Brisbane base section headquarters to establish a chemical warfare school for all American forces. Since no authority existed for such an establishment, Burke

[9] CMLHO Biographical Sketches. Copthorne was also Acting Adjutant General, USAFIA, from March to May 1942.
[10] Copthorne to Wilson, 13 Jul 42.

officially assumed the operation of the base section school while in fact preparing for the establishment of a SWPA CWS school. The first class with thirty-three unit gas officer students was in session before the school was approved in August, and the third class, also of unit gas officers, was ready to graduate before September, when the school officially became a theater activity as part of the Chemical Warfare Service Training Center.[11]

Burke started his school in a converted private residence with one officer and two enlisted assistants. He called on Willis, soon promoted to lieutenant colonel, on officers of the laboratory company, the 62d Chemical Depot Company, and on the 10th Chemical Maintenance Company to assist him with instruction. In the following year, with a peak staff of five officers, the CW school conducted thirty courses, including those for unit gas officers, unit gas noncommissioned officers, and special, technical, decontaminating, and demonstration courses for other soldiers. These courses, usually of two weeks' duration, graduated nearly 1,000 students.[12] But even this accomplishment was not equal to the task at hand of training and retraining SWPA forces in defense against gas warfare. Even before the school started, Copthorne drew upon his meager supply of officers, again supplementing them with details from the chemical service units, to establish four mobile training teams for the purpose of instructing widely dispersed units in chemical warfare defense. In driving home instruction these training teams demonstrated chemical warfare defensive and decontaminating equipment and tested procedures in which live toxic agents were used. The demonstrations and tests were usually given at company level for selected officers and NCO's. Length of instruction varied from a few hours to two days, according to the company's needs and schedules.[13]

The training teams, like the school, were attached to the Chemical Warfare Service Training Center, which was supported by the base section headquarters at Brisbane. The training center, in addition to administering the school and the teams, also arranged or conducted special co-operative instruction and demonstrations which called for

---

[11] (1) Interv, Hist Off with Lt Col Carl V. Burke, 28 Jan 46. (2) Summary of Past History of the Cml Warfare School, APO 923 (hereafter cited as History, Cml Warfare School). Orgn Files, AFWESPAC, Folder USASOS History of Cml Warfare School, APO 923. (3) Willis-Gay Interv, 12 Jun 50.

[12] History, Cml Warfare School.

[13] (1) History, Cml Sec USASOS. (2) Burke Interv, 28 Jan 46. (3) Copthorne Comments, 13 Jan 61.

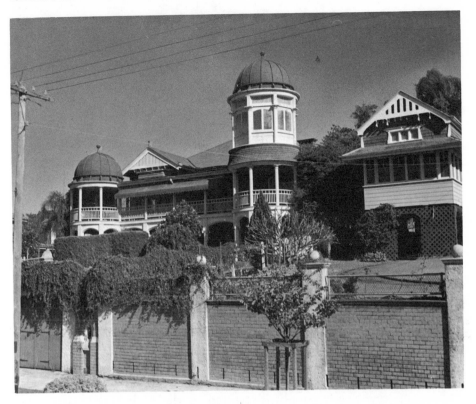

ANNEX BUILDING, CHEMICAL WARFARE SCHOOL, BRISBANE, AUSTRALIA

more equipment or a greater instruction load than the school or the teams could handle individually. Standard U.S. training aids and equipment were not available. Major Enz acquired a small laboratory at the University of Melbourne and manufactured gas identification sets using commercial materials and toxics furnished by the Australian and American Armies. Instructors or chemical service units fabricated other equipment and aids. The school got very little instruction and no materials from the United States, but it did benefit by an exchange of information with the Australian Antigas School near Toowoomba.[14]

The newly established training facilities were used by the 32d and 41st Infantry Divisions, first American tactical ground forces organizations in the theater. The 41st Division had reached Australia on 7 April 1942, and the 32d Division on 14 May 1942. Both organizations

[14] Burke Interv, 28 Jan 46.

included chemical sections, the 41st section headed by Maj. Frank M. Arthur, and the 32d section by Capt. Edward H. Sandell. Both of these officers established division chemical warfare schools.[15]

When General MacArthur converted USAFIA into USASOS on 20 July 1942, general and special staffs retained their responsibilities virtually unchanged. Such reorganization as was accomplished was apparently intended to bring USASOS into line with a War Department directive for theater communications zone organization.[16] Copthorne felt that there should be a chemical officer in General Mac-Arthur's GHQ, but, he also felt that for the time being his location in USASOS permitted him close supervision of the matters in which the CWS had the greatest immediate concern.[17] A position in GHQ would presumably have been an Allied staff position similar to the one which Shadle had just taken over in AFHQ. Since there was no World War I precedent and since Shadle's was the only such CWS appointment in World War II, a like appointment in GHQ would have been unusual.

CWS Functions

CWS functions of immediate concern were those of personnel, supply, and training, as they had been earlier; but now Copthorne also had reason to become deeply interested in the technical preparations for gas warfare. As theater chemical officers the world over were then discovering or were about to discover, he had found that they had "almost an independent Chemical Warfare Service out here."[18] The manifestation of this independence in SWPA was not, as in other theaters, in the realm of supply, but rather in the provision of technical chemical information to all forces in the theater and in the exchange of information with the Allies. As far as supply was concerned, the time lag between the United States and the theater was so great that the individual service could as yet do little to influence shipments. Distribution within the theater was tightly controlled by USASOS since critically short transportation had to be centrally controlled. In technical matters, however, Copthorne had charge of the only full-fledged laboratory in the theater, and he strongly believed that it was

[15] Ibid.
[16] History, USASOS, pp. 27–29.
[17] Personal Ltr, Copthorne to Porter, 17 Aug 42.
[18] Ibid.

to the advantage of the service for this laboratory to handle any technical problem referred to it. Since the Japanese had reportedly employed gas in China, since they were apparently logistically capable of mounting a gas attack, and since it would be to their advantage to initiate such an attack before the American defenses were organized, Copthorne also believed that the Japanese might initiate gas warfare at any time. This possibility, he felt, called for active intelligence work and extensive technical investigation of the characteristics of available muni-

COLONEL RIEGELMAN

tions in the theater's tropical environment. He also saw the need for improvising new munitions and techniques to be used before supplies and information became available from the United States.[19]

In order to meet the technical portion of his functions, Copthorne had set up a Technical Advisory Board to maintain scientific liaison with the British, the Australians, and within the U.S. forces, and to advise the laboratories. Also, several of Copthorne's subordinates had begun munitions testing. Two of them, Capt. Richard H. Cone and Lt. James W. Parker were killed in an air accident while carrying out experiments to determine whether incendiary bombs could be improvised from training bombs, using gasoline thickened with crude rubber as a filling.[20]

In September 1942 the chemical section went along with USASOS headquarters to Sydney, but the change in location made little change in the section's operation. In the following month the chemical section began circulating a mimeographed Chemical Warfare information bulletin designed to apprise officers in the field of technical and intelligence developments.[21] Also, during this period Headquarters, I Corps, under the command of Lt. Gen. Robert L. Eichelberger, arrived in

[19] *Ibid.*
[20] *Ibid.*
[21] History, Cml Sec USASOS.

Australia to become the senior tactical American ground command. The I Corps chemical officer was Col. Harold Riegelman, a distinguished New York attorney who had served in World War I as a gas officer and had since been prominent in Reserve activities. In the words of his commander, he was "a loyal efficient staff officer with an analytical brain who pursued his work with diligence." [22] Riegelman's section included an officer assistant, a warrant officer, and six enlisted men.[23] On arrival in Australia, Colonel Riegelman at once began to lay plans with Major Arthur of the 41st Division, and to await an opportunity to confer with Captain Sandell of the 32d Division.

CWS Baptism—The Papua Campaign

This opportunity never arose. Two regiments of the 32d Division had been ordered forward to New Guinea in September, and on 18 October Sandell, T/Sgt. John K. King, and Sgt. Raymond F. Dasman, as the advance detail of the chemical section, reported to their commanding general at Port Moresby on the southern tip of New Guinea.[24] Sandell's was among the first chemical sections to participate in combat in World War II after the fall of the Philippines. The duties performed by the 32d Division Chemical Section, while they might not be categorized as either administrative or staff work, which were theoretically the section's main responsibilities, demonstrate the ingenuity with which chemical sections in many combat elements in all parts of the world approached and defined their tasks.[25]

Sandell and his sergeants spent a few days in the Port Moresby area locating the chemical equipment which the regiments had discarded on landing. Most of the equipment was in a deplorable state, having been scattered in odd piles about Port Moresby and exposed to the elements. The gas masks, approximately 5,000, had been collected and put under cover. USASOS had established a forward base at Port Moresby, but the base chemical officer, inexperienced and recuperating from malaria, had been unable to locate either the labor or the materials

[22] Gen Robert L. Eichelberger, USA (Ret.), "A Prefatory Note," in Harold Riegelman, Caves of Biak (New York: Dial, 1955).

[23] Riegelman, Caves of Biak, pp. 3–4.

[24] For a complete account of the Papua Campaign, see Samuel Milner, Victory in Papua, UNITED STATES ARMY IN WORLD WAR II (Washington, 1957).

[25] The following account of the initial activities of the 32d Division Chemical Section is based on: Acting Div CmlO to CG 32d Inf Div, 18 Feb 43, sub: Rpt on the Activities of the 32d Inf Div Cml Sec During the Papuan Campaign.

to build storage places and to collect and store other equipment.
Nearly all troops in the area had been fighting to repel the Japanese
invasion until a short time before Sandell's arrival.

Sandell managed to get a 10-man detail from the 107th Quartermaster Battalion, then assigned to the Port Moresby base, and with
this help he and his men gathered, inspected, and stored any matériel
that gave promise of serviceability. Sandell and his men were also given
the mission of searching the jungle to discover if any native garden
or jungle foods could be found to supplement the ration. From 8 to 21
November Sandell attended the New Guinea Force school on jungle
tactics as a student and presented briefings on chemical warfare as an
instructor.

On 27 November Sandell was ordered forward to the Buna-Gona
area, where an assault had been launched ten days earlier, to see if
chemical smoke or incendiary supplies would be useful in pushing the
attack. The assault was going badly because locating the enemy in
his cleverly camouflaged positions was difficult and driving him from
well-fortified bunkers with the weapons available was almost impossible. To get a line on enemy fortifications and master the assault
problem, Sandell led a patrol to a point south of the Buna Mission.[26]
He returned to Port Moresby, joined forces with Sergeants King and
Dasman, and together they collected HC smoke pots, Australian rifle
smoke grenades, thermite aerial bombs, blasting powder, gelignite,
safety fuzes, detonators, and friction tape. Back in the fighting zone
on 4 December, they set to work improvising hand grenades from the
rifle smoke grenades. They had some difficulty persuading infantrymen
to use them until an infantry captain demonstrated that it was safe
to pass through the smoke released by two grenades thrown directly
in front of an active bunker. The grenades were then much in demand.

On 7 December 1942 men of the 114th Engineer Combat Battalion
brought forward the first two portable flame throwers to arrive in the
combat area. Despite King's one attempt to put the flame throwers
in operating condition, they failed to fire properly. Flame throwers
were not again used in the Papua Campaign.[27] After receiving chemical
and ordnance supplies on 11 December, King and Dasman refined their
modified smoke grenade. Persisting in spite of a number of false starts,
they also produced a dependable Molotov cocktail and developed a

---

[26] For this patrol action Captain Sandell was awarded a Silver Star.
[27] See below, Chapter XIV, for full account of this failure.

hand-thrown concussion torpedo capable of killing all the occupants of a large bunker. After combat testing the improvised weapon, the 127th Infantry requested all the torpedoes the CWS sergeants could manufacture.

Captain Sandell was killed in action on 26 December 1942, and Dasman became a victim of malaria. King carried on at the front until the division was relieved late in January 1943.[28] The initiative and resourcefulness of Sandell and his men fitted in well with the concept of the CWS developed by Fries and Porter.

The Principal Mission—1943

Preparedness for Chemical Warfare

In February 1943 Riegelman visited New Guinea to assess the combat situation. He felt that Sandell and his men had done a fine job under extremely difficult circumstances, but he was disturbed by the lack of chemical weapons and the evidences of the poor use of smoke in the whole campaign. Like Copthorne, he was firmly convinced that the chemical officers should learn what effect gas would have in the tropics, and he agreed with Copthorne that the best place to find out was on the spot. While he believed defensive training was better than it had been in World War I, he was still concerned about the adequacy of both training and equipment since he believed the Japanese to be capable of using gas, and feared that even if they did not, some of the jungle odors might cause gas scares, which like an actual attack would result in panic if more specific training was not given. Riegelman reported his observations to his superiors and set to work in corps headquarters to provide remedies to the problems he foresaw.[29]

Copthorne likewise continued to be much concerned with the tactical problems of preparedness, but he believed that his position in USASOS prevented him from acting adequately in the tactical and planning field. In February 1943 he and his section moved up to the newly reconstituted U.S. Army Forces in the Far East, a headquarters somewhat comparable to the army theater headquarters in Europe and North Africa. He took with him to Brisbane Lt. Col. John C. Morgan,

---

[28] King was later commissioned and served in the Sixth Army Chemical Section.

[29] (1) Riegelman, *Caves of Biak*, pp. 26–30. (2) Personal Ltrs, Riegelman to Waitt, 26 Jan 43, and Riegelman to Porter, 26 Feb 43. CWS 314.7 Pers Ltrs of Colonel Riegelman.

recently promoted, Major Enz, and three other officer assistants. Lt.
Col. John C. Morcock, Jr., became Chemical Officer, USASOS, serving
with Captain Williams and two other officer assistants.

Copthorne still felt that he should be in GHQ where the chief
engineer and chief signal officer resided but recognized that although
the new USAFFE was a headquarters without tactical functions, it at
least promised to offer a better place for gas warfare preparedness
planning than USASOS.[30] USAFFE headquarters did not offer channels for formal co-ordination of the preparedness effort with Australian
chemical warfare authorities. Although informal relationships with
the Australians were good, Copthorne strongly felt that there should
be a formal relationship, particularly since the Australians found it
possible to communicate through their technical channels with the
chemical warfare establishment in England, and thereby with the
CWS and with the U.S. Chemical Warfare Committee in the United
States. Copthorne himself had found neither a command nor a technical channel which permitted easy communication with the technical
and planning authorities in the United States.[31] The Australians had
established a Chemical Warfare Service early in 1942 which like the
British counterpart was a joint effort of their army, navy, and air
force. Lt. Col. F. S. Gorrill of the British establishment was on duty
in Australia, and in 1943 he undertook an investigation of gas warfare
in the tropics.[32]

Staffing Problems

The move to higher headquarters and the completion of the first
theater gas warfare plan in March [33] again brought to the fore the
problem, which had been troublesome from the beginning, of providing
a chemical staff. Copthorne had still received no allotment of officers
in which each officer was earmarked for the kind of job he was intended
to fill. The only officers with appropriate rank, military education,
and experience to fill the top positions were Col. Carl L. Marriott who
arrived in April as Chemical Officer, Sixth Army, and Colonel Riegel-

[30] (1) History, Cml Sec USASOS.   (2) Ltr, Copthorne to Hist Off, 22 May 51.
[31] Interv, Hist Off with Copthorne, 26 Apr 61.
[32] D. P. Mellor, "Australia in the War of 1939–45," *The Role of Science and Industry* (Canberra:
Australian War Memorial, 1958) pp. 372–76.
[33] Ltr, CinC GHQ SWPA to TAG, 7 Apr 43, sub: Theater Plans for Cml Warfare. GHQ AG 381
(12–8–42)C.

man. Both men already had important posts and were unavailable to the theater organization. By the end of July 1943, no requisition for CWS personnel channeled through the USAFFE G–1 had yet been filled. Copthorne took the view that most of the young Reserve officers assisting him were doing excellent, and in some cases, outstanding work, but in implementing and revising the theater gas warfare plan and the training responsibilities which were growing daily, he had no one with sufficient rank and experience to handle the operations (planning) tasks. Furthermore, a large part of offensive gas warfare planning had to originate with the air forces where preparation for the retaliatory effort would be concentrated. Neither in USASOS nor in USAFFE did Copthorne have any power to control the Fifth Air Force, which reported to GHQ through Allied Air Forces. His relationship with Maj. Walter C. Weber, Fifth Air Force Air Staff chemical officer, was so cordial that he could practically consider him as an assistant, but Weber, then the only field-grade chemical officer in the Fifth Air Force, had his hands too full with supply and service functions to give any deep consideration to long-range planning.[34]

In the face of such problems, Copthorne increased his strength as best he could. It had been demonstrated by the time of the move to USAFFE that the existing organization for securing chemical technical intelligence through unit gas officers and NCO's was ineffective. Copthorne accordingly assigned Maj. John A. Riddick, who had been Enz's assistant, to head a new Intelligence Section in his office. He charged Riddick with securing six junior officers and twelve NCO's to organize and train six technical intelligence teams. Riddick found the officers and men and brought them into the USAFFE Chemical Section for training. At the same time the headquarters rule that all captured equipment must be channeled to the Australians was relaxed. The teams soon went out on attachment to combat units. Riddick compiled their findings, together with laboratory analyses and descriptions of captured enemy equipment, and forwarded the resulting report to chemical officers and unit gas officers as well as to the headquarters of other theaters and areas in contact with the Japanese.[35]

At the same time the CWS SWPA began to rotate chemical officers among assignments so that as many officers as possible could have field

---

[34] Personal Ltrs, Copthorne to Waitt, 14 Jul 43; Copthorne to Porter, 27, 28 Jul 43.
[35] (1) Copthorne Comments, 13 Jan 61. (2) Morgan, Comments, 9 Feb 61.

and staff experience. Lt. Col. Robert W. Smith became Morcock's executive, and Maj. Irving R. Mollen came from Base Section 3 to be his supply officer. The Melbourne base section chemical officer came in to be supply officer in the USAFFE section for a few months and then returned to Melbourne. Another field officer was assigned to a brief tour as operations and training officer in the Chemical Section, USAFFE, before becoming commandant of the school. Maj. Carl V. Burke replaced Colonel Morgan as executive officer in the USAFFE section after Morgan became CWS

COLONEL MARRIOTT *examining Japanese gas mask.*

Liaison Officer with the Australian Army, a position established in place of formal co-ordination. Colonel Willis moved from Brisbane to Townsville since Townsville was the base most actively in support of forward operations. He then served a short tour in the Advance Section, USASOS, in New Guinea, and returned to Townsville. Morcock moved out to become chemical officer of the Advance Section and Colonel Smith took his place in USASOS.[36]

Co-ordinating the Theater CWS

Copthorne felt the CWS in the United States should provide gas warfare technical and preparedness doctrine for the tropics, or else that it should assist him and his colleagues in the Pacific areas in formulating such doctrine, but he was not satisfied that his appeals for help had received sufficient attention in the United States.[37] He found communication with the Central Pacific Area chemical staff too difficult in 1943 to offer adequate opportunity for co-ordinated study of chemical problems, but his colleagues in the South Pacific were closer

---

[36] (1) Information Bull, CWS Hqs USAFFE Nos. 8–16, 10 May–10 Sep 43. (2) Morgan Interv, 10 Oct 45. (3) Burke Interv, 28 Jan 46.
[37] Copthorne Interv, 26 Apr 61.

and had more experience with tropical warfare so there the opportunities for exchange of information seemed better. The Chemical
Section, U.S. Army Forces in the South Pacific Area (USAFISPA),
had been organized by Col. Leonard J. Greeley in August 1942. In
November 1942 Greeley was designated Deputy Chief of Staff,
USAFISPA, and Lt. Col. Joel L. Burkitt became chemical officer.
While the USAFISPA Chemical Section had been hampered by shortage of manpower, lack of chemical materials, and the perpetual Pacific
problems of difficulties in communication and transportation, its staff,
as Copthorne knew, had kept in close touch with the combat organization chemical officers.[38]

Copthorne decided that he might be able to accomplish gas warfare
doctrinal formulation by "committee." He accordingly invited
Greeley and Burkitt along with the principal chemical officers in
SWPA to a conference at the SWPA CWS school from 1-3 July 1943.
Col. Robert N. Gay, Chemical Officer, XIV Corps, then in SOPAC,
joined Greeley and Burkitt. From SWPA came Marriott, Riegelman,
Lt. Col. Lyle A. Clough, Chemical Officer, 32d Division, Lt. Col.
James O. Andes, who was soon to replace Clough, and Major Arthur,
along with principal members of the USAFFE and USASOS staffs.
The conference first "defined" the tropics in terms of the effect of prevailing meteorological conditions and terrain on gas warfare. Next
the conferees observed demonstrations of incendiary, flame, and smoke
weapons and munitions. They then spent a day on tactical gas warfare
requirements and a half a day on tactics of smoke employment. The
meeting concluded with a half-day session on ammunition supply
requirements. The principal value of the conference appears to have
been that the chemical officers were able to agree on what they did
and did not know. What they did know or were able to conclude
concerning the performance of available munitions in the tropics was
stated as area tactical doctrine for the employment of chemical agents
and weapons. A list of items related to munitions performance characteristics about which they were in doubt was drawn up for investigation in the theater or referral to OCCWS.[39]

As Riegelman expressed his views on the conference, "Everybody

---

[38] (1) CMLHO Biographical Sketches. (2) 1st Ind, CG USAFISPA to TAG, 1 Apr 43, on Ltr,
TAG to CG USAFISPA, 19 Dec 42, sub: Theater Plans for Cml Warfare. AG 381 (12-8-42) OB-S-
E-M. (3) Interv, Hist Off with Col Nelson McKaig, USA (Ret.), 27 Apr 61.
[39] Rpt of Conf of Cml Warfare Officers, 1, 2, 3 Jul 43, Cml Sec USAFFE, n.d.

profited enormously. Everybody contributed values from his own experience." [40] But in retrospect, the conference was more significant than its immediate value in providing a forum for the exchange of experience and as a means of formulating temporary doctrine would indicate. Its significance lay in the fact that it presented practically the only means of integrating the CWS in SWPA. It accomplished for Copthorne a measure of the co-ordination of effort which Rowan achieved in the ETO through supply control and continuous personal liaison. It was less successful as a means of control than Rowan's because a conference is a transitory affair, and in the SWPA the means of sustaining its co-ordinating benefits were few. The organization of the SWPA forces, the tremendous physical distances over which the forces in the theater had to move troops and matériel, and the continuing difficulty of communication within the theater and with the United States all militated against maintaining a continuously co-ordinated effort. Copthorne could only hope to provide a link between research and the firing line by enlarging and continuously revitalizing his two greatest sources of strength, control of technical intelligence and authority to advise on, and sometimes even to make, CWS personnel assignments. He also still sought to build up the function of formulating supply policy and the capability of planning within his own staff.

A temporary hitch in the operation of Copthorne's plans came in September 1943 when he and the other service chiefs were transferred back to USASOS. Except for about two weeks' confusion attendant upon the move, the transfer had little impact on Copthorne's functions because the promise of improved prestige and capability and of better lines of communication in USAFFE had not been fulfilled. An officer remained in the G–4 office in USAFFE as CWS representative. The reorganized USASOS office included Enz, Burke, and Riddick in their respective technical, training, and intelligence positions. Smith became supply officer and Mollen remained as his assistant. A lieutenant colonel recently arrived from the United States became operations and training officer. Two other officers and two warrant officers completed the section. Intelligence trainees were transferred to the 42d Laboratory for further training.[41]

[40] Personal Ltr, Riegelman to Waitt, 9 Jul 43.
[41] Info Bull, CWS USASOS, No. 18, 25 Oct 43.

Preparedness—The Theater CWS Situation at the End of 1943

After the period of adjustment, prospects for the chemical section became brighter. Lt. Col. John P. Youngman, a supply officer with considerable background and experience whom Copthorne had long wanted in the theater, arrived from the United States to take over the supply position. Colonel Smith became Copthorne's deputy. Maj. Jack F. Lane, a young officer with a training background, arrived to take a training center assignment. Lt. Col. Augustin M. Prentiss, Jr., a vigorous, young (28 years old) Military Academy graduate with infantry, CWS, and air experience, also arrived from the United States to become Chemical Officer, Fifth Air Force. Major Weber became Chemical Officer, V Air Force Service Command, thus giving Prentiss an opportunity to devote his time to planning and policy.[42]

Lt. Col. Donald G. Grothaus and Maj. Richard T. Brady of the Field Operations staff, OCCWS, agreed with Copthorne's estimate of his problems and accomplishments during their visit to the theater late in 1943 and early in 1944. Grothaus agreed with Copthorne that the Pacific was the most likely area for the initiation of gas warfare, and he pointed out, as Copthorne had, that the CWS deficiency of knowledge as to the employment of gas in the tropics was a serious drawback in planning and could well be a vital defect should actual gas operations commence.[43] He also noted that Prentiss was hampered in planning for gas warfare retaliation by a lack of information on the effectiveness of toxic munitions in a tropical environment.

Grothaus praised Copthorne's policy of setting the service units, such as the chemical laboratory, to work on any technical problem within their range of competence whether the solution would have chemical significance or not. He believed that these services performed for a number of theater elements had added significantly to the respect for and acceptance of the CWS in the theater. Other factors increasing respect resulted from four successful Fifth Air Force smoke operations

---

[42] (1) Info Bull, CWS USASOS, No. 19, 25 Nov 43.   (2) Personal Ltr, Copthorne to Porter, 24 Nov 43.

[43] The following remarks on Grothaus' and Brady's estimate of the situation are drawn from: Grothaus and Brady, OCCWS to CCWS through ACCWS Field Opns, 29 Mar 44, Rpt on Visit to SWPA, SOPAC, and CENPAC (hereafter cited as Grothaus-Brady Rpt). CWS 314.7 Observer Rpts. While Grothaus and Brady worked part of the time as a team, Brady was charged only with the investigation of technical intelligence and wrote only that portion of the report.

in New Guinea,[44] and from excellent liaison with the Australian forces. One CWS officer, Capt. Howard E. Skipper, had been sent to work in the Australian Chemical Warfare experimental station, and Grothaus believed that the CWS should provide more help, both in manpower and materials, to further the Australian experiments on gas in the tropics. Another source of increased respect was the record of the 4.2-inch chemical mortar battalion in the South Pacific Area. In the United States this mortar battalion had been assigned to SWPA, but since the SWPA chemical staff was not informed that the unit was authorized to fire high-explosive shells nor that such shells were available, the battalion had been given so low a movement priority as a gas warfare unit that it was diverted to SOPAC.[45] Reports filtering into SWPA on the effectiveness of the chemical mortar using high-explosive shells made several ground commanders eager to obtain battalions for their own employment. On the debit side, Grothaus, again as Copthorne had, deplored the poor condition of CWS matériel arriving in the theater and indicated that OCCWS action to improve the situation was imperative. Also, despite some recent improvements in the manpower situation, SWPA still had a greater shortage of experienced officers than any other major theater. While strict theater personnel ceilings prevented large additions to the theater CWS complement, Grothaus was of the opinion that in future shipments OCCWS could do much to make up in quality what was lacking in quantity.

Major Brady, whose specific mission was to investigate intelligence, was so impressed with Major Riddick's accomplishments that he forwarded to OCCWS Riddick's schedule for training technical intelligence teams. Brady recommended that these teams be trained in the United States. He visited some of the teams which had begun to operate in forward areas with command sanction early in November and approved their activities.[46] The intelligence teams were a valuable aid to the CWS SWPA for the remainder of the war. Copthorne later

---

[44] (1) Prentiss personally supervised these four operations and flew in the lead plane on the first one. Prentiss Interv, 25 Oct 61. (2) For details on one of these operations at Lae, see below, Chapter X.

[45] Copthorne Comments, 13 Jan 61.

[46] Personal Ltr, Riddick to Morgan, 14 Nov 43, inclosing: (1) Ltr, AG USAFFE to CG USASOS, 9 Nov 43, sub: Responsibility for Technical Intelligence, FEGC 323.361; (2) Memo for Rcd, Riddick, 12 Nov 43, sub: Conf with Col E. R. Thorpe, ACofS G-2 USAFFE.

commented that the organization for intelligence was so effective that it should stand as an example for all similar theater activities.[47]

CWS, *Southwest Pacific Area, 1944–45*

The year 1944 was somewhat paradoxical for the Office of the Chief Chemical Officer, USASOS. On the one hand, the supply situation was good; the condition of equipment had improved; planning capabilities improved throughout the year; training was progressing smoothly; technical intelligence was working well; and technical investigations continued to produce worthwhile information. On the other hand, until late in the year, the advance of forces toward the Philippines put increasingly greater distances between Copthorne's immediate staff and the CWS in the field, thereby making communication increasingly more difficult. Even the advanced echelons of USASOS communicated more readily with the combat forces than with their own main echelon. Thus, while the USASOS Chemical Section was successfully accomplishing its aims and missions, the chief chemical officer, because of the organization of the theater and its physical setup, had a less important role in the operation of the theater CWS as a whole. (*Chart 7*)

A Solution for Technical Planning Problems

Copthorne made a trip to Washington in the spring of 1944 for consultations in OCCWS, where he gave special attention to his manpower and planning problems. Lt. Col. William A. Johnson, an officer whom Copthorne had several times requested, arrived in the theater during Copthorne's absence to take over the operations and training functions. In June the theater gas warfare plan was revised, and the revision indicated a considerable improvement in the theater situation both with respect to supply and plans. Technical and munitions performance information was still deficient, but a team of two officers sent out to SWPA by OCCWS had made a preliminary survey of requirements for information on gas warfare in the tropics just before Copthorne's departure, and OCCWS was soon to set up a project for assessment of gas in tropical situations in the western hemisphere.[48]

---

[47] Copthorne to Hist Off, 22 May 51.
[48] (1) Info Bulls, CWS USASOS, Nos. 24 and 25, 25 Apr and 25 May 44. (2) History of the Cml Sec USASOS, Mar 44–Jul 45. USASOS Mil History Rpts.

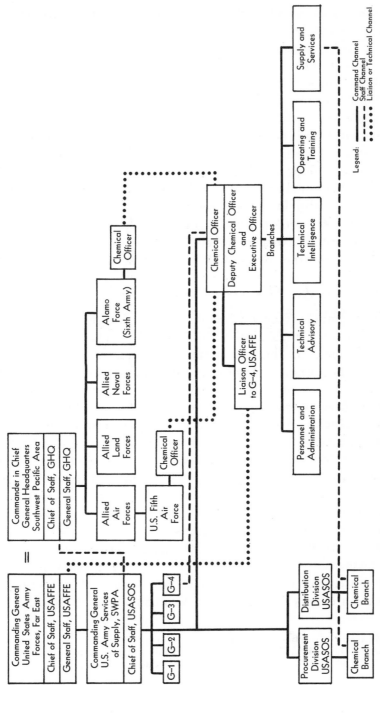

CHART 7—ORGANIZATION OF CHEMICAL SECTION, HEADQUARTERS, UNITED STATES ARMY SERVICES OF SUPPLY SOUTHWEST PACIFIC AREA, 1 JUNE 1944

Legend:
Command Channel
Staff Channel
Liaison or Technical Channel

Source: Adapted from: SWPA Personnel and Administration, CWS 314.7; Organizational Manual, U.S. Army Services of Supply, SWPA, revised 1 Jun 44, ASF 200; Cannon, Leyte: Return to the Philippines, p. 25.

By the end of 1944 the SWPA gas warfare planning enterprise at last reached the echelon where it had been in theory but not in fact for three years.[49] Copthorne personally went on temporary duty with G–3, GHQ, to make another revision of the gas warfare plan. This superior headquarters could co-ordinate the activities of the ground, naval, air, and service commands affecting plans for gas warfare. The remaining technical problems were also approaching solution. In November 1944 the theater and the Allies concurred in a proposal forwarded to the theater by General Waitt for the establishment of a Far Eastern Technical Unit (FETU) to investigate the performance of toxics and toxic munitions in the theater. Enz had originally suggested such an establishment to OCCWS. FETU, under the command of Lt. Col. John D. Reagh, completed its tests and analyses during 1945 and in the process furnished needed planning data to the theater. The unit employed officers and civilian scientists from the United States and drew upon the theater CWS for assistance, service, and supply.[50]

Theater Training—Final Phase

The Chemical Warfare Service training center continued to be a SWPA focus for chemical training during 1944 although corps and division courses had become common in the latter half of 1943. Early in 1944 the distance of most combat units from Australia made it impractical to send large groups back to Brisbane. A new Chemical Warfare Service training center was therefore established at Oro Bay in New Guinea. At first the school remained at Brisbane, but gave some assistance in conducting courses at Oro Bay. About the middle of 1944, a little less than two years after its establishment at Brisbane, the school moved to Oro Bay where it remained until early in 1945. The Chemical Warfare Service Training Center and the school were subsequently re-established in the Manila area, but the war ended before the school was in full operation.[51]

In the Oro Bay location, the training center and school came under the jurisdiction of the Chemical Officer, Intermediate Section, USASOS. Intermediate Section (later New Guinea Base Section) was a forward area service and supply command with jurisdiction over all

---

[49] SWPA gas warfare plans from the first officially emanated from GHQ.
[50] (1) History, Cml Sec USASOS, 44–45. (2) FETU's Rpts and Corresp. CWS 314.7 FETU.
[51] (1) History, Cml Sec USASOS, 44–45. (2) Burke Interv, 28 Jan 46.

but the most forward bases. Copthorne had secured the transfer of Colonel Gay from SOPAC to SWPA in December 1943 to be Chemical Officer, Intermediate Section. In January 1944 Colonel Gay became chemical officer of an advanced headquarters of USASOS and Burke, recently promoted to lieutenant colonel, became Intermediate Section chemical officer. In this position, Burke was in charge of direct support to the combat forces as supplied by the New Guinea bases. This was a difficult position since the occupant in effect served two masters. General instructions and command came from USASOS, but decisions on allocation of resources and requests for supply, services, and training came primarily from Sixth Army.[52]

The CWS in the Combat Forces, 1944–45

The SWPA combat forces had from the beginning enjoyed a greater degree of independence than most similar forces elsewhere in the world because the nature of the area, as noted earlier, made closely co-ordinated operation extremely difficult. The independence, at least with respect to chemical matters, increased throughout 1944. Sixth Army was the principal U.S. Army ground combat organization in the theater in 1944, although Eighth Army was to be organized late in 1944 and to become operational in 1945.[53] Colonel Marriott presided over the Sixth Army chemical establishment. Maj. Leonard L. McKinney was assistant, deputy, and frequently operations officer, for Colonel Marriott.[54] The Sixth Army Chemical Section included a supply officer with one or sometimes two assistants, and usually an operations officer. Colonel Marriott was invalided home in mid-1944 and was replaced by Col. John R. Burns.[55]

The Sixth Army Chemical Section had a major hand in determining tactical policy, and it not only allocated incoming resources among the supporting bases, but also allocated resources among subordinate combat organizations. The allocation duties meant distributing to Sixth Army organizations such combat units as the chemical mortar

---

[52] (1) Ltr, CmlO Intermediate Sec USASOS to CmlO's Bases A, B, D, E, F, 1 Apr 44, sub: Ltr of Instr. ISCW 300 in Unit Files, 93d Cml Composite Co. (2) Burke Interv, 28 Jan 46. (3) Willis-Gay Interv, 12 Jun 50.

[53] See Robert Ross Smith, *The Approach to the Philippines*, UNITED STATES ARMY IN WORLD WAR II (Washington, 1953), pp. 278, 450n.

[54] (1) Col Harold Riegelman, MS, Admin of CW Functions in Theaters of Opns—SWPA. (2) CMLHO Biographical Sketches.

[55] CMLHO Biographical Sketches.

battalions, which belatedly became available to the theater with the activation of one battalion and the arrival of another in mid-1944, and of such service units as were available. But service units were not readily available. When, late in 1943, Marriott asked Copthorne how he might obtain one of Copthorne's service units, Copthorne wrote, "you might just as well have nonchalantly asked me how you could get my right arm or even my bed at Lennon's." [56] Copthorne was understandably reluctant to give up any service unit since USASOS units were already thinly spread in detachments in an attempt to meet supply and service requirements. But even had he been willing and able to release a unit, the organizational cleavage between service and combat forces was so deep that USASOS did not feel that it was responsible for supplying units to the combat forces. It was USASOS policy to retain its badly needed units.[57] Eventually, USASOS policy was changed to permit the release of one unit in January.[58] Sixth Army parceled out this unit, and later others, in detachments to divisions to service flame throwers, recondition shell, and handle supply. These detachments were subsequently converted into cellular units, that is, units composed of smaller self-supporting elements, to perform the same functions.

Colonel Burns and Col. Ralph C. Benner, Chemical Officer, Eighth Army, continued to work on the problems of chemical tactical policy and of allocation of men, units, and materials for the remainder of the war in the Pacific. They had the job of receiving and evaluating plans and requirements which originated in echelons subordinate to the army headquarters. They, in turn, translated these plans and requirements into the concepts of the whole organization, co-ordinated them through staff in their own headquarters, and dispatched them through command channels to GHQ. Using both technical and command channels, the Army chemical officers received reports of chemical activities and problems and maintained continuous inspections to insure the greatest possible effectiveness at field levels.[59]

Below army level, 1944 and 1945 saw the culmination of a great change which had taken place since the tragic and heroic improvisa-

---

[56] Personal Ltr, Copthorne to Marriott, 19 Nov 43. Sixth Army Cml Sec Memos. (Lennon's was the best hotel in Brisbane and a highly prized officer's billet.)

[57] *Ibid.*

[58] History, Cml Sec USASOS, 44–45.

[59] (1) Riegelman, Admin of Cml Warfare Functions in Theaters of Operations—SWPA. (2) Interv, Hist Off with Lt Col Leonard L. McKinney, 12 Jan 46.

tions of the 32d Division Chemical Section in the Papua Campaign. USASOS and Sixth Army managed during 1943 and early in 1944 to obtain a sufficient supply of essentials such as smoke pots, hand grenades, 4.2-inch chemical mortar shells, and individual protective equipment. Colonel Riegelman in I Corps and his subordinates in the divisions plunged into training and tactical work, and by the time of the Hollandia operation early in 1944, they had defensive training of the individual soldier well in hand.[60] I Corps had also officially adopted a policy of using smoke shell to provide a target area marking system. Riegelman secured approval for the concept of attaching a mortar company to each assaulting division under the operational control of the division chemical officer. The misuse of smoke concealment which Riegelman had found in his first tour in New Guinea had been corrected by troop training and by orienting commanders.[61]

Flame thrower techniques had also been perfected, and the weapon itself had been improved through the extraordinary efforts of both USASOS and field chemical officers and men. The weapon still had its faults and maintenance and repair problems were to plague SWPA forces for the duration of the war. With respect to tactical employment of the flame thrower, Sixth Army declared that the weapon logically belonged with the infantry rather than with the engineers, who had brought it into the Pacific. Both Sixth Army and I Corps developed an infantry team for the tactical employment of the flame thrower, and Sixth Army officially set up a team training program which was materially aided by a roving demonstration team organized by Colonel Gay in the USASOS advanced echelon.[62]

Other corps chemical officers, Col. Francis H. Phipps, X Corps, Lt. Col. John L. Bartlett, XI Corps, and Lt. Col. Richard R. Danek, XIV Corps,[63] like Riegelman who was replaced by Col. Frank M. Arthur in 1945, for the most part performed tactical and training functions. They concerned themselves with supply only with respect to critical

---

[60] For information on the campaigns in this period, see Smith, *The Approach to the Philippines.*

[61] (1) Riegelman, *Caves of Biak,* pp. 64–65, 70–74, 87–96.   (2) Interv, Hist Off with Col Harold Riegelman, USAR (Ret.), 10 Oct 56.

[62] (1) Riegelman, Admin of Cml Warfare Functions in Theaters of Opns—SWPA.   (2) Willis-Gay Interv, 12 Jun 50.   (3) Burke Interv. 28 Jan 46.

[63] XIV Corps transferred from SOPAC to SWPA.   Col. Hugh M. Milton II, corps chemical officer in SOPAC, became corps ACofS, G–4, and subsequently corps chief of staff. Col R. N. Gay, XIV Corps chemical officer, was succeeded by Lt. Col. William H. Shimonek who returned to the United States in 1944 and who was replaced by Danek.

items, such as the gas mask and 4.2-inch mortar shell, or in emergency
situations. Depending on the training and talents of each officer, corps
chemical officers also performed a variety of staff and operating tasks
not directly related to chemical warfare or completely unrelated,
depending upon their capabilities. Riegelman, who had been an
infantry officer as well as a gas officer in World War I, did a study
on the reduction of Japanese cave defenses on the island of Biak, an
operation which had combined infantry and chemical techniques.[64]

Division chemical officers had their hands full.[65] As their top priority
function, they were directly responsible for gas warfare training of
every man in the division. They accomplished what training they
could through their own sections and also made use of traveling training teams. By these means and by sending quotas (ideally, one officer
per company and one noncommissioned officer per platoon) of unit
gas officers and gas noncommissioned officers to theater and other
schools, they could train UGO's and UGNCO's and in turn help them
establish unit schools and training periods. The training activity was
a constant one since malaria, battle casualties, and ordinary shifts in
personnel frequently necessitated the establishment of an entire new
roster of UGO's and UGNCO's who would likewise be required to
give instruction down to the last private in the last squad. Corps
chemical officers and command inspectors checked on divisional chemical training periodically.

The division chemical officer's duty of next priority was supply.
He cleared requirements statements for gas masks and other protective
supplies, smoke pots, grenades, mortar shell, and various items of chemical equipment with the division G–4, and, if necessary, with the
Ordnance and Quartermaster officers. When supplies were received

---

[64] (1) Riegelman, Admin of Cml Warfare Functions in Theaters of Opns—SWPA. (2) Riegelman,
Caves of Biak, pp. 140–55. (3) USAFFE Board, n.d., Rpt 126 (Japanese Cave Defenses).

[65] This account of the duties of the division chemical officer is based on: (1) Riegelman, Admin of
Cml Warfare Functions in Theaters of Opns—SWPA; (2) Memo, Arthur for Hist Off, 21 Nov 45,
sub: Review of Col Riegelman's Paper, Admin of Cml Warfare Functions in Theaters of Opns—SWPA
(Colonel Arthur was Chemical Officer, 41st Infantry Division and I Corps); (3) Memo, Lt Col
Maurice A. Peerenboom for Hist Off, n.d. (Colonel Peerenboom served as Chemical Officer, 32d Infantry
Division in 1943); (4) Personal Ltr, Maj David D. Hulsey to Waitt, 3 Jun 45, in CWS 314.7 Pers Ltr
File (Misc) WESPAC, AFPAC, SPBC (Maj Hulsey was Chemical Officer, 6th Infantry Division);
(5) Interv, Hist Off with Lt Col James P. Sutton, 18 Dec 45 (Colonel Sutton was assistant chemical
officer and assistant to the Chief of Staff, I Corps, and subsequently the 32d Division chemical officer);
(6) Memo, Capt John M. McDonald, OpnsO, for Col Burns, CmlO Sixth Army [1 May 45], in
Sixth Army 333 Inspections; (7) Riegelman, *Caves of Biak, passim;* (8) Riegelman Interv, 10
Oct 56.

or in transit, the chemical schedule in loading, storage, issue, and service plans had to be cleared again with general and special staff officers, and the actual operation of supply followed down to the regimental and special staff levels. Division chemical officers in the Pacific found that co-operative plans, sometimes employed in other theaters, for combining chemical issue and service operations with those of ordnance or engineer sections seldom worked since these services normally used their own resources to the limit. Since, in such combined arrangements, the chemical sections relied heavily on the facilities and services which Ordnance and Engineers provided in the Pacific, the division chemical officer acquired the additional duty of securing and supervising his own service detachments which occasionally worked as far forward as regimental supply to issue chemical materials, service flame throwers, and handle mortar shell. The assistant division chemical officer often devoted full time to supply and service which included field improvisation or adaptation of matériel.

Planning, staff, and advisory functions also occupied the chemical officer—at least part of the time. Some of this work was chemical; some was not. The division chemical officer might find himself assigned to liaison, reconnaissance, or observer duties, or he might move out of the staff field into the supervision of combat loading or beach discharge of cargo. Lt. Col. Nelson McKaig, 25th Division chemical officer, an agricultural chemist in civilian life, inspected and supervised divisional food preparation and spent a considerable period setting up a divisional rest camp on Luzon. There were always the additional details that every staff member drew, such as sitting on courts-martial, assisting in command inspections, acting as fire hazards inspector, savings bond officer, and the like. There was an initial impression that the chemical officer had little to do in the absence of gas warfare, so that the division chemical officers may have been assigned a proportionately larger number of staff, command, and operating details than their colleagues. Some division chemical officers, like their colleagues in Europe, welcomed such details because of the opportunity, lacking in the course of ordinary chemical activities, to keep in touch with members of the staff and subordinate units. Some believed, as did Colonel Copthorne, that any service rendered by the CWS increased the prestige and acceptability of the service.

COLONEL COPTHORNE (LEFT) WITH GENERAL WAITT *at Colonel Copthorne's Oro Bay quarters in October 1944.*

A Second Theater CWS Conference

To return to the theater level, the respect for the service was increasing, and after the middle of 1944, Copthorne again laid plans for co-ordinating the chemical warfare effort for the Pacific through the best means available to him—a service conference such as the one which had been so successful in 1943. The second theater CWS conference, held from 10–13 October at Oro Bay under the official direction of Maj. Gen. J. L. Frink, Commanding General, USASOS, was considerably more extensive in scope than the previous conference, but the theme was still the tactical employment of chemical warfare, including aerial and land smokes and incendiaries, the chemical mortar, and the flame thrower.[66]

General Waitt and Lt. Col. Jacob K. Javits attended as representatives of OCCWS. Col. George F. Unmacht, Chief Chemical Officer, U.S. Army Forces, Pacific Ocean Areas, and Colonel Greeley represented POA, while Colonel Kellogg and others represented the China-Burma-India theater. The Australian Army, the American corps, divisions, and chemical mortar battalions also sent chemical officer delegates as did USAFFE and USASOS. The Navy sent some of its officers having chemical duties. Colonel Prentiss, now Chemical Officer, Far East Air Forces (a headquarters supervising the Fifth and Thirteenth Air Forces) attended with other representatives of the air forces. Also present were Dr. W. A. Noyes and several other civilian scientists of the National Defense Research Committee.

The conference made a series of recommendations that were considerably more authoritative than those of the earlier conference. The

[66] This paragraph and the following account are based on: Rpt, CWS Conf, USASOS SWPA. CWS 314.7.

Chemical Warfare Officers During the Oro Bay Conference, October 1944

conferees sought a simple table of toxic ammunition requirements based on operational trials under tropical conditions. This, as already indicated, they were soon to get.[67] They asked for new aerial toxic munitions, impregnated clothing with increased durability, new gas grenades, and tactical training material reflecting the behavior of chemical agents in the tropics. Other requests were for more manpower for mortar battalions, improved mortars, more spare parts, more and improved field equipment and munitions. But the significance of this conference, as of the previous one, was not so much in what was recommended and requested as it was in the indication of joint effort and the revelation of considerable technical knowledge, much of which had been accumulated through considerable effort and three years of theater experience. General Waitt was particularly impressed by the fact that the conference permitted an exchange of views and experiences among chemical officers of all the Pacific areas, and he noted that the presence of individuals from the United States tended to lessen the view held by some theater officers that they had been neglected by OCCWS.[68]

The Office of the Chief Chemical Officer—Final Phase

In September 1944 Colonel Copthorne and a part of his section moved to Hollandia and in October the remainder of the section followed from Australia. This office in Hollandia served as the base for setting up the Philippine operation. Copthorne visited Leyte during the campaign in December, and early in February moved his office to that island. These moves placed the USASOS Chemical Section nearer the nerve center of the theater and considerably eased communication with the forward elements. But even better things were to come. At the end of March the office of the chief chemical officer moved with the advanced echelon of USASOS to Luzon. Here command, service, and supply activities were being centered, and, while the chief chemical officer still had no official control or function outside of USASOS, his technical ties and his supervision of theater gas warfare planning at last gave him a very effective tool for controlling the theater CWS.[69]

---

[67] See above, pp. 208–10.

[68] Waitt, 25 Nov 44, Preliminary Rpt on Situation in POA and SWPA Based on Visit to SWPA and POA, 24 Sep–21 Nov 44.

[69] History, Cml Sec USASOS, 44–45.

General MacArthur was named, after the return to the Philippines, to command the U.S. Army Forces, Pacific (AFPAC), with jurisdiction over all Pacific theaters. In July 1945 Copthorne achieved what since April 1942 he had considered to be his rightful place—he was named Chief Chemical Officer, AFPAC. He finally had technical control of the CWS not only in the service command but also in the air forces and the ground forces.[70] Of the theater chemical officers in World War II only General Shadle as Chief Chemical Officer, AFHQ, enjoyed a comparable official position.

The war in the Pacific ended in September. Most of the officers who had served Copthorne during the long period of the war had already returned to the United States, but he remained as Chief Chemical Officer, AFPAC, until October 1945 when he was succeeded in turn by Col. Sterling E. Whitesides, Jr., and by General Loucks, both of whom served brief tours. Brig. Gen. Egbert F. Bullene served from July 1945 to March 1946 as Chemical Officer, Army Forces, Western Pacific—the administrative, supply, and service command which was organized to succeed USASOS in supporting the invasion of Japan but which was diverted instead to closing out the activities of SWPA or rebuilding them to suit occupation needs. Until his departure Copthorne worked, in a new context, on the same kind of problems which had occupied his attention since February 1942; he requested and assigned personnel, made plans, traced supplies, sought information, established intelligence procedures, and tried to put the CWS component of the occupation forces on a firm technical footing.[71]

Organizing the Chemical Warfare Service, Hawaiian Department

The Emergency

Lt. Col. George F. Unmacht, Chemical Officer, Hawaiian Department, was having breakfast on the morning of 7 December 1941 when

---

[70] (1) GHQ AFPAC GO 73, 26 Jul 45. (2) GHQ AFPAC Staff Memo 15, 14 Jul 45. (3) Ltr, CCmlO AFPAC to CmlO's, Sixth, Eighth, and Tenth Armies, FEAF, AFWESPAC, 2 Aug 45, sub: Corresp with the CCWS. AFPAC CW 312.3 in CWS 314.7 Misc Files, WESPAC, AFPAC, SPBC.

[71] (1) Personal Ltrs, Waitt to Copthorne, 4, 17, 29 Aug, 25 Sep, 4, 5 Oct 45. (2) Personal Ltrs, Copthorne to Waitt, 17, 19, 29 Aug 45. (3) Ltr, CCWS to CCmlO AFPAC, 23 Aug 45, sub: Request for Publications. (4) Ltr, CCmlO AFPAC to CCWS, 12 Aug 45, sub: Japanese Sniff Set. AFPAC CW 386.3. (5) Ltr, CCWS to CCmlO AFPAC, 25 Sep 45, sub: Post-Hostilities Cml Warfare Mission. (6) Ltr, CCmlO AFPAC to CCWS, 31 Oct 45, sub: Misc Info. AFPAC CW 350 (31 Oct 45). (3), (4), (5), and (6) in CWS 314.7 Misc Files WESPAC, AFPAC, SPBC.

he saw Japanese planes dropping bombs.[72] Within half an hour, Unmacht reported to the department headquarters from his office at Fort Shafter and directed Maj. James M. McMillin, Commanding Officer, Hawaiian Chemical Warfare Depot, Schofield Barracks, to begin issuing service gas masks to departmental troops then equipped with training masks. Lt. James E. Reilly and the men of the 5th Chemical Service Company (Aviation) on duty at Hickam Field also saw the attack and sprang into action. They shot down one of the attacking planes.[73]

Hawaiian Department authorities at the time feared that other air attacks would be made and that these attacks would include the use of gas. Unmacht's first responsibility, therefore, was to prepare against aerial gas attack. Leaving M/Sgt. Ralph I. Libby in charge of the Fort Shafter office, Unmacht reported to the departmental advance command post at Aliamanu crater. By noon he had telephoned all CWS staff officers and units on Oahu and had made sure that all were preparing for gas attack. The CWS officer ranking next to Unmacht, Lt. Col. Maurice E. Jennings, Chemical Officer, Hawaiian Air Force, also reported to the advance command post, with an enlisted assistant. Lieutenant Reilly and Lt. Melvin F. Fincke remained at Hickam Field while Lt. Willard H. Blohm took up duty at Wheeler Field. The CWS officers with the air force had the assistance of the chemical aviation company. Major McMillin and 1st Lt. William J. Tanner continued to operate the depot at Schofield Barracks where Capt. Howard S. Leach, Commanding Officer, Company A, 1st Separate Chemical Battalion, was, in addition to his other duties, post chemical officer. The men of Company A, whose second in command was 1st Lt. Rubert D. Chapman, were assigned to guard the depot, haul munitions, and furnish details for the post.

Maj. John H. Becque, Chemical Officer, 25th Infantry Division, was on duty at the Aliamanu crater post with the division staff. Unmacht secured the appointment of 1st Lt. Woodson C. Tucker as Acting Chemical Officer, 24th Infantry Division, which lacked a

---

[72] Unless otherwise noted, this and the following sections are based on History of the Chemical Warfare Service in the Middle Pacific, a 5-volume collection of journals, historical reports, and documents compiled and edited under the direction of Capt. Jerome K. Holmes, Chief, Intelligence and Technical Division, Chemical Office, Headquarters U.S. Army Forces, Middle Pacific, 1946, OCMH.

[73] Chronological history of the chemical office, Hawaiian Department to Middle Pacific, History of Cml Sec, USAFMIDPAC, vol. I, sec. II. Lieutenant Reilly was awarded the Legion of Merit for his performance on 7 December 1941.

chemical section, on the afternoon of 7 December. Unmacht was himself joined that afternoon by 1st Sgt. Roland P. Fournier and one other enlisted man. These 11 officers and approximately 375 enlisted men made up the CWS, Hawaiian Department, until 11 December when 2 Reserve officers reported for duty.

During those first few days the CWS established several supply points in addition to the depot and, with the help of a Civilian Conservation Corps company, completed the issue of service masks. McMillin also put into operation a reconditioned impregnating plant, a chloride of lime production plant, and a toxic land mine and shell-filling plant, all of which had been refurbished in the month before the attack.[74] One Reserve officer at once began converting a plant of the Pacific Guano and Fertilizer Company, of which he had been an employee, to the production of bleach.

Civil Defense

Since the CWS had the only available supply of sirens and horns, intended to be used as gas alarms, these were distributed as warnings for air attack pending the acquisition of an air alert system from continental United States. The CWS reconditioned training masks turned in by troops and reissued them to the home guard, civil defense officials, police, firemen, public utilities employees, and other civilians in key positions. At the cabled request of the Hawaiian Department, the Chief CWS gathered 478,000 new and used training masks in the United States and shipped them to Hawaii. When these masks began to arrive early in 1942, Unmacht's men set civilian crews to work reconditioning the masks and modifying them with sponge rubber padding to fit oriental faces and the faces of children. Civilian masks were issued through first aid stations.

Unmacht and nearly all of his officers, including several newcomers in the theater, together with 2d Lt. Edouard R. L. Doty, who gave up the post of territorial civil defense director to be commissioned, became involved in extensive civil defense training. Unmacht, promoted to colonel on 12 December 1941 and made territorial co-ordinator for gas defense in January, gave almost 300 public talks and radio broadcasts. A total of 68,000 civilians attended schools for specialized chemical warfare defense. After the middle of 1942 civil defense ac-

---

[74] Personal Ltr, Unmacht to Porter, 10 Nov 41. CWS 210.3/234.

tivities began to decrease, but civil defense training continued until mid-1943.[75]

Organization—Departmental Chemical Office

Meanwhile, in February 1942, Unmacht reorganized his immediate office, which in December had consisted only of Libby's Administrative Section, to include an Administrative Section under a civilian employee, Miss M. Allegra Clifton, a Training and Civil Defense liaison Section under Lieutenant Doty and a Supply Section under Lieutenant Libby, recently commissioned. In July a further reorganization introduced an executive officer, Capt. James H. Batte, changed Doty's section to Plans and Training, and put 2d Lt. Roland P. Fournier, who had been commissioned with 2d Lt. Ralph I. Libby, in charge of supply. This reorganization in part reflected the addition of responsibilities and individuals to handle them, but it also helped prepare for the strategic and organizational decisions then being made in the Pacific theater. The Hawaiian Department organization, after the organization of the Pacific areas, continued to be the senior Army command for the Central Pacific Area. There was at the time no chemical representative on Admiral Nimitz' joint and Allied POA staff nor on his Pacific fleet staff. The supreme command and the fleet command were based in the Hawaiian Islands.

Early Training

The July 1942 organization remained in effect during the second half of 1942. In this period emphasis shifted from immediate defensive preparations to preparation for combat in the Central Pacific Area. The area mission up to that time had been indirect support of operations in SOPAC and SWPA, and Hawaii had operated as a staging point for units bound south of the equator. This responsibility had entailed checking supply and training and providing either or both when required for troops outward bound. After the middle of 1942 it became increasingly evident that Hawaii would serve as a base for mounting forces for combat in the Central Pacific under CENPAC or POA command. The CWS, Hawaiian Department, stepped up troop training as its immediate share in the expected CENPAC re-

---

[75] Unmacht, Summary of Activities of CWS in POA, 19 Feb 45. CWS 314.7.

COLONEL UNMACHT WATCHING TRAINEES WASH GAS FROM CLOTHING, *Hawaii.*

sponsibilities. Unmacht did not establish a theater school as Copthorne had done in SWPA, but he inaugurated a series of gas officer and gas NCO courses for various elements of the department and for combat organizations. While the first informal instruction had been given to a group of air wardens only a few days after the attack on Pearl Harbor, the first course, for 278 UGO's and UGNCO's, was given 17–18 August 1942 in the Fort Shafter gymnasium. Two more advanced courses were given in September and October, and training for the year was brought to a rousing finish during three days in December when the departmental CWS staged a chemical warfare maneuver with 1,295 participants.

Position of the Theater Chemical Officer

At the end of 1942 the Hawaiian Department reorganized from an advance and rear echelon structure in which both echelons were responsible for all functions under the direction of the rear echelon, to a more conventional combat forces, service forces, and air forces pattern and added an echelon for military government since the territory was still under military control. Unmacht remained the department chemical officer with responsibilities in all four fields. His position was unique among chief chemical officers overseas in that he was both staff officer and commander of the chemical warfare troops not assigned to other organizations.[76]

In actually commanding troops, Unmacht came closer to the manual definition of a chief of service than any other chief chemical officer. But this was not the only way in which Unmacht's position differed from the positions of the other chief chemical officers. The Hawaiian Department and its successor commands, U.S. Army Forces, Central Pacific Area (USAFICPA), U.S. Army Forces, Pacific Ocean Areas (USAFPOA), and U.S. Army Forces, Middle Pacific (USAFMID-PAC), were in fact theater headquarters of the kind envisioned in the War Department organization manuals, and in these headquarters, unlike those in Europe, North Africa, and the Southwest Pacific, a commander, who did not double also as a supreme commander, was resident.[77] Unmacht therefore had more opportunity to present his

---

[76] Hawaiian Dept GO 110, 29 Jul 43.

[77] The Central Pacific Army headquarters was not technically a theater headquarters since no over-all Pacific theater command was organized and since the Central Pacific Army headquarters was supervised by POA, a superior headquarters with a larger jurisdiction.

proposals directly to his commander, Lt. Gen. Delos C. Emmons, until May 1943 and Lt. Gen. Robert C. Richardson, Jr., thereafter, than did chief chemical officers in other theaters and areas. As Unmacht himself phrased the relationship, "We receive a lot of encouragement and impetus from topside." [78] With the theater naval command, which stood in a position roughly comparable to supreme headquarters in other theaters, Unmacht had a good relationship although the Navy took little interest in chemical warfare until combat experience proved the value of the chemical mortar and flame throwers. Navy and Marine Corps officers assigned to chemical duties were usually junior, but commanders frequently consulted Unmacht on chemical supply and training. A reciprocal agreement was worked out whereby the CWS would use the Navy impregnation plant at Pearl Harbor in return for impregnating Navy uniforms. When in the summer of 1944 Navy interest in chemical warfare quickened, Admiral Nimitz, in his capacity as Commander in Chief, Pacific Fleet, appointed a chemical officer to his own staff—Capt. Tom B. Hill, USN, who worked in close cooperation with Unmacht.[79]

The Offensive Period in the Central Pacific

Organization of the Theater Chemical Office, 1943–45

On the eve of combat operations in the Central Pacific, Unmacht twice reorganized his office to reflect the increase in activities relating to combat planning and training. In January 1943 Captain Doty, recently promoted, became executive officer and chief of a new Intelligence Division. Reilly, now a captain, became chief of Plans and Training Division and was assigned an officer assistant. Except for redesignation as divisions, administration and supply remained unchanged from the 1942 organization. At the end of June 1943, with an increased workload and greater availability of officers, Unmacht again reorganized his office on a pattern very similar to that prescribed in prewar planning for a theater chemical office. Doty, now a major, became operations and executive officer. Intelligence Division was given the added duty of supervising technical functions. Unmacht

---

[78] Personal Ltr, Unmacht to Waitt, 29 Oct 42. CWS 314.7 Pers Files, MIDPAC.
[79] Waitt and Javits to CCWS, 15 Dec 44, Rpt of Trip to POA and SWPA. CWS 314.7 Observer Rpts.

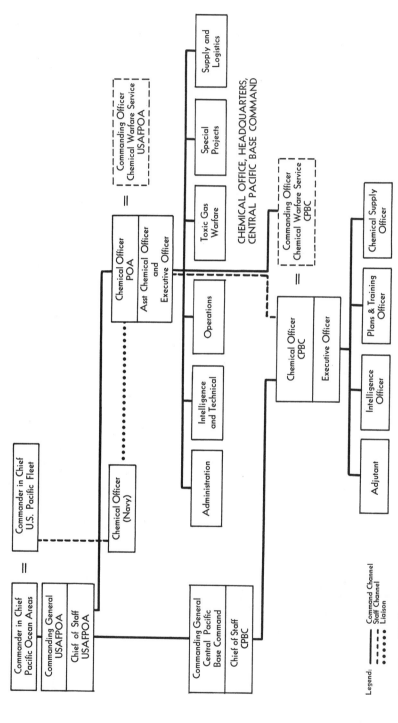

CHEMICAL OFFICE, HEADQUARTERS,
CENTRAL PACIFIC BASE COMMAND

Legend: ———— Command Channel
        ▪▪▪▪▪▪ Staff Channel
        ●●●●●● Liaison

Source: History, CWS USAFMIDPAC, Annexes Ia and IIa.

had detailed a few men with technical experience to set up a small laboratory with locally obtained equipment and supplies. At the end of 1943 a laboratory company arrived to assume technical duties. The Plans and Training Division was enlarged and redesignated Operations and Training Division.

The June 1943 reorganization established the form from which the theater chemical section varied but slightly until 1945. At that time an organization consisting of five policy and supervisory divisions and one administration division was approved. (*Chart 8*) Lt. Col. Edouard R. L. Doty, again promoted, remained as executive officer with duties as assistant chemical officer, supervisor of the theater chemical plan, and liaison officer to field chemical sections and the Navy. Operational planning, base development, personnel and unit assignments, and redevelopment planning were assigned to the Operations Division. Capt. Jerome K. Holmes, in civilian life a chemist, headed the Intelligence and Technical Division which supervised intelligence and laboratory operations and which prepared or supervised the preparation of all technical and intelligence reports. Maj. R. Beverly Caldwell headed the Special Projects Division which was charged with training, inspections, supervision of, and planning for, defense against biological warfare, and technical developments outside the usual laboratory sphere. The Toxic Gas Warfare Division was assigned supervision of gas warfare doctrine development, surveillance of toxic munitions, and liaison with the air forces, which in this theater, as in the rest of the world, had become virtually independent of the local Army command.

Colonel Unmacht delegated operating supply functions and detailed supply planning to the Chemical Office, Central Pacific Base Command, which had been organized under Maj. Roland P. Fournier on 1 July 1944. In his own office, Unmacht retained the Supply and Logistics Division. To this division the CWS chief assigned policy functions relating to operational projects and forecasts for requirements and transportation and analysis functions relating to supply reporting.

Gas Warfare Preparedness

The Chemical Section, Hawaiian Department, like the chemical sections all over the world, had a paramount interest in gas warfare preparedness. Although Unmacht had devoted most of his attention after the Pearl Harbor attack to immediate individual and collective protection, he also surveyed the department's ability to retaliate in the case of gas warfare. There were some toxics in the area, but the means of retaliation, like the possibility of being able to reach any enemy force, were indeed slim in 1942. Even had they been ample, however, the nearest target was so far away as to make the immediate possibility of retaliation a remote one. Unmacht set about improving the supply status and at the same time inaugurated both offensive and defensive training. He also arranged to check on both methods of training.

In June and July 1942 the War Department ordered chemical offensive training in the theaters, and the CWS in the Central Pacific complied by providing training for CWS units and chemical sections.[80] In August the department CWS initiated a schedule for spot-check inspections of Army units in the Central Pacific to determine their readiness for gas warfare. Of the 522 units inspected by the end of October, 12 percent proved to be thoroughly prepared, 69 percent satisfactorily prepared, and 19 percent partially prepared or without any preparation. Renewed training, especially of UGO's and UGNCO's, and new issues of supplies soon enabled all units to come up to acceptable standards of preparedness. While these preparedness measures were being accomplished, the War Department in December 1942 called for the submission of a gas warfare plan.[81]

The first Hawaiian Department gas warfare plan, which was coordinated with the local Navy and Marine Corps commands, was dispatched to the War Department on 8 February 1943. The plan simply indicated that in the event of gas warfare maximum use of available weapons and equipment would be made, and no request for special supplies was included. The heart of the plan consisted of a detailed plea for the immediate provision of chemical units and manpower, including a chemical weapons regiment, air and ground service troops, and chemical staff personnel.[82] The War Department at first indicated that no troops were available but in July requested restudy and resubmission of the troop request.[83] Unmacht replied by reviewing the problems of preparedness. In his opinion these were: (1) lack of

---

[80] Ltr, Unmacht to CG Hawaiian Dept, 7 Jan 43, sub: Theater Plans for Cml Warfare. CWS 314.7 Central Pacific Theater.

[81] *Ibid.*

[82] Ltr, CG Hawaiian Dept to TAG, 8 Feb 43, sub: Theater Plans for Cml Warfare. Hawaiian Dept AG 381.

[83] Ltr, Unmacht to CG Hawaiian Dept, 17 Aug 43, sub: Theater Plans for Cml Warfare. CWS 314.7 Central Pacific Theater.

suitable aircraft and trained airmen for toxic spray missions; (2) lack
of chemical troops for ground retaliation and for providing artificial
smoke protection; (3) inadequate decontamination troops and lack
of centralized control over decontamination squads in the Seventh
Air Force; and (4) insufficient manpower for service operations.
Unmacht asked first priority for service units and a smoke generator
battalion since such troops were urgently needed. He assigned a lower
priority to, but still cited an urgent need for, nine CWS staff officers
in addition to the fifteen authorized, and a chemical mortar battalion.[84]

During the period from the August 1943 reappraisal until November
of 1944, most of the service, smoke, and mortar units that the Central
Pacific CWS required in the absence of gas warfare were received from
the continental United States or were acquired when the South Pacific
Area organization was consolidated with the Central Pacific.[85] Also
during that period Unmacht was delegated the responsibility for co-
ordinating and consolidating all gas warfare plans for Army (including
Army Air Forces), Navy, Marine, and Coast Guard elements in the
Pacific Ocean Areas. Since the POA administrative organization had
long permitted Unmacht to work with all of these elements, he and
his staff were well acquainted with the needs and capabilities of each.
The consolidated gas warfare plan, formulated in June and July, was
consequently extensive and specific, even including an annex listing
and describing selected aerial objectives for possible retaliatory gas
attacks on the enemy. The first concern now was not service units or
weapons since the POA was well equipped or had the promise of being
well equipped early in 1945, but, rather, the strategic plan.[86] Also of
concern was the supply of toxics which, considering the scope of the
plan, still existed only in token quantities.

The strategic planning question was to be answered through the
co-ordination of the Pacific area plans by the United States Chemical
Warfare Committee. In General Porter's opinion the CWS would
have been ready for gas warfare in the Pacific had it broken out in
1944 or 1945[87] No new duties were indicated for the CWS POA by
the strategic plans. Unmacht continued his emphasis on gas warfare

[84] *Ibid.*

[85] Memo, Unmacht for Waitt, 4 Nov 44. CWS 314.7 Central Pacific Theater.

[86] Ltr, Unmacht to CCWS, 8 Jul 44, sub: Theater Plans for Cml Warfare. USAFCPA CWS 381 in
CWS 314.7 Central Pacific Theater.

[87] (1) Porter Interv, 24 Aug 61. (2) See Brophy and Fisher, *Organizing for War,* ch. IV.

and nongas warfare chemical training, on technical intelligence, and on the special projects assigned to his service.

Training in the Offensive Period

Divisional duties in the 1945 organization reflected the activities of the CWS in the Central Pacific in the period 1943–45. The tempo of training, as noted above, increased greatly during these years. During 1943, the CWS presented chemical warfare courses including four for various Marine Corps elements, two for Navy commands, and eight for Army combat organization UGO's and UGNCO's. Another chemical field maneuver with 1,376 participants was held 28–31 July. According to the G–3 report, this maneuver included:

... use of smoke, use and types of smoke-producing equipment, use of chemical land mines and minefields including students' laying of minefields, firing of chemical munitions from all types of weapons, decontamination methods and problems, use of protective clothing and equipment, demonstration of field hospital methods of handling gas casualties by Medical Corps personnel, tactical use of flame throwers, incendiaries, filling of airplane spray tanks, and spray attack on column [of students on a] road.[88]

The same report indicated that participants were favorably impressed by the maneuver.

In September 1943, two months before the first Central Pacific forces assault on Makin Atoll, the CWS presented the first course of instruction in the operation of the portable flame thrower. Many similar courses followed since in the Central Pacific as in the South and Southwest Pacific, the flame thrower became a valued infantry weapon and a particular favorite of the Marine Corps. From January to May 1944, Unmacht's immediate staff prepared a total of thirty-two courses, including, for the first time in February 1944, a course on the vehicle-mounted flame thrower developed and manufactured by the CWS, Navy, and Marines in Hawaii.

In July 1944, after giving courses or demonstrations for nearly 37,000 students, Unmacht's office turned over the operating training responsibility to the Chemical Officer, Central Pacific Base Command. Between 1 July 1944 and 31 August 1945 the CPBC office conducted

---

[88] Memo, Capt G. L. Quigley, CAC, for Col Keliher, OACofS G–3, Hawaiian Dept, 4 Aug 43, sub: Rpt on Dept Cml Field Exercise. Reproduced as an. I–c, History of Cml Sec USAFMIDPAC.

gas courses, lectures, and demonstrations for 38,933 students. In view of the fact that all of this instruction was given at the highest area Army (and sometimes Navy) level and that the usual organization and unit schools continued to be conducted, the training record of the CWS in the Central Pacific was a particularly outstanding one. The CENPAC CWS took full advantage of the fact that the Hawaiian Islands were used as a staging area through which many units and combat organizations were being rotated and given advanced training. Lt. Col. James E. Reilly, Unmacht's training officer for most of the active period, received the Legion of Merit for his accomplishments.

Chemical Warfare Intelligence

The intelligence activities of the Central Pacific chemical office actually began in January 1943 when Maj. Nelson McKaig, formerly a member of Unmacht's staff and then Chemical Officer, 25th Infantry Division, sent in from the South Pacific a Japanese gas mask. The staff of the improvised laboratory immediately set to work analyzing the mask. In February McKaig sent a shipment of Japanese chemical warfare materials. Since chemical intelligence combat teams did not begin to function in SWPA until the following November, Central Pacific laboratory analyses of such materials were among the earliest although the 42d Chemical Laboratory Company in SWPA had obtained some items.[89] Thereafter, a fairly regular flow of captured chemical items came to the theater CWS, mostly through intelligence channels. Lt. Robert E. Wingard, the first Intelligence Division chief who was able to devote most of his attention to the task, set up the chemical office as a clearinghouse for intelligence information. He both received information from and transmitted it to the theater intelligence authorities, OCCWS, the laboratory, and field chemical officers. In November 1943, Unmacht also assigned Wingard to the supervision of the CWS portion of an Army-Navy project for the study of micro-meteorological conditions in advanced Pacific bases. The data thus collected became a part of theater gas warfare planning, and the study was continued for the duration of the war. The Intelligence Division trained CWS field officers to collect meteorological data, and CWS elements of island garrison forces contributed to this collection.

---

[89] (1) See above, pp. 197, 202. (2) For an account of laboratory work, see below, Chapter VII.

Holmes succeeded Wingard in July 1944. Holmes concentrated on widening the field of intelligence liaison and on building up an extensive file of intelligence information not only of theater origin but also of that originating in other theaters or from allied sources. The Intelligence Division also compiled catalogs of enemy matériel for ready field reference. The section staff interviewed CWS officers returning from combat in order to find out and publish lessons learned. Holmes combed the entire catalog compilation for the most significant gas warfare data which he included in an annex to the theater gas warfare plan.

Special Projects and Technical Activities

The CWS in the Central Pacific devoted a major part of its attention during World War II to special projects and technical developments. The first special project, as recounted above, was the equipping and training of civilians in gas defense. In connection with this first project, CWS officers, Medical Corps officers, and civil defense officials developed, tested, and supervised the manufacture of gas protective hoods for small children. The hoods were made more attractive for children by the addition of "bunny" ears. Officials also supplied the "bunny" hood to patients in the leper colony on Molokai Island.

As the combat period approached, Colonel Unmacht and his staff turned their attention from numerous projects in gas warfare defense and decontamination to the nontoxic chemical weapons and munitions. Their work on the flame thrower tank, and later on stabilized flame thrower fuels, was the outstanding overseas development work of the worldwide CWS.[90] Unmacht was a strong proponent of the use of the 4.2-inch chemical mortar with high-explosive shell, and the development, testing, and combat supply of a landing craft mortar mounting for Pacific amphibious operations represented one of his achievements in the field of combat support. The mortar gun boat development was also a noteworthy example of Army-Navy co-operation.

As did the chief chemical officers in the European and North African theaters, Unmacht treated defense against biological warfare (BW) on a special project basis. During the period 1941–44, he co-operated with the theater surgeon, Brig. Gen. Edgar King, as well as other

[90] See Brophy, Miles, and Cochrane, *From Laboratory to Field*, ch. VII.

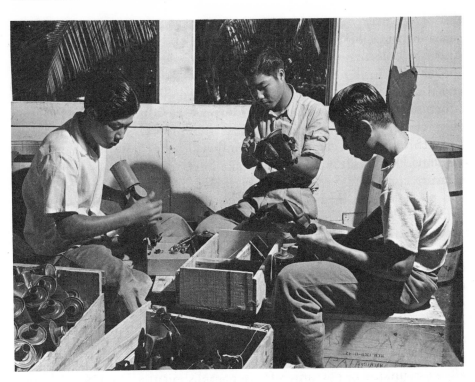

HONOLULU HIGH SCHOOL BOYS REPAIRING GAS MASKS FOR CIVILIAN USE

service chiefs in inspecting water, ice, and food supplies. CWS units participated in insect and rodent control. These measures were extended to the forward bases through garrison force medical officers. In August 1944, Unmacht was designated to succeed the surgeon as theater bacteriological warfare officer in keeping with the assignment of that function to the CWS on a global basis. Major Caldwell, as Unmacht's representative, then arranged a co-operative plan with the surgeon under which the CWS accepted the primary responsibility for BW intelligence, the physical protection and training of troops, and strategic and tactical BW defense planning. The Medical Department reassumed the primary responsibility for inspection of food and water, the biological protection of troops, epidemiological control, and the care and treatment of casualties. Caldwell, subsequently promoted to lieutenant colonel, and Maj. John O. Clements of CPBC performed the CWS tasks and worked with the medical officers in the performance of their duties. A War Department observer reported in April 1945 that the theater was "quite BW conscious," and he found that intelligence information and defensive plans met the required standard.[91]

Colonel Unmacht was an unusually dynamic officer who was not afraid to use his energy in any way he felt might contribute to the war effort. Few other chemical officers would have believed possible the overseas development, much less the assembly, of a main armament flame thrower tank. Unmacht not only believed it possible—he got the job done. His willingness to undertake large responsibilities in no small measure contributed to the success of the CWS in the Central Pacific and to the esteem in which the service was held. The Central Pacific situation also contributed because the commander, not being also a supreme commander as in other theaters, had the time to give support to his services. The Central Pacific Army commander did not command combat operations, but his support as senior Army commander in the theater for most of the war made easier the operation of the CWS.[92] The CWS also enjoyed an excellent relationship with the POA and Navy commands in the area because it was able to provide services and weapons support when the Navy and the Marine Corps wanted them. The Central Pacific Area and the military facilities in the area offered a unique opportunity for accomplishment. The CWS administration in the theater was almost ideally suited to these circumstances.

The environment and the area command situation in SWPA, by contrast, were not amenable to the CWS. The chemical officers in SWPA strove mightily and ingeniously to provide chemical weapons and equipment and to insure preparedness. Their contributions were significant, especially in connection with portable flame throwers and mortars, but distances and difficulties of communication hampered them. Even more hampering was the disadvantageous position of the highest CWS echelon in the SWPA service and supply organization. While Copthorne maintained that the CWS SWPA was well regarded in the theater throughout the war, the CWS until late in the war faced the obstacles in performing its gas warfare preparedness duties of working through two superior echelons. Gas warfare preparedness in the United States, in North Africa, and in Europe, was a joint and Allied

---

[91] Rpt, Lt Col W. S. Moore to CMIS, Apr 45, as cited in History, Cml Sec USAFMIDPAC.
[92] The commander of the Tenth Army, which formed in Hawaii for the Ryukyu Campaign, was senior to General Richardson, Central Pacific commander.

concern, but in SWPA there was no joint or Allied agency through which Copthorne could work formally.

Copthorne and his subordinates evolved some excellent, indirect methods, such as the conferences and the intelligence and training teams, for presenting the contributions of the CWS. Through the use of these methods, Copthorne accomplished co-ordination of his service. Unmacht accomplished a similar co-ordination through his relationships with his superior commands. Rowan achieved his co-ordination through a combination of personal diplomacy and supply control. Shadle in the MTO did not see the necessity for a close control of his service. He accordingly emphasized a lesser co-ordination than the other chief chemical officers through staff work in his own headquarters and supply troubleshooting on problems which strong field chemical sections could not handle.

CHAPTER VI

Theater Supply: Pacific

Foundation of Chemical Supply in Australia

Forming a Theater Stock

Chemical warfare supplies available to the United States Army Forces in Australia in December 1941 consisted of 14,000 empty 100-pound bomb casings, a small amount of protective equipment in the hands of troops, and the maintenance allowances brought in by the 3d Chemical Laboratory Company. This company was equipped with the training gas mask, a light, snout-type mask with canister directly attached to the facepiece,[1] some 1½-quart decontaminating apparatus, and a little antigas protective ointment. The unit possessed no non-corrosive decontaminating agent for use in the apparatus, no bleach (chloride of lime) for area decontamination, and no antigas shoe impregnite. Units and individuals subsequently arriving in Australia did have personal protective items and decontaminating materials. Units also arrived with small maintenance stocks.[2]

USAFIA chemical officers collected the maintenance stocks from incoming organizations and units and these constituted the first theater chemical warfare supply. Even Task Force 6814, soon to be the American Division, added to this stock when it stopped over in Melbourne on the way to New Caledonia.[3] The 32d and 41st Infantry Divisions, on arriving in Australia in the spring of 1942, also contributed. The chemical stockpile further increased as the War Depart-

---

[1] For description of the various CWS gas masks, see Brophy, Miles, and Cochrane, *From Laboratory to Field*, Chapter XIV.

[2] Morgan Interv, 1 Oct 45.

[3] Task force 6814 and the American Division are identified in John Miller, jr., *Guadalcanal: The First Offensive*, UNITED STATES ARMY IN WORLD WAR II (Washington, 1949), p. 215.

ment diverted to Australia supplies which could not be landed in the Philippines and as theater chemical supply officers bought what they could in the local market. The USAFIA CWS carefully hoarded all equipment for the use of forces which at any moment might move out to fight the enemy. Issues were kept to a minimum in the rear areas, and some issues of Australian gas masks were made. By 30 June 1942 the CWS inventory stood at 2,098 short tons.[4]

War Department Policy for the Southwest Pacific Area

The CWS in SWPA was not yet aware, at the end of June, of the War Department supply policy; they had heard nothing at all from the United States in the first four months after the establishment of the USAFIA and were to have no word from the Office of the Chief, Chemical Warfare Service, until July.[5] The basic War Department plan was dated 22 January 1942, and the specific plan for the forces in Australia was dated 2 February 1942. The specific War Department plan called for 90 days' supply of all classes other than ammunition, computed on the standard tables of basic allowances (TBA); 90 days' supply of ground ammunition, computed on the basis of a special ammunition day of supply for weapons in the theater; and five months' supply of aerial bombs, ammunition, and pyrotechnics, computed according to a special allowance per aircraft in Australia and the Netherlands East Indies. The Adjutant General instructed the technical services in the United States to compute allowances and set up shipments to the San Francisco Port of Embarkation, which was charged with shipment to the theater. The chiefs of the technical services were also charged with allotting funds to the theater for the operation of their services in the theater and for the local procurement of matériel.[6]

OCCWS immediately began to set up shipments against the War Department plan in accordance with strength figures furnished. It

---

[4] (1) Interv, Hist Off with Maj Arthur H. Williams, Jr., 23 Jan 46. (2) Office of the Chief of Engineers, GHQ, AFPAC, *Engineers of the Southwest Pacific*, vol. VII, *Engineer Supply* (Washington, 1949), Table 5, p. 58.

[5] (1) Morgan Interv, 1 Oct 45. (2) Personal Ltr, Copthorne, CCmlO USAFIA, to Wilson, Chief Field Serv OCCWS, 13 Jul 42. CWS 319.1 1942.

[6] (1) Ltr, TAG to CG USAFIA, Chiefs Supply Arms and Servs, *et al.*, 22 Jan 42, sub: Sup of Overseas Depts, Theaters, and Separate Bases. AG 400 (1–17–42)MSC–D–M. (Later to be revised as WD Memo W–700–8–42, 10 Oct 42. See above, ch. III). (2) Ltr, AG to CG USAFIA, Chiefs Sup Arms and Servs, 2 Feb 42, sub: Sup of U.S. Army Forces in the Australian Area. AG 400(1–31–42)MSC–D–M.

calculated requirements for toxics according to the allowances for ammunition and aerial bombs. Only mustard gas was available for immediate supply. CWS supply authorities questioned the shipment of mustard gas without the specific authority which had always been necessary for toxic shipments. They also questioned the quantity to be shipped because they lacked aircraft strength figures on which aerial toxic requirements computations were based. General Brett, USAFIA commander, who was probably unaware of these questions within the War Department, nevertheless answered them by cabling a request for 1,000 tons of mustard. The Chief of Staff queried General MacArthur as to his desires and, receiving a confirmation of Brett's request, in April directed the shipment. The Services of Supply reduced the quantity to 870 tons because of shipping space shortage. OCCWS effected shipment on 15 April 1942.[7]

At the time the mustard was being shipped, the theater forces were compiling a matériel status report which reached the United States at the end of May. According to OCCWS figures, most items were in excess of allowances and only one item, the chemical land mine, was in short supply. OCCWS attributed excesses to the shipments diverted from the Philippines and to cabled special requirements, such as the one for mustard and another for incendiary bombs which the Commanding General, Army Air Forces, had ordered shipped.[8] In fact, OCCWS apologies for excesses were misleading. Theater chemical officers still considered the supply short because, although they had no exact knowledge of strength in the theater or supplies in the hands of troops, they rightly anticipated a considerable build-up in theater strength.[9] Later War Department plans for other theaters provided for substantial build-up on the basis of anticipated strength far in excess of current strength, but not until the end of the war in Europe was in sight did a build-up concept apply to the Pacific. To illustrate, OCCWS computed the July 1942 report of chemical materials in Australia according to the theater strength and estimated that the

---

[7] (1) Ltr, Chief Field Serv OCCWS to TAG, 15 Feb 42, sub: Shipment of Mustard Gas to Australia. CWS 320.2/45-79. (2) Memo, ACofS OPD for TAG, 28 Mar 42, sub: Mustard Gas in Australia. OPD 475.92 sec. 1. (3) Memo, Actg Chief Distr Br SOS for CCWS, 19 Apr 42, Shipment of Mustard Gas to Australia. ASF SP 400(4-19-42). (4) Msg, CCWS to CG USAFIA, 15 Apr 42. CM-OUT 1296, also in CWS 320.2/54-79.

[8] Memo, ACCWS for CG SOS, Attn: Chief Distr Br, 14 Jun 42, sub: Status of Matériel in Australia. CWS 320.2/75 (6-14-42).

[9] (1) Ltr, Copthorne to Wilson, 13 Jul 42. (2) Williams Interv, 23 Jan 46.

chemical stock had reached 98 percent of the authorized level. There were, at that time, 95,021 service gas masks for the United States forces in Australia, and this quantity was estimated to be 9,000 more than the allowance. Yet, also in July 1942, the Army Service Forces asked the chiefs of the technical services if they were prepared to support 1,000,000 men in the Pacific.[10] On the assumption that at least half of this strength would be assigned to SWPA, this would mean approximately one mask for every five men as opposed to the European theater planning ratio of one mask in stock for each individual who would already have an initial issue mask.[11] Even though masks and shipping space were not available at the time, some method of supply planning that would have anticipated SWPA needs in advance of an increase in strength would have caused less confusion.

Theater Retaliatory Preparedness for Gas Warfare

There was little that Colonel Copthorne, Chief Chemical Officer, USAFIA, and in July USASOS, could do to order enough supplies to meet an increase in SWPA strength except to ask that supplies be sent in quantities greater than the SWPA allowance. Under War Department supply procedures he could make requests to exceed allowances only by explaining at length that unusual circumstances would result in the use of extra supplies or that service operations would require supplies not listed in the War Department plan for SWPA. The supplies which prepared SWPA for retaliation in case gas warfare should start were mostly obtained, like the first shipment of mustard gas, by such requests to exceed the allowances. The CWS SWPA needed toxic-filling plants, which were not on the allowance list, to handle this first shipment. Copthorne accordingly cabled an order for plants. The plants arrived in Australia in July but drawings and assembly instructions, which were not available in Australia, did not accompany them. The mustard shipment reached Australia in August. In order to store the gas in newly established toxic gas yards at Darra, Queensland, and Geelong, Victoria, CWS officers assembled the filling plants

---

[10] (1) Monthly Matériel Status Rpt 403, USAFIA, as of 15 Jul 42, ACofS G-4 WDGS to CCWS, 20 Aug 42. CWS 320.5/54-79.   (2) Memo, ACofS Opns SOS for Chiefs of Engrs, CWS, *et al.*, 24 Jul 42, sub: Storage Facilities for Pacific Opns. AFS SPOPN 486.1; also in CWS 320.2/23-26.

[11] The European ratio was determined by comparing 1943 mask authorization (Baldwin, Bingham, and Pritchard, Readiness for Gas Warfare in the Theaters of Operations) with theater projected strength (Ruppenthal, *Logistical Support of the Armies*, I, 128-29).

by guesswork. The 14,000 100-pound bomb casings were available for filling only because USAFIA had been unable to ship them to their original destination, the Philippines. While most of the mustard was used in filling these bombs, some of it was set aside for filling toxic land mines which had been procured in Australia. M10 aircraft spray tanks, which came from War Department allowance to SWPA, arrived without accessories and mounting instructions. The War Department also shipped some toxic-filled artillery shell from allowances.[12]

In March of 1943, when the first gas warfare plan was produced, toxics had been further dispersed to six toxic storage yards. One, near Charters Towers, Queensland, contained 115 tons of bulk agents, 5,900 filled 100-pound bombs, about 1,000 empty spray tanks, and 600 empty bombs. Another, at Kangaroo, north of Townsville, contained 5,500 mustard-filled 100-pound bombs and more than 20,000 artillery shells. The enlarged Darra yard held nearly 435 tons of bulk agents, nearly 90,000 artillery rounds, a small supply of toxic smoke candles, and empty bombs, spray tanks, and land mines. A new Columboola yard 200 miles west of Brisbane held 11,000 mustard-filled 100-pound bombs, and a new yard at Kingswood near Sydney stored only artillery shell (approximately 53,000 rounds). The original yard at Geelong stored 400 tons of bulk mustard and 3,160 toxic smoke candles. The CWS SWPA estimated that in the event of gas warfare the stock at Charters Towers would be sufficient for an immediate retaliatory strike. Then, within seven hours, spray tanks could be filled and delivered for a 16-plane spray mission. The spray mission could thereafter be sustained from other stocks for 63 plane missions. More missions could be flown only if some spray tanks were returned after the flights and this was not expected because spray tanks were normally jettisoned. The artillery shell could not be used prior to movement to forward areas, and no time estimate was given for that movement, presumably because the time could not be calculated in the face of uncertainty as to the available forms of transport. There was at the time no assurance that forward artillery would be on hand to fire the shell since only one American artillery piece had gone forward for the recently ended Papua Campaign.[13]

---

[12] (1) Ltr, Copthorne to Wilson, 13 Jul 42. (2) Morgan Interv, 1 Oct 45. (3) Williams Interv, 23 Jan 46.

[13] CinC GHQ SWPA to TAG, 7 Apr 43, Rpt, Theater Plans for Cml Warfare (hereafter cited as Theater Plans, Mar 43). GHQ AG 381 (12-8-42)C.

Theater Defense Preparedness for Gas Warfare

On the defensive side, as noted above, every individual in the theater was allotted a gas mask, and there was a small reserve, adequate on the TBA basis, of service masks.[14] In the opinion of the chemical officers, one undoubtedly shared by the troops, the 5-pound service mask was of very limited utility in the tropics. It could not be worn for any length of time in a hot climate with even an acceptable degree of discomfort, and it was too heavy and bulky to be carried by troops, who could function efficiently only under a minimum burden. The SWPA Chemical Section accordingly requisitioned 228,000 training masks or lightweight substitutes for the equipment of, at least, all assault echelons, and the 2,000 training masks in the theater were earmarked for this purpose.[15] OCCWS shipped 139,000 training masks which represented the available supply since training masks were also in demand elsewhere. The masks arrived, as requested, waterproofed; that is, both ends of the canister were sealed. The difficulty with the waterproofing job done in the United States was that the seals were paper and had to be torn off to put the mask in ready condition. The seals could not be restored by the individual user of the mask even if the materials had been provided. SWPA chemical officers thereupon set out to design restorable seals. Capt. Stephen Penler, commander of the 412th (later 62d) Chemical Depot Company, suggested a "milk bottle cap" for the valve (outer) end of the canister.[16] A Sydney paper manufacturer succeeded, after several attempts, in producing the bottle cap seal. These seals were packed in small cans and the can inserted into a pocket sewn into the mask carrier. The open (mask end) of the canister was sealed with a rubber plug, and Capt. John Senter designed a quick acting clamp for securing the canister to the facepiece. Both plug and clamp were also locally procured. The 10th Chemical Maintenance Company set up a production line and performed the not inconsiderable task of modifying masks and carriers.[17] More than a year later the CWS in the United States provided a reusable rubber cap which could be attached to the valve end of the canister.

[14] Theater Plans, Mar 43.

[15] Ibid.

[16] Captain Penler was killed in an air accident in December 1942.

[17] (1) Ltr, Copthorne to Hist Off, 16 Feb 51. (2) Lt Col Irving R. Mollen, Chemical Warfare Sup—SWPA, World War II, 16 May 52. MS in CMLHO. This article also appeared in *Armed Forces Chemical Journal*, vol. XI, No. 2 (March–April, 1957), pp. 34–36, and No. 3 (May–June, 1957), pp. 31–33.

Furnishing protective clothing was an even greater problem than supplying the mask. In SWPA, as elsewhere in the world, protective clothing storage and issue was a quartermaster responsibility, but impregnating the clothing with antigas chemicals was a CWS responsibility.[18] Also in SWPA, as elsewhere, the CWS and the Quartermaster Corps worked in close co-operation. The first supply of protective clothing came from the United States in July 1942. Because fighting would be in the tropics, it was unfortunate that much of the clothing, including underwear, was woolen. Just as the supply arrived instructions were received that all garments must be modified by the insertion of gussets and double flies to afford increased protection at trousers and shirt openings.[19] Quartermaster employees made the gussets and flies and inserted them; the CWS rented a dry-cleaning establishment in Melbourne for the dual purpose of impregnating the gussets and flies and of testing an improvised impregnating process. Copthorne secured the formula for the American impregnite from the Australians who got it from the chemical warfare experimental station in England. The direct channels of communication with the United States had again failed.[20]

The experience in the rented dry-cleaning plant proved the improvised impregnating process acceptable. The CWS acquired two English-made Maja trichlorethylene dry-cleaning plants and three commercial laundry dryers, and by the middle of October had this equipment in operation in a factory in Sydney. There the CWS impregnated such clothing as the quartermaster had in stock.[21]

Copthorne, writing to Brig. Gen. Alexander Wilson in OCCWS, questioned the sense of providing prescribed double-layer (long underwear, outer garments, gloves, sox, leggings, and hood) protection in a climate where that much clothing could certainly not be worn.[22] Wilson replied that the War Department was working on worldwide protective policy and that, for the time being, the SWPA CWS could

---

[18] See Alvin P. Stauffer, *The Quartermaster Corps: Operations in the War Against Japan*, UNITED STATES ARMY IN WORLD WAR II (Washington, 1956), pp. 202–03.

[19] Ltr, TAG to CINC SWPA *et al.*, 14 Jul 42, sub: Cml Warfare Protective Clothing. AG 420 (5 Jul 42) MS–SPOPS–M.

[20] (1) Ltr, Copthorne to Hist Off, 16 Feb 51.   (2) Personal Ltr, Copthorne to Porter, 14 Oct 42.

[21] Ltr, Copthorne to Porter, 14 Aug 42.

[22] A survey made in 1943 disclosed that 38 percent of rear area troops in New Guinea wore no underwear whereas the figure for combat area troops who dispensed with these items was 100 percent. Grothaus and Brady to CCWS, 29 Mar 44, Rpt on Visit to Southwest, South and Central Pacific Areas. CWS 314.7 Observer Rpts.)

only furnish the prescribed level under the assumption that the area commander would weigh the risk of gas warfare against the efficiency of the soldier and instruct subordinate commanders as to his policy on wearing protective clothing. The question of policy was never settled to theater satisfaction. The March 1943 SWPA gas warfare plans provided only that outer garments and leggings would be stocked in forward areas while underwear was held in rear reserve.[23] The world-wide policy adopted over a year later, in April 1944, provided that only 15 percent of SWPA soldiers would have double-layer protection available.[24] Other forward area combat and service troops, or 35 per-cent of the area command, were given one and a half layer (outer garments, gloves, leggings, and hood, plus cotton drawers) protection, and the rear area troops, estimated at 50 percent of the command, were not provided with any protective clothing.[25] Copthorne believed that mid-thigh length knit cotton shorts would afford nearly as good pro-tection as the cotton drawers and would be bearable in the tropics.[26] The 1944 plan permitted the use of knit shorts, when available, for one and a half layer protection.

Other items of protection against gas warfare were the decontami-nants and the equipment to disperse them. The decontaminants in-cluded personal protective ointment, noncorrosive decontaminant for vehicles and equipment, and bleach, the area decontaminant. Since the M1 protective ointment was in short supply and regarded by SWPA officers as of doubtful effectiveness, the CWS SWPA improvised an individual protective kit consisting of swabs, kerosene (a solvent for vesicant gases), an alkaline soft soap produced locally, and a half measure of M1 ointment.[27] General Porter advised Copthorne that the M1 ointment had been reappraised and redesignated M4 and that new techniques for its use had been evolved. OCCWS at the time considered the M4 ointment effective without a solvent or soap to accompany it.[28] The solvent and soap in the SWPA kit served as a substitute for oint-ment until a sufficient quantity of M4 ointment was received late in

[23] Theater Plans, Mar 43.

[24] Ltr, TAG to CINC SWPA et al., 24 Apr 44, sub: Cml Warfare Protective Clothing Accessories and Equip. AG 420 (28 Mar 44) OB–S–SPOPP–M.

[25] See Brophy and Fisher, Organizing for War, ch. IV.

[26] Ltr, CCmlO USASOS to CCWS, 29 Jan 43, sub: Use of Jockey Midway Shorts. CWS USASOS 422.

[27] Copthorne to Porter, 14 Oct 42.

[28] Pers Ltr, Porter to Copthorne, 12 Nov 42.

1942. The War Department at the same time sent enough noncorrosive decontaminating agent and its disperser, the 1½-quart apparatus. Bleach supplies were growing, but the theater was still short of full allowance. Chemical officers believed that bleach would deteriorate in the tropics. Although the first tests proved that American bleach was standing up well, SWPA officers found after a few months that both the bleach and its containers deteriorated. To fill shortages, the CWS bought bleach from the Australians. The supply men discovered a double benefit in this procurement. Not only was the bleach more readily obtained, but also it was more stable in the tropics and the containers could better withstand the inevitable rough handling. The supply was unfortunately limited by the small production of chlorine in Australia. As for the dispersing equipment—the 3-gallon hand decontaminating apparatus and the 400-gallon power-driven apparatus —the hand apparatus was available in considerable quantity, more than a thousand in excess of allowance in February 1943, and the stock of powered apparatus, 115 in February, was sufficient for critical needs even though 18 short of allowance. It is very doubtful that much area decontamination would have been possible in the jungle in any case. Gas detection devices and gas alarms were not available although the latter could be improvised.[29]

The one protective item of which there was a definite overage was the gasproof curtain. The curtain was designed for World War I trench warfare and was still issued on a World War I basis of two curtains for 20 men. The SWPA CWS asked the San Francisco port to stop shipping curtains and suggested to area forces that those on hand might be used for foxhole covers in event of vesicant gas attack, since the individual protective cover was not yet available to serve that purpose. OCCWS soon changed the basis of issue to two per 200 men and designated the curtains for use at command posts, communications centers, and medical installations.[30]

[29] (1) Copthorne to Wilson, 13 Jul 42. (2) Copthorne to Porter, 14 Oct 42. (3) Mollen, Cml Warfare Sup—SWPA, World War II. (4) Monthly Matériel Status Rpt 403, USAFIA, as of 15 Jul 42. (5) Theater Plans, Mar 43. (6) Baldwin, Bingham, and Pritchard, Readiness for Gas Warfare in Theaters of Opns, app. B.

[30] (1) Copthorne to Porter, 14 Oct 42. (2) Porter to Copthorne, 12 Nov 42.

Theater Chemical Supply Status—End of the Preparatory Phase

In sum, the CWS SWPA had by the end of 1942 reached the status of gas warfare supply, both offensive and defensive, reflected in the area gas warfare plans reported to the War Department on March 1943. That is, except for gas detection, SWPA could defend against any gas warfare emergency involving troops likely to be in direct contact with the enemy. Offensively, the air forces could make an immediate retaliatory strike and although they could sustain retaliation for only a brief period, this might have been sufficient considering the distances which isolated individual enemy forces in the theater. The big problem was service in the event of gas warfare. The only available facility for clothing impregnation was the improvised Sydney plant. The CWS estimated that in the event of gas warfare, it would need several chemical impregnating companies, three additional air service units, and one chemical composite company per forward area division. The ability of services other than the CWS to handle gas warfare was also dependent upon increasing service capability. For example, Australian hospitals would have to bear the load of gas casualty treatment because the American hospitals did not then have enough manpower and facilities. Forward area medical service would have been sadly deficient for the same reasons although the chief chemical officer and the SWPA surgeon had co-operated in improvising a field gas treatment kit which would have afforded assistance to medical officers in the field.[31]

While the SWPA supply of most gas warfare items could be considered adequate, the supply of nongas warfare chemical items was clearly inadequate. There were few hand grenades and little smoke equipment. In fact, smoke munitions were so scarce that Colonel Copthorne ordered the improvisation and testing of a smoke apparatus using FS mixture procured in Australia. There were some flame throwers of the kind that had proved unemployable in the Papua Campaign, but there were no mortars and only 1,000 rounds of mortar shell. The general chemical inventory, which from July to December 1942 had grown from 2,098 short tons to 5,093 short tons, was therefore mostly gas warfare items. The greatest gain, from 299 to 1,641 tons, had been in Class V, ammunition, the class into which the toxics

---

[31] (1) Ltr, CCmlO USASOS to CWS, 26 Jan 43, sub: Directions for Use of Cml Warfare Sups. CWS USASOS 461 APO 501 (Directions). (2) Williams Interv, 23 Jan 46. (3) Theater Plans, Mar 43.

fell. During the last six months of 1942, the CWS had received 4,983 short tons of matériel. The bulk of this total, 4,645 short tons, came from imports, mostly from the United States, but 139 tons, the greater portion of which was laboratory equipment and production supplies, had come from distress cargoes (cargoes landed in Australia because they could not reach destinations in the combat zone), and 199 tons came from local procurement. Although the latter figure was small, its size is not the measure of its importance since most of the items so procured were critical.[32]

The Tyranny of Climate and Distance

Establishment of a New Guinea base in August 1942 and the events of the Papua Campaign brought sharply into focus the problems dealing with the condition of both gas warfare and nongas warfare chemical matériel. SWPA chemical officers had been aware from the first that much of the equipment received was rushed production not of the highest quality, but conditions of storage and issue in New Guinea demonstrated that every weakness in design, manufacture, inspection, packaging, and shipment was magnified many times when items were subjected to the extremes of heat, humidity, and rough handling unavoidable in the tropics and semitropics. Sometimes these problems could be resolved or reduced to manageable proportions in SWPA; sometimes they could be met by improvements in the United States; sometimes area forces simply had to adjust to living with the problems. Often a combination of these solutions applied, as in the case of the flame throwers, for example.

Bleach

The deterioration of bleach, mentioned above, was another problem which called forth a joint effort but which was never solved with complete satisfaction. SWPA received and stored bleach in light-gauge, painted and unpainted steel drums of 70-, 100-, 140-, and 300-pound capacity. Handling the larger drums was a problem, but it became apparent, late in 1942, that the handling difficulty was insignificant compared to the problem arising from corrosion of the containers and

---

[32] (1) Morgan Interv, 1 Oct 45.   (2) Copthorne to Porter, 14 Oct 42.   (3) Office of the Chief of Engineers, GHQ, AFPAC, *Engineer Supply*, pp. 57–58, Tables 4 and 5.

deterioration of the bleach. Copthorne in December 1942 ordered a
survey of bleach in semitropical and tropical storage to determine how
great the loss might be. Base section chemical officers found that all
the 100-pound nonpainted drums surveyed had corroded and that the
bleach had deteriorated below the standard acceptable for decontamination. Corrosion of larger unpainted drums, for some unexplained
reason, was negligible while 77.2 percent of 100-pound drums painted
brown had corroded. Orange-painted drums in both 70- and 100-
pound sizes had stood up well. In all, the CWS turned over 25 tons
of deteriorated bleach to the engineers for water purification use. A
few weeks later the New Guinea base reported corroding drums and
deteriorating bleach. Copthorne could only advise that, since there was
probably no solution other than the impractical one of lacquering the
drums inside and out, deteriorated bleach should be turned over to
other services and replacement requisitioned. A part of the replacement could come from Australian sources, but the bulk would have
to come from the United States.[33]

OCCWS was at work on the problem when Copthorne informed it
of his experience. The War Department CWS finally succeeded in
obtaining a more stable bleach and in improving the container,[34] but
the tropical climate continued to take its toll in every storage place
from Australia to the Philippines. Fortunately, the deteriorated bleach
was still adequate for the hygienic uses to which the Quartermaster
Corps and the Corps of Engineers could put it. Because of this secondary use, the demands on critically short transportation were no greater
than they would have been had each service obtained its own supply.
The CWS SWPA was forced to adjust to the demands of continuous
survey of stocks and handling transfers.[35]

Noncorrosive Decontaminating Agent

Another decontaminant problem concerned the noncorrosive decontaminating agent (DANC). The agent was a mixture of solvent,
acetylene tetrachloride, and a dry chemical known as RH 195. The

---

[33] (1) Ltr, CCmlO USASOS to CCWS, 10 Dec 42, sub: Corrosion of Chloride of Lime Containers
(CWS USASOS 470.6), and 1st Ind, CCWS to CCmlO USASOS, 24 Feb 43. CWS SPCVO 470.6
(12-10-42). (2) Ltr, CWO Serv Comd APO 502 to CCmlO USASOS, 14 Jan 43, no sub, and 1st
Ind, CCmlO USASOS to CWO Serv Comd APO 502, 2 Feb 43.

[34] Brophy, Miles, and Cochrane, *From Laboratory to Field*, ch XVI.

[35] Mollen, Cml Warfare Sup—SWPA, World War II.

two components were shipped and stored unmixed in a 2-compartment 6-gallon drum with the RH 195 packed in the compartment above the acetylene tetrachloride. The dry chemical apparently corroded the seal between the two compartments allowing the contents to mix; the resulting mixure had a life of about three months. Drums dented in shipment almost inevitably corroded because the lacquer on interior surfaces scaled off around the dent. After the first discovery of this packaging deficiency in October 1942, base section chemical depot troops opened dented drums and transferred serviceable RH 195 to bottles. If the chemical had combined with the solvent, the mixture was stored for its serviceable life, and when manpower and equipment were available the solvent was reclaimed at the end of that life. The area CWS obtained a crimping machine to reseal drums containing new and reclaimed solvent. The War Department CWS strengthened the RH 195 compartment, made it of a metal more receptive to preservative lacquer, provided a corrosion-proof plastic gasket between compartments, and, eventually, designed a new dual container. But still the CWS in the Pacific had trouble—the old container continued to come through the supply system. One base section received 14,000 old containers in the four months ending in September 1943. The noncorrosive decontaminating agent problem was one that the CWS SWPA learned to live with.[36]

The one and a half quart decontaminating apparatus for dispersing the noncorrosive decontaminant and the 3-gallon apparatus were poorly crated. The crate consisted of a wooden frame with a cardboard liner; both cardboard and wood frequently failed with almost disastrous results when the crates were used as a base in warehouse stocks.[37] Another minor but annoying packaging defect was in the pack for shoe impregnite. The War Department CWS shipped the preparation in small cans packed in cardboard boxes. The boxes were too heavy for one man to handle, and the cardboard simply disintegrated after brief exposure to the weather. The CWS solved this problem by switching to small wooden boxes.[38]

---

[36] (1) Ltr, CCmlO USASOS to CCWS, 16 Nov 42, sub: Deterioration of RH 195 Containers. CWS USASOS GSCW 400.2. (2) Ltr, CCWS to CCmlO USASOS, 18 Dec 42, sub: Deterioration of RH 195 Containers. CWS SPCVO 470.6 (12–18–42). (3) Ltr, CCmlO USASOS to CCWS, 29 Sep 43, sub: Defective DANC Containers (CWS USASOS GSCW), with 1st Ind, ACCWS Field Opns to CCmlO USASOS, 25 Oct 43. CWS SPCVO 457 APO 501 (29 Sep 43). (4) Grothaus-Brady Rpt.
[37] Grothaus-Brady Rpt.
[38] Morgan Interv, 1 Oct 45.

The Gas Mask

A considerably more serious problem arose from the effect of the jungle climate on gas masks and carriers. Fungi attacked the glass lens of the Australian gas masks which American troops were using. Molds and mildew covered and rotted gas mask carriers and the harness of the mask itself. Rust and corrosion ate away canisters, buckles, and rivets. In the 41st Infantry Division the chemical officer, Colonel Arthur, prescribed a daily brushing of the carrier, but this only retarded the growth of mold and mildew. Furthermore, brushing was possible only for masks kept by individuals, who usually had them only for short periods. Assault troops carried masks in landing and dropped them as soon as the risk of initiation of gas warfare was determined to be slight. These masks were uncared for until chemical officers could assemble details or obtain service troops to collect, inspect, and store them. In early operations losses were large, as much as 45 percent in one assault, and the number of recovered masks rendered unserviceable was also large. Better recovery techniques, especially those evolved when service detachments landed with assault troops, reduced losses to 5 percent and greatly increased the number of serviceable masks recovered.[39]

OCCWS believed that the SWPA mask problems might be solved by the introduction of the lightweight service mask in 1943. The lightweight mask and its carrier were more rugged than the training mask then in use in SWPA, and the carrier was water resistant and therefore was more resistant to mold and mildew. Also, the CWS provided an adhesive tape waterproofing for the canister. Colonel Arthur set up a wearing test of the mask in the 41st Division. The facepiece was plainly superior to that of the training mask, but the canister rusted as badly, and the adhesive tape waterproofing tended to remove the paint, thus accelerating rusting. With waterproofing clamp in place the rubber hose from canister to facepiece softened and distorted in twelve days, and the adhesive tape waterproofing proved of doubtful value under tropical conditions. Also, the carrier, although apparently more resistant to deterioration, proved somewhat bulky to

---

[39] (1) Ltr, CmlO 41st Inf Div to CmlO USAFFE, 7 Jun 43, sub: Mold on Gas Mask Carriers. Sixth Army 475—Weapons for Jungle Warfare. (2) Mollen, Cml Warfare Sup—SWPA, World War II. (3) Ltr, CO 42d Cml Lab Co SWPA to Chief Tech Div OCCWS, 1 Sep 43, sub: Transmittal of Mold Cultures.

wear and, as in Normandy, offered a target for sharpshooters. Arthur recommended that the SWPA-devised training mask and waterproofing be retained but that the lightweight facepiece be substituted for the training facepiece. The War Department approved Arthur's suggested modification of the training mask, and supplies were furnished to make theater modifications. The CWS tried again with an assault mask with cheek-mounted canister, but no significant number of these masks became available in the theater before the end of the war. In sum, this was again a problem that the SWPA CWS tried to overcome with various expedients but without a real solution, for it was unable to find a means of preventing mold, mildew, and corrosion.[40]

Protective Clothing

As noted above, storage and issue of antigas protective clothing was a quartermaster responsibility, but the CWS was vitally involved in providing impregnation services and in prescribing the use and care of protective clothing. The SWPA chief quartermaster issued instructions, in the name of the Commanding General, USASOS, on protective clothing in December 1942, in January 1943, and in March 1943. The last of these instructions repeated the then current War Department policy of providing as yet undesignated "double layer" protection based on the cotton herringbone twill "fatigue" uniform as "minimum" and with an additional impregnated woolen or cotton khaki uniform as "complete" protection.[41]

Patently, complete protection was beyond the SWPA capacity, and the instructions provided that only one set of outer garments plus accessories per individual should be issued or should be held in forward depots for issue to combat troops. Forward depots were also authorized to hold normal replacement quantities to be called forward when needed by operational organizations. The instructions also prescribed storage and maintenance procedures including provision for CWS inspection of clothing in storage.[42]

---

[40] (1) Ltr, CmlO 41st Inf Div to CmlO I Corps, 16 Jun 43, sub: Rpt on Field Test of M4–10–6 Gas Mask (41st Div 470.6), with 2d Ind, forwarded by Ltr, CCmlO USAFFE to CCWS, 9 Jul 43, sub: Lightweight Service Masks. USAFFE FECW 470.72. (2) Ltr, CCmlO USASOS to CG Sixth Army, 22 Oct 43, sub: Wearing Tests on New Type Masks. Sixth Army AG 470.72—Protective Apparatus.

[41] Ltr, AG USASOS to CG's Sixth Army et al., 26 Mar 43, sub: Cml Warfare Protective Clothing. USASOS GSQMS 421 in Sixth Army 422.3 Protective Clothing.

[42] Ibid.

USASOS elaborated the storage, requisition, and issue procedures for protective clothing in May 1943. At the end of the month, the commanding officer of the subbase at Oro Bay, which had officially opened late in April, informed the Commanding General, 41st Infantry Division, that 70 percent of the base protective clothing stock, most of which was held for the division, was unserviceable.[43] The unserviceable clothing had rotted or the fabric had lost its tensile strength. Much of the unserviceable clothing was that dyed jungle green on which chemical service units in Australia had expended so much effort. Since CWS officers had made the serviceability tests, the CWS SWPA was aware of the problem. In a little more than a week after the first notification, Copthorne asked Sixth Army to determine the extent of damage. Sixth Army replied that almost all clothing in loose storage or in the hands of individuals had deteriorated. Clothing received from the United States and stored in its original waterproof bales and packages off the ground and under cover had not deteriorated. Similarly, those sets of clothing in the hands of individual soldiers which had been stored, as prescribed, in the bottoms of barracks bags hung so that air would circulate under the bag had not deteriorated. Since all troops did not have the opportunity to hang barracks bags in positions where air would circulate, Sixth Army ordered protective clothing withdrawn from individuals for storage in unit supply, but storage conditions in unit supply were far from ideal. The best that unit storage could accomplish was slightly to prolong garment life and, perhaps more importantly, to make garments available for regular serviceability inspection.[44]

CWS officers soon learned that the effective life of protective clothing was likely to be six months and that the best which could be expected was a year.[45] Colonel Smith, then chief of the USASOS Chemical Section and later Copthorne's deputy, undertook the direct supervision of protective clothing distribution plans and liaison with quartermaster

---

[43] Ltr, CO Advance Subbase B to CG 41st Div, 30 May 43, sub: Impregnated Clothing. USAFFE Advance Subbase B 422 in Sixth Army 422.3 Protective Clothing.

[44] (1) Ltr, CCmlO USAFFE to CG Sixth Army, 9 Jun 43, sub: Impregnated Clothing. USAFFE FECW 420, cited in Ltr, CG Sixth Army to CG USAFFE, 29 Jun 43, sub: Impregnated Clothing. Sixth Army AG 420W in Sixth Army 422.3 Protective Clothing. (2) Ltr, CmlO 41st Div to CG 41st Div, 22 Jun 43, sub: Inspection of Impregnated Clothing. 41st Inf Div 470.6 in Sixth Army 422.3 Protective Clothing. (3) Memo, CmlO Sixth Army CO Hq Co Sixth Army, 23 Jun 43, no sub. In Sixth Army 422.3 Protective Clothing.

[45] Also see Stauffer, *Operations in the War Against Japan*, p. 202.

on the subject. In the circumstance, Smith had no choice but to provide protective clothing for forward area troops and to plan replacing it every six months. Replacement was provided either from the United States or from stocks impregnated in SWPA. In order to carry on impregnation in the area, processing units were required. The 105th Chemical Processing Company arrived in SWPA in June 1943 just as the extent of the clothing problem was becoming known. Since the unit did not receive its own plants for another six months, it worked at processing in the improvised theater plant to rebuild the theater reserve. Copthorne and Smith sought to move the 105th and the eighteen companies received in 1944 into forward areas so that impregnating facilities, both for building up clothing reserves and for reimpregnation in the event of gas warfare, could be close to the organizations with the greatest need, but obtaining USAFFE or GHQ authority and transportation for these forward moves was extremely difficult.[46]

The SWPA protective clothing reserve problem diminished during late 1944 and early 1945 as stocks were continuously reconstituted by shipments from the United States. Anticipated reserve demands were also reduced by the War Department directive of April 1944 which assigned protective clothing only to 50 percent of the area force. Clothing still deteriorated although better packaging and the use of the M2 water emulsion impregnating process somewhat lengthened the serviceability period. The CWS still sought to move processing units forward as reimpregnation insurance against a gas warfare emergency, and the units, even in forward areas, were diverted to secondary missions which would permit readiness to operate in such emergency.[47]

In the last year of the war, most of the area protective clothing reserve was stored in the Hollandia, New Guinea, base while organizational allowances were carried in unit supply when commanders would permit, or in forward bases when they would not. The forward bases also stored organizational maintenance stocks. As the fighting progressed farther and farther from Hollandia transportation for resupply became more difficult to obtain, and, in event of gas warfare, the transportation situation might have been desperate. Chemical officers were confident, however, that had gas warfare been initiated there would have been sufficient air transportation available in the interim before the process-

[46] Interv, Hist Off with Lt Col Irving R. Mollen, 28 Apr 53.
[47] Ibid.

ing companies could move forward and commence operation. Certainly SWPA was adequately supplied with processing units. Because of the SWPA storage problems and the estimated threat of gas warfare in forward areas, SWPA had more units than any other theater.[48]

Defective Equipment and Spare Parts

Some SWPA chemical supply problems were common to all theaters. For example, the power-driven decontaminating apparatus was widely used for water carrying and giving showers, but the parts supply, as elsewhere, was critical. No spare parts of any description arrived in the theater before Colonel Morgan returned to the United States after the middle of 1943. Even when parts did begin to arrive, there were few for the large apparatus. Some vehicles were cannibalized to keep others in operation, but even this expedient failed because many parts were not interchangeable among the four different makes of apparatus and because the same type of parts wore out on all apparatus. CWS officers arranged with their Ordnance colleagues, late in the war, to replace worn-out decontamination motors with jeep motors, and this local adaptation permitted some apparatus to be returned to service.[49] Other munitions also failed because of faulty manufacturing, faulty inspection, or poor packaging in the United States. Examples are the early shipments of the M33 smoke tank, which air chemical units rebuilt, and of M14 and M8 chemical hand grenades of which such a large percentage malfunctioned that Colonel Grothaus, the OCCWS observer, recommended the destruction of entire lots.[50] Another major problem which was at least aggravated by SWPA storage conditions was that concerning the 100-pound toxic bomb.

Toxic Munitions

As noted above, bombs were early stored in three toxic gas yards in Australia. Leakers were soon discovered among the thin-cased bombs, and sizable detachments from two service units were required to segregate the leakers, decontaminate the storage areas, and vent and paint nonleaking bombs. After a time it became evident that the

---

[48] (1) Mollen Interv, 28 Apr 53. (2) For information on processing company assignments, see Brophy and Fisher, *Organizing for War*, app. H–11.

[49] (1) Morgan Interv, 1 Oct 45. (2) Grothaus-Brady Rpt. (3) Mollen, Cml Warfare Sup—SWPA, World War II.

[50] Grothaus-Brady Rpt.

mustard filling of some bombs was itself deteriorating. Copthorne asked for replacement by distilled mustard, which was not so much subject to deterioration, but OCCWS replied that the production authorities in the United States could not afford the time and effort to distill mustard when the undistilled product proved satisfactory elsewhere. Concentrated SWPA CWS effort kept most of the bombs in serviceable condition. Copthorne was anxious, as the war progressed, to move the bombs closer to the scene of fighting. Finally, in 1944, transportation was secured to establish a considerable stock in New Guinea. When Copthorne's own section moved to Leyte, he again attempted to move the bombs forward, but transportation could not be obtained. Toward the end of hostilities, after a toxic gas yard had been established in the Philippines, another effort was made to move the stock forward, but a detailed inspection revealed that few bombs were then serviceable, and the Chemical Section, Western Pacific, arranged for the disposal of bombs remaining in Australia and New Guinea.[51]

The deterioration of stocks did not mean that SWPA was without supplies for gas warfare retaliation. General MacArthur requested that stockage be maintained on the west coast pending the availability of shipping. Shipping would have been allotted at once in case of emergency. Also, bombs and other toxic munitions declared unserviceable were replaced so that minimum area reserves were maintained until near the end of the war. The area reserves, equal to four or five days' retaliation, were in any case inadequate since the plans made late in the war were based on the west coast stock.[52]

Chemical Warfare Tactical Supply, Southwest Pacific Area

Tactical Supply Policy

Just as many problems in chemical supply in SWPA arose from the difficulties imposed by climate, terrain, and distances, so was the

---

[51] (1) Morgan Interv, 1 Oct 45. (2) Grothaus-Brady Rpt. (3) Personal Ltr, Waitt to Copthorne, 13 Jan 45. (4) Ltr, CCmlO AFWESPAC to CWS, 2 Sep 45, sub: Destruction of M47A2 H–Filled Bombs, with 4th Ind. AFWESPAC CSCW 470.6 (2 Sep 45) in CWS 314.7 Misc files, WESPAC, AFPAC, SPBC. (5) Baldwin, Bingham, and Pritchard, Readiness for Gas Warfare in Theaters of Opns, pp. 474–75. (6) Mollen, History of Cml Warfare Sup—SWPA, World War II.

[52] (1) Ltr, CINC GHQ SWPA to TAG, 19 Dec 43, sub: Revised Theater Plans for Gas Warfare. GHQ AG 381 (19 Dec 43) APO 500 in OPD 385 CWP sec. II–B. (2) Baldwin, Bingham, and Pritchard, Readiness for Gas Warfare in Theaters of Opns, pp. 457–75. (3) Mollen, History of Cml Warfare Sup—SWPA, World War II.

organization for supply dictated by these conditions. Other factors, such as War Department priority, perpetual shortage of manpower, and the nature of the SWPA organization also played a part. In theory SWPA supply operated just as it did in other theaters. SWPA was first concerned with insuring TBA and tables of organization and equipment allowances for all its organizations and units. It was secondly interested in establishing regular maintenance quotas, usually 30 days' supply, which moved forward with combat units, or were held in rear area depots or unit supply for rear area units. A third task was establishing theater reserves set at 60, 90, 150, or 180 days' supply by the War Department (OPD), as calculated against the War Department approved troop basis. All this was the normal business of supply which was handled and computed in just about the same way by SWPA personnel, by the office of the chief of the War Department technical service, and by the responsible port of embarkation.

In the CWS SWPA, as mentioned above, once the initial problems of determining area strength and authorizations and initial supply status of units and organizations had been solved, "normal" supply became a matter of forwarding requisitions for shortages in initial equipment, maintenance, and area reserves. The complication here became one of knowing what to ask for since poor communication frequently left SWPA chemical officers in the dark as to what was available, or what changes had been made in equipment and allowances, or what new items had been added to the system. Part of this burden was removed by the port of embarkation which automatically filled shortages disclosed by the theater's matériel status reports, but this and other automatic supply created problems in unwanted equipment such as gasproof curtains, and 20,000 horse gas masks in a virtually horseless area.[53] Matériel status report supply also frequently arrived in the theater so many months after the report went forward that the conditions cited and basis for stockage no longer existed.[54] But these "normal" supply problems existed in every theater and were only more difficult in degree in SWPA because of serious shortages and failures of communications. Much more difficult were the special requisitions problems.

Again in the special requisitions area, the theaters operated on the same basis. All theater chemical officers submitted special requisitions

[53] Grothaus-Brady Rpt.
[54] Ibid.

771–608 O–66—18

to build up gas warfare preparedness, and in all theaters special requisitions or special projects originating with combat organizations were the very basis of tactical supply. In the North African–Mediterranean theater special requisitions sometimes brought wanted tactical requirements, but when special requisitions failed, organization chemical officers like Colonel Barker, with the help of service chemical officers like Colonel Coblentz, improvised their own requirements and handled them through their own channels. In the European theater special requisitions seldom brought the items the theater wanted from the United States, but General Rowan and his staff controlled chemical supply through an individual system that had matured for two years before it was put to the test of combat. Rowan and his staff could call upon the comparatively abundant resources of the European build-up and of the British allies. The chemical special operational projects in Europe were evolved in close co-ordination between combat and service elements, and the bulk of supply came from theater stocks managed in the theater by the service elements. For example, base section chemical officers could come in for weekly conferences with their theater chief, and, on the Continent, service elements, such as Colonel Stubbs's ADSEC Chemical Section, were in daily contact with the combat organizations. Transportation and communication in Europe were overburdened, but the distances were shorter and the road and other facilities vastly superior to those of the Pacific. The differences in degree in SWPA were so great as to be almost differences in kind.

When Sixth Army became the major SWPA American ground element, on a level co-ordinate with USASOS, in February 1943, it assumed responsibility for tactical supply. Colonel C. L. Marriott, Sixth Army chemical officer, arrived in Australia with the second echelon of the army in April but remained only a short time before moving forward to Milne Bay with ALAMO Force, a task force created in June 1943 from Sixth Army troops, and in fact a forward echelon of the army. Marriott's office was thus separated by 1,200 air miles from Copthorne's. Marriott's assistant, Major McKinney, remained in the Sixth Army headquarters. The only expeditious means of communication was by radio, but with such heavy demands on the radio net, normal communication was by letter or informal memo.[55]

[55] (1) Mary H. Williams, *Chronology 1941–1945*, UNITED STATES ARMY IN WORLD WAR II (Washington, 1960), pp. 93, 114. (2) General Walter Krueger, *From Down Under to Nippon* (Washington: Combat Forces Press, 1953), pp. 6–10, and app. 1.

Responsibility for CWS operational supply projects rested with Marriott. Since he had very little assistance and since, after the move to ALAMO Force at Milne Bay, even his own section was divided, most of the supply policy load fell directly upon his own shoulders. But even this was not difficulty enough in the difficult Pacific area. He lacked the logistic information and means of transportation, and his ability to improvise locally was practically nil, since there was no available civilian source of transportation and no substitute line of communication to Allied forces such as many field chemical officers had. New Guinea had no motor roads, no industry, and only a little unskilled manpower. Air transportation carried very high priority and water transportation was at a premium. Until 15 November 1943, he could deal with the Chemical Officer, Advance Section, USASOS, at Port Moresby. From 15 November until 31 March 1944 he dealt with chemical officers of Advance Section at Lae and Intermediate Section at Port Moresby. But miles of water or air lay between the USASOS sections and his office in ALAMO Force headquarters, which was at Milne Bay until October, at Goodenough Island until December, and near Finschhafen until May 1944.[56]

Requirements and Transportation

Marriott spent much of his time in 1943 simply in determining how SWPA interpreted chemical supply, what channels existed, how much subordinate elements wanted, and where to store the immediate supply demands of organizations. In June 1943 USASOS provided that requisitions for TBA equipment should be submitted to base section chemical officers who could fill them without further reference. Requisitions for supplies in excess of TBA had to be approved by Marriott and forwarded to USASOS. The availability of non-TBA items in USASOS depended upon the ability of the USASOS Chemical Section supply officers to predict unusual issues and to persuade the United States authorities to ship them. Transportation could be obtained either by theater allotment of space, which was controlled in GHQ, or by San Francisco Port of Embarkation allotment. USASOS sometimes issued credits for controlled (non-TBA or scarce) items to Sixth Army for Marriott's suballotment, but each issue against credit had to be approved

---

[56] (1) Krueger, *From Down Under to Nippon*, pp. 12–15. (2) Mollen, History of Cml Warfare Sup—SWPA, World War II.

by USASOS through the issuing base.[57] Unusual issues of TBA, such as for the 1st Marine Division which arrived from South Pacific area fighting minus much of its equipment, were approved through USAFFE, Sixth Army's administrative (not operational) command channel, to USASOS.[58]

Sixth Army forwarded operational projects to GHQ SWPA and in the course of preparing such a project in June, Marriott, bypassing technical channels, pointed out to the supreme command that confusion existed as to the meaning of the term *CWS supplies*.[59] He indicated that the prohibition against the use of toxics led some staff officers to believe that smoke and incendiary shells and grenades, chemical ammunition then issued by Ordnance, were also prohibited. The belief also existed that protective equipment and chemical ammunition were restricted to a 30 days' supply, and problems arose because some protective equipment (such as protective clothing and covers) were issued by Quartermaster on a 90 days' supply basis while other equipment (gas mask, protective ointment, and shoe impregnite) were issued by CWS, apparently on a 30 days' basis. USAFFE, where Copthorne's office was then located, replied without reference to GHQ that the Ordnance-issued items were to be used since they were not toxics. The theater administrative headquarters also indicated that tactical planning should encompass TBA plus 30 days' maintenance and 30 days' reserve for Classes II and IV. For ammunition supply USAFFE prescribed basic units of fire for initial issue and provided that maintenance and reserves be calculated in days of supply.[60] Reserves were parceled out among intermediate bases by the combat organizations. The headquarters regretted confusion resulting from the issue of protective equipment by two services and indicated that action had been initiated to make all protective equipment the responsibility of one service.[61]

With the possible exception of information on specific day of

---

[57] Ltr, CmlO USASOS to Base Sec and Subbase CmlO's, 6 Jun 43, sub: Requisition Channels for CWS Sups. USASOS GSCW 400.312 in Sixth Army 400 Sups (General).

[58] Ltr, CG Sixth Army to CG USASOS through CG USAFFE, 18 Jun 43, sub: Cml Warfare Equip for 1st Marine Div (Sixth Army AG 400W), with 1st Ind, CG USAFFE to CG USASOS, 27 Jun 43 (USAFFE FECW 470.6), and 2d Ind CG USASOS through CG USAFFE to CG Sixth Army, n.d. (USASOS GSCW 457/29). All in Sixth Army 400 Sups (General).

[59] Ltr, CG Sixth Army to CG SWPA through CG USAFFE.

[60] For definitions of days of supply, units of fire, and classes of supply, see above, Chapter III.

[61] 1st Ind, CG USAFFE to CG Sixth Army, 27 Jun 43, on basic Ltr above. USAFFE FECW 475 in Sixth Army 400 Sups (General).

supply and unit of fire allowances, Marriott certainly learned nothing he did not already know. His letter was undoubtedly prompted by a desire to "get something on paper" which would establish an operational planning base and at the same time set headquarters thinking about the assignment of responsibilities. The responsibility for protective items, despite the USAFFE assurance, remained divided between CWS and Quartermaster, but the SWPA responsibility for storage and issue of chemical grenades was transferred from Ordnance to CWS in September. Chemical and incendiary bombs remained an Ordnance responsibility, but the CWS was newly charged with inspection and servicing of the munitions.[62] If Marriott had indeed sought a transfer of responsibility for all chemical items to CWS supply authority, he learned, as the following events demonstrated, to regret it, because he found that the CWS had acquired so much responsibility as to make handling the forward supply job a huge burden.

Supply Procedures and Their Application

Just two days before the transfer of responsibility from Ordnance to CWS, ALAMO Force prescribed supply procedures for combat troops. Each special staff section was assigned to prepare requirements and to oversee and record distribution of the items in its province. The USASOS requisition procedure was followed in that units would requisition directly on base commanders while approval channels were through the army staff section.[63] Marriott was launched into a hectic period of dealing with loading and unloading, storage, maintenance, and combat replacement of the small quantities of the comparatively few chemical items which were so easily misplaced, misappropriated, and misspent among the vast quantities of material moving over the vast distances of the Pacific.

Probably as much at Marriott's behest as for his own use, Copthorne attempted, also in September 1943, to obtain the latest logistics tables, TBA's, and TOE's from the CCWS.[64] This information was not imme-

---

[62] Ltr, CG USAFFE to CG's Sixth Army, Fifth Air Force, and USASOS, 8 Sep 43, sub: Allocation of Ordnance and Cml Warfare Functions (USAFFE ECW 321.011), with 1st Ind, CG Sixth Army to Distr, 22 Sep 43 (Sixth Army AG 322-W), in Sixth Army 400 Sups (General).

[63] CG ALAMO Force to Distr, 6 Sep 43, sub: SOP for the Sup and Resup of Outlying Forces. Sixth Army 400.311—Req–Proc and Sup.

[64] Ltr, CCmlO USAFFE to CCWS, 25 Sep 43, sub: Logistic Planning Tables, CWS. USAFFE FECW 400.301.

diately forthcoming, but McKinney did get USAFFE unit of fire data which he sent to Marriott and subordinate chemical officers on 4 October, and Marriott promptly issued an ALAMO Force version.[65] But he still lacked information on grenades. A month later he wrote to McKinney that it was embarrassing not to know the particulars on these items for which he was responsible. Declaring that someone must have the information, he briefly ordered, "Shell out." [66]

Preparations for the forthcoming Arawe-Cape Gloucester-Saidor offensive were more important than obtaining a set of logistical data. Organizations were about to move out from Australia. McKinney, at a conference in Copthorne's office (Copthorne had now returned from USAFFE to USASOS) apparently charged that not enough was being done for the combat forces. He particularly urged that division chemical officers be given advance information on their supply status.[67] Copthorne's men, who were older hands at fighting the battle of Pacific transportation, must have appeared un-co-operative since there was little they could do that had not already been done. USASOS elements had only limited ability to provide transportation and no official power to assess tactical supply preparations. Movement and allotment priorities must come from Sixth Army, and, since supply was strictly interpreted as a command function in SWPA, only Sixth Army could furnish supply status data to combat organizations. Furthermore, USASOS chemical officers never knew when matériel would move. It was their legitimate practice to ship maintenance with outgoing units so that it might be withdrawn to stock forward bases. There it would be available to supply the same units or others in critical need. The point was that conditions of movement and storage in SWPA were so poor that the area command could not afford to permit combat organizations to attempt to carry along all their supplies into an assault. The only result would be wastage, and wastage as high as 90 percent of protective items had already been experienced in assaults.[68]

Sixth Army was not long in seeing the point. On 12 October 1943, Marriott notified the Chemical Officer, Advanced Echelon, USASOS,

---

[65] (1) Ltr, ACmlO Sixth Army to CmlO ALAMO Force et al., 4 Oct 43, sub: Cml Warfare Unit of Fire Table. Sixth Army 400.314 Estimated Rqmts. (2) Memo, CmlO ALAMO Force, 13 Oct 43, sub: Approved Unit of Fire Table for Cml Warfare Ammunition. OCmlO Sixth Army—Memos from Forward Echelon.

[66] Memo, Marriott for McKinney, 14 Nov 43. Sixth Army AG 300.6 Misc Memos.

[67] Memo, McKinney for Marriott, 3 Oct 43. Sixth Army AG 300.6 Misc Memos.

[68] (1) Mollen, Cml Warfare Sup—SWPA, World War II. (2) Grothaus-Brady Rpt.

of his intended distribution of Sixth Army ammunition supplies among the New Guinea subbases, and he indicated the initial issues that would be required from each base.[69] McKinney's principal task then became getting the transportation that USASOS could not get. Base section chemical officers had become adept at locating and using any nook or cranny not spoken for in any kind of shipping headed for New Guinea, but supply of the scope required by Sixth Army called for more space than they could find. McKinney appealed to the Regulating Officer, GHQ, who was in charge of all SWPA transportation allottments, and also appealed to Sixth Army general staff members to assist in obtaining priorities for chemical items.[70]

Procedures Questioned

Marriott was naturally concerned about having McKinney do a transportation job which he felt should be done automatically in connection with operational planning. He further objected to being separated from his own section by 1,200 miles and to doing business with the USASOS main echelon from the same distance. Copthorne made a tour of New Guinea bases at this time and talked these points over with Marriott. Copthorne agreed that Marriott should deal with the chemical element of Intermediate Section at once and with that of Advanced Section as soon as that section was set up to handle his requests. Copthorne emphasized, both while in New Guinea and in a letter upon his return, that under the circumstances planning must come from Marriott and that only Marriott was in a position to clear information to the combat elements on the one hand and to the USASOS base elements on the other. He forcefully pointed out that the base elements could be prepared to meet demands upon them only if they knew the complete supply plan—how much material had been issued, how much was to be issued and maintained, and who was authorized to receive supplies. During his trip Copthorne discovered that one base chemical officer had reissued ammunition TBA to a division since he did not know that the division had already received it. Another division refused to relinquish an overage of flame thrower fuel

[69] Ltr, CmlO ALAMO Force to CmlO Adv Echelon USASOS, 12 Oct 43, sub: Stockage of CWS Class V Items. Sixth Army 475 Weapons for Jungle Warfare.

[70] (1) Mollen, Cml Warfare Sup—SWPA, World War II. (2) Memo, Cml Sec for ACofS G–4 through ACofS G–3 Sixth Army, 12 Nov 43, no sub. Sixth Army 400 Sups (General). (3) Memo, McKinney for Marriott, 14 Nov 43. Sixth Army AG 300.6 Misc Memos.

because it feared future unavailability. At least part of this fear was justified, but if every organization was not supplied on the same basis, the supply system would soon fail. Copthorne had neither the authority nor the channels to correct these situations. Marriott chided Copthorne for ordering base chemical officers to suspend issue in some cases, but Copthorne could do no less in trying to prevent misapportionment of resources.[71]

Except for the instances of maladjustment in issue and lack of knowledge by the base chemical officers of specific resupply requirements for ammunition, the base supply status met minimum requirements (30 days' for Sixth Army's 180,000 strength) at the time of Copthorne's visit. The only items deficient were the 1½-quart decontaminating apparatus (19.9 days) and the M15 white phosphorus grenade, of which there were none.[72] The WP grenade deficiency was not a local failure; there were no stocks in any theater. When WP grenades did become available SWPA got them first, and a supply of these was in the forward bases by 15 December.[73] The Oro Bay base was below 30 days' Class II supply in October and just above 30 days in November, but, presumably at Marriott's direction, the Port Moresby base compensated with 67 days in October and 76 days in November.[74] The only supply complaint noted in the period was one from the 24th Infantry Division pointing out a shortage of SWPA-modified training masks, but again this was not a local failure. The 10th Chemical Maintenance Company was awaiting the arrival of new canisters from the United States in order to begin waterproofing.[75] During the combat operations a shortage of hydrogen cylinders for flame throwers developed, but this too was a problem which was not solved locally for some time since there was no regular channel of supply for commercial gases.[76]

---

[71] (1) Memo, Marriott for McKinney, 27 Oct 43, no sub. OCmlO Sixth Army Memos from Forward Echelon. (2) Memo, Marriott for McKinney, 1 Nov 43, no sub. (3) Personal Ltr, Copthorne to Marriott, 13 Nov 43. (4) Memo, Marriott for McKinney, 21 Nov 43, no sub. All in Sixth Army AG 300.6 Misc Memos.

[72] Memo, CmlO Intermediate Sec USASOS, for G-4 Intermediate Sec, 24 Nov 43. USASOS Intermediate Sec 400.314 in Sixth Army 400.314 Estimated Rqmts.

[73] Memo, ACmlO Intermediate Sec USASOS for G-4 Intermediate Sec USASOS, 17 Dec 43, no sub. Intermediate Sec 400.314 in Sixth Army 400.314 Estimated Rqmts.

[74] Ibid.

[75] Ltr, CmlO Sixth Army to CmlO 24th Div, 23 Nov 43, sub: Training Masks, Waterproofed for 24th Infantry Div. Sixth Army Cml Warfare 470.72 in Sixth Army 470.72, Gas Masks No. 4.

[76] Memo, ACmlO Intermediate Sec USASOS for G-4 Intermediate Sec USASOS, 17 Dec 43, no sub. Intermediate Sec 400.314 in Sixth Army 400.314 Estimated Rqmts.

Tactical Procedures Set

By the end of the first week in December there was little more that Marriott and McKinney could do. Fighting in the Pacific was savage and intense but usually brief, so that once forces were committed in a campaign there was practically no hope of getting even resupply from distant bases or from the United States unless it was already on the way. Sixth Army Chemical Section planning turned to supplying training munitions for the next break in combat, and support of the combat forces consisted of juggling supplies at the forward bases to permit maximum availability.[77]

Marriott took the occasion to write to chemical officers at subordinate echelons asking that statements of requirements for future operations come early and in full detail. The only way to avoid the last-minute hustle which had just been experienced was to plan far enough ahead so that CWS claims on shipping and storage could be entered months in advance. Marriott realized that the supply element of Copthorne's office should not be placed in the position of having to outguess the combat elements in order to place requisitions on the United States in time to receive any material.[78]

As new campaigns began in early 1944, it became obvious that it was no longer possible to start from scratch. In order to keep supplies moving, the Sixth Army Chemical Section had to know what had been expended and what was on hand. Marriott and McKinney experienced considerable difficulty in obtaining expenditure and status reports from task forces in widely scattered locations. This failure was particularly frustrating since, at the expense of much effort, they had secured service detachments or at least junior officers to accompany those task forces without chemical sections. The primary duty of these detachments was flame thrower service, but the officers were also charged

---

[77] (1) Memo, Cml Sec ALAMO Force for CmlO Advance Base A, 7 Dec 43, no sub. Sixth Army 300.6 Memos (ALAMO Supply Point No. 1). (2) Ltr, CmlO ALAMO Force to CmlO Advance Base B, 1 Dec 43, sub: Routing of Requisitions. Sixth Army 400.311 Requisitions. (3) Ltr, CmlO ALAMO Force to CWSO BACKHANDER Task Force, 2 Dec 43, sub: Routing of Requisitions. Sixth Army 400.311 Requisitions. (4) Memo, Marriott for Riegelman, CmlO I Corps, 13 Dec 43, no sub. Sixth Army AG 300.6 Memos—I Corps. (5) Ltr, CCmlO USASOS to CmlO ADSOS, 30 Dec 43, sub: Shipment of Sups by ALAMO Force. Sixth Army AG 300.6 Memos—ADSOS.

[78] (1) Memo, Marriott for Lt Col K. W. Haas, CmlO 1st Cavalry Div, 30 Nov 43. (2) Memo, Marriott for Riegelman, 30 Nov 43. Both in Sixth Army AG 300.6 Memos.

with handling supply. It was finally necessary to secure a command letter to get some of the reports.[79]

By the end of February 1944 Marriott was thoroughly disgusted with the detailed supply operation which had been the lot of the Sixth Army Chemical Section. He wrote to Copthorne that he had come to the conclusion that "we were sweeping water up hill." [80] Considering the small quantity of chemical supply, he believed that Ordnance would feel no additional strain on handling chemical ammunition, and he felt that Ordnance would not need a separate system as did the CWS. He wanted more time to devote to tactical policy and gas warfare protection and he felt he could get the time only by disposing of a part of his supply burden.[81]

There was some justice in Marriott's comments. The quantity of chemical supply was very small, but perhaps precisely for that reason, chemical materials tended to be lost when handled by another service. But Marriott was not to be relieved of his supply burden; if anything, it increased. USASOS did offer some help. The Distribution Division, USASOS, had been created in January specifically to handle Sixth Army's most vexing problems—transportation and distribution policy. The veteran CWS supply manager, Maj. Arthur H. Williams, Jr., moved into the position of Chemical Officer, Distribution Division. The Distribution Division operated as a field element of USASOS and it moved forward ahead of the main echelons.[82] The USASOS commander, Maj. Gen. John L. Frink, also redefined the duties of USASOS Advance and Intermediate Sections. Effective 1 March 1944, Advance Section became a transportation and handling agency and Intermediate Section took over the command of all forward bases and the supervision of supply policy.[83] Since the Distribution Division soon moved into Intermediate Section, the Sixth Army Chemical Section at last had

[79] (1) Ltr, ACmlO ALAMO Force to CmlO US Forces APO 321, 21 Jan 44, sub: CWS Resup MICHAELMAS. Sixth Army 471.6 Grenades. (2) Memo, McKinney for CmlO ALAMO Base 2, 21 Jan 44, no sub. Sixth Army 400 Sup. (3) Ltr, ACmlO ALAMO Force to CCmlO USASOS, 25 Jan 44, sub: Ammunition Status Rpts. Sixth Army 471 Ammunition. (4) Memo, Col Marriott for Col R. N. Gay, CmlO ADSOS, 31 Jan 44, sub: CWS Units. Sixth Army AG 300.6 Memos. (5) Ltr, CG ALAMO Force to CG Dir Task Force, 2 Feb 44, sub: Cml Ammunition Rpts. Sixth AG 471W in Sixth Army 470.71 Ammunition.

[80] Personal Ltr, Marriott to Copthorne, 26 Feb 44. Sixth Army 472.4—4.2 inch Cml Mortar.

[81] Ibid.

[82] History of Distr Div USASOS. OCMH MS.

[83] Ltr, CG USASOS to CG's ADSOS and Intermediate Sec, 25 Feb 44, sub: Functions and Responsibilities of ADSOS and Intermediate Sec. Sixth Army 323.31 Development of Bases.

USASOS officers with considerable resources close at hand. Still, the Sixth Army Chemical Section devoted much of its time to supply and service.

Marriott issued a new unit of fire table on 1 March because he was still responsible for tactical requirements and planning.[84] Also, now that some support problems were handled by USASOS, the forward area problems increased. The inexperienced, young junior officers with the task forces lacked the knowledge to handle supply, and Marriott's office was frequently called upon to give detailed instructions at the regimental combat team level. In many cases Marriott sent out the officers of his own section to inspect or to clear up a field supply problem.[85]

The introduction of chemical mortar battalions to the Pacific and the increased use of the flame thrower also added to supply duties. Every task force chemical section whether of divisional size or smaller was now more than ever engaged in combat loading and unloading, in collecting supplies on beachheads, and in furnishing support, such as flame thrower fuel mixing, in forward areas. These elements all reported expenditures and special requirements and problems. In each case the Sixth Army Chemical Section had a function of planning, reviewing, or directing operations.[86]

By the middle of 1944 replacement factors had been increased, supply was more plentiful, and items received were in better shape. The first block-loaded ships were then being prepared in San Francisco, and the Sixth Army Chemical Section took advantage of this means to resupply ammunition. Block-loaded ships were those vessels with loads specially designed to support a task force with a balanced variety of supplies. The matériel was loaded so that discharge could be effected easily and expeditiously, and loads were so marked that accounting and reporting problems were greatly reduced. Each block-loaded ship came into a USASOS base and waited there to be called forward for the support

[84] Ltr, CG Sixth Army to Distr, 1 Mar 44, sub: Unit of Fire Table for Cml Warfare Ammunition. Sixth Army AG 471W.

[85] (1) Memo, SupO Sixth Army Cml Sec for CmlO ALAMO Force, 24 Mar 44, no sub. (2) Memo, CmlO ALAMO Sup Point No. 1 for CmlO ALAMO Force. (3) Memo, Marriott for Riegelman, 11 Apr 44. (4) Memo, CmlO ALAMO Sup Point No. 1 for CmlO ALAMO Force, 3 May 44. All in Sixth Army AG 300.6 Memos. (5) Ltr, CmlO ALAMO Force to CO Det 93d Cml Composite Co, 8 Mar 44, sub: Maintenance Factors. Sixth Army 470.72 Protective Equip.

[86] (1) CmlO 41st Inf Div, n.d., Rpt, Cml Phase and Sec Hist Rcd of HORLICKS [Biak] Opn. Sixth Army 350.05 Biak.

of an appropriate task force. The block-loaded procedure facilitated supply on Leyte.[87]

Colonel Marriott was invalided home in July 1944, so that he did not see the effect of the block-loaded ships upon his supply operation. By the time of his departure the pattern of supply was well set, and although there were problems, such as the inability of USASOS to move bases forward fast enough when combat reached the southern Philippines and a critical supply shortage late in 1944, there was no essential change in the chemical tactical supply operation until the end of the war.[88]

Chemical officers in the Southwest Pacific faced the most difficult supply task experienced by the CWS during World War II. The hardships faced by chemical officers in other theaters—lack of supply information, immensely complicated requirements, requisitioning, and review systems, shortage of critical items, and the early poor condition of equipment—were all compounded by distance, tropical conditions, and lack of channels and facilities in SWPA. As a result SWPA chemical officers developed a series of expedients which were at times unusual and often ingenious. By employing these expedients they did build up area reserves and they did provide the combat forces with both matériel and service. It does seem possible in retrospect that their task, which was never an easy one because of the unpredictable and almost overwhelming difficulties of tropical warfare, might have been somewhat more simply and more expeditiously handled had logistical planning received more emphasis both in the theater and in the War Department.

The Theater Supply System, Central Pacific

Supply in the Emergency Period

The CWS Hawaiian Department in December 1941 stocked more chemical items than any other overseas element of the Army.[89] Major

---

[87] (1) Memo, Cml Sec Sixth Army for Mollen, 30 Jun 44, no sub. In Sixth Army 400 Supplies. (2) Mollen, Cml Warfare Sup—SWPA, World War II.

[88] (1) Mollen, Cml Warfare Sup—SWPA, World War II. (2) Ltr, CmlO Base K to Distr, 4 Dec 44, sub: Critical Items CWS Class II and IV. Base K KCWS 400.301 in Sixth Army 401.1 Critical Items. (3) Ltr, CmlO Base K to CmlO Subbase K and Cml SupO Base K, 5 Dec 44, sub: Issue of Cml Warfare Equip and Sups. Sixth Army 400 Supplies.

[89] Unless otherwise noted, this and the following sections are based on the History of the CWS in the Middle Pacific.

McMillin, Chemical Officer, Hawaiian Chemical Depot, was prepared to issue 60,000 service gas masks when, less than an hour after the Japanese attack on Pearl Harbor began, Colonel Unmacht, department chemical officer, ordered distribution. The departmental CWS also stocked about 90 tons of bleach, 110 tons of chemicals for impregnating permeable protective clothing, and nearly 25,000 gallons of noncorrosive decontaminating agent. Several thousand hand decontaminating apparatus and a completely inadequate supply of personal protective ointment completed the defensive stock.[90]

The CWS stored some ammunition, smoke agents, and toxic agents, about eleven tons of FS smoke, 3,000 HC smoke pots, and nearly 500 tons of bulk toxics almost evenly divided between persistent and nonpersistent gases. The departmental ordnance officers stored some toxic and smoke-filled ammunition. The departmental CWS carefully hoarded 32 4.2-inch chemical mortars, aware that the whole Army had only 44.[91]

Since Unmacht's first responsibility was to insure gas warfare protection and a defensive potential for troops, as noted above, he at once directed that impregnating and bleach production operations start, and he also set out to procure cans to be filled as chemical land mines. On 10 December 1941 he cabled the Chief, CWS, for funds to procure materials and to operate and to convert plants. The theater CWS assumed that the War Department would immediately ship TBA equipment for the known troop strength in the Hawaiian Department, but in case such material should not be en route, Unmacht on 17 December cabled for 60,000 suits of protective clothing, 25 tons of impregnite, nearly 200,000 tubes each of shoe impregnite and protective ointment, and training masks, dust respirators, gasproof curtains, and chemical mortar shell. The request was amended on the following day to include more mortar shell, bleach, children's masks, and respirators for babies.

By the end of December most of the protective equipment on hand, including all but about 5,000 service masks and 5,000 training masks, had been issued to troops, and issues to civilians began. The War Department emergency shipments including training masks for civilians began to arrive in January. Within ten days 15,673 masks had been

---

[90] Weekly Rpt for the CofS, CWS Munitions on Hand as of 12 Dec 41, OC CWS, dated 20 Dec 41. CWS 319.1/2249.
[91] Ibid.

issued to civilians, and by 1 March 1942 393,680 of the eventual 425,699 had been distributed. Local workers added nearly 38,000 "bunny" hoods, substitutes for nonavailable children's masks, to the total.

Chemical Supply Reserve

The first department report on supply status to the War Department G–4 in October 1942 revealed no serious supply problem except the lack of service personnel. The depot was severely handicapped in the operation of 3 subdepots on Oahu, 3 in outlying islands, and 5 production plants. In Unmacht's opinion the one chemical depot company activated in the theater in March and the one decontamination company which arrived in June were already overburdened. Theater stock was not up to the prescribed 75-day reserve level, but the San Francisco port was keeping the theater informed on the progress of requisitioned shipments, and automatic supply on less important items was steadily building toward the stockage goal. There is little sense of urgency in the report, probably because the department was enjoying a lull between the emergency period and the combat period.

The March 1943 report does reflect a sense of urgency. Requisitioning responsibility had been transferred from the depot to the departmental chemical office because supply planning for CENPAC combat forces was now in prospect. The failure to maintain authorized stock levels had become serious because large-scale issues of TBA equipment contemplated would deplete area reserves. The departmental CWS had run into the problem of requisitions edited in the United States, a problem which plagued all theater chemical officers. The port had supplied in the requested quantity only two items of a 19-item requisition placed in November 1942; fourteen items were disapproved without statement of cause. Even more serious in the view of departmental chemical officers was the fact that training ammunition supplies were running out in a period of intensive training.

The CWS in Hawaii could report no improvement in June, but in September 1943 the theater reported that relief had been received. The War Department authorized for the Central Pacific Area a 60-day operating level in addition to the 75-day reserve level, and the port authorized an additional "pipeline" factor. The "pipeline" factor allowed the Hawaiian Department to requisition additional supplies to maintain levels during order and shipping time. TBA issues for combat forces, of which the first was then mounting, could then be handled without difficulty.

On 1 July 1944 the Chemical Office, Central Pacific Base Command (CPBC), assumed the logistics functions except for broad policy and long-range planning which remained the province of Unmacht's chemical office. This transfer placed stock level and TBA issue problems in CPBC hands. It also gave the Chemical Office, CPBC, supervision of the combat supply and resupply system which had been inaugurated for the earliest theater operation against the enemy in the Gilbert Islands in November 1943.

Toxic Supply

Another reserve problem was that of toxic supply. As the first gas warfare plan indicated, the 500 tons of toxic on hand at the time of the Pearl Harbor attack would have been sufficient, taking into account the retaliation then possible. As strength grew and weapons and aircraft became available, the CWS in CENPAC realized that 500 tons represented hardly a token amount for retaliation even under the assumption that retaliation would take place on one of the small Pacific islands. The CWS consequently persuaded Army and Army Air Forces commands to requisition toxics. Some were received and stored by Ordnance with CWS maintaining the responsibility for inspecting munitions in storage. Between July and November of 1944 the peak stock of 498.5 short tons of bulk lewisite was on hand as well as the peak stockage of 1,126.5 tons of toxics that went into bombs. Other peak stockages for bulk mustard, artillery shell, and chemical mortar shell were attained in the first half of 1945.

CWS officers judged the 100-pound mustard-filled bomb as the most important munition for retaliation. The peak stock on this item, attained in July 1944, was 15,244 bombs with 541.2 tons of toxic filling. This supply was token only. If, for example, this entire supply had been used on Iwo Jima, which had an area of seven and one-half square miles, it would only have contaminated a little more than half, or four and one-half square miles.[92] Considering the vapor effect of mustard and the fact that the entire island would not have been regarded as a target, the stock would have been sufficient for one contamination. In

---

[92] These computations were made using the standard World War II manuals.

the opinion of most chemical officers one contamination would have been enough to end all enemy resistance on the island. The question of resupply for other objectives would then arise. According to Generals Porter and Waitt an actual initiation of gas warfare would have given the CWS sufficient priorities to effect resupply, by air if necessary, from the west coast.[93]

From the point of view of supply on hand the CWS in CENPAC was only prepared to make an initial gas warfare strike. But, since CENPAC had better lines of communication to the United States than most overseas areas, gas warfare could have been sustained.

Chemical Warfare Tactical Supply, Central Pacific

Tactical Supply Policy

The essence of the combat supply and resupply lay in the nature of Central Pacific combat. The Joint Chiefs of Staff scheduled area forces to take a number of small and fiercely defended islands and atolls lying across the expanse of the Pacific. Early supply base development in most of these objectives was out of the question—they were too small and too far away from main bases, or even if they were large enough for base development the distance between them was so great that it was impossible to establish a string of forward bases in the SWPA pattern. Each ground and sea combat operation had to be complete in itself. The assigned combat force took the objective as rapidly as possible and withdrew leaving a small or, in the case of Marshalls and Marianas, a large garrison to clean up and prepare the objective for such use as could be made of it. Any resupply was destined for the garrison only. These island garrisons sometimes built large bases but they usually served the air forces rather than ground combat forces.

The U.S. Army Forces in the Central Pacific formed seven provisional garrison battalions before a single objective was taken. Each supply plan was made on the assumption, which proved correct, that the ordinary requisition or allotment procedures used in other theaters would not work. All supply for the combat forces must be at sea before the forces arrived at their objective, and garrison force supply had to be in the area as soon as garrison forces could receive it. In this

---

[93] (1) Porter Interv, 24 Aug 61.   (2) Waitt Interv, 13 May 61.

circumstance, supply could hardly be a function of the combat command. Logistic plans for each operation were a joint product of combat, garrison force, and theater planners. Tight logistical control was essential. Consequently, supply plans were originated by the combat staffs working with the technical service staffs. These preliminary plans were approved and co-ordinated at general staff echelons and forwarded to the Commander in Chief, POA, for the strategic, tactical, and logistical last word. The tight control came from the management of transportation by the Commander in Chief, POA. Every inch of transport space had to be allocated by strict priorities since shipping was short, since all essentials had to be carried, and since an amphibious force operating at such distances from a base had to be of an easily manageable size.

The First Test—The Gilberts Operation

In the Gilberts operation assaulting troops carried full initial allowances plus 30 days' essential maintenance and five units of fire computed according to War Department replacement factors.[94] An additional 30 days' maintenance accompanied garrison force troops. Then additional shipments were set up to give the garrison forces a 30-day operating level and a 60-day reserve by D-day plus 60 days. The CWS computations were involved because each of these levels had to be computed on the basis of troop strength expected to be at the objective when supplies arrived. Since strength would decline rapidly with the withdrawal of combat forces once the objective was taken, a descending schedule of strength was drawn up.

All CWS supplies for the Gilberts operation were loaded in Hawaii. Shipments totaled 93 measurement tons (40 cubic feet per ton), most of it for the Marine Corps assault forces. There were no serious CWS supply problems, but there were a number of lessons for the future. Assaulting forces wanted more flame throwers and more smoke in forthcoming operations although the CWS made a special allowance of smoke pots for the Gilberts.

Assault troops on the Gilberts used the power driven and 3-gallon decontaminating apparatus to spray sodium arsenite on the dead since it was impossible to provide mortuary services in the assault. The

---

[94] For an account of the Gilberts operation, see: Philip A. Crowl and Edmund G. Love, *Seizure of the Gilberts and Marshalls,* UNITED STATES ARMY IN WORLD WAR II (Washington, 1955).

chemical aided in control of disease-bearing insects and the arresting of nauseous odors.[95] An extra allowance of the apparatus was indicated.

The Gilberts operation also pointed up some handling problems. Combat troops found flame thrower fuel mixing and repair difficult, partly because 55-gallon drums of fuel were too heavy to handle, and partly because repair parts could not be adequately distributed and used during tactical operations. The Navy and the marines requested the installation of racks on landing craft so that smoke pots could be carried in a ready position for immediate firing. The Army's 27th Division chemical officers indicated that chemical supplies were insufficiently waterproofed.

Supply System Refinement

The USAFICPA CWS took these problems from the Gilberts into account in planning the Marshall Islands invasion for January, February, and March of 1944. Flame fuel was provided in 5-gallon cans. Waterproofing was improved and allowances for smoke and flame munitions and for the decontaminating apparatus were raised. Even the basic supply system underwent refinement. USAFICPA set up block loads to be shipped directly from the United States to the Marshalls. The CWS shared in the theater system revision by computing a block-load on the basis of 20 days' supply for 1,000 men. Since War Department factors were usually stated on a 30-day basis and were often not computed in a per-man requirement, CWS USAFICPA was forced to convert War Department figures into per-man-per-day requirements according to theater experience in order to determine the more convenient 20-day block. Chemical officers worked up shipment blocks which would provide 90 days' supply for the garrison forces on D-day plus 90 days in the Marshalls.

In the actual Marshalls operation, the tactical commander held resupply offshore until he could determine that it could be landed without clogging the beaches. The only CWS supply problem arising in the Marshalls was that so many portable flame throwers were provided that not all could be used. The allowance per division for subsequent operations was cut from 192 to 141 weapons. The physical condition and handling of supplies otherwise met demands, demonstrating that the CWS had learned to operate its share of the theater supply

[95] Stauffer, *Operations in the War Against Japan*, pp. 252–55.

system. For example, the CWS supplied only end-item replacements to the combat echelons since it was apparent that spare parts could not be handled and used until the garrison forces were set up. Waterproofed packaging and palletized loads assembled by the Hawaiian Chemical Depot and the combat troops themselves before the operation proved to answer other equipment and handling needs. Although space could not be provided for chemical service troops to handle supply, the sanitation problem was so great that the excess decontaminating apparatus were provided and manned by troops of the 29th Chemical Decontamination Company under the supervision of a medical officer.

The theater and CWS supply system was substantially complete at the end of the Marshalls operation. In subsequent operations, the only major refinement was a differentiation between assault and garrison resupply. The practice previous to the Marianas operation in June was to provide resupply on a per-man basis without regard to whether the men supplied were in combat or garrison echelons. POA experience made it clear, however, that combat troops would not be in any area long enough to need resupply on some items, such as gas mask repair kits and gasproof curtains, even in the event of gas warfare. The garrison forces who collected and reconditioned equipment would be in greater need of reconditioning supplies and base development supplies. The CWS USAFICPA accordingly determined assault and garrison resupply blocks on the basis of probable need and scheduled shipment of these blocks so that assault forces would handle only essential resupply.

The Final Test—Okinawa

The great test of the Central Pacific supply system came with invasion of Okinawa in April 1945. Tenth Army was organized in Hawaii in preparation for the Ryukyus Campaign of which the Okinawa invasion was a part, and the Tenth Army Chemical Section, then under Col. Thomas A. Doxey and later under Col. John H. Harper, set to work with the theater (now U.S. Army Forces, Pacific Ocean Areas—USAFPOA) and CPBC Chemical Sections. CWS supply troubles both in providing basic equipment and in resupply were intensified because units and organizations scheduled for the operation were mounting in places varying from the west coast of the United States to the recently captured Palaus and some were still committed in other operations. The CWS planners prepared supply plans which could be rapidly adjusted to new situations. They provided this flexibility by planning for "type" units and organizations rather than for specific named units and organizations, according to earlier practice. The theater command arranged that requisitions for "type" unit supplies could be placed on the San Francisco port. The port then forwarded supplies to holding and reconsignment points to await theater designation of receiving organizations. The theater further directed the assemblage of an emergency reserve stock in the Marianas to be used in event the "type" supplies fell short of filling basic requirements for the designated specific unit. The CWS logisticians, on the basis of their own experience, estimated shortages for organizations which were known but which could not be consulted because they were still committed to combat. The logisticians computed resupply blocks according to the theater system as usual.

The chemical service manpower requirement was greater than the theater had ever experienced. There were not enough service units available in the theater, and repeated pleas to the United States resulted in the scheduling of two chemical service units on redeployment from the European theater and one unit from the United States. But these units could not arrive before the operation was well under way, so Unmacht activated two service companies and a provisional chemical detachment in Hawaii. He also secured the assignment of a quartermaster service company to chemical work pending the arrival of other units in the target area.[96]

Assault on Okinawa's Hagushi beaches began on Easter Sunday morning, 1 April 1945. Contrary to expectations, no significant resistance was encountered, and a much larger area was taken than had been originally planned in the first three days. As far as the CWS was concerned, the easy advance immediately posed the problem of collecting chemical equipment dropped on the beachhead by incoming troops. Initially, division personnel established beach dumps. On L-day plus three, XXIV Corps took over the operation of the dumps, and the 4342d Quartermaster Service Company which had been assigned to the CWS arrived with the 1st Provisional POA Chemical Detachment (later the 411th). Elements of the service company and the detach-

[96] (1) Cml unit files, 147th and 148th Cml General Serv Cos and 231st Cml Depot Co. (2) Ltr, CG Tenth Army to CG Island Comd, 20 Jan 45, sub: Plan for CWS Sup. Tenth Army AG 475 Cml.

ment were attached to division chemical sections to assist in dump operation. On 10 April 1945 Island Command, the garrison force for Okinawa, whose chemical officer was Lt. Col. Emory A. Lewis, took over the supervision of the dumps and service personnel.[97] Island Command Chemical Section and its service units had the mission of receiving, storing, and issuing CWS matériel to service echelons and to Tenth Army ASP's and dumps.

The most serious problem of the CWS which developed during the Okinawa operation was the shortage of 4.2-inch mortar ammunition. The 4.2-inch chemical mortar was increasingly acknowledged by commanders and troops alike as a valuable weapon. Because of extensive use, especially in such operations as the Battle of the Bulge, 4.2 ammunition was in short supply in the zone of interior and in all theaters of operations when the Okinawa operation was being formulated. The USAFPOA CWS had planned on having ammunition resupply for Okinawa arrive in the block-loaded ships from the west coast, but because of the shortage, ammunition had to be collected in the Hawaiian Islands and the Marianas and then forwarded to Okinawa. In all, approximately 50,000 rounds of heavy M4 shell were forwarded and another 20,000 rounds of M3 shell were acquired from the Navy at the target. The M4 shell weighed 35 pounds as opposed to 25 pounds for the M3 HE and WP shell. The heavier shell decreased mortar range by 1,000 yards and caused greater strain and wear upon the guns. Breakdowns occurred and a greater replacement of parts than had been anticipated was required. It was a case, however, of using the M4 shell or having none. Fortunately, the end-item and spare parts replacement allowances were sufficient to cover necessary repairs, but this was not the end of the shell problem.[98]

The mortar units in combat soon discovered that fuzes had corroded in many of the shells, causing premature bursts. Tenth Army called for replacement fuzes. The USAFPOA responded to eleven emergency requests by air, shipping 46,502 pounds of fuzes from the United States and from Hawaii.

---

[97] (1) Roy E. Appleman, James M. Burns, Russell A. Gugeler, and John Stevens, *Okinawa: The Last Battle*, UNITED STATES ARMY IN WORLD WAR II (Washington, 1948), pp. 68–76. (2) Action Rpt, XXIV Corps, Ryukyus Campaign, 1 Apr 45, dated 30 Jun 45, Incl to Barker to CCWS, 28 Sep 45, Rpt, Visit to Okinawa, Ryukyu Islands. CWS 314.7 Observer Rpts.

[98] 1st Lt John A. Landt, CO B 88th Cml Mortar Bn to CG 1st Marine Div, Opnl Rpt of Action With the 1st Marine Div on Okinawa, 30 June 45.

Neither ammunition nor fuze problems could be attributed to the USAFPOA chemical supply system, for shells and fuzes were not available in the United States according to plan. It is possible that the requirements stated for ammunition resupply were low, but since there was a shell shortage this point could not be proved. On the whole, the system worked well for the Okinawa operation.

The administration of all CWS activities in the Central Pacific proved to be more effectively and economically handled than in other theaters because circumstances in the area permitted greater centralization of procedures and more command support of the CWS. The CWS supply system in the area also reflected this administrative efficiency. In supply the CWS did not have the independence in the Central Pacific that it had in other theaters—the service had to work through the well-oiled Army-Navy machine. But under Central Pacific conditions this lack of independence was not a significant drawback, for it brought the benefits of working as a part of, rather than in spite of, the theater organization. Independence in other theaters, on the other hand, brought the frustrating problems of trying to operate a very small supply service in a company of giants. In final analysis the CWS supply job was accomplished both through the independent CWS supply systems evolved in other theaters and through the centralized system of the Central Pacific and neither type of system proved to be perfect. But the Central Pacific system which provided logistical control from the top, although it was less responsive to the desires of field commanders, offered the CWS the best and most consistent employment of theater resources and talents.

CHAPTER VII

Chemical Warfare Service Units

The Chemical Warfare Service provided service units for all theaters of operations during World War II. In so doing, it had in mind primarily its responsibility for providing the United States Armed Forces with the capability of defending themselves against gas attack and retaliating effectively in kind. The task of maintaining readiness for gas warfare in the field embraced a number of contributory missions. Chemical warfare matériel, whether defensive, like gas masks and protective clothing, or offensive, like toxic agents and the munitions to deliver them, had to be provided through depots and dumps; this required units trained to handle, repair, and issue such items. Teams trained and equipped for the systematic decontamination of service area installations after gas attack were essential in a gas warfare situation. Defensive measures also included the availability of freshly processed permeable protective clothing for troops called on to execute missions in a contaminated area; hence the need for processing teams and equipment to insure an adequate supply of impregnated uniforms. Gas warfare intelligence was dependent on the presence in theaters of technicians and laboratories capable of determining the nature of gas attacks and assessing the significance of captured matériel. Finally, the prosecution of a gas offensive demanded close maintenance and supply support for the combat elements responsible, whether they were mortar battalions or Air Forces bombers.

The needs of gas warfare readiness, therefore, set the pattern for prewar CWS planning for service units. The prescribed standard for a wartime situation, in which the existence or at least the imminence of gas warfare was taken for granted, called for the assignment of a chemical depot company, decontamination company, laboratory company, impregnating company (as the processing company was then called), and maintenance company to each field army, with additional base depot chemical facilities under the control of the army communications zone.[1] By the time the United States entered the war, the CWS had come, perforce, to adjust its standards to meet the needs of gas warfare preparedness in situations which, for the time being, at least, did not include gas. The normal basis of assigning maintenance companies remained the field army, but the other units were henceforth to be assigned to theaters of operation, either for retention under direct theater control or for further assignment to agencies within the theater. CWS air service units were provided for assignment to theater air forces. In addition to these specialized companies, the CWS began at the outset of the war to provide composite companies capable of undertaking all of these service missions for field armies through a system of specialized teams of platoon size or less.

Somewhat more than a year after Pearl Harbor, with large-scale land action against the enemy taking place as yet only in the Southwest Pacific and North Africa, a CWS report showed a total of 19 service units of all types sent to all overseas destinations, including some in the Western Hemisphere. Of these 19, the Southwest Pacific had received a composite company, 2 decontamination companies, a laboratory, a maintenance, and a depot company. A depot company, a maintenance company, and a decontamination platoon had gone to North Africa. Only 2 processing companies had left the zone of interior; both were in the United Kingdom.[2] By the middle of 1944, with major Allied offensive campaigns in process all over the world, the current troop basis included an authorization for 128 CWS ground service units, about 25 more than the total number included in theater CWS plans, so far as these had been formulated. There were 102 service units actually in the theaters as of 31 July 1944, compared with the 101 deemed necessary by the Chief, CWS, for a nongas situation. A total of 64 additional CWS units were on duty overseas with the Army Air Forces. In general, the supply of CWS service units was adequate for "insurance" purposes, considering the fact that gas had not been used by the enemy and that there was no particular indication of a sudden change in that situation. Had there been a sudden shift to gas warfare conditions, service unit requirements would have been seriously above existing theater capabilities in some instances, most

---

[1] FM 3–15, Sup and Field Serv, 17 Feb 41.
[2] USCWC, Rpt on Gas Warfare Preparedness, U.S. Army, 2 Feb 43.

notably in the need for processing companies. The European and Mediterranean theaters alone would have required a total of two dozen additional processing companies to meet an all-out resort to gas warfare by Germany.[3]

But with gas warfare no more than a grim possibility, it was not surprising that theaters were willing to spread their chemical service units somewhat thin. It was inevitable, also, that those service missions which were not directly dependent on the presence or threat of gas should come to the fore. Two of these, both unanticipated in prewar planning, came to be of particular importance: the provision of close maintenance and supply support for 4.2-inch mortars firing HE and the storing, mixing, filling, and loading of airborne incendiary munitions. The hard-won acceptance of the flame thrower as an effective weapon in the Pacific theaters brought with it the need for flame thrower maintenance and fuel supply. The demonstrated value of CWS screening smokes led to the requirement for stockage of smoke mixtures and maintenance of smoke generators. The immediate relevance of all these services to the needs of combat gave them prominence, but the basic gas warfare readiness mission was not forgotten. Depot companies continued to see to it that a gas mask in good working order was available for every soldier, processing companies maintained theater reserve stocks of impregnated clothing, and laboratory companies worked steadily at the tasks of evaluating enemy chemical warfare matériel and providing technical surveillance for American stocks.

As one of the consequences of serving as insurance against the outbreak of gas warfare CWS service units acquired an assortment of responsibilities of immediate urgency, but often unrelated to their basic missions. The decontamination companies, which never functioned as such overseas, were particularly prone to this sort of development. Their equipment, which lent itself to the carrying and dispensing of water, became the basis for their utilization as shower units, among other things. Similarly, the impregnating plants of the processing companies bore enough of a functional relationship to laundry machinery to enable companies to supplement quartermaster laundry service when their own processing mission was in abeyance. Sometimes it was CWS training rather than organic equipment that seemed to point the way to new missions for service units. More than one chemical

---

[3] USCWC, Rpt of Readiness for Cml Warfare as of 1 Jul 44.

service company found itself, after a brief training period, operating smoke lines, and in two cases CWS service troops joined mortar units. Laboratory companies turned to developing or testing field expedients ranging from camouflage dye to flame thrower tanks and found time to perform an impressive variety of miscellaneous technical chores for other services.

The development of new missions, even more than the ordinary exigencies of active theaters, frequently demanded a high degree of flexibility in CWS service units. More often than not, flexibility in response was obtained at the expense of the proper organization of the unit and consequently with a good deal of difficulty. For the most part, each type of company was set up to operate as a unit under the control of the company commander. Each subordinate element was organized, manned, and equipped for a specific range of specialized tasks contributory to the main task. *Ad hoc* rearrangement of manpower and equipment to meet new demands resulted in administrative problems which often interfered with the unit's effectiveness. The requirement for flexibility was met to some degree by the formation of the composite companies, with their cellular structure designed to permit each cell to operate independently of the others. The experience of the Pacific theaters was to lead to greater reliance on these all-purpose organizations and to demands for still more flexibility of structure and employment. In this respect this experience pointed the way toward postwar doctrine.

The Chemical Laboratory

Seven Chemical Warfare Service laboratory companies saw service overseas between 1941 and 1945. The essential mission of the laboratory company in the field was to analyze and evaluate enemy chemical matériel and to maintain technical surveillance over CWS supplies. These functions made it a major source of technical intelligence, both as to enemy capabilities for chemical warfare and the storage life of CWS ammunition and protective items. At first conceived of as a more or less mobile entity capable of following an army in the field, it was in practice treated as a semifixed installation of a theater communications zone, a status better suited to its more than ten tons of laboratory equipment.

However bulky its equipment, a laboratory company was not a large unit. Its prescribed strength at the time the United States entered World War II was only 86—14 officers and 72 enlisted men—and the tendency of subsequent years was toward a still more restricted personnel roster. Indeed, the first laboratory company to go overseas, en route at the time of the Pearl Harbor attack, was authorized no more than 78 officers and men in its movement orders.[4] By the end of 1943, in accordance with a TOE of the preceding July, laboratory companies were reorganized to consist of 8 officers and 51 enlisted men. The enlisted strength was set at 50 the following year.[5] The original laboratory company was organized rather loosely into headquarters, chemical, and physical sections, the headquarters organization including, in addition to the major commanding, an officer in charge of chemical intelligence. The 1943 reorganization, while cutting the strength of the company, doubled the number of its subdivisions. There were, henceforth, in addition to the headquarters unit, sections designated organic, analytical, chemical engineering, toxicology, and intelligence. This setup was designed for a more effective division of labor in handling the work facing a company in the field.

Once established and operating, usually in or near a major urban center, the chemical laboratory company acted as a research center and technical clearinghouse for the entire theater. In performance of its principal mission, it examined captured enemy chemical munitions and protective items, studied the behavior of American chemical matériel under theater conditions, surveyed items in storage for possible deterioration, collected chemical intelligence from captured enemy personnel and documents, and made regular reports of its various findings and activities to OCCWS. It was from the reports of the 45th Chemical Laboratory Company in the spring of 1945 that the Chemical Warfare Service first learned of the existence and structure of the new German nerve gases, the so-called G agents. When not engaged in its principal chemical mission, the laboratory served the theater as a general-purpose research establishment, carrying out whatever projects its equipment and technical personnel were capable of handling.

---

[4] History of the 42d Cml Lab Co.
[5] TOE 3–97, 6 Jul 43 and 3 Jun 44.

These tasks ranged from tests of Army Air Forces engine coolants to manufacture of a camouflage skin dye for jungle troops.[6]

The oldest of the laboratory companies was typical in its overseas experience. The 41st Chemical Laboratory had begun its existence as the 1st Chemical Company (Laboratory) in 1940 in the days before the laboratories were assigned the forties for numerical designation. From its ranks while in training at Edgewood Arsenal had come cadres for the second and third laboratories to be activated. In the spring of 1943 the company took ship for North Africa, arriving at Mers el Kébir near Oran early in May, as the Tunisia Campaign was approaching its end. Assigned at first to Fifth Army, the company spent several months at Marina, Algeria, just over the border from Fifth Army's Moroccan headquarters, working under the supervision of the Fifth's Chemical Officer, Colonel Barker. When Fifth Army embarked for Italy in September 1943, the 41st was retained in Africa at the disposal of theater headquarters in Algiers. After several weeks in a staging area near Oran, under assignment to Mediterranean Base Section, the company moved to more permanent quarters at Sidi Ferruch, near Algiers, and took up its role as a theater laboratory assigned to AFHQ. It remained there until after the fall of Rome.[7]

The principal business of the 41st in North Africa turned out to be surveillance of CWS matériel held in storage. When stored items developed unexpected reactions to aging in depots the laboratory was called upon for an explanation. An instance of this occurred in the spring of 1944 when the chemical officer of Seventh Army asked for an investigation of certain phosgene detector tubes, which had turned black. The 41st determined that the tubes, taken from the detector kit, M9, contained a highly unstable indicator chemical which had decomposed, and recommended replacement with tubes of a newer type.[8] For the most part, though, surveillance consisted of sending inspection teams to the depots. A typical team might consist of an officer and two enlisted men.[9] A surveillance program drawn up by the 41st in the spring of 1944 and scheduled for accomplishment before

---

[6] (1) Ltr, ACCWS Field Opns to Theater CmlO's, 10 Jun 44, sub: Rpts of Lab Units.   (2) 42d Cml Lab Co, 29 Oct 43, Rpt, Problems Submitted to the 42d Cml Lab Co.   Both in CWS 314.7 Unit Files.

[7] History of the 41st Cml Lab Co.

[8] Tech Rpt 30, 41st Cml Lab Co, 8 Jun 44 .

[9] Memo, CmlO Fifth Army for CmlO AFHQ, 14 Jun 43, no sub.   CWS MTOUSA 400.112 Analyses, Tests, Trials, Equivalents, Experiments.

the end of the year included thirty-four item examinations, ranging from bulk mustard to antidim sticks (for preventing mist on gas mask eyepieces).[10]

In July 1944 a few weeks after the fall of Rome, the 41st moved from its Algerian home to new quarters in the Italian capital. There it shared with a British Expeditionary Forces outfit, the South African 23d Antigas Laboratory, the facilities of the Italian Military Chemical Institute. The surveillance responsibilities continued, including now a program for the test firing of mustard-filled mortar shells, instituted for the purpose of checking the ballistic properties of chemical ammunition kept in storage over long periods.[11] Intelligence reports increased as more chemical equipment from enemy depots in Italy fell into American hands. Captured items included not only German matériel but also defensive chemical warfare items from countries occupied or controlled by the Germans. The 41st had the opportunity of studying and reporting on individual gas mask canisters, decontamination kits, and the like from Czechoslovakia, Hungary, Rumania, and Yugoslavia in addition to German and Italian matériel. Nevertheless, as might have been expected in a less extensive theater, the intelligence functions of the 41st did not match in magnitude those of some of the laboratory companies in western Europe and the Pacific.[12]

In contrast to the comparatively routine transfer overseas of the 41st Laboratory, the process of getting the 3d Chemical Field Laboratory Company (later redesignated the 42d Chemical Laboratory Company) to a theater of operations was far from typical. The company came into being at Edgewood, Md., on 15 May 1941 with a complement of Reserve officers and a cadre drawn largely from the 1st Laboratory. After filling out its ranks with newly inducted selectees, the unit spent the summer and early fall in basic and specialized training. Rather suddenly, at the end of October 1941, it was ordered to the west coast to prepare for shipment overseas. On 21 November, the company embarked and sailed westward, the first CWS unit of the war to be dispatched overseas. The destination was given simply as PLUM, but it was not reached on schedule. PLUM was the Philippines,

[10] Ltr, CO 41st Cml Lab Co to CCmlO NATOUSA, 24 May 44, sub: Surveillance Program for U.S. Cml Warfare Matériel. CWS MTOUSA 400.112 Analyses, Tests, Trials, Equivalents, Experiments.

[11] Interv, Hist Off with Maj James B. Goodson, CO 41st Cml Lab Co, 14 Aug 59.

[12] CWS Technical Notes for Laboratories (a series of monthly compilations of major laboratory field reports and other items of interest, published monthly from July 1944 until the end of the war by CWS Technical Command).

and the troops were still at sea when the Japanese turned the Philippines into a theater of war. The convoy received orders diverting it to Australia and, as indicated above, docked at Brisbane on 22 December. The company was not to reach the Philippines for three and a half years.

In Brisbane the company settled down to work as a unit of Base Section 3, U.S. Army Forces in Australia. By the end of February the laboratory equipment had been set up in permanent quarters and organized technical work was under way. At first a substantial number of laboratory personnel were detailed for general duty with base section headquarters, but these demands slackened after the first few months and by midyear the company was able to pursue its mission at approximately full strength. It had become in the interim the 42d Chemical Laboratory Company by redesignation effective April 12, 1942, and had moved to new quarters in buildings formerly occupied by a Brisbane hospital.[13]

According to one of its commanding officers, the 42d possessed neither a clearly defined mission nor an effective training for field operations when it arrived in Australia.[14] This did not prevent the company from serving as an all-purpose technical unit from the very outset. Before it had finished unpacking its equipment, it had received and responded to Air Corps queries on oxygen and rust inhibiters, Australian Army problems with Kieselguhr water filters, and base section demands for an ant exterminator. Not long thereafter it was at work on practical studies of petroleum bomb fillings. In September 1942, the 42d took on a major assignment for the Quartermaster Corps—turning 100,000 pounds of fatigue uniforms into jungle green camouflage suits. A formula and procedure for dyeing the uniforms were developed in the course of a day by a 5-man team, and the dyeing itself was carried out under the supervision of company personnel.

By midsummer the 42d, in addition to its routine analytical work, was engaged in several CWS research problems of a more generalized nature, including studies of nitrogen mustard, low temperature studies of mustard for high altitude spraying, and tests of the action of mustard and impregnite on fabric. Colonel Copthorne, chief chemical officer of USASOS, regarded this type of work as a necessary supplement to

---

[13] History of the 42d Cml Lab Co.
[14] Interv, Hist Off with Maj Hugh W. Hillis, CO 42d Cml Lab Co (1942-44), 25 Sep 45.

the technical information he was receiving from the United States, so much so that he recommended to General Porter that field laboratory companies be declared branches of the Technical Division of Edgewood Arsenal. This attempt to formalize a research and development mission for the laboratory companies was met with a prompt and firm reminder that the mission of field laboratories was properly confined to testing friendly and captured chemical warfare equipment and identifying enemy toxic agents, should any be used. While this reminder may have served to set the record straight, it had little direct application to the multitude of miscellaneous technical problems which the 42d by now regarded as its responsibilities. In a subsequent letter General Porter admitted as much; pure research aside, he said, the work of the 42d could not be precisely circumscribed so as to deprive SWPA of the services it was performing.[15]

Fortified with official approval, the 42d Chemical Laboratory Company increasingly continued to handle the theater's laboratory needs. A report prepared in October 1943, summarizing the problems outside the normal mission area which the 42d had undertaken since its arrival, listed over fifty tasks performed for the other technical services and the Air Corps. Some of these were of considerable magnitude. A skin dye for camouflage purposes was developed to meet a Quartermaster Corps requirement, and enough of it was manufactured to fill 150,000 2-ounce bottles. For Ordnance a considerable amount of analysis of defective items was done: propellant cartridges, mortar charges, and AN–M103 bomb fuzes. In addition, captured enemy explosives were analyzed, both for Ordnance and for the Navy. Counter Intelligence Corps received help from the laboratory in checking on several instances of suspected sabotage. Industrial analyses of many types were made— steels for the Air Corps, sand for the Engineers, soldering flux for Ordnance, soaps for Quartermaster. Even the Chemical Warfare Service benefited from the 42d's nonmission labors, if the manufacture of some 3,500 detonation tubes of assorted toxic agents for troop training be so considered.[16]

The miscellaneous field work of the 42d, varied as it was, did not

[15] (1) Ltr, CCmlO Hq USASOS SWPA to CCWS, no sub, 17 Aug 42. (2) Ltr, CCWS to CCmlO Hq USASOS SWPA, no sub, 17 Sep 42. (3) Ltr, CCmlO HQ USASOS SWPA to CCWS, no sub, 24 Nov 42. (4) Ltr, CCWS to CCmlO Hq USASOS SWPA, no sub, 14 Jan 43. All in CWS 314.7 Pers Files.

[16] 52d Cml Lab Co, 29 Oct 43, Rpt, Problems Submitted to the 42d Cml Lab Co. CWS 314.7 Unit Files.

prevent the company from carrying out the primary responsibilities of its mission. Its regular technical intelligence reports on captured Japanese chemical equipment began to appear as soon as its laboratory was set up, and continued thereafter, to the number of nearly fifty, during the two and a half years that elapsed before it prepared to leave Australia. Surveillance of theater stocks of CWS equipment was a continuing responsibility.[17]

Toward the end of September 1944 the 42d was instructed to prepare itself and its equipment for transfer forward. Much of the regular laboratory work was accordingly discontinued, and the company spent the following months largely on garrison duty while waiting for movement orders. For a time it conducted advanced chemistry courses for its own personnel. Finally, in June 1945, with the reconquest of the Philippines nearly complete, the 42d embarked for Luzon. It arrived in Manila on 21 June. By the time the laboratory was set up once again, the war had come to an end.[18]

Just as the experience of the 42d demonstrated a tendency for the work of the laboratory in an isolated theater to broaden, the 43d Chemical Laboratory, in a somewhat comparable situation, exemplified to a striking degree the ability of such a unit to extend its usefulness. In this case the functions of the unit were construed by the theater, at least in practice, to include a measure of research and development. Despite the official CWS policy which regarded development as the prerogative of the Technical Division at Edgewood, the 43d, in the course of its work on "field expedients," tended to make itself a development unit in the field.

The 43d Chemical Laboratory Company, activated at Edgewood Arsenal on 26 August 1942,[19] was ordered to Hawaii in December of 1943. Upon its arrival it was assigned to theater headquarters (Central Pacific Area) and stationed at Schofield Barracks, where the theater chemical officer, Colonel Unmacht, had laboratory facilities (manned by 8th Chemical Depot Company personnel) already in operation. The 43d took over the existing laboratory functions, added its own equipment, and set to work.[20] The immediate tasks were predominantly within the intelligence portion of the mission—the study and descrip-

---

[17] History of the 42d Cml Lab Co.
[18] Ibid.
[19] Hq CWS Edgewood Arsenal GO 17, 26 Aug 42.
[20] History of Cml Sec AFMIDPAC, I, an. I-b, 8–11.

tion of captured Japanese chemical equipment. Nearly one hundred technical reports on captured matériel were to be made by the 43d in the succeeding twenty months. Surveillance of theater chemical stocks led the company into a detailed study of deterioration in impregnated clothing. But before long larger problems began to absorb its attention.

At the time the 43d arrived in the Pacific theater, Army, Navy, and Marine Corps personnel were becoming increasingly anxious to acquire armored vehicles equipped with flame throwers for use against Japanese island emplacements. Rather than wait for Edgewood Arsenal, entangled in conflicting priorities and requirements, to provide the weapons, the theater went ahead on its own.[21] The work was in its early stages when the 43d appeared on the scene. In February 1944, after tests of the Anglo-Canadian Ronson flame thrower mounted on a Bren gun carrier had proved inconclusive, the project was placed in the hands of Colonel Unmacht, who assigned it to the 43d. A task force from the company succeeded in redesigning the Ronson to make it a practical main armament weapon for the M3 tank. Mounted in a shroud simulating a howitzer, the Ronson flame thrower turned the quondam M3 into the Satan. By mid-May 1944, the task force had supervised the completion, test firing, and combat readying of twenty-four Satans for use by the marines in the Marianas.[22]

From flame throwers the 43d moved on to an extensive consideration of flame thrower fuels. The development of thickened fuel—gasoline thickened to jelly by the addition of certain aluminum soaps—had proved to be essential to the effectiveness of flame throwers in the field. Napalm had been adopted as a standard thickener during the war, but in practice it appeared that field-thickened fuels tended to vary in characteristics and performance. Flame thrower fuels mixed in Hawaii and sent to the front lines, for example, were sometimes found to have had their viscosity more or less reduced by absorbed water, and any substantial change in viscosity involved an unacceptable lack of certainty of flame thrower range and performance. Assigned this problem, the 43d determined that drying gasoline before mixing, and adding finely divided activated silica gel to the mix, would produce a fuel stabilized enough to be packaged, stored, and shipped successfully. This work, accompanied by a series of papers on the theory and manufacture of stabilized fuel, was completed in the summer of 1945, whereupon the

[21] See Brophy, Miles, and Cochrane, *From Laboratory to Field*, ch. VII. See also, below, ch. XIV.
[22] History of Cml Sec AFMIDPAC, II, an. II–c, 2–6.

771–608 O–66—20

company proceeded to supervise the building of an activating plant at the chemical warfare depot and the mixing of 150,000 gallons of fuel, using silica gel salvaged from packaged motors, in which it had been enclosed as a desiccant.[23]

The research and development activity which these accomplishments characterized went beyond the specific mission of the laboratory, but was typical of the manner in which Colonel Unmacht as head of the theater CWS encouraged independent action to meet theater needs. It played a major role in winning for the 43d a Meritorious Service Unit Award at the conclusion of hostilities.[24]

The Chemical Maintenance Company

Twenty maintenance companies were supplied to the ground forces overseas by the CWS before the end of the war. Though designed to serve field armies, they could also be, and frequently were, assigned to the Communications Zone. Their mission was third and fourth echelon maintenance of all CWS equipment and matériel, which could and did include everything from salvaging discarded gas masks to manufacturing parts for the 4.2-inch mortar. While maintenance companies were intended to function as salvage and repair centers near CWS Class II and IV depots, in practice some maintenance units assigned to field armies found it necessary to send their men forward beyond the army service area for close support of the front, in order to keep mortars and smoke generators in combat condition.

T/O 3–47, 1 April 1942, set the authorized strength of a maintenance company at 4 officers and 119 enlisted men, organized into a headquarters outfit, a 3-unit repair platoon, and a salvage platoon. The repair platoon was supposed to include all of the company's skilled mechanics not assigned directly to headquarters, leaving the salvage platoon to operate principally with laborers. A revised organization table published in November 1944 showed a maintenance company pared down to 93 officers and men. The two platoons were redesignated gas mask repair and equipment repair, respectively, and nearly all the enlisted personnel authorized were classified according to specific skills.

---

[23] (1) *Ibid.*, pp. 35–37. (2) 43d Cml Lab Co Tech Rpts 81, 10 Jul 45, and 90, 22 Aug 45. CWS 314.7, Unit Files.

[24] Ltr, CO 14th Cml Sv Bn to CG CPBC, 22 Aug 45, sub: Recommendation for the Meritorious Service Unit Award. CWS 314.7 Unit Files.

The platoons were organized into functional sections.[25] Nevertheless, experience in the field throughout the war showed that under the pressure of combat requirements the work of maintenance companies often left prescribed organizational patterns behind.

One of the more noteworthy service records of the war was that of the 12th Chemical Maintenance Company, which acquired eight battle credits in the course of assignments ranging from Tunisia through Sicily and Italy to central Europe. Activated 1 May 1942 at Fort Custer, Mich., the 12th went overseas in March 1943, landing at Casablanca on the 18th. It was assigned to Atlantic Base Section and its first job was running CWS supply dumps. In the last month of the Tunisia Campaign it operated in conjunction with advanced supply depots at Bône and Ouled Rahmoun in eastern Algeria and at Tabarka in Tunisia. It began to undertake more orthodox maintenance work—salvage and repair—in the days after the Tunisia Campaign ended.[26]

An advance detachment of the 12th, assigned to 3d Division, landed in Sicily on 10 July 1943 at the outset of the invasion, in order to get a CWS supply dump functioning as soon as possible near the combat area. The rest of the company was in Sicily by the middle of July. During the month or so of fighting that followed before Sicily was won, the company provided the first example of close maintenance support of combat units by the CWS. The 12th's maintenance and repair officer, Lieutenant Notorangelo, took a 10-man detachment into the combat zone near Sant'Agata in the second week of August to carry out on-the-spot maintenance for the 4.2-inch mortars of the 2d Chemical Battalion. The battalion was supporting the infantry advance along the north coast of Sicily on the left wing of Seventh Army. The maintenance detachment later proceeded south to Randazzo, on the right wing, to perform the same service for the 3d Chemical Battalion, after getting needed parts from a rear depot. At the same time, Lieutenant Notorangelo utilized this experience to provide the Chemical Officer, Seventh Army, with the first detailed figures available on attrition rates of mortar parts in combat.[27]

After a period of salvage and repair work in Palermo, marked by a concerted effort to get the required number of serviceable gas masks

[25] TOE 3-47, 22 Nov 44.
[26] Hist of the 12th Cml Maint Co.
[27] Draft Ltr, CO 12th Cml Maint Co to CG NATOUSA, 17 Nov 43, sub: Recommendation for Award. CWS 314.7 Unit Files.

ready for the coming campaign, the 12th followed the Allied forces into Italy early in November 1943. Setting up shop at the Fontanello Caves near Naples, the company reverted to its role of depot operator, storing incoming CWS supplies for Peninsular Base Section. It found time to re-establish its gas mask repair line, though, with the aid of some Italian civilian labor. In December the 12th responded to an emergency report from Fifth Army that mortar propellant charges were too damp to give accurate ranging. Discontinuing its gas mask line, the company set to work improvising a powder ring dryer and a shell reconditioning line and repacking the propellant rings in water-proofed cases. Two weeks after the operation began an explosion and fire wrecked the shops, though fortunately there were no major casual-ties. The 12th put its equipment together again at another depot near Casandrino, devised a more reliable powder ring dryer, and had its lines operating again within a week.[28]

Meanwhile, a mortar repair detachment had settled at Capua to service the mortar battalions attached to Fifth Army. In April 1944, the remainder of the company also moved to Capua. There they found the weapons repair section, commanded by Lieutenant Notorangelo, established at the erstwhile Royal Italian Arsenal, which the retreating Germans had wrecked before moving out. The section had joined other Fifth Army service troops in getting the installation in working order by salvaging usable machinery and acquiring additional equipment, Italian, American, or German, wherever possible. In effect, the 12th now had an arsenal of its own. It was fortunate that this was so, for the demands for smoke generator and mortar spare parts rose sharply under the pressure of the bitter Italian campaign of 1943–44. When the depots could not supply enough parts, the 12th's Capua arsenal manufactured them. The Weapons Repair Section, making full use of the skills of a large working force of Italian civilian machinists, inaugurated this new mission with the fabrication of mortar cup forks. A number of other items were soon added to the list as the rugged terrain, long usage, and high ranges took their toll of the overworked 4.2-inch mortars. Shock absorber slides proved especially vulnerable. To keep the mortars in working condition, the 12th cast and machined new slides of bronze—after liberating the bronze from Italian naval

---

[28] (1) History of the 12th Cml Maint Co.   (2) 12th Cml Maint Co, Activities During the Italian Campaign, 1943–44. CWS 314.7 Unit Files.

CAPUA ARSENAL, AS THE GERMANS LEFT IT. *Within thirty days it was producing mortar parts for the Fifth Army.*

vessels in Naples harbor—which subsequently proved to be more durable than the brass slides they replaced. Tube caps and steel recoil springs were also prominent in the mortar parts output of the Capua arsenal. For the mechanical smoke generators and the power-driven decontaminating apparatus the weapons repairmen fabricated sprocket gears of several types, along with nuts, couplings, and the like.

The usual repair functions of a maintenance company were carried on side by side with the manufacture of spare parts. The Capua arsenal, as reconstructed by the 12th, contained a cradle rack for repairing 400-gallon tanks from power-driven decontaminating apparatus, a welding shop, a repair shop for vehicular components and chemical handling trucks, and sections for work on Esso and Besler mechanical smoke generators. The 12th's gas mask repair sections occupied a shop of its own, with two production lines for the disassembly, repair, and reassembly of damaged or salvaged masks. A group of Italian soldiers assisted in the operation of this facility, which turned out over 150,000 reconditioned masks in less than five months.

In September 1944, the 12th was assigned to Seventh Army, then engaged in pushing up the Rhône Valley from the coast of southern France to join the armies in the European Theater of Operations. By the end of the month, the company was in Dijon, serving as a unit of Continental Advance Section. A weapons repair group, designated as Detachment A, moved on to Épinal to resume close support of the mortar battalions. More work was done to improve the Capua shock absorber slide, including the addition of small amounts of phosphoric tin to the original bronze alloy. Mortar cup forks continued to be made. Portable flame throwers were reconditioned. By December the rest of the company reached Épinal, whereupon a reorganized and somewhat smaller Detachment A moved out to the front. It took up quarters near the command post of the 99th Chemical Mortar Battalion, then supporting Third Division on the Colmar front. Here, within range of German artillery, the detachment kept the battalion's mortars in operating condition. The detachment remained with the battalion throughout the winter, and in March 1945, moving forward across the Saar with the front, became the first portion of the 12th to enter Germany. Before the end of the month it was across the Rhine. By the time the Germans surrendered, it had accompanied combat troops deep into southern Bavaria.[29]

A second close support group, Detachment B, left the main body of the 12th in mid-March to join the 87th Chemical Mortar Battalion in Germany. The 87th had begun to take part in the advance across the Rhineland, and the detachment had to carry out its mission between rapid movements forward. Once across the Rhine, and before moving ahead to the 96th Chemical Mortar Battalion, Detachment B performed a final individual maintenance mission for the 87th on the eve of the battalion's transfer to First Army. Together with the other forward elements of Seventh Army it had penetrated Austria before hostilities ended.[30]

Chemical maintenance companies were not as extensively utilized in the Pacific war as they were in Europe. Only two maintenance companies got west of Hawaii, and one of these, the 10th, ended the war

---

[29] Hist of 12th Cml Maint Co.
[30] Ibid.

as a CWS general service company, a type of all-purpose support organization much favored in the Southwest Pacific Area. Before its conversion, however, the company had made important contributions in its original role. The 10th Chemical Maintenance Company, activated 1 July 1940 at Edgewood Arsenal, was sent overseas three months after Pearl Harbor as part of the forces assigned to rebuild Allied power in the Southwest Pacific. It reached Australia early in April 1942, and like the 42d Chemical Laboratory Company joined Base Section 3 in Brisbane.

As an early arrival in the theater, one of the 10th's original tasks was to assist the 62d Chemical Depot Company in the operation of CWS depots in Australia. It was not long before special maintenance problems resulting from waging war in a tropical environment began to dominate the scene. A major example was the discouraging failure in combat of the M1A1 portable flame thrower in the course of the Papua Campaign. The 10th spent the greater part of 1943 putting the discredited weapon through an extensive series of tests, in the course of which all flame throwers in the SWPA were thoroughly overhauled.[31] It became clear that tropical heat and humidity were the flame thrower's chief enemies. Pinhole corrosion of the nitrogen, hydrogen, and fuel cylinders, occurring in 75 percent of the weapons examined, led to leakage, low pressure, and consequent failure in the field. Corrosion resulting from moisture attacked other components as well, and batteries deteriorated readily when exposed to jungle climate.[32]

The 10th set to work to clear up as many of these defects as possible. There was no quick solution for the problem of pinholes in the cylinders. All that could be done was to repair those cylinders which were not excessively corroded and replace the rest, insofar as supplies permitted. In order to make it possible for troops to spot flame throwers with defective cylinders before attempting to use them in combat, pressure gages and adapters to fit all types of commercial pressure

---

[31] (1) Ltr, CmlO USASOS SWPA to CmlO's Base Secs 2, 3, 4, and 7 and CO 10th Cml Maint Co, 16 May 43, sub: Flame Throwers. Sixth Army Rcds, 470.71 Flame Thrower. (2) Ltr, CG USASOS SWPA to CO 10th Cml Maint Co, 6 Feb 44, sub: Commendation. History of the 10th Cml Maint Co.
[32] (1) Ltr, CCmlO USAFFE to CmlO USASOS SWPA, 12 Apr 43, sub: Auxiliary Equip for Flame Throwers. FECW 470.71/6 in CWS SPCVO 470.71 APO 501. (2) 3d Ind, CO 10th Cml Maint Co to CCmlO USASOS SWPA, 29 Dec 43. Sixth Army Rcds, 470.71 Flame Thrower.

cylinders were added to the flame thrower service kits.[33] The problems resulting from wet electrical systems were met by waterproofing the weapon effectively enough to enable it to stand total immersion and still retain its usefulness. The company's own tests of the results of its waterproofing project included the firing during rainfall of random samples of waterproofed weapons after keeping them under water for about seventeen hours. It was able to report by October of 1943 that, given adequate pressure in the cylinders, the flame throwers which it had waterproofed and checked would function as intended regardless of moisture.[34]

While the work on flame throwers was of major importance, it was far from constituting the only large-scale project of the 10th in Australia. Reconditioning of depot stocks was a continuing task. Providing waterproof seals for gas mask canisters kept the company busy on more than one occasion. Some 180,000 canisters of one type were waterproofed in late 1943 and early 1944; the company historian permitted himself the remark that the job had become somewhat monotonous after the first hundred thousand. By April 1944, however, the 10th found itself somewhat short of CWS assignments and tending more and more toward ordinary garrison details as the focus of war moved northward toward the Philippines. At last the company itself moved northward, to New Guinea, in August 1944, and shortly thereafter was reorganized. Pressure toward the streamlining of rear area service units in the theater had been reflected in proposals to replace the CWS depot, maintenance, and decontamination units with general service companies capable of meeting all of these requirements as they arose. Though the European theater commanders had been unimpressed with the idea, it seemed sufficiently attractive in the special circumstances of the Southwest Pacific to cause it to be adopted in the case of a few selected units, as soon as an appropriate table of organization was published. This event occurred in the summer of 1944, and the 10th, just arrived in New Guinea and past the critical period in its

---

[33] Ltr, CCmlO USAFFE to CmlO USASOS SWPA, 10 Jun 43, sub: Flame Thrower Testing Equip. Sixth Army Cml Sec Rcds, 470.71 Flame Thrower.

[34] (1) 10th Cml Maint Co, Instrs for Changing the Battery in the Flame Thrower and Rewaterproofing, 28 May 43. Sixth Army Rcds, 470.71 Flame Thrower. (2) Rpt, CO 10th Cml Maint Co to CCmlO USASOS SWPA, 25 Oct 43, sub: Rpt of Serviceability of Flame Thrower, Portable, M1A1, Waterproofed. CWS 314.7 Unit Files. (3) Ltr, Maj John J. Shaffer, USAR, to Hist Off, 19 Sep 56. Major Shaffer, then a captain, commanded the 10th Chemical Maintenance Company for the greater part of its service in Australia.

maintenance mission, was one of the units to experience the change. As of 1 November 1944 it was reorganized as the 10th Chemical Warfare General Service Company. The remainder of its war service, including an additional eight months in New Guinea and the last month of the war in Luzon, was spent under that name.[35]

The Chemical Depot Company

Chemical depot companies played a key role in the movement of CWS matériel in the overseas theaters. The basic mission of these units, some twenty of which saw overseas service, was to act as CWS supply centers, either for field armies or for communications zone commands. This included receiving, storing, and issuing chemical supplies, certain salvage operations, and operating filling lines for certain chemical munitions. A depot company was a good-sized outfit, with a total strength of almost 200 men. When in the field, it was not unusual for a company to resolve itself into a group of detachments handling a series of assignments simultaneously. A company assigned to a theater headquarters, on the other hand, was also capable of serving many needs, ranging from technical training to theater supply.

As organized under TOE 3–67, 28 May 1942, the 184 officers and men of a depot company constituted a small headquarters unit, an administration platoon controlling three record, storage, and maintenance sections, and three service platoons for guard and labor functions. This plan was substantially altered by the next edition of the TOE, 6 October 1943, which shifted administrative functions to an enlarged headquarters unit, turned the former administrative platoon into a 52-man maintenance organization, and assigned all remaining storage, surveillance, and handling responsibilities to the service platoons, now reduced to two. By the end of the following year emphasis was being placed on the supply and munitions filling missions, with a consequent conversion to a uniform 3-platoon organization totaling 155 officers and men.[36] Operating under a headquarters unit charged with basic administration, the three service platoons, each divided into ammunition, toxic gas, and general supply sections, were nonetheless capable

---

[35] (1) History of the 10th Cml Maint Co.   (2) Draft Memo, CCWS to CofS, attn: ACofS G–3, 7 Jan 44, sub: Proposed Cml Warfare General Serv Co. CWS 314.7 Unit Files.   (3) TOE 3–137S, Cml Warfare General Serv Co, 9 Aug 44.

[36] (1) FM 3–65, Cml Depot Co, 1 Dec 44.   (2) TOE 3–67, 6 Jan 45.

of acting independently if the need arose, providing the company commander with three ready-made units for detached service.

The 8th Chemical Depot Company had a notable record as one such theater supply agency. It was activated at Fort Shafter in March of 1942 for the specific purpose of operating the supply functions of the Hawaiian Chemical Warfare Depot for the department chemical officer. These were of considerable magnitude. Under Colonel Unmacht's vigorous leadership, the depot had already completed the substantial task of obtaining and distributing enough service gas masks to provide adequate protection to troops in the event of a new Pearl Harbor in chemical warfare.[37] By the time the 8th was activated the depot was in full swing as the only central distribution agency in the department for CWS supplies. It maintained subdepots for local troops on the islands of Hawaii, Kauai, and Maui. In addition to discharging its supply mission, the depot served as a third and fourth echelon maintenance center, a function performed in 1944–45 by the 20th Chemical Maintenance Company.[38]

Along with its other responsibilities, the 8th found itself on activation with an impregnating plant already in full operation. Colonel Unmacht had had an experimental impregnating plant—one shipped to Hawaii at some earlier date—put in operating condition shortly before Pearl Harbor. One of his first acts after the attack was to order the plant into active operation, in order to provide protective clothing for the troops then in Hawaii. The plant, designated No. 5, was manned by men of Company A, 1st Separate Chemical Battalion, the only force then available for the purpose. When Colonel Unmacht got his depot company activated, it was given the additional duty of running No. 5 until an impregnating company should arrive. As Plant No. 5 demonstrated a high degree of mechanical unreliability, the depot company was generally engaged in emergency repairs. For a time it took over and operated two small Navy impregnating plants at Pearl Harbor. By January 1943 a new plant, No. 8, had been shipped to the Islands, and a new building had been constructed to house it. The new facilities tended to ease the task of the depot company somewhat, but not until January 1944 was the 8th finally able to turn this unscheduled responsibility over to a newly arrived unit,

---

[37] See above, pp. 220, 267.
[38] History of Cml Sec AFMIDPAC, II, an. I–d, 2–23.

the 110th Chemical Processing Company, and concentrate on its supply mission.[39]

As a supply unit, the 8th was responsible for seeing to it that all troops sent forward from Hawaii were properly equipped with CWS matériel. It kept subdepots and forward areas supplied. The unit sometimes found it necessary to handle bulk toxics in operations involving transfer from damaged containers, or from ton containers to drums. In the course of these handling operations, three enlisted men of the 8th designed and built a handling cart for more expeditiously moving 150-pound cylinders.[40]

The 8th assisted the 43d Laboratory Company in manufacturing the first batches of the stabilized flame thrower fuel (napalm plus activated silica gel) developed by the latter unit in 1945. In the summer of that year the Hawaiian Chemical Warfare Depot built its own unit for the activation of the silica gel. The 8th had this unit operating at a rate of one ton per day during the last weeks of the war. Between May and August of 1945 the depot manufactured a total of 226,343 gallons of fuel.[41]

Of great importance to the theater CWS was the 8th's secondary mission of training cadres for new units. Among these were supply detachments activated to help shoulder the burden of CWS depot management in Hawaii and general service companies destined for combat support in the Western Pacific. In the last year of the war the 8th trained and supplied to other units enough officers and enlisted men to have doubled its own authorized strength.

In contrast to the role of the 8th as a theater headquarters supply element was that of the 6th Chemical Depot Company, a unit which operated many installations without ever permanently establishing itself at any of them. It was a depot company on the move, following American combat forces from England to Germany by way of North Africa, Italy, and France.

The 6th was activated at Fort Sam Houston on 25 March 1942. After a brief training period, the company embarked for an overseas assignment on the 1st of July and arrived in Scotland on the 12th. Within a few days the company, the first of its kind to reach the European theater, was in quarters at two points in southwestern Eng-

[39] *Ibid.*, V, an. II-k, 1-6.
[40] *Ibid.*, V, an. III-a, 50-51.
[41] *Ibid.*, pp. 104, 107.

land, under assignment to the newly created Southern Base Section of the theater Services of Supply. It set to work almost at once, sending out detachments to establish chemical sections at general depots for handling Class II and IV CWS supplies, as well as for constructing two depots for chemical munitions. This procedure of operating several installations at once through self-sufficient detachments was to be a consistent pattern in the operation of the 6th throughout its service overseas.[42]

The 6th was the CWS unit depot assigned to II Corps in the fall of 1942 for operations in North Africa. It arrived in Oran from England early in December 1942, and immediately took over a depot previously established by corps headquarters. As the North African campaign developed, the 6th began setting up new installations, after the manner of its English experience. The Oran depot, for Class II and IV supplies, remained company headquarters for the time being, while detachments set up and operated depots eastward along the North African seaboard as far as the Tunisian border, turning them over in due course to relieving units. The company used anything available for storage—garages, factories, sheds—and resorted to open storage when necessary. For chemical munitions, however, open storage was the rule, rather than the exception.[43]

The 6th remained in North Africa during the month-long Sicilian campaign, but was reassigned to Fifth Army immediately afterwards in anticipation of the invasion of Italy. Nine of the company's enlisted men, temporarily attached to the 531st Engineer Shore Regiment, went ashore at Salerno on D-day, 9 September 1943, with the assault troops. Operating in two groups, they took charge of identifying, storing, and issuing CWS matériel brought over the beaches on the first three days of the invasion. By the 8th of October the 6th was in Naples.

The 6th spent almost a year in Italy, in the course of which it was at one time or another responsible for over thirty supply points. It had general responsibility for all chemical depot needs of Fifth Army. Company headquarters, originally in the Naples area, was shifted northward repeatedly, reaching Piombino in northern Tuscany by midsummer of 1944. In the interval the company supplied two de-

---

[42] (1) History of the 6th Cml Depot Co.   (2) Ltr, Maj Levin W. Lane to CmlC Hist Off, 28 Mar 50.   Major Lane was commanding officer of the 6th, 1943–45.
[43] History of the 6th Cml Depot Co.

tachments for service with the Anzio-Nettuno assault force. The first of these landed at Nettuno on D-day, 22 January 1944, the second joined it on 23 January. During the months of bitter fighting that followed, the beachhead detachment of the 6th, augmented from time to time, handled 12,000 tons of CWS munitions. In the same period, Headquarters Detachment was enlarging the scope of its usual duties by manufacturing some 10,000 Molotov cocktails out of napalm and glass bottles.[44]

In July 1944, the 6th was assigned to Seventh Army, in order to participate for a third time in an invasion—in this case the assault on the Mediterranean coast of France. Three detachments, attached respectively to the 3rd, 36th, and 45th Divisions, VI Corps, landed with the initial assault forces on 15 August and carried out the unusual mission of organizing chemical supply on the beaches. Company headquarters followed two weeks later and moved northward almost at once to Grenoble, where it set up a depot for Class II and IV CWS supplies before moving forward again. Meanwhile a detachment had gotten a base depot at Marseille under way for Continental Base Command, the supply and service agency of the invasion period. Other detachments handled CWS supply at successive ammunition supply points as Seventh Army advanced toward Alsace.[45]

The 6th remained with Seventh Army through the winter of 1944–45 (during which the partial withdrawal of American forces in Alsace to meet the threat of the German counteroffensive in the Ardennes temporarily forced the 6th, like some other forward units, to move its headquarters back), and advanced with it into Germany in the spring. In the meantime, it found time to organize and conduct a training program to convert a French smoke generator company to a chemical depot unit.[46] The end of the war found the company operating several depots in the Seventh Army area of the southern Rhineland. Immediately after the end of hostilities, the 6th set up Rheinau CWS Depot before preparing to go home.[47]

---

[44] (1) *Ibid.* (2) Lane Ltr, 28 Mar 50.

[45] History of 6th Cml Depot Co.

[46] Ltr, CO 6th Cml Depot Co to CG Seventh Army (Through CmlO Seventh Army), 9 Nov 44, sub: Rpt on Cml Warfare Depot School . . . CWS 314.7 Unit Files.

[47] Hist of the 6th Cml Depot Co.

The Chemical Decontamination Company

The chemical decontamination company was a specialized organization designed to counter the threat of crippling gas attacks on rear area service facilities. While the services of a company were expected to be available to combat troops under gas attack if the situation permitted, the primary mission was confined to installations in the service area, on the assumption that combat units should have the capability to meet a tactical gas situation with their own resources. Deconamination companies were not assigned by any precise formula (the recommended ratio was one company per 100,000 strength) and were intended, while maintaining a headquarters in a service area, to send out detachments to either service or combat zones at their own discretion. As organized under TOE 3–217 (1 April 1942), a company included 4 officers and 200 enlisted men, functioning as three 60-man platoons of three sections apiece, plus company headquarters. The table was changed on 12 October 1943 to provide for four 33-man platoons, reducing the total company strength to 170, and making the 10-man section the smallest operating unit, instead of having a further subdivision into squads, as formerly provided. The basic function of the section was to operate a 400-gallon power-driven decontaminating apparatus, a truck-mounted sprayer designed to heat and distribute a slurry of bleaching powder and water.

The abstention of the belligerents from gas warfare left the decontamination companies without a primary mission to perform. In consequence, while keeping themselves in readiness for possible future gas emergencies, the companies sent overseas found themselves assigned to a variety of tasks. Theater and army chemical officers welcomed their presence when CWS-trained units were needed for munitions handling, smoke screening, or depot labor. Other elements of the armed forces discovered that the power-driven decontaminating apparatus had more than one use; thereafter, decontamination units were sometimes engaged in giving showers, handling water, and wetting down dusty roads. Occasionally, decontamination companies were pressed into service totally unrelated to their training or equipment. One such unit eventually became part of a G–2 task force in ETO.

The 21st Chemical Decontamination Company was one of the most active of those whose overseas service lay principally in the CWS mission area. The 21st, activated at Camp Bowie, Tex., in March 1942, began its overseas experience when its 1st Platoon, detached for the purpose, joined Western Task Force in Casablanca on 18 November of the same year, ten days after the first assault forces had landed in North Africa. The task force chemical officer, Colonel Barker, used the platoon to set up his CWS depot. The platoon had had no specific training for this mission, but with the administrative aid of a detail from the task force chemical section it set up a depot nonetheless. By January 1943 it was able to find the additional time to assist in the program of CW schooling begun by Colonel Barker.[48]

In May 1943 the rest of the 21st reached Casablanca. By that time the company's 1st Platoon had gone forward to Algeria, and the company itself followed within a month. The company and platoon alike were destined for the Sicily Campaign and accordingly were earmarked for assignment to Seventh Army.[49] They arrived in Sicily during July, the 1st Platoon going direct to Palermo (which had been occupied on the 22d), the remainder of the company landing on the south shore. By August the company had been reunited at Palermo, but only to split up into detachments stationed along the Sicilian north coast where they handled CWS supplies. Together with elements of the 63d Chemical Depot Company and the 12th Chemical Maintenance Company, the several platoons of the 21st implemented the CWS supply plan by setting up and operating a series of ammunition supply points extending as far east as Campofelice, some thirty miles beyond Palermo.[50] The 21st also supervised the operation of the CWS Class II depot in Palermo until relieved by the 63d Depot Company in October.

The 21st remained in Sicily for about ten months after the conclusion of the Sicily Campaign, under assignment to Island Base Section. During the period it was kept busy on various CWS tasks under the supervision of the IBS chemical officer, including such work as gas mask reconditioning and the maintenance of a smoke line as part of the defense plan for Palermo harbor.[51] By June of 1944 CWS stocks in Sicily had been closed out, and the 21st went to Italy to prepare for reassignment to Seventh Army and the campaign in southern France.

The role of the 21st in the Seventh Army's campaign from the beaches of the Riviera to the heart of Germany was to be that of a

---

[48] Hist of the 21st Decontamination Co. Seventh Army 322.
[49] Seventh Army Rpt of Opns in Sicilian Campaign, an. H.
[50] *Ibid.*
[51] History of IBS.

smoke unit. There was time for only a brief training period before the company joined the assault forces. In the initial assault, a platoon of the 21st accompanied each of the three assault divisions, company headquarters and the remaining platoon being held in reserve.[52] The mission in this instance was to provide smoke cover for supply dumps on and near the beaches, as needed. On D-day, August 15, groups of men from the 21st went ashore with the first assault wave carrying (or towing) smoke pots with them. Smoke lines were set up several hundred yards inland as soon as possible. Two weeks later the 21st was moved, in two installments, to Marseille to provide smoke cover for the port. For its work on the beaches, the company received a commendation.[53]

As the campaign advanced northward toward Alsace and Germany, the 21st continued to function as a smoke generator outfit. Equipped with smoke pots and M2 mechanical smoke generators, it provided detachments for smoke coverage throughout the autumn of 1944 for the Army supply routes. Toward the close of the winter campaign in Alsace, the company once again found itself in a battle zone when it provided screening for the troops, American and French, of the XXI Corps front during the final cleaning up of the Colmar Pocket.[54]

Though the 21st had become accustomed to its smoke mission by the spring of 1945, it had reverted to its original role by the end of the war. As American troops drove across Germany in April and May of 1945, they seized intact a number of chemical warfare depots. The task of safeguarding and managing these important and potentially hazardous acquisitions was an appropriate one for a decontamination company. Accordingly, a detachment of the 21st took over initial gas security and munition inventory responsibility at the Wildflecken site in April. By the time the war ended, the company was in charge of gas security for the principal German chemical depot at St. Georgen, deep in Bavaria.[55]

The overseas experience of the 31st Chemical Decontamination Company was in decided contrast to that of the 21st. Both gained

[52] Seventh CWS Staff Sec Rpt, 1 Jan–13 Oct 44.
[53] GO 64, Hq Seventh Army, 24 Feb 45.
[54] CO 21st Cml Decontamination Co to CmlO Seventh Army, 25 Feb 45, Rpts, (1) Opns with XXI Corps and 75th Infantry Div, (2) Opns with the 3d Inf Div. CWS 314.7 Unit Files.
[55] (1) Memo, CmlO Seventh Army to CO 21st Cml Decontamination Co, 20 Apr 45, no sub. (2) Memo, Div CmlO 42d Inf Div to CmlO Seventh Army, 14 May 45, sub: Opn of 21st Cml Co (Decontamination). Both in CWS 314.7 Unit Files.

honors for front-line combat. But while the 21st served in direct support of CWS missions as supply and smoke troops when not fulfilling their original purpose, the secondary missions ultimately acquired by the 31st turned out to be somewhat farther afield.

The 31st was activated at Camp Bowie, Tex., in July 1942. After a training period which included some instruction in amphibious operations, it embarked for Great Britain, arriving early in January 1944. Its assignment was to First Army's 6th Engineer Special Brigade, a collection of units destined for the assault wave of the Normandy invasion. With them it underwent further training in invasion tactics throughout most of the two months immediately preceding the start of the campaign.

Shortly after noon on D-day a 25-man detachment from the 31st landed in Normandy with the 149th Engineer Combat Battalion and joined the battle which had been in progress on OMAHA Beach since dawn, its primary mission being reconnaissance against the possible gassing of the landing site by the Germans. By the time the remainder of the company landed on the following day, seven of the detachment's personnel, including its commander, 1st Lt. Stanley Boggs, had been wounded. When the absence of gas warfare had been confirmed, the company joined other service troops in policing the beach and unloading ammunition. It was able to move to a bivouac area on 12 June (D plus 6), by which time it was busy with a variety of emergency tasks— assembling supply dumps, guarding prisoners, and finding new uses for its big power-driven decontaminating tanks. It employed them to wet down dust, to haul water, to fight fires, and to provide showers.[56]

In the last week of July the battle moved out of Normandy, and by mid-August the Germans were rapidly retreating across France. As the German policy of abstention from gas warfare continued to be confirmed by events, the necessity for the retention of decontamination units by the engineer special brigades declined. On August 20th, the 31st was reassigned, this time to an unexpected destination. It was detailed to Headquarters, Special Troops, 12th Army Group, to serve as headquarters troops for a special intelligence force being organized by the 12th Army Group G–2. This so-called T-Force was designed to operate as a front-line agency directly behind the advancing combat troops, where they were to seize enemy documents and round up agents

[56] History of the 31st Cml Decontamination Co.

and collaborators before they escaped.[57] The 31st turned in all its CWS unit equipment, including its decontamination tanks, drew in exchange an additional supply of cargo trucks and jeeps, and departed, for practical purposes no longer a CWS unit, for the first T-Force objective—Paris. On August 23, it reached the front line at Rambouillet. The objective was entered on August 25th, in the vanguard of the Allied troops. The 31st, one of the first American service units in the liberated capital, had T-Force headquarters set up in the Petit Palais before midnight of that day. That action marked the beginning of more than eight months of constant movement. T-Force headquarters left Paris for the east on 7 September. Between that date and the German surrender the following May, the 31st occupied fourteen successive stations in France, Luxembourg, Belgium, and Germany. It had all the usual headquarters administrative duties to keep it occupied—operating messes, providing mail and payroll services, supplying the force with clerks, maintaining a motor pool, and assuring internal security.

The 31st continued in its new role until T-Force ceased to function on 6 May 1945, the day before the instrument of surrender was signed at Reims. The company was en route for Wiesbaden at the time. On its arrival it joined 12th Army Group's Special Troops and performed such missions as operating trucks and guarding prisoners of war for three weeks until it was returned to the United States for redeployment to the Pacific. It was training for that purpose when the war ended.[58]

The Chemical Processing Company

The chemical processing company was a basic element in defense against gas warfare. Its primary mission was to keep available to theater chemical officers a supply of permeable protective clothing adequately and recently impregnated with chlorinating compounds so as to protect the wearer from the effects of vesicant vapor or droplets. Companies were designed for assignment to theaters for location in the communications zone, generally near a chemical depot.

A company consisted of a total of 146 men, organized on a 2-platoon basis. Each platoon was the organizational equivalent of a processing plant and contained three functional sections for continuous 3-shift

[57] 12th Army Group Rpt of Opns, IV, 3–6.
[58] Hist of the 31st Cml Decontamination Co.

operation. Accordingly, the company possessed two impregnating plants (either the M1 type employing acetylene tetrachloride as a solvent or the M2 water suspension type).[59] The impregnating plants were semifixed industrial installations of impressive size, not unlike commercial laundries. An M1 plant, for example, included two 400-gallon solution tanks, a predryer, two final dryers, and an impregnator, recognizably related to laundry-type drying and washing machines respectively, solvent recovery apparatus, a steam generator unit, complete with boiler and oil burner, an electric generator unit, a fuel tank, a water pump, and such auxiliary items as work tables, tool kits, and spare parts—the total equipment load approximating fifty tons. It could be installed only in a building with a floor heavy enough to support it and large enough to provide adequate work space. In practice, this meant a building with the equivalent of a 4-inch reinforced concrete floor and about 3,600 square feet of floor space. Installation required the skills and labor needed to handle heavy machinery, four or five separate piping systems, and electrical wiring.[60] The equipment and techniques involved in the impregnation of clothing were enough like those of quartermaster laundries to provide the processing companies with ready-made secondary missions—laundering, dry-cleaning, waterproofing, dyeing, and comparable service functions —which were to keep many companies profitably occupied during periods when their primary mission was not in requisition. But less obvious duties were not wanting. Like other service troops, processing companies were drawn upon for whatever labors were required at the time. Depot assignments were not uncommon. Two units, the 113th and the 120th Chemical Processing Companies, had nearly all their men detailed for a time to the 87th and 81st Chemical Mortar Battalions respectively to provide additional support for the mortar teams. They served with the battalions throughout the Normandy and Northern France Campaigns. Another, the 109th, did construction work with the engineers. But a due regard for the possible outbreak of gas warfare and the corresponding requirement in every theater for reserve supplies of impregnated clothing kept processing companies occupied with their primary mission fairly often.

The experience of the 105th Chemical Processing Company may be cited to demonstrate the work of a typical unit. The 105th was ac-

[59] TOE 3-77, 1 Mar 44.
[60] TM 3-270, Clothing Impregnating Plant M1 (Theater of Opns), 4 Feb 44.

PLANT OF 105TH CHEMICAL PROCESSING COMPANY, BRISBANE, AUSTRALIA

tivated in August 1942 at Edgewood Arsenal and trained there and at
Camp Sibert. In mid-May 1943, the company embarked from New
York for Brisbane, Australia, via the Panama Canal. It arrived a
month later, marched out to Camp Doomben, and went to work for
the chemical warfare depot and base section headquarters pending
arrival of its impregnation plants.[61]

Personnel of the 105th got their first taste of processing in the field
when the bulk of the company's first platoon went to Sydney to help
the theater provide a reserve of some 70,000 protective uniforms for
its troops. The 62d Chemical Depot Company was in charge of the
effort, which consisted of getting a nonoperating improvised impregnating plant in working condition. The detachment spent a week on
the task before the setup, manufactured from standard laundry equipment, was ready for its first load. Thenceforth, the unit kept the
plant running at full prescribed rates, some 8,000 pounds of clothing
per 24-hour run. It remained on the job until mid-February 1944,

---

[61] History of the 105th Cml Processing Co.

when, with the mission virtually complete, it rejoined the rest of the company.[62]

The rest of the 105th had been kept busy, meanwhile, on details for the theater chemical officer. One detachment, for example, went to Columboola, two hundred miles west of Brisbane, to provide storage and perform surveillance for 29,000 mustard-filled bombs, a task involving a good deal of decontamination work when leakers were found. The company's first organic impregnating plant, an M1, arrived in January 1944, and the men went to work to provide a building for it at the CWS center near Brisbane. Before the end of March, after essential piping was finally acquired, the plant was ready for operation, and the 105th proceeded with its primary mission.

Not long thereafter the 1st Platoon was again detached, this time for duty at Base A, Milne Bay, New Guinea. At this more forward base it set up an impregnating plant to help protect the combat forces clearing the way to the Philippines against possible gas attack. The 2d Platoon continued operating the company's M1 plant in Brisbane, for the most part on a 24-hour basis. Its output of protective clothing continued until the beginning of October 1944, when it was ordered to cease operations and prepare for movement. For the next few months, while awaiting movement orders, the 105th kept itself busy with miscellaneous jobs for the 62d Chemical Service Company and the local Ordnance service center. At Milne Bay, meanwhile, the company's 1st Detachment, now well behind the new front in Leyte, had been diverted to laundry and dry-cleaning operations, together with depot work.[63]

In mid-June 1945, the 105th finally received its long delayed orders and moved forward to Luzon. At the same time the 1st Detachment left Milne Bay and rejoined the company at the CWS training center near Manila. The training center needed them, but not for processing; it was in the midst of a hurried construction program to house a CWS school and garrison. The 105th, well accustomed to construction jobs, pitched in and was hard at work building facilities when hostilities ended.

Another processing company in the Southwest Pacific Area, the 103d, though its overseas experience was much like that of the 105th,

---

[62] (1) *Ibid.* (2) History of Cml Sec Hq USASOS SWPA. Orgn Files, AFWESPAC, Folder USASOS History of Cml Warfare School, APO 923, Jul 42–May 44.

[63] History of 105th Cml Processing Co.

found itself for a time with a new mission. The 103d, which had also been activated at Edgewood in August 1942, was sent to Hollandia, New Guinea, in July 1944. There, at a base captured from the Japanese only three months before, it was to be comparatively close to combat organizations.

An immediate need of the combat troops was protection against mite-born scrub typhus. The answer appeared to be impregnation of uniforms with an insecticide. Accordingly, the 103d, once it had its two impregnating plants set up, was put to work mite-proofing all available uniforms with dimethyl phthalate. Not until this task was complete, in mid-October, did the company turn to its normal processing missions. But by that time theater requirements for protective clothing were taking second place to more routine needs. The base quartermaster required assistance in meeting his laundering mission, so that the 103d began devoting the bulk of its time to laundry. By December 1944, the company's plants were working full time as laundries for base units and hospitals. These duties, continued for the next six months at rates in excess of 150,000 pounds of laundry per month, earned the 103d a Meritorious Service Unit Plaque before it went to Luzon for miscellaneous service assignments just before the Japanese surrender.[64]

The Chemical Service Company

For the greater part of the war the type of unit ultimately designated as a chemical service company was known as a chemical composite company.[65] The purpose of the composite company was to provide field organizations of divisional size with a CWS service organization capable of simultaneously operating supply points, doing third and fourth echelon maintenance, running a field laboratory and a field impregnating program, and providing at least a nucleus of trained men for decontamination. Furthermore, the composite company was expected to be able to put its entire manpower of over 200 into any one of these tasks should the situation require. The goal was flexibility: a versatile unit, not too tightly organized, which could meet CWS service needs for smaller combat forces or isolated fronts. The war in the Pacific was emphatically of such a nature, and it was in the Pacific that most composite companies saw service.

[64] History of the 103d Cml Processing Co.
[65] Composite companies were redesignated service companies in March 1945.

The first organizational scheme for composite companies provided for specialized sections of considerable bulk, averaging almost forty men apiece, fairly closely tied in to company headquarters, and presumably meant to remain intact during operations.[66] Within a short time reports from the Southwest Pacific declared that more flexibility was needed and that in actual practice existing units were usually split up into smaller groups. Such detachments usually suffered from the lack of an appropriate administrative organization and organic equipment. The problem was that the concept of cellular structure had been modified by too great a dependence on the administrative and internal support capabilities of the unit as a whole. The cells were not self-sufficient, and clearly they needed to be. In July 1943 a new organization plan was devised, making more explicit use of the principle of cellular structure—that is, of flexible organization based on small specialized teams capable of extended independent operations —than had previously been the case. The new pattern, applicable alike for separate platoons, companies, or battalions, was promulgated by TOE 3–500, 19 July 1943, and provided a choice of several types of such teams, varying in size from one to sixty-six men, for the CWS functions of maintenance, depot operations, decontamination, processing, and laboratory work. The War Department also authorized teams which could operate as headquarters for units composed of operational teams and support teams to operate messes and to provide automotive maintenance. Separate equipment allowances were listed for each type of team. This arrangement was intended to make possible the formation of composite units of a size directly related to the type of mission required and the size of the force to be supported. A further refinement of cellular organization was made when the TOE was reissued in December 1944 in order to provide still greater flexibility, principally in the area of administrative and maintenance teams.[67]

Hence, the service units that the CWS placed overseas, for the most part in the Pacific, were far from uniform in size, makeup, or functions. In some cases, rather than maintain company organizations for scattered service detachments, companies were inactivated and their

---

[66] TOE 3–277, Cml Composite Co, 1 Apr 42.

[67] (1) Ltrs, CCmlO USASOS to CCWS, 27 Jan 43 and 6 Mar 43, sub: Cml Composite Cos. CWS 320.2 CWS Units. (2) TOE 3–500, Cml Warfare Serv Orgns, 19 Jul 43, 15 Dec 44.

93D CHEMICAL COMPOSITE COMPANY TESTING FLAME THROWER FUELS, *Milne Bay, New Guinea.*

elements reconstituted as separate service platoons, as TOE 3–500 had provided for.[68] Sixth Army, in the course of its campaign on Luzon in 1945, attached chemical service platoons to its divisions; the missions of such a divisional platoon included reconditioning 4.2-inch mortar ammunition (the checking and cleaning of shells being of particular importance in the corrosive environment of the tropics), service and maintenance of portable flame throwers (together with training their operators), manning a smoke pot line, repairing gas masks, preparing napalm, performing second and third echelon maintenance of mortars, providing chemical warfare intelligence, and using the power-driven decontaminating apparatus as a water carrier and portable shower. Such an attached platoon was regarded by Sixth Army as an essential part of the combat division.[69]

[68] The 94th Chemical Composite Company, for example, assigned to SWPA in the fall of 1943, operated as four separate units from January 1944 onward and was at length disbanded in November 1944 to form the 272d, 273d, 274th, and 275th Composite Platoons.

[69] Ltr, CG Sixth Army to CG USAFFE, 26 Dec 44, sub: Shortage of Cml Serv Troops. Sixth Army 322 CWS Orgns.

One of the few exceptions to the rule that CWS composite companies went to the Pacific was the 92d Chemical Composite Company. Activated at the end of 1942 at Camp Sibert, the 92d was organized on the basis of TOE 3–277 when it went overseas the following spring. It was destined for the North African theater. Its debarkation point, reached on 10 May 1943, was Casablanca, but it soon moved forward to Mateur in newly won Tunisia. There its depot section took over the CWS section of General Depot 6, Eastern Base Section, and its impregnation section set up an open storage depot. The laboratory section assembled its equipment in a garage and went to work on captured chemical matériel. The maintenance section set up a repair shop and began work on gas masks, flame throwers, and decontaminators, both portable and power driven. During the summer the units followed EBS headquarters from Mateur to Bizerte but otherwise they maintained their activities through 1943 uninterrupted, save for an occasional air raid. The company formed a principal CWS rear echelon support for both the Sicilian and the Italian invasions.

In February 1944 the 92d was reorganized under the new TOE 3–500, utilizing an organizational scheme under which the laboratory section was discontinued entirely, leaving the company with a repair team, a maintenance and salvage section, a decontamination team, and three supply (depot) teams, as well as a headquarters and mess.[70] The following month, despite the new organization, a detachment amounting to about half of one of the supply teams (and taking about half of the team's equipment) left for depot duties with Northern Base Section in Corsica, not to rejoin the company until January 1945. Another depot team, together with the decontamination team, was sent, as Detachment A, to Island Base Section in Palermo. The bulk of the company spent a few weeks closing out its depot and maintenance installations before being itself transferred in May to Mediterranean Base Section at Oran.[71]

The 92d's mission at Oran was primarily the creation of a consolidated CWS depot near MBS headquarters. Four outlying depots were closed out and their stocks moved to the new central installation, a former engineer storage center with ample facilities. It took more than a month to get the 4,000 tons of CWS matériel crated, consoli-

[70] Ltr, AGO to CG NATO, 17 Feb 44, sub: Reorgn of 92d Cml Composite Co. AG 322 (14 Feb 44) OB–I–SPMOU–M.
[71] History, 92d Cml Composite Co.

A CHEMICAL SERVICE COMPANY LABORATORY, NEW GUINEA

dated, stored, and properly maintained. When the job was complete and the depot, plus an attached CWS maintenance shop, was in good running order, the 92d turned the facilities over to another unit and prepared to leave for its next assignment, Peninsular Base Section in Italy.[72]

In Italy the 92d served again primarily as a depot unit. Upon its arrival in mid-August 1944, it was sent to the CWS depot near Bagnoli; Detachment A had already arrived from Sicily to take over the depot at Santa Maria and move its stocks to Bagnoli for consolidation. The maintenance mission was resumed in September, when a detachment went north to set up and run a CWS maintenance shop at PBS Forward Echelon, Leghorn. This left the rest of the company with the Bagnoli depot as its sole responsibility, except for the gas mask repair section, which operated in conjunction with the storage facility. The decontamination team had become, in effect, another depot team. Depot administration, however, came to include training

[72] *Ibid.*

as well. An Italian service battalion was stationed at the depot under control of the 92d for training in depot operation, as well as for the sake of the additional labor supply. Depot work included both Class II and IV storage at the main installations and open storage of Class V matériel at a site near Naples. The provision of trained security details for shipment and storage of toxic munitions gave men of the decontamination team recurring practice in their primary mission. A less common opportunity for the use of their skills came in spring, when the team decontaminated the area used by the 41st Chemical Laboratory Company for testing mustard-filled mortar shells.[73]

The 92d remained on the job as a depot-maintenance outfit at Bagnoli and Leghorn for the remainder of the war. The cessation of hostilities in Europe did not reduce the company's workload for some time. The Leghorn detachment, much depleted by personnel transfers, acquired control of a German prisoner of war battalion to help it rehabilitate, box, and ship matériel to the Far East, a task accomplished ahead of schedule. The Bagnoli portion of the company celebrated the end of the war by disposing of its supply of toxics through the winter of 1945–46, sinking the matériel in deep water off the island of Ischia. It was not until the spring of 1946 that the 92d, by then possessed of a Meritorious Service Unit Plaque, was ready for inactivation.

More typical of the experience of composite companies was the overseas record of the 240th. Activated in August 1943, at Camp Sibert, the 240th Chemical Composite Company was reorganized under TOE 3–500 the following February. Under this setup, the company had a total of no less than twenty-two cellular teams, including at least one for each of the following CWS service missions: maintenance, supply, decontamination, and processing. The last of these was represented by only a single unit, and the laboratory function was omitted altogether, leaving the company organized primarily for depot and maintenance work, with decontamination capabilities when needed. The 240th, after reorganization, had a total strength of just over 200 men. Toward the end of May 1944, it embarked from Portland, Ore., for the Southwest Pacific Area, and arrived in Finschhafen, New Guinea, a month later for assignment to Sixth Army.

On arrival, the 240th went into bivouac at Cape Cretin and began functioning for the time being as a depot unit, helping out with the

[73] *Ibid.*

operation of the CWS depot at Finschhafen's Base F. Meanwhile, the Chemical Officer, Sixth Army, decided that the 240th, like other composite companies so assigned, could be best utilized as four separate service units, of a size and composition suitable to the support of a reinforced division. Accordingly, in mid-August, the company became the parent of Units 1 through 4. Unit 1 was weighted toward the maintenance and depot functions, as was Unit 4, though the latter also had impregnation specialists. Unit 2 was largely drawn from the impregnation team, with smaller numbers representing the other service missions. Unit 3 was almost entirely a maintenance outfit, except for one small depot team. Company headquarters personnel were divided between units 1, 2, and 4.[74] All four units were destined to participate as divisional support elements in amphibious assaults.

Unit 1, suitably enough, was the first to be committed. Toward the end of August it was earmarked for the mid-September invasion of Morotai, midway between New Guinea and the Philippines. Its mission was to set up CWS supply dumps on the beaches to collect, store, and salvage CWS matériel and to provide second and third echelon maintenance for chemical equipment.[75] The Morotai task force, named TRADEWIND, assembled for staging at Maffin Bay in Wakde-Sarmi sector of northwestern New Guinea before the end of August. On 11 September the unit's depot team, including five maintenance men attached to infantry regiments to support flame thrower operations, embarked with the assault forces and landed with them on Morotai on the morning of 15 September. There was little organized Japanese resistance on the island as the combat troops moved rapidly forward and the service units, after some initial trouble with the approaches to the beaches, began organizing support areas.[76] The depot team of Unit 1 of the 240th, working like the rest of the task force under sporadic enemy air attack, brought up ammunition to a CWS mortar platoon, set up its bivouac area, and arranged for its dump to be situated near the ordnance supply site. It was busy for the next few days locating and storing matériel, principally signal and incendiary grenades.[77]

---

[74] History of the 240th Cml Composite Co.
[75] An. 5, Admin Order 1, Hq TRADEWIND Task Force, 23 Aug 44, cited in History of the 240th Cml Composite Co.
[76] See Smith, *Approach to the Philippines*, pp. 480–93.
[77] History of the 240th Cml Composite Co.

The remainder of Unit 1 joined the depot team on Morotai on 11 October, by which time the operation had been declared over and the work of building an air base was well under way. The unit continued operation of the CWS dump, put up warehouses with space for maintenance operations, and did a brisk business in picking up and reconditioning gas masks. The unit remained in place on Morotai, attached to the 31st Division, until the last week in January 1945, when it joined the 33d Division and embarked for Luzon.[78]

Unit 2's first mission was not long behind that of Unit 1. This unit left New Guinea for Los Negros in the Admiralties at the beginning of October 1944, to join the 1st Cavalry Division as part of Sixth Army's invasion force for the reconquest of the Philippines. It promptly reembarked to join the Leyte invasion convoy. A-day for Leyte was 20 October, and that morning the 1st Cavalry Division landed as the northernmost element of the assault, securing White Beach just south of Tacloban, the island's capital. Unit 2 reached Leyte and landed at White Beach on A plus 2, 22 October, by which time the division was driving the enemy out of the Tacloban area. The unit's first task was getting 4.2-inch mortar ammunition to the 85th Chemical Mortar Battalion, in the course of which operation it ran a beach ammunition dump. By mid-November it was in Tacloban, setting up a divisional CWS depot. The operation of this supply point constituted Unit 2's mission for the remainder of the Leyte Campaign. At the end of January 1945 the unit was attached to XI Corps, which joined Sixth Army's Luzon Campaign by landing near San Narciso on 29 January to cut off Bataan. Unit 2 landed with the corps and set up a corps chemical warfare depot.

Unit 3, after being first assigned to and then withdrawn from the Morotai invasion force, remained at the Maffin Bay staging area for the time being, providing depot support and flame thrower maintenance for the 123d Regimental Combat Team, then engaged in local operations against the Japanese. In mid-November the unit went to Sansapor, at the northwest tip of New Guinea, to join the 6th Division, part of the force being staged for the invasion of Luzon. It spent the next weeks loading mortar shells and other CWS supplies on ships; inspecting, reconditioning, and test firing flame throwers; and training. The task force of which it was a part embarked on 30 December 1944.

[78] *Ibid.*

On the morning of 9 January 1945 the combat troops landed on the shores of Lingayen Gulf, north of Manila, 6th Division holding the center of the beachhead. There was no immediate enemy opposition. The men of Unit 3 began reaching the beaches some three hours after the first assault and immediately set to work organizing a CWS beach dump. A consolidated chemical dump for the 6th Division's beachhead was in operation by the next morning, supporting the division's 4.2-inch mortar companies. Five days later a detachment set up an advance depot fifteen miles inland, and the task of moving mortar shells, grenades, and flame thrower fuel off the beaches was begun. A second inland depot was set up the following week, replacing the first. Regular forward movements of supply points followed at intervals of a few days. The unit's repairmen were kept busy maintaining the division's flame throwers. Supply and maintenance operations in close support of 6th Division continued without a break until the division was relieved on 30 April after three and a half months in action.[79]

Unit 4 remained at Cape Cretin, New Guinea, until mid-November 1944. At that time, having been attached to the 40th Division, it proceeded to the division's stage area at Cape Gloucester, New Britain. The 40th, like the 6th, was scheduled to participate in the Luzon landings, and Unit 4, like Unit 3, spent the last weeks of November 1944 checking and loading mortar ammunition. The unit also placed 15-man teams on detached duty with each of two mortar companies attached to the division. The 40th Division landed on the southwestern flank of Sixth Army's assault on the shore of Lingayen Gulf on the morning of 9 January. Two hours after the first assault wave hit the beach, personnel of Unit 4 began arriving ashore. The unit soon had a depot for Class II and Class IV CWS supplies in the town of Lingayen and an ammunition dump operating in conjunction with the divisional ordnance supply point. Both depot and ammunition dump were moved forward after two weeks, by which time the detachments had rejoined the main group, bringing Unit 4 up to its full strength. It continued in support of the 40th Division throughout February 1945.[80]

By that time the 240th Chemical Composite Company had long ceased to be a unit in any operational sense. Its four segments were

[79] History of the 237th Cml Serv Platoon.
[80] History of the 238th Cml Serv Platoon.

all on Luzon, but each was in support of a different outfit. Sixth Army had already come to the conclusion that it required nothing of composite companies save the provision of platoon-size detachments for close divisional support. Under the circumstances there was little reason to retain company organization, especially in view of the fact that the basic TOE 3–500 could apply as well to an independent platoon as to a company. As had already happened in other cases, the decision was made to disband the 240th as a company and activate its units as separate composite platoons. Accordingly, as of 12 February 1945 the 240th Chemical Composite Company ceased to exist. In its place there appeared, organized under the current TOE 3–500 (15 December 1944), the 240th Chemical Service Platoon, formerly Unit 1, and the 236th, 237th, and 238th Chemical Service Platoons, the erstwhile Units 2, 3, and 4, respectively. From then on the four platoons were for all practical purposes divisional chemical warfare elements and served through the remainder of the Philippines campaign in that capacity.[81]

Chemical Air Service Companies

As in other respects, so in the field of chemical service operations the Army Air Forces functioned as a separate entity. The Air Forces had major CWS functions, as a potential principal user of toxic agents in the event of gas warfare, as a participant in smoke missions, and as the utilizer of the new CWS strategic weapon, the incendiary bomb. To assist in the execution of these chemical missions, the CWS organized and sent into the field several types of service units especially designed for Air Forces needs. Included among those seeing overseas service were chemical depot companies, chemical maintenance companies (both types bearing the additional designation "Aviation"), and the many chemical companies designated simply "Air Operations," one hundred of which were activated between 1942 and 1945. Half of these saw service in overseas theaters. Four of the fourteen maintenance companies, aviation, and all of the twenty depot companies, aviation, also went overseas.

The air depot companies, like their ground counterparts, had as their principal mission the storage, surveillance, and preparation for issue

---

[81] The 236th (formerly Unit 2) was attached to the 38th Division, an element of XI Corps, on 23 March 45.

LOADING LIQUID SMOKE INTO AN M10 SMOKE TANK FOR AIRCRAFT, *New Guinea.*

of CWS matériel, in this case primarily bulk toxics, smoke mixtures, and incendiaries. Normal assignment was on the basis of one per AAF general depot when, as was usually the case, the depot in consideration was intended for storage and issue of chemical supply in appreciable quantities. A typical air depot company, the 754th, assigned to the VIII Air Force Service Command in England, had four sections: administrative, chemical, incendiary, and security maintenance.[52] The last three of these were respectively in charge of storage, surveillance, and filling of chemicals and chemical ammunition, storage and surveillance of incendiaries, and repair, maintenance, defense, and security details for the depot. The proper execution of these tasks called for a good deal of technical proficiency, especially in the handling and surveillance of toxics. Another air depot company in that command, the

[52] T/O 3–418, 28 Feb 42.

763d, found that a depot company might be responsible not only for filling mustard bombs but for making up such items as M47A1 incendiary bombs as well, using bomb casings, gasoline, and thickener.[83]

Chemical companies, air operations, in their organization and mission presented certain parallels to the composite companies of the ground forces. Like the latter, they were meant for close support of combat units and were organized on a cellular basis, with platoons (four to the company) capable of performing like missions on a self-sustaining basis when attached separately to units of appropriate size. The major missions of air operations companies were to maintain CWS ammunition storage dumps, to prepare and arm chemical munitions for combat use and (in practice) to load such munitions on the using aircraft. The recommended normal basis of assignment was one air operations company per group or one platoon per squadron. A platoon consisted of a headquarters team and four identical operations teams, which were essentially toxic-filling outfits. In addition to its headquarters and its four platoons, the air operations company included a distributing point section to operate its dump; this group included at least two men trained in decontamination techniques and equipped with a power-driven decontaminating apparatus.[84] The processes involved in handling, arming, and loading CWS bombs, bomb clusters, and spray tanks required a good deal of technical training and special equipment.[85]

Air operations companies were not infrequently faced with unanticipated tasks. For example, companies in the SWPA used a newly developed spray tank (the E2B25, produced by the Far East Air Force Service Command) not only for smoke operations but for the spraying of DDT over areas rendered hazardous by the presence of insect-borne malaria or typhus.[86]

In the last months of the Pacific war aerial incendiaries played an increasingly important role in both the strategical and tactical spheres. The assault on Iwo Jima, for example, was preceded by a 10-week bombardment by planes based in the Marianas; incendiary bomb clusters formed a significant part of their load. Air operations com-

---

[83] Conf Rpt, The Opn, Duties, and Function of a Cml Depot Co, Avn, 22–23 Feb 43. Eighth AF 520.805–Nov 43.

[84] TOE 3–457, 29 Sep 44. An earlier version, 1 July 1942, differed in providing for platoons with two large operations teams apiece.

[85] Capt Louis E. Schueler, 876th Cml Co AO, The Cml Co, Air Opns. Eighth AF 520.805–Nov 43.

[86] Col Augustin M. Prentiss, Jr., Cml Warfare History of Fifth Air Force–Far East Air Forces. CWS 314.7 Fifth AF.

panies supporting the bomber formations increased the supply of incendiaries by improvising fire bombs from 55-gallon drums filled with napalm and armed with an M15 WP grenade and an all-ways fuze. The fuzing of this unfamiliar weapon was the source of so much concern to the air crews that at first they insisted that CWS personnel accompany the flights to keep an eye on the incendiaries. The air operations companies always loaded incendiaries into planes and, when necessary, were called upon to modify bomb bays to accommodate particular types of incendiary bomb clusters.[87] In the early months of 1945 incendiary raids on a vast scale carried the war direct to the industrial centers of Japan. In their support of these crippling blows, the air operations companies contributed significantly to the final victory.

[87] Interv, Hist Off with Lt Col Alfred J. Green, USAR, 15 Sep 59.

CHAPTER VIII

Large Area Smoke Screens in the MTO

It was the fate of the Chemical Warfare Service to enter World War II with rather ill-defined responsibilities, a circumstance accented by the absence of its most clearly defined mission—gas warfare. As a consequence, responsibilities were delineated and missions took shape as the necessity for meeting new conditions actually arose in the theaters of operations. A case in point was large area screening. The tremendous development in air power between the world wars produced a situation which made the concealment of ground targets a prime necessity. Clues pointing to this development were apparent in the 1930's but for various reasons little had been done to prepare for large area screening. The first adequate American smoke generator did not appear until 1942. Once the generators were in the theaters, a chain of circumstances created smoke missions which were unknown even in the tentative doctrine of the prewar period.

Background of Large Area Screening

Experiment and Trial

Although the employment of small quantities of smoke in combat was an ancient military technique, its use to conceal extended areas was a twentieth century innovation. The term *large area screen* is quite imprecise. The size of a large area screen depends upon the nature and size of the target to be obscured. The screen had to be large enough to baffle enemy bombardiers; if it were too small it would merely pinpoint vital areas. The technical aspects of large-scale smoke screening had been a CWS concern from the time that service received the smoke mission in 1920. The most immediate interest was in the development of agents and munitions to support tactical operations. Because initial CWS experiments in area screening along the Panama

Canal were unsuccessful, the search for agents and means of disseminating area screens continued sporadically until 1936 when the War Department decided that with the means available large area screening was not practicable.[1]

The high importance placed on hemisphere defense by the RAINBOW plans of 1939 [2] revived War Department interest in providing passive defense for the vulnerable areas of the Panama Canal. On 1 July 1940 the War Department directed Maj. Gen. Walter C. Baker, Chief, Chemical Warfare Service, to submit an estimate of the costs of development, installation, and maintenance of smoke screening apparatus required for concealing the three locks. By the end of the month the War Department sent this estimate to the commanding general, Panama Canal Department, for comments. The Air Corps commander in the Canal Zone favored the project in principle but had some reservations. The commanding general of the Panama antiaircraft defenses opposed any extensive use of smoke which might nullify the effectiveness of antiaircraft fire. The department chemical officer advised his commander that in view of the lack of information about the effectiveness of large area screens it would be unwise to plan a costly screening installation for the three locks. The matter was held in abeyance.[3] Nevertheless, two points had emerged from the Panama studies. First, technical means for generating artificial clouds were inadequate. Second, there was serious opposition by commanders to the employment of smoke during air raids. Until a better means of smoke production was devised, a mutually satisfactory decision about smoke employment was impossible.

At that time, the war in Europe provided actual combat tests of the use of smoke. Before mid-1940 British interest in large area screening had been rather theoretical—an interesting proposition but hardly practicable.[4] When the German invasion of the Low Countries and

---

[1] (1) Phosphorus, chlorosulfonic acid, and hexachlorethane (HC) had been the agents tested. (2) For a review of large area smoke tests at Panama from 1921 to 1939, see OCCWS Tech Study 23, Use of Smoke to Screen Panama Canal Locks, 18 Jul 40 (rewritten 9 Jul 41). (3) Special Folder on Smoke Screen Experiments in Panama [1921–31]. CWS Ret 470.6/2491.

[2] Matloff and Snell, *Strategic Planning for Coalition Warfare, 1941–42*, pp. 7–8.

[3] (1) Ltr, CmlO Panama Canal Dept to CCWS, 1 Oct 40, sub: Use of Smoke to Screen Panama Canal Locks. (2) Memo, CmlO PCD for ExecO OCCWS, 8 Oct 40, no sub. Both in CWS Ret 470.6/57–231.

[4] (1) Statement, Dir of Weapons and Vehicles (Br) for Asst Chief Imperial General Staff, ca. 1 May 43. CWS 314.7 Smoke Opns. (2) The various smoke devices developed by the British are discussed in TDMR 396, Jun 42. Tech Lib ACmlC, Md.

France in the spring of 1940 provided the Luftwaffe with airfields within easy reach of the United Kingdom, the British gave serious attention to the possibility of using smoke to conceal vital installations. At first, the British Ministry of Home Security, responsible for screening vulnerable targets, provided oil-burning orchard smudge pots for targets in Birmingham and Coventry. It waived smoke abatement orders so as to increase the industrial haze, no longer the public nuisance it had been in time of peace. The Admiralty Fuel Experimental Station at Haslar, England, later developed the first large-capacity oil-burner generator, cumbersome and inefficient but the best smoke producer available at the time.

The typical British large area smoke installation in 1941 consisted of several thousand stationary smudge-type oil pots and a few Hasler generators which gave body to the screen from upwind positions. Although requirements for oil, all of which had to be imported, and manpower were heavy, area screening proved well worthwhile. In addition to military advantage, smoke became an important factor in maintaining the morale of factory workers, especially in munitions plants. Employees sometimes demanded smoke, despite its inconvenience, as the price of continuing to work at night.[5]

Beginnings of Large Area Screening in the United States

The gradual transition of area screening from theory to practice was observed with interest in the United States. The Chemical Warfare Service carefully surveyed the development of European equipment and screening techniques and, with the Army Air Corps and other Army elements, investigated the problems which would accompany the development of large area screening.

In mid-1940 the only smoke-producing munitions available to the U.S. Army were smoke shells, pots, grenades, and airplane smoke tanks. These munitions were satisfactory for establishing transitory curtains and could be used to a limited extent for blanketing enemy positions, but they were unsuitable for maintaining smoke screens over wide areas of friendly terrain because of the limited amount of smoke they produced and because artillery and mortar shells could not be impacted

[5] (1) Thomas K. Sherwood, NDRC, Div B, Rpt 197 (OSRD 435), Rpt on Screening Smokes, CWS-17, 3 Mar 42, passim. Tech Lib ACmlC, Md. (2) British Historical Monograph, Special Weapons and Types of Warfare, Part II A, gives a complete picture of the development of smoke missions and munitions in Great Britain.

near friendly troops. Moreover, smoke from the HC-filled pots was harassing at best and in concentrated amounts could be quite toxic. Following the British lead, the CWS adapted the commercial smudge pot which was standardized as the M1 stationary oil generator. CWS scientists and later those of the National Defense Research Committee (NDRC) became interested in more efficient smoke production techniques. In 1942 there appeared an entirely new type of smoke generator, one which emitted a "smoke" composed of small particles of oil created when a superheated oil-vapor mixture condensed upon ejection into the air. Production began on this generator in September 1942, and it was standardized as the M1 mechanical smoke generator (often called the Esso, after the company which produced it) in the following December.[6]

In December 1941 the Chemical Warfare Board undertook a study of large area smoke concealment with particular application to Edgewood Arsenal. Within a few days after the Pearl Harbor attack General Porter instructed the board to expand its objectives to include the general principles and techniques of screening, a project which was given highest priority.[7] The investigations of the Chemical Warfare Board soon had proceeded far enough to establish several tentative principles of rear area screening. Observation from the air revealed that smoke at night changed the appearance of both natural and artificial terrain features. Smoke was of less value during daylight and might even accentuate vital targets. Blackouts would still have to be maintained at night because bright lights were visible through the smoke; in other words, rear area screening was supplementary to the blackout, not a substitute for it. And, finally, screening, while appreciably reducing visibility, would not eliminate observation from the air.[8]

After the completion of the Edgewood tests, the CWS felt better prepared to provide technical supervision of smoke installations in the zone of interior, which the Operations Division, War Department General Staff, was finding difficult to establish because of shortages of

---

[6] (1) See Brophy, Miles, and Cochrane, *From Laboratory to Field*, for a detailed account of research and development activities and technical details of these generators. (2) James P. Baxter 3d, *Scientists Against Time* (Boston: Little, Brown and Co., 1947), pp. 282–89. (3) Barker Ltr, 13 Dec 58.

[7] Ltr, Chief Field Serv OCCWS to President Cml Warfare Bd, through CG Edgewood Arsenal, 19 Dec 41, sub: Study of Large Area Smoke Screen Technique. CWS 470.6/1554 CWB Proj 251.

[8] Ltr, President Cml Warfare Bd to Chief Phila Ord Dist, 2 Jan 42, sub: Smoke as Protective Concealment. CWS 470.6/1554 CWB Proj 251. Further tests early in 1942 substantiated these findings.

men and matériel. The commanding generals of the several defense commands forwarded screening requests, arranged in order of importance, to the War Department, which compiled all requests, giving each a priority rating. The CWS aided OPD in this task by performing feasibility surveys for each proposed installation.[9]

Meanwhile, the CWS recommended the activation of thirty-four chemical smoke generator companies. On 8 April the first three units (the 75th, 76th, and 77th Companies) were formed and, before their training was completed, received the mission of concealing aircraft plants in California. By the end of May the War Department had authorized the activation of 11 companies to be stationed as follows: 6 with the Western Defense Command; 3 in Panama; one at the Sault Ste. Marie Locks; and one, an experimental unit, at Edgewood Arsenal.[10] By 20 July a total of 14 companies had been activated, 9 located on the west coast of the United States.

Each of these early smoke units, organized under a table of organization calling for 4 officers and 196 enlisted men and 3,600 M1 stationary smoke generators (the smudge pot type)[11] was capable of blanketing an area of about four square miles. Generators were employed in two or more concentric smoke lines which completely surrounded the vital area, allowing for wind from any direction. By the proper placement of additional generators and by use of an electrical ignition system, a substantial amount of smoke could be formed in about ten minutes.

When the United States entered the war the long-standing Panama Canal screening project was immediately revived. At the time, the smoke pot was the only screening munition available and it required too many men to make a Panama smoke installation feasible.[12] The stationary generator proved more satisfactory, and, as a consequence, Lt. Gen. Frank M. Andrews, Caribbean Defense Command, recommended that plans for screening in the Department be implemented as soon as possible.[13] By 1 January 1943 two smoke generator companies had

---

[9] Memo, Maj D. R. King, OCCWS, for Col James W. Rice, Cml Warfare Bd, 5 May 42, sub: WD Policy With Reference to Rear Area Smoke Screens.   CWS 470.6/1554 CWB Proj 251.

[10] Ltr, TAG to CCWS, 25 May 42, sub: Request for Authority for Activation of Cml Smoke Generator Cos, and 1st Ind.   CWS Ret 320.2/207.

[11] T/O 3–267, 1 Apr 42.

[12] Interv, Hist Off with Lt Col Harold Walmsley, 23 Feb 48.

[13] Ltr, CG AGF to CG SOS, 19 Jun 42, sub: Stationary Smoke Generators for Large Area Screen, and 2d Ind, CCWS to CG SOS.   CWS Ret 470.6/2711–2754.   An electrical ignition system further reduced the necessary manpower.

arrived in Panama equipped with the M1 mechanical generator. Used in conjunction with the stationary generator, this new equipment greatly eased the situation on the smoke lines.

In July 1942, with a practical means of screening assured, General Porter made several recommendations on plans for rear area screening which were approved by the General Staff. The War Department ordered that additional smoke generator companies be activated to bring the total to 42. These new units were to train at the CWS Replacement Training Center at Camp Sibert, where large area screening exercises could be freely conducted.[14] By August 1942 troop basis planning provided for the employment of 12 companies in theaters of operations, 3 in Panama, and 14 by the defense commands in the zone of interior. Activation of chemical smoke generator companies continued at the rate of about 3 a month until February 1943, when a total of 40 had been organized.

Defensive screening operations during 1942 consisted of the establishment of zone of interior smoke installations and the development of screening readiness in Panama. Operations at the Sault Ste. Marie locks [15] and at Camp Edwards, Mass., were primarily for experimental purposes, both tactical and technical. The requirement for smoke installations in the Western Defense Command began to decline after the defeat of the Japanese fleet in the Battle of Midway in June 1942 and ended with the increase in American air power during the early months of 1943. Smoke was never made in anger in the United States. But the anxious period after 7 December 1941 provided the impetus for rapid progress in the development of matériel and the organization of units. This was a necessary prelude to overseas screening operations.

Initial Operations: The Northwest African Ports

Early on the morning of 8 November 1942 British and American forces attacked Northwest Africa. The assault operations consisted of three distinct parts. The Western Task Force, entirely American and combat loaded in the United States, struck the coast of French Morocco in the vicinity of Casablanca. The Center and Eastern Task

---

[14] (1) Memo, CCWS for ACofS OPD WDGS, 20 Jul 42, sub: 1942 Over-all Plan for Rear Area Smoke Screen Protection. (2) 1st Ind, ACofS for Opns SOS to CCWS, 11 Aug 42. Both in CWS Ret 320.2/207.

[15] Originally the purpose of smoke operations at Sault Ste. Marie was protection, not testing. Memo, Capt Howard P. McCormick, CWS, for Gen Wilson, 31 Mar 42.

Forces, mounted in Great Britain, had as their respective targets the Mediterranean ports of Oran and Algiers.[16] The initial French resistance soon ceased, and the British-American forces turned east toward Tunisia.

By then the United States Army had attained a capability in large area screening which a year earlier would have seemed impossible. A new generator, the M1, had been devised, units were being activated to operate it, and the doctrine for its employment—the concealment of vital rear area installations—had become an accepted feature in the defense against air attack. The Northwest African campaign was to provide the crucial test of combat for this generator, these units, and this mission.

Although the Luftwaffe failed to react to the landings in Northwest Africa, enemy planes in the succeeding months raided Algiers and other ports to the east in an effort to disrupt Allied supply lines. Both the United States and Great Britain supplied troops and munitions for the large area screening mission. Shortly before, the British No. 24 smoke pot had been dubbed "the savior of Malta" for its part in shielding the island's harbor from concentrated enemy air attacks.[17] The Americans provided the M1 smoke pot and the M1 mechanical smoke generator, smaller and more efficient and maneuverable than the large British Haslar.[18] These two generators, the primary equipment of the units performing the smoke mission, were to form the nucleus of the smoke installations at the Northwest African ports.

Because smoke was not required, no American smoke units participated in the initial landings, a fortunate circumstance in view of the limited number of available units. Elements of the 78th Smoke Generator Company did arrive at Casablanca on 13 November, five days after the shooting began.[19] The company set up a smoke installation on 23 November which served principally for demonstration purposes.[20]

---

[16] Howe, *Northwest Africa*, provides the complete story of the Northwest African campaign.

[17] London Mil Attaché Rpt 56781, 12 May 43, sub: Area Smoke Screening, app. B.

[18] The M1 mechanical generator weighed 3,000 pounds empty and 5,400 pounds when filled, that is, complete with fog oil, fuel oil, and water. Troops could operate in its smoke with no adverse effects. The M1 smoke pot contained 10 pounds of HC smoke mixture and burned from 5 to 10 minutes. An improved model, the M1A1, appeared in 1944. The longer burning M5 pot was developed later in the war.

[19] 78th Cml Smoke Generator Co History, 1942, p. 1. This detachment of the 78th embarked in six different vessels and had smoke generators ready for emergency use.

[20] Ltr, CO 78th Smoke Generator Co to CmlO Western Task Force, 30 Nov 42, sub: Report of Test Run.... CWS 314.7.

The first smoke company to see action in Northwest Africa was the 69th Smoke Generator Company. It landed at Oran on 25 December, and on the following day it relieved a detachment of engineer troops which, using British No. 24 smoke pots, had maintained a smoke line in the harbor since 9 November.[21] By February 1943 both the 78th and the 69th Companies were at Algiers where they successfully operated their M1 mechanical generators in conjunction with a British company equipped with Haslars.[22]

All told, ten major North African ports had the benefit of smoke installations manned by troops from the United States, Great Britain, and France.[23] These operations were not simultaneous but represented a steady movement eastward as the Allied troops, in conjunction with those under Generals Sir Harold R. L. G. Alexander and Montgomery, converged on the Axis concentrations in Tunisia. Bizerte, although captured just before complete victory in Northwest Africa, served as one of the chief marshaling ports for the invasion of Sicily and later Italy, thus becoming one of the Mediterranean's most heavily screened ports. A British smoke unit was waiting on the outskirts of Bizerte on 7 May as the II U.S. Corps was capturing the city, and within twelve hours the port was screened. By the end of June all four of the American smoke generator companies in the theater were providing the smoke defenses for Bizerte. In addition to the 69th and 78th these were the 168th and 172d, just arrived from the United States and still without generators.[24]

Smoke installations usually consisted of two rings, the size of which depended upon the area to be screened. An inner ring of smoke pots provided for the quick concealment of vital targets while an outer ring of mechanical generators built the main element of the smoke blanket. Pots were also used to fill in gaps in a blanket caused by shifting winds or by other unforeseen conditions. Smoke was made at night only; during the day fighter aircraft provided protection for the dock areas of the harbors.

---

[21] 69th Cml Smoke Generator Co History, Jun 42–Apr 44, p. 2.

[22] CWS TofO Ltr No. 12, 31 Mar 44, Incl. 4.

[23] A detailed account of the screening operations in Northwest Africa as well as of those in Italy, described later in this chapter, can be found in Paul W. Pritchard, CmlC Hist Study No. 1, Smoke Generator Opns in the Mediterranean and European Theaters of Opn, 1949, pp. 36–83.

[24] Also arriving in June were the 24th and 25th Chemical Decontamination Companies, in the theater as insurance against the introduction of gas by the enemy but well trained in the smoke mission.

Early on the morning of 6 July 1943, with Bizerte's port, channel, outer harbor, and bay crowded with ships for the impending invasion of Sicily, the Luftwaffe attacked with a force of more than sixty aircraft. The smoke units had nine minutes warning. At 0409 the German bombers began their run on the smoke-obscured targets. Despite intense antiaircraft fire the enemy kept up an almost uninterrupted attack for thirty-six minutes. At 0445 the bombers withdrew, and the order to "cease smoke" came shortly after. During the 65-minute smoking period the units expended 4,135 gallons of fog oil and 535 British smoke pots. Although the enemy bombed several dumps and inflicted about a score of casualties outside the screen, no bombs fell within the vital area. The ships and docks were untouched and the channel remained open.[25]

In August two of the four American smoke units were alerted for the Sicilian operation. In September the remaining American companies sailed for Italy, and British troops manned the Bizerte screen until their relief by French units in January 1944.

By concealing the harbors and port facilities from Algiers to Sfax from enemy air bombardment, American and British smoke companies played a limited yet important part in the Northwest African campaign. The extent of the smoke operations depended upon the clearness of the night, the military traffic at a port facility, and the degree of enemy air activity. The Luftwaffe succeeded in sinking a few ships in these harbors and caused some damage to port installations, but its attacks on the ports in Northwest Africa were largely without effect.[26]

This first combat experience entirely justified the hopes of the designers of the mechanical generator. It produced substantial clouds of persistent white "smoke" with comparative speed. Although the weight of the generator required vehicular transportation and its fuel requirements were substantial, these were but modest logistical considerations compared with the results obtained.

Perfecting the Technique: The Italian Ports

The port of Naples was the initial Allied objective after Anglo-American forces had secured a foothold in southern Italy. The logistical

---

[25] (1) 69th Cml Smoke Generator Co History, Jun 42–Apr 44. (2) 78th Cml Smoke Generator Co History, 1943.

[26] Logistical History of NATOUSA-MTOUSA, 30 Nov 45, pp. 106–07.

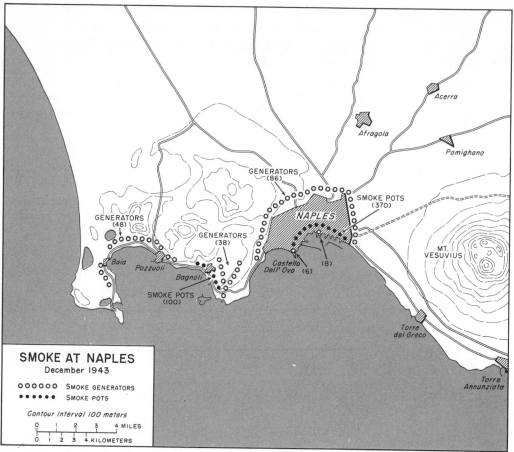

SMOKE AT NAPLES
December 1943

ooooooo   SMOKE GENERATORS
••••••   SMOKE POTS

Contour Interval 100 meters

0 1 2 3 4 MILES
0 1 2 3 4 KILOMETERS

D. Holmes, Jr.

MAP 3

considerations that demanded taking the port city naturally required
the uninterrupted flow of supplies into its spacious harbor. The smoke
installation that aided in this task was the most comprehensive of its
kind in the war. And it had the benefit of the experience gained in
screening the ports of Northwest Africa.

The vital shipping area at Naples included the port and harbor of
the city itself, the port area at suburban Bagnoli, and the fine harbor
at Pozzuoli in the Bay of Baiae. (*Map 3*) The smoke installation
began operations in October 1943, reached a climax late in the year,
and tapered off by the following summer as Allied successes farther
to the north helped reduce the possibility of heavy enemy air attacks.

At its height the smoke lines were manned by the 163d, 164th, 168th, 172d, and 179th Smoke Generator Companies, the 24th Decontamination Company, and the British 807th (SM) Company—in all, about 1,000 officers and enlisted men.

At first, no common headquarters existed to direct the activities of these units, a fact which soon led to the establishment of a provisional smoke generator battalion headquarters.[27] Although an improvement, this "provisional" headquarters was not the answer. The lack of status and the inadequate capability of this provisional unit, led by the senior smoke generator company commander, finally impelled the theater in March 1944 to request the assignment of a headquarters and headquarters detachment, chemical smoke generator battalion. This unit was urgently needed, the theater said, to provide centralized control over the several smoke companies in such matters as technical operations and administrative and logistical support. As a result, Headquarters and Headquarters Detachment, 22d Chemical Smoke Generator Battalion, was activated on 5 May 1944.[28]

The smoke installation in the Naples complex included three sectors, each with inner and outer rings. The inner ring at Naples proper consisted of 370 British smoke pot positions and 14 Besler generators, a Navy generator, small, efficient, and much like the Army's M2 which would appear later. The outer ring, about six miles long, included 86 mechanical generators. The Bagnoli sector had 100 smoke pot and 38 mechanical generator positions, the Pozzouli, 48 mechanical generators. The smoke from these installations blended into one massive screen extending at times for a distance of twenty miles. As in the case of the North African ports, smoke was used during the night and during the periods of twilight. The prevalent winds at these times were offshore, an ideal condition for the land-based generators, although ten craft loaded with floating M4 smoke pots were ready to cover any gaps caused by occasional breezes from the sea. Air turbulence from two nearby land masses created constant difficulty in the development of an adequate screen. One of these was the volcano Vesuvius whose mass and glow, according to captured German pilots, provided the

[27] Technical and administrative problems of the American companies initially were handled by Colonel Barker, Fifth Army chemical officer, and later by Colonel Coblentz of the Peninsular Base Section.

[28] (1) CM–IN 13125, 18 Mar 44. (2) Ltr, TAG to CG NATO, 30 Mar 44, sub: Constitution and Activation of Hq and Hq Detachment, 22d Cml Smoke Generator Bn. AG 322 (28 Mar 44) OB–L–SPMOU–M. (3) GO 80, Peninsular Base Sec, 4 May 44.

additional disservice of furnishing guides to attacking enemy bombers.[29] Smoke orders came from the British 45th AA Brigade charged with the port defense.[30]

Enemy air raids were frequent and heavy at Naples, but its defenses —fighters, flak, and smoke—combined to blunt the effectiveness of the attacks. On the night of 26 November, for example, the screen confused and delayed the enemy flare laying aircraft to such an extent that the bomber formation released its load without benefit of flares. As a result, none of the bombs did damage, most of them falling into the bay.[31]

Although there was a letup in the number of air raids on Naples during the last half of March and April 1944, the tempo increased in May with the Allied drive on Rome, and the port was screened fourteen times. During one of the spring raids about 113 merchant ships and 60 naval craft were shielded by smoke in the ports and anchorages at Naples, all of which escaped damage.[32] According to the AFHQ intelligence bulletins this was not exceptional; the screening activities at Naples were generally effective.[33]

As the Germans fell back before the Allied offensive their air attacks against Naples practically ceased. The smoke installation was gradually reduced to a single ring of pots around the harbor, manned by Italian personnel. Some of the American smoke units began to prepare for operation against southern France; others moved north to new ports, now that Naples was no longer able to supply efficiently the troops above Rome. During the advance northward the Fifth Army captured Civitavecchia, Piombino, and Leghorn, ports which upon repair were pressed into service to relieve the supply situation. Civitavecchia required but a small screen and that for a short time. The 179th Smoke Generator Company saw brief service there before moving to Piombino, where in June it joined with the 172d Company in manning the smoke installation.[34]

[29] Colonel Barker toyed with the idea of concealing Vesuvius with 4.2-inch mortar shell, a plan soon discarded as impracticable.

[30] Fifth Army Cml Sec Daily Jnl, 18 Dec 43.

[31] CWS TofO Ltr No. 12, 31 Mar 44, p. 48.

[32] AFHQ, History of AA and Tactical Smoke Screening in North Africa and Italian Theaters Between 1 Jan and 31 Dec 44, pp. 7–8.

[33] An evaluation based upon about fifty AA intelligence bulletins issued between October 1943 and May 1944 by the 12th Antiaircraft Artillery Brigade.

[34] AFHQ, History of AA and Tactical Smoke Screening in North Africa and Italian Theaters Between 1 Jan and 31 Dec 44, p. 8.

SMOKE SCREEN SHIELDS UNLOADING OPERATIONS DURING AIR RAID ALERT, *Salerno.*

Activity at both of these ports subsided when the facilities at Leghorn, captured on 19 July, were repaired and gradually put into operation. Within a week the 179th Smoke Generator Company, to be joined shortly by three British companies, erected a screen at Leghorn. Initially, Leghorn represented a unique example of rear area screening in that it remained for some time within range of enemy artillery on the north bank of the Arno River. On 28 July the 172d Company moved up from Piombino and deployed in a 7-mile arc at a distance approximately five miles north and northeast of the city. The haze from the generators, just as in the Anzio operation,[35] denied to the enemy observation of port and road traffic. The company maintained the line, sometimes despite the objections of the Royal Navy in the port, for thirty-eight days, by which time the enemy had with-

---

[35] See below, pp. 336–40.

drawn from his Arno River positions. The smoke installation at the port itself was continued until April 1945.[36]

Leghorn marked the end of American participation in port screening in the Mediterranean Theater of Operations. Rear area missions gradually petered out with the diminished effectiveness of the Luftwaffe. The 172d and 179th Smoke Generator Companies, by now the only U.S. smoke units in Italy, turned to a type of employment that had evolved earlier in the theater—the use of smoke in forward areas. But before the development of that mission smoke units had been used in assault landings.

The Changing Mission: Smoke in Amphibious and Beachhead Operations

Salerno

The fighting in Italy proper saw an immediate extension of what had been the normal mission of smoke units. Thus far, in doctrine and experience, large area screens had concealed rear area installations exclusively. At Salerno smoke troops landed on D-day in support of the combat elements.[37]

The Fifth Army landings in the Gulf of Salerno, just around the Sorrento Peninsula from Naples, represented the first foothold of American troops on the mainland of Europe. Two corps participated in the attack—the British 10 on the left and the U.S. VI on the right. The 36th Infantry Division, forming the assault element of the American corps, drew as its objective the beaches near the town of Paestum.[38]

Each of the assault battalions, storming ashore early on 9 September 1943, carried about 200 M4 smoke pots.[39] Dropped in the water by

[36] (1) Ltr, CO 172d Cml Smoke Generator Co to CG Adv Hq Allied Armies in Italy, 13 Sep 44, sub: Report on Smoke Haze North of Leghorn. (2) Fifth Army Cml Sec Daily Jnl 28 Jul 44. (3) AFHQ, History of AA and Tactical Smoke Screening in North African and Italian Theaters Between 1 Jan and 31 Dec 44, pp. 8–9, 11–12.

[37] The Salerno action is based on: (1) Fifth Army Cml Sec Daily Jnl, 9, 10, 25 Sep 43, CMLHO; (2) Memo, Barker for CMLHO, 4 Feb 47, sub: Answers to Questions; (3) Lt Harrie A. James, USNR, Observations During Opn AVALANCHE, Center Task Force Southern Task Force, 24 Oct 43, CWS 314.7 Smoke Opns.

[38] Details of this operation may be found in Martin Blumenson, Salerno to Cassino, a volume in preparation for the series UNITED STATES ARMY IN WORLD WAR II.

[39] The M4 floating smoke pot (and improved models M4A1 and M4A2) consisted of a 5-gallon pail containing twenty-six pounds of HC. This amount filled but one-third of the container, thus creating the necessary buoyancy.

infantrymen, the floating munitions helped conceal succeeding landing craft; placed on the beaches they screened exposed flanks. Navy personnel also employed smoke. Some support craft dropped pots; others were equipped with the Navy Besler smoke generator. This artificial smoke, combined with the morning mist and the haze of battle, created limited visibility. As a consequence, the enemy, with limited observation, resorted to a curtain of unobserved fire placed just off the beaches. This was in decided contrast to the initial situation wherein individual landing craft were reported to have been sniped at by enemy 8-inch guns.[40]

One CWS unit landed on D plus 2 as part of the beach force of VI Corps. The 24th Decontamination Company, under the direction of the naval task force, used M1 and M4 smoke pots to screen the beaches and anchorages. Later, the Navy gave the unit eight Besler generators, a number gradually increased to thirty-six. Standard practice during the first week, when the issue was often in doubt, was to create smoke during the hours of evening and morning twilight and during moonlight, favorite times for German bombers to attack. During air raid alerts the smoke of the 24th Company usually was abetted by generators on naval craft. So effective was the smoke screen that beach and harbor were often concealed within three minutes of the alert. During the nights smoke came to assume the primary position among antiaircraft defenses.

Average daily expenditures during the first week on the Salerno beaches were 250 M1 and 100 M4 smoke pots and 5,000 gallons of fog oil. One of the principal difficulties encountered was the burning glow of the smoke pots which often served as aiming points for enemy bombers.[41]

Despite this handicap the smoke mission received new respect in the strongly contested battle for the Salerno beachhead. Troops and landing craft welcomed anything that would make them less vulnerable, and the pots and generators manned by infantrymen, sailors, and CWS

---

[40] (1) James, Observations During Operation AVALANCHE. (2) Professor Morison does not mention smoke in his account of the battle although he includes a photograph (opposite page 282) of a PT (patrol boat, motor torpedo boat) boat laying smoke. (Samuel Eliot Morison, "History of United States Naval Operations in World War II," vol. IX, Sicily–Salerno–Anzio, January 1943–June 1944 (Boston: Little, Brown and Co., 1954).

[41] This objection was voiced by several Navy observers as cited in CWS Theater of Operations Letter No. 15, 21 June 1944, pages 26–27.

troops provided effective concealment from enemy fire.[42] It was the opinion of naval officers with the shore control party at Salerno that the smoke screen saved many lives and landing craft.[43]

Anzio

The bold end run of Fifth Army's VI Corps at Anzio has provoked much debate among postwar strategists, both armchair and professional. At the time, its planners felt that this maneuver would be the best way to break the stalemate encountered in front of the formidable German defenses which formed the Gustav Line. Unfortunately, Operation SHINGLE fell far short of expectations. The enemy responded quickly to the "abscess" in its flank and contained the beachhead in beleagured impotency from its establishment on 22 January 1944 until the Allied breakout in the following May.[44]

As at Salerno, provision was made for a large area screen for the Anzio beachhead. Again as at Salerno, the 24th Decontamination Company was assigned this mission. The company, equipped with M1 and M4 pots and with eight Navy Besler generators, landed on D-day. On its first night ashore the unit smoked the beaches and anchorage, and within two days it had set up a smoke line almost two miles long. As the beachhead forces were augmented, other smoke troops, including a British unit and the U.S. 179th Smoke Generator Company, moved to Anzio to increase the size of the screen.[45]

Initially, smoke at Anzio was intended to be part of the antiaircraft screen. Experience had shown that a favorite enemy tactic was low level bomber attacks at dawn and at dusk. Consequently, it soon became standard practice to screen the port each day during the periods of dawn and dusk. The smoke troops also operated during red alerts at night, for smoke again proved to be the best antiaircraft defense during the hours of darkness. Throughout the first three weeks the Luftwaffe made at least one raid each night. Flares dropped by

---

[42] (1) AGF Board Rpt, pt. V, NATO, 10 Nov 43, cited in CWS TofO Ltr No. 9, 31 Dec 43, p. 10. (2) CWS TofO Ltr No. 12, 31 Mar 44, p. 32.

[43] James, Observations During Opn AVALANCHE.

[44] Nevertheless, the Anzio landing had a concrete effect on the over-all German war strategy, for the enemy interpreted it as the first of a series of peripheral attacks aimed at dispersing German reserve forces in Europe. The enemy also reacted with special vigor in order to gain the prestige of destroying an Allied beachhead. Harrison, *Cross-Channel Attack*, pp. 232–33, 234.

[45] (1) Fifth Army History of Activities, 22 Jan 43. (2) AFHQ, History of AA and Tactical Smoke Screening in North African and Italian Theaters Between 1 Jan and 31 Dec 44, p. 11.

lead planes seemed to be extinguished as they dropped into the screen. During daylight raids antiaircraft artillery and fighter planes constituted the sole defense.[46]

The decrease in the number of enemy air raids after mid-February, caused by effective antiaircraft defenses, brought little relief to the port and beachhead at Anzio, for the reduction of air attacks was accompanied by an increase in long-range artillery fire. Along the periphery of the beachhead and in the bordering mountains were innumerable enemy observation posts. Farm houses suspected of harboring German observers were demolished with 8-inch howitzers, and towers and nearby ridges were blanketed by chemical mortar and artillery smoke shell. But the mountains in the background continued to afford the enemy unrestricted view of beach installations and ships in the harbor. Although the entire Allied beachhead lay within range of enemy guns, the air defense, artillery, and naval commanders at first objected to smoking the beach and harbor during daytime because of possible interference with observation for friendly gunfire and with the unloading of the ships in the anchorage. This valid complaint was something to be reckoned with. Yet the losses incurred from enemy bombers and artillery were also worth taking into account. From 22 January through 10 February, for example, a daily average of almost twenty-eight tons of Allied ammunition was blown up by these means.[47]

To resolve this problem chemical officers, with the approval of Maj. Gen. Lucian K. Truscott, Jr., the corps commander, came up with a new technique for the mechanical smoke generator—the production of a light haze in the area between the harbor and the front lines, thin enough to permit normal operations within it, thick enough to prevent German observation from the encircling hills.[48]

To apply this technique the 179th Smoke Generator Company on 18 March moved from the harbor area toward the forward positions. The smoke line, now forming a 15-mile arc around the port, included nineteen generator positions on land and two generators mounted on Navy patrol craft in the harbor. (Map 4) The latter prevented enemy observation from the flanks of the concave contour of the coast line.

---

[46] Col Walter A. Guild, "That Damned Smoke Again," vol. LIV, No. 10, *Infantry Journal* (October, 1944) pp. 25–28. (Colonel Guild served as VI Corps chemical officer during the Anzio operation.)

[47] *Anzio Beachhead*, AMERICAN FORCES IN ACTION SERIES (Washington, 1947), p. 110.

[48] (1) Ltr, CmlO AFHQ to OCCWS, 11 Mar 44, sub: Smoke at Anzio Bridgehead. (2) Guild, "That Damned Smoke Again," *Infantry Journal* (October, 1944).

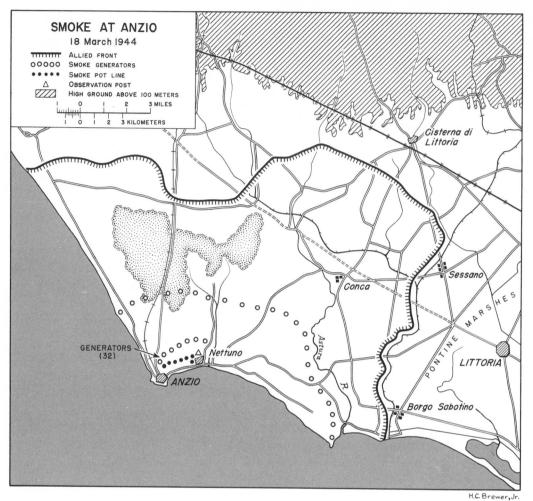

MAP 4

After a period of trial, error, and compromise the smoke line was established just beyond the antiaircraft positions of the port and just short of the field artillery observation posts. The line was divided into four sections with generators spaced at 1,000-yard intervals. Smoke positions were connected by telephones, and each section had radio communication with the command post. The amount of smoke needed was determined by an observation tower in Nettuno, abetted at times by liaison planes borrowed from the artillery. Each hour an Air Forces meteorology section provided weather data. Operations began one-half hour before dawn and ended one-half hour after sunset.[49]

The result was a light haze which, regardless of wind direction, denied observation to the enemy without restricting movement within the beachhead. Under concealment of this haze trucks were driven off LST's (landing ships, tank) onto the beach, unloaded, and returned to the ships unmolested. This was a particularly important operation as the Allied troops at Anzio received an average of 3,500 tons of supplies a day for the 6 months after the January landings.[50]

Radio interception disclosed that German artillery was on the alert during daylight hours to take advantage of sudden wind changes which afforded brief views through the screen. Objections to the daylight screen which commanders had raised during the planning stage disappeared after the smoke operation began. Allied artillery units even requested and obtained additional daylight screening to hide the flash of guns, thus inaugurating a new mission for smoke generators.[51] Another unusual mission of the 179th was in the interest of health. Generators, run at a reduced temperature for fifteen minutes during the morning and evening, spread a thin film of oil over the area. This oil film settled on the water and killed the larvae of the malarial mosquito, long a menace in the area.[52]

Soldiers going ashore at Anzio sometimes did not realize that smoke was being used. Lt. Raymond C. Stillger, who landed with the 34th Infantry Division three days after the daylight screening began, thought that the haze was a result of either a natural morning mist or smoke and dust from the battlefield. He noted that the mountain ranges were not visible from the harbor and that the artillery fire which dropped offshore was ineffective. When his unit moved forward, Stillger saw that the haze rarely drifted to within a mile of his position, usually remaining well to the rear. This was good; the infantry did not want the smoke to its front lest the Germans counterattack under cover of the screen. During the two months which Stillger spent in the line, it

---

[49] (1) Guild, "That Damned Smoke Again," *Infantry Journal* (October, 1944). (2) 179th Smoke Generator Co, Opnl Memo No. 1, 1 Aug 44, sub: Method and Lessons Learned on the Anzio Beachhead. (3) Interv, Hist Off with Capt Morris W. Lofton, 13 Mar 46. (Captain Lofton, the author of the operational memo, served as operations officer of the 179th at Anzio.)

[50] Logistical History of NATOUSA–MTOUSA, 30 Nov 45, p. 106. Beach gradients at Anzio permitted this ship-to-shore unloading.

[51] Ltr, CmlO Fifth Army to CCWS, 14 Apr 44, sub: Status of Cml Units in the Fifth Army.

[52] Opnl Memo No. 1, 179th Smoke Generator Co.

was necessary to request a reduction of smoke in his sector on only two occasions. At the rear it was a different story. After fighting in the mountains of southern Italy, the average infantryman felt uncovered on the Anzio plain and welcomed the concealment of smoke haze.[53]

While the large area screen at Anzio was not as decisive as some commentators would have one believe—"It [the mechanical smoke generator] probably saved the Anzio beachhead. . . ."—[54] its value was nonetheless considerable. General Truscott commented on the effectiveness of the smoke, which was used extensively "to limit German observation and reduce the effectiveness of their artillery fires."[55] German sources after the war testified to the effectiveness of the "well prepared and conducted" screening operations at Anzio which obstructed observation and interfered with defensive and direct fire.[56] Perhaps the situation was best summed up in the observations of Bill Mauldin's incomparable Willie and Joe.

The Invasion of Southern France

With the successful completion of the Sicilian operation in the summer of 1943 the Seventh U.S. Army became nonoperational, its headquarters reduced to caretaker status.[57] Then in January 1944 Allied Force Headquarters directed it to form a planning group for an operation against southern France to be mounted sometime in the following May. After considerable debate at the highest echelons DRAGOON (it was first called ANVIL) was given a definite time, place, and implementing force. These were 15 August 1944, a series of beaches east of Toulon, and Seventh Army's VI Corps.[58] The corps got three experienced infantry divisions for the operation, the 3d, 45th, and 36th.

Because of the mountains bordering the narrow beaches of the assault areas, the enemy could have excellent observation of the landing

---

[53] Interv, Hist Off with Capt Raymond C. Stillger, 29 Nov 50.

[54] Baxter, *Scientists Against Time*, p. 287.

[55] Lt. Gen. Lucian K. Truscott, Jr., *Command Missions: A Personal Story* (New York: E. P. Dutton, 1954), p. 457.

[56] Herman Ochsner (formerly a major general in the German Army), CmlC Hist Study No. 2, History of German Cml Warfare in World War II, pt. I, The Military Aspect, p. 30.

[57] For a complete account of the invasion of southern France, see Robert Ross Smith, The Riviera to the Rhine, a volume in preparation for the series UNITED STATES ARMY IN WORLD WAR II.

[58] *Report of Operations—The Seventh United States Army in France and Germany, 1944–1945* (hereafter cited as *Seventh Army Opns in ETO*) (Heidelberg, Germany: Heidelberg Gutenberg Printing Co., May 1946), I, chs. I–V, 1–115.

"*My God! There we wuz an' here they wuz.*"

force. Cognizant of the terrain and with the experience of Salerno and Anzio behind it, the Navy was eager to screen the assault force and anchorage from artillery fire and bomber aircraft. Its smoke plan, drawn up to provide concealment for beach and bay, was quite complete. Each Navy and merchant vessel had several means of producing smoke—with smoke pots, liquid smoke, and fog oil for the Besler generators furnished by Seventh Army's Chemical Section.[59] CWS troops attached to the assault divisions were prepared to land at H-hour, screen the flanks of the several beachheads, and be ready to conceal the assault boats in case of offshore winds. Once the landings were secure these CWS parties, under control of the engineer shore groups, would be ready to shield supply dumps and anchorage from air attack.[60]

The smoke troops again were to come from a chemical decontamination company, this time the 21st. On 25 March 1944 the unit's 2d Platoon moved from Palermo to a beach near Oran, where it was attached to the 40th Engineer Combat Regiment to prepare for the invasion. Practice in assault landings and in the erection of beachhead smoke lines constituted the bulk of this unit's training. In turn, the Engineers gained the experience of working in a haze limiting visibility to fifty yards. By June the platoon rejoined the 21st in Italy where it passed on its recently acquired amphibious experience to its three sister platoons.[61]

During the last weeks of July and the first week of August the three divisions which were to make the assault and their supporting troops underwent brief but effective practice for the appointed task.[62] The culminating point was a full dress exercise in which the conditions expected on the beaches of southern France were realistically duplicated. Live ammunition, beach obstacles, and smoke screens helped to achieve authenticity.[63]

---

[59] Seventh Army Cml Sec, Hist Rpt, 1 Jan 44 to 31 Oct 44. A unique employment of the liquid smoke saw LCM's (landing craft, mechanized) equipped with a contraption which forced the FS smoke through an ejection pipe where it was dispersed in a cloud by the blast of an airplane propeller.

[60] (1) *Ibid.* (2) Cml Annex to Field Order, 40th Engineer Combat Regt, 23 Jul 44 (included as an. 4 to the Seventh Army report.)

[61] Seventh Army Cml Sec Hist Rpt, 1 Jan—31 Oct 44, an. 199, in R. G. 207.3.

[62] Assignment of the platoons of the 21st Chemical Decontamination Company was as follows: the 1st Platoon to the 36th Engineer Shore Group, 3d Division; the 2d to the 40th Engineer Shore Group, 45th Division; and the 3d to the 540th Engineer Shore Group, 36th Division. The 4th Platoon was held in corps reserve. (1) *Ibid.* (2) *Seventh Army Opns in ETO,* III, 909-10.

[63] *Seventh Army Opns in ETO,* I, 71-89.

The 1st Platoon, 21st Decontamination Company, received an extra amount of training because the 3d Division had detailed plans for the use of ground smoke during the initial phases. The additional work for the platoon, and for a detail of two officers and thirty enlisted men from the 3d Chemical Mortar Battalion which augmented the division's smoke troops, was aimed at producing physical hardness, self-reliance, and proficiency in tactics of the infantryman.

The 3d Division's target area was the St. Tropez Peninsula. Elevations here reached 1,000 to 1,500 feet, providing the defenders with excellent observation of the sea, the beaches, and the narrow strip of wooded dunes. The 3d Division's assault areas on the peninsula, designated Red Beach and Yellow Beach, were both flanked by capes, a situation which enhanced the possibilities of German observation and provided the motive for the flanking screens of the attacking force. But if the terrain was unpropitious, its defense was another matter. Intelligence sources indicated that the enemy would not defend the area too strongly because of commitments in northwest France. Moreover, the rather skimpy fixed defenses of the area were manned by non-German and limited service troops.[64]

Preceded by heavy naval and air bombardment the VI Corps landed on 15 August against light resistance. During the actual assault the Navy used smoke only in the 3d Division sector. Here smoke pots and generators in landing craft screened the flanks of the boat lanes and concealed incoming craft from enemy fire. Each of the four smoke details, two per beach, was to land at H-hour in an LCT. Training trials had demonstrated that under favorable conditions the detachments with their allotments of 1,200 M1 smoke pots could unload in about five minutes. It was hoped that the final stage of the trip to the beach would take place in specially buoyed medium tanks which were on the LCT's. If this were not possible the pots were to be floated ashore in rubber boats, or, in an extreme case, the packing boxes

---

[64] The account of smoke operations in the 3d Division sector is based on: (1) Ltr, CmlO 3d Div to CmlO Seventh Army, 20 Sep 44, sub: Ground Use of Smoke Pots, M1A1, During Opn DRAGOON; (2) Ltr, ACmlO 3d Div to CmlO 3d Div, 18 Sep 44, sub: Use of Smoke on Red Beach for the DRAGOON Opn; (3) Ltr, Platoon Leader, 2d Platoon, 21st Cml Decontamination Co to CO 21st Cml Decontamination Co, 16 Sep 44, sub: Platoon Opn; (4) Ltr, Platoon Leader, 1st Platoon, 21st Cml Decontamination Co to CO 21st Cml Decontamination Co, 16 Sep 44, sub: Opns of 1st Platoon, 21st Cml Decontamination Co, 15–30 Aug 44; (5) 3d Cml Mortar Bn, Histories, Italy, 1–14 Aug 44, and Campaign of Southern France, 15–31 Aug 44.

with the pots enclosed could be tied in tandem and towed ashore by hand.

The smoke detail on the left flank of Red Beach was led by Lt. Frank J. Thomas, commanding the 1st Platoon, 21st Company. According to plan, four amphibious tanks carried the men across the beach to the railroad about 150 yards beyond. Fanning out to four positions at 100-yard intervals, the detail began operations within ten minutes of landing. The smoke line was gradually pushed inland to a road 250 yards from the beach. Until this time the smoke troops had not received enemy fire, but now mortar and small arms fire caused one casualty. No casualties were suffered in the heavily mined woods through which the smoke troops passed to reach the road.

The detachment from the 1st Platoon, which landed on the right flank of Red Beach, was led by Capt. Sam Kesner, assistant chemical officer of the 3d Division. For some reason the landing craft dropped its amphibious tanks some 1,000 yards from shore. Consequently, Kesner's party, which remained in the LCT, had to unload its pots the hard way. Some were thrown into two 6-man rubber boats and towed to the beach. The rest of the smoke munitions were tossed overboard and floated ashore in their crates, an expedient made necessary by the pressure of enemy small arms fire. The situation was made more difficult because the LCT had landed 400 yards to the right of its assigned area in order to avoid mines. The smoke plan called for four positions on the beach, a number soon increased to twelve because of the adverse winds. The smoke detail soon pushed inland about 100 yards, suffering four casualties in the early hours.

The two smoke details in 3d Division's Yellow Beach came from the 3d Chemical Mortar Battalion. Each of the one officer–fifteen enlisted men details landed at H-hour, meeting conditions not unlike those found on Red Beach. Because of the offshore mines, the LCT carrying the right flank party beached south of the assigned area. The group worked northward into position using smoke grenades for concealment from small arms fire. Opposition was heavier near the center of the beach but the smoke screen helped to eliminate observation, with the result that enemy fire became erratic, ceasing about H plus 30 minutes. The total length of the two screens on Yellow Beach was 2,000 yards.

Although the smoke mission for DRAGOON was extremely well planned and executed there was still room for improvement. Captain

Kesner felt that the eggs should not have been placed in so few baskets—
that a larger number of craft should have carried the members of the
smoke details during the assault. In this way the sinking of any LCT
would not have been an irreparable disaster. Maj. Albert L. Safine,
Chemical Officer, 3d Division, suggested that in landings where enemy
opposition would be substantial (resistance at DRAGOON was weak)
the smoke detail should land at H plus 30 and that the equipment
include amphibious mounted generators.

Smoke in Normal Forward Area Operations

In the struggle for Italy it seemed that the dice were always loaded
in favor of the defense. As a rule the German defenders controlled
the high ground which typified the Italian terrain and thereby kept
the Allies under excellent observation. Such a situation called for a
considerable amount of smoke.

There were several methods for laying smoke under such circumstances. The firing of artillery smoke shells upon enemy observation
points was an old technique, abetted by the introduction of the efficient
4.2-inch mortar. The trouble in Italy was the abundance of observation points, making the blanketing of all of them impracticable.
Another method of preventing enemy observation was the somewhat
difficult job of placing a curtain of smoke between the opposing forces.
More feasible was the covering of friendly positions and movements
by smoke, a technique obviously requiring emplaced rather than projected smoke. Smoke pots were immediately available for this type
of mission, although the harassing, if not toxic, nature of the HC
filling hardly commended them for extensive or extended use. More
often a combination of pots and shells was used. To illustrate, early
on the morning of 13 October 1943, as VI Corps' 3d and 34th Divisions
attacked across the swift moving Volturno River, the 2d and 84th
Chemical Mortar Battalions routinely fired smoke shells on enemy
observation towers in the distant hills. More unusual was the detail
from the 84th Battalion which manned smoke pots for the concealment of bridging sites and exposed approaches. The mission was not
uniformly successful. On the evening of 13 October, for example,
smoke pots set off to conceal bridge building activities drew enemy
artillery fire to the area, a circumstance which made construction impossible. Even though smoke in some cases, particularly in inadequate

amounts, could thus be a mixed blessing, Company D, 84th Chemical Mortar Battalion, kept alerted a 100-man detail equipped with 1,000 smoke pots to cover bridge sites.[65]

Another example of a screen formed by pots and shells occurred in mid-January 1944. II Corps captured the high ground east of the Rapido River and began to move up troops and supplies in preparation for an assault crossing. Because the main supply route, Highway No. 6, passed through relatively level terrain, it was exposed for a considerable distance to observed artillery fire from enemy positions on the mountain heights beyond the Rapido.[66] On 18 January troops from the headquarters of the 2d Chemical Mortar Battalion, under the supervision of Colonel Burn, II Corps chemical officer, screened a section of the highway with M1 smoke pots. At noon this force was supplemented by three smoke pot stations manned by troops from one of the firing companies of the battalion. During that day more than 1,000 enemy shells fell into the screened area with practically no damage and little interruption of traffic. Although the smoke interfered with the observation of American artillery, the corps commander considered the screen essential, and an entire company of the 3d Battalion went forward with 185 tons of smoke pots.[67]

These two examples demonstrated the need that existed for concealment in the forward areas in Italy and the immediate steps taken to adapt the smoke pot to the large area mission. These initial attempts, while generally successful, called attention to the possibilities of the use of the mechanical generator in similar situations—possibilities which were soon to be realized.

Smoke on the Garigliano

On 9 March the 88th Infantry Division relieved a British unit on Fifth Army's extreme left. The sector included the area southeast of the town of Minturno where Highway No. 7 crossed the Garigliano not far from where the river emptied into the Tyrrhenian Sea. About

---

[65] (1) *From the Volturno to the Winter Line,* AMERICAN FORCES IN ACTION SERIES (Washington, 1944), p. 48. (2) Co D 84th Cml Mortar Bn, Field Jnl, 10–17 Oct 43. (3) Memo, Barker for Hist Off, 4 Feb 47. (4) Interv, Hist Off with Capt Ernest H. Davis, former CO Co C 84th Cml Mortar Bn, 27 Jun 45.

[66] See *Fifth Army at the Winter Line,* AMERICAN FORCES IN ACTION SERIES (Washington, 1945), illustration, p. 66.

[67] (1) 2d Cml Bn S-3, Jnl, Jan 44. (2) CWS TofO Ltr No. 11, 9 Mar 44, p. 15. (3) Fifth Army Cml Sec Daily Jnl, 19 Jan 44. (4) Co C 2d Cml Bn Jnl, 19 Jan 44.

EFFECT OF SMOKE CURTAIN, ITALY. *Bridge site before screening (above). Same bridge after screening, with background obliterated (below).*

CARRYING SMOKE POTS INTO POSITION IN THE RAPIDO RIVER AREA

five miles up the coast stood Mount Scouri which, with the hill masses above Minturno, provided the Germans with excellent observation of the road network in the valley. Particularly vulnerable was Highway 7 along which passed all troops and supplies for the II Corps front. The British had used smoke pots around the river's main bridge, a practice continued by American troops. On 28 March the 172d Smoke Generator Company, recently freed from duty at Naples, undertook the large area smoke mission in this area.[68] The new smoke installation also centered on the bridge. (*Map 5*) This vital point was encircled by a ring of 10 smoke pot positions having a 200-yard radius. The nucleus of the screen was a circle of mechanical generators 600 yards from the bridge. Just offshore, generators in small craft lent substance

[68] The account of the Garigliano screen is based on: (1) Fifth Army Cml Sec Rpt, n.d. (ca. April 44), sub: Defensive Smoke in Current Fifth Army Opns; (2) Col. Maurice E. Barker, "Smoke for River Crossings," *Infantry Journal*, LVIII, No. 1 (January, 1946), 37–41; (3) Interv, Hist Off with Maj Richard C. Burn, formerly CO 172d Smoke Generator Co, 30 Jan 47.

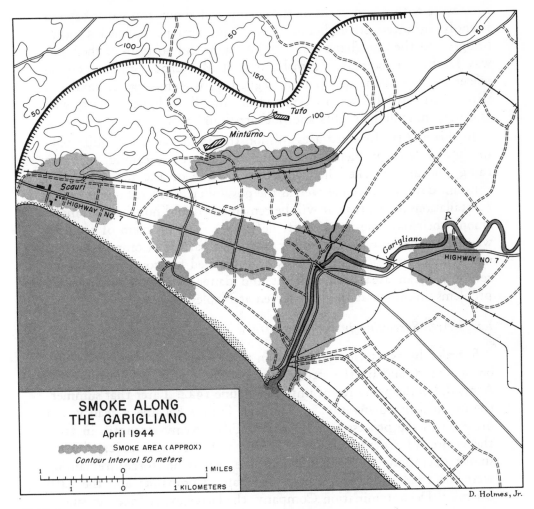

SMOKE ALONG
THE GARIGLIANO
April 1944
SMOKE AREA (APPROX)
Contour Interval 50 meters
1 MILES
1 KILOMETERS

D. Holmes, Jr.

MAP 5

to the left flank of the screen, an expedient made necessary by the
prevailing onshore winds.

In an effort to nullify the effectiveness of enemy artillery each generator had three prepared positions. Under cover of darkness the crews
moved their generators from position to position always eschewing
regularity and pattern in a generally successful attempt at hiding exact
locations. The area between the river and the enemy lines was dotted
with other pot and generator positions picked primarily to deny observation between the bridge and Minturno. The most advanced of

these were within 500 yards of the enemy and about 200 yards beyond friendly infantry strongholds. Lesser installations concealed other bridges over the Garigliano and road junctions and portions of the highway farther to the rear. From his post at Minturno a smoke control officer supervised the installation, regulating the emission of smoke so that a uniform haze was maintained during all daylight hours as well as during moonlight nights and nocturnal air raids.

In this its first forward area mission the 172d Company quite naturally met with problems not found in rear area screening. For one thing, the unit worked in two shifts because of the necessity of a constant daytime screen as well as the possibility of operations at night. (Installations at the rear, it will be remembered, did not include smoke among their daytime antiaircraft defenses.) The problem of security was greater because of the danger of enemy patrols. Communications maintenance increased appreciably and the need for continuous fog oil resupply in an area both difficult and dangerous to reach involved problems unknown at the port screen at Naples.

Large Area Screening in Northern Italy

Stymied by swift German reaction to Operation SHINGLE (Anzio) on one hand, and by the strong Gustav Line on the other, the Fifth Army did not capture Rome until early June 1944. Later that summer, the much debated invasion of southern France became a reality and drew off in the process a large part of Fifth Army strength, in fact, the entire VI Corps. Six of the nine CWS companies capable of smoke operations were included in the departing force; remaining were the 172d and 179th Smoke Generator Companies and the 24th Chemical Decontamination Company, the latter experienced in smoke operations but soon diverted to chemical depot operations. As a result, the means to pursue a successful forward area smoke mission were seriously impaired, especially when the recently won ports of Civitavecchia, Piombino, and Leghorn were requiring what were to be the last vestiges of port screening in the Italian campaign. By September the 172d and 179th were released from the Leghorn operation and placed in support of II and IV Corps, respectively, attachments which were to last until the end of the war.

That same month saw the beginning of a concerted effort by the 15th Army Group to penetrate the Gothic Line to which the Axis had withdrawn after the fall of Rome. The natural strength of this position, which crossed Italy between Florence and Bologna, combined with the weakened state of the Allied forces, resulted, after an initial Fifth Army penetration, in eventual stalemate.

During the first month of the offensive the 172d Company concealed bridge sites on the Sieve and Santerno Rivers. In each case, accurate German artillery fire became ineffective once smoke was employed.[69] The divisions in the II Corps sector at first made spectacular gains, reaching a point on Highway No. 65 above Livergnano within twelve miles of Bologna. Here the advance stopped, and there was to be little change in the front line until the following April. On the left shoulder of this penetration, strong German resistance denied Fifth Army Mount Adone and the hill mass at Monterumici, with the resultant variation on a familiar theme—from these vantage points the enemy retained direct observation of Highway No. 65, the main supply route for the section.[70]

In partial answer to this threat on the supply route, the 172d Smoke Generator Company maintained a smoke line from 16 October 1944 until 14 April 1945. For 181 days, except when the weather made screening unnecessary or when II Corps for one reason or another needed perfect visibility in the area, the smoke haze concealed friendly movements along a 2-mile stretch of the highway. Periods of bright moonlight sometimes forced the 172d to operate on a 24-hour basis.

Although the enemy was only about two miles away vehicles drove along the road without difficulty. The smoke was also of value to patrols and other troops moving across exposed areas. By reducing the danger and dread of observed fire the operation on Highway No. 65—the longest continuous forward area smoke screen in World War II—was both a material and psychological aid.

The 172d, with some outside help, performed another important mission while at Livergnano. From 25 January to 27 March 1945 a detachment from the company screened the road network in the Sillaro Valley which supplied both the U.S. II Corps and British Eighth Army sectors. The most vital part of this network was the

---

[69] See photographs on page 347, above.

[70] This section on operations in northern Italy is based on: (1) 172d and 179th Smoke Generator Co Journals; (2) Fifth Army Cml Sec Jnl, 25 Feb–3 Mar 45; (3) Lt. Col. Houston Joyner, CWS, "They Couldn't See Down Into the Valley," *Armed Forces Chemical Journal*, III, No. 2 (October, 1948).

SMOKE SCREEN CONCEALS MOVEMENTS ALONG HIGHWAY

crossroads at San Clemente, the site of a smoke pot screen manned first by the 88th Division and then by British troops, since the capture of the town in October. The undesirable characteristics of the HC pots led to a successful January trial of a smoke installation featuring the recently developed M2 mechanical generator. Captured enemy patrols admitted the effectiveness of this installation which concealed vehicular traffic, troop concentrations, supply dumps, and artillery positions of American and British forces.

On the IV Corps front the 179th Company supported operations ranging from the Ligurian coast to the Serchio Valley and Highway No. 64. Because of the distance between these missions—in the IV Corps sector Highway 64 was over forty miles from the sea—the unit's two platoons operated separately. The 1st Platoon, between Highway No. 1 and the sea, screened the coastal plain north of Viareggio. Detachments from the platoon were split off to fulfill other missions: screens for bridge sites and tank attacks and hazes for daylight patrols.

On 5 November, the 2d Platoon began a 102-day haze to cover an exposed stretch of Highway 64, as well as several supply installations, in the right sector of IV Corps. Just as in the case of Highway 65 south of Bologna, before the haze daytime traffic on the road always drew fire. Afterward, the amount of enemy fire noticeably decreased, bridges were built and strengthened without interruption, and traffic passed with little interference.

As World War II began, the large area screen was designed to conceal rear area installations. American and British smoke units and equipment in North Africa successfully demonstrated the validity of this mission and the adequacy of the smoke munitions. Once the scene of fighting shifted to the mainland of Italy doctrine for large area screens saw a drastic expansion. True, the old mission remained—as witness the smoke installation at the Naples complex, the largest of its kind of the war. But added to this was the use of smoke in assault landings and during the more conventional type of front-line operations. The evolution of the front-line mission was dependent upon several factors. First was the peculiar nature of the terrain in Italy, where circumstances and geography conspired to have the Allied forces continually advance under the superior observation of the enemy and against his deadly fire. The second factor was the limitations of conventional front-line smoke munitions—artillery and mortar shells and the smoke pots. And last, the gradual diminution of the power of the Luftwaffe and the consequent lessening of the need for port screening released smoke units, never in abundance in Italy, for the fulfillment of the new mission.

Forward area screening encountered the stiff and legitimate objections of such diverse sources as the field artillery and the supporting naval units. The problem, of course, was observation. Smoke did contend with these effective and established elements, and CWS officers took great care to see that the nature of these smoke screens was complementing, not competing.

CHAPTER IX

Large Area Smoke Screens in the ETO

The Invasion of Normandy

Almost from the very beginning of their labors Allied planners for the cross-Channel attack contemplated the use of smoke for the beaches in France and the ports that were to be developed there. In 1942 the combined British-American planning organization included an anti-aircraft committee which, in turn, had a smoke subcommittee. The logistical computations for the British Haslar generator, the best model then available to the Allies, indicated such large requirements for oil as seriously to limit extensive use of the technique of large area screening. Fortunately, at this time the National Defense Research Committee brought out the M1 mechanical generator, news of which sent a mission hurrying from England to the United States. Colonel Montgomery, the American representative, reported that the new generator was five times as efficient as any existing smoke device. Substitution of the M1 for the Haslar enabled smoke planners to draw up oil requirements which were far more reasonable.[1]

The development of the new generator prompted attempts by CWS staff officers in England to get a smoke generator company for the theater. War Department inquiries about the requirements for such units got little response from the Eighth Air Force, which came to the conclusion that the advantages of airdrome concealment were equaled or outweighed by the interference of smoke with operations. But SOS authorities in the theater showed interest in smoke as a means of concealing supply installations and later included the ports in

---

[1] (1) Interv, Hist Off with Col MacArthur, 23 Nov 45. MacArthur participated in the smoke planning for the invasion, later becoming Chemical Officer, 12th Army Group. (2) Col Montgomery to CG ETO, 14 Oct 42, Rpt of American Representatives, British-American Large Area Smoke Mission to the U.S. CWS Ret 470.7–2815.

Great Britain through which flowed the build-up of troops and supplies from the United States. Diminishing German air raids reduced theater interest in this type of activity, although during mid-1943 planners envisioned the use of some twenty or twenty-four smoke companies to conceal continental ports once the invasion was under way.[2]

With the return of General Eisenhower to London from the Mediterranean area in January 1944, planning for the cross-Channel attack began to take final shape. The troop basis for U.S. smoke generator troops now totaled twelve companies, organized into three battalions. Although these were originally listed as SOS units with a primary mission of rear area screening, Colonel MacArthur, CWS representative in the planning group, insisted that one smoke battalion be earmarked for tactical employment with the combat forces.[3] And it was to be in this role, rather than through their part in the concealment of rear areas, that smoke units were to make their most effective contribution.

Brigadier G. H. Pennycock, director of chemical warfare for the British 21 Army Group, co-ordinated Allied smoke screening plans for the initial phase of the invasion. Colonel Coughlan, FUSA chemical officer, was in turn responsible for the operational plans for American forces. One problem which had been troubling First Army, the difficulty of landing the heavy M1 generators on the Normandy beaches, was eliminated almost on the eve of the assault with the arrival of the M2 generator which had a dry weight of only 172 pounds. Smoke troops received the first M2 on 13 May, 7 more on 24 May, 50 on the 28th, and 27 between that date and 3 June.[4]

Final plans for the use of large area smoke screens during the cross-Channel attack provided for smoke over the ports of England from which the invasion would be mounted and smoke over OMAHA and UTAH beaches in Normandy. In both cases the screens would be used as a means of concealing activity from German aircraft. The companies of the 24th and 25th Smoke Generator Battalions received the English port assignment; the 23d Battalion, commanded by Lt. Col. William M. Fiske and including the 79th, 80th, 84th, and 161st Smoke Generator Companies, was earmarked for duty at OMAHA Beach, but not

[2] Pritchard, Smoke Generator Opns in MTO and ETO, pp. 85–87. This monograph contains a detailed account of smoke planning and operations in the European theater.

[3] MacArthur Interv, 23 Nov 45.

[4] 23d Cml Smoke Generator Bn Unit Diary, 18 Apr–3 Jun 43.

for the first three days of the operation. Chemical decontamination troops, scheduled to go ashore with the initial landings, were at first to use smoke pots and M2 generators to provide any necessary smoke. The 23d Battalion, with two companies on land and two on offshore trawlers, would assume responsibility for the antiaircraft smoke at OMAHA Beach on D plus 3.[5]

Once these general plans for smoke operations were completed, the units which were to take part could begin realistic training for their projected tasks. The 30th, 31st, and 33d Decontamination Companies received such training and were attached to engineer special brigades for the operation. The 79th and 80th Smoke Generator Companies, designated as the sea group of the 23d Battalion, had to become accustomed to working and living on trawlers. Their offshore employment also presented communications problems which had to be worked out by the battalion. In order to insure the necessary timing and co-ordination the 23d was attached to the 49th Antiaircraft Artillery Brigade which had control of smoke although subject to the approval of the naval command and the veto of the tactical air command.

The two smoke generator battalions assigned to the English ports naturally began operations before the actual day of the invasion. The 25th, comprising the 85th, 86th, 165th, and 171st Smoke Generator Companies, furnished smoke in the Weymouth-Portland area. During the last part of May the Luftwaffe attacked the area three different times inflicting damage only during raids when the battalion was not ordered to make smoke. The 24th Battalion (81st, 82d, 87th, and 167th Smoke Generator Companies), part of which saw action in the vicinity of Brixham, made smoke on fewer occasions than did the 25th.[6]

The 33d Chemical Decontamination Company landed on UTAH Beach on D-day with the multiple mission of decontamination reconnaissance, smoke, and CWS supply.[7] Although by that afternoon the unit was prepared to provide smoke on call from VII Corps, the German Air Force failed to appear in strength and the need for smoke never materialized. As a consequence, the 33d's main mission became that of supply; the CWS dump maintained by the unit handled over

---

[5] Final area smoke plans for the invation appear on FUSA Rpt of Opns, 20 Oct 43–1 Aug 44, an. 17, Cml Warfare Sec.

[6] Pritchard, Smoke Generator Opns in MTO and ETO, pp. 93–94.

[7] For details of the invasion, see Harrison, *Cross-Channel Attack.*

5,000 tons of CWS Class II and IV supplies during the first three weeks on the beachhead.[8]

Both the 30th and 31st Decontamination Companies saw action on OMAHA Beach. The former's 1st Platoon landed at H plus 16 minutes in the midst of the most rugged fighting of the invasion with the missions of decontamination, smoke, and supply. At first, the platoon fought along side the infantry using small arms and grenades and later, when the beachhead was secured, it aided in evacuating wounded and in clearing mine fields. During the afternoon the portable generators that had been lost in the surf at the time of the landings were retrieved and put into operating condition. As at UTAH, there were no calls for smoke. The 1st Platoon suffered 25 percent casualties on D-day and was cited for outstanding performance of duty.[9] At 1300 the 3d Platoon landed on OMAHA to be joined by the remainder of the 30th Company on D plus 1. A 25-man detachment of the 31st Decontamination Company came ashore at H plus 7 hours on 6 June and was reunited with the rest of the company on the next day. In activities which followed the pattern set by the other decontamination companies, the men of the 31st performed a series of secondary duties in the absence of gas warfare and the need for smoke.[10]

According to plan, the companies of the 23d Smoke Generator Battalion were to have assumed the smoke mission at OMAHA on D plus 3. The land contingent of the battalion, the 84th and 161st Companies, arrived off the beach on the afternoon of D plus 2 and came ashore that evening. Both companies experienced a great deal of difficulty. Men and equipment became separated; some roads indicated on the map were nonexistent and others were heavily mined or subject to enemy fire. Fortunately, few German planes appeared over the area and smoke was not required.[11]

The 79th and 80th Smoke Generator Companies, with their men and MI smoke generators aboard thirty of His Majesty's trawlers, on 9 June arrived off OMAHA Beach, where they served as the offshore element of the 23d Battalion smoke installation. But they received no requests for smoke. The great storm of 18–21 June wrecked some of

---

[8] (1) 33d Cml Decontamination Co Hist Résumé. CMLHO. (2) Pritchard, Smoke Generator Opns in MTO and ETO, p. 94.

[9] (1) WD GO 21, 30 Mar 45. (2) The 1st Platoon also received the French Croix de Guerre with Silver-Gilt Star. DA GO 24, 10 Dec 47.

[10] 31st Cml Decontamination Co, Hist Résumé.

[11] 23d Cml Smoke Generator Bn Unit Diary, June 44.

M2 SMOKE GENERATOR

the trawlers and others returned to England for repair and refueling, never to return to OMAHA. Some offshore smoke troops did provide screens at Port en Bessin where both British and Americans were bringing ashore fuel oil and lubricants. Here, in co-ordination with the British, the smoke trawlers stood ready to provide screens at twilight and during nocturnal red alerts as long as this important facility seemed threatened.[12]

During the critical period while the Allies were fighting to secure a firm foothold in Normandy, the landing beaches were virtually free from bombing from the air, and the need for beachhead and port screening did not materialize. Equipped with M1 generators, the companies of one smoke battalion did take positions around Cherbourg and remained on the alert until mid-August, although the need for smoke never arose. Under circumstances such as these, smoke units received

---

[12] (1) 23d Cml Smoke Generator Bn Unit Diary, Jun–Jul 44.   (2) 79th and 80th Smoke Generator Cos Unit Diaries, Jun 44.

unrelated secondary missions, mostly involving trucking duties. Consequently, when an opportune time did arise for using smoke in close support of tactical operations the companies were busy performing other tasks.

The Generators, Units, and Missions

The most influential factor in the development of the mission of forward area screening in the European theater was the appearance of the M2 mechanical smoke generator. This compact, efficient generator enabled chemical troops to establish effective smoke installations in those areas of the battlefield subject to enemy small arms fire. For example, the M2 could be emplaced on the near bank in an assault river crossing and ferried to the far side as soon as that area was cleared of enemy opposition. The M2 mechanical generator, as already mentioned, weighed only 172 pounds as compared to the ton and a half figure of the M1. Employing the same principle as its predecessor, the M2 drew its fog oil from an external source, usually a 55-gallon drum, and was capable of producing smoke one minute after it started operation, whereas it took the M1 five minutes. The new model consumed about fifty gallons of fog oil in an hour compared to twice that amount for its predecessor.[13]

A total of five smoke generator battalions saw action in the European Theater of Operations. The need for some organization for the administration and control of several smoke generator companies became evident in Italy in connection with the complex Naples installation with its several smoke companies. Consequently, three battalion headquarters and headquarters detachments, the 23d, 24th, and 25th, were organized just before the cross-Channel attack. Later the 22d Smoke Generator Battalion entered the theater as a supporting unit of Seventh Army, and the 27th Battalion, activated in the zone of interior in July 1944, was placed in support of Ninth Army.

The basic smoke unit was the smoke generator company, 15 of which saw action in the European theater. A smoke company consisted of a company headquarters, headquarters platoon, and operations platoon. The operations platoon comprised 4 sections, each section having 6 squads. A company equipped with M2's had a total of 50 generators,

---

[13] For more on the development and characteristics of the several CWS mechanical smoke generators, see Brophy, Miles, and Cochrane, *From Laboratory to Field*.

2 per operations squad and 2 with company headquarters. Personnel of this smoke company numbered 4 officers and 131 enlisted men.[14] The same company with the identical number of troops would have been equipped with only 24 M1 generators, or one per operations squad.

The mission which smoke units had originally considered their most important, the concealment of ports, never materialized in the European Theater of Operations. Experience at the time of the cross-Channel attack indicated that the Luftwaffe was not strong enough to jeopardize these basic supply installations, and this situation did not change throughout the rest of the war. Seventh Army did maintain a rather extensive smoke installation at Marseille during the period September to November 1944, but at no time did the Luftwaffe seriously threaten the port.[15]

The large area screening mission in the European theater did not undergo the slow transition from rear to forward areas that had marked the fighting in North Africa and Italy. The absence of any great threat by the enemy air force and the development of a mobile generator meant almost from the first that the smoke companies in the ETO would play their most significant role in the forward areas, that is, if they were to play a smoke role at all. Initially, when the German air threat failed to materialize, the smoke units found themselves assigned to a series of secondary missions— transportation, guard, and security details. Early in the fall of 1944 only four of the twelve companies assigned to the theater were available for forward area smoke operations.[16] While at times the assignment of smoke companies to other missions was understandable in the absence of tactical situations which called for concealment, in other cases the transfer was not justified. The First Army, for example, could often have used smoke units in forward operations but refused to do so until the time of the Rhine crossings.

But gradually smoke companies began fulfilling forward area missions as the situation warranted. These could be of several kinds. Screens were used to conceal main supply routes. Seventh Army employed smoke units in this manner as much as any other army in the

---

[14] TOE 3–267, 4 May 44.

[15] (1) See Pritchard, Smoke Generator Opns in MTO and ETO, pp. 215–19. (2) Two U.S. smoke companies operated with the British at Antwerp for more than two months and smoked the Scheldt River and the approaches to the city.

[16] Ltr, CCmlO ETO COMZ to CCWS, 20 Sep 44, sub: Tactical Use of Smoke Generator Cos. CWS 314.7.

theater, perhaps because of its previous experience in Italy. Commanders occasionally used smoke haze to cover the advance or withdrawal of troops or to cover a unit attacking a fortified position.[17] But there can be no doubt whatever that mechanical smoke generators played their most important role in the theater by concealing American troops as they crossed many of the rivers which had temporarily blocked the way to eventual victory. The first such operation took place early in September at the Moselle River.

The Use of Smoke at River Crossings

General Patton's Third U.S. Army became operational on 1 August 1944 and shortly thereafter began its rapid advance across France. By the end of August its forward units, outrunning their supplies of oil and gasoline, ground to a halt east of the Meuse. When the advance resumed early in September, Third Army faced an enemy with a second wind and rather good defensive positions behind the Moselle River.

As long as the Third Army had been rolling forward it doubtless had been more concerned with fuel oil than fog oil. Its rapid advance of August left little room for the tactics of concealment, smoke or otherwise. Consequently, those smoke troops which had been assigned to Third Army had left their generators and turned to transportation duties on the supply line, whose tail extended clear back to the Normandy beaches.

On 6 September Patton's XX Corps renewed the advance with the 7th Armored Division in the van, its mission the seizure of crossing sites over the Moselle. The 5th Infantry Division, following hard on the heels of the 7th, prepared to force a crossing if the armored attack failed. On 7 September the corps commander, Maj. Gen. Walton Walker, ordered the 5th Division to pass through the 7th Armored and establish a bridgehead on the east bank of the Moselle at Dornot, six miles southeast of the fortress city of Metz. This initial attack across the Moselle proved abortive and two days later, 10 September, the 5th Division abandoned the precarious bridgehead. On the same

---

[17] For details of these operations, see Pritchard, Smoke Generator Opns in MTO and ETO.

day the 10th Infantry, 5th Division, crossed the Moselle at Arnaville, three miles south of the site of the unsuccessful crossing.[18]

The Arnaville Crossing

The 84th Smoke Generator Company was hastily recalled from its transportation duties to support the Arnaville crossing. The excellence of German artillery and observation was such as to recommend the possibilities of smoke as a means of concealing the exposed crossing site. At this time the possibilities of the M2 generator were not widely known in Third Army; in fact large area smoke screens in tactical situations had evolved rather recently. This screen at the Arnaville assault and bridging sites was thus to provide new experiences for the various people involved—the infantry, the engineers, and the men of the smoke company.[19]

At the site of the crossing in the narrow valley of the Moselle, a railroad, a canal, and the river roughly parallel each other in a 500-yard belt. A small stream, the Rupt de Mad, flows through the Arnaville gap, passes under the railroad and canal, and empties into the river. East of the river lay a strip of open land beyond which rose the hills which were occupied by the enemy. North-south roads on each side of the river mark the division between river flats and the beginning of the hills. On clear days the Germans had observation of the Arnaville area from 5 or 6 miles down (north) the river and from 3 or 4 miles up the valley.

---

[18] Two other volumes in the series U.S. ARMY IN WORLD WAR II provide additional material on this battle and on the campaign of which it was a part. Hugh M. Cole's excellent *The Lorraine Campaign* (Washington, 1959) deals with Third Army Operations in Lorraine during the period September–December 1944. In the volume *Three Battles: Arnaville, Altuzzo, and Schmidt*, by Charles B. MacDonald and Sidney T. Mathews (Washington, 1952), MacDonald gives a detailed and graphic account of the Arnaville crossings. Both can be profitable to a reader desiring further information on operations of Third Army in the Lorraine Campaign. For additional details on the use of smoke at Arnaville, see again Pritchard, Smoke Generator Operations in the MTO and ETO, pages 107–25, a work on which this present account relied heavily.

[19] Chief sources for this account are: (1) CO 84th Cml Smoke Generator Co, Opn Rpt, Vicinity Arnaville, France, 17 Sep 44; (2) CO 84th Cml Smoke Generator Co, Final Opns Rpt, Arnaville, France, 10–21 Sep 44; (3) Lt Col Levin B. Cottingham, Employ of a Smoke Generator Co in an Assault Crossing of the Moselle River, n.d. (ca. 21 Sep 44); (4) 12th Army Group Immediate Rpt No. 68, I, Use of Smoke in Crossing of the Moselle River, 28 Sep 44; (5) Intervs, Cottingham (formerly CmlO 5th Inf Div), 1 Oct 45, 9 Oct 45, 19 Mar 46, 25 Sep 46; (6) Rpt of Lt Col William H. Greene (formerly CmlO XX Corps) on the smoking operations at Arnaville, France, 10 Sep 44, dated 11 Nov 47, all in CMLHO; (7) TUSA AAR, I, 68–81; (8) 5th Inf Div G–3 AAR, Sep 44, Orgn Files, ETO; (9) 5th Division Historical Section, *The Fifth Division in the ETO* (Atlanta: Albert Love Enterprises, 1945).

Early on 9 September Col. Robert P. Bell, commanding the 10th Infantry, and a party went forward to examine the crossing site. Despite the presence of enemy mines they were able to select suitable approaches and found two footbridges over the canal. They also determined that the river banks were suitable for the launching of assault boats and the erection of adequate bridges once the area was secured.

In quest of surprise, the artillery plan stipulated that there would be no preparatory fire preceding the crossing. But smoke from the generators of the 84th Company was expected to conceal the crossing sites as dawn broke on the 10th. Lt. Col. Levin B. Cottingham, chemical officer of the 5th Division, arranged for a meteorological study of the area as an aid to the smoke operations. He scanned the daily weather reports of the Air Forces and the local weather supplements of the division artillery. Arnaville residents verified that the prevailing winds were westerly and of low velocity. After a reconnaissance Cottingham and the commander of the 84th Smoke Generator Company decided on a line of generators behind Hill 303, some 2,300 yards west of the crossing site. (Map 6). They expected that the prevailing winds would carry the smoke from these positions over the crossing sites and over the flat areas on the far side of the river. Concealed from enemy air and ground operations, engineers could erect and maintain the necessary bridges in support of the operation. Generators were not placed at the crossing site at first because of the unlikelihood of wind change and because of the 84th's lack of experience under fire. Hill 303 protected the generators from direct enemy artillery and small arms fire, an important consideration for smoke troops who, far from battle hardened, had been driving trucks across a quiet countryside only a few days before. One smoke observation post was established at the OP of the 10th Infantry's Cannon Company on the crest of Hill 331, south of Arnaville. Another was located on Hill 303. Cottingham, the smoke control officer at the crossing site, used radio to keep in touch with the observation posts. The 1103d Engineer Combat Group, commanded by Lt. Col. George E. Walker, charged with the bridge building operation, had tactical control of the screen.

Fog oil for the M2 generators was available at the Third Army depot at Troyes, 180 miles to the rear. Because the organic transportation of a smoke company was inadequate to cope with such lengthy supply lines, the division quartermaster lent the trucks for fetching the fog

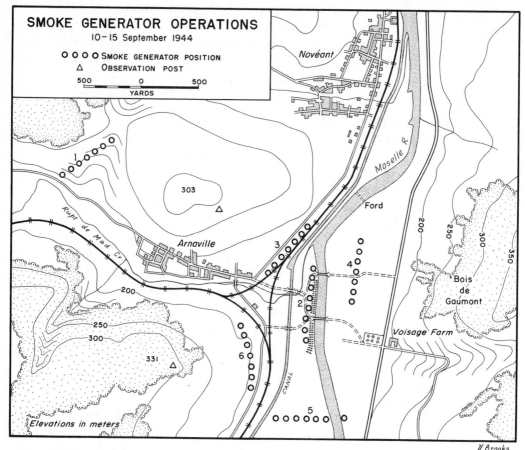

SMOKE GENERATOR OPERATIONS
10–15 September 1944

O O O O SMOKE GENERATOR POSITION
△   OBSERVATION POST

500   O   500
YARDS

MAP 6

oil to a company supply area four miles to the rear of the forward
dump behind Hill 303. Company vehicles hauled the oil drums the
rest of the way. In addition to generator smoke, the 84th had a supply
of M1 and M4 smoke pots to be used for patching gaps in generator
smoke and for supplemental screening.

The 84th moved into its positions during the night of 9–10 September and was ready to produce smoke at dawn. Initially the company
set up only twelve generators at Position 1, a number which could be
increased or decreased as the situation demanded since the full complement of fifty generators was available.

At 0115 on 10 September troops of the 1st Battalion, 10th Infantry,
began loading into the boats on the near bank of the Moselle. They

SMOKE SCREEN BEGINS TO FORM ON THE MOSELLE RIVER

encountered scattered small arms fire immediately and machine gun and mortar fire as they advanced over the flat open terrain across the river, but the first German artillery fire did not fall until daybreak. By this time the 2d Battalion had also begun its crossing, assisted by the smoke of the M2 generators which opened up at 0600. Under this concealment the 2d Battalion completed its crossing, the wounded were evacuated from the far shore, and supplies and ammunition were sent across to the embattled troops. By 0800, after close fighting and heavy casualties, the two battalions had taken two hills. Suddenly at 1000 the wind shifted, causing the screen to dissipate. Enemy artillery concentrated on the crossing site, now laid bare.

Within an hour Colonel Cottingham and Lt. Frank W. Young, of the 84th Company, moved four generators down to the side of an abandoned railroad embankment (Position 2 on the map). Smoke pots helped conceal the generators as they began to build up a screen, and by 1200 the crossing site was again covered by smoke. Shortly before noon Brig. Gen. Alan D. Warnock, assistant division commander, and Cottingham looked for the commanding officer of the 84th Smoke Generator Company to tell him to keep the generators running continuously. 1st Lt. George R. Lamb, the company executive officer, was across the river reconnoitering for new emplacements, and Lieutenant Young continued to direct operations along the near bank. The company commander could not be found. At this point, Col. William H. Greene, XX Corps chemical officer, present to inspect the screening operation, joined Cottingham in a search for company personnel. There were many barrels for fog oil at the dump west of Arnaville, but no sign of smoke generator troops. The two CWS officers eventually located a group under control of the 1st sergeant who, not without difficulty, organized details to move generators and fog oil to the crossing site. Without preparation for this type of operation and without company leadership, a number of the smoke troops had to be urged to take up positions down by the river bank. Upon making his appearance in the late afternoon, the company commander was relieved and replaced by Lieutenant Lamb.

The number of generator positions was soon increased in order that an effective screen might be maintained, regardless of the direction of the wind. Position 3 paralleled a short stretch of the Arnaville-Noveant road and was later augmented by a jeep-mounted generator which patrolled the road on the lookout for any gaps in the screen. That night eight generator crews crossed the Moselle with their equipment, dug in their generators, and were ready to start operations at Position 4 at dawn of 11 September. The new smoke plan also included emergency Positions 5 and 6, located south of Arnaville, but these were never needed in the operation.[20]

At daybreak on 11 September the 84th began smoking operations at Position 3 on the far bank of the river. For several hours activity at the bridgehead was essentially unmolested; enemy shelling had practically ceased. The engineers had hauled several pieces of heavy equipment to the near bank and were about to begin bridge construction. Around 0900 an unidentified engineer, doubtlessly influenced by the absence of opposition and the interference of smoke with bridging

---

[20] It was also during the night of 10–11 September that the smoke company tested the feasibility of a screen against artillery observation and air bombardment on moonlight nights, although the bridgehead was neither bombed or strafed during any night of the operation.

activities, ordered the smoke generators to shut down.[21] As soon as the screen dissipated, hell broke loose on the bridge site. German artillery made direct hits on two pieces of heavy engineer equipment and killed or wounded several engineers. Cottingham ordered the screen re-established at once, and the engineers shifted their efforts 300 yards downstream inasmuch as the enemy had pinpointed the original bridge site. To avoid any future interference with smoking activity, the division commander assumed control at the bridge site, to be exercised by his chemical officer.

The engineers rated the value of smoke at Arnaville less highly than did the participating chemical officers. After the war, Colonel Walker expressed the view that enemy fire on the crossing site was limited more by a shortage of ammunition than by American smoke.[22] Undoubtedly the enemy did suffer from a limited supply of ammunition and could not make lavish use of shells for missions of harassment and interdiction. But his interest in lucrative targets of opportunity, as evidenced by this experience on 10 and 11 September, was enough to convince the 5th Division that a smoke screen should be maintained.

A 15-hour screen on 12 September was featured by the use of a jeep-mounted generator on the valley road east of the river. About noon engineers completed a treadway bridge at the north site but had to withdraw temporarily because of heavy shelling. The screen continued on 13 September although from time to time enemy fire made the location almost untenable. That day German guns inflicted four casualties and destroyed two generators of the 84th Company and two of its trucks.

Again on the 14th enemy fire forced the engineers to evacuate the bridge site from time to time. Fluctuating winds frequently exposed generator emplacements to direct enemy observation, and the crews hurriedly moved their generators after such an exposure. Smoke pots hid upwind generators, filled gaps in the line, and maintained the screen while crews replaced or repaired generators. Enemy fire killed one man of the smoke company and wounded another. Late on the 14th, engineers completed the bridge at the south site making possible one-

---

[21] (1) Colonel Walker of the 1103d Engineer Combat Group was not the officer who gave the order. *Three Battles*, p. 74n. (2) Some engineer accounts place the time of heavy shelling several hours earlier, but MacDonald in his Arnaville account, after a careful study of the after action reports, agrees that 0900, the time set by Cottingham, must have been the approximate hour. *Ibid.*, p. 74.

[22] MacDonald in *Three Battles*, page 67, cites this opinion by Colonel Walker.

way traffic across the Moselle. That day there was some decrease in enemy fire. On the 15th the 5th Division captured the dominating hill in the area, and German artillery fire further diminished with the advance of the infantry and armor. Thus the bridgehead was secured at a cost of 725 casualties in the 10th Infantry, 13 killed and 100 wounded in the 1103d Engineer Combat Group, and 2 killed and 7 wounded in the 84th Smoke Generator Company.

Securing the bridgehead did not eliminate the need for smoke, for the Arnaville bridges, which became integral parts of the main supply route for succeeding operations of XX Corps, remained under German observation from Fort Driant and neighboring points in the vicinity of Metz. The 161st Smoke Generator Company, under the command of Capt. Charles D. Underwood, relieved the 84th on 21 September and maintained a screen at Arnaville until the 25th, when XX Corps decided that smoke was no longer necessary. Enemy artillery promptly destroyed the treadway bridge and damaged the ponton structure, stopping all traffic. In response to an engineer request for the resumption of the screen a section of the 84th returned on the 29th and established "a very comforting smoke screen." [23] Enemy guns at Fort Driant, with much of the Moselle Valley in range, continued to fire indiscriminately but failed to damage seriously the heavy ponton bridge.[24]

The Lessons Learned at Arnaville

The operation at Arnaville demonstrated for the first time in the European theater that smoke generators could give effective support to an opposed river crossing. The experience also served notice that certain improvements were desirable.

Even before the operation began it was evident that a smoke company had enough organic vehicles for transporting fog oil and supplies from company dumps to forward positions, but too few 2½-ton trucks to haul oil from the army supply point. The 5th Division solved the problem of fetching oil from the army supply by augmenting the five company trucks with additional vehicles. This matter of limited organic transportation and its effect on resupply remained a constant

[23] Col. William C. Hall, CE, "Harassing Fire," *The Field Artillery Journal*, vol. 35, No. 2 (February, 1945), pp. 68–69.
[24] TUSA AAR, vol. II, pt. III, p.

problem for smoke generator companies in the fighting in France and Germany.[25] The Arnaville experience also pointed out that definite plans had to be made to get generators and fog oil across the river at an early hour. This meant making an initial assignment of boats and rafts to the smoke company for that specific purpose, an assignment which quite possibly would have been made if a section of the 84th Chemical Smoke Generator Company had been a component part of the river crossing assault team.

The operation focused attention on the need for definite control of area screening. Tactical control of the screen by the engineer unit responsible for the bridge appeared logical at first. But the action of the engineers in shutting down the screen in the course of the operation caused all elements to suffer and demonstrated that in certain tactical situations it was highly desirable to clear smoke interference complaints through division headquarters where a decision could best be made. In fact, in subsequent river crossing operations the 5th Division kept control of the screen in the hands of the commanding general until his rear boundary had advanced beyond the bridge. If screening was still necessary, as it was at Arnaville, control reverted to the corps engineer unit charged with maintaining the bridge.

One of the most important lessons learned at the Moselle was the fallacy of depending upon prevailing winds and the necessity of planning for winds from any quarter. On 10 September the prevailing wind remained constant for the first four hours and then turned variable and remained so for several days. Five valleys converged near the vital point, and at times the smoke from generators only several hundred yards apart drifted in opposite directions. Matters were made worse by difficulties in the observation and adjustment of the Arnaville screen. Colonel Cottingham decided to experiment with aerial observation because the hills which rose beyond the far bank were too insecurely held for the establishment of observation posts. Beginning on 14 September he made at least three flights daily: one at 0800, another at 1300 when convection currents began raising havoc with the screen, and the last at 1700 when the air temperature began dropping. Aerial observation revealed defects which could not be noticed from the ground, enabling the observer to anticipate the

---

[25] (1) Pritchard, Smoke Generator Opns in MTO and ETO, p. 119;   (2) USFET Study 69, Smoke Generator Opns and Orgns, pp. 10–11.

effects of wind change. He could note smoke drift from fires in villages and streamers from artillery smoke shell and thus direct generator shifts before the development of any serious gaps. Usually such a trip in a liaison plane, borrowed from the artillery, took about fifteen minutes, but on one trip conditions were so miserable that the necessary adjustments required almost two hours.

Maintenance proved a problem despite the fact that a continuous screen required only a few generators operating simultaneously and that the average generator hours of operation in a day was only forty-four. Experience indicated that extra generators, strategically placed, obviated the need of shifting others when variations and veerings appeared in the wind or when a generator failed to operate. And as a rule three generators a day were replaced because of mechanical failures, burned-out coils for the most part. Consequently, before the end of the operation all forty-eight generators had to be employed. In subsequent operations, assignment to the division of mechanics from a chemical maintenance company brought about improvement in maintenance.

The experience at Arnaville indicated the need for additional smoke generator operators. One man per generator sufficed for rear area screening but the conditions encountered in the front lines made two operators mandatory. The additional man enabled proper reliefs and insured that someone was available for relaying messages to the next position along the smoke line. In case of a casualty, one operator could administer first aid and keep the generator operating. And two men at a position were better for morale.

Troops coming directly from the communications zone into a sector under enemy artillery and small arms fire had to make a rapid mental and emotional adjustment. A few men cracked under the strain, but the majority held up well. Nonetheless, this initial experience demonstrated that a smoke company should have combat training and a period of indoctrination before commitment to an assault crossing operation.[26]

The 84th Chemical Smoke Generator Company began its Arnaville operations under the additional handicap of inefficient direction before its attachment to the 5th Division. Both personal and organizational

---

[26] The 90th Division chemical officer reached the same conclusion about another smoke generator unit. See Ltr, CmlO 90th Div to CCmlO ETO, 20 Jan 45, sub: Opns of Smoke Generator Company in Support of River Crossing. CWS 314.7.

equipment were below standard, with a number of men lacking articles of clothing, rifle belts, helmets, and canteens. Some trailers had been left at the last bivouac before reaching the division. Training in the important areas of communications and map reading was below standard. All these factors, combined with the examples of poor leadership on the part of the company commander once the 84th was committed to action, contributed to make more difficult the company's introduction to combat. A few shifts in leadership and the example set by officers and men who did respond to demands of the situation helped mold the unit into an efficient team. That the performance of the 84th improved is indicated by the fact that General Walker awarded Bronze Star medals to an officer and four enlisted men and by the statement of the 5th Division Assistant Chief of Staff, G–3, after the operation, that "a Smoke Generator Company must be included in making a river crossing.[27]

The Third Army Crossing of the Saar River

After the successful campaign against Metz, which fell in late November 1944, XX Corps was ready to begin its advance into Germany.[28] By 1 December the corps had reached the west bank of the Saar River and was preparing to establish bridgeheads on the east bank, in the face of the West Wall defenses of the enemy. Before reaching the West Wall, one of the most strongly fortified areas in Europe, Third Army would have to cross the open river flats, a tactical situation which could well call for a considerable use of smoke.[29]

The XX Corps plan for the Saar operation called for assault crossings in the Dillingen-Saarlautern sector by the 90th and 95th Divisions while the 10th Armored Division feinted a crossing near Hilbringen. The 161st Smoke Generator Company, attached to the 10th Armored Division, was ordered to screen the vicinity of the partially destroyed Merzig bridge, which, for all the enemy could know, might already have been repaired for a crossing operation.[30] Beginning on 4 December the 84th Smoke Generator Company screened both flanks of the 95th

---

[27] 5th Inf Div G–3 AAR, Sep 44. Orgn Files, ETO.

[28] The Metz campaign involved assault crossings of the Moselle, Seille, and Nied Rivers, all of which were effectively supported by the 84th and 161st Smoke Generator Companies. For a discussion of the use of smoke in these operations, see Pritchard, Smoke Generator Opns in the MTO and ETO.

[29] Elements of XII Corps crossed the Saar on the right of XX Corps.

[30] (1) TUSA AAR, II, pt. II, 9.   (2) 10th Armored Div CWS Sec AAR, 1–31 Dec 44.

Division as it crossed the river in the vicinity of Saarlautern. The division also called for generator smoke on the captured bridge at Saarlautern and over the construction activities at Lisdorf.[31]

The most extended screening missions of the Saar crossing were those in the Dillingen-Pachten area, several miles north of Saarlautern, in support of the 90th Division. These operations involved the 84th and 161st Smoke Generator Companies, and elements of the 81st Chemical Mortar Battalion. The infantry began crossing before dawn on 6 December, and smoke operations began at daybreak. Entrenched behind the West Wall on the far side of the Saar River, the Germans could observe all feasible crossing sites and the road nets leading to them. Artillery and mortar fire hit throughout the river area during the whole period of the operation, and in the early phase enemy small arms fire covered the crossing sites. The smoke troops at the ferry site were still within range of small arms fire as late as 10 December.[32] So heavy was hostile fire that for the sixteen days of the assault, engineers of the 90th Division were unable to erect a vehicular bridge and operated ferry traffic only with great difficulty. The variable winds which prevailed for the first six days tore gaps in the screen, so that mortar and artillery smoke shells had to be used as supplements.[33]

On 19 December the 90th Division began to withdraw from the east bank as part of Third Army regroupment to oppose the German breakthrough in the Ardennes. This maneuver involved the movement of nine battalions of infantry and more than 100 vehicles through a restricted crossing site which was still within range of enemy artillery and which was serviced by only a single ferry, one foot-bridge, and a few assault boats. The 84th and 161st Smoke Generator Companies screened the withdrawal successfully and were among the last troops to return to the near bank.

Screens for the crossing and withdrawal at the Saar resulted in expenditures of 151,000 gallons of fog oil and 8,500 HC smoke pots. The smoke line near Dillingen had extended for more than 2,000 yards

---

[31] (1) 84th Cml Smoke Generator Co, Summary of Smoke Opns in the ETO, 12 May 45. (2) For an account of the spectacular capture of this bridge by the 1st Battalion, 379th Infantry, see Cole, *The Lorraine Campaign*, pages 517-19.

[32] During these operations seven enlisted men of the 161st and one officer and three men of the 84th received a total of two Silver Star and nine Bronze Star medals for valor under fire.

[33] (1) 90th Inf Div, Rpt of Opns, Dec 44, pp. 7-26. Orgn Files, ETO. This report furnishes a detailed account of the difficulties of screening and bridging the Saar River at Dillingen during both the assault and the withdrawal phases. (2) Ltr, Div CmlO 90th Inf Div to CCmlO ETO, 20 Jan 45. (3) 81st Cml Mortar Bn AAR, Dec 44.

and covered troops and vehicles moving up to, as well as across, the Saar River and had effectively concealed traffic along roads to Saarlautern and other points. Enemy sources reported that U.S. "artificial fog" along the Saar interfered with German observation and diminished the effectiveness of his artillery fire.[34]

Smoke Operations at the Roer

As early as December 1944 Ninth Army was aware of the desirability of smoke support for its contemplated Roer River crossing, and it was at this time that it had secured the services of the 74th and 83d Smoke Generator Companies.[35] These units, commanded respectively by Capt. George B. Warren, Jr. ,and Capt. Augustus H. Shaw, Jr., were attached to XIII and XIX Corps. Both companies underwent training for front-line operations since preparations in the zone of interior had been directed toward the rear area mission. The German counteroffensive in the Ardennes delayed the scheduled Roer crossing. During this interval Ninth Army held smoke demonstrations in the rear area of the 29th Division to acquaint infantry and engineer commanders with the capabilities and limitations of the mechanical generator.[36]

With the defeat of the Germans in the Ardennes, the Allies again focused their attention on the Rhine. But the immediate objective was to cross the Roer, and Ninth Army, flanked on the right by the First Army, was to launch an assault crossing of that river and advance northeast to join forces with the First Canadian Army, which was to drive southward along the Rhine and clear its west bank. The Ninth Army sector was a broad, flat region cut by the Roer and other streams which flow generally in a northward direction. Entrenched on the far bank the enemy had excellent observation of the western approaches to the river. He also was able to flood the Ninth Army sector by the controlled release of water from the dams up the valley. As a consequence, the 10 February target date for the crossing was postponed until 23 February when Ninth Army assaulted on a 2-corps front—the

---

[34] Interv, Hist Div ETOUSA with Maj Gen Kurt von Muehlen (former commander of *Kampfgruppe Muehlen*), Apr 46. MS # A–972 in OCMH.

[35] These were the first smoke units assigned to the Ninth Army which became operational on 5 September 1944.

[36] (1) 83d Cml Smoke Generator Co Opns Rpt, 19–30 Dec 44. (2) 29th Div AAR, Dec 44.

XIII on the left near Linnich and the XIX on the right in the vicinity of Jülich.

The 74th Smoke Generator Company supported the crossing of the 84th Division in the XIII Corps sector. On the night of 22–23 February the 74th used smoke pots from 2000 to 0315 while engineer and infantry troops concentrated on the near bank; the assault began at the latter hour under concealment of smoke which drifted toward the far side. At first, the smoke company used only pots for fear that the noise and placement of the mechanical generators would disclose the position and intention of the infantry, separated from the enemy only by the Roer River. But after the crossing the 74th used both mechanical generators and pots in smoking the bridge sites. Each day it stood by prepared to smoke on call. Each night from 1700 to 0700 hours it screened several bridges in the vicinity of Linnich from enemy aircraft. The 74th continued these missions until 3 March, first in support of the 102d Division and then while attached to the 19th Antiaircraft Artillery Group. The screening at Linnich was generally successful despite understandable complaints about the irritating effect of HC smoke and some interference with traffic and friendly artillery observation. The smoke materially aided bridging operations and, according to infantrymen of the 1st Battalion, 333d Infantry, effectively concealed the flash from their 60-mm. mortars.[37]

While the Linnich assault was in progress, XIX Corps crossed the Roer upstream on a 2-division front, the 29th Division on the left at Jülich and the 30th Division on the right in the Pier-Schophoven area. Corps assigned the 83d Smoke Generator Company (less one section) to the 29th Division which in turn attached it to the 121st Engineer Combat Battalion. The smoke plan for the operation stipulated that Company A, 92d Chemical Mortar Battalion, use white phosphorus shells to supplement the generator smoke in the event of unfavorable winds. Screening began at 0350, twenty minutes after the initial assault, along a 2-mile smoke line opposite Jülich. Under cover of this smoke engineers worked with little hindrance by the enemy. A request by the division engineer that smoke be continued after daybreak to keep observed enemy fire away from the bridge sites was overruled by corps because

---

[37] (1) 74th Cml Smoke Generator Co Rpt of Smoke Generator Opns (5 Feb–3 Mar 45), 9 Mar 45. (2) Ltr, CO 27th Smoke Generator Bn to CmlO Ninth Army, 25 Feb 45, sub: Smoke Opns of the 74th Smoke Generator Co. (3) 84th Inf Div AAR, Feb 45, pp. 13–25. Orgn Files, ETO.

of interference with the observation of corps artillery.[38] Shortly after the screen lifted hostile artillery fire destroyed one of the bridges under construction. It was the opinion of the division engineer that smoke might well have saved the bridge, and the XIX Corps staff was convinced that better smoke co-ordination was needed in future operations.[39]

Several miles upstream the 30th Division planned to cross the Roer River in the vicinity of Schophoven and Pier and drive north to the Cologne-Jülich highway along which the enemy might launch a counterattack against the Jülich bridgehead of the 29th Division. It expected that the crossing would be difficult because of the swollen channels, the many pools of water from the recent floods, the spongy soil, and the lack of cover. In fact, during November Ninth Army had considered a crossing in that vicinity impracticable.[40]

The infantry began the crossing by boat at 0330 23 February after a 45-minute artillery preparation reported to have been one of the heaviest concentrations of fire experienced in the European theater.[41] Along the 8,000-yard division front 246 artillery pieces, 35 mortars of the 92d Chemical Mortar Battalion, and 36 guns of the 823d Tank Destroyer Battalion participated in the preparation. The initial assault force encountered only light opposition. The 119th Infantry crossed at the north site, opposite Schophoven, while one battalion of the 120th Infantry crossed to the south, opposite Pier. A mile of low, boggy ground and water separated the two sites.

The smoke plan called for screens over both these sites, as well as over the area between them, during the twelve daylight hours of 23 February. If conditions should prevent the effective screening of both bridge sites, the northern bridge was to have priority. The division commander maintained control of the use of smoke, while the division chemical officer supervised its operation. The critical observation posts of the enemy were in the towns on the far bank and along the low ridge of hills to the northeast. At first, only one section (twelve gen-

---

[38] (1) Ltr, Col John B. Cobb to Hist Off, 18 Jan 50. (2) Ltr, Col Charles H. Gerhardt to Hist Off, 9 Feb 51. Gerhardt, as a major general in command of the 29th Division during this operation, wanted the screen continued during daylight hours but was overruled by corps.

[39] (1) Cobb Ltr, 18 Jan 50. (2) Ltr, CmlO 29th Div to CmlO XIX Corps, 7 Mar 45, sub: Smoke Generator Opn in Roer River Crossing. CMLHO. (3) 83d Cml Smoke Generator Co, Notes on Roer River Screening, Koslar, Germany, 23 Feb 45, n.d.

[40] Robert L. Hewitt, *Work Horse of the Western Front: The Story of the 30th Infantry Division* (Washington: Infantry Journal Press, 1946), pp. 212-13.

[41] *Ibid.*, pp. 215-16.

erators and crews) of the 83d Smoke Generator Company was available, supplemented by a detachment of seventeen infantrymen, several mechanics from the 57th Chemical Maintenance Company, and two men from the division chemical section. For several nights preceding the jump-off, smoke troops went forward and dug foxholes, established supply dumps, and prepared generator emplacements.[42]

The smoke troops moved into position at 0245 on 23 February. The din of the heavy artillery preparation drowned the noise of movement and darkness hid the exact location of the bridging area. Smoking began at 0630. The generators provided good concealment at the northern site but unexpected winds at the south site tore gaps in the screen. The smoke line was extended to the southeast. In mid-morning engineers ceased construction on the south bridge because of accurate artillery fire, which was probably adjusted when gaps appeared in the screen. After one battalion crossed on boats and Alligators, the 120th Infantry transferred its effort to the northern site where the 119th, under effective smoke concealment, was crossing without much difficulty.

Smoke concealed the northern crossing throughout the day. While engineers worked on a treadway bridge, infantrymen crossed a foot bridge and overran enemy positions on the east bank of the river. Maj. Gen. Leland S. Hobbs, commanding the 30th Division, ordered the screen continued during the coming night and the next day. The request for the night screen was prompted by the Luftwaffe which had been rather active during the previous two nights and which was using a number of jet-propelled planes. Another section of the smoke company came from the 29th Division at Jülich to help maintain the screen.

During the night of 23–24 February the 30th Division extended the bridgehead to the northeast, capturing the towns of Hambach and Niederzier and eliminating enemy observation of bridge sites from the east. The northern bridge was opened to passage of armor at midnight. By dawn the wind was from the north and smoke troops established pot positions on the far bank along the western edge of the Krauthausen-Selgersdorf road. Troops and armor advancing over this route were exposed to observed fire from the woods beyond Hambach, so the smoke line was moved eastward across the road, 100 yards into the

---

[42] CmlO 30th Div Rpt on Roer River Smoke Screen, Schophoven, Germany, 23–24 Feb 45, n.d. This report covers in detail the planning and operational phases of screening for the 30th Division at the Roer crossing, and is the chief source for the discussion of that crossing.

fields. For the same reason, other smoke positions were established north of the Selgersdorf-Daubenrath road. Chemical troops captured four prisoners while setting up these final positions in an area infested with enemy mines.

Division headquarters ordered smoke over both the northern and the southern bridges for the night of 24–25 February. But the supply of smoke pots was exhausted by about 1530 hours and the M2 generators were in need of repair after a long period of continuous operation. Moreover, the crews were fatigued from thirty-three hours of continuous duty. Consequently, the decision to use smoke that night was canceled. By morning the 30th Division had driven the enemy beyond range of observation, and smoke was no longer necessary.

Large area screening activities along the Roer contributed to the success of 30th Division operations in several ways. Smoke over the northern area enabled the engineers to start construction of a vehicular bridge five hours earlier than had been anticipated. The enemy never had an opportunity to deliver observed fire, a circumstance that enabled the 295th Engineer Combat Battalion to maintain uninterrupted bridging operations. In fact, there was not a single engineer casualty from enemy fire at the northern bridge. As a result of this building feat, the first armor moved across the Roer River at H plus 21, fifteen hours ahead of schedule.[43] Another benefit of the screen was the concealment of infantry and armor units moving up to, across, and beyond the river, particularly those units in the vicinity of Selgersdorf. In two instances the infantry called for extension of the smoke coverage near the front line. Captured prisoners stated that, while they believed the Roer offensive was imminent, the darkness at the time of the initial attack and the subsequent screening confused the Germans as to the exact location of the American effort. The plan for the Roer crossing had called for only twelve hours of smoke, but during operations screening continued without cessation for thirty-three hours. This extension was indicative of the effectiveness of the screen and the value which General Hobbs placed upon smoke.[44]

First Army crossed the Roer on the right of Ninth Army. The VII Corps, on the left, crossed near Düren and advanced northeastward

[43] Combat Observer XIX Corps to CG ETOUSA, 28 Feb 45, Observers Rpt No. 155 (Roer River Crossing).

[44] (1) CmlO 30th Div Rpt on Roer River Smoke Screen, Schophoven, Germany, 23–24 Feb 45, n.d. (2) Hewitt, *Work Horse of the Western Front*, p. 221.

to protect the right flank of Ninth Army. The 104th and 8th Divisions spearheaded the corps attack. The other two corps of First Army, the III in the center and the V on the right, initially remained on the defensive but were prepared to advance on or after D plus 2.[45]

Forward area screening developed slowly in the First Army. There was none during 1944, with the exception of an August operation at Mayenne, France, which shielded a bridge against enemy air bombardment. But the smoke tests that Col. Kenneth A. Cunin, army chemical officer, ran at Liège in late 1944 impressed at least one high ranking commander, Maj. Gen. J. Lawton Collins, commanding VII Corps. Collins and his engineer officer, Col. Mason Young, both saw great possibilities in using the mechanical smoke generator in assault river crossings and the general attempted to get some to support his corps' assault of the Roer. Circumstances prevented the use of smoke generators in the Roer crossing. Col. Jack A. Barnes, VII Corps chemical officer, had too little time to collect the equipment or to assemble suitable trained troops. In fact, the only trained smoke units were the 79th and 80th Smoke Generator Companies and these, the First Army commander decided, could not be released from the secondary duties to which they had been assigned. Any screening operation would therefore have to depend upon the smoke pot and the white phosphorus shells of the chemical mortar. The plan for using smoke in the sector of the 104th Division was abandoned when its artillery commander objected to possible interference with observation.[46]

The 8th Division planned to cross south of Düren with the 28th Infantry on the right at Lendersdorf and the 13th Infantry on the left. After the crossing, the 28th Infantry was to protect the corps right flank until III Corps entered the fight. The 13th Infantry did not plan to employ smoke at the crossing, but the 28th Infantry made provisions for using HC pots to conceal the initial assault and the subsequent bridge construction. S/Sgt. Robert J. Cesari of the 80th Smoke Generator Company gave training in smoke tactics to the infantrymen of the reserve battalion who were to man the pots. On the eve of the attack Capt. Kirk J. Ruger, commanding the 80th, was attached to the division as smoke observer and adviser. He was especially concerned with screens planned for the two bridges which were

---

[45] FUSA Rpt of Opns, 1 Aug 44–22 Feb 45, p. 160.

[46] Interv, Hist Off with Barnes, 27 Jun 50. Barnes believed that division objection to smoke would have been overruled had mechanical generators been available.

to be built by the 294th Engineer Combat Battalion in the vicinity of Lendersdorf.[47]

The 28th Infantry jumped off near Lendersdorf early on 23 February. The smoke from HC pots, the haze from shell fire, and the morning mist concealed the crossing site until shortly after 1000. During this phase the two bridge sites (Nos. 9 and 10) received sporadic and unobserved small arms and mortar fire. But at 1000 the west wind ceased, the screen lifted, and accurate enemy artillery fire began to come in on bridge site 10. Captain Ruger's suggestion to have Company D, 87th Chemical Mortar Battalion, fire WP shells against enemy positions on the right flank across the river was ruled out for fear that friendly troops might be in the impact area. In the absence of wind the use of smoke pots would have been ineffective.

There was also trouble at the bridge site No. 9, visited by Ruger in midafternoon. Engineers had suspended all activity on this treadway bridge because of the direct fire from an enemy self-propelled gun on the opposite bank, accompanied by small arms fire. The division's assistant commander, Brig. Gen. Charles D. W. Canham, insisted that the bridge be started promptly, regardless of cost, and asked Ruger to recommend the use of smoke so as to conceal renewed attempts at construction. A light northwesterly wind had set in by this time and Ruger suggested a smoke installation through Lendersdorf augmented by floating pots which, because of the curve in the stream, would establish a semicircular smoke line around the crossing site. But in the meantime enemy fire had increased so much that all work was postponed at this site and concentrated on bridge No. 10. Company D, 87th Chemical Mortar Battalion, was then ordered to establish a smoke screen on the far bank where the Roer River intersected the III–VII Corps boundary. Sergeant Cesari had already set up a smoke line around bridge No. 10 and his smoke detail of ten men from the 28th Infantry had placed the pots. The heavy fire, however, had scattered the detail and Cesari had to light the pots himself. The smoke drew additional fire, but the engineers were able to resume work on the footbridge. Chemical troops maintained HC and WP screens

---

[47] (1) 2d Ind, CmlO First Army to CmlO 12th Army Group, 5 Apr 45, on Ltr, CO 80th Smoke Generator Co to CO 23d Smoke Generator Bn, 28 Feb 45, sub: Rpt on Smoke Opns 23d, 24th, 25th Feb, Roer River Assault and Crossing. CWS Unit Files, 23d SG Bn. CMLHO. (2) 23d Cml Smoke Generator Bn Unit Diary, 18–24 Feb 45. (3) 294th Engr Combat Bn AAR, 1–28 Feb. 45. Orgn Files, ETO.

from 1630 until darkness. That night the Luftwaffe bombed and strafed the bridge site while enemy artillery continued to fire into the area.[48] Next morning the commanding officer, 28th Infantry, on the advice of Captain Ruger, ordered Company D, 87th Chemical Mortar Battalion, to continue the screen on the high ground to the southeast. German artillery fire on the bridge sites lessened but did not cease. Obviously the enemy knew the location of the engineers. Later in the day jet fighters strafed the bridge sites, by now without smoke probably because the pot supply was exhausted. That night enemy planes dropped flares and continued to bomb and strafe the area, damaging the bridge at site No. 9 and some engineer equipment. The air effort which continued until noon of the 25th had as many as twenty planes over the area at one time.[49]

Smoke was not effectively used to support the Roer crossing of the 28th Infantry. VII Corps correctly estimated during the planning stage that the enemy could seriously oppose any crossing in the 28th Infantry sector for at least three days. The two bridge sites remained within mortar range of an enemy-held area on the right flank which was not engaged by American forces until 26 February, or three days after the 28th Infantry attack. Projected smoke could have been employed here profitably, as Captain Ruger suggested, if suitable coordination had existed. Under the prevailing northwest wind mechanical generators could have concealed the bridges effectively without seriously interfering with infantry or artillery operations. For the most part, the smoke would have drifted into enemy-held territory opposite III Corps. The area to be covered was too large to be effectively hidden by smoke pots. The 4.2-inch chemical mortars placed smoke on observation points to the southeast, but only after the enemy had ranged in on the bridges. And none of these screens could conceal the bridge sites from an attack. German artillery fire and bombing delayed the construction of the two bridges, so that they were not finished until more than forty-eight hours after the fighting began, and then at a cost of 23 wounded engineers.[50] Smoke, if properly employed, undoubtedly would have reduced enemy observation and probably

[48] Interv, 2d Info and Hist Serv, First Army, with Ruger and Cesari, 1 Mar 45.

[49] (1) Ibid. (2) Ltr, CO 80th Cml Smoke Generator Co to CO 23d Cml Smoke Generator Bn, 28 Feb 45, sub: Rpt on Smoke Opns, 23d, 24th, 25th Feb 45, Roer River Assault and Crossing.

[50] Part of the delay was due to the rapid current and high water. At other crossings of VII Corps, however, bridges were completed much sooner. Just a few miles down the Roer the 30th Division (Ninth Army) completed a vehicular bridge in twenty-one hours under the cover of smoke.

would have lessened the time required for construction and the number of engineer casualties suffered in the process.[51]

The Use of Smoke at the Rhine River Crossings

When the Allies terminated the Rhineland Campaign on 21 March 1945 they found themselves, with one exception, poised along the west bank of the Rhine, ready for the final assault. The exception was the Remagen bridgehead in the First U.S. Army sector, where a combination of fortuitous circumstances and aggressive action by the leaders and men of Combat Command B, 9th Armored Division, secured on 7 March the only Rhine River bridge taken intact by the Allies. During the fourth week in March the Ninth, Third, and Seventh U.S. Armies successfully assaulted the Rhine. In each case, units of the four armies used smoke generator companies to conceal either their actual assault crossing or the crossing sites during the period of build-up.

The unexpected capture of the Ludendorf railroad bridge on 7 March and the rapid expansion of the bridgehead radically changed the First Army plans for the Rhine crossings. Under the new plan VII Corps would expand the Remagen bridgehead northward to the Sieg River. As army forces cleared the far bank of the Rhine, its engineers, under the concealment of smoke, would build bridges first at Rolandseck, then Konigswinter, then Bonn. Because of success at Remagen, conventional assault crossings in the VII Corps sector were unnecessary. Bridge sites might be subject to artillery and mortar fire but not to any serious amount of small arms fire.[52]

The day after the capture of the Ludendorf bridge the engineers at the bridge site requested a smoke generator unit. When First Army replied that none was immediately available the engineers at Remagen had to depend upon whatever pots they could hurriedly gather. Finally, on 10 March, First Army relieved its smoke units from other duties and gave them five days to be ready for screening missions, whereupon the 79th and 80th Smoke Generator Companies retrieved their smoke

[51] (1) Interv, Hist Off with Maj Martin F. Massoglia, formerly ExecO 238th Engr Bn, 2 Dec 49. (2) History of VII Corps During Opns in Belgium and Germany, 1–28 Feb 45. Orgn Files, ETO. (3) 294th Engr Combat Bn AAR 1–28 Feb 45. Orgn Files, ETO. (4) Ltr, CO 80th Cml Smoke Generator Co to CO 23d Cml Smoke Generator Bn, 28 Feb 45, sub: Rpt on Smoke Opns, 23d, 24th, 25th Feb 45, Roer River Assault and Crossing.

[52] (1) 3d Ind, Deputy CCmlO ETO, 26 Apr 45 on Ltr, CmlO VII Corps to CmlO FUSA 7 Apr 45, sub: VII Corps Smoke Opns for Bridging the Rhine River. CMLHO. (2) History of VII Corps, 1–31 Mar 45. Orgn Files, ETO.

equipment from its six months' storage. On 15 March the two units received march orders and, early next morning, the 79th departed for Remagen and the 80th Company headed for VII Corps in the vicinity of Rolandseck.[53]

During the early phase of the Remagen operation the Germans held the high ground on the east bank with observation over the bridges and the approaches thereto. Artillery fire continually impeded, and at times halted, the movement of First Army troops through the area.[54] To provide for the increased traffic, III Corps engineers built two bridges which the enemy attempted to destroy by artillery and mortar fire, by bombing, and even by demolitions. Mechanical smoke generators would have expedited the erection of the bridges, according to an engineer officer, but by 16 March, when the 79th Smoke Generator Company (Capt. Morris W. Kane) arrived, the urgent need for smoke had ended.[55]

The first VII Corps units passed through the Remagen bridgehead on 15 March and within two days they had cleared the area opposite Rolandseck. Engineers started bridging the Rhine at Rolandseck on the night of 16–17 March and at dawn the 80th Smoke Generator Company began concealing the bridge site. The next afternoon most of the company departed for another bridge site at Konigswinter although several squads remained at Rolandseck until 23 March. Meanwhile, the 79th Company had moved from Remagen to Konigswinter and set up generators on the east bank of the Rhine. Smoke operations at this site, featured by the use of boat-mounted generators, also ended on 23 March.[56]

An extensive First Army screening operation took place along the Rhine at the southern outskirts of Bonn. Under technical control of the 23d Smoke Generator Battalion, smoke was started at 0501, 21 March, and continued without interruption for sixty-one hours. After

[53] (1) Armor School Research and Evaluation Div, Study: The Remagen Bridgehead, 7–17 Mar 45. CmlC School. (2) 23d Cml Smoke Generator Bn Unit Diary, 11–24 Mar 45. (3) Ltr, Cunin to Hist Off, 1 Feb 50.

[54] Capt. John F. Hyde, CMP, "Armored Bridgehead Operation," Armored Cavalry Journal, LVIII, No. 4 (July–August 1949), 37–38.

[55] (1) Massoglia Interv, 2 Dec 49. (2) 23d Cml Smoke Generator Bn Unit Diary, 10–24 Mar 45.

[56] (1) Ltr, CmlO VII Corps to CmlO FUSA, 7 Apr 45, sub: VII Corps Smoke Opn for Bridging the Rhine River. (2) 79th Cml Smoke Generator Co S–3 Rpt 51, Mehlem, Germany, 18–24 Mar 45, dated 25 Mar 45. (3) 80th Cml Smoke Generator Co S–3 Rpt 30, Bonn, Germany, 18–24 Mar 45, dated 25 Mar 45.

23 March the smoke troops remained alerted for five days, ready to operate against bombers, but the threat never was to materialize.

By 21 March the Third Army had reduced the Saar-Palatinate triangle, except for the mopping-up phase, and three of its corps had reached the Rhine. General Patton insisted that the enemy be given no chance to recover from the defeat in the Palatinate. Third Army planned to secure crossings over the Rhine River promptly and then advance to the northeast. The VIII Corps, on the left, would attack between Koblenz and Bingen and XII Corps was to cross the Rhine between Bingen and Worms. XX Corps, on the right flank, would continue mopping-up activities and then cross through the bridgehead of either VIII or XII Corps.[57]

The XII Corps attached the 84th and 161st Smoke Generator Companies to the 5th and 90th Divisions, respectively, for the assault crossings. The 162d Smoke Generator Company was to support the 87th and 89th Divisions of VIII Corps operating north of Bingen. The 81st Company was trucking for XX Corps but would be available for smoke operations on short notice. With four smoke generator units on hand, the Third Army could not only use smoke at the crossings but could also lay deceptive screens. There was some thought of placing a large dummy screen at Mainz because the enemy apparently believed that an initial crossing attempt would be made at that point.[58]

Previous Third Army smoke generator operations had emphasized concealment from artillery observation, as enemy aircraft had been relatively inactive. During February, for example, only thirty-two enemy planes were reported over the entire Third Army zone, and of these only two made attacks, both of them strafing.[59] But as the Army approached the Rhine, enemy air activity increased. On 20 March large numbers of German aircraft, including the new jet-propelled Me262, attempted to bomb bridges and strafe troops. On that date the Luftwaffe made a total of 314 sorties in the XII Corps zone alone.[60] This increased enemy air activity, even though temporary, was a distinct threat to the Rhine bridging operations and suggested that the crossing sites be screened against air as well as against artillery observation.

---

[57] TUSA AAR, I, 311–12.
[58] George S. Patton, Jr., *War As I Knew It* (Boston: Houghton, Mifflin Co, 1947), p. 266.
[59] TUSA AAR, I, 279.
[60] *Ibid.*, I, 310.

The 5th Division made the first crossing of the Rhine for the Third Army on the night of 22–23 March in the Oppenheim-Nierstein area. Two regiments had already crossed when, at dawn, the 84th Smoke Generator Company provided smoke from both sides of the river. Each day thereafter the 84th established a heavy screen at dawn and dusk, the periods when the engineer bridges were most vulnerable from the air. During the night the 84th maintained a haze which could be readily thickened in case of attack. In daylight, fighter planes and AA guns fought off enemy aircraft. A number of the generator positions along the near bank were atop a hill and the smoke, although blanketing the bridges from the air, was not dense enough on the ground to hinder traffic.[61] Additional generators were mounted on Dukws, but were not needed.

The importance of screening the Oppenheim-Nierstein area can be judged by the traffic which crossed the Rhine at that point. Five divisions, with supplies and supporting troops, passed over its three bridges between 23 and 27 March. And between 24 and 31 March, 60,000 vehicles crossed in support of the XII Corps assault. The smoke screen which initially concealed this area was approximately two and a half miles long and three-quarters of a mile wide. None of the bridges sustained damage during the area's four major air attacks.[62]

For several days after the crossing at Oppenheim-Nierstein the increased activity of enemy aircraft necessitated the continuance of smoke generator operations. On 24 March, 138 enemy planes attacked bridges, installations, and troop concentrations in the XII Corps sector. During the next day the sorties increased to 231. Heavy enemy aircraft losses and the overrunning of many fighter fields by the Third Army's advance soon reduced the threat posed by the Luftwaffe, and on 26 March only three German planes appeared over the XII Corps.[63] As a matter of precaution, smoke generator operations continued at Oppenheim-Nierstein until 31 March.

While the 5th Division was crossing at Oppenheim, the 90th Division was cleaning up Mainz and threatening to cross the Rhine either there or to the north. In support of this feint the 161st Smoke Generator

---

[61] 84th Cml Smoke Generator Co, Summary of Smoke Opns in the ETO, 12 May 45.

[62] Brig Gen P. H. Timothy, The Rhine Crossing—Twelfth Army Group Engineer Operations (Hereafter cited as The Rhine Crossing), (Ft Belvoir, Va., Jul 46), p. 38.

[63] TUSA AAR, I, 315–17. Another factor in the sudden reduction of Luftwaffe activity may have been the shifting of enemy planes to the crossing sites of other Allied armies.

Company, on 23 March, made smoke at several points between Bingen and Mainz. On the same day the 90th Division swung south, crossed the Rhine at Nierstein, and assumed control of the southern portion of the 5th Division bridgehead, an action which obviated the need for smoking the Rhine between Mainz and Bingen. Two days later a detachment of the 161st moved into Nierstein and extended the smoke line which the 84th Smoke Generator Company had already established there.[64] By 26 March all major units of XII Corps were well beyond the Rhine and were attacking points along the Main River in the vicinity of Frankfurt. The 161st Smoke Generator Company then moved forward and screened the bridges.

The divisions of VIII Corps crossed the Rhine between Bingen and Koblenz. The precise sites were Rhens and Boppard in the 87th Division sector, and Oberwesel, St. Goar, and Wellmich in the sector of the 89th Division. The 162d Smoke Generator Company divided its generators and crews between the two divisions. The smoke plan at Boppard called for screens for the assault crossing of the 345th Infantry and for the ponton bridge building activities of the 1102d Engineer Combat Group. The 162d made the first smoke at Boppard on 25 March from 0620 to 0635, just before the 345th Infantry attack. The generators smoked again at 0650 and remained in operation until late that night. With a favorable wind, the cloud traveled across the river and filled the valley. That night the wind shifted from south-southeast to northeast and the 162d, in order to conceal the bridge operations, moved its generators across the river. The smoke crews continued the screen throughout the next day, 26 March, under a steady rain of enemy artillery, mortar, and machine gun fire. The operation ended 26 March.[65]

Meanwhile, on the night of 24 March one section of the 162d set up a smoke screen in support of a deceptive move made by the 353d Infantry, 89th Division. The ruse was successful in that the enemy directed a large amount of artillery and small arms fire into the screened, but unoccupied area. The actual assault came early on 26 March; smoke operations ceased after half an hour because of inter-

---

[64] TUSA AAR, I, 314–22; II, pt. 11, 15.

[65] (1) 162d Cml Smoke Generator Co, Final Opn Rpt, Boppard, 24–27 March 45. (2) Smoke was not employed in the crossing of the 347th Infantry, 87th Division, at Rhens.

ference with forward observation. The crews of the 162d remained in position, until 28 March, in case the enemy shelled the bridge site.[66]

The 162d Smoke Generator Company also provided smoke for the assault of the 354th Infantry, 89th Division, opposite Wellmich, on the morning of 26 March from 0600 to 0630. Enemy artillery and small arms fire at the time of the successful crossing was heavy but unobserved.[67] At the same time, the company set up five generator positions near Oberwesel for the crossing of the 355th Infantry, 89th Division, and smoked from 0550 to 1700 hours, 26 March, while two battalions crossed the river. The screen not only covered the crossing site but also denied observation to enemy forces located at Kaub, upstream on the far side of the Rhine.[68] The Luftwaffe was not as active against VIII Corps bridge sites as it was against those of XII Corps although artillery and small arms fire were heavier. But despite heavy initial resistance the 87th and 89th Divisions advanced rapidly to the east, and by 28 March the Rhine mission of 162d Smoke Generator Company was over.

The 81st Smoke Generator Company supported XX Corps, which did not enter the picture until 27 March, when the 80th Division attacked across the Rhine and Main just southeast of Mainz and cleared the area around Kastel and at the junction of the two rivers. As soon as the infantry cleared the far bank, the smoke company screened the bridging operations, with half of the unit on either side of the river. Under smoke, the Third Army engineers built a 1,896-foot steel treadway bridge, probably the longest floating tactical bridge of the war.[69] The 81st continued to operate at Mainz until the evening of 1 April.[70]

Early in March 1945 the 3d and 45th Divisions of Seventh Army began preparations for the Rhine crossings. These divisions and various supporting organizations converged on Lunéville, France, to make use of the several lakes in the area for specialized training. Among the units supporting the 3d Division was the 540th Engineer Combat

---

[66] 162d Cml Smoke Generator Co Final Opn Rpt, St. Goar, 25–28 Mar 45. CMLHO. Col. James V. Montgomery, VIII Corps chemical officer, was killed during this operation.

[67] 162d Cml Smoke Generator Co, Final Opn Rpt, Wellmich [Germany], 25–26 Mar 45. CMLHO. There were no bridging activities at Wellmich.

[68] (1) 162d Cml Smoke Generator Co, Final Opn Rpt, Oberwesel [Germany], 25–27 Mar 45. CMLHO. There were no bridging operations at Oberwesel. (2) Timothy, The Rhine Crossing, p. 42.

[69] Timothy, The Rhine Crossing, p. 40.

[70] TUSA AAR, I, 322; II, pt. 11, 15.

Group with the 69th Smoke Generator Company attached. Supporting troops of the 45th Division included the 40th Engineer Combat Group and the 78th Smoke Generator Company. These attachments were to carry through the entire period of the Rhine crossings so that trained and co-ordinated teams would be ready to support the assault.[71]

Divisions of XV Corps led the Seventh Army assault across the Rhine. The initial crossings were to be made between Gernsheim and Ludwigshaven by the 45th Division on the left and the 3d Division on the right, the first crossing north, the second south of the city of Worms.[72] All five companies of the 22d Smoke Generator Battalion received screening assignments for the assault crossing, the first time all had been committed to the same forward area operation. Battalion headquarters was relieved from all other duties on the eve of the crossing and placed under direct control of the Seventh Army chemical officer. Previously, the battalion commander had occasionally participated in the Rhine crossing preparations, but generally his headquarters had performed other duties. As it turned out, the most important battalion function at the Rhine was logistical, the co-ordination of the supply of fog oil to the various smoke companies.[73]

Early on 26 March, for a brief period just before as well as during the assault crossings, the 163d and 168th Smoke Generator Companies drew German attention from the actual sites by maintaining feint screens in the sectors of the 71st and 36th Divisions. Meanwhile, the 45th and 3d Divisions crossed the river in the Worms areas on 2-regiment fronts. Enemy opposition to the 45th Division petered out quickly and no smoke was needed although the 78th was in position. This was not the case with the 3d Division in its Ludwigshaven-Worms sector. Here initial resistance to the early morning attack was weak, but by 0400, an hour and a half after the assault began, hostile artillery pinned down all troops in the area, and engineer operations at the upstream crossing site stopped. One engineer company suffered fifty-four casualties. Although German artillery fire hit three smoke company vehicles, the unit lost no men to enemy action. The intense

---

[71] (1) The same two smoke generator companies had attended an engineer school at La Valbonne, near Lyon, during the previous October, with the mission of screening engineer river operations. (2) 69th Cml Smoke Generator Co, History (May–Dec 44). (3) 78th Cml Smoke Generator Co, History, 1 Oct–31 Oct 44, 12 Nov 44. Both in Orgn Files, ETO. (4) Seventh Army Cml Sec History, 1 Jan–31 Oct 44.

[72] *Seventh Army Opns in ETO*, III, 741–45.

[73] Seventh Army Cml Sec History, Mar 45.

artillery fire did prevent a platoon trying to take over smoke pots in assault boats from reaching the west bank. Fortunately, the southwest winds eliminated the need for pots across the river. At 0700 the 1st Platoon, from positions in the near bank generated a fog oil screen between the enemy on Friesenheimer Island and the crossing site, a maneuver which effectively blocked German observation of troop and boat movement. At 1030 the 1st Platoon with six generators crossed the river in Dukws only to be pinned down for several hours by enemy fire with four generators still on the craft. The two that were gotten off maintained a haze between Sandhoffen and the crossing site which "greatly reduced the accuracy of enemy fire on the engineer operations.[74]

The two assault battalions in the 30th Infantry sector completed their crossings by 0305, and the 2d Platoon, 69th Smoke Generator Company, set up a smoke pot line on the far bank two and a half hours later. Just before daylight smoke began to pour from the pots across the river and from mechanical generators on the near shore. The variant winds caused smoke to be needed on all sides. The smoke haze denied observation to German troops on an island in the river which held out until several hours after daylight. Because the infantrymen took over the storm boats which had been allotted to the smoke troops, their own being destroyed by enemy artillery, the supply of smoke pots and the crossing of the generators were both delayed. By 0930 the smoke troops had four generators in operation across the river and half an hour later a wind shift to the southwest minimized the problem of smoke supply to the far bank.[75]

During the day the commanding general, 3d Division, ordered that smoke be made over both sites on a 24-hour basis. After 27 March the Luftwaffe, not hostile artillery, became the greater threat. The 2d Platoon, 69th Smoke Generator Company, continued to smoke the ponton and treadway bridges, which the engineers built near Worms, until 31 March. The 1st Platoon concealed the heavy ferry site with smoke until 30 March then moved to Ludwigshaven and screened the

---

[74] (1) 2832d Engr Combat Bn Opns Rpt, Mar 45. Orgn Files, ETO. (2) 69th Smoke Generator Co Opns Rpt No. 3, 5-31 Mar 45. Except for the omission of meteorological information and data on expenditures, this is a model report. It outlines the general situation, the special training, the special organization of the company for the operation, the preliminary moves, the operations of both platoons, and includes a discussion, an evaluation, and overlays of the smoke lines.

[75] (1) 69th Smoke Generator Co Opns Rpt No. 3, 5-31 Mar 45. (2) 2833d Engr Combat Bn Journal, Mar 45. Orgn Files, ETO.

bridge which connected that city with Mannheim. The 78th Smoke Generator Company moved to Mannheim on 1 April and set up a smoke line around the bridge which was erected over the Neckar River, but smoke was not needed. CWS troops maintained both installations until 5 April.[76]

On the eve of the Rhine crossing the Ninth U.S. Army was still with the British 21 Army Group, an attachment which had taken place at the time of the German counteroffensive. On its left was the British Second Army with a boundary near Wesel; on its right, just upstream from Dusseldorf, was the First U.S. Army, holding the left sector of General Bradley's 12th Army Group. Ninth Army designated its XVI Corps to make an assault crossing in the sector between Orsoy and Buderich. Initially, XIII and XIX Corps were to hold the west bank of the Rhine opposite the Ruhr, later to follow through the XVI Corps bridgehead. Chemical units available to XVI Corps for screening operations included the 27th Smoke Generator Battalion and the 74th and 83d Smoke Generator Companies. The 89th and 93d Chemical Mortar Battalions also were to contribute to the smoke mission.

Ninth Army screening operations along the Rhine River were divided into two phases, those before the crossing and those in connection with the assault. The purpose of smoke in the first phase was to conceal movement on the west bank and confuse the enemy as to Army intentions and crossing preparations. For eight days before the assault, smoke intermittently covered sixty-eight miles of the front north of Dusseldorf held jointly by British and American troops. The plan provided for "smoking" days and "nonsmoking" days, according to a schedule which was co-ordinated with air reconnaissance activities. In the Ninth Army sector the 74th and 83d Smoke Generator Companies and provisional personnel performed these preliminary missions with smoke pots, the mechanical generators being conserved for the main crossing effort. Enemy reaction to the employment of smoke during the first phase was varied. Prisoners stated that at first the Germans expected the assault after each smoke operation, but after continued feints they became confused as to Allied intentions. In some localities the Germans were extremely sensitive to smoke and

[76] (1) *Ibid.*   (2) 69th Smoke Generator Co History, Mar 45.   (3) XV Corps, AAR, Mar 45, pp. 71ff.   Orgn Files, ETO.   (4) Memo, CO 22d Smoke Generator Bn to CmlO Seventh Army, 29 Mar 45. Orgn Files, ETO.   (5) Cml Sec Seventh Army History, Mar 45.

replied promptly with inconsequential fire. A German radio broadcast boasted that an American attempt to cross the Rhine under smoke had been repulsed. On the whole, however, the enemy showed little reaction. A more important result of the smoke was expediting Allied troop and supply movements, particularly in the British and Canadian sectors where many dumps were located in exposed areas.[77]

The XVI Corps plans for the Rhine operation called for a 2-division crossing in the vicinity of Wallach, Mehrum, and Milchplatz. Naval craft were available for the initial assault and the engineers were ready to bridge the Rhine, a task which they anticipated would be no more difficult than that of bridging the Roer River under flooded conditions. After the crossing, the Ninth Army was to drive eastward, contain the enemy in the Ruhr pocket to the south, and maintain contact with the British Second Army on the left.

Smoke plans for the crossings provided for concealing the bridge sites for forty-eight continuous hours, if necessary. Under no circumstances was smoke to interfere with the airdrop of the First Allied Airborne Army at Wesel, scheduled to begin at 1000 hours on the first day. Maj. Robert H. Kennedy, commanding the 27th Smoke Generator Battalion, supervised the activities of the two smoke generator companies and operated the corps smoke control center. The artillery agreed to furnish liaison planes for observation of the screen. With the additional assistance from the artillery meteorological sections, the smoke control center would be advised of screening conditions anywhere in the army area at any particular moment. Any complaints about the interference of smoke with operations were to be referred to the smoke control center, with the matter reconciled by the G-3. Elements of the 89th Chemical Mortar Battalion would screen the right flank of the corps sector, opposite Orsoy, along the Rhein-Herne Canal.[78] The 83d Smoke Generator Company and two sections of the

---

[77] This account is based upon: (1) Lt Col W. R. Sawyer, GSO 1 Rpt on Smoke Screens Carried Out by First Canadian Army (R) (printed in the field by 1 Canadian Mobile Printing Sec RCASC, 15 Jul 45), pp. 33–34; (2) 21 Army Group, Cml Warfare Liaison Ltrs, No. 8, 25 Mar 45, No. 9, 24 Jul 45, CmlC School 461/2514; (3) Interv, Hist Off with Col Harold Walmsley (formerly CmlO Ninth Army) and Capt Joel B. Marangella (formerly IntellO Cml Sec Ninth Army), 14 Feb 47; (4) Ltr, CO 74th Cml Smoke Generator Co to CG Ninth Army, 23 Mar 45, sub: Rpt of Smoke Opns; (5) Ltr, CG 84th Div to CG XIII Corps, 7 Apr 45, sub: Smoke Opns; (6) Ltr, ACmlO 102d Div to CmlO XIII Corps, 7 Apr 45, sub: AAR on Smoke Used on Rhine River, all in CMLHO; (7) Hewitt, *Work Horse of the Western Front*, pp. 234–38.

[78] (1) Interv, Hist Off with Lt Col Andrew M. Bishop, Lt Col Joseph C. Prentice, Capt Clyde H. Westbrook, Capt Ralph R. Wance, and Mr Charles E. Miller, 1 Mar 50. (2) For more information on chemical mortar smoke operations, see below, Ch. XII.

74th would conceal the crossing sites of the 30th Division near Wallach and Mehrum, while the other two sections of the 74th Smoke Generator Company were to smoke at Milchplatz for the 79th Division crossing. Generator positions, as far as practicable, were to take advantage of the protection afforded by the dike on the west bank. Where necessary, the smoke troops were to use pots over the low land between the dike and the river. The first smoke was to appear at dawn on 24 March.[79]

The Ninth Army assault crossing of the Rhine River began on the night of 23–24 March. After heavy preparatory fire the initial waves of the 30th and 79th Divisions jumped off at 0200 and 0300 hours, respectively. Resistance was not serious and by daybreak thirteen battalions of infantry had crossed and secured four bridgeheads, several thousand yards deep. Within twenty-four hours the front lines had advanced approximately six miles beyond the Rhine.[80]

At dawn, smoke from the generators along the dike line concealed the ferrying operations of the assault boats from enemy ground and air observation. Fear that the haze might drift over the Wesel airdrop area and impede paratroop operation proved groundless. In midmorning the wind shifted from west to east, through south, and the smoke troops moved pots and generators across the river and screened from the far bank. Smoke continued on the first day until after dark. On 25 and 26 March smoke covered the bridges in the 30th Division sector during the daylight hours. But at Milchplatz, in the sector of the 79th Division, the generators remained idle until enemy guns had ranged in on the bridge site.[81] From 27 to 31 March the smoke troops operated only during the periods from 0500 to 0800 and from 1700 to 2000 hours, when the bridges were most vulnerable to air attack. Enemy aircraft strafed the generator lines during the nights of 24, 25, and 26 March, and artillery fire lasted through 24 and 25 March, but the smoke troops suffered only two casualties. The only damage to smoke equipment occurred during the movement of Alligators and tank destroyers during the hours of darkness of the initial assault. Smoke was not required after 31 March.[82]

[79] (1) Ltr, CmlO XVI Corps to CmlO Ninth Army, 1 Apr 45, sub: Smoke Opns—FLASHPOINT. Reproduced in Pritchard, Smoke Generator Opns in MTO and ETO, pp. 313–15. (2) Walmsley-Marangella Interv, 14 Feb 47.

[80] (1) Hewitt, Work Horse of the Western Front, pp. 238–42. (2) 30th Inf Div G-3 After Battle Report, Mar 45, pp. 4–5. Orgn Files, ETO.

[81] Interv, Hist Off with Capt Warren (formerly CO, 74th Smoke Generator Co), 27 Jun 50.

[82] Ltr, CmlO XVI Corps to CmlO Ninth Army, 1 Apr 45, sub: Smoke Opns—FLASHPOINT.

Planned as a 48-hour operation, smoke actually was used at the Rhine crossings for a period of eight days. During the first two days of the crossing the frequent shifts of wind direction made screening difficult, especially at Milchplatz, although the concealment of crossing activities was generally effective.[83]

Summary

The outstanding mission of the chemical smoke generator company for all armies in the European theater was the concealment of bridge and river crossing sites. Next in importance was the screening of main supply routes. Only as the Allies approached the Rhine did the Luftwaffe become a threat to operations. There were no calls for smoke to hide the flash of friendly artillery, as had been the case in Italy. Occasionally, an area screen concealed a flank of an armored or infantry advance or withdrawal.

Smoke generator companies generally operated as a unit, under the control of either the division or of the engineer unit charged with the bridging activities. When the need for area screening was anticipated, the division commander secured one or more smoke units from either corps or Army. Only in rare instances was the smoke generator kept available at regimental level, or lower, to be used as an instrument of opportunity.

European experience in large area screening revealed several principles which govern successful smoke operations. First, adequate time should be allowed during the planning of any operation to insure thorough reconnaissance and supply. Second, the control of a screen should be in the hands of the commander of the highest echelon concerned. Smoke can be a two-edged sword, simultaneously harmful and beneficial. A high level arbiter is necessary to balance its benefits against its disadvantages and come up with a decision most likely to insure ultimate success. Third, a smoke plan should provide for a smoke installation which completely surrounds the vital area, a factor which requires the planned transfer of men and equipment to the far bank

---

[83] (1) Hewitt, *Work Horse of the Western Front*, pp. 238–42. (2) 30th Inf Div G–3 After Battle Report, Mar 45, pp. 13. (3) Lt. Col. John C. Dalrymple, "Engineer Combat Group in the Rhine River Crossing," *Military Review*, XXVIII (August 1949), 5. (4) Ltr, CO 57th Cml Maintenance Co to CmlO Ninth Army, 29 Mar 45, sub: Maintenance of M2 Smoke Generators During Opns (Rhine River). CWS 314.7 Unit Files, 57th Cml Maint Co.

during the initial plan of a river crossing operation. And, finally, screening operations should begin before the enemy observes activity in the vital area and should cover considerably more territory than that area.

American armies gradually applied these principles to their European smoke operations. At first, the divisions of Seventh Army were more adept in the technique because of their experience in Italy. But before long the Third Army units resorted to corps area screens even more often than those of Seventh Army. Of the four armies in the European theater only the First failed to employ area screening when the occasion seemed to demand it, due in large part to a policy which kept smoke units at other tasks from which they could not be quickly relieved. On the whole, American forces in Europe learned the technique and principles of forward area screening rather quickly, especially considering the late development of the M2 generator which enhanced the possibilities of such employment.

CHAPTER X

Large Area Smoke Screens
in the Pacific

Large area smoke operations in the Pacific contrasted sharply with those in Italy, France, and Germany. By concealing rear area installations and forward area operations, CWS smoke generators in Europe had performed a vital service. The few smoke units in the Pacific, on the other hand, were inactivated while still in the training stage. The role of smoke in the Pacific was restricted mainly by geography and by the decision which gave the war against Germany priority over the Japanese conflict. Geography was an especially limiting factor. It dictated that a good deal of the fighting in the Pacific would be done by the naval arm. The most effective use of smoke in the Pacific was in the form of anchorage screens maintained by the Navy to conceal the vulnerable vessels involved in the numerous island hopping campaigns so typical of the war against Japan.

Early Attempts To Introduce Area Screening in SWPA

In the early phases of the war in the Southwest Pacific Area commanders who considered area screening as a means of concealing airfields from enemy air attack ran up against several serious problems.[1] These included not only a lack of a suitable means for static screening and a shortage of smoke materials but also a scarcity in shipping, both within the immediate area and from the United States to SWPA. If smoke was to be used the means and material would have to be devised locally.

When an industrial survey disclosed that large quantities of the FS smoke material could be produced in Australia, Colonel Copthorne, Chief Chemical Officer, USASOS SWPA, assigned the 42d Chemical

---

[1] Ltr, CCmlO USASOS to CCWS, 16 Nov 42, sub: Tech and Intell Work. AGO CWS Ret 319.1/3006. This letter reviews the background of the early requests for screening.

Laboratory, then in Brisbane, the mission of developing both a large and a small smoke generator which could employ this chemical smoke. Tests in the summer of 1942 revealed deficiencies in the large model which was dropped entirely later in the year after word came that the newly developed mechanical smoke generator would soon be made available to the theater. The 42d Laboratory Company went on to develop a small smoke generator which was to see limited use in the theater.

In January 1943 the Commanding General, USASOS SWPA, approved a project for concealing an advanced base or port with smoke and requisitioned two smoke generator companies from the United States to carry out the project. The harbor at Port Moresby, New Guinea, was chosen as the site for the first smoke installation, although military authorities realized that another port might be more critical by the time the smoke units arrived. After an on-the-spot survey of Port Moresby, Colonel Copthorne recommended that some generators be mounted on barges or power boats to insure adequate smoke coverage.[2]

In May 1943 the theater asked the Chief, CWS, to comment on its tentative plans for a smoke installation at Milne Bay, which, as had been foreseen, was now a more exposed harbor than Port Moresby. These plans, which included the employment of generators both on land and on water to conceal shipping activity in the harbor, suffered from a lack of power boats on which to mount the generators which were to be waterborne. The theater requested the War Department to send several craft suitable for this purpose along with the two smoke companies requisitioned earlier in the year.[3]

In July SWPA pressed the War Department for the immediate shipment of the two smoke companies and speculated on the reduced requirement for smoke pots if three smoke generator battalions were assigned.[4] People in the Southwest Pacific Area were also concerned with the possibility that the two companies, which by September had not yet arrived, would be equipped with the 3,000-pound M1 generator, instead of the new lightweight M2.[5] Meanwhile, in response to the

[2] Ltr, CCmlO USASOS to CCWS, 30 Jan 43, sub: Rear Area Smoke Screens. CWS 314.7.

[3] Ltr, CCmlO USAFFE to CCWS, 21 Jul 43, sub: Smoke Generator Cos. AGO CWS Ret 320.2–USAF in the Far East.

[4] (1) CM–IN 257, Brisbane to WAR, 1 Jul 43. (2) CM–IN 7666, Brisbane to WAR, 11 Jul 43.

[5] CM–IN 1601, Brisbane to WAR, 3 Sep 43.

SMOKE GENERATOR IN A DUKW ON MILNE BAY

theater's interest in large area screening, General Porter in August 1943, sent Maj. Roy E. Halverson, a trained smoke officer, to the Southwest Pacific Area.[6] Major Halverson made surveys at Milne Bay, Oro Bay, and Goodenough Island, concluding that the establishment of smoke installations at any of these locations would be a difficult proposition. He confirmed Colonel Copthorne's view that the lack of road nets at advanced ports would entail heavy dependence upon water transportation. Not only were appropriate craft in short supply but the M1 smoke generator was rather bulky for this type of employment. In fact, the successful screening of port facilities in the Southwest Pacific seemed to require an amphibious smoke unit, a type that so far had not been foreseen by planners in Washington.[7]

By mid-1943 the Japanese were raiding Goodenough Island regularly and Milne Bay, New Guinea, occasionally. The theater proceeded with its plans to station the two smoke generator units temporarily at Milne Bay where they could be adapted to island employment and

[6] CWS USAFFE, Info Bull, No. 15, 24 Aug 43.
[7] (1) Interv, Hist Off with Morgan, former theater CWS liaison officer with the Australian Army, 30 Jan 46. (2) Interv, Burke, former CmlO Base A, Milne Bay, New Guinea, 30 Jan 46.

trained for more difficult operations at a more advanced port.[8] But the 70th and 170th Smoke Generator Companies landed at Sydney, instead of Milne Bay. Shortage of shipping and the higher priority of other units precluded the immediate transshipment of these units to Milne Bay, and the two companies remained in Australia for almost two full months after their arrival in October 1943. As a result, smoke company training at Milne Bay did not begin until January 1944 and then only under the greatest difficulties. The base commander could not permit a considerable amount of smoke over the area because his installation was operating under pressure, day and night. Of even greater importance was the lack of craft on which to mount the smoke generators. Boats could be borrowed for short periods, but none could be assigned to the smoke troops. General Porter, Chief, CWS, arranged to ship four J boats which, shortly after arrival, were severely damaged by a storm.

By April 1944 it was evident that smoke training operations would have to be shifted to a less active port. Chosen was Base E at Lae, on the northeastern coast of New Guinea, where ships anchored while awaiting a call to a more exposed port[9] and, consequently, where practice screens would not interfere with normal port operations. Another advantage was the short distance to the air base at Nadzab, up the Markham River from Lae. The air base was an ideal place to test screening of air installations and a source of aircraft from which to observe the practice screens. The companies moved to their new location in mid-July and immediately experienced greater success with their training program. The road net facilitated land training, and boats were available for working out problems in the bay. In mid-August Headquarters and Headquarters Detachment, 26th Smoke Generator Battalion, under the command of Maj. Allen H. Williams, arrived from the United States and took charge of the two smoke companies.[10]

A Question of Mission

In June 1944 the commanding general, USASOS, recommended to General MacArthur the employment of smoke generator units during the early stages of an amphibious operation for screening supply dumps

[8] Burke Interv, 30 Jan 46.
[9] Interv, Hist Off with Lt Col Joseph S. Terrell, Jan 46.
[10] (1) Ibid. (2) Burke Interv, 30 Jan 46.

as well as for concealing ships engaged in unloading.[11] He proposed that the 70th and 170th Smoke Generator Companies be equipped with suitable craft and trained to use the new lightweight M2 generators, then en route to the theater. General MacArthur agreed that the smoke troops could be profitably employed in future operations and suggested the transfer of the two companies to the Sixth Army for amphibious training under an engineer special brigade.[12]

Col. Carl L. Marriott, Sixth Army chemical officer, opposed this suggestion, indicating that the USASOS recommendation was merely an admission that it had been unable to interest the 14th Antiaircraft Command in the value of the smoke units. Reasons given by Colonel Marriott for this lack of interest included inappropriate equipment, the fact that the Esso generators were too unwieldy, and the reputation of the two smoke companies at Milne Bay for "smashing up" their equipment.[13] CWS officers at Milne Bay refuted this last argument, attributing damaged equipment to the work of the elements, not to careless maintenance.[14] In arguing against the assignment of the two smoke companies to Sixth Army, Marriott also brought up the matter of control. In an assault landing these units initially would be controlled by the naval task force commander. On the other hand, smoke operations to conceal ships just off the beaches would have to be co-ordinated by a second agency, the one charged with the control of antiaircraft artillery and fighter aircraft. Marriott recommended that USAFFE should clarify the question of control and assign the smoke units to the 14th Antiaircraft Command, a troop unit not under Sixth Army.[15]

Early in September 1944, and before any decision was reached on the control of the smoke units, a group of Sixth Army officers witnessed a smoke demonstration at Lae which featured the recently arrived M2 mechanical generator, smaller and more economical and efficient than its predecessor. Without exception, the officers were most enthusiastic about the capabilities of the new mechanical gen-

---

[11] Ltr, CG USASOS to CG USAFFE, 4 Jun 44, sub: Assignment of Craft to Provisional Smoke Generator Bn. Sixth Army, 470.71–SG.

[12] 1st Ind, CG USAFFE to CG Sixth Army, 11 Jul 44.

[13] Memo, CmlO Sixth Army for G–3 Sixth Army, 16 Jul 44. Sixth Army 470.71–SG.

[14] Ltr, Lt Col Joseph S. Terrell to Hist Off, 19 May 1950.

[15] Memo, CmlO Sixth Army for G–3 Sixth Army, 16 Jul 44. Sixth Army 470.71–SG.

erator and requested that every effort be made to obtain smoke companies for Sixth Army to be used on beachheads and airstrips.[16]

It seems that the final decision regarding the assignment of the CWS smoke companies pleased no one. The two companies were not assigned to the Sixth Army, nor to an antiaircraft artillery command, as recommended by Colonel Marriott. In October the commander of the USA Services of Supply, Southwest Pacific Area, unaccountably ordered that the 70th and 170th Chemical Smoke Generator Companies be inactivated and that the personnel so released be used to activate two quartermaster truck companies.[17] This decision marked the end of efforts to prepare the two units for combat and prompted Navy officers to question the wisdom of eliminating the smoke units in face of the increasing need for smoke in beach operations.[18]

The officers and men of the headquarters of the recently arrived smoke generator battalion received assignments with the chemical warfare school at Oro Bay. There they taught and prepared studies for the employment of smoke in future operations. The new lightweight M2 generators, which arrived in the theater in August, were turned over to the Navy along with the supply of fog oil and most of the floating smoke pots.[19]

Renewed Interest in Smoke

The smoke companies had hardly been inactivated before ground commanders in the area began inquiring about their availability. The XI Corps, for example, became interested in smoke after learning of the successful employment of the mechanical generator at Anzio.[20] Chemical officers at the CWS conference at Oro Bay wanted to know how long it would take to train combat troops in the use of the lightweight M2 generator for forward area operations. At this time, October 1944, about 100 of these generators were in or en route to the theater.[21] A month later Lt. Col. David D. Hulsey, Chemical Officer,

---

[16] Interv, Hist Off with Lt Col Allen H. Williams, formerly CO 26th Smoke Generator Bn, 5 Jun 50.
[17] (1) Ltr, Secy War to CINCSWPA, 16 Oct 44, sub: Disbandment, Constitution and Activation of Certain Units. AG 322 (12 Oct 44). (2) CM–IN 12423 (13 Nov 44) CG USAFFE, 12 Nov 44.
[18] Williams Interv, 5 Jun 50.
[19] Burke Interv, 30 Jan 46.
[20] Ltr, CmlO XI Corps to CmlO Sixth Army, 22 Aug 44, sub: Smoke Generators, and 1st Ind thereto, CG Sixth Army to CG XI Corps, 30 Aug 44. ORB Sixth Army 470.71–SG.
[21] CCmlO USASOS, Rpt of CWS Conf, 10–13 Oct 44, p. 30.

6th Infantry Division, asked Col. Harold Riegelman, Chemical Officer, I Corps, whether any smoke troops were available to screen river crossings. The answer was: in the absence of smoke units ground troops would continue to rely on mortar smoke shell and smoke pots for that type of mission.[22]

Meanwhile, various units of the Sixth Army resorted to limited area screening with whatever smoke weapons or equipment was available. The 2d Engineer Special Brigade used the small FS generator developed by the 42d Chemical Laboratory Company to conceal LCM's unloading at Colasion Point from rifle and machine gun fire.[23] But the M1 and M4 smoke pots proved to be the mainstays for area screening. Smoke from these munitions successfully concealed the Tacloban airstrip on Leyte from Japanese bombers during the full moon period of November 1944.[24] In the Zamboanga operation in western Mindanao Colonel Arthur, chemical officer of the 41st Infantry Division, organized a smoke pot line along one side of an airstrip then under construction after Japanese artillery had damaged heavy engineer equipment.[25] During the Luzon Campaign, the Sixth Army used smoke pots far more extensively than previously to conceal road and bridge construction from enemy observers.[26] The increased use of smoke in the Sixth Army resulted from the stepped-up activity of the Japanese air force; the shift to larger land masses for maneuvering, along with a decrease in the amount of jungle fighting; the availability of smoke weapons and munitions; recent emphasis by commanders and chemical officers on the importance of smoke in combat; and the fact that the use of smoke had proved beneficial in saving lives and equipment.

Another possible mission for large area screening, the concealment of airfields, was beginning to take shape in the Pacific Ocean Areas.

---

[22] Ltr, CmlO I Corps to CmlO 6th Inf Div, 8 Dec 44. In Riegelman's private files.

[23] (1) Memo, Actg CmlO for ACofS Sixth Army, 23 Nov 44. Sixth Army 470.6–Smoke. (2) In the Biak operation, I Corps had used this same item for harassing effect; when the generators were placed in the windward openings of caves, the smoke not only drove out the Japanese but disclosed other entrances to the cave. CG I Corps, History of Biak Opn 15–27 Jun 44, G–3 Rpt, an. 2, Cml, p. 47. AGO HRS 201–11.4 (15459). General Krueger cites the testimony of Japanese generals after the Philippines campaign attesting to the usefulness of smoke and white phosphorus in driving Japanese soldiers out of their caves. *From Down Under to Nippon*, p. 327.

[24] Comdr Amphib Group 8 Seventh Fleet Action Rpt, Leyte Opn, pt. V (D), Special Comments, Smoke.

[25] Interv, Hist Off with Col Frank M. Arthur, former chemical officer of the 41st Division and I Corps, 1 Jul 46.

[26] Sixth U.S. Army, Rpt of the Luzon Campaign, 9 Jan 45–30 Jun 45, III, Rpts of the General and Special Staff Secs, Rpt of the Cml Warfare Officer, 90.

In the summer of 1944 United States forces captured Guam, Tinian, and Saipan in the Marianas group and immediately began constructing airfields from which to stage bombing attacks against Japan. These bases became operational in the fall and early winter of 1944, and B–29's of the XXI Bomber Command began their assault on the Japanese homeland.[27] In turn, these airfields in the Marianas were subjected to enemy air raids, infrequent and largely ineffective, but nonetheless "an expensive nuisance, which, if unchecked, could have become more costly." [28]

Even as the Advanced Echelon, XXI Bomber Command, was staging at Hickam Field, Oahu, its chemical officer, Maj. John Barrows suggested the use of smoke generators to conceal the B–29's when they reached the Marianas. The Commander in Chief, POA, turned down this request on the ground that the available shipping space was needed for more vital supplies.[29] General Waitt, Assistant Chief CWS for Field Operations, brought the subject up again during his November 1944 visit to Saipan. Noting the vulnerability of the B–29's to Japanese attack—several of the planes had already been destroyed by enemy air action—Waitt insisted that the use of smoke could conceal the expensive aircraft without interfering with the antiaircraft screen. Later on in Hawaii, he urged Admiral Nimitz and General Richardson to adopt this plan.[30] Despite the merits of the case, and the fact that eleven B–29's had been destroyed and forty-three others damaged, the plan for screening the Marianas airfields against enemy attack never got off the ground. The interests of the strong antiaircraft artillery defenses were considered paramount.[31] In any event, enemy air attacks ceased early in 1945 when Iwo Jima with its air bases fell to U.S. Marine forces, thus eliminating the trouble at its source.

The question of employing smoke troops at airfields arose again in

---

[27] The XXI Bomber Command was an element of the Twentieth Air Force, which, under Joint Chiefs of Staff control, had as its mission the strategic bombing of Japan. For the complete picture of these operations, see Wesley Frank Craven and James Lea Cate, eds., THE ARMY FORCES IN WORLD WAR II, vol. V, *The Pacific: Matterhorn to Nagasaki, June 1944 to August 1945* (Chicago: University of Chicago Press, 1953).

[28] Craven and Cate, eds., *Matterhorn to Nagasaki*, p. 582.

[29] Interv, Hist Off with Grothaus, former CmlO, Seventh Air Force, 27 Apr 50.

[30] Rpt on Trip of Waitt and Javits to POA and SWPA, 24 Sep–21 Nov 44, dated 15 Dec 44. CWS 314.7 Observer Rpts.

[31] (1) CM–IN 930, CG AAFPOA to WD, 1 Dec 44. (2) Grothaus Interv, 27 Apr 50. Colonel Grothaus felt that the shortage of available shipping remained a factor in the decision not to employ smoke.

connection with Operation ICEBERG, the campaign against the Ryukyus chain. Because of the proximity of the islands to the Japanese homeland, American planners correctly anticipated that their assault would provoke a great amount of enemy air action. The Navy made excellent use of smoke at Hagushi Beach, Okinawa, during the earlier phases of the operation, but withdrew its smoke personnel in the postamphibious phase when Lt. Gen. Simon B. Buckner, commanding Tenth Army, assumed leadership ashore of the land forces of the operation. Originally, the Army planned to use smoke generators to conceal airfields and beaches during Phases II and III of ICEBERG, during the occupation of Ie Shima and the establishment of control over northern Okinawa, and during the seizure of additional islands in the Nansei Shoto. The 28th Smoke Generator Battalion, comprised of the 67th, 68th, and 71st Smoke Generator Companies, received the Okinawa assignment. Unfortunately, the 71st Smoke Generator Company was not available in time for operations on Ie Shima. Although the Headquarters and Headquarters Detachment, 28th Chemical Smoke Generator Battalion, and elements of the 67th and 68th Smoke Generator Companies arrived at Okinawa on 12 June, Phase III of the operation was canceled. The remainder of the two companies arrived on Okinawa early in July, but Japanese air activity had diminished considerably, and the need for smoke no longer existed.[32]

Although the planning for the invasion of Kyushu, the southernmost island of the homeland of the enemy, had not been completed when Japan surrendered, it appeared certain that smoke generator troops would have seen extensive use had the invasion been mounted. Colonel Copthorne, now Chemical Officer, Army Forces, Pacific, arranged with representatives of the operations officer of his headquarters and with the commander of Amphibious Forces, Pacific Fleet, for the use of five chemical smoke generator companies during the early stages of OLYMPIC, as the operation was dubbed. Earmarked for the eastern shore of Kyushu were the three companies of the 28th Smoke Generator Battalion. The two quartermaster truck companies which had formerly been the 70th and 170th Smoke Generator Companies were to be reconverted to smoke units and earmarked for operations on the western shore of Kyushu. During the initial stage of the operation

---

[32] (1) Unit records in CmlC Hist Off. (2) Interv, Hist Off with Maj Lucius F. Lincoln, formerly ExecO 28th Smoke Generator Bn, 12 May 50. (3) CG Tenth Army Action Rpt, Ryukyus, 26 Mar-30 Jun 45, vol I, ch. 11, sec. XIII, par 1a(2).

and under control of the Navy, the companies were to screen ship concentrations, harbors, and beaches. Once the invasion forces had successfully landed, smoke troops would revert to Army control. How these units were to be assigned in support of tactical operations on Kyushu was still a matter of conjecture when the war came to an end. Upon orders of AFPAC, Eighth Army prepared a study on the use of smoke troops in land operations on the island. It recommended in July 1945 that twelve M2 mechanical generators be issued to the chemical service platoon assigned to each combat division and that two smoke generator battalions, each with four companies, be redeployed from Europe and assigned, one each, to the two invading armies.[33]

Colonel Copthorne approved the idea of giving mechanical smoke generators to chemical service platoons, calling attention to the growing tendency of combat troops to demand larger and larger smoke screens and arguing that the use of fog oil by the service platoon would reduce the tonnage of mortar and artillery smoke ammunition. The chemical officer of Sixth Army, Colonel Burns, opposed the plan. He felt that the chemical service platoons had neither the men nor the transportation for the conduct of screening operations. Moreover, he considered impractical any attempt to substitute a fog oil screen for a projected smoke screen because they served "different tactical purposes."[34] There could be no doubt that chemical service platoons in the combat area were fully occupied in the supply and maintenance of chemical supplies and were already short of transportation facilities. But Burns's statement concerning tactical screening ran counter to the experience of U.S. forces in Europe who frequently used fog oil to save mortar and artillery ammunition. V–J Day found still unanswered this question of how the combat divisions in the Pacific could best be supported by smoke generator personnel.

---

[33] (1) Interv, Hist Off with Williams, 5 Jun 50. Colonel Williams of the AFPAC Chemical Section had a part in this smoke planning. (2) Lt Col William R. Maull to CCWS, 28 Sep 45, Rpt of Official Travel, pp. 35–36. CMLHO. Colonel Maull stated that AFPAC was to activate only one additional smoke company.

[34] Ltr, CCmlO AFPAC to CmlO Sixth Army, 4 Aug 45, sub: Smoke Generators as Additional Equip for Cml Serv Platoons, and 1st Ind CmlO Sixth Army to CCmlO AFPAC, 11 Aug 45. Sixth Army 400.34—Equipment—Special T/E & T/BA.

The Navy's Use of Smoke

Naval operations in Pacific waters, particularly in the last two years of the war, were accompanied by an extensive use of smoke. Although the Navy had its own arsenal of smoke munitions, including HC pots and the Besler mechanical generator, its use of CWS equipment was not uncommon. CWS personnel also contributed to the fulfillment of the Navy's smoke mission.

The question of concealing Pearl Harbor with smoke was one of long standing, and the Army, before World War II, had discouraged at least one Navy suggestion for screening that most important installation.[35] It was natural that the matter would assume a much greater significance after 7 December 1941. Although early in 1942 a special smoke board set up by Admiral Nimitz recommended against screening the Pearl Harbor area, the M1 mechanical smoke generator was scarcely off the assembly line before the Navy obtained fifteen of the items for use in the Hawaiian Islands.[36] Knowing little or nothing about the generators, Navy officials at Pearl Harbor requested Colonel Unmacht to service and demonstrate the machines. By March 1943 he had gotten possession of all fifteen generators, trained men from the 91st Chemical Mortar Company in their operation, started a program for training Navy personnel, and had demonstrated the generators along the Honolulu waterfront and at Pearl Harbor.[37]

The Navy's interest in area screening prompted General Richardson, commanding the Hawaiian Department, to take a renewed interest in smoke equipment. Earlier, he had attempted unsuccessfully to secure fifty generators without taking any smoke troops. The Chief, Chemical Warfare Service, had strongly opposed this suggestion, arguing that the efficient operation of the generators required trained men available on a 24-hour basis.[38] Richardson was still unwilling to substitute smoke generator troops for others on his troop basis for Hawaii. Again the War Department replied that the Hawaiian Department could not have the equipment without the troops, although as a compromise it was willing to send a cadre of smoke specialists, provided that General

---

[35] Watson, *Prewar Plans and Preparations*, pp. 470–71.
[36] Ltr, Waitt to Unmacht, 18 Nov 42. CWS 314.7 Personal Ltr file, AFMIDPAC.
[37] Ltrs, Unmacht to Waitt, 11 Dec 42, 3 Mar, 5 Mar 43.
[38] Ltr, Waitt to Unmacht, CmlO Hawaiian Dept, 18 Nov 42.

Richardson activate a smoke unit within the theater.[39] During the negotiations, Colonel Unmacht argued that the need for smoke was far greater in Hawaii than along the west coast of the United States, where smoke units were then stationed. He believed that the situation justified 500 smoke troops despite the presence at Honolulu and Pearl Harbor of 10,000 men assigned to fighter, antiaircraft, and barrage balloon units. Unmacht's arguments that smoke troops, man for man, contributed more to antiaircraft defense than those of any other service were not persuasive enough to cause the Hawaiian Department to substitute smoke troops for other types.[40]

The Navy made one more attempt to secure a smoke installation for Pearl Harbor, suggesting that its facilities be screened with existing equipment—15 mechanical generators and 1,100 obsolete stationary generators. General Richardson referred the proposal to Colonel Unmacht who pointed out that, in comparison with mechanical generators, the stationary models consumed too much oil and required too many men to operate. Besides, he argued, there was not enough equipment on hand to screen Pearl Harbor effectively. Unmacht used this opportunity to try again to convince the Hawaiian Department to ask for smoke generator companies.[41] The diminishing need for smoke at the islands served to nullify this last attempt to get a full-scale smoke installation at Pearl Harbor.

After mid-1943 smoke screening activities in the Pacific Ocean Areas were confined to the combat zones. The first of the island campaigns in the Central Pacific Area was the V Amphibious Corps' assault on the Gilberts. Plans for Tarawa, the objective of the 2d Marine Division, called for curtains of smoke laid by carrier planes, as well as the use of Army M1 and M4 smoke pots loaded on landing craft, to conceal mine sweeper activity and the assault waves of marines as they rendezvoused for the final run. The actual operation saw limited use of smoke. The aircraft screens were deemed unnecessary, although the pots on the landing craft did obscure the assault craft from enemy observation. Smoke activity during the difficult days after the assault proved to be of more importance. Six landing craft, stationed at various positions to the windward, used smoke pots

---

[39] Ltr, CG Hawaiian to CG ASF WD, 23 Apr 43, sub: Smoke Generator Equip and 1st Ind, Secy War to CG Hawaiian Dept.   AG 400 (4–23–43) OB–S–E.
[40] Ltr, Unmacht to Waitt, 30 Mar 43.   CMLHO.
[41] Ltr, Unmacht to Waitt, 13 Jul 43.   CMLHO.

to shield ships anchored in the lagoon during enemy night air attacks, at times aided by LST's equipped with smoke pots.[42]

Area screening of anchorages became accepted procedure for operations in the Marshall Islands, the next step up the island ladder. The Navy rehearsed the planned smoke procedures during January 1944 and put them into practice during the invasions of Kwajalein, Roi-Namur, and Eniwetok. In brief, small craft burned M1 and M4 HC pots, furnished by the CWS depot in Hawaii, while the cargo and personnel ships employed the Navy's Besler mechanical smoke generators for the first time. The glare from the pots and their fire hazard emphasized the need for a small lightweight generator which could be mounted on small craft for this type of operation.[43]

The Marianas campaign in the summer of 1944 saw further Navy successes with anchorage screening. Between 15 June (D-day) and 7 July, the Saipan anchorage had a total of 19 hours of smoke entailing 57,000 gallons of fog oil and 11,400 smoke pots. The commander of the Joint Expeditionary Force called it "the greatest factor in the extremely effective defense of the transport area against air attack. During the repeated attacks 100 bombs were dropped in the vicinity of the transport area, but were obviously dropped blindly. . . ."[44]

The Navy set up a most complete smoke installation at Guam. Emplaced mechanical generators lined the landlocked harbor while small craft with mounted generators patrolled the entrance. Resembling those established during 1943–44 at Bizerte, Naples, and Anzio in the Mediterranean theater, this was one of the few smoke installations in the Pacific which depended upon land-based mechanical generators as the primary means of screening. Ironically, enemy air forces never tested the smoke defenses.[45]

[42] (1) Comdr TF 53, app. 3 to an. A to CTF 53 OPORD A 104–43 (revised). CMLHO. (2) Comdr, Transport Div 4 Tarawa, in Extracts from Naval Rpts on Use of Smoke by the Navy in Amphib Opns to Date, Jan 44. Sixth Army 470.6—Smoke. (3) Rpt of Tarawa Opn (AGO 370.2 (31 Dec 43)), cited in CWS TofO Ltr 11, 9 Mar 44, p. 12. (4) Crowl and Love, Seizure of the Gilberts and Marshalls, p. 129. (5) Capt. James R. Stockman, USMC, The Battle for Tarawa (Washington, 1947), p. 13.

[43] (1) Extracts from Naval Rpts on Use of Smoke by the Navy in Amphib Opns to Date Marshall Islands Opn. Sixth Army 470.6—Smoke. (2) Ltr, CmlO Sixth Army to Div CG's, 24 Jun 44, sub: Marshall Islands Campaign. Sixth Army 314.7—Rpts, Hist.

[44] CWS TofO Ltr 22, 28 February 1945, pages 23–24, cites comments made by the Commander of the Joint Expeditionary Force in Report of Amphibious Operations for the Capture of the Marianas Islands, 25 August 1944.

[45] (1) Lt. Comdr. V. C. Alexander, USNR, "Area Smoke Screen in Harbor Defense," Naval Harbor Defense (OPNAV 30–3–A), No. 3, May 1945, pp. 11–15. (2) Interv, Hist Off OCCmlO with Comdr Alexander, member of the Amphib Smoke Committee, 25 Sep 45. CMLHO.

On 20 October 1944 Sixth Army launched its operations against the Philippine Islands with the assault on Leyte. The Japanese response was immediate, including the commitment of a substantial part of Japan's air reserves.[46] During the first stage of the operation U.S. carrier-based planes twice laid screens over the invasion beaches of X and XXIV Corps. Floating smoke pots enabled two beached LST's to resume unloading after an interruption caused by enemy mortar fire. For the first four days the Japanese concentrated their air activity during the hours of daylight. Antiaircraft defenses during this period consisted for the most part of U.S. carrier-based fighters which prevented any serious damage to the ships or the targets onshore. This procedure restricted smoke to the twilight periods and night alerts. In the next four days, when enemy planes averaged 175 sorties, the Navy used smoke extensively during day as well as twilight and night attacks. After 27 October the smoke again was restricted to twilight, moonlight, and nocturnal alerts. This return to former tactics, which were continued in operations at Lingayen Gulf and Okinawa, came about for several reasons: the ineffectiveness of the daytime screens except under ideal low-speed wind conditions, the fear that the smoke generators would not hold up under extended use, a shortage of fog oil, the establishment of an airstrip at nearby Tacloban, and the fact that daytime smoke precluded observation by the antiaircraft batteries at the same time that it allowed enemy aircraft glimpses of the masts of the assembled ships.[47]

Antiaircraft defenses at Leyte Gulf were largely successful. Few, if any, ships received hits while hidden by smoke although several destroyers outside the screen suffered damage. This accomplishment was the greater because Leyte marked the first appearance in force of the Japanese kamikaze planes. By preventing Japanese pilots from sighting individual targets, smoke did much to reduce the effectiveness of these suicide missions. After the operation the commander of Southern Attack Force commented that "area smoke, properly employed, is

---

[46] CG Sixth Army, Rpt of the Leyte Opn, 20 Oct–25 Dec 44, pp. 40–41. CMLHO.

[47] (1) Ltr, Comdr TF 79 to Comdr Seventh Fleet, sub: Seizure of Leyte—Rpt of Participation of TF 79. Bur Yards & Docks File No. FFI–D–NB (503). (2) Comdr Amphib Group 6, Pacific Fleet, TF 79.2, Rpt of Leyte Opn, 4 Nov 44. CMLHO. (3) Comdr Amphib Group 8, Seventh Fleet Action Rpt—Leyte Opn—Rpt On, pt. V, Special Comments (d) Smoke (extract undated). Both in CMLHO.

invaluable for protecting a transport area from enemy air attack at night or at twilight." [48]

The landings at Lingayen Gulf in Luzon saw some use of smoke pots to conceal the beaches from direct observation by enemy artillery until American counterbattery fire could silence the opposition. [49] Once the beachhead was secured the Navy regularly screened the anchorage at dawn and dusk for a daily total of about two hours. The Leyte experience led to improvements in the screens at Lingayen Gulf. Smoke boats arranged in lines at distances of 500, 1,000, and 2,000 yards windward from the ships resulted in a more uniform screen than had been the case at Leyte. Ships under smoke at Lingayen suffered no damage from the dawn and dusk air raids, despite the frequent 15- to 20-knot sea breeze. Denied observation of the anchorage, the Japanese planes made several hits on destroyers and escorts patrolling outside the concealed area. The supply situation at Lingayen Gulf was much better than that at Leyte which had seen the near depletion of fog oil and smoke pots. [50]

The naval commander at Lingayen Gulf strongly recommended that LCVP (landing craft, vehicle and personnel) smoke boats should be fitted with the CWS lightweight smoke generator as soon as possible. The smoke cloud produced by this mechanical generator not only was more persistent, but it was without the toxicity of HC smoke. Frequently, both at Leyte and at Lingayen, men aboard ships became ill when ventilating systems drew in the HC-laden air. And there was always the storage problem and fire hazard presented by smoke pots. [51]

In preparing for the campaigns of Iwo Jima and Okinawa, the Navy in the Pacific received technical assistance from members of the Amphibious Smoke Committee. Capt. N. F. Chamberlain, CWS, and three naval officers of the committee reported to the Commander, Amphibious Forces, U.S. Pacific Fleet, on 5 November 1944 for

---

[48] (1) Comdr Southern Attack Force (TF 79), Rpt of Philippine Opn: Tactical Use of Smoke 13 Nov 44. Bur Yards & Docks, FFI–D–NB (503) (AL). (2) CmlO X Corps, Hist Data, Leyte–Samar Campaign, app. G, n.d. Sixth Army 319.1—Leyte Opn.

[49] Ltr, CmlO 43d Inf Div to CmlO I Corps, 23 Jan 45, sub: Misc Summary Rpt, 23 Jan 45. Sixth Army 319.1—Weekly Activity Rpts, Divs.

[50] (1) Rpt, Comdr TF 79, Lingayen Gulf Opn, n.d., sub: Tactical Use of Smoke. Bur Yards & Docks FFI–D–NB (503) (AL–1), and in ORB Sixth Army 370.2–Luzon Opns Rpts. (2) Ltr, Copthorne to Hist Off, 23 May 50. Naval officers remarked to Colonel Copthorne that smoke operations at Lingayen Gulf showed a great improvement in technique.

[51] (1) Ibid. (2) Capt Walter Karig, Battle Report: Victory in the Pacific (New York: Rinehart & Co., 1949), pp. 30–31.

temporary duty as smoke specialists. In Hawaii they lectured on the experimental work done at the Amphibious Training Base, Fort Pierce, Fla.,[52] trained air and naval crews and infantry troops in the employment of smoke munitions and equipment, prepared training directives, and assisted in writing smoke plans for scheduled operations. The committee appeared in Hawaii at a rather opportune moment, for interest in smoke screening had reached a high point with the news of how kamikaze pilots had been baffled at Leyte.[53]

On 22 December 1944 the committee, before many high-ranking combat commanders in the POA, including ten admirals and a number of Marine and Army generals, successfully staged in Hawaii a large-scale demonstration on the use of smoke in landings. Vice Adm. Richmond K. Turner, Commander, Amphibious Forces, Pacific Fleet, was among those impressed by the capabilities of smoke. As a result of the demonstration members of the smoke committee were requested to participate in subsequent landing operations as smoke advisers.[54]

At Iwo Jima the Navy used a limited quantity of smoke during the initial assault, including screens laid by carrier-based planes as the first wave approached the beach.[55] Later, screens concealed ships in the anchorage from kamikaze planes during sixteen different night raids. No vessel under the screen suffered damage, although five enemy bombs straddled the USS *Auburn*.[56] Beach and shore party personnel had been specially trained for the employment of portable smoke generators on the island, but none actually made the landing.[57] The satisfactory performance of waterborne generators negated the need for landing the palletized generators, an operation which would have been imperiled by the heavy sea and currents.

The most extensive and prolonged area screening operation in the Pacific took place at Okinawa. Anticipating that the Japanese air forces would desperately oppose any landing so close to the homeland, framers of the task force smoke plan specifically provided for night coverage of the anchorage and further directed the commanders of

[52] The naval doctrine on use of smoke in amphibious operations was published in Commander in Chief, U.S. Fleet, Smoke Screens for Amphibious Operations, 8 Nov 44.

[53] Memo, Chamberlain for CO Research and Development Center Amphib Tng Comd U.S. Atlantic Fleet, 22 Jun 45, sub: Summary of Activities of the Amphib Comd in Forward Areas. CMLHO.

[54] (1) *Ibid.* (2) Ltr, CmlO POA to ACCWS for Field Opns, 23 Dec 44. CWS 314.7 Personal Ltr file, AFMIDPAC.

[55] Karig, *Battle Report: Victory in the Pacific*, p. 303.

[56] Comdr Amphib Group 2, Iwo Jima, Action Rpt, pt. VIII, Smoke. CMLHO.

[57] *Ibid.*, pt. X, Force Beachmaster's Rpt, sec. B (K), Smoke Generators.

attack forces and groups to draw up detailed plans for other uses of
smoke. The latter provision resulted in limited use of smoke in connection with underwater demolition team activities, landing feints,
the assault on Ie Shima, and mine-sweeping activities. But the anchorage screens were another matter. Okinawa saw the kamikaze campaign
reach a crescendo,[58] and in an effort to minimize the terrible destruction caused by these riders of the "heavenly wind" the Navy expended
more fog oil and smoke pots at the Hagushi Beach anchorage than in
any other single operation of World War II.[59]

In addition to the customary means of smoking from small craft
and ships the Navy on L-day plus 1 took ashore forty-five mechanical
generators and divided them between the north and south sectors of
Hagushi Beach. Next day these generators went into operation. The
southern line, commanded by Captain Chamberlain of the Amphibious
Smoke Committee, had twenty-five emplacements; the northern line
had about fifteen. Limited training of the generator operators did
not prevent the shore contingent from maintaining an adequate screen
over the anchorage.[60]

A word about the operation of the screen. The senior officer present
afloat ordered smoke when unidentified planes, as shown by the radar
screen, seemed likely to attack. All ships under the screen withheld
antiaircraft fire, because smoke was an ample safeguard against the
few planes which penetrated the outside fighter defense and because
AA fire might disclose the location of the ships.[61] During the night of
L-day (1 April) smoke covered the anchorage for a total of 6 hours
and 32 minutes. Smoke concealed the anchorage and beaches during
40 of the 46 nights between L-day and 16 May, with the average screen
lasting slightly more than 2 hours. From 17 May until 21 June, the
day the island was secured, the Navy resorted to smoke practically

[58] For details on the kamikaze attacks, see: (1) Appleman *et al.*, *Okinawa: The Last Battle*, pp.
97–101; (2) Maj Charles S. Nichols, Jr., and Henry I. Shaw, Jr., *Okinawa: Victory in the Pacific*
(Washington, 1955), pp. 82–86.

[59] (1) Comdr (Adm Turner) Amphib Forces Pacific Fleet, Action Rpt, Okinawa Gunto, pt. V,
Special Rpts; sec. C, Naval Ordnance and Gunnery; IV—Protective Smoke Cover (1 Apr–16 May 45).
CMLHO. (2) Memo, Chamberlain for CO Research and Development Center Amphib Tng Comd,
U.S. Atlantic Fleet, 22 Jun 45, sub: Summary of Activities of the Amphib Comd in Forward Areas.

[60] (1) Beachmaster Hagushi Beaches to Comdr Amphib Group 12, Rpt, Smoke Generator Opn,
Hagushi Beaches, Okinawa. (2) Comdr (Turner) Amphib Forces Pacific Fleet, Action Rpt, Okinawa
Gunto, pt. V, Special Rpts; sec. C, Naval Ordnance and Gunnery; IV—Protective Smoke Cover (1 Apr–
16 May 45).

[61] Ltr, Maj N. F. Chamberlain, CmlC Res, to Hist Off, 1 May 50.

every night for an average of one hour and 27 minutes, although one night of unusual Japanese air activity resulted in an 8-hour screen. Estimated expenditures of smoke materials for the Okinawa operation were 2,475,000 gallons of fog oil, 35,000 land smoke pots, and 47,500 floating smoke pots, or floats as they were known to the Navy.[62]

Comments on smoke operations at Okinawa were of special importance because of their influence on planning for the invasion of Japan. Captain Chamberlain reported that the initial skepticism among ship captains as to the value of smoke over the anchorage quickly changed "to an almost frantic clamor for smoke cover when it was found that only those ships *outside* the smoke screen were being hit by suicide planes." [63]

Admiral Turner made a number of recommendations for future smoke operations, which, for the most part, concerned logistics. Again, planning for the Okinawa operation had not provided adequate quantities of fog oil and pots, either in the forward area or in reserve. Consequently, supplies were almost exhausted several times during an operation. He advocated equipping all merchant ships with fog oil generators and expanding the maintenance facilities for smoke equipment. Both measures would further increase the requirements for fog oil to 8,000 barrels (approximately 400,000 gallons), an amount he considered a minimum for planning an operation the size of the one at Okinawa. This weekly replenishment figure was double that requested (although not always supplied) for Okinawa. Turner also emphasized that smoke personnel should be recognized as specialists and urged that CWS smoke generators units be provided for onshore assistance.[64] It seems that if the Pacific war had continued, smoke would have played an important role on sea as well as on land.

Screens for Airborne Operations

Airborne operations in the Pacific differed considerably from those in the war against Germany. The difference was largely a matter of

[62] (1) Comdr (Turner) Amphib Forces Pacific Fleet, Action Rpt, Okinawa Gunto, pt. V Special Rpts; sec. C, Naval Ordnance and Gunnery: IV—Protective Smoke Cover (1 Apr–16 May 45). (2) Comdr V Amphib Force, CTF 51, Rpt of Capture of Okinawa Gunto, Phases I and II (17 May–21 Jun 45).

[63] Memo, Capt Chamberlain for CO Research and Development Center Amphib Tng Comd U.S. Atlantic Fleet, 22 Jun 45, sub: Summary of Activities of the Amphib Comd in Forward Areas.

[64] Comdr (Turner) Amphib Forces Pacific Fleet, Action Rpt, Okinawa Gunto, pt. V, special Rpts; sec. C, Naval Ordnance and Gunnery; IV—Protective Smoke Cover (1 Apr—16 May 45).

size; the geography of the Pacific area, as noted earlier, dictated that most ground operations there would be on a smaller scale than those on the land mass of Europe. The forces in the Pacific received more modest allotments of men and matériel than did those in Europe. Perhaps the very small size of the Pacific airborne operations made them more suitable for support by air-land smoke screens. In any event, in contrast with experience in Europe, half of the six airborne operations in the war against Japan had the benefit of smoke.[65]

The first of the air-screened paratroop landings, indeed the first airborne operation in the Pacific, took place in eastern New Guinea at the airstrip near Nadzab, a village some twenty-five miles up the Markham River from the coastal town of Lae.[66] The landing at the Nadzab strip, an overgrown facility about a half a mile north of the river, took place on the morning of 5 September 1943, the day after an Australian-American amphibious task force went ashore near Lae. The successful completion of these missions would lead to control of New Guinea's Huon Peninsula and increased control of the straits between New Guinea and New Britain. More immediately, the seizure of Nadzab would prevent Japanese reinforcement from the Wewak area and would enable C-47's to fly in the Australian 7th Division for a move down the Markham River to Lae.[67]

The 503d Parachute Infantry regiment made the jump at Nadzab. Little enemy opposition was expected, but because the Japanese did have troops in the vicinity of Lae and at the Heath Plantation, between Lae and the immediate objective, there was some chance of encountering one of the daily patrols which scouted the Nadzab area. To take care of any such possibility the airdrop was preceded by B-25's which worked over the area with .50-caliber machine guns and parachute fragmentation bombs. Seven A-20's followed armed with smoke tanks to screen each of the three drop zones from possible enemy observation. (Map 7) Eighty-one C-47's fell in behind the smoke-laying A-20's. The troops began jumping at 1020 and within five minutes the entire

---

[65] For a detailed account of the use of smoke in Pacific airdrops, see John Christianson, "The Use of Smoke with Parachute Operations," *Military Affairs*, XXV, No. 3 (Fall, 1961) 47–56.

[66] For a full treatment of this operation and the general strategic picture of operations in eastern New Guinea, see John Miller jr., *CARTWHEEL: The Reduction of Rabaul*, UNITED STATES ARMY IN WORLD WAR II (Washington, 1959), pp. 189–221. See also, Wesley Frank Craven and James Lea Cate, eds., "The Army Air Forces in World War II," vol. IV, *The Pacific: Guadalcanal to Saipan* (Chicago: The University of Chicago Press, 1950), pp. 180–86.

[67] Miller, *CARTWHEEL: The Reduction of Rabaul*, pp. 189, 194.

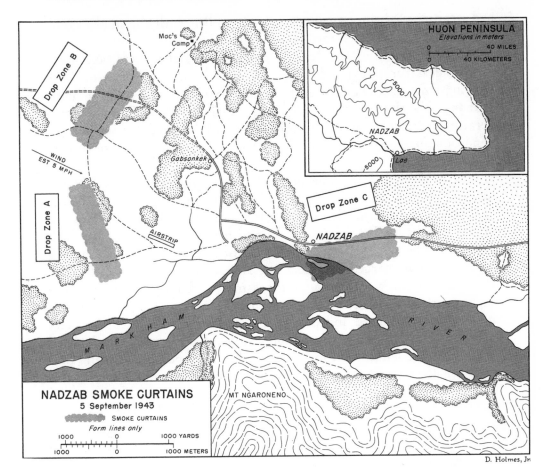

MAP 7

force was on the ground. No Japanese were encountered; casualties were minor.[68] No doubt the distinct success of the landings was the result of the total lack of opposition at Nadzab.

The smoke phase of the operation, while generally successful, revealed the expected inadequacies in procedure which accompany any such pioneering effort. Each of the seven A–20's carried four M10 smoke tanks, a versatile munition which served also as a spray tank for toxic agents. Slung under the wings of aircraft, the M10 tank

---

[68] (1) *Ibid.*, p. 208.   (2) General George C. Kenney in *General Kenney Reports, A Personal History of the Pacific War* (New York: Duell, Sloan and Pearce, 1943), page 293, states there were ninety-six C–47's in the Nadzab operation.

had a capacity of thirty gallons and when filled with the smoke agent
FS weighed a total of almost 550 pounds.[69]

On the morning of the Nadzab operation weather conditions were
almost ideal for putting down a curtain of smoke. The wind was
blowing from northwest to southeast at an estimated five miles an hour.
Although the sky was clear there was a high overcast. The 80° temperature was accompanied by a humidity of 85 percent, a favorable
condition for a good curtain, dependent as FS is on the moisture in
the atmosphere.[70]

In 2 groups of 2 and one of 3, the A–20 attack aircraft laid the
screens over Nadzab at an altitude of 250 feet and a speed of 225 miles
an hour. Each of the tanks was filled with 19 gallons of the agent,
or a total for the 28 tanks of approximately 532 gallons. In each
formation the pilot of the lead plane discharged 2 tanks, counted 4
seconds, and discharged the remaining 2. Staggered slightly to the rear,
the other A–20 went through the same procedure, allowing for a
slight overlap to insure the continuity of the screen. The smoke settled
quickly to the ground and then rose to an average height of 400 feet
along each of the three 4,500-foot screens. Each screen lasted about
2 minutes, the length of time prescribed in the operational plan. Still
effective after 5 minutes, the smoke rose, bunched, and dispersed after
10 more minutes had passed.

How effective would these smoke curtains have been if the paratroopers had landed in the face of enemy opposition? Maj. Tristram J.
Cummins, Jr., Chemical Officer, Fifth Air Force, felt that two of the
screens were too close to the wooded areas to have screened the observation of Japanese had they been located in the outer fringes of the woods.
If the screen had been placed 2,000 feet from the woods, the troopers
could have landed and organized with a potential enemy still cloaked
by the drifting smoke. The operation also disclosed shortcomings in
filling equipment and difficulty with the attachment of tanks to the
aircraft.

It seems that little use was made of the lessons learned at Nadzab
in the application of air smoke to the next Pacific airborne operation—

---

[69] FS, a solution of sulphur trioxide in chlorosulfonic acid, was a standard smoke agent. When
atomized it reacted with water vapor present in the air to form a dense cloud of droplets of sulphuric
acid.

[70] Cml Warfare Opns Rpt 1, CmlO Fifth AF, 14 Sep 43. Sixth Army 470.6 Smoke. The remainder
of the Nadzab account is based upon this report.

SMOKE SHIELDS A PARATROOP DROP, NEW GUINEA

the jump at Kamiri airdrome on the island of Noemfoor. Capture of the island, which lay just off the coast of northwestern New Guinea, would neutralize the Japanese on nearby Biak and provide airstrips for the Allied advance on the Vogelkop Peninsula. Again, the jump was made by paratroopers of the 503d Parachute Infantry regiment; their 3 July 1944 airborne attack followed by one day the amphibious landing of the 158th Regimental Combat Team (RCT).[71] Because of the success of the assault landing, the troopers of the 503d landed without encountering enemy opposition. Two smoke missions preceded the airdrop. B–25's used M47A2 white phosphorus bombs to blanket nearby Kornasoren airdrome and its antiaircraft batteries. Then three A–20 attack bombers, each with two M10 smoke tanks, moved in the van of the C–47's with their cargo of paratroopers.

---

[71] Smith, in *Approach to the Philippines*, pages 397–424, presents a detailed description of the Noemfoor operation.

771–608 O–66—28

The weather, similar to that at Nadzab but with a bit more humidity, favored the use of smoke. But the six smoke tanks on the three attack bombers, not enough to lay a screen for the required two and a half miles, produced a patchy, hole-filled curtain over the airdrome. Consequently, the troopers jumped into a undeveloped screen and were still jumping as the smoke began to dissipate and as a southeasterly wind blew it directly over the drop zone, creating hazard and confusion. The hard surface of the airstrip, the debris with which it was cluttered, and the low altitude from which the jump was made combined to produce casualties totaling 10 percent, an abnormally high rate. Next day another battalion jumped onto the same airstrip, this time without a smoke screen. Casualties were 8 percent, high enough for the task force commander to call off a scheduled third jump.[72]

By way of explanation for the rather shoddy smoke operation, the Fifth Air Force chemical officer cited insufficient notice of the impending mission and the lack of opportunity for the wing chemical officer to participate in the operation's logistical planning. Whatever the fault, the fact remained that not only was smoke for the mission inadequate but no planes were in reserve to patch up the screen once it got spotty.[73]

The last use of smoke in Pacific airborne operations took place on 23 June 1945 over the Camalaniugan airstrip in northern Luzon. The airdrop, carried out by a reinforced battalion of the 511th Parachute Infantry, coincided with a drive down the Cagayan River valley by Sixth Army's 37th Division and the occupation of the coastal town of Aparri by a Ranger task force. Lt. Gen. Walter Krueger, Army commander, expected that this combination of actions would pinch out the remaining Japanese forces in northern Luzon.[74]

Smoke was needed to conceal the troopers from the observation of Japanese forces suspected to be in positions in the wooded hills four miles to the southeast of the airstrip. Three B–25's, each equipped with a single tank, laid down an intervening screen. The E1 tank, developed in the Southwest Pacific by the V Air Force Service Command,

---

[72] Smith, *Approach to the Philippines,* pp. 413–16.

[73] (1) Cml Warfare Opns Rpt 5, CmlO Fifth AF, n.d., no sub. (2) See also unsigned report, Use of Smoke at Noemfoor Island. Both in CWS 314.7 Air Smoke.

[74] Robert Ross Smith, in *Triumph in the Philippines,* finds fault with General Krueger's conclusion, pointing out that most of the contemporary intelligence sources, which proved to be right, indicated that the Japanese forces were not retreating down the valley but into the mountains both east and west of the valley.

carried 167 gallons of liquid FS smoke and featured a discharge valve which could be opened and closed during the course of a mission.[75] This was in decided contrast with the M10 smoke tank, used at Nadzab and Noemfoor, which expended smoke all at one time.

The weather over northern Luzon was ideal for the smoke mission. The three B–25's took off from an airfield to the south and arrived over the target at 0855. A pair of planes made the initial run, one a scant 10 feet above the grassy surface, the other, 25 feet. They flew parallel to one another, 30 yards apart and one echeloned 100 feet to the rear, at speeds between 230 and 240 miles an hour. After an interval of several minutes the third plane reinforced the screen by laying smoke between the existing streamers at an altitude of 50 feet. Within a matter of minutes the original planes made a return run, this time at altitudes of 75 and 110 feet. The third B–25 completed the mission by making its second pass at 120 feet. The net result was a dense screen which was effective for over an hour. The first wave of C–47's dropped its paratroopers a little after 0900, and within half an hour the second and third waves landed. The operation was featured by seven gliders which brought in artillery and heavy equipment. Jump casualties came to 7 percent of the participating force. There was no enemy opposition.[76]

All of the air screening operations in the Pacific were carried out unhampered by enemy opposition, certainly a factor which contributed to their over-all success. But this much can be garnered from the Pacific experience: given proper planning, an adequate amount of smoke correctly placed, and good weather conditions, smoke delivered by air could add great insurance to the success of any airborne operation.

[75] Ltr, ACCmlO for Field Opns to CmlO FEAF, 29 Jan 45, sub: Airplane Spray Tank E–1 for B–25 Aircraft. CWS 314.7 Air Smoke.

[76] (1) Rpt, CmlO 309th Bomb Wing to CmlO Fifth AF, 26 Jun 45, sub: Cml Warfare Tactical Opns Rpt. CWS 314.7 Air Smoke. (2) Smith, *Triumph in the Philippines*, pp. 29–30.

CHAPTER XI

The 4.2-Inch Mortar in the MTO

On 10 July 1943 American, British, and Canadian forces landed on the southern and eastern coasts of Sicily, and in the ensuing 38-day campaign the 4.2-inch chemical mortar met its first test in combat. This CWS weapon, still untried in battle nineteen months after the entry of the United States into the war, by 1945 was to become an important part of the Army's arsenal.

The 4.2-inch chemical mortar was a multiple-purpose weapon employed in close support of ground troops. Its versatility was indicated by its ability to fire toxic agents, smoke, and high explosives. In original tactical concept it was a basic ground weapon for offensive gas warfare. No other weapon approached the gas-delivering capacity of the 4.2-inch mortar; eight of them could fire over a ton of toxic agent in a span of two minutes.[1] The smoke mission was also a part of the original tactical concept of mortar employment and was one of the reasons for its success in World War II. But the real key to the popularity of the weapon was its ability to fire high explosive shell, a johnny-come-lately as far as chemical mortar missions were concerned.

The 4.2-inch mortar was the culmination of attempts to improve the 4-inch British Stokes Brandt (SB) mortar. With American-made SB mortars and with shell and propellants purchased from the British after World War I, the CWS sought to obtain increased range, accuracy, and mobility.[2] By 1924, experiments under the direction of Capt. Lewis M. McBride (later colonel) produced the rifled 4.2-inch chemical mortar with a range of over 2,000 yards, and by the end of World War II this distance had been doubled.[3]

The Chemical Warfare Service saw the 4.2-inch mortar as a weapon which possessed mobility and flexibility, which could go in and out of

---

[1] Memo, CCWS for AcofS G–3, 13 Apr 36.

[2] Chemical Mortars, 4-inch and 4.2-inch, in Summary of Activities of the Mechanical Division, Edgewood Arsenal, 1920–1928 (hereafter cited as EATR 189) Proj E8a 29 May 35, p. 63.

[3] (1) EATR 189, p. 62. (2) For a full description of the research and development of the 4.2-inch mortar, see Brophy, Miles, and Cochrane, *From Laboratory to Field.*

action quickly, and which was capable of delivering mass fire in an unusually short time. Compilation of firing data was simple, and the communications system was efficient and rapid. Its high angle enabled it to reach targets in defiladed positions, inaccessible to most types of artillery. The short minimum range of the mortar and its mobility enabled it to give support to infantry units. The low silhouette of this easily concealed weapon offered a difficult target to the enemy.[4]

Despite the potentialities of the 4.2-inch mortar the War Department showed little interest in the weapon and in 1935 suspended its manufacture. For about a year preceding September 1941 the 81-mm. mortar and not the 4.2-inch was the authorized weapon for the chemical battalions. These developments were typical and help reveal the over-all status of the CWS during the 1930's. Later, during the war, a theater chemical officer was to maintain: "It can be readily understood that our service cannot be too greatly criticized, for at no time during the days of peace were we permitted to try out our equipment during field maneuvers, etc., which would have given us a great amount of experience," [5] an opinion concurred in by General Porter, Chief of the CWS.

The Authorization of the High Explosive Mission

If the high explosive mission had not been authorized, activity of chemical mortar units in a nongas war probably would have been confined to screening operations.[6] While the CWS saw the chief function of the mortar as firing gas shells, it did not overlook the possibility of using the weapon to fire high explosives. As early as 1934 these shells were fired in experiments.[7] After the outbreak of World War II the infantry's need for a good medium-range close support weapon became evident, and General Porter and his staff took vigorous steps to get the HE shell standardized and to make the firing of such a shell a major mission of the chemical mortar battalions.

[4] Memo, ExecO OCCWS for CCWS, 17 Dec 34.   CmlC Bd.

[5] (1) Ltr, CCmlO AFHQ to Chief Opns Div CWS, 26 May 43. (2) Ltr, CCWS to CCmlO NATOUSA, 4 Jun 43. Both in CWS 314.7 Personal Ltr files, NATOUSA.

[6] For an expanded account of the matter of authorization of the HE mission and the early activation of mortar units, see (1) Opnl History of Cml Bns and the 4.2-Inch Mortar in World War II, pt. I, To the End of the Sicilian Campaign (Aug 43); (2) Brophy and Fisher, *Organizing for War*, pp. 302–04.

[7] Memo, Lt Col Rollo C. Ditto ExecO OCCWS for CCWS, 17 Dec 34, in Mortars (4.2-Inch), Development of Mechanized Transportation. CRDL Tech Library, Edgewood Arsenal.

The determination, mentioned above, to convert the chemical weapons units to the 81-mm. mortar naturally interrupted negotiations regarding the HE 4.2 mortar shell. A personal conference between General Porter and General Marshall, Army Chief of Staff, resolved the issue in favor of the 4.2-inch mortar, a decision followed by steps to equip the mortar battalions with the approved weapon.[8] Later came the authorization to produce a high explosive filling for the 4.2-inch mortar shell.[9]

This was only half the battle. There remained the double problem of securing War Department approval for the necessary doctrinal change and convincing the ground commanders that mortar battalions were worthy inclusions on troop lists that already must have looked pathetically thin. The doctrinal matter involved the revision of FM 100–5, Field Service Regulations, Operations. Actually, the manual change would merely reflect the tacit approval of the War Department of the new mission for the 4.2-inch mortar. The CWS presented its case at a February 1943 conference with representatives of the Army Ground Forces and the Services of Supply. The latter agreed with the CWS point of view but the Army Ground Forces demurred, advocating a Field Artillery Board test of the mortar. If it passed, the weapon should be given to the Field Artillery to be employed only in those theaters which were without 105-mm. howitzers, just about eliminating any effective employment of the mortar.[10]

The Training Division, Services of Supply, in a strong statement of nonconcurrence, called attention to the substantial increase in firepower which would be enjoyed by a division supported by 4.2-inch mortars. For example, the mortar could place almost four and a half times as much high explosive on a target in a given period of time as could the 105-mm. howitzer, albeit at shorter ranges. The mortar weighed 305 pounds, the howitzer over 2 tons. And mortar units were extremely economical in demands upon manpower. To support its case by actual combat experience, SOS cited the excellent war record of the British chemical mortar with its high explosive mission.[11]

[8] Memo, Chief Field Serv OCCWS for CmlO GHQ, 19 Jan 42. Cited in CWS, Monograph, Opnl Hist of Cml Bns and the 4.2-inch Mortar in WW II, pt. 1, p. 19.

[9] (1) CWTC Item 515, 26 Apr 42. (2) Brophy and Fisher, Organizing for War, p. 45.

[10] (1) Interv, Hist Off with Lt Col Graydon C. Essman, 30 Oct 44. (2) Memo, Dir of Tng SOS for CofS SOS, 27 Feb 43. (3) Memo, CG AGF for CofS, 13 Feb 43. All in CMLHO.

[11] (1) Memo, CofS SOS for CofS, 27 Feb 43. CMLHO. (2) The 12,000-yard range of the 105-mm. howitzer was three times that of the 4.2-inch mortar.

Opposition to the CWS SOS point of view gradually waned, and on 19 March 1943 the War Department authorized the use of HE by the 4.2-inch mortar and directed that necessary amendments be made in the tactical doctrine.[12]

There remained the difficulty of selling the mortar battalion to the field commanders. To them the idea of firing high explosives from the chemical mortar was untried and unproven. An accompanying difficulty was the fact that the 4.2-inch mortar was a chemical weapon. The general impression of most ground force officers was that the functions of CWS were confined to "gas and gas masks and . . . smelly clothing." [13] These officers were surprised and dubious about including in the troop basis chemical units which would fire WP and HE in close support of the infantry.

Obviously, CWS officers had a job on their hands, particularly those staff officers assigned to commands just entering combat. In North Africa Colonel Barker, chemical officer of the Western Task Force, was effective in convincing ground commanders of the worth of the 4.2-inch mortar. Barker pressed for chemical mortar units for support of the North African operations, calling attention to the tactical demands for such a weapon. "This country (and north) is mostly open except for farmhouses and country villas which are in fact rather strong little forts. Trenches within these rock walls give lots of protection to the inhabitants thereof and [machine guns] in such places command a lot of ground." [14] Barker was not to get his mortar units in time for North African operations, but as Fifth Army chemical officer he got four chemical mortar battalions with which to begin the Italian campaign, fought in terrain even better suited for use of the 4.2-inch weapon.

Activation of Chemical Mortar Units

In mid-1941 there was only a handful of mortar units, consisting of regiments, separate battalions, and companies. The 1st and 2d Chemical Regiments had only one active company between them; the two separate battalions, also the 1st and 2d, each had an active company. Completing the roster were two separate chemical companies, one of

[12] Memo for Rcd, 18 Mar 43, by Essman, on Memo, CofS SOS for CofS. CMLHO.
[13] Ltr, CmlO Atlantic Base Sec NATO to Chief Opns Div, 25 Feb 43.
[14] Ltr, CmlO Fifth Army to CCWS, 9 Jan 43. CWS 314.7 Personal Ltr files, Barker, 1942–43.

which was to be lost on Bataan and the other to be inactivated shortly after the United States entered the war.[15] This unimpressive list, with its regiments, battalions, and companies, indicated some indecision about the size of the basic type of weapons unit. Indeed, the brigade also had its supporters. By 1941 it had been pretty well decided that the basic unit of the mortar organization would be the battalion, composed of organic companies. The exception was the several separate mortar companies which saw action in the Pacific fighting.

As of January 1942 there were two chemical mortar battalions, the 2d and 3d, on active duty.[16] Four more, the 81st, 82d, 83d, and 84th were activated by mid-year.[17] During the ten-month interval from June 1942 until May 1943 the number of mortar battalions remained at six.

Meanwhile, the series of plans prepared in the United Kingdom for the cross-Channel attack included the possibility of chemical weapon support.[18] The 1942 plan, for example, which called for a force of a million men included a recommendation for twenty mortar battalions.[19] While there was far less than this number available, the lack of reality between plans for the use of mortar battalions and the number of units on hand was tempered by several factors. At that time the mission of these units was restricted to gas and smoke, and thus far it was a gasless war. Moreover, ground force commanders, operating within the limits of the troop basis, were reluctant to give up units of known potential for a type untested in combat.

By March 1943 the persistent work done by the Chemical Warfare Service in selling its battalions was beginning to prove embarrassing because by this time theater requests for weapons battalions exceeded the 6 on hand. The CWS pointed out that, unless other activations

---

[15] See Brophy and Fisher, *Organizing for War,* app. H.

[16] Chemical mortar battalion was the designation prescribed by the last of several wartime tables of organization. Earlier names included separate chemical battalions, chemical battalions (separate), and chemical battalions (motorized). For the sake of simplicity, the designation chemical mortar battalion will be used throughout the text.

[17] (1) Ltr, TAG to CG Third Army and CG SOS, 25 Mar 42. (2) 1st Ind, Asst AG to CCWS, 7 Apr 42. (3) Ltr, Asst AG Third Army to Chief CWS, 11 Apr 42. (4) 83d Cml Bn GO 1, 10 Jun 42. (5) The War Department General Staff based future activations on a schedule which called for a total of 6 battalions by the end of 1942, 12 more in 1943, and another 12 in 1944. Except for 1943, when only five battalions were activated, this schedule was met. Memo, Troops Div OCCWS for Chief Field Serv, 28 Mar 42.

[18] Memo, McCormick for Chief Troops Div, 2 Apr 42.

[19] Memo, Chief Planning Br Opns Div SOS for Supply Arms and Services, 7 May 1942.

4.2-INCH CHEMICAL MORTAR CREW IN ACTION *during the Italian campaign.*

were authorized before the existing units were shipped, there would be no battalions in the United States, trained or in training, and no sources of cadres for units activated later. As all of the 6 existing battalions were committed for the months of March and May 1943, the CWS urgently recommended that 19 additional battalions be activated by the end of 1943, 6 of them at once to replace a like number being sent overseas.[20] Soon after the final decision to commit four battalions for operations in Sicily, the War Department authorized the activation of four additional battalions—the 86th, 87th, and 88th in May and the 85th in June.[21]

[20] Ltr, Actg CCWS to OPD WDGS, 11 Mar 43.
[21] (1) Memo, Chief Field Rqmts Br OCCWS for Chief Sup Br, 16 Apr 43. (2) TAG Ltr, 4 May 43. AG 320.2 (5–1–43). (3) CWS Units Activated, 1 Oct 44. CMLHO.

Sicily

Preparation for Combat

The mortar battalions selected for participation in HUSKY, the invasion of Sicily, were the 2d, 3d, 83d, and 84th.[22] The latter three sailed almost immediately, arriving in North Africa early in May. These battalions finished their training in the theater although about half of the available time was spent in acquiring their full complement of organizational equipment and in staging. At this time the 3d, 83d, and 84th Battalions were placed in support of the 3d, 1st, and 9th Infantry Divisions, respectively.[23]

Unfortunately, the pressure of preinvasion activities and the late date of attachments left little time for the kind of training most urgently needed by the mortar battalions—combined exercises with the infantry units to which they were attached. Most mortar units also lacked amphibious training. Of the early arriving battalions, only two companies of the 3d, commanded by Lt. Col. Edgar D. Stark, had received this specialized training before leaving the United States, and that was limited to a few weeks at the Amphibious Training Center, Camp Carrabelle, Fla., later known as Camp Gordon Johnston.[24] The three battalions received "only sketchy preparation for the problem of amphibious maneuvers" at the Fifth Army Invasion Training Center after they arrived in North Africa.[25]

The fourth mortar unit earmarked for Sicily fared better in its preparations. While undergoing training at Fort Bragg, N. C., the 2d Battalion, commanded by Lt. Col. Robert W. Breaks, had been able to arrange locally for joint training with infantry units also located at Fort Bragg. The 2d Battalion was attached to the 45th Infantry Division in February 1943 during final training preparations for overseas movement, preparations which included work in mountain and amphibious operations. This experience constituted what until then

---

[22] Unless otherwise noted, the section on Sicily is based upon the combat reports of the participating battalions: (1) Journal of 2d Cml Bn (Motorized) in World War II, to 10 Aug 1943; (2) History of 3d Cml Bn in Campaign of Sicily, 10 Jul 43–30 Aug 43; 83d Cml Bn, Battle Rpt, The Battle for Sicily, 5 Nov 1943. See also: (4) Lt Col Albert N. Garland and Howard McGaw Smyth, Sicily and the Surrender of Italy, UNITED STATES ARMY IN WORLD WAR II (Washington, 1965).

[23] Rpt of Seventh Army in Sicily.

[24] (1) Rpt of Seventh Army in Sicily, p. H–1. (2) Interv, Hist Off with Lt Col Robert W. Breaks and Col Fellenz, 23 Oct 44. (3) Brophy and Fisher, Organizing for War, ch. XIII.

[25] Rpt of Seventh Army in Sicily, p. H–1.

were probably the only cases of joint 4.2-inch mortar–infantry training in the United States. The 45th and its supporting units sailed for
North Africa combat-loaded, arriving near Oran just twelve days
before embarkation for Sicily. During this brief stay the 2d Battalion
completed a 15-day training program in less than half the allotted
time.[26]

CWS officers in North Africa exerted every effort to acquaint infantry commanders with the chemical mission, including the 4.2-inch
mortar and its proper employment. Even before the arrival of the
chemical battalions they conducted demonstrations with 4.2-inch
mortar WP shells, colored grenades, and flame throwers. With the
arrival of the first three battalions CWS officers were able to hold
mortar demonstrations for the chief of staff of Seventh Army and other
high ranking officers.[27]

Despite the limited time to prepare for the invasion the participating
infantry divisions gave some thought and effort to use of mortar units
during the assault phase. Three platoons of the 3d Battalion mounted
mortars on landing craft and actually accompanied the assault waves
of three of the four landing teams of the 3d Infantry Division. Complete surprise in that sector eliminated any need for the 4.2-inch
mortars.[28] Plans to use 2d Battalions mortars in the assault phase were
canceled because of the limited number of landing craft. No thought
was given to the amphibious employment of the 83d Battalion because
of that unit's lack of specialized training.[29] The 84th Battalion was
not committed to the fighting in Sicily, but was kept in reserve.

The experience in Sicily prompted some of the participating CWS
officers to predict the unlikelihood of mortar employment in subsequent
landing operations.[30] The Fifth Army chemical officer felt that "when
one is making a landing at a distance from his base, shipping space is
so precious that I doubt if it will ever be possible to mount the 4.2-inch

---

[26] (1) Journal of 2d Cml Bn. (2) Col. Breaks Comments on draft of this volume, 3 Feb 61,
declared that senior commanders such as Maj. Gen. Omar Bradley and Maj. Gen. Troy Middleton
gained an early appreciation of the 4.2-inch mortar from observing these exercises.

[27] (1) CWS TofO Ltr No. 5, 3 Sep 43 and Incl. 1, p. 2. (2) Rpt of Seventh Army in Sicily,
p. A-4.

[28] History of 3d Cml Bn in Campaign of Sicily, 10 Jul 43–30 Aug 43. (2) CWS TofO Ltr No. 6,
8 Oct 43, p. 14.

[29] (1) Breaks-Fellenz Interv. (2) CWS TofO Ltr No. 6, 8 Oct 43, p. 14.

[30] (1) Ltr, CO 83d Cml Bn to ACCWS for Field Opns, 12 Sep 43. CWS 314.7 Personal Ltr files,
NATOUSA. (2) Breaks-Fellenz Interv.

on landing craft," [31] a correct prediction for the war against Germany, if not for the operations in the Pacific theaters.

Upon entry in combat each of the mortar battalions was composed of 1,010 men: 36 officers, 1 warrant officer, and 973 enlisted men, [32] distributed among a headquarters, a headquarters company, a medical detachment, and four weapons companies. Each company had 2 platoons, each platoon 2 sections, and each section 3 squads. On the basis of one mortar per squad, the battalion complement of mortars was 48. Transportation of the battalion consisted of 88 2½-ton trucks and 36 vehicles of varying smaller sizes. Chemical mortar carts were present in case of rough terrain. Side arms for the battalion included 820 .45-caliber automatics.[33]

The Initial Test of Battle

H-hour for HUSKY was 0230, 10 July 1943. With one exception the mortar units landed in their assigned sectors without incident. The exception was the 83d Battalion, commanded by Colonel Cunin, three companies of which supported a Ranger task force which was attached to the 1st Infantry Division and which had as its objective the coastal town of Gela, with its complex of strong defenses.[34] The three mortar companies encountered false beaches in front of the true landing area. Although the assault craft carrying Company A managed to push across the sandbar and reach its proper objective, the vessels carrying the other two companies extricated themselves only with difficulty.

During the first days of the battle chemical mortars fired against every type of target that presented itself. Some of the hardest fighting took place at Gela where a series of enemy tank thrusts threatened Ranger units, and, surprisingly enough, where 4.2-inch mortar fire was used with a great deal of success against armor. On D-day mortar fire from Company C, 83d Battalion, helped throw back a tank-infantry attack, and later a group of Italian light tanks broke into town only to be repulsed by antitank guns, bazookas, and pole charges.

---

[31] Ltr, CmlO Fifth Army to ACCWS for Fld Opns, 26 Sep 43.

[32] T/O 3-25, Cml Motorized Bn (Separate), 1 Apr 42.

[33] The 2d Battalion substituted .30 carbines for the .45's in order to have a better local defense capability. Breaks Comments, 3 Feb 61.

[34] (1) 83d Cml Bn, Battle Rpt, The Battle for Sicily, 5 Nov 43, pp. 2-5. (2) Maj. William S. Hutchinson, Jr., "Use of the 4.2-Inch Mortar in the Invasion of Sicily," *Chemical Warfare Bulletin*, vol. 29, No. 8 (December, 1943-January, 1944).

PULLING A 4.2-INCH MORTAR CART OVER RUGGED TERRAIN

In this skirmish the bazooka team of Company A disabled one tank which was immediately blown up by a Ranger with a pole charge.[35] Next day chemical mortars, firing without aiming stakes or prepared emplacements, were not quite accurate enough to destroy any of a group of nine tanks but were threatening enough to force the tanks to withdraw to positions where they were dispatched by friendly artillery and naval gunfire.[36]

Actually, the chemical mortars had the necessary accuracy to engage targets as small as a tracked vehicle. Just before dawn on one of the early days of the Sicily campaign, a temporarily disabled German tank began harassing an infantry position with automatic fire as the crew made repairs. Asked for help by the infantry, a 2d Chemical Battalion company commander called for one sensing round and then for a volley of eight. The tank was silenced. Daylight examination of the tank found all mortar rounds within an area fifteen yards in diameter, with

[35] Hutchinson, "Use of the 4.2-Inch Mortar in the Invasion of Sicily," *Chemical Warfare Bulletin*, vol. 29, No. 8 (December, 1945–January, 1944).

[36] (1) *Ibid.* (2) 83d Cml Bn, Battle for Sicily, 5 Nov 43.

one of them down the open turret of the vehicle.[37] Once the beach-heads were consolidated, chemical mortars fired preparations preceding infantry attacks, interdicted enemy lines of communications, and fired on machine guns, mortars, ammunition dumps, and barracks.[38]

One of the most significant chemical mortar smoke missions in Sicily was a series of screens fired for the 3d Infantry Division during the period 6–8 August. The Germans held a strong ridge line east of the Furiano River, which flows northward to the sea. The 7th Infantry received the mission of seizing the heights dominated by Hill 715. The 2d Mortar Battalion supported the attack with smoke and high explosives; Companies A and D fired HE concentrations and Company B carried out the smoke mission.[39] From 0530 to approximately 0900 on 6 August B Company maintained a 3,500-yard screen to conceal the advancing infantry. Firing from positions west of the river the mortarmen gradually increased the range of the smoke curtain from 1,000 to 3,200 yards to keep pace with the progress of the attacking troops. The smoke mission terminated upon orders of the commander of the assault infantry battalion. At about 1000, as the mortars were firing on call, enemy artillery began pounding the American positions. Enemy shells hit 4 of the 6 mortar positions (knocking over 3 weapons, but damaging only 1), 2 platoon-size ammunition dumps, and generally raised havoc with the wire communications of the battalion. That afternoon D Company fired a smoke mission which helped 2 infantry battalions under heavy counterattacks to withdraw to the west side of the river.

Early next morning the infantry tried again, and one B Company platoon concealed the advance to the attack position with a 1,000-yard screen. The mortars maintained this screen for almost fourteen hours despite difficulties caused by shifting winds.[40] Once the screen was established it was kept up by two WP rounds a minute, although for a short period around noon weather conditions made it necessary to raise this number to five. The mortar crews lifted the screen several

[37] Journal of 2d Cml Bn, 14 Jul 43. (2) Lt Col Robert C. Breaks, "My Men Had Guts," *Chemical Warfare Bulletin*, vol. 30, No. 1 (February–March, 1944), (3) The journals of the three battalions contain frequent references of the direct or indirect destruction of tanks by 4.2-inch mortar fire.

[38] Ltr, ACmlO 45th Div to CmlO 45th Div, 31 Jul 43.

[39] Because of its proficiency in dispatching enemy troops the 4.2-inch mortar in Sicily acquired the nickname Goon Gun. As a tribute to the part these mortars played in this operation, Hill 715 became known as Goon Gun Hill, at least in CWS circles. The infantry called it Million Dollar Hill because of the large number of rounds fired on it. The artillery also participated in the smoke mission.

[40] Rpt of Seventh Army in Sicily, p. B-18.

times during the day to permit friendly dive bomber attacks on the enemy positions. On the third day the infantry succeeded in taking the heights east of the Furiano, again with the help of chemical mortar smoke and high explosives.[41]

Of the three mortar units committed to HUSKY the 2d Chemical Battalion saw the most action. In fact, it was said to have been the only combat unit on the island that saw no relief during the entire operation.[42] After reaching Palermo the 3d Battalion was transferred to II Corps, an attachment which terminated its combat activities for the campaign. Thereafter the battalion performed a number of rear area duties, principally those dealing with transportation. It also guarded prisoners of war and ammunition dumps, collected ammunition, and generally participated in assignments which failed to utilize its capabilities as a mortar unit.[43] On the other hand, the limited activity of the 83d Battalion, attached to both the 2d Armored and 82d Airborne Divisions after the initial stages of the campaign, resulted primarily from a lack of suitable targets.[44]

Despite early difficulties faced by the chemical mortar battalions in their first combat action, they made a creditable record during the Sicily Campaign. The absence of established doctrine and, with the exception of the 2d Battalion, the lack of joint infantry-mortar training, resulted not only in some misuse of the battalions but in the failure to use them "where they could have been employed to exceptional advantage." [45]

Nevertheless, reaction of ground commanders who had been supported by the chemical mortars was generally favorable, and most of them advocated chemical mortar support for all divisions committed to action.[46] Among their comments were "the equivalent of real artillery," which the chemical mortar was not, and "the most effective single weapon used in support of infantry," [47] a statement to which it had fair claim.

---

[41] Breaks, "My Men Had Guts," *Chemical Warfare Bulletin*, vol. 30, No. 1 (February–March, 1944).

[42] (1) *Ibid.* (2) Upon its relief from attachment to the 45th Division, the 2d Battalion was attached to the 3d Division.

[43] (1) History of 3d Cml Bn in Sicily. (2) Rpt of Seventh Army in Sicily, pp. H–1—3.

[44] Rpt of Seventh Army in Sicily, pp. H–1—3.

[45] CmlO Seventh Army, Rpt of Cml Warfare Opns—Sicilian Campaign, 24 Sep 43.

[46] Ltr, CO 83d Cml Bn to ACCWS for Field Opns, 12 Sep 43.

[47] Extracts from Training Notes from the Sicilian Campaign, in Ltr, CCmlO NATOUSA to ACCWS for Field Opns, 6 Nov 43. CWS 314.7 Personal Ltr files, NATOUSA.

The Problem of Transportation

General Shadle, Chief Chemical Officer, NATOUSA, put his finger on one of the main shortcomings revealed by this first test of combat when he said there was nothing seriously wrong with the 4.2-inch mortar or the chemical battalion except transportation.[48] The principal means of motor transport in the mortar battalion was the 2½-ton truck, often too big and too conspicuous to operate adequately in positions as near the front as the 4.2-inch mortars were emplaced. The ¼-ton truck and trailer seemed more appropriate, and at times infantry commanders gave up some of their own jeeps in order to insure chemical mortar support.[49] Because man-handling the mortar carts was an arduous task, crews sometimes attached them to jeeps, an unsatisfactory practice because of damage to the wheels and handles of the smaller vehicle. Once an infantry battalion commander directed his reserve riflemen to help mortar crews struggling with their carts, an unorthodox move which illustrated as well as anything how highly infantrymen esteemed the mortar.[50] Often mortar crews commandeered mules in order to keep up with the infantry advance. These animals not only made up for inadequate basic transportation but reached places inaccessible to vehicles,[51] a fact that led General Patton to opine at the end of the campaign that the pack animal still had a role in modern warfare.[52]

The mortar battalion tables of organization and equipment published shortly after the Sicilian campaign provided for ¼-ton trucks and trailers as the basic means of transportation. But because of delays in acquiring the new vehicles and because of the type of terrain and fighting encountered in Italy, this change did not prove to be the expected panacea.

Efforts To Increase the Range

The other serious difficulty encountered in the first combat employment of the mortar was that of its range. The introduction of the

---

[48] Ltr, CCmlO NATOUSA to ACCWS for Field Opns, 26 Aug 43. CWS 314.7 Personal Ltr files, NATOUSA.
[49] Journal of 2d Cml Bn.
[50] Breaks, "My Men Had Guts," *Chemical Warfare Bulletin*, vol. 30, No. 1 (February–March, 1944).
[51] Journal of 2d Cml Bn.
[52] Notes on the Sicilian Campaign.

M5A1 propellant in January 1943 increased the range of the mortar from 2,400 to 3,200 yards.[53] The M6 propellant, standardized in March 1943, raised the maximum range to 4,500 yards although the item was not in production in time for use in Sicily. Meanwhile, in July 1943 OCCWS froze the range of the 4.2-inch mortar at 3,200 yards, despite repeated requests from North Africa for increased range. Washington headquarters answered: "It has been decided, for practical purposes, and in view of manufacturing and materiel difficulties, the chemical mortar is to be considered as having a maximum range of 3,200 yards. . . . It is considered that this is a satisfactory range, and any additional work done is to be confined to further perfecting the performance of this weapon within this range." [54]

At the end of hostilities in Sicily a conference of Seventh Army CWS officers agreed that a range of 4,500 was required,[55] an opinion which was reflected in the other important reports of the Sicilian campaign.[56] These recommendations, combined with an urgent request from theater headquarters for a chemical mortar range of at least 4,500 yards, led the OCCWS to reverse its decision.[57] Shortages of certain ingredients for the M6 propellant added to the delay involved in getting the Army Ground Forces blessing for the increased range, so that supplies of the M6 propellant did not reach the theater until the end of the year.

Among the lesser problems arising in Sicily were certain shortcomings of the M2 mortar sight. This piece of equipment was unsatisfactory for night employment because it lacked a means of illumination. Moreover, it could not be employed from deeply defiladed positions. In these positions sighting stakes had to be placed to the rear of the mortar position rather than to the front, because of the small traverse (200 mils) of the M2 sight. This limited traverse also caused excessive re-emplacements. Captured Italian 81-mm. mortar sights with 360° traverse proved much superior to the American model.[58]

---

[53] CWS TofO Ltr No. 1, 3 Mar 43.

[54] CWS TofO Ltr No. 3, 23 Jun 43.

[55] Conf of Cml Warfare Officers of Seventh Army. CMLHO.

[56] (1) Rpt of Cml Warfare Opns, Sicilian Campaign, 24 Sep 43. (2) Notes on the Sicilian Campaign.

[57] (1) CM–IN 18330, 24 Aug 43. (2) CM–OUT 11648, 28 Aug 43. (3) IOM, ACCWS to ACCWS Field Opns, 26 Aug 43.

[58] (1) Ltr, CO 83d Cml Bn to ACCWS Field Opns, 12 Sep 43. (2) Conf of Cml Warfare Officers of Seventh Army. (3) Memo, ACmlO Seventh Army for CmlO Seventh Army, 23 Aug 43. CMLHO.

There was little difficulty with mortar maintenance during the operation as the equipment was new and not seriously overtaxed. Ammunition was in good supply in Sicily although inadequate waterproofing initially resulted in numerous corroded fuzes.[59] And transportation difficulties resulted in low ammunition reserves at forward positions, even though the over-all supply of mortar shell in Sicily was ample.[60]

The Salerno Landings

The 2d, 83d, and 84th Chemical Mortar Battalions took part in the fighting at Salerno, the first of a series of punishing campaigns fought in the rugged terrain of Italy.[61] Companies C and D of the 83d supported American Rangers and British Commandos of the 10 British Corps, Fifth Army's left unit during its assault at Salerno. Originally, the 84th Chemical Battalion was to have supported the 36th Division, the assault force of the VI U.S. Corps on the army's right. These plans went awry. According to the battalion commander, Lt. Col. Harrison Markham, Seventh Army orders releasing the 84th to VI Corps were lost, and by the time the confusion cleared no shipping space was available with the 36th Division. Three companies of the battalion did find room with corps reserves and eventually fired for the 45th Division, which also had the support of the 2d Chemical Battalion.[62]

Although the enemy reacted vigorously to the Salerno landings, so that a period of sanguinary fighting resulted in which the fate of the beachhead was sometimes uncertain, the attack began auspiciously. Company A, 2d Chemical Battalion, landed at 0300, 10 September, (D plus 1) with the 179th Infantry, 45th Division.[63] Next day violent enemy counterattacks pushed the American force back from its advanced position, and in the course of the withdrawal Company A's 1st Platoon lost eleven men. Company B, in support of elements of

---

[59] (1) Rpt of Seventh Army in Sicily, p. H-1.   (2) CM-IN 4819, 8 Jun 43.

[60] See Journal of 2d Cml Bn, pp. 28, 33, 40, 52.

[61] For general accounts of the fighting in Italy, see (1) Blumenson, Salerno to Cassino, and Ernest F. Fisher, Cassino to the Alps, volumes in preparation for the series U.S. ARMY IN WORLD WAR II; (2) see also, Garland and Smyth, *Sicily and the Surrender of Italy.*

[62] (1) Interv, Hist Off with Markham, 16 Jan 45.   (2) Opnl History of Cml Bns and the 4.2-Inch Mortar in World War II, pt. II, The Italian Campaign, p. 53.   This is a detailed study of chemical mortar operations in Italy.

[63] Unless otherwise noted, the 2d Chemical Battalion S-3 Journal serves as the basis for the account of that unit's operations in Italy.

another regiment of the 45th Division near the town of Persano, also
ran into trouble. Suddenly faced with direct enemy fire, the mortarmen
had no alternative but to pull back. In the confusion that followed
some of the mortars were left behind, to be recovered, fortunately, at
a later time. Company C supported the 157th Infantry, 45th Division;
for some unaccountable reason Company D remained in reserve during
the entire Salerno operation.[64]

The first troops of the 84th Battalion came ashore near Paestum on
D-day, but congestion in shipping space forced them to land without
equipment. It was not until 12 September that these companies received
their full complement of men and mortars.[65] By this time the situation
of the Fifth Army was serious. The German attack which had turned
the right flank of the 45th Division also cut off elements of the 36th
Division north of the Calore River.[66] Orders received by a company
commander of the 2d Mortar Battalion indicated the grave plight of
the American forces. If the enemy should come too close for effective
mortar fire, the mortar troops were directed to stand fast and defend
their positions with rifle fire and, if necessary, bayonets.[67]

Virtually every available American element was thrown into the
line on 14 September when the enemy renewed his heavy infantry and
tank attack. One of the companies of the 2d Chemical Battalion fired
1,152 rounds during the day. Over 500 of these were white phosphorus used to set fire to the dry brush, making those areas untenable
to the enemy. Early that afternoon the company helped repulse an
enemy tank attack in an action which saw the mortar forward observer
direct artillery fire as well as that of his own weapons. The stalwart
defense on 14 September blunted the German counterattack and secured the beachhead.

Meanwhile, companies of the 83d Battalion supported the American
Rangers and British Commandos in action in the 10 Corps sector.[68]
On Sicily this mortar unit had earned the sobriquet Artillery of the
Rangers. This expression was equally apt for the unit's service with
the Commandos, who also operated without organic heavy weapons.

---

[64] (1) Co A 2d Cml Bn, Rcd of Events.   (2) 2d Cml Bn Casualty Rpt, 11 Sep 43.   (3) Fifth Army
Cml Warfare Sec Journal, 26 Sep 43.   (4) Ltr, Fifth Army CmlO to CCWS, 25 Sep 43.

[65] Unless otherwise noted, the operations of the 84th are based on the battalion field journal.

[66] VI Corps Opns Rpt, Sep 43.

[67] Co C 2d Cml Bn Unit Journal.

[68] Unless otherwise noted, the 83d Battalion Operations Report is the basis for account of unit operations in Italy.

The Commandos and Company D landed at Vietri sul Mari at 0400, 9 September, with the task of blocking the northern approaches to Salerno. In addition to performing missions of harassment and interdiction, the 4.2-inch mortars fired on troops, tanks, and emplacements. An impressive action took place on 18 September when D Company fired a preparatory barrage of 1,194 rounds on two strongly defended hills north of Salerno. The hard fighting in the Vietri area continued for about ten days until the Germans began their withdrawal.[69]

At this juncture, the Commandos, having suffered casualties of almost 75 percent, were pulled from the line. Company D stayed on, reinforcing Company C, which had landed at Mairoi on D-day in support of the three battalions of American Rangers. This small, elite force of 1,500 advanced inland and seized Chiunzi Pass and Mt. St. Angelo, which commanded the German supply route south of Naples. Charged with holding the entire peninsula the Ranger force held out for three weeks against attacks in which the enemy sometimes had a numerical superiority of eight to one. As a consequence, the Rangers were so thinly spread that mortar units not only performed their own mission as artillery of the Rangers but also held front-line positions as regular infantry. Sometimes mortar crews were stripped down to one or two men and the rest sent to repel counterattacks or on patrol. These crews engaged enemy 88-mm. guns and 240-mm. howitzers at distances 2,000 yards or more beyond the authorized range of their mortars. Companies C and D of the 83d fired over 14,000 rounds in the first two weeks of the campaign, a total, according to Colonel Barker, which equaled that of all the other mortar units.[70] One result of this heavy firing at excessive ranges was the rapid breakdown of the weapons. In spite of the combined efforts of both CWS and ordnance maintenance units, at the end of the first three weeks in Italy there were only three mortars in action in one company and six in the other.[71]

Naples fell to the British 10 Corps on 1 October and the first phase of the Italian fighting was over. The important role of 4.2-inch mortars in the over-all success is indicated by Col. William Darby of the Rangers who reported that his forces were able to hold Chiunzi Pass "largely due to the chemical mortar battalion attached to the unit." [72]

[69] Interv, Hist Off with Lt Col William S. Hutchinson, Jr., 26 Jan 45.
[70] Ltr, CmlO Fifth Army to CCWS, 25 Sep 43.
[71] (1) *Ibid.* (2) Hutchinson Interv, 26 Jan 45.
[72] Notes on Interv with Darby, 18 May 44. AG–OB–S, Log 2704.

From the Volturno to the Winter Line

Crossing the Volturno

By 6 October the Fifth Army had advanced to a line running generally along the south banks of the Volturno and Calore Rivers inland to the town of Benevento. The British 10 Corps held the western part of this front, the U.S. VI Corps the eastern sector. These units crossed the Volturno on the night of 12–13 October. The 84th Chemical Mortar Battalion (less Company A) supported the 3d Division and Company A, 2d Battalion, supported the 34th Division.

Of these mortar units, the 84th Battalion probably received the most calls for support. Company D fired both screening and high explosive missions for a regimental crossing and later screened bridge-building activity of the engineers. During the daylight hours of 13 October Company B used 2,805 rounds of white phosphorus to conceal the corps left flank from enemy observation from the heights above the town of Triflisco. The mortarmen carried out this mission by firing the WP directly on these heights using the maximum authorized range of the 4.2-inch mortar—3,200 yards. At first, Company B employed one platoon of four mortars for the screening operation but the required rapid rate of fire made barrels so hot that propellants ignited before the rounds reached the firing pin. The commitment of another platoon reduced the rate of fire and eliminated the trouble.[73] In addition to these normal mortar missions, the 84th Battalion furnished a detail of 3 officers and 100 men which expended 400 M1 smoke pots to conceal bridging sites and their exposed approaches.[74]

Fifth Army carried the assault of the Volturno with swiftness and skill, and for a brief time thereafter chemical mortar activity was characterized by relatively light firing. It was during this period that problems arose which were to confront mortar units throughout most of the Italian campaign. One of these involved communications. Mortar battalions used a tremendous amount of wire to maintain contact among units, the radio playing a secondary role because of the excessive amount of dead space typical in mountainous terrain and because of the danger that its use would reveal exact positions to the enemy. Mortarmen usually laid two lines of wire from the company

---

[73] (1) Fifth Army Chemical Warfare Sec Journal, 16 Oct 43. (2) Markham Interv, 16 Jan 45.
[74] For an account of the use of smoke pots by mortar units, see above, Chapter VIII.

command post to the platoon firing positions and at least two lines (by different routes) from each gun position to the observation post. In heavy fighting enemy fire frequently shot up the wire—the communication lines of one mortar platoon were interrupted six times during a single day in the Mount Acero region, permitting it to fire only two missions with a total expenditure of eighteen rounds.[75] The wire-cutting capabilities of friendly vehicles, particularly those with tracks, also proved discouraging to good communications. In fast-moving situations there was no alternative to the radio. The SCR–284, used principally between battalion and company command posts, proved reasonably satisfactory but poor performances by SCR's 193 and 194 brought a great many complaints.[76]

It was also at this time that the need for animal transport began to increase. Poor roads characterized the rocky, mountainous terrain in which the fighting took place, forcing the 84th to use oxen to haul its mortars over the steep slopes near Venafro. Mules were the usual beasts of burden. Upon crossing the Volturno, the 84th Battalion, failing to get these animals from the 3d Division to which it was attached, captured its own mules and successfully improvised pack saddles. Because the U.S. Army mule pack was too large and heavy for the local animals, the Italian model became the pack usually employed.[77]

Early Fighting in the Winter Line

After being driven from positions north of the Volturno the enemy fell back to his Winter Line which extended along the Garigliano River and thence into the mountainous region from Mignano to Venafro and on toward Isernia. This series of defensive positions was designed to hold Fifth Army's advance and allow the Germans to fortify further the more formidable Gustav Line. Allied forces reached the Winter Line during the first week of November, but the rather rapid advance ground to a halt in front of stiffened resistance and in face of the increased difficulties caused by winter weather.[78]

The initial attack on the Winter Line saw all four chemical mortar battalions committed to action. The 3d Battalion, which had remained

[75] Co C 2d Cml Bn Unit Diary, 15 Oct 43.

[76] (1) History of 3d Cml Bn, Jan 44, pp. 10–11. (2) ASF Bd Rpt, NATO, No. 71, 6 Nov 43, Rpt of 45th Inf Div. (3) Breaks-Fellenz Interv, 23 Oct 44. (4) Markham Interv, 16 Jan 45.

[77] (1) Markham Interv, 16 Jan 45. (2) AGF Bd Rpt, NATO, No. A–112, 23 Dec 43.

[78] Fifth Army History, II, 47.

behind in Sicily, joined the Fifth Army on 30 October. Company A of the 84th and Companies A and B of the 83d rejoined their parent units for the first time on Italian soil.[79] Until then the operations of the Fifth Army had not been marked by extended static situations, and the chemical mortar units were of only limited value in rapidly moving situations. Strong enemy defenses and the approach of winter promised a different sort of campaign, one which would make good use of the capabilities of the 4.2-inch mortar.

The key position in the American sector opposite the Winter Line was a gap in the mountains at Mignano through which ran Highway 6. This presented an avenue to the Liri Valley, called the Gateway to Rome, and the ultimate objective of the operations. To the left of the Mignano gap loomed Mount Camino and to the right, Mount Sammucro. In between were several lesser land masses which effectively served as "stoppers" for the break in the east-west mountain chain.[80]

The VI Corps had reached the Winter Line in early November and had bloodied its nose in its attempt to break through. In the various engagements in the Mount Difensa–Mount Sammucro–Mount Santa Croce area the 2d and 83d Chemical Mortar Battalions saw action in support of the 3d Division and Ranger and parachute troops. The mortars fired preparatory barrages, sometimes followed by screens for the advancing infantry. On 12 November one platoon of Company C, 2d Battalion, in conjunction with the artillery and in support of a 3d Division attack on Mount Difensa, laid down a preliminary barrage on a point just beyond the summit, an area which could not have been reached by the artillery. During the last three minutes of the barrage, the platoon fired forty-nine rounds of WP to conceal the infantry assault. Twenty-four rounds of white phosphorus screened the American withdrawal when the attack failed.[81]

On 13 November a German counterattack against the 4th Ranger foothold on Mount Sammucro initially rolled back that unit's right and left flank. Some of the shells of the protective concentrations of Company B, 83d Battalion, fell within 100 yards of friendly positions. The company fired 3,605 rounds of HE and 163 WP so rapidly that one of the mortar firing pins became fused. In the course of this fighting German artillery scored two direct hits on Company B ammu-

[79] Fifth Army Cml Warfare Sec Journal, 1, 9, 22, 30 Oct 43.

[80] *Fifth Army at the Winter Line*, p. 8.

[81] Co C 2d Cml Bn Unit Diary.

nition dumps, destroying 1,000 rounds of ammunition.[82] The Rangers thwarted the attack, and artillery, mortar, and small arms fire prevented the enemy from reorganizing for another assault.[83]

In mid-November Fifth Army paused to regroup. II Corps moved to the middle of the line, and VI Corps shifted to the right. For two weeks, while army planned for a continuation of the assault on the Winter Line, its troops remained on the defensive. The missions of the 4.2-inch mortars—the prevention of enemy observation and disruption of his troop concentrations and counterattacks—reflected this lull in operations. It was during this period that water-damaged propellants became a serious problem. In the 84th Battalion 80 percent of these items were found to have moisture enough to cause shorts or "poop outs." An investigation of this condition by the chemical officer of the Fifth Army led to the manufacture and operation of a dryer for propellants by the 12th Chemical Maintenance Company at Capua.[84]

Fifth Army plans for overcoming the Winter Line defenses consisted of three phases: an attack on Mount Camino on the left of the Mignano gap; an attack on Mount Sammucro on the right of the gap; and, finally, the drive into the Liri Valley. The first phase, appropriately called Operation RAINCOAT, combined assaults by the British 10 and the American II Corps on Mount Camino and its neighboring peaks, Mounts Difensa and Maggiore. Company A of the 83d Battalion and Company B of the 2d supported the 1st Special Service Force[85] and the 142d Infantry, 36th Division, in this operation. The second phase, the attack on the Mount Sammucro complex, began on 8 December. During this difficult fighting Company B, 83d Chemical Battalion, supported the 3d Ranger Battalion in an attack against Hill 950, a lesser land mass adjacent to the main objective. Although at first successful, the Rangers were finally swept off the hill by a violent enemy counterattack. Company B mortarmen placed heavy concentrations on the hill in rebuttal, attracting intense enemy artillery and mortar fire in the process. This concentration killed two men, wounded ten, hit the company ammunition dump, and temporarily put one platoon

[82] 83d Cml Bn Casualty Rpt, 14 Nov 43.
[83] Co B 83d Cml Bn Action Rpt, 23 Nov 43.
[84] (1) Fifth Army Cml Warfare Sec Journal, 10 Dec 43. (2) See above, Chapter VII, for more on the Capua facility.
[85] Composed of Canadians and Americans, this regiment-sized unit was a specially trained task force and not, as the name implies, a service force in the normal sense.

out of action. Next morning the Rangers again took Hill 950, abetted by heavy artillery and 4.2-inch mortar preparations, but their losses were so heavy that they were replaced by the 504th Parachute Infantry regiment. The 4.2-inch mortar company remained in position and supported the new unit until 23 December, by which time Mount Sammucro was in American hands.

Problems and Improvisations

On 15 December the 36th Division attacked the remaining enemy-held heights of Mount Sammucro and the stronghold of San Pietro, a town located off the southwest slope of the mountain. The four companies of the 2d Battalion ran into trouble in supporting this attack with smoke and high explosives. Tanks broke the communication wire of two companies, and spongy soil caused the mortars of another to bounce so badly that they had to be re-emplaced every five or six rounds. Mortar breakage was a serious problem; when Company A completed its mission on 16 December only three mortars remained in action, and the elevating screw of each of these was locked.[86] Much of the breakage resulted from frequent use of mortars against German heavy mortars and *Nebelwerfers*, whose ranges exceeded that of the American weapon. Firing at excessive range caused failure of many parts of the mortar—elevating and traversing screws bent, the brass barrel housings split, locking forks bent, base plates broke, and recoil springs lost their resilience.[87] The new M6 propellant, promised during the Sicily Campaign, and a strengthened base plate combined to increase the maximum authorized range of the 4.2-inch mortar from 3,200 to 4,400 yards. The battalions in Italy began receiving the new propellants in December 1943, and their successful tests prompted the Fifth Army chemical officer to request that all future shipments of propellants be of this type.[88]

A feature of the fight for San Pietro was the introduction of a self-propelled 4.2-inch mortar, designed to provide the infantry with a means of more mobile support and armored units with a weapon with a high angle of fire. Developed by Colonel Barker and the 36th Division ordnance officer, at the instigation of the latter's commander,

---

[86] (1) Co C 2d Cml Bn Unit History, 15 Dec 43. (2) Co A 2d Cml Bn Rcd of Events.

[87] Ltr, CmlO Fifth Army to CCWS, 24 Nov 43. CMLHO.

[88] (1) 3d Cml Bn Journal, 5 Dec 43. (2) Fifth Army Cml Warfare Sec Journal, 5 Dec 43, 21 Jan 44. (3) Ltr, CmlO Fifth Army to CCWS, 22 Jan 44. (4) CM–IN 20511, 31 Jan 44.

this roving gun was simply a 4.2-inch mortar mounted on an M7 half-track. Upon first lumbering into position at San Pietro, its noise brought down a heavy enemy artillery concentration. Moving to a defiladed position the self-propelled mortar fired with good results fifty rounds of WP at a range of 3,000 yards.

The weapon and chassis came through this initial test with moderate success. The mortar mount suffered some damage and the blast effect against the sides of the vehicle proved exceedingly uncomfortable to the gun crew. But it appears that little subsequent use was made of the self-propelled mortar. Its size and silhouette precluded emplacement where close support weapons were needed. And any weapon which attracted too much enemy fire was not popular with the infantry.[89]

While II Corps was overcoming the stubborn German defenses around Mignano, VI Corps, occupying the right flank of Fifth Army, found the going equally rough in the mountains to the north. Heaviest fighting in the 45th Division sector took place near the village of Lagone. In an engagement on 15 December a forward observer for Company B, 84th Battalion, attached to the 180th Infantry, sighted the enemy forming for a counterattack in the sector of the adjacent regiment. The 209 rounds of high explosive and 454 rounds of white phosphorus shell dumped upon this formation aided in throwing back the enemy assault. One prisoner disclosed that the attack was going well until the German troops suddenly encountered intense mortar fire which killed the prisoner's officer and a number of his fellow soldiers. "We wanted to surrender . . .," the German continued, and the "mortar fire scattered our troops all over the hill and gave us a chance to get away and give ourselves up." [90]

Mount Pantano was the scene of the heaviest action in the sector of the other VI Corps division, the 34th. Fighting seesawed among the four knobs of the mountaintop for days, supported on the American side by the effective fire of a company and a half of the 3d Chemical Battalion. During a 2-day period at the end of November the mortar crews used so much ammunition, over 1,500 rounds, that fire was temporarily suspended. This was one of the few cases of such curtailment in the Italian campaign.[91]

[89] Fifth Army Cml Warfare Sec Journal, 5, 7, 8, 11, 16 Dec 43.

[90] 84th Cml Bn Field Journal, 15 Dec 43.

[91] (1) History of 3d Cml Bn, Nov 43.   (2) Co D 3d Cml Bn Journal 29, 30 Nov 43.

Action With the French Expeditionary Corps

The capture of the heights of Mount Sammucro, to the northwest, and of Mount Lungo, to the southeast, made San Pietro untenable for the Germans. The 36th Division occupied the destroyed and deserted village on 17 December. There remained the third phase of the Fifth Army attack on the Winter Line, a II Corps drive to the Rapido, accompanied by a similar move through the mountains to the river by the French Expeditionary Corps (FEC) on the north. The fighting here provided a unique attachment for the 3d Chemical Mortar Battalion. The FEC, composed of a Moroccan and an Algerian division, replaced the VI U.S. Corps early in January 1944 when the corps withdrew from the right sector of Fifth Army to prepare for the impending Anzio operation. The 3d Chemical Mortar Battalion joined the FEC in an attachment which, with brief exceptions, lasted until June 1944. Preparatory to this attachment Fifth Army screened the four mortar battalions in Italy for French-speaking personnel, assigning those who qualified to the 3d Battalion. The mortar unit carried out its assignment well, being only mildly affected by the difficulties of adjusting to the operational procedures of the French.[92] Its troubles came from another quarter.

On 12 January the French Expeditionary Corps began a 3-day attack which successfully carried it through the northeastern vestiges of the Winter Line. Initially, Company B supported a regiment of the 2d Moroccan Division. During the course of the morning's firing a shell exploded in a mortar barrel, killing one of the crew and wounding three others. As it turned out, this was but a prelude for worse things to come. The command post of Company C, 3d Battalion, was located in the town of Cerasuolo, a focal point for action in that particular sector. Colonel Stark, the battalion commander, was at this command post to insure the necessary close mortar support and to co-ordinate the fire of Companies C and D. At 1430 12 January Colonel Stark held an impromptu conference, attended by two company commanders, two acting company commanders, and a company executive officer. Eighteen minutes after these officers assembled enemy aircraft bombed the town. The command post sustained at least one direct hit. All the attending officers and seven enlisted men died instantly. Despite the virtual elimination of the command element of the battalion, prompt

[92] 3d Cml Bn Journal, Dec 43, Jun 44.

reorganization permitted the unit to continue its mission, in fact, Company C fired 157 rounds within two hours of the bombardment. The next day, however, the battalion reverted to Army control and went to a rest area near Naples.[93]

The Gustav Line

While defending the Winter Line the enemy had been working furiously on his positions behind the Rapido and Garigliano Rivers. Known as the Gustav Line, these defenses extended from Mount Marrone on the northeast, through the mountains to Belvedere Hill, and south to Cassino. The line then followed the Rapido and Garigliano Rivers across the Liri Valley and continued along a formidable mountain barrier curving back to its terminus, Mount Scouri, on the Tyrrhenian Sea. The mountains on both ends of the Gustav Line, tremendous obstacles in themselves, were supplemented by well-emplaced weapons and mine fields. The center of the line, although lacking natural impediments, was a skilfully organized defense of mine fields and wire, pillboxes, and automatic weapon emplacements, all of which were covered by enemy artillery farther up the valley. The Fifth Army History succinctly summarizes the strength of the position: "The area of the Gustav Line had long provided the Italian General Staff with ideal terrain for field exercises. In these problems forces representing the enemy had never been able to penetrate the defense. The Italians considered the area as an impregnable obstacle to any army attempting to capture Rome from the south. The Germans were determined to prove the validity of that assumption." [94]

On 15 January the enemy line before II Corps extended from Belvedere Hill along the right bank of the Rapido and Garigliano Rivers to the junction of the Liri and the Garigliano. Highway 6, the road to Rome, passed through the level terrain in the center of the corps sector, exposed as far back as Mount Lungo to observed artillery fire from enemy positions on the mountain heights in back of Cassino.[95] The 2d Chemical Battalion used smoke pots to conceal this vulnerable area

---

[93] 3d Cml Bn Opns Rpt, Jan 44.
[94] Fifth Army History, VI, 7–8.
[95] See *Fifth Army at the Winter Line*, illustration on p. 66.

during the build-up for the II Corps attack across the Rapido, the initial American thrust against the Gustav Line.[96]

The Fifth Army plan for its drive on Rome consisted of two parts: a 3-corps attack against the Gustav Line followed a few days later by an amphibious maneuver south of Rome and in back of the Gustav Line defenses—the SHINGLE operation at Anzio. Army planners hoped that the pressure on the main German position, combined with the threat to his rear, would force the enemy into a general withdrawal.

The assault on the Gustav Line began on 17 January when the British 10 Corps attacked across the Rapido. Successful on the left and in the center, the British forces were unable to win their objective on the right. So it was that when II Corps attacked three days later, it did so with an exposed left flank. South of Cassino the Rapido is a narrow, swift-moving stream varying in depth from nine to twelve feet. Sant'Angelo, the objective of the 36th Division, the assault force of II Corps, stands on a 40-foot bluff above the west bank of the river. The 141st Infantry, supported by Company A of the 2d Chemical Battalion, was ordered to cross the Rapido north of the town and then attack south and west. Companies B and C of the mortar battalion fired for the 143d Infantry which was to cross the river south of the town and then, after reaching initial objectives, assist the 141st in the seizure of Sant'Angelo. Company D, assigned to a regiment of the 34th Division, was located in a position from which it could support the 141st Infantry.

The night of 20 January was one of pandemonium. Attacking at 2000 without surprise through mine fields and the fire of artillery, mortars and automatic weapons, both regiments encountered terrific resistance. All four mortar companies fired barrages just before or immediately after the time of attack. One half hour before the assault, Company A used 400 rounds of white phosphorus to lay down a smoke screen which, in the total absence of wind, rose to a height of 150 feet. Between 2030 and 2100 Company C placed 119 rounds of WP on enemy positions. Next day Company A laid down smoke screens for the men of the 141st who had been stranded on the far bank of the Rapido while Company C fired 204 rounds of WP to cover the withdrawal of elements of the 143d Infantry which had been given up for

---

[96] For an account of these screening activities by the 2d Battalion, see above, Chapter VIII.

lost on the previous night. That afternoon, on the resumption of the attack, further 4.2-inch mortar fire supported the infantry units.[97]

One of Company C's forward observers participated in this action as a member of the command post party of the 1st Battalion, 143d Infantry. Meeting with heavy German rocket and automatic weapons fire on the near side of the river, the battalion commander ordered a barrage of 4.2-inch white phosphorus. At midnight the small party crossed the Rapido. The battalion commander was wounded, and the lieutenant who took charge ordered the men to dig in for the night. At dawn he went in search of the missing infantry Companies A and B and upon his return announced that they were the only ones remaining. With the radio out, the small group made its way back across the Rapido under cover of fog. It was a thorough defeat; the regimental commander reported that the combat efficiency of his unit was destroyed.[98]

The situation was just as bad with the 141st Infantry. Mortar Company A fired smoke missions on 21 and 22 January to screen two infantry battalions on the far side of the river. Next day the company expended 441 rounds of WP on a screen to cover the withdrawal of some forty men of the 141st Infantry. The abortive attack had been costly.[99]

Unfortunately, the smoke screen mission fired for the men stranded on the far bank of the Rapido seriously interfered with the observation of the corps artillery. With communications out and with infantry positions unknown, effective artillery support was impossible.[100] There were also misunderstandings regarding the use of smoke. In a 23 January conference between the 36th Division chemical officer and Capt. James O. Quimby, Jr., commanding Company A, 2d Chemical Battalion, the former commented on the density of enemy smoke at the site of the bridgehead. Quimby had to explain that this was his smoke, not German, a fact unknown to division as well as corps.[101]

A 24 January mission of Company C demonstrated that some commanders receiving support continued to be unfamiliar with the cap-

---

[97] (1) 2d Cml Bn Journal, 15–20 Jan 44.   (2) Co C 2d Cml Bn Unit Diary, 20–21 Jan 44.   (3) Co A 2d Cml Bn Unit Diary, 21 Jan 44.
[98] (1) Co C 2d Cml Mortar Bn Unit Diary, 21 Jan 44.   (2) 143d Inf Opns Rpt, Jan 44.
[99] (1) Co A 2d Cml Bn Rcd of Events, 22 Jan 44.   (2) 141st Inf Opns Rpt, Jan 44.
[100] Fifth Army History, IV, 47.
[101] Statement, Maj James O. Quimby, Jr., to CMLHO, 17 May 50.

abilities of the chemical mortar. The infantry battalion commander, for example, called for smoke to screen a patrol which was about to feel out enemy defenses and search for American wounded. Several times during the course of this mission he called for target changes requiring gun re-emplacements and once he wanted it without cessation of fire. The commander also requested an increase in the rate of fire at a time when mortarmen were already firing twenty-one rounds per mortar per minute. When the smoke ascended directly into the air, he called upon the mortar commander to rectify the situation. In the words of the custodian of the company diary: "We are still wondering if he wanted us to come down and blow on it." [102] Reactions to this impromptu mission were mixed. The captain with the infantry patrol, which brought back two wounded American soldiers, praised Company C for the effective screen. On the other hand, II Corps immediately informed the mortar company that no more smoke was to be fired without its approval.[103]

The Anzio Beachhead

Fifth Army launched the second phase of its winter offensive on 22 January on the beaches near Anzio and Nettuno, seaside resort towns located barely thirty air miles south of Rome. The objective of VI Corps was to cut the historic roadway known as the Appian Way and Highway 7, as well as other German supply routes. With these severed, the enemy in the Gustav Line would be left to choose between extermination and withdrawal. Two mortar battalions saw action at Anzio, the 83d, initially in support of Colonel Darby's Ranger forces, and the 84th, which landed late on D-day with the 3d Infantry Division.

The 83d had undergone a month of training in preparation for the assault. Companies A and B, loaded in Dukws, went in with the second wave but received no calls for fire until H plus 6 because of the achievement of complete surprise. An enemy 88-mm. gun which had been shelling the beach supplied the mortars with their first target. In firing on this gun at a range of 2,000 yards and forcing it to withdraw, Company B provided an excellent example of its usefulness at times when the artillery had not yet come into position.[104] That the mortars

---

[102] Co C 2d Cml Bn Unit Diary, 24 Jan 44.

[103] Ibid.

[104] (1) 83d Cml Bn Opns Rpt, Jan 44.   (2) Hutchinson Interv, 26 Jan 45.

did not need specific targets to be effective was well illustrated at Anzio by the tactics of the Ranger commander. Colonel Darby, who had received mortar support both on Sicily and at Salerno, met the first elements of the 83d Battalion with orders to set up weapons and start firing in the general direction of the Germans. His logic was: "I want the bastards to know I have something heavy, so they will start digging in. That will give me a chance to maneuver." [105]

On the morning of D plus 1 Company B moved into position 2,000 yards north of Anzio to support the advance of the Rangers, while in the afternoon Company A advanced to a position 10,000 yards north of the town on the east side of the Anzio-Rome highway. From 24 to 28 January these companies fired on wooded areas and troop concentrations, on roads and rail junctions, and on houses and haystacks in support of Ranger attacks on Carocetta and Aprillo. Bedeviled by excessive mortar breakage from emplacements in the spongy ground, Lt. Col. William S. Hutchinson, Jr., commanding the 83d, ruefully concluded that the 4.2-inch mortar was far better suited to mountain fighting than for operations "in the mucky, ill-drained soil of the Anzio beachhead." [106]

Although it landed on D-day, the 84th Chemical Battalion did not undertake its first missions until three days later, 25 January, when Company A, with its mortars emplaced on an abandoned railway bed, fired 100 rounds against houses, haystacks, roads, and ditches, all places that were suspected of concealing Germans. Two days later the same unit expended 750 rounds of ammunition, hindered all the while by excessive mortar breakage.[107]

Meanwhile, on 26 January Companies C and D met with tragedy. While en route from Naples to the beachhead the LST carrying these units struck a mine and caught fire. The explosion of mortar ammunition magnified the danger. Many of the survivors who escaped this small hell were picked up by an LCI (landing craft, infantry) which in turn hit a mine and went down with all on board. The two companies lost a total of 293 officers and enlisted men; the survivors were taken to a rest camp near Naples.[108] Augmented, reorganized, and retrained,

---

[105] Cml Warfare School Tng Memo No. 6, 31 Oct 44.
[106] 83d Cml Bn Opns Rpt, Jan 44.
[107] 84th Cml Bn Field Journal, 25, 27 Jan 44.
[108] 83d Cml Bn Unit Journal, 31 Jan 44.

these units were to see some combat action with the 88th Division near Minturno before joining the parent battalion at Anzio in mid-April.

One of the objectives of the 30 January drive by VI Corps toward the Alban Hills was cutting Highway 7 at the point where it passes through Cisterna. The 1st and 3d Ranger Battalions set off toward the town at 0100, an hour before the main effort, which would be made by the 4th Ranger Battalion and elements of the 3d Infantry Division. Companies A and B, 83d Chemical Battalion, were in support of the Ranger battalions. Creeping along a ditch which led to Cisterna, the Rangers reached the outskirts of town by dawn. There they fell into an enemy ambush. The units making the main effort failed to advance sufficiently to be of any aid to the embattled Ranger forces. Company B placed mortar fire on the encircling Germans in a vain attempt to cover a withdrawal. Only six Rangers made it back.[109]

Not only did the VI Corps attack fail but it was soon clear that a German counterattack was imminent. From 1 February until the eventual breakout in May, the corps mission was essentially defensive. Both mortar battalions were called upon for heavy fire against enemy attacks and were subjected to frequent enemy artillery and mortar shelling and air bombardment. Because of excellent German observation of the beachhead and all routes leading to Allied positions, there was a great demand for smoke screens laid by mortars, pots, and generators.[110]

During the period of containment at Anzio it was usual for three mortar companies to stay in the line, while one remained in reserve near battalion headquarters. Unlike the situation near Venafro and San Pietro on the southern front, rear areas at Anzio were well within the range of enemy artillery. Reports were that some men preferred their emplacements to the battalion areas on the beaches. Nevertheless, rotation did give the men a change of scene and diet and also allowed commanders to inspect equipment and to supervise the integration of replacements.

From the time of the landing until 20 May the 84th Battalion fired 50,166 rounds (8,019 WP) of ammunition; the 83d from February

[109] (1) Company A supported the 4th Ranger Battalion on 30 January in its attempt to relieve its sister units at Cisterna. (2) Rounds Away!—The Story of the 83d Cml Bn, pp 8–9. CWS 314.7 Unit Files. (3) Hutchinson Interv, 26 Jan 45. (4) CmlO Fifth Army Rpt of Cml Warfare Activities, 8 Jan–21 Jan 44.

[110] See above, Chapter VIII, for smoke generator operations at Anzio.

until 20 May expended 14,326 rounds (4,716 WP). Casualties for the two battalions in the Anzio beachhead were 30 dead and 87 wounded.[111]

Cassino

With the failure of the 36th Division attack across the Rapido, General Clark directed II Corps to shift to the north, with the town of Cassino, Monte Cassino, and the eventual drive into the Liri Valley as its objectives. By 1 February the 34th Division, which was to serve as the main striking force, had established a bridgehead across the Rapido near the town of Cairo, about two miles north of Cassino.

The town of Cassino lies on Highway 6 at the foot of the main mountain barriers to the Allied advance through the Liri Valley. Rising behind Cassino is Castle Hill, an elevation of some 633 feet. Overshadowing both is Monte Cassino upon which stands the historic monastery. Together they offered the enemy excellent observation of the movements of the Allied army in its attempt to break into the Liri Valley. A few miles north of Cassino were the towns of Cairo and Villa, the latter being the site of a group of Italian barracks which at different times in the tug of war which followed were to shelter both German and American forces. Four miles northeast of Monte Cassino massive Mount Cairo towers 5,500 feet above sea level. This small area to the north and west of Cassino was to be the scene of some of the bitterest battles fought during the Italian campaign, for it was here that the German forces battled to protect Monte Cassino and the entrance to the Liri Valley.[112]

Commanded now by Maj. James R. Chapman, the 2d Chemical Battalion supported the 34th Division in the February attacks against the Cassino defenses. On 1 February Company D fired ninety-seven rounds of WP before a successful infantry assault on the barracks area at Villa. But next day the lack of communications and the absence of adequate observation precluded mortar support for men of the 135th Infantry as they worked their way southward along a ridge line. This situation repeated itself during the period 4–6 February in the bitter engagement on the headland and plateau north of the abbey. In three days of costly fighting the infantry won Hill 593 (Abaneta Farm)

---

[111] (1) 84th Cml Bn Opns Rpt, Jan–May 44.   (2) 83d Cml Bn Opns Rpt, Feb–May 44.
[112] Fred Majdalany, *The Battle of Cassino* (Boston: Houghton Mifflin Co., 1957), gives a graphic account of this action.

which dominates the approaches to the abbey but the fluid, even confused, situation dictated that there could be little or no mortar support. In further attacks toward the abbey on 8 February Companies B and D did fire 840 rounds in casualty and screening missions. On the same day Company A used limited amounts of WP to screen the advance of supporting tanks, a mission abruptly halted when the smoke spread over infantry positions on the flats near the river.[113] On 11 February, in rain, sleet, and snow, the troops of II Corps made another effort to take Monte Cassino. Companies B, C, and D, hampered by the weather and disrupted communications, supported individual regiments of the 34th and 36th Divisions. Fighting in the craggy terrain before the abbey was at such close quarters that Company C received no calls from the regiment it supported. The other two mortar companies fired less than 100 rounds each.[114]

Mid-February saw British, New Zealand, and Indian troops committed to the fighting around Monte Cassino. Allied bombers struck the famous abbey on 15 February in an operation conspicious for its lack of positive results. In fact, Allied troops moved back from the hard-won Hill 593 just before the bombardment, and it was the German forces that reoccupied the position when the air strike was over. It took three days for British and Gurkha troops to retake the hill, during which time the British requested and received support from Company C, 2d Chemical Battalion. The mortar unit delivered a 20-minute barrage of 246 rounds against a row of trees near the abbey among which the enemy had emplaced a number of machine guns. After completion of this mission the commanding officer of the 141st Infantry, to which the mortar company was attached, telephoned his congratulations and those of the British to the mortarmen of Company C. This gesture, as well as expression of thanks upon the relief of Company C on 27 February, was particularly gratifying for the mortarmen since this same infantry officer had previously announced, when a short mortar round fell within fifty yards of his command post, that he would never again request a mission from a chemical mortar unit.[115]

During the last days in February all of the weapons companies of

[113] (1) 2d Cml Bn Opns Rpts, 1, 2, 4, 5, 6 Feb 44.   (2) 135th Inf Opns Rpt, 2 Feb 44.   (3) 2d Cml Bn S-3 Journal, 8 Feb 44.   (4) Co A 2d Cml Bn Rcd of Events, 8 Feb 44.   (5) 133d Inf Opns Rpt, Feb 44.
[114] (1) Co C 2d Cml Bn Unit Diary, 10 Feb 44.   (2) 2d Cml Bn Opns Rpt, 11 Feb 44.
[115] (1) Co C 2d Cml Bn Unit Diary, 14, 18, 20 Feb 44.   (2) Co C 2d Cml Bn Rcd of Events, 17, 18, 27 Feb 44.

the 2d Chemical Battalion reverted to the control of the parent unit. One hundred and seventy consecutive days in the line had been culminated by the difficult fighting at Cassino, the roughest time experienced by the battalion to date. The Germans were not the only enemy; the terrain, the weather, the lack of shelter, and the limited supply of suitable clothing combined to make life miserable.[116]

Small satisfaction was gained at Cassino from the over-all contribution of the mortars. There were times when disrupted communications and the fluid nature of the fighting meant that the chemical companies could offer only limited support.

The Drive on Rome

During March and April 1944 the Allied forces in Italy paused, trained, refitted, and regrouped in preparation for another assault against the Gustav Line defenses. A greatly contracted Fifth Army held a narrow sector from the Tyrrhenian coast to the Liri River; II Corps, composed of the recently arrived 85th and 88th Divisions, was on the left and the French Expeditionary Corps was on the right. The sector of the British Eighth Army now extended from the Liri River to the Adriatic, including the strong German defenses which centered at Monte Cassino.

The 2d and 3d Chemical Battalions maintained their attachments to the II Corps and the FEC. After leaving the lines at Cassino in late February, the 2d Battalion passed into II Corps reserve for a period of rest, training, and repair and replacement of equipment. On 13 March Company D joined the 88th Division in its quiet zone near Minturno for a 2-week attachment that served to familiarize the new unit with the 4.2-inch mortar and its capabilities. During April the entire battalion, again in corps reserve, underwent a vigorous training program. Elements of the 3d Battalion participated in smoking operations on the upper Garigliano in the FEC sector. Abetted by a detail from the 172d Smoke Generator Company, successive companies of the mortar battalion maintained an extensive smoke installation in the vicinity of the Tiger Bridge across the Garigliano.[117]

On the eve of Fifth Army's 11 May attack on the Gustav Line 3d Battalion communication equipment was augmented by the issue of

---

[116] *History of Second Mortar Battallion* (Salzburg, Austria, n.d.) p. 24. CMLHO.
[117] 3d Cml Bn Opns Rpts, 30 Apr 1–13 May 44.

sixteen SCR–300's. The successful use of this radio prompted the battalion commander to regard it as the only set which might tend to reduce the telephone to the rank of a secondary means of communication in battle. The exchange just before the attack of 10 2½-ton trucks for 32 jeeps and 48 ¼-ton trailers increased the mobility of the mortar battalion and its ability to get ammunition forward.

The 3d Battalion fired 7,000 rounds of ammunition in twelve hours of preparatory fire. Each of the four companies supported a French division, three of them by direct attachment to the infantry and the fourth through the control of division artillery. The latter company did the least firing, primarily because of delays encountered in securing firing data, a circumstance which prompted the battalion commander to recommend strongly that this company also be placed under infantry control.[118] The enemy lines broke by the middle of the second day, and mortar support decreased. By 27 May the pursuit became so rapid that the battalion was placed in corps reserve and remained there until relieved from attachment to the FEC on 11 June.

The 2d Chemical Battalion went into action on the Minturno front on 11 May in support of II Corps' 85th and 88th Divisions. After expending more than 10,000 rounds in a 7-hour preparation, the battalion fired missions for the two divisions as the situation required.[119] For example, the initial objective of the 339th Infantry, 85th Division, was San Martino Hill which had an importance all out of proportion to its modest height of 200 feet because it dominated an important enemy supply route. Within a 15-minute period late on 11 May the battalion fired 1,267 rounds against this objective.[120] The fight for San Martino Hill lasted several days. On 13 May all four mortar companies fired high-explosive and smoke missions in support of the attacking infantry. The hill fell next day, and II Corps placed the 2d Battalion in support of the 88th Division attacking Santa Maria Infante. In this engagement the mortars made good use of smoke to blind enemy observation from nearby Pulcherini. In fact, WP made up about one-third of the 13,575 rounds fired by the battalion between 11 and 14 May. Generalfeldmarschall Albert Kesselring, the German commander in Italy, commented on the effectiveness of these American screens. Be-

---

[118] Hist of 3d Cml Bn, May 44.

[119] Col. Maurice E. Barker, "Mortars Are the Man-Killers," *Chemical Warfare Bulletin*, vol. 30, No. 4 (August, September, October, 1944).

[120] 2d Cml Bn Opns Rpt, May 44.

cause of the extensive use of smoke along the Garigliano, he wrote, German artillery had to fire on American river crossings "without the least observation." [121]

The May experiences of Company A may be taken as typical of those of the entire 2d Chemical Battalion once Allied forces breached the Gustav Line defenses. On the 14th the company moved forward by jeep with a regiment of the 88th Division, firing 191 rounds of white phosphorus in midafternoon. Two days later the company used a pack mule train to move overland with the infantry; even then it took overnight marches to keep up with the assault battalions. During the period 21–22 May Company A fired 165 rounds against enemy troops. There were more marches, more difficult terrain to traverse, more changes in position and attachment. All in all, events and units moved so swiftly that there could be little employment of the 4.2-inch mortars.[122]

Fifth Army co-ordinated the VI Corps breakout of the beachhead at Anzio with the southern front's attack on the Gustav Line. Companies A and B, 83d Chemical Battalion, supported the 1st Armored Division and Companies C and D, the 45th Infantry Division. All four companies fired mass concentrations in support of the initial attack, those with the 45th Division aiding greatly in the successful resistance to two German counterattacks. Once the breakthrough was achieved the mortar units supporting the armored division found they could keep pace only by frequent displacements. Consequently, corps placed these companies in support of the 36th Division, which had moved to Anzio by sea, for the drive that broke the German line at Velletri, twenty miles southeast of Rome.[123]

Meanwhile, the 84th Chemical Battalion on 23 May expended 3,081 rounds in support of 3d Division. After the initial breakthrough the 84th Battalion, as had the 83d, found it impossible to keep up with the infantry. The battalion commander blamed this on the large and unwieldly 2½-ton trucks and the scarcity of jeeps and trailers. Communications also broke down during the swift movement, for there was no time to lay wire and the SCR–284 proved unreliable. But

---

[121] Quoted in Fifth Army History, V, 204.

[122] Co A 2d Cml Bn Rcd of Events, May 44.

[123] (1) The Story of the 83d Cml Bn, pp. 10–11. (2) Lt. Col. William S. Hutchinson, "The Forgotten Front," vol. 31, No. 1 Chemical Warfare Bulletin (January, February, 1945). (3) Hutchinson Interv, 26 Jan 45.

these complications mattered little; the rapid retreat of the enemy meant that the mortars found little use. As the 83d Chemical Battalion commander summarized it: "The pursuit was so fast-moving and resistance so weak that the use of the 4.2-inch mortars was unwarranted." [124]

Both mortar battalions participated briefly in the pursuit beyond Rome before reverting to army control on 10 June. The 2d and 3d Battalions returned to army control a day later. After about a month's rest three of the battalions, the 2d, 3d, and 83d, went with VI Corps from the Fifth Army to the Seventh Army and began training for the invasion of southern France.[125]

The Invasion of Southern France

The three chemical mortar battalions which participated in the assault on the beaches of southern France were veteran units which had taken part in one or more amphibious landings in Sicily and Italy.[126] Consequently, preparations for DRAGOON for the most part consisted of perfecting teamwork with the infantry. The exceptions were Company A, 2d Chemical Battalion, and Company D, 83d Battalion, which were part of an airborne task force created especially for the operation. Activated in July, this force included American and British parachute and glider units.[127] The mortar companies received their assignment to the airborne task force on 11 July and moved to training sites at airfields in the vicinity of Rome. Here they trained in glider operations and prepared loading lists for personnel, equipment, and vehicles.[128]

Late on the afternoon of D-day, 15 August, the two airborne mortar companies landed in the vicinity of Leluc, France, with the glider units of the provisional airborne task force. None of the gliders was lost through enemy air or antiaircraft action but many were wrecked by the sawed-off utility poles—Goering asparagus—with which the Germans studded some of the most likely landing sites. One glider hit

---

[124] (1) 84th Cml Bn Opns Rpt, May 44.   (2) 83d Cml Bn Opns Rpt, Jun 44.

[125] (1) Hist of 3d Cml Bn, Jul 44, incl 5.   (2) Markham Interv, 16 Jan 45.

[126] For a detailed description of the invasion of southern France, see Smith, Riviera to the Rhine.

[127] Rpt of Opns, Seventh U.S. Army in France and Germany (hereafter cited as Rpt of Opns, Seventh Army), I, 110–11. Other supporting units were antitank, engineer, signal, and medical companies.

[128] CWS TofO Ltr No. 23, 3 Apr 45. This document includes the loading lists and tables of individual equipment.

with such impact that the jeep load in its nose catapulted through the front end of the aircraft, seriously injuring the three men sitting in the vehicle.

Elements of Company A, landing between 1845 and 1900, had assembled at their predesignated area by 2130 and were prepared to fire on the town of Le Muy. Next morning the company fired 200 rounds of HE on the town and 48 rounds of WP on its southern exits. Le Muy fell by midafternoon. Later that day the airborne troops made contact with reconnaissance elements of the 45th Division. After this junction the mortar companies remained attached to the task force as it pushed to the French-Italian border, being relieved from this attachment on 17 September at Nice, France.[129]

The gliders of Company D, 83d Chemical Battalion, were released over the drop zone near Le Muy at seven minutes after seven on the morning of D-day. Fourteen mortarmen received light injuries during the landings. The company did not fire on that first day but expended 650 rounds in support of the 517th Infantry on 16 August. The mortar unit remained in support of this unit until the end of the month doing relatively little firing in the drive to the Italian border.[130]

A mortar company accustomed to normal attachments encountered problems in adapting itself to glider operations. Techniques of loading and securing equipment had to be formulated and mastered. Men and equipment had to be distributed in such a way as to allocate weight equally among the several gliders. Moreover, it was necessary to allocate the material so that the loss of one glider would not destroy all the equipment of the same type. The exigencies of glider operations caused a number of changes in the normal organization and equipment of a mortar company based mostly on the fact that a company, landing by gliders, often had to operate as an independent unit until such time as contact could be made with other elements. Because of this fact medical aidmen joined each mortar platoon and automatic weapons were added to provide means for independent defense. In the table of equipment for an airborne mortar company drawn up after DRAGOON by Capt. Raymond J. Lakey of the 83d Battalion, the responsibility for unit security accounted for all additions to the complement of weapons. Captain Lakey recommended that 4 light machine guns, 8

---

[129] (1) Rpt of Opns, Seventh Army, I, 110–14. (2) CWS TofO Ltr No. 23, 3 Apr 45. (3) Co A 2d Cml Bn Rcd of Events.
[130] 83d Bn Rpt of Action, Aug 44.

BAR's, 16 tommy guns, and 18 .45-caliber pistols be added to the arsenal of an airborne company. And whereas the table of equipment of a motorized company called for 5 bazookas, 7 should be carried by a glider-borne company.[131]

Since the assault operation against the beaches of southern France met only light opposition, the mortar battalions found they had relatively few missions to fire as they accompanied their divisions to the west and north.[132] Because fire was not needed in such a rapid advance, some of the units were given jobs involving supply. A company of the 83d Battalion established and operated a railhead to St. Maximin in order to ease the serious logistical problems of the 45th Division. And at one time companies of the 2d Battalion hauled supplies for the 36th Division.[133] For the 3d Battalion August was a period of long, fast movements with little fighting. The low rate of ammunition expenditure mitigated the shell supply problem which otherwise would have been acute since army supply dumps were frequently 100 miles to the rear.[134]

These mortar battalions continued to support the troops of the Seventh Army as they fought to the north and northeast—the Vosges, Belfort, Bitche, Colmar were familiar names to the mortarmen. Some mortar units fired for divisions of the 1st French Army which, with the U.S. Seventh, made up Lt. Gen. Jacob L. Dever's 6th Army Group. Offensive action came to a temporary halt in mid-December 1944 when the Germans launched their Ardennes counteroffensive.[135]

The Fighting Ends in Italy

The departure of the 2d, 3d, and 83d Chemical Mortar Battalion for southern France left only the 84th in support of the divisions of Fifth Army from July until the end of October 1944. This unit found itself scattered along the entire army front.[136] In an effort to make up for this lost support the theater in June 1944 converted two antiaircraft

---

[131] Capt Raymond J. Lakey, Rpt on 4.2-Inch Mortar Airborne Company, pt. II, 15 Oct 44. CmlC School Lib.

[132] For an account of mortar battalion participation in the D-day screening, see above, Chapter VIII.

[133] (1) *Rounds Away: Two Years of Combat with Eighty-Third Chemical Mortar Battalion* (Innsbruck, 1945), pp. 41–42. (2) History of Second Chemical Mortar Battalion, pp. 33–34.

[134] 3d Cml Bn Rpt of Opns, Aug 44.

[135] See below, Chapter XII, for details on the German counteroffensive.

[136] Ltr, CCmlO NATOUSA to CCWS, 26 Oct 44. CWS 314.7 Personal Ltr files, NATOUSA.

artillery automatic weapons units to the 99th and 100th Chemical Mortar Battalions. After completing a period of intensive training under the direction of Colonel Hutchinson, a former commander of the 83rd, the 99th, commanded by Lt. Col. Gordon A. Dixon, left for France and the 100th, commanded by Lt. Col. Russell E. McMurray, joined Fifth Army in Italy.[137]

July had seen the 84th reorganize under the long ignored tables of organization and equipment of September 1943, a move which reduced the number of officers and enlisted men of a mortar battalion from 1,010 to 622. The new tables also cut the number of $2\frac{1}{2}$-ton trucks and increased the number of $\frac{1}{4}$-ton trucks (jeeps) assigned to a battalion. The long delay between the publication of the tables and actual reorganization was the result of several factors. For one thing, mortar battalions in Italy had scant time away from the front line to put the required changes into effect. Moreover, for a long while there were not enough jeeps to make the substitution in vehicles. Finally, mortar commanders feared that because of the cut in personnel their units would find it impossible to operate efficiently if reorganization took place.[138]

While the Italian campaign was in progress the War Department drew up still another TOE based upon the recommendations received from battle-experienced CWS officers.[139] The salient feature of this revision was the elimination of one weapons company, a move which placed the battalion on the triangular basis characteristic of the infantry division.[140] The new organization became effective in September 1944, and two months later the 84th and 100th Battalions reorganized accordingly.[141]

After his rapid retreat above Rome, the enemy defended positions north of the Arno River, called the Gothic Line, which were not

---

[137] (1) *Ibid.*   (2) 100th Cml Bn Opns Rpts, Jul–Nov 44.

[138] (1) Hist of 3d Cml Bn, Jun 44, p. 44.   (2) Markham Interv, 16 Jan 45.   (3) See Opnl History of Cml Bns and the 4.2-inch Mortar in World War II, pt. II, The Italian Campaign, pp. 101–19.   (4) The fighting in Italy had altered mortar commanders' views as to the desirability of the $\frac{1}{4}$-ton truck. Too much had been expected of these vehicles. The $2\frac{1}{2}$-ton trucks were still needed to haul ammunition from army supply points to the mortar battalion dumps and on to company dumps. Earlier thoughts on transportation had been conditioned by the experience of the fast-moving Sicilian campaign; operations in Italy, characterized by slow movements and static situations, brought about the change. Opnl History of Cml Bns and the 4.2–inch Mortar in World War II, p. II, Italian Campaign, p. 106.

[139] Ltr, ACCWS for Field Opns to CCmlO NATOUSA, 12 Feb 44.

[140] Other features of this TOE are discussed in Chapter XII, below.

[141] CWS TofO Ltr No. 21, 31 Jan 45, p. 35.

breached by Allied forces until late September 1944. During that month the 84th Battalion expended about 6,500 rounds of ammunition, over half of which was white phosphorus. New infantry divisions, unfamiliar with the mortars and particularly their high-explosive mission, seemed to make more frequent calls for smoke. Each of the four companies of the 84th supported a different division of II Corps, which was fighting its way northward through the mountains. Despite transportation difficulties, the 84th gave heavy support during October, firing some 16,000 rounds (5,000 HE), mainly against enemy counterattacks and emplacements and also as a screen for American positions and supply routes.[142] On 31 October the 84th Chemical Battalion passed into Fifth Army reserve to be replaced by the 100th Battalion, companies of which supported, at one time or another, each of the infantry divisions of II Corps.[143]

In January 1945 Fifth Army received reports of the hardships encountered in other theaters and in the United States with the fuzes for the M3 4.2-inch mortar ammunition which, unfortunately, made up the bulk of 4.2-inch ammunition in the theater. Nonetheless, during February the 84th and 100th Battalions used over 11,000 rounds of the suspected ammunition without particular difficulty. On 9 March a shell burst three feet from the barrel of one mortar, killing one man and wounding four others. Thereafter, mortar crews used lanyards to fire suspected ammunition, a precaution which at first reduced the efficiency of mortar crews.[144]

From the conclusion of the Gothic Line fighting in the fall of 1944 until the spring of 1945 Fifth Army troops remained in relatively the same positions. April saw an army offensive which cracked German defenses in a matter of a week. The 84th and 100th Battalions supported the IV and II Corps, respectively, in this operation until the infantry advance was too swift for effective support. It was at this time that 4.2-inch mortar operations in the Mediterranean theater came to an end.[145]

[142] 84th Cml Bn Opns Rpts, Sep, Oct 44.

[143] 100th Cml Bn Opns (for Nov 44), 5 Dec 44.

[144] (1) 84th Cml Mortar Bn Opns Rpt, Feb, Mar 45. (2) 100th Cml Mortar Bn Opns Rpts, Feb 45. (3) 84th Cml Mortar Bn Field Journal, 9 Mar 45. (4) Fifth Army Cml Sec, Cml Warfare Activities, 11–17 Mar 45.

[145] (1) 84th Cml Mortar Bn Opns Rpt, Apr 45. (2) 100th Cml Mortar Bn Opns Rpt, Apr 45.

Fighting in Italy was as bitter and the enemy defenses as stubborn as any experienced by American forces in World War II. The mountainous Italian terrain, with its abundance of defiladed positions inaccessible to artillery fire, placed a heavy demand on high trajectory weapons, particularly the 4.2-inch mortar. In addition, 4.2-inch mortar units were indispensable to Ranger and Commando units which lacked organic heavy weapons. Most infantry commanders were at first unaware of the potential of the 4.2-inch mortar, but once they had seen the weapon in action they were usually anxious for mortar support. In Italy the chemical mortar truly came of age.

CHAPTER XII

The Chemical Mortar in the ETO

Getting chemical mortar battalions for the European Theater of Operations, U.S. Army, proved to be a complicated and difficult problem. Colonel Rowan, chief chemical officer in the theater, had recommended a total of 24 battalions for the theater troop list, a figure based upon the formula of 2 battalions per corps (18) and 2 additional battalions per army (6). His commander approved this recommendation, including the figure in the over-all troop list, which was forwarded to Washington early in 1943.[1]

The War Department took no action on the troop basis recommended by the theater commander. In November 1943 it sent an officer to England to inform the theater commander on War Department troop basis policy—the establishment of an over-all theater personnel ceiling within which the theater commander could set up his own troop basis. The officer produced a list of those units which were immediately available, those which were in training, and those which were scheduled for activation. He stated that the theater commander could take his pick, staying, of course, within his over-all ceiling. Because the list admittedly had no relation to the one submitted by the ETO, a situation which negated a large amount of detailed theater planning, the War Department agreed to activate and train units not on the list, with the understanding that this would take additional time. Unfortunately, there were only seven chemical mortar battalions on the list.

Lt. Gen. Omar N. Bradley, commander of the U.S. army group in the theater, received the job of determining the final troop list. Rowan pointed out to General Bradley that the seven chemical mortar battalions bore no logical numerical relation to the number of armies and corps on the list, that they could not be distributed equitably,

---

[1] (1) Ltr, ACCWS for Field Opns to CCmlO ETOUSA, 16 Nov 43. (2) Ltr, Rowan to Hist Off, 3 Dec 51. CWS 314.7.

and that they were far too few to achieve their full potential. Rowan then asked Bradley for the twenty-four mortar battalions of the original troop list. Bradley replied that he would like to have more mortar units but, because the troop ceiling had just about been reached, adding them would mean giving up other units that were equally valuable. This he was reluctant to do.

At the time of these negotiations the only mortar battalion located in the European theater was the 81st. Attempts to secure one of the four combat-experienced units from the North Africa Theater of Operations were turned down as "impossible and impracticable"; the mortar battalions in Italy already were overworked. Colonel Shadle, chief chemical officer of that theater, stated that the battalions were so highly regarded that "the sticking of my fingers into this question would be practically the same as putting them in a 'bandsaw'." [2]

A change in the table of organization for the mortar battalion promised an unexpected source of men. Under the existing table the authorized strength was 1,010; a revised table of September 1943 reduced this number to 622.[3] Colonel Rowan was informed that the battalions in the United States were organized under the older table. Taking into consideration the battalions then existing and those which could be formed from the men excess by reorganization under the new table, Colonel Rowan came up with a total of eleven potentially available battalions. If General Bradley asked for but one battalion in addition to the War Department troop list, there would be enough to equal just half of the original request, or one per corps and army. General Bradley acceded, requesting twelve mortar battalions for the theater troop list.

Although it began auspiciously, the plan for capitalizing on battalion reorganization as a source for new units soon turned sour. The theater received permission in December to activate a mortar battalion in England manned in large part by the men freed in the reorganization of the 81st Battalion.[4] But Rowan learned to his dismay that the battalions in the United States earmarked for his theater had already been reorganized under the new table of organization, thus cutting off an important supply of personnel.

With only two battalions in England as late as February 1944 the

---

[2] Ltr, CCmlO NATO to ACCWS for Field Opns, 2 Dec 43.
[3] See above, ch. XI.
[4] (1) CM–IN 7606, 12 Dec 43.   (2) CM–OUT 7110 16 Dec 43.

shortage of such units became critical. Although the troop basis for the ETO now included 12 battalions, only 7 were listed as available in 1944. What was worse, only 4 of these would be in the theater in time for the Normandy landings—the 81st, the 92d, activated in England, and the 86th and 87th, both of which arrived in April.[5]

Preparations for OVERLORD

Of these four battalions the 92d was least prepared for combat operations in France. The other three units concentrated on amphibious training in the winter and spring of 1944, having undergone basic and unit training in the United States. The 92d, activated in England in February 1944, had to start from scratch.[6]

From the beginning the training activities of the battalion were hampered by the type of men it received. Of the first 373 assigned to the unit, 308 were of average intelligence or less. Fifty-six had AWOL records, 22 had been court-martialed for other offenses, and 12 had had VD. About 15 of the group were suffering from some disability or were on limited service; 13 others went immediately to the hospital. Throughout its period of activation the 92d usually received those men declared surplus by other units.[7]

The battalion devoted the last two weeks of February to making its camp at least partially fit for human habitation. The first part of March saw the enlisted men screened for a selection of potential NCO material and subjected to a review of all basic subjects. Small arms instruction, mortar drill, and the training of 162 drivers followed. By the end of March companies had been organized, squads knew something about their mortars, and the battalion was able to pack and move with some degree of order. Training intensified in April, with special emphasis on field work and marksmanship. Morale reached its lowest point at this time; few realized that the rigorous conditioning was necessary for their own survival. Work on mortar ranges began on 10 April and continued into May. The month of

[5] (1) Memo, MacArthur, CmlO FUSAG, for Brig Gen James E. Wharton, ACofS G-1 FUSAG, 25 Mar 44. (2) CM-OUT 1365 3 Feb 44.

[6] The only other mortar battalions activated overseas were the 99th and 100th, converted from antiaircraft artillery units in Italy, and the 98th converted from a tank destroyer battalion on New Guinea.

[7] Unless otherwise noted, the unit material in this chapter has been taken from the histories, journals, and after action reports of the several mortar battalions.

May also saw the battalion undergo a two-and-a-half-week period of intensive training while attached to a field artillery group. There was no time for amphibious training before the invasion, and as a consequence the 92d did not participate in the initial landings. Nor did the 86th Battalion receive assault training in time for D-day activity.

The 81st Battalion was the chemical unit most adequately prepared for the D-day operation. It had trained at the amphibious center at Camp Gordon Johnston, Fla., before leaving the United States. From December 1943 until the following April it participated in intensive exercises at the Assault Training Center in Devonshire and in other maneuvers along the western and southern coasts of England. The 87th Battalion was also well prepared for the invasion; thoroughly trained in the United States, it took part in two amphibious exercises in England that spring. The latter training had indicated that the increased problems in communications and supply in amphibious operations made greater demands on unit personnel. (Battalion commanders already were finding that the reduced complement of men in the new TOE was inadequate to keep forty-eight mortars in action even in normal operations.) Consequently, each of the two mortar battalions earmarked for the invasion was temporarily fattened by 125-man detachments from two chemical processing companies.

The Normandy Campaign

The 81st and 87th Chemical Mortar Battalions landed in Normandy early on D-day in support of the V and VII Corps, respectively, on OMAHA and UTAH Beaches. Companies A and C of the 81st were attached to battalions of the 16th Infantry, 1st Division, and Companies B and D landed with battalions of the 116th Infantry, 29th Division. As it approached the shore, the landing craft carrying the forward battalion group received heavy shelling which killed a sergeant and seriously wounded the battalion commander, Lt. Col. Thomas H. James. Without benefit of engine or rudder the craft drifted aimlessly until currents providentially beached it at a protected spot along the shore.

Company A, landing at H plus 50, lost some of its equipment in the heavy seas. Even worse, Capt. Thomas P. Moundres, its commander, was mortally wounded before reaching the beach. The senior lieutenant assumed command and succeeded in getting the platoons into firing

SMOKE SCREEN DURING THE OMAHA BEACH LANDINGS

positions. First day missions included a smoke screen for advancing infantry and the destruction of an enemy machine gun. Company C did not land until midafternoon because the infantrymen in preceding waves were pinned down on the edge of the beach. The unit finally got ashore at 1500 and made its way to positions about 200 yards inland. It received no requests for supporting fire.

The four LCVP's carrying Company B were unable to find a route through the heavy obstacles in their assigned sector, and two of these vessels were disabled by artillery fire as they headed toward another landing area. Despite a heavy sea and enemy opposition, all troops and equipment aboard the stricken craft were transferred to an empty LCT. Company D landed between H plus 50 and H plus 60, but its commander, Capt. Philip J. Gaffney, was killed when his landing craft struck a mine. Before finding an outlet off the dangerous strip of beach the unit changed its position three times and fired one mission. Night found the mortars dug in at St. Laurent-sur-Mer. Thus, on 6 June

CHEMICAL MORTARS AT UTAH BEACH

1944 3 officers of the 81st were killed and 2 others, including the battalion commander, were seriously wounded. One company lost its total complement of transportation while each of the other three companies lost two vehicles.

Trouble developed on D plus 1 as enemy snipers allowed leading infantry elements to pass through, firing on units which followed. To meet this threat the battalion formed details to wipe out the sniper nests. The mortarmen learned another trick of combat during these early days in Normandy. The enemy, having retreated from the area in which American mortars were to be set up, had marked on its firing charts all logical positions for these weapons. The men of the 81st soon found it was best to avoid reverse slopes and similar accepted mortar sites in favor of unconventional open terrain.

The 87th Chemical Battalion, commanded by Lt. Col. James H. Batte, was attached to VII Corps in the D-day assault of UTAH Beach. Three of the firing companies supported the three battalions of the

8th Infantry, 4th Division, and the fourth company supported a battalion of the 22d Infantry of the same division. Forward observers of the mortar companies landed with the initial waves of infantry, and the units themselves came in at H plus 50. Shortly after landing, the battalion fired 140 rounds and then followed the infantry in moving off the beach. For almost six hours the 4.2-inch mortars were the only ground weapons capable of delivering heavy fire support.[8] Targets during the first twenty-four hours of action were enemy machine gun emplacements, concrete emplacements, and pillboxes.

Quinville Ridge, some ten miles northwest of UTAH Beach and a D-day objective for VII Corps, was not taken until 14 June. The companies of the 87th Battalion supported the 4th Division in the fight for this objective, expending 16,870 rounds and suffering 36 casualties in the process. The mortar units continued in support of the 4th Division as it drove north to Cherbourg. On 23 June Company C fired a spectacular rolling barrage in support of a battalion attack which prompted Brig. Gen. Theodore Roosevelt to telephone his congratulations back to the mortar positions.[9]

The attack on Cherbourg included several other noteworthy 4.2-inch mortar missions. On 23 June Company A blended its fire so that white phosphorus showered German troops just routed from their positions by high explosives. That evening twenty men from Company D fought as infantry troops while the rest of the unit delivered heavy fire against an enemy counterattack. On 24 June the mortars of Company B successfully dueled with German artillery, assumed to be 88-mm. guns, which had been shelling an American regimental command post. On the same day, Company C aided in repelling a vigorous enemy counterattack by getting off 300 rounds before the division artillery could come into action. Expressing his view that the two mortar companies with his division had materially aided the success of the advance, Col. Kramer Thomas, chief of staff of the 79th Division, emphasized an inherent characteristic of the mortars—that of quick response to a given mission. On several occasions, he stated, the chemical mortars, because of the rapidity with which they went into action and the availability of ammunition at gun positions, were the only artillery-type support available.[10]

---

[8] 87th Cml Bn Journal, 6 Jun 44.
[9] 87th Cml Bn Opns Rpt, 6–15 Jul 44.
[10] 87th Cml Bn Journal, From D Day to D plus 20.

After the fall of the port of Cherbourg half of the battalion supported the 9th Division during the several days required to mop up the Cap de la Hague. By 1 July, when this operation ended, the 87th Battalion had been in continuous combat for twenty-five days. Nineteen man had been killed and 75 had been wounded; battalion ammunition expenditures totaled 19,129 rounds of HE and 11,899 rounds of white phosphorus.

The nature of the fighting in Normandy was determined by the predominant feature of the Norman terrain, the hedgerow. As described by Colonel MacArthur, Chemical Officer, 12th Army Group: "The country is gently rolling grazing land, consisting of rectangular grass fields generally about 100 yards deep in the direction of our advance and 150 to 200 yards wide." The colonel stated that these hedgerows were actually earth walls about four feet high surmounted with bushes and dotted with small trees. They were natural obstacles which could be put to excellent use in warfare, and the enemy fully exploited their defensive possibilities. Machine gun emplacements were located at the corners of hedgerows, and their lengths bristled with machine pistols, rifles, and antitank weapons. Mines with trip wires sometimes supplemented the already imposing defenses. Naturally, an advance over this ground was as slow as it was dangerous; units measured their progress by hedgerows, not miles. This was a form of position warfare with *bocage* replacing the traditional role of trenches.[11]

The terrain was particularly dangerous for mortar forward observers, a fact emphasized by the following notation from the journal of the 87th Battalion for 13 July 1944: "Scarcely a day passes that some one, if not all the forward observer party, are either wounded or killed. Yet, all officers of this battalion operate as forward observers and there are always volunteers among the men."

The 86th Battalion arrived in Normandy on 29 June. Attached to First Army, the companies of this unit initially supported elements of the 90th Infantry and 82d Airborne Divisions. Company B was an exception. The ship which was taking this unit across the Channel sank after either striking a mine or being struck by a torpedo. One man was listed as missing and 26 were injured; most of the equipment was lost. Refitted in England, the unit rejoined the 86th on 18 July.

---

[11] Memo, MacArthur for ACofS G–3 Hq 12th Army Group, 28 Jul 44, p. 2. CWS 314.7 Unit Files. CMLHO.

Although created for combat support, chemical mortar battalions found themselves at times in something other than a supporting role. The experience of Company A of the 86th on the night of 6–7 July is a case in point. One of its platoons was firing for a battalion of the 359th Infantry; another was in the immediate vicinity. Wire connected the mortar company with the infantry battalion. The mortar company liaison officer at the forward infantry observation post reported that the situation there was uncertain and appeared to be getting out of control. An urgent mission, requested by an adjacent battalion, prompted the mortar company commander to withdraw his security element and send it for more ammunition. Although three infantry companies were thought to be in front of the mortars, enemy machine gun fire suddenly pierced the air above the mortar crews. The mortar company commander called the infantry battalion but could get no definite word about the situation. The infantry battalion agreed that a mortar barrage would probably help, and the two platoons fired at a range of 700 yards. When the machine gun fire crept closer, the commander again tried to contact the infantry command post. Finding it had moved, he ordered one of his platoons to withdraw, a maneuver accomplished with difficulty because of the heat of the barrels and the firm emplacement of the base plates. Soon the mortar positions were swept by enemy machine gun fire and the other platoon received the march order. As the company withdrew, 5 men fell into enemy hands, escaping when the Germans were driven off by the company's sole remaining .50-caliber machine gun. The next morning all equipment was recovered with the exception of one destroyed jeep.[12]

Although not involved in D-day operations, the 92d Chemical Battalion soon participated in the Normandy fighting. Attached to XIX Corps and supporting the 30th Division, the unit first saw action in the opening days of July along the Vire River. On 8 July the 92d supported the 29th Division which was spearheading the XIX Corps drive on the centers of German resistance around St. Lô. This and one other attack proved unsuccessful; fourteen days and two attachments later the battalion was poised for the breakthrough operation.

COBRA, the offensive to break out of Normandy, began on 25 July. The VII Corps, with three divisions abreast, led the attack. Companies A and B, 92d Battalion, were firing preparatory missions in support

[12] 86th Cml Bn AAR, 1 Jul–31 Jul 44, pp. 5–6.

of units of the 30th Division when Allied heavy bombers droned in to soften German resistance. To the dismay of the American troops, about 35 of the planes dropped their bomb loads within friendly lines.[13] Nearly 200 bombs fell in the 92d Battalion area alone. Lt. Gen. Lesley J. McNair, Army Ground Forces commander, was instantly killed while observing the action from a point just in front of Company A. Battalion losses were 5 dead and 23 wounded. Company A lost 9 mortars, half of its ammunition, and all of its vehicles. Company B fared better, managing to salvage 8 of its 12 mortars. On the following day Company C relieved Company A and the latter unit drew back to reorganize; three days later Company A, in turn, relieved Company B. By 3 August all units returned to the battalion area for rest and refitting.

Operational Problems

Despite the complaints heard throughout the Normandy Campaign about the lack of trained mortar battalion replacements, there was no over-all shortage of CWS officers in the European theater. Colonel St. John, Chemical Adviser, G–3, SHAEF, reported in June 1944 that so many CWS officers were in the theater that they were "sitting in each other's laps and standing on each other's feet." [14]

The root of the trouble was the existence of two distinct types of CWS officers, technical and combat, whose roles were usually not interchangeable. Misassignment not only resulted in a waste of talent but usually in a substandard performance. An officer whose training and background fitted him for a chemical laboratory assignment probably made a poor mortar platoon leader. Because these facts were understood neither by the Ground Forces Replacement Command in England, nor by the personnel officers of the higher commands, it was not unusual for trained mortar officers to find themselves in depots or in branch immaterial positions, while the mortar battalions had to settle for unqualified replacements.[15]

This situation was verified by the commander of one of the mortar units which saw action in Normandy. Colonel Batte reported that during the course of one week in the latter part of June he received

---

[13] Craven and Cate, eds., *Europe: ARGUMENT to V–E Day*, pp. 231–34.

[14] Rpt, St. John for CCWS, 28 Jun 44.

[15] (1) *Ibid*. (2) Ltr, Rowan to Waitt, 24 Feb 45, no sub. CWS 314.7 Personal Ltr files, ETO. (3) Rowan Interv, 26 Sep 58.

two CWS officers and one infantry officer as battalion replacements. Batte stated: "The two CWS officers admitted they had never so much as touched a mortar in their entire army experience; before entering OCS they were in the Medical Corps. The greater part of their service in CWS after finishing OCS had been in pools and at the Military Police Training Center, Ft. Custer, Mich." [16] The accuracy of these comments made by graduates of the CWS officer candidate school might be open to question, since the OCS curriculum included fifty hours of 4.2-inch mortar training.[17] But whatever the explanation, these men were not psychologically prepared to enter combat.[18]

They probably lacked technical proficiency, as well, for the Chemical Warfare School came to consider fifty hours as an inadequate period of mortar training, and in the summer of 1943 inaugurated a Battalion Officers Course, with the specific purpose of producing qualified mortar battalion officers. Because the battalions in combat were not receiving these officers as replacements, Colonel Batte had been requesting and usually getting infantrymen.[19] Similar problems were encountered with enlisted men. Lt. Col. William B. Hamilton, commanding the 86th Battalion, stated that the replacements received by his unit were not trained CWS mortarmen but were "basics from the infantry or most any other branch." [20]

Efforts were made to overcome the lack of suitable mortar battalion replacements. General Rowan established a Chemical Training Battalion in England which began operations in August 1944. Until its termination in October 1944 this unit, which doubled as a replacement organization, trained 125 officers and 700 enlisted men for assignment with mortar battalions. This fine record was in part vitiated by two factors: the heavy demands permitted only a fraction of these troops to receive all of the prescribed three weeks of training, and despite

---

[16] Memo, Batte to Porter, 26 Jun 44.   CWS 314.7 Personal Ltr files, ETO.

[17] See Brophy and Fisher, *Organizing for War*, ch. XV.

[18] Colonel Batte had some first lieutenants who actually broke down and cried at the prospect of being sent into battle. Ltr, Batte to CMLHO, 28 Jul 60.

[19] Memo, Rowan, no addressee, 26 Aug 44, sub: Notes on Trip to Far Shore, in Ltr, Rowan to Waitt, 2 Sep 44.

[20] Ltr, CO 86th Cml Bn to CCWS, 18 Jul 44, sub: Employ of Cml Combat Bn.

all precautions these men continued to become lost in the Ground Forces Replacement Command.[21]

The personnel situation remained critical throughout the winter of 1944-45. December found the mortar battalions in the 12th Army Group understrength by twenty-five officers and the theater replacement center seemingly devoid of qualified chemical mortar officers.[22] The 92d Battalion, earlier unaffected by replacement problems, now reported that "trained officer and enlisted replacements have been unavailable and consequently a continuous training program has been found necessary." [23]

An urgent message from the theater to the War Department in February 1945 called attention to the need for chemical mortar officers. Within the theater further steps were taken to rectify the replacement situation. All CWS officers assigned outside the service had been located and a number of them were now serving in their proper capacities. Also, the willingness of the Ground Forces Replacement Command to work with the informal advice of General Rowan's office lessened greatly the chance of misassignment of officers.[24]

A personnel problem of a different sort had existed even before the battalions entered combat. The revised table of organization of September 1943, it will be recalled, reduced the battalion strength from 1,010 to 622. Battalion commanders were of the opinion that this number was below that required to man, supply, and provide communications for the forty-eight mortars within the unit. Although there was disagreement as to the composition of an appropriate table of organization, all of the commanders considered the 6-man squad too small to keep a mortar in action. A popular remedy was to withdraw several mortars and reinforce the remaining squads with the men thus freed. Lt. Col. Ronald LeV. Martin took more drastic measures with the 92d Battalion. He received permission to eliminate one of the four companies of his unit, thus anticipating the revised

---

[21] (1) Ltr, Maj Otis P. Gray to CCmlO ETOUSA, 15 Jan 45, sub: Rpt on Cml Training Bn, Incl to History of Plans and Tng Div Cml Sec ETOUSA, 6 Jun 44–9 May 45. Admin File 545B, Hq ETO, WW II Div NA. (2) Memo, St. John for Comdt Cml Warfare School, 21 Sep 44. (3) Ltr, Rowan to Waitt, 22 Dec 44, no sub. CWS 314.7 Personal Ltr files, ETOUSA.

[22] Ltr, CmlO 12th Army Group to CCWS, 11 Dec 44, no sub.

[23] 92d Cml Bn AAR, Dec 44.

[24] (1) CM–IN 22090, 22 Feb 45. (2) Ltr, Rowan to Waitt, 24 Feb 45, no sub. CWS 314.7 Personal Ltr files, ETO.

table of organization which was to become effective in the fall of 1944.[25]

Another difficulty which emerged in Normandy involved the tactical employment of chemical mortar units, or more precisely, the matter of mortar battalion control. The resulting controversy provoked two schools of thought, one holding that mortar units should be directly responsible to the infantry which they supported, the other maintaining that they should operate under artillery control. Influential in this dispute was the background and training of the participants. The commander of the 92d, for example, had been a field artillery officer until transferring to the CWS; moreover, the last training phase of his unit had been supervised by the artillery officer of the corps to which the battalion was attached. It was not strange that this battalion commander became a leading exponent of the artillery control school.

One of the main benefits of the artillery control system was the efficiency with which the battalion could operate as a unit. In defensive situations mortar fire could be readily massed, and the unit's fire could be effectively integrated with that of the artillery. In the European theater, however, the limited number of mortar battalions generally precluded the maintenance of battalion integrity.[26]

Most of those concerned, CWS and otherwise, favored the close infantry support method. This fact was confirmed in a CWS theater of operations letter which stated that although applicable artillery techniques and practices should be used, the normal role of the chemical battalion "should be considered as part of the Infantry team . . . furnishing close support with a heavy and powerful mortar."[27]

The Drive Toward Germany

The Fall of Aachen

After the breakout at Avranches, the Allied advance to the east sharply accelerated. The tactical value of the 4.2-inch mortar usually decreased in fast-moving situations, and such was the case during most

---

[25] (1) Brig. Gen. Hugh W. Rowan, "Mortars in Normandy," *Chemical Warfare Bulletin* (January–February, 1945). (2) 92d Bn History.

[26] (1) Rowan, "Mortars in Normandy," *Chemical Warfare Bulletin* (January–February, 1945). (2) Memo, CCmlO 12th Army Group for G-3 12th Army Group, 28 Jul 44. CWS 314.7 (3) Rowan Interv, 26 Sep 58.

[27] (1) CWS TofO Ltr No. 18, 14 Sep 44, p. 3. (2) This view was substantiated by a postwar study in chemical mortar battalions by the General Board, U.S. Forces European Theater.

of the campaign in northern France. Although there were periods of intense action, most of the mortar battalions enjoyed a breathing spell. Some battalions temporarily acted as trucking units to help ease logistical problems which accompany any army in rapid movement. Time was available for rest, rehabilitation, and training, as well as for the opportunity to enjoy the enthusiastic reception of the liberated French people. It was a well-deserved respite coming between two taxing campaigns.

The American forces first came into contact with the Siegfried Line in September 1944. At that time there were still only four chemical battalions assigned to the 12th Army Group, an insignificant number for such a formidable force. And the stiffening enemy bore little resemblance to the German troops who had recently fled across northern France. First Army, lacking the logistical support it had recently enjoyed, began a series of limited probes against the German defenses. The objective of one of these attacks was Aachen.

The 92d and 87th Chemical Mortar Battalions supported First Army in this difficult operation which took the form of a double envelopment. The 92d Battalion fired for the 30th Division in the XIX Corps drive to the north, and the 87th supported elements of VII Corps in the southern sector.

The attack on Aachen, set for September, was delayed by the wet, miserable weather until early October. During the ensuing lull the 92d improved its gun positions, perfected plans for prearranged missions, and fired a number of probing missions. Finally, on 2 October, the 30th Division attacked the Siegfried Line in the direction of Übach, Germany. In preparation for the assault the 92d Battalion placed a destructive barrage upon wire barriers of concertinas and double aprons which lay in the route of advance of two infantry regiments. Over 1,200 high-explosive shells fell in these two areas whose combined size measured 1,700 by 300 yards, cutting broad swaths through the obstacles. The mortars then kept a rolling barrage 150 yards ahead of the advancing troops. Subsequent missions included those of interdiction, harassment, general support, and smoke screens on the flanks to hamper enemy observation. Targets of opportunity were numerous. One forward observer used mortar fire to chase a German weapons platoon into a pillbox and then adjusted 8-inch artillery fire to bring about the destruction of the concrete fortification.

The battalion expended 25,000 rounds of ammunition and suffered 30 casualties in the Aachen operation, which ended with the fall of the city on 23 October.[28]

The 87th Battalion supported the 1st and 9th Divisions in the lower jaw of the pincers attack against Aachen. Frequent re-emplacements of the mortars resulted because of the soft, wet ground, a condition which also contributed to the heavy breakage of parts. Missions of interdiction were frequent; tanks, personnel, machine guns, and mortars were targets of opportunity for the 4.2-inch weapons. White phosphorus effectively screened observation from the formidable enemy positions which protected Aachen. Later, mortar fire was placed upon the enemy's vigorous counterattacks as he attempted to fight out of the beleaguered city. Against one counterattack on 16 October Company B disabled 2 tanks, knocked out 1 self-propelled gun, and killed between 70 and 80 of the enemy. The captain of the infantry company thus aided declared that the mortar support prevented the enemy from overrunning his unit. Against another counterattack the chemical mortars fired white phosphorus shells behind the supporting enemy tanks, silhouetting them for the benefit of American tank destroyers. One German tank was knocked out, two others were damaged, and the rest withdrew. Maj. Gen. Clarence R. Huebner, commanding the 1st Division, praised the chemical mortars for the part they played in stopping these counterattacks.[29]

The 81st Chemical Mortar Battalion at Metz

While assigned to the First Army, the 81st Battalion crossed northeastern France into Belgium and Luxembourg, and in September got its first taste of fighting among the fortifications of the Siegfried Line. Here it learned that while the prepared concrete and steel positions were impervious to mortar shell, smoke did prove effective in preventing observation from these strongpoints.[30]

---

[28] (1) 92d Cml Mortar Bn, History, 1944. (2) History of 30th Inf Div Arty, 1–31 Oct 44. (3) Col. Ronald L. Martin, "92d Chemical Mortar Battalion History," Armed Forces Chemical Journal (October, 1951).

[29] 87th Cml Bn Rcd of Events, pp. 87, 91.

[30] (1) The Eighty-First Chemical Mortar Battalion (booklet, 1945), pp. 44–51. (2) 12th Army Group, Battle Experiences No. 88, 9 Nov 44. White phosphorus shell, apart from its utility as a screening agent, sometimes had a psychological effect when used against enemy fortifications. The crew of at least one enemy pillbox, for example, surrendered when one of its members, seeing the WP smoke, called out, "Gas!"

In mid-September the battalion was reassigned to the Third Army, also recently halted by logistical difficulties. Lt. Gen. George S. Patton ordered a series of limited operations which would place his forces in a more favorable position once the drive to the Rhine was resumed. Attached to XX Corps, the 81st Battalion was in the vicinity of Metz, preparing to support the 5th and 90th Divisions in attacks against Fort Driant and Maizieres-les-Metz, an industrial town located north of the city.[31]

The first attempt against Fort Driant was made on 27 September by the 2d Battalion, 11th Infantry, 5th Division. This hurriedly planned attack proved abortive, primarily because the strength of the objective was not fully appreciated. Located on the dominant height in the area south of Metz, Fort Driant was one of the most important elements of the fortifications which encircled the city. It consisted of four casemates and a central fort whose concrete walls were 7 feet thick and whose various components were connected by a labyrinth of underground tunnels. Wire obstacles and a dry moat, 60 feet wide and 30 feet deep, surrounded the over-all complex.

The infantry battalion attacked the fort under a pall of smoke which Company D, 81st Battalion, placed on the installation and on the observation posts behind it. By late afternoon the futility of the attack was fully revealed, and the infantry troops were ordered to withdraw. Plans were immediately made by the division commander for a more systematic attack on the fortification.

Company D was to remain in support of the 11th Infantry, but its attachment was changed from the regiment itself to the supporting 19th Field Artillery Battalion. From positions two miles north of the town of Onville, the mortars began to register on targets in the Fort Driant area in preparation for the coming attack. Occasionally, other missions were fired. Targets of opportunity included mortar and machine gun positions and harassing rounds were placed on the road network. In turn, the mortar positions were subjected to sporadic but effective enemy artillery fire.

On the evening of 2 October Capt. Arthur R. Marshall, the company commander, attended several conferences with artillery officers to settle certain details of the attack. Late that night two 2½-ton trucks

---

[31] Cole, *Lorraine Campaign*, pp. 257–75. This volume contains an excellent description of the Fort Driant action.

brought an extra 866 rounds of white phosphorus to a forward position where they were met by jeeps and trailers from the company. A platoon from Company C was attached to Company D for the operation.

A great deal more planning went into the 3 October attack on Fort Driant, again made by the 2d Battalion, 11th Regiment, than was given to the one a week earlier. Tankdozers were called on to fill in portions of the encircling moat, and "snakes"—long pipes filled with explosives—were brought forward to be used against the wire obstacles in front of the fort. Again, fighter bombers attacked the fort and corps and division artillery battered its concrete defenses. More mortar smoke was used than in the earlier attack.

H-hour for the second Fort Driant attack was 1100. Company D and its attached platoon immediately began the smoke screen in order to prevent enemy observation of the assault. An irregular 15-mile-an-hour wind made this an extremely difficult mission. At times four distinct screens had to be maintained in order to achieve the proper placement of smoke. Company D continued the screen for five and one half hours, expending 1,600 rounds of white phosphorus ammunition. Despite these well-laid plans the infantry had but limited success. One company did reach positions within the fort, but the enemy reacted strongly, making reinforcement impossible. Again on 11 October Company D's mortars maintained a 7-hour, 1,400-yard smoke screen, this time with 1,975 rounds of white phosphorus. Elements of the 11th Infantry fought on and around Fort Driant until the night of 12–13 October, when a decision was reached to withdraw. No other large screens were required in the ensuing days although target of opportunity and harassment missions were frequent.

The high-explosive shell fired by the mortar company proved just as ineffective against the fortifications around Metz as it had against Siegfried Line installation at Aachen. This result was not surprising; 500 and 1,000-pound aerial bombs also bounced harmlessly off the concrete and steel of the fortifications.[32]

One of the handicaps under which the 81st Battalion operated in front of Fort Driant was the high incidence of mortar breakage. Not only did the weaker parts of the mortar (the recoil slides and elevating screws) give way, but the sturdier components (the base plates and the

---

[32] 81st Bn, Metz Campaign, 18 Sep–21 Nov 44.

standards) as well. During the afternoon of 5 October, for example, the breakage became so severe that only one mortar per platoon was available for firing. On that day 10 base plates, 6 standards, 1 barrel, 1 elevating screw, and 1 collar were damaged. Blame for this equipment failure was attributed to the extreme range at which missions were fired and to the mixed rock and shale in which the base plates were emplaced, resulting in uneven pressures and a consequent shearing effect.[33]

Meanwhile, Company A of the 81st Battalion supported the 35th Infantry, 90th Division, in an attack on Maizieres-les-Metz. The mortars laid smoke to screen friendly attacks and to cloud enemy observation while mine fields were being removed. Other missions included those of interdiction and targets of opportunity.

The operation against the town proceeded slowly. At one point the infantry was content to use the situation as a realistic training ground, each day setting up platoon and squad attack problems against a house or two.[34] Company A accomplished an extraordinary mission during the house-to-house fighting. When an infantry battalion was held up by a single enemy machine gun, the battalion commander, located in a cellar across the street from the enemy position, called for 4.2-inch mortar fire. Company A adjusted a single mortar on the machine gun; its fourth or fifth round landed directly on the sill of the second story window from which the enemy weapon was firing.[35]

Maizieres-les-Metz fell on 30 October, and the all-out drive on the city of Metz began early in November. As at Aachen, the attack took the form of a double envelopment, each arm of which was supported by companies of the 81st Battalion. In this operation Company C found itself attached to Team Cherry of the 10th Armored Division, a most unusual arrangement. During the initial stages of the attachment mine fields and roadblocks kept the advance at a relatively slow pace, and the mortar company was able to assume its normal role. But as the pace quickened, the problems of the supporting unit increased. In order to insure constant support, the two mortar platoons leapfrogged forward, one of them ready to fire while the other advanced to the next appropriate position. A liaison officer stayed with the team commander to insure prompt response to any calls for fire. This leap-

---

[33] (1) Co A 81st Bn War Diary, 1–7 Oct 44.   (2) 81st Bn, Hist Rpt, 24–30 Sep 44.

[34] Cole, *Lorraine Campaign,* p. 278.

[35] Memo for Rcd, Maj James H. Watts, 5 Mar 52.

frogging technique was abandoned when Team Cherry split in two, and a platoon joined each of the new elements.

This employment of a mortar unit in support of an armored team was not altogether satisfactory. The battalion commander, Lt. Col. Jack W. Lipphardt, questioned the practice, calling attention to the difficulties of replacing mortar parts and of resupplying ammunition in fast-moving situations and to the relative vulnerability of mortar equipment.[36] As the battalion operations officer, who accompanied Company C during this attachment, put it: "The mortar is a close support weapon for the doughboy and is of much more value to the infantry regiment than to a combat command."[37]

In support of the entire Metz operation the 81st Chemical Battalion fired 51,118 rounds of ammunition. During part of the time a shortage of artillery shell enhanced the role of the 4.2-inch mortar.[38]

Mortar Parts and Their Maintenance

Maintenance of the 4.2-inch mortar, which became such a grave problem during the autumn fighting along the Siegfried Line, had bothered battalion commanders since the Normandy landing. In the early days of fighting in France the chemical mortar assumed an important role as a primary means of heavy weapon support. Missions were fired from undesirable positions at ranges far in excess of the 4,500 yards for which the mortar was designed, a circumstance which contributed in a large way to mortar part breakage.

The 87th Chemical Battalion, during its first twenty days in Normandy, for example, expended 114 complete sets of springs and bent 100 elevating screws beyond repair.[39] The failure of the springs was not entirely the result of equipment fatigue and firing at excessive ranges. According to Colonel Batte the difficulties experienced with the mortar springs were "due to faulty and inferior material and workmanship." New springs were known to stay contracted an inch or so under normal length after only five or six rounds had been fired. This weakness compounded the over-all vulnerability of the mortar,

---

[36] 81st Bn, Hist Rpt, 5–11 Nov 44.

[37] Co C 81st Cml B, Metz Campaign, 18 Sep–21 Nov 44.

[38] (1) The Eighty-First Chemical Mortar Battalion, p. 60. (2) 81st Bn Hist Rpt, 5–11 Nov 44.

[39] Ltr, Batte to CG First Army, 25 Jun 44, sub: Replacement of Parts for 4.2-inch Mortar. CWS 314.7 Personal Ltr files, ETO.

for other parts—shock absorber slides, elevating screws, and even standards—suffered when springs functioned improperly.[40] The situation was greatly alleviated when the CWS devised new and stronger rectangular springs.[41]

Mortar breakage was not confined to Normandy but continued through the campaigns of northern France and the Rhineland. A number of circumstances accounted for such breakage. For one thing, in the fast-moving fighting across northern France, which was more in the nature of pursuit than combat, mortars were almost always called on to perform at excessive ranges.[42] Another factor was the emplacement of weapons in soft ground, a situation which plagued the 86th Battalion, in September and October. In some cases, the mortar crews of the 86th, after firing only two or three rounds, had to dig through the mud to the base plate and haul it out with a jeep.[43] A similar problem was the presence of hard shale rock in the soft clay which provided uneven support for the base plate and produced a shearing effect. The 81st Battalion particularly experienced this difficulty. But as the damage was much less frequent with the new mortar than with the old, part of the weapon mortality must have resulted from equipment fatigue.[44]

As mortar parts continued to break, battalion commanders began to criticize the design and construction of the weapon, claiming that it should be able to withstand the rigors of combat without an extraordinary amount of repairs and replacement.[45] They were especially critical of the construction of the base plate. The standard base plate weighed 150 pounds, a heavy item when carried by hand. In the European theater where hand-carry was at a minimum (the weapons and ammunition were usually conveyed by jeep trailer) it would have been practicable to have a heavier base plate if the additional weight would have added to its strength.

Upon the recommendation of Colonel Batte of the 87th Battalion steps were taken to devise such a base plate. One model, constructed

[40] (1) *Ibid.* (2) Rowan Interv, 26 Sep 58.

[41] (1) Ltr, Waitt to CCWS ETOUSA, 14 Aug 44. (2) Memo, Col Harry A. Kuhn for CG ASF, 7 Aug 44, sub: G–4 Per Report ETO, Quarter Ending 30 Jun 44. CWS 319.1. (3) 81st Cml Bn AAR, 4 Nov 44 (for Oct 44), p. 4.

[42] 81st Cml Bn Hist Rpt, 30 Jul–5 Aug, 13–19 Aug, 10–16 Sep 44.

[43] 86th Cml Bn Hist, 11 Oct 44.

[44] 81st Cml Bn Hist Rpt, 1–7 Oct 44.

[45] (1) Ltr, CCmlO ETO to CCWS, 21 Feb 45, sub: Bn Comdrs' Comments on the Cml Mortar Bn and Its Equip. (2) 92d Cml Bn AAR, Dec 44, Battle Lessons and Conclusions.

in a Belgian steel mill, weighed 275 pounds and was 7 inches longer and broader than the standard item. Several were issued to mortar units of the First Army, where the reaction among the crews was favorable. The use of this base plate resulted in fewer re-emplacements, in better accuracy, and in less damage to other parts of the mortar. Modifications were also made in the tie rod. Instead of welding this part to the standard, it was secured by a loop, nut, and belt arrangement which, by allowing greater flexibility, resulted in less breakage.[46]

Manufacture of the base plate in Europe resulted from a search for improvement, but other parts were produced there for the specific purpose of relieving shortages.[47] Among these items were cup forks, elevating and traversing screws, connector rods, standards, base and tube caps, shock absorber and traversing slides, and spring guides. Unfortunately, no manufacturers could be found for the most critical mortar part, the spring.[48] The Seventh Army also made spare parts for CWS equipment, preventing at one time, at least, a crisis in the resupply of certain items. This work took place at Épinal at an army maintenance installation which used the students and facilities of a former vocational school.[49]

The shortage of mortar spare parts harassed battalion commanders from the early days of the Normandy fighting and remained unsolved throughout most of the European operations. The solution of this problem was a primary mission of a CWS spare parts team which visited the Continent during the winter of 1944–45. In its final report the Spare Parts Team praised the work done by the chemical maintenance companies on the component parts of the mortar. With ingenuity and versatility these companies improvised, cannibalized, and even manufactured sufficient spare parts to permit the continued

---

[46] (1) Ltr, CmlO First Army to CCWS, 11 May 45. (2) Ltr, CmlO First Army to CCmlO ETOUSA, 1 May 45, sub: Shipment of Strengthened ADSEC COMZ 4.2" Cml Mortar Baseplates to Edgewood Arsenal for Test. (3) Memo, Batte for Hist Off, 4 Apr 52.

[47] (1) Memo, Capt Robert O. Myers for CmlO Seventh Army, 17 Jan 45. (2) Ltr, Lt Col Ingalls S. Bradley, Deputy CWO ADSEC COMZ to CCWO ETOUSA, 9 Jan 45, sub: Procurement of Spare Parts for 4.2-inch Cml Mortar. (3) One of the plants at which mortars were produced was located about twenty-five miles north of Namur, Belgium. Full advantage was taken of local skilled labor and the mass production facilities of the plant. Ltr, CO 11th Cml Maint Co to CmlO Seventh Army, 16 Feb 45.

[48] (1) OCCWS, Final Rpt, Spare Parts Team in MTO and ETO, pp 108–09. CMLHO. (2) Ltr, Bradley to CCWS ETOUSA, 9 Jan 45, sub: Procurement of Spare Parts for 4.2-inch Cml Mortars. (3) Rowan, panel comments.

[49] Seventh Army Cml Sec Hist Rpt, 1–31 Dec 44.

operation of the mortar battalions.[50] Despite occasional criticism
about the distance between the
mortar battalions and the maintenance companies,[51] effective liaison was generally maintained between these units. Seventh Army
insured prompt maintenance by
the unprecedented device of attaching 17-man detachments of
the chemical maintenance companies directly to the mortar battalions under army control. The
rest of these companies were responsible for the maintenance of
other chemical equipment, as well
as of mortar carts and ammunition, and for fourth and fifth
echelon maintenance on the mortars themselves.[52]

PREPARING A 4.2-INCH MORTAR
SHELL FOR FIRING, *Ardennes counter-offensive.*

The German Winter Offensive

Progress of the Allied armies, slow and costly during the fall of 1944,
came to a complete halt on 16 December as the Germans launched
their surprise winter offensive through the Ardennes. In one of the
many readjustments hurriedly made to meet the threat of the Bulge,
the 3d Chemical Battalion was shifted from the 6th to the 12th Army
Group.[53] There it fought with Third Army's III Corps to relieve the

---

[50] (1) OCCWS, Final Rpt, CWS Spare Parts Team in the MTO and ETO, p. 11. (2) The 11th
Chemical Maintenance Company (Seventh Army) developed and manufactured a pneumatic shock
absorber which aided in the reduction of breakage of mortar parts. Hist Rpt, Cml Sec Seventh Army,
1–30 Dec 44.

[51] In November, Lt. Col. Ronald LeV. Martin of the 92d Battalion requested that the maintenance
company be moved farther forward as it took a day to take damaged parts to the rear for repair. The
colonel also considered excessive the length of time taken to make the repairs. Ninth Army Cml Sec,
p. 1, Notes on Visit, 28 Nov 44, by Lt Joel B. Marangella and Capt Cooney.

[52] Ltr, Maj J. J. Heffner, Office of CmlO Seventh Army, to CO 11th Cml Maint Co and CO 12th
Maint Co, 22 Dec 44, sub: Responsibilities of Seventh Army CWS Maintenance Cos. App. A, Hist
Rpt Cml Sec Hqs Seventh Army, 1 Dec–31 Dec 44).

[53] The 2d, 3d, and 83d Chemical Mortar Battalions participated in the Seventh Army invasion of
southern France and eventually were assigned to the 6th Army Group. The 99th Battalion, activated
in Italy, joined the 6th Army Group in December 1944.

encircled forces at Bastogne. Mortar companies initially were attached to 2 infantry divisions, an armored division, and a cavalry squadron. During December units of the battalion operated under 2 armies, 2 corps, 6 infantry divisions, and a cavalry group. They expended 17,499 rounds of ammunition and, surprisingly enough, suffered no casualties.[54]

Farther to the north the 86th Chemical Battalion supported V Corps in the First Army sector. There it was touch and go. The enemy had broken through a neighboring unit and had then cut into the V Corps sector. German paratroopers landed in the corps rear area intent on the disruption of communications and the seizure of installations. 86th Battalion headquarters organized eight patrols to comb the area for these enemy troops. The patrols found no paratroopers, but they did come across a house with a cache of enemy equipment and weapons.

The rear area of Company D was overrun during the confusion of the breakthrough, and 14 of its men were listed as missing in action. Company C of the 86th lay in the direct path of the German drive. Never had the unit experienced such a critical situation; never had its efficiency, morale, discipline, and resourcefulness been so tested. Units which had protected the mortar company suddenly turned to it for protection. Mortar fire halted enemy advances and covered friendly movements; mortarmen maintained communications for and with isolated and threatened units and stayed at their guns while these units withdrew to safety. One mission fired on 19 December enabled a hard-pressed infantry company to withdraw safely from a position that had become untenable. The mortarmen placed smoke and high-explosive shell in a narrow gap which separated the infantry unit from the enemy and continued to fire while all other units passed to the rear. Then they, themselves, withdrew. At times during this period division artillery, armor, and infantry withdrew under Company C's protective fire—fire which "was largely responsible for holding up the enemy advance and almost solely responsible for the safe manner in which these withdrawals, were effected.[55]

During the first week of the Ardennes offensive the 86th Battalion expended 7,380 rounds of ammunition. However, the service given by the battalion could not be measured in rounds. Its value during

---

[54] (1) Hist, Hqs 3d Cml Bn, 25 Dec 44, p. 20.   (2) 3d Cml Bn Rpt of Opns, 1–31 Dec 44, p. 2. Both in 3d Cml Bn History, Dec 44.

[55] 86th Cml Bn Hist, 17–23 Dec 44, p. 4.

those trying days can be appreciated only with the knowledge that the 4.2-inch mortar was an important source of artillery-type fire—fire which enabled the infantry in its sector to gain some order out of the chaos caused by the German attack.

During December the mortar battalions began to reorganize under new tables of organization and equipment. Dated 29 September, the revised TOE triangularized the battalion by eliminating Company D. This change had long been advocated by CWS officers, although there had been a recent move to retain the fourth company as a replacement and training unit.[56] The designation of the three companies was changed from "weapons" to "mortar." Each had 3 platoons of 4 mortars, or a total of 36 for a battalion; the previous organization provided for 4 companies, each with 2 platoons of 6 mortars, or a total of 48.

Battalion commanders had long complained of insufficient men; now, despite the reduction in the number of weapons, battalion strength rose from 622 to 672. What formerly had been the headquarters detachment with 63 men was changed to a headquarters company with 155. The inclusion of nine $1\frac{1}{2}$-ton trucks in the new TOE provided a slight increase in the amount of organic transportation.

All of the chemical mortar battalions (they previously had been designated "chemical battalions, motorized") did not convert to the new organization immediately but did so throughout the winter of 1944–45 and the following spring, as they enjoyed an infrequent relief from front-line activity. The 2d and 92d, for example, converted in December, the 91st in January, and the 87th in May.

Mortar Shell Malfunctions

The period of the Ardennes counteroffensive saw the start of a series of mortar shell malfunctions which were to plague the battalions for most of the winter of 1944–45. These malfunctions were of two types: barrel bursts, in which the round prematurely exploded within the barrel; and muzzle bursts, in which the round exploded after leaving the barrel but still within the vicinity of the mortar emplacement.

In December 1944 ETOUSA impounded several lots of chemical mortar ammunition suspected of containing faulty shells. Periodically thereafter, as muzzle and barrel bursts occurred, other ammunition

---

[56] (1) CM–OUT 19799, 28 Mar 44.   (2) CM–OUT 8007, 19 Mar 44.   (3) 12th Army Group Immediate Rpt 39, Batte Interv.   (4) St. John, Chemical Opns in France.

was withdrawn from supply channels. By the middle of January 1945 a combined list of restricted ammunition included 90 percent of the available supply. Sometimes the pressure of the tactical situation forced the release of suspected ammunition. In these cases the mortar crews took particular precautions to minimize danger; some chemical mortar battalions fired their weapons with the use of lanyards and others built sandbag emplacements along side of the mortars.[57]

A conference of mortar battalion commanders of both the 12th and 6th Army Groups was held in January in the office of General Rowan, with defective 4.2-inch mortar shell as one of the main topics of discussion. Consensus was that most of the blame for malfunctions was attributable to the mortar fuze. One solution initiated by Seventh Army was the substitution of an artillery fuze for the suspected CWS item. Test firing of shells with this alteration proved successful, and 30,000 of these fuzes were obtained for the conversion of an equal number of impounded mortar shells. A difference in threads made the substitution of fuzes no easy job. One big advantage resulted from the new combination; the artillery fuze included a delayed action setting (not found in the CWS M3) which had long been sought by chemical units for use against buildings, pillboxes, and other structures.[58]

Mortar shell misfires reached a peak in January 1945. In one 10-day period two mortar battalions attached to First Army experienced a total of five barrel or muzzle bursts resulting in serious injury to four men. These accidents happened despite careful checking and the observance of precautionary measures. One serious result of these malfunctions was that mortar crews were beginning to show fear of their weapon.[59]

Concern for this serious situation in the theater naturally extended to the Office of the Chief, CWS, in Washington. The few zone of interior malfunctions had been thoroughly investigated and were found to have been caused in practically every case by a faulty fuze. The increase of misfires overseas prompted General Porter in January 1945 to send to Europe an investigating mission headed by General Bullene. A definite correlation between extreme cold weather and

[57] (1) Seventh Army Cml Sec Hist Rpt, 1–31 Jan 44, 25 Feb 45, p. 4.   (2) OCCWS Rpt of Malfunction of the 4.2″ Cml Mortar Ammunition, Their Cause, Effect and Measures Taken to Correct Deficiencies (hereafter cited as Rpt of Malfunctions), 12 Aug 46, VIII, 75.

[58] Seventh Army Cml Sec Hist Rpt, 1–31 Jan 45; 1–28 Feb 45.

[59] Rpt on Malfunctions, VIII, 55.

malfunctions, particularly barrel bursts, had been established by tests in the zone of interior. The experience in Europe substantiated these findings, as there were no more barrel bursts after 29 January when the cold spell ended. The Bullene mission attributed the muzzle bursts, which were not related to the temperature, to a series of weaknesses and defects in the mortar fuze. Corrective measures were recommended in all cases, some of which had been anticipated by the zone of interior investigations.

Actually, the over-all malfunction record of 4.2-inch mortar ammunition during World War II was not bad. Of the approximately four million rounds expended both in training and in combat a total of 63 exploded prematurely, causing the death of 38 and the injury of 127 American soldiers. This averaged 1.58 premature rounds in every 100,000 fired.[60]

The Final Drive

By the end of January 1945 the Allies had regained the ground lost during the enemy's Ardennes offensive. In February the 12th Army Group prepared for attack along the Roer and Sauer Rivers, an attack whose impetus would carry to the Rhine. This latter obstacle, the last great defensive barrier for the enemy, was surmounted in March. After that, victory was but a matter of time.

Much of the fighting of February and March involved river crossings. The Roer, the Erft, the Sauer, the Moselle, the Rhine—these were the larger rivers which blocked the American forces in their drive to the east. The chemical mortar battalions, by both smoke and high explosive missions, provided valuable support in this series of important operations.

One of the most spectacular smoke operations in Europe involving chemical mortar battalions was staged in the Third Army sector during the XII Corps attack across the Sauer and Our Rivers. This attack, which began on 7 February 1945, was supported by the 91st Chemical

---

[60] Rpt of Malfunctions, Abstract, pp. I–II. (2) See Brophy, Miles, and Cochrane, *From Laboratory to Field*, Chapter XV, for more on mortar shell malfunction.

Mortar Battalion, commanded by Lt. Col. Roy W. Muth.[61] Companies
B and C fired for regiments of the 5th Division; Company D supported
the 417th Infantry, 76th Division, attached to the 5th Division for
the operation; and the two platoons of Company A supported, respectively, the 905th and 314th Field Artillery Battalions of the 80th
Division.

These mortar units moved to positions to the west and south of the
Our-Sauer Rivers line several days before the attack was to begin.[62]
This movement in itself was difficult. The roads, heavy with traffic in
support of the impending attack, were subject to enemy fire from the
heights east of the rivers. The positions of Company D were in the
town of Echternach on the south bank of the Sauer, an area which
had not been occupied in strength by American forces because the
commanding ground just across the river was studded with pillboxes
of the Siegfried Line. This fact was driven home when the mortar
officers who reconnoitered Echternach quickly attracted enemy machine gun fire. The company moved into the town, two vehicles at a
time, under the cover of darkness and with chains and reflectors removed from the jeeps and trucks.

Company B, in support of the 10th Infantry, had less trouble getting
to its attack position despite the traffic-clogged roads leading to the
river. Four hours after receiving march orders on the morning of
5 February, the platoons of the unit traveled ten miles and set up
their mortars in the town of Berdorf. Company C supported the
11th Infantry also from positions near Berdorf. Anticipating heavy
enemy artillery opposition, the unit placed its switchboard and fire
direction centers near the mortars to reduce the expected difficulty in
keeping wire communications intact.

The XII Corps met strong resistance along the Our and the Sauer.
The Germans, ensconced in the strong defenses on the heights on the
east, dominated the valley. The swift-moving rivers were additional

[61] The 91st Battalion was committed to action in December 1944, a month which saw the beginning
of a steady influx of new mortar battalions. By the end of the war the 12th Army Group had a
total of twelve, the number previously decided upon for the European theater. In addition to those
units already mentioned in the text, the following chemical mortar battalions saw action with the
12th Army Group: the 89th, commanded by Lt. Col. Donald E. Yanka; the 90th, Lt. Col. Edgar V. H.
Bell; the 93d, Lt. Col. Jacquard Rothschild; the 94th, Lt. Col Benjamin D. Williams, Jr.; the 95th,
Lt. Col. Earl L. Shepherd; the 96th, Lt. Col. Farleigh E. Smith; and the 97th, Lt. Col. Edwin S. S.
Hays, Jr. The 6th Army Group had four battalions.

[62] The Our River branched off from the Sauer River about ten miles or so below the town of
Echternach, making the two, in effect, a continuous waterway.

obstacles. Given the excellent German observation and the relative impregnability of his positions, it is understandable that smoke missions assumed a great importance in the XII Corps operation.

All four of the companies fired screening missions for the American attack. The 10th Infantry found the going exceedingly rough. On the second day of the attack Company B maintained two major screens to obscure enemy observation, one parallel to the front and one perpendicular to it. In addition, one of the platoons successfully blanketed an enemy observation post and placed fire on several troop concentrations. In all, 2,357 rounds of WP were fired that day. Operations were impeded by abnormal wind conditions which caused the smoke to rise vertically, a phenomenon called "pillaring." On the following day the company expended 2,232 rounds of white phosphorus on a 9-hour smoke screen. At one point the screen was lifted and the effectiveness of smoke was dramatically demonstrated as enemy artillery and machine guns opened fire on American troops. The screen was resumed at once, and the enemy activity abruptly ceased. During the two days action just described the 1st Platoon alone expended 3,287 rounds of white phosphorus, or roughly 41½ tons.

One platoon of the smoke generator company attached to corps supported the Echternach crossing. After a short period of operation the smoke troops claimed that twelve generators were out of order and their unit commander sent the equipment back to a maintenance company for repair. There the generators were examined by Colonel Cottingham who found all but one to be in perfect operating condition. And the exception was in need of very minor adjustment. Apparently, the lack of training, discipline, and leadership prompted the smoke troops to take this action in an effort to be relieved from front-line duty. At Bollendorf, to the west, smoke generator troops effectively established a curtain between the crossing site and the high ground to the northwest from which the Germans had excellent observation.[63]

Among the problems confronting the 91st Battalion during the Sauer-Our operation was the dirty ammunition with which the battalion was supplied. During the two days of intense firing reported above, all available officers and men, from cook to company commander,

---

[63] (1) Pritchard, Smoke Generator Opns in MTO and ETO, p. 140. (2) According to Colonel Cottingham, XII Corps, after Echternach, requested Third Army to see to it that the smoke company not be attached to it in future operations until the company had proper training and leadership. Cottingham Interv, 17 Dec 56.

were compelled to assist in cleaning the rounds and preparing them for firing. Communication was likewise a problem. The wire and radio communication of a platoon of A Company, for example, was also used by two engineer units and the medical detachment and heavy mortar platoon of an infantry battalion. Even the matter of feeding the men proved difficult. The road leading into Echternach was a gantlet that had to be run daily by the mess personnel of Company D. Pfc. Richard Stubblefield had two jeep tires shot out from under him by shell fragments during one such mission, but continued to take hot food to the men.

As evidence of the severity of fighting against the obstacles of the Sauer and Our Rivers and the Siegfried Line, the companies of the 91st fired for five days from their initial positions. During this period units of the battalion completed twenty-four smoke missions ranging in duration from thirty minutes to nine hours and requiring almost 10,000 rounds of shell.

In another February operation the 87th Battalion supported VII Corps in the First Army attack across the Roer River in the vicinity of Düren. Early in the month the battalion's four mortar companies, two attached to the 8th Division and two to the 104th, moved into firing positions on the west side of the river. Here they waited for two weeks. The Germans, before relinquishing control of the area, destroyed the sluice valves of the Roer River dams. The raging waters of the river rose five feet, forcing postponement of the attack until 23 February.

The period of waiting was not idly spent by the mortar companies. Some fired on targets of opportunity and others interdicted road junctions. Company D, during the last days before the attack, set up feint smoke screens in the hope that the enemy would be less apprehensive when screens appeared for the actual crossing. On the night before the attack the company blanketed the eastern bank of the Roer to cover four patrols sent out to clear mines from the far side of the river. Smoke was necessary because of the bright moonlight.

Supporting fire for the First Army attack began early on the morning of 23 February. After the assault began the mortar companies laid smoke screens to cover the infantry in its drive across the river. One company fired four smoke screens which progressively covered an attacking battalion, enabling it to cross the river and an expanse of flat terrain with negligible casualties. Again moonlight made this

ROER RIVER BRIDGE BEHIND A SMOKE SCREEN

concealment necessary. Company C for over fifteen hours maintained a continuous 1,500-yard screen which blocked enemy observation from the high ground near Düren and allowed ferrying and bridge construction operations to continue without the hazard of observed artillery fire. On this first day alone the 87th Mortar Battalion fired over 4,000 rounds of ammunition.

The VII Corps, spearheading the First Army's advance to the Rhine, eliminated all enemy resistance in its zone on the west side of the river by 9 March. On the following day the 87th Battalion received word that it was to be sent from the First to the Seventh Army, which on 15 March was to initiate a drive through the imporant Saar-Palatinate triangle.[64] This operation was to involve the penetration of the Sieg-

---

[64] The 87th Battalion made this move as a unit, the first time it had assembled or moved as a battalion entity since it had left England. The 162-vehicle convoy covered the 317 miles and was in position with mortars ready to fire in 33 hours. Only 3 vehicles failed to complete the move because of mechanical failures. (1) 87th Cml Bn Rcd of Events, 13–14 Mar 45. (2) Ltr, Batte to Hist Off, 25 Jul 60.

fried Line and the drive to and the ultimate crossing of the Rhine. Twice before the 87th had supported divisions which penetrated the Siegfried Line—near Aachen in September 1944 and near Malmédy in February 1945. And, as before, the battalion supported a vanguard corps, this time the XV. By 23 March divisions of the corps had penetrated the Siegfried Line and were ready for the Rhine crossing. All four companies of the 87th Battalion were in support of the 3d Division which was to cross in the vicinity of Worms. Intense artillery and mortar preparations preceded the assault across the 1,000-foot-wide river.

Companies A and B consolidated their fire in support of the 7th Infantry. Between 0200 and 0315 on 26 March they fired twenty-three concentrations entailing 1,200 rounds of ammunition. Thereafter various targets of opportunity—machine guns, self-propelled guns, mortars—were hit by the 4.2-inch mortars. At dawn the combined companies laid two 10-hour screens (600 and 2,200 yards) which concealed bridge-building operations from direct enemy observation. Companies A and B expended 3,615 rounds of WP and 462 rounds of HE during the first day of the attack.[65] The effectiveness of the fire was made a matter of record by the operations officer of the 3d Division.

The Ninth Army, north of First Army and still under control of 21 Army Group, crossed the Rhine in an area just north of the Ruhr Valley. The army attack was concentrated on the XVI Corps front, with another corps poised to exploit initial successes, and a third lending support by fire and demonstration. In keeping with the decision temporarily to bypass the great Ruhr industrial area, XVI Corps attacked with an exposed right flank. To prevent enemy observation from the many potential observation posts in the Ruhr Valley, Ninth Army called for a 2-mile smoke screen along its exposed right flank.

The XVI Corps attacked with two divisions abreast, the 30th on the left and the 79th on the right. The 89th Chemical Mortar Battalion, Colonel Yanka commanding, supported the 79th Division.[66] Colonel Yanka initially divided his battalion into two parts, one for each of the attacking regiments of the 79th. Company A, with the 3d Platoon of Company B attached, supported the 313th Infantry on the division's right; Company C, augmented by the other two platoons of Company

---

[65] Company C was not called upon for fire on 26 March and Company D expended only 457 rounds. Both units crossed the river on the first day.

[66] The 92d Battalion was attached to the 30th Division.

ARTIFICIAL HAZE OBSCURES VEHICLES CROSSING THE RHINE

B, fired for the 315th Infantry on the left. These inflated companies reported to their respective regiments on 12 March. As this mortar battalion was without experience in river crossings, forward observer teams, two of which were to cross with the assault elements, joined the infantry for specialized training.

The 79th Division began to cross the Rhine in the Milchplatz-Orsoy area at 0300 on 24 March. Companies A and C of the 89th Chemical Mortar Battalion joined artillery units in pre-H-hour preparations and then, for seventy-five minutes after the attack began, fired prearranged concentrations. Upon completion of the preparatory fire the platoons of B Company reverted to company control. At 0600 Company A, firing from Orsoy, began its 3,500-yard screen along the division's right flank. Each mortar fired a volley of fifteen rounds to establish the screen and then fired a round every fifteen seconds to maintain it. This rate was found to be excessive and was reduced to an average of one shell per mortar per minute. At times the screen thinned, and additional rounds were fired. The screen was maintained until dark.

One mortar was reserved for any targets of opportunity reported by the forward observers. Late in the day Company C crossed the river as did the first platoon of Company B, now in support of the 314th Infantry. Company A remained in position.[67]

Several problems arose during the first day. The soil gave way under rapid fire, causing frequent re-emplacement of base plates. The heavy rate of fire also caused considerable damage to mortar parts. Over-heated barrels caused premature ignitions; in one instance a barrel became so hot that it bent. Shock absorber mechanisms broke down, base cap pins sheared, and locking forks broke or bent. On the other hand, tie rods and standards held up well.

On the morning of D plus 1 (25 March) heavy enemy fire from the right hastened the resumption of the flanking smoke screen. During that day the length of the screen was reduced by 700 yards because of the high rate of attrition of mortar parts. The next afternoon Capt. Clyde H. Westbrook, commander of Company A, reconnoitered the east bank of the Rhine for new mortar positions. That night the company crossed the river on Alligators and floating bridge sections and continued the smoke screen at dawn the next day. On 27 March the tactical situation was such that the use of smoke on the right flank was no longer required.[68]

With the Rhine behind them the Allies pushed deeper into German territory, and although there was some bitter resistance left in the enemy, it was to be only sporadic. Chemical mortar battalions accompanied the armies in their advance but much of the time, as in northern France, the rapid movement eliminated the need for their employment. And so, as the European war came to an end, some of these battalions were already serving in nonoperational and occupational capacities. This was as it should have been; they had done their measure of fighting and had acquitted themselves well.

[67] Part of the 74th Smoke Generator Company supported the 315th Infantry at Milchplatz. There were no generators at Orsoy until 26 March. See above, Chapter IX, for details of smoke generator activities during the Rhine crossing.

[68] (1) Notes of Conf Held at Hist Off, 1 March 50, sub: 89th Cml Bn and the Rhine Crossing. (2) 89th Cml Mortar Bn History, 24 Mar 45.

CHAPTER XIII

The Chemical Mortar in the Pacific

The employment of chemical mortar units in the Pacific differed considerably from that in the Mediterranean and European theaters. With the halt of the general Japanese advance at Guadalcanal, Allied forces faced the prospect of subjugating or bypassing the many island groups that lay between them and Japan. Because some of the islands were not very large certain of the campaigns were to be fought by small task forces, with a single mortar platoon attached to a regimental combat team. The islands also dictated that there would be a great many amphibious operations in which the 4.2-inch mortar, mounted on landing craft, was gradually to assume an important role. In many cases the advancing Allies were confronted by thick jungle growth which hindered the use of artillery and enhanced the value of the more mobile 4.2-inch mortar. This terrain, consisting of dense vegetation broken only by an occasional path, created problems of observation and transportation even for chemical mortar units. The climate of the Pacific added to the difficulties of mortar operations; the heavy rain, intense heat, and high humidity of the tropics made it difficult to insure effective employment of the mortar and proper maintenance of the weapon and its ammunition.

South Pacific Area

The initial combat employment of chemical mortar units in the war against Japan took place in September 1943 during the fight for New Georgia in the South Pacific Area.[1] It must be re-emphasized that the CWS did not receive authorization for the high explosive mission for 4.2-inch mortars until 19 March 1943, nearly seven months

---

[1] The South Pacific Area lay south of the Equator, east of longitude 159° east, and west of longitude 110° west. It was a vast expanse and included more than one million square miles of ocean and thousands of islands, among them New Zealand, New Caledonia, the New Hebrides, and the Santa Cruz, Fiji, Samoan, Tongan, Cook, and Society Island.

after U.S. forces first landed on Guadalcanal. For the Allies the Guadalcanal operation was the beginning of the road back. More immediately it had the mission of blunting the Japanese advance and protecting the vital lifeline between Australia and the United States.[2] With Guadalcanal secured, American forces looked northwest up the Solomon Island chain that led to New Britain and the important Japanese base at Rabaul. The Russell Islands fell first; then came the New Georgia campaign with its focal point at Munda, the site of an enemy airfield. The attack on the island of New Georgia began on 2 July 1943.

The 82nd Mortar Battalion was the first and only battalion in the South Pacific Area. Under command of Lt. Col. William H. Shimonek, the unit arrived at New Caledonia on 19 July 1943, too late to see action in the Munda operation. After a few weeks of training on Guadalcanal, elements of the 82d Battalion entered the mopping-up operation on Arundel and Kolombangara Islands in the New Georgia group. Assigned to XIV Corps and attached to the 43d Infantry Division, a platoon of B Company landed on what was to be known as Mortar Island in the Stima Lagoon area. This platoon fired its first combat rounds on the morning of 10 September when, under control of the division artillery, it delivered harassing and interdictory fire against the enemy, some of it on enemy barges operating between Kolombangara and Sagekarasa Islands.[3]

Meanwhile, in close support of the 27th Infantry, 25th Division, another platoon of the mortar battalion, moved up to Bamboe Peninsula on Arundel Island. The men used jeeps, hand carry, and a variety of boats to negotiate the difficult terrain. Once in position the mortars fired at enemy barges and troops. Despite the extreme range mortar fire destroyed three barges, causing the loss of enemy troops and supplies. From 25 September to 4 October the mortars placed cross-channel fire on the airfield on Kolombangara Island and on enemy shipping in the narrow waters between the islands.

These initial mortar operations were accompanied by certain problems, notably those involving transportation and supply. Major Mc-

---

[2] For details on the Guadalcanal operation, see Miller, *Guadalcanal: The First Offensive.*

[3] Unless otherwise noted, material for this section was based on the after action reports and unit files of the 82d Chemical Mortar Battalion and supported units. The latter include XIV Corps, 43d, 37th and 25th Divisions, 182d and 24th RCT's, and 135th Field Artillery Battalion. These records may be found in the Sixth Army Rcds, CMLHO. Military Intelligence Division, War Department, World War II, A Chronology, and CWS Theater of Operations Letters, 7, 10, 18, 19, have also been used.

Kaig, chemical officer of the 25th Division, improvised methods to provide the transportation and manpower necessary to resupply mortar units. Shipped from Guadalcanal to New Georgia by LST and from New Georgia to the northern end of Arundel Island by LCT (landing craft, tank), the ammunition was then transferred by LCM's to a battalion dump at the west end of Sagekarasa Island. From there engineer ponton boats took the ammunition across a lagoon to the mortar platoon's unloading points at the other end of the island.[4]

Although infantry commanders were unfamiliar with the capabilities and limitations of the mortar, most troops recognized the satisfactory performance of both the mortar crews and the weapon. And it was the opinion of a prisoner of war that the Japanese feared mortar barrages more than those of the artillery. One criticism by supported units was the great number of tree bursts which occurred in the heavy jungle canopy and which resulted from a lack of a delayed action fuze.[5]

The 82d Battalion next saw action on Bougainville, the largest of the Solomon group. Operations on this island began on the first day of November 1943 when the 3d Marine Division spearheaded the assault landings of the I Marine Amphibious Corps, with the 37th Infantry Division landing a week later. The XIV Army Corps, composed of the 37th and American Divisions, took over from the marines on 15 December. The corps commander, Maj. Gen. Oscar W. Griswold, indicated his desire to employ chemical mortar units in place of corps artillery in situations where the use of the latter was impracticable.

During and after the all-out enemy counterattacks on the American perimeter around Empress Augusta Bay in March 1944, infantry divisions attached mortar platoons to regiments or battalions. Control of the weapon varied. In the American Division mortar units operated directly under the supported infantry organizations, while in the 37th Division the mortarmen received firing instructions through the fire direction center of the artillery battalion to which they were attached. Both methods were satisfactory, but direct contact with the supported infantry seemed preferable since it allowed greater responsiveness during changing situations and provided closer liaison with responsible

---

[4] Ltr, Col McKaig to Hist Off, 27 Dec 50.

[5] (1) Ltr, Dir Intell ASF to Distr, 21 Jan 44, sub: Opns Against Treasury Island and Munda. CWS 319.1–Treasury Island. (2) Ltr, CO Co B 82d Cml Bn to CCWS, 2 Oct 43. (3) 43d Inf Div Rpt of Opns During Arundel Campaign (29 Aug–23 Sep 43).

commanders.[6] Heavy barrage missions were normally co-ordinated with corps and division artillery.

The jungle foliage on Bougainville was so thick that forward observers, compelled to employ sound-sensing methods of observation, were often located only 30 yards from the enemy and directed fire to within 20 yards of their own observation post and of the front lines. During the height of one enemy attack, the mortars placed smoke shell directly in front of enemy forward elements while troops of the 182d Infantry, only 30 yards away, withdrew without casualties. This was one of the few uses of WP on Bougainville, since the smoke further reduced the jungle's limited visibility.

Infantry commanders soon recognized that the mortars could engage, with a weight of shell comparable to that of 105-mm. artillery, many targets which could not be reached by the 105's and 155's. To insure adequate fire coverage of the entire 13-mile perimeter, thirty mortar positions were established which were linked together by more than 150 miles of communications wire. The necessity for this unusual number of gun positions was well demonstrated during one 4-day period in March by simultaneous requests from the 129th, 145th, and 182d Infantry for supporting fire from the platoons of Company A.

Daily battalion expenditure of mortar shell on Bougainville during March was extremely heavy; during the last three weeks of the month Company A alone expended 20,250 rounds in defense of a hill held by elements of the Americal Division. In an 11 March mission Companies A and D massed fire with 75-mm. and 105-mm. howitzers and with 60-mm. and 81-mm. mortars in a preparation which helped repel an enemy attack. Twelve days later Companies C and D joined with seven artillery battalions and two cannon companies in the heaviest general supporting fire laid down in the South Pacific fighting.

Field artillery officers were impressed by the amount of effective fire produced by a chemical mortar company as compared to that of an artillery unit. Maj. John D. Tolman, who commanded the 82d Chemical Mortar Battalion from 26 April until the close of the Luzon Campaign, disclosed that infantry commanders felt they could not "properly accomplish [their] mission [without] 4.2-inch mortar sup-

---

[6] XIV Corps, Extracts, Rpt on Lessons Learned in Bougainville Opn (hereafter cited as XIV Corps, Extracts, Rpt on Bougainville), p. 3. CMLHO.

port." [7] The 37th Division considered the 4.2-inch mortar "a powerful and devastating supplement to the division's artillery and mortar fires," and commanders of the Americal Division, while recommending reduction of the minimum range to increase the weapon's flexibility, commented on the effectiveness of the chemical mortar in perimeter defense and for fire on reverse slopes. [8] Captured Japanese documents revealed the enemy's fear of the weapon; enemy artillery was instructed to concentrate on American mortars. [9]

Infantry and chemical battalion commanders on Bougainville indicated that they were unfamiliar with each other's organization, tactics, and procedures and recognized the need for joint unit training. This reciprocal unfamiliarity continued to be a problem whenever a mortar unit was committed for its first engagement or a division had a chemical mortar unit attached to it for the first time. [10]

Beginning at Bougainville securing mortar crews against enemy infiltrations became a serious problem, particularly during night missions. Because of the absence of infantry perimeter guards and the frequency of enemy infiltrations, the battalion provided for day and night shifts both at the gun positions and at forward observation posts. Single and double apron fences surrounded emplacements. Automatic rifles and grenades were the chief means of repulsing Japanese attempts to overrun mortar positions.

The relatively static nature of the battle for the perimeter around Empress Augusta Bay eased the problem of maintenance. On the coral rock soil of Arundel, Company B had broken five base plates, bent five or six tie rods, and cracked several barrel cups and base plate spades. On Bougainville, despite the heavy and continuous fire, the softer ground and the fact that time was available to construct adequate emplacements resulted in a minimum of damage to mortar parts. The torrential rains, high humidity, and intense heat of South Pacific islands created serious problems both in the maintenance of mortar shell and its

---

[7] (1) Ltr, CO 82d Cml Mortar Bn to ACCWS for Field Opns, 22 Apr 44, p. 4.   (2) CWS TofO Ltr No. 19, 24 Oct 44, p. 38.

[8] (1) Ltr, CG 37th Div to CO 82d Cml Mortar Bn, 20 Apr 44, sub: Commendation.   (2) XIV Corps, Extracts, Rpt on Bougainville, pp. 2, 9,

[9] (1) Ltr, CO 82d Cml Mortar Bn to ACCWS for Field Opns, 22 Apr 44.   (2) TofO Ltr No. 15, 21 Jun 44, pp. 3–4.

[10] (1) 37th Div AAR Bougainville, 8 Nov 43–30 Apr 44, p. 59.   (2) Lt. Col. Orbie Bostick (formerly CmlO SOPAC), "Twenty-one Months in the South Pacific," *Chemical Warfare Bulletin*, vol. 29, No. 8 (December, 1943—January, 1944).

components. During the heaviest downpours, firing ceased because excessive water in the barrel resulted in "poop-outs." The extreme heat melted the filling of white phosphorus shells, creating a lateral void for those rounds stored in a horizontal position. These rounds tumbled badly when fired. A lack of adequate waterproofing combined with dampness caused the malfunction of cartridges and propellants and corrosion of fuzes while shells were in storage. In an attempt to minimize these difficulties on Bougainville mortarmen placed their ammunition dump, featured by sheltered racks and a double-decked roof, as far inland as possible. Even then ammunition had to be checked and rechecked, particularly the fuzes. Although heat, rain, and dampness continued to be a problem throughout operations in the South and Southwest Pacific, the situation improved in late 1944 with the introduction of metallic containers for propellants and cartridges.

At least one difficulty with mortar shells was not brought on by the weather. This was the occasional absence of the steel balls which prevented the premature arming of the fuze. Despite close inspection of mortar ammunition short rounds and premature bursts resulted in several casualties to both mortarmen and infantry.[11]

Southwest Pacific Area

New Guinea

Early in 1943 the Chemical Warfare Service,[12] the War Department, and Southwest Pacific Area headquarters considered the possibility of shipping chemical mortar units to the Southwest Pacific.[13] The area's demand for these units grew more insistent after a weapons demonstration held in October 1943. At the demonstration General Krueger, Commanding General, Sixth Army, told Maj. Gen. William H. Gill, Commanding General, 32d Infantry Division, that the 4.2-inch chemical mortar was the weapon needed to clean the enemy out of tenaciously

---

[11] (1) Ltr, CG USAFISPA to CCWS, 10 Apr 44, sub: Faulty 4.2 Cml Mortar Shell Fuzes. CWS 314.7 Unit Files. CMLHO. (2) Rad CM-OUT 24933, 19 Apr 44. (3) Rad CM-IN 14685, 20 Apr 44. (4) The 82d remained on Bougainville until December 1944, when it sailed for Luzon. 82d Cml Mort Bn, Hist Data Cards.

[12] References used for this section, unless otherwise noted, include: (1) Unit Rcds, 98th Cml Mortar Bn (CMLHO); (2) Sixth Army AAR's (Sixth Army Rcds, ORB, CMLHO).

[13] (1) Ltr, CmlO USASOS to ExecO OCCWS, 18 Jan 43. (2) Personal Ltr, CmlO I Corps to ACCWS for Field Opns, 26 Jan 43. (3) Ltr, ACCWS for Field Opns to Chief OPD WDGS, 11 Mar 43, no sub. All three in CMLHO.

held positions.[14] Several other high-ranking commanders who had participated in the Buna campaign in Papua, where mortar battalions had not been available, echoed this opinion. They suggested that a chemical mortar battalion be made a part of army troops for attachment to corps and divisions.[15]

In April 1944 General MacArthur launched a new offensive along the northern coast of New Guinea in a series of operations which, in collaboration with Admiral Nimitz' drive through the Central Pacific, would place American forces in a position to retake the Philippine Islands. On 22 April MacArthur's initial objectives, Hollandia and Aitape, were attacked by I Corps operating as RECKLESS Task Force.[16]

The elements of RECKLESS Task Force had chemical mortar support for the Hollandia operation, but this support came from a rather odd source. Because of a shortage of mortar units in the zone of interior the War Department in February 1944 authorized the SWPA to convert a tank destroyer battalion to a chemical mortar battalion at the earliest practicable date. Almost immediately the theater reorganized the 641st Tank Destroyer Battalion which, after a brief period of training, participated in the Hollandia operation, under command of Lt. Col. Alexander Batlin. But redesignation waited until June 1944, producing the anomalous situation of a so-called tank destroyer unit firing 4.2-inch chemical mortars.[17]

The mortars played an extremely minor role at Hollandia, the entire four companies firing less than 350 rounds during about one week in the line. At the request of a regimental commander one company dragged a single mortar and 120 shells on carts for twelve miles along a narrow, muddy mountain trail, across a 2,000-foot ridge, through swamps, and over three rivers—only to arrive too late to support the fight for Hollandia Airdome. It was fortunate that expenditures were low because ammunition was limited. On the night of 23 April enemy planes bombed the beachhead dumps at Humboldt Bay destroying 6,550

---

[14] Memo, ACmlO Sixth Army for CmlO ALAMO Force, 8 Oct 43. 300.6—Misc Memos and Ltrs, Sixth Army Rcds.

[15] Excerpt from AGF Bd Rpt on SWPA, No. 31, 25 Feb 44. CMLHO.

[16] For details of the strategic decisions and tactical aspects of these operations along New Guinea's northern coast, see Smith, *Approach to the Philippines.*

[17] (1) Rad, CM–IN 8408, 12 Feb 44. (2) Ltr, AG to CINCSWPA, 25 Feb 44, sub: Reorgn and Redesignation of 641st Tank Destroyer Bn. (3) CM–IN 0238Z, Jul 44.

rounds of 4.2-inch mortar shell, or about 78 percent of the available supply.[18]

Subsequent New Guinea operations utilized but one mortar company at a time. Company B of the 98th, commanded by 1st Lt. Vernon E. Woebbeking and attached to the 191st Field Artillery Group, successively supported the 163d, 158th, and 20th Infantry Regiments during the Wakde Islands–Maffin Bay fighting which took place in May 1944. During the assault phase of this operation, the LCM's carrying the 4.2-inch shell grounded over fifty yards from the beach and the mortar crews had to carry their cargo through chest-deep water.[19] During the cross-channel firing on the Wakde group the chemical mortars massed fires with the 81-mm. mortars and with the artillery from the mainland. When attached to artillery units the mortar platoons were divided into 2-gun sections with weapons placed approximately 1,000 yards apart. Chemical officers and Sixth Army headquarters vigorously criticized this practice because it prevented the units from massing their fires and giving close support to the infantry. They insisted that platoons be employed as units under direct infantry control.[20] Later, mortar units were assigned to the infantry and remained so attached for the rest of the operation.

In June 1944 HURRICANE Task Force, principally composed of two of the three regiments of the 41st Division, assaulted the island of Biak, located west of Wakde off New Guinea's northern coast.[21] The Allied forces wanted the island, as they had Wakde, as a site for airfields for bombing operations against the enemy. Company D, 98th Battalion, commanded by Capt. Jalmar Gertulla, supported the attacking forces with missions for perimeter defense, beachhead extension, and harassment. On one occasion the 2d Platoon covered the withdrawal by water of a tank-led infantry battalion and then, after destroying their mortars and ammunition, withdrew itself. Early in June observers of the mortar platoon directed fire from landing craft on cave mouths

---

[18] (1) AGF Bd Rpt on SWPA, No. 74, 9 Jun 44, Employ of 4.2″ Cml Mortars. (2) Cml Sec 41st Div, n.d., Hist Rpt, LETTERPRESS Opn (22 Apr–5 May 44). AGRO-H (7945) 341–11.7. (3) Smith, *Approach to the Philippines*, p. 66. (4) Lt. Col. John E. Clarke, "The Longest 12 Miles on Earth," *Chemical Warfare Bulletin*, vol. 31, No. 1 (January–February, 1945), pp. 47–49.

[19] Personal Ltr, CmlO TORNADO TF to CmlO Sixth Army, 22 May 44. 300.6—Memos to and from APO 565 Unit 1, Sixth Army Rcds.

[20] Ltr, Cml Warfare Intell Team 4 to CmlO USASOS, 24 Jun 44, sub: Rpt on Use of Cml Warfare Weapons and Munitions.

[21] See Riegelman, *Caves of Biak*, for a personal account of the Biak operation. During World War II Colonel Riegleman served as I Corps chemical officer.

invisible to both air and ground observers. Unfortunately, when the 1st Platoon fired 180 rounds of high explosive at cave mouths for an antitank company on 7 June, 10 out of 12 rounds with T-89 delay fuzes were duds, while other rounds with point-detonating fuzes exploded as tree bursts above the caves.

What might be considered classic examples of combined all-mortar preparations took place on 16 and 27 June. Chemical mortar barrages preceded advances of the 186th Infantry near the village of Mokmer on Biak; this fire was then lifted and was followed sucessively by the 81-mm. and the 60-mm. mortars. On both dates, the infantry advanced against minor resistance to objectives which, before these preparations, had been vigorously defended.[22]

With the Wakde experience in mind the 20th Infantry inquired whether a chemical mortar company could be assigned to the 6th Infantry Division. After Biak, supported battalions in the 162d and 186th Infantry Regiments stated that because of its greater range and blast effect on area targets, the 4.2-inch mortar filled the gap between the 81-mm. mortar and artillery. Because of the higher angle of fire, the infantry preferred the 4.2-inch mortar to 75-mm. and 105-mm. howitzers for firing on sharply defiladed and densely wooded terrain. In open terrain the mortar was equal in effectiveness, if not range, to the 105-mm. howitzer. On the other hand, two battalion commanders considered the 4.2-inch mortar less accurate than the 81-mm. weapon and complained of the slow displacement of the former over rough terrain during a fast-moving advance.[23]

The 98th Battalion encountered some of the same tribulations on New Guinea that had marked the fighting in the South Pacific Area. These included the unfamiliarity of infantry commanders with the capabilities and limitations of the weapon, the inadequate training of mortar personnel in infantry tactics and procedures, the excessive length of time firing personnel remained in the line without relief, and the deleterious effects of dampness on mortar shell components and their containers. The disadvantages of attaching mortar units to artillery

---

[22] Ltr, CmlO U.S. Forces to CmlO ALAMO Force, 19 Jul 44, sub: Preliminary Tech Rpt 5, p. 6. 350.05-Biak, Sixth Army Rcds, ORB.

[23] (1) Ltr, CmlO TORNADO TF to CmlO Sixth Army, 22 Jun 44. 472.4—4.2″ Cml Mortar, Sixth Army Rcds, ORB. (2) Ltr, CmlO 41st Inf Div to CmlO ALAMO Force, 27 Jul 44, sub: Preliminary Tech Rpt 16, pp. 1–2. 350.05—Biak, Sixth Army Rcds, ORB.

organizations, realized in the South Pacific, were emphasized in the Southwest Pacific.[24]

Beginning with the fighting on New Guinea, one of the most persistent of the bottlenecks facing mortar units was the lack of adequate motor transportation. Several times the units were unable to keep up with supported infantry in fast-moving actions. At Hollandia and on Wakde ship-to-shore movement suffered seriously from a shortage of amphibious vehicles. In the former operation, one company failed to land in time to carry out its mission in support of an infantry regiment. The value of adequate motorized equipment from ship to shore and from the shore inland was again illustrated on Biak where assignment to the company of 4 Dukws and 3 additional 2½-ton 6 x 6 trucks insured prompt and speedy landing of men, weapons, and shell; facilitated leapfrogging of platoons during movement of the company along beach areas; and resulted in satisfactory ammunition resupply. Colonel Arthur, Chemical Officer, 41st Division, as well as the G-3 of I Corps, felt that mortar units should be committed with complete organic transportation and urged that the companies be provided with either 2 LVT's (landing vehicles, tracked) or 4 Dukws for amphibious movement.[25]

Leyte

In September 1944, with the northwest coast of New Guinea in the hands of General MacArthur and with the Marianas Islands secured by Admiral Nimitz, the Joint Chiefs of Staff, deciding to skip three planned intermediate objectives, set their sights directly on the island of Leyte in the Philippines.[26] In a move that speeded up the Pacific time

[24] (1) Cml Sec 41st Div, n.d., Hist Rpt, LETTERPRESS Opn (22 Apr–5 May 44), p. 10. (2) CmlO 41st Inf Div, n.d., Hist Rcd, Cml Sec 41st Inf Div, p. 4. CMLHO. (3) An. 2 to G–3 I Corps, History of Biak Opn, 15–27 Jun 44, n.d., p. 40. (4) Ltrs, CmlO PERSECUTION TF to CmlO Sixth Army, 27 Apr, 22 May 44. 300.6—Memos to and from APO 565 Unit I, Sixth Army Rcds, ORB. (5) CM–IN 14904, 17 Aug 44.

[25] (1) An. 2 to G–3 I Corps, History of Biak Opn, 15–27 Jun 44, p. 40. (2) Ltr, CmlO 41st Inf Div to CmlO ALAMO Force, 12 May 44, sub: Cml Phase of LETTERPRESS Opn. (3) Sixth Army Cml Warfare Activities During the Biak Opn, pp. 6–7. 350.05, Sixth Army Rcds, ORB.

[26] Unless otherwise noted, references for the Leyte operation include: (1) Unit Histories, Rpts, and Rcds of 85th and 88th Cml Mortar Bns, in Sixth Army Rcds; (2) Sixth Army, Rpt of Leyte Opn, 30 Nov 45, and Rpt of G–4 and Cml Sec of same headquarters; (3) CmlO X Corps, Rpt of Leyte Campaign, 3 Jan 45, in Sixth Army Rcds; (4) Ltr, CG 24th Div to CG X Corps, 18 Dec 44, sub: Rpt, Chemical Warfare Activities Leyte Opn, CMLHO; (5) 19th Inf Hist Rcd, Leyte Campaign, 8 Sep–22 Nov 44.

table by exactly two months, they directed MacArthur and Nimitz to assault Leyte on 20 October.[27]

At the time of the Leyte invasion Sixth Army included X Corps and XXIV Corps. The latter had been at Pearl Harbor preparing for the assault on the island of Yap when the change of plans eliminated that particular operation. Thereupon Admiral Nimitz turned over the XXIV Corps to General MacArthur. Major elements of XXIV Corps were the 77th and 96th Divisions, having among their supporting units the 88th Chemical Mortar Battalion (less companies C and D), and the 7th Division, supported by the 91st Chemical Company. The latter, one of two *separate* mortar companies to see action in World War II, had been stationed for some years at Schofield Barracks on Hawaii.[28]

Chemical mortar units already with Sixth Army were the 98th and the 85th Battalions. The former, having participated in the Wakde and Biak fighting, had entered a period of rest and rehabilitation. The 85th Chemical Mortar Battalion, a recent arrival from the United States, supported X Corps in the Leyte operation, specifically the 1st Cavalry and 24th Infantry Divisions.

Commanded by Lt. Col. Kenneth K. MacDonald, the 85th Battalion landed on the beaches of Leyte with the early waves of the 20 October assault. The battalion was divided into two groups, corresponding with its attachments—the headquarters detachment and Companies A and B with the 1st Cavalry and Companies C and D with the 24th Division. Company C ran into immediate difficulty. Coming in with the fourth wave the two landing craft carrying the 3d Platoon received direct hits from enemy fire. One man was killed and 10 others were wounded. But in general, enemy resistance was light, and this circumstance, combined with a lack of transportation, limited initial activity for the companies of the 85th Battalion. Companies C and D had landed without organic vehicles and were to operate under that handicap for the entire campaign.

During the second and third weeks of November, Company C supported the 21st Infantry, 24th Division, in the extremely bitter fighting for Breakneck Ridge, southwest of the town of Pinamopoan located on the northern coast of Leyte. The Japanese defended this position

---

[27] See M. Hamlin Cannon, *Leyte: The Return to the Philippines*, UNITED STATES ARMY IN WORLD WAR II (Washington, 1954), for the strategy behind this decision and for an account of the actual operation.

[28] See Brophy and Fisher, *Organizing for War*, app. H.

with a tenacity that gave the hill formation its nickname. For a time the rugged terrain limited artillery support, a situation which enhanced the value of the CWS weapon. The mortar platoons fired nearly 2,800 rounds of ammunition during the period 7–15 November, including missions against troop concentrations, entrenchments, pillboxes, mortars, machine guns, and light artillery.

On 14 November the 32d Division relieved the 24th Division and, as so often was the case, Company C of the 85th Battalion remained in the line in support of a new infantry regiment, this time the 128th. Within four days an incident occurred which marred good relations between the supporting and supported units. On the morning of 18 November the mortars of Company C, along with other supporting weapons, fired about 375 rounds against an enemy strongpoint. Despite the testimony of the mortar forward observer, the division chemical officer, and the regimental commander himself, Company C was charged with a short round burst that killed one infantryman of the 128th and wounded seven others. The X Corps commander, Maj. Gen. Franklin C. Sibert, ordered the relief of the mortar company, an action which took place six days later with the arrival of Company B. Unfortunately, this incident destroyed the confidence of the infantry in the chemical mortar; for quite a while thereafter the division employed the 4.2-inch mortar only for road interdiction.[29]

Company B, 88th Chemical Mortar Battalion, commanded by Capt. Henry A. Kitselman, came ashore with elements of 96th Division (XXIV Corps) over the beaches near Dulag.[30] During the first two weeks of combat the platoons of the company operated separately in support of infantry battalions in attacks in the vicinity of the landing beaches, against enemy positions on Labiranan Head, Labir, and Catmon Hill, and inland near the villages of Tabontabon and Dagami. Initially, the swamp and poor transportation prevented the mortars from getting inland and thereafter transportation proved to be a major problem. During this period, which coincided with the rainy season, the vehicles of the mortar company became mired, while advancing infantrymen

---

[29] (1) It was a matter of small irony that General Sibert was the son of the first Chief, Chemical Warfare Service, Maj. Gen. William L. Sibert.   (2) Ltr, CG 32d Div to CG X Corps, 19 Dec 44, sub: Rpt of Cml Warfare Activities in the Leyte Opn. Sixth Army Rcds, 319.1 Leyte Opn Rpts. (3) Lt John K. King, Rpt of Inspection of Forward Position during A+27 – A+31, Nov 1944. Sixth Army Rcds, 333 Inspection Rpts.

[30] The troops of XXIV Corps also had the support of eight mortar boats.

were calling for fire now beyond mortar range. The mortars did complete some missions. On 22 October one of the mortar platoons repulsed an attack of a Japanese patrol killing 52 of the enemy and itself suffering 2 killed and 6 wounded. Later, on 27 and 28 October, the mortars silenced enemy 75-mm. mortars in defilade on Catmon Hill, burned four sniper-infested pillboxes, and screened the withdrawal of an infantry company pinned down on Catmon Hill.

From 5 to 20 November Company B, firing as a unit, supported the 382d Infantry and then, until 28 November, the 381st, which was slowly advancing through the swamps, rice paddies, and hilly terrain west of Dagami. Mortarmen, with the aid of Filipinos, carried their weapons and ammunition by hand, or placed them on the backs of plodding carabao. The intense rain continued to hamper all ground operations. It caused base plates to sink into the soft mud and resulted in mortar breakage and the consequent suspension of firing.

Company A, 88th Chemical Mortar Battalion, landed with the 77th Division early in December 1944 and remained with that unit for two months. The 91st Chemical Mortar Company supported the 7th Division throughout the Leyte Campaign. Although placed under control of division artillery, each of its three platoons supported one of the three regiments of the division. During this 41-day commitment, two platoons used artillery forward observers and one used its own. In the drive on Ormoc the division artillery assumed control of the mortar company. Although no missions took place under this arrangement the platoon fired for registration every evening. In mid-December two of the platoons reverted to regimental attachment, a step which in the opinion of the company commander, Capt. Eugene F. Them, resulted in a far better utilization of the unit.[31]

The performance of the 4.2-inch mortars on Leyte was not an unqualified success. Infantrymen frequently complained that the mortar units could not keep pace with them in rapid advances over rough terrain, a situation resulting as much from the rainy season in which the operation took place as from the lack of complete organic transportation among the mortar units. This lack stemmed directly from the infantry's unfamiliarity with the needs of mortar units—only one of the six divisions which saw action had had previous chemical mortar support. As a result, most of them failed to allot sufficient shipping

---

[31] Ltr, CO 91st Cml Co (Motorized) to CmlO XXIV Corps, 14 Dec 44, sub: Rpt of Mortar Co Activities. Sixth Army Rcds, 319.1 Leyte Opn Rpts.

space for the mortar units and most organic vehicles were not taken aboard.[32] Only when the supported divisions and regiments assigned additional transportation to the mortar companies did the latter recover their mobility.[33] At the conclusion of the Leyte operation chemical officers not only recommended the use of Dukws for mortar units in assault landings, but also the employment of tracked vehicles in swampy terrain.[34]

Luzon

Turning his attention from Leyte, where he left the newly activated Eighth Army, to Luzon, General MacArthur directed General Krueger to seize a beachhead on Lingayen Gulf, drive southward and free Manila, and, eventually, liberate the entire island.[35] The decision to take Luzon had come only after prolonged debate at the highest level of strategic planning. S-day for the operation was 9 January 1945.[36]

Sixth Army operations on Luzon had the support of three mortar battalions.[37] The 98th Chemical Mortar Battalion supported I Corps on the left of Sixth Army's beachhead and the 82d fired for the divisions of XIV Corps on the right. The 85th Battalion was released from the Eighth Army later in January and attached to XIV Corps. These three mortar battalions provided continuous close support throughout the fighting on Luzon. As on Leyte, the corps normally reattached mortar companies to divisions which, in turn, assigned platoons to assault regiments.

Initially, XIV Corps faced but token resistance as it headed down the central plain of Luzon toward Manila. Enemy opposition increased in the last week of January, particularly in the Zambales Mountains on

[32] (1) Ltr, CG Sixth Army to Distr, 25 Nov 44, sub: Rpt on Mistakes Made and Lessons Learned in K-2 Opns, pp. 20-21. 314.7 Hist Rpts, Sixth Army Rcds, ORB. (2) Ltr, ACmlO Sixth Army to CmlO I Corps, 29 Oct 44. 300.6 Memos, I Corps, Sixth Army Rcds, ORB.

[33] (1)Ltr, CG Sixth Army to Distr, 25 Nov 44, sub: Rpt on Mistakes Made and Lessons Learned in K-2 Opns, pp. 20-21. (2) Co A 88th Cml Mortar Bn Journal, Leyte.

[34] Ltr, CmlO POA to CCWS, 4 Apr 45, sub: Observer Rpt of Action of Co B 88th Cml Mortar Bn on Leyte. CMLHO.

[35] Sources for this section include: Unit Histories and Rpts of 82d, 85th, 88th, and 98th Cml Mortar Bns, in Sixth Army Rcds ORB and CMLHO; XIV Corps M-7 and M-1 Opns, Luzon; Rpts of 25th, 32d, 33d, 37th, and 43d Divs, of 5th, 7th, and of 8th Cav Regts, and 20th and 63d Inf Regts.

[36] For details on the strategy behind the Luzon decision as well as for a comprehensive account of the entire campaign, see Robert Ross Smith, *Triumph in the Philippines*, UNITED STATES ARMY IN WORLD WAR II (Washington, 1963).

[37] As in the case of Leyte the assault troops of I and XIV Corps were accompanied by 4.2-inch mortar boats.

the right flank of the corps. After a week marked by effective mortar fire against personnel, weapons, tanks, and supply dumps, three companies of the 82d turned southward to join in the struggle for Manila. The fourth, Company B, remained behind in the hills west of Fort Stotsenburg, successively supporting elements of the 40th, 43d, and 38th Divisions from 28 January to 18 March. Mortar operations in support of a 40th Division attack on Snake Hill North were featured by some unusual action on the part of forward observers. On 7 February, after enemy fire wounded a platoon forward observer, Cpl. Edward A. Yehle of the mortar observation party successfully directed chemical mortar and artillery fire against enemy opposition in front of a battalion of the 160th Infantry. Next morning another mortarman, Pvt. Herbert H. League, took charge in a similar situation, simultaneously directing 4.2-inch mortar, 81-mm. mortar, and artillery fire in action which resulted in the destruction of at least one enemy machine gun and which served as a screen for the evacuation of friendly casualties. Later, League directed similar fire which proved instrumental in the death of 40 Japanese and in repulsing an enemy attack.

Meanwhile, the main body of the 82d supported the 37th Division as XIV Corps pushed down Route 5 toward Manila. The approach to the city was uneventful in comparison to the resistance encountered once the American forces entered Manila. Fire missions for the mortars picked up immediately. The weapon screened regimental crossings of the Pasig River, which bisects the city, and fired support, incendiary, and neutralization missions, mostly in conjunction with infantry mortars and the artillery. After witnessing the chemical mortars in action before the High Commissioner's residence, the Assistant Chief of Staff, G–3, 37th Division, declared that "direct support infantry weapons, particularly 4.2-inch mortars, falling close to our own lines, were found to neutralize the enemy where penetration took place."

The 85th Battalion was triangularized just prior to landing near San Fabian in the Lingayen Gulf on 28 January with the 1st Cavalry Division.[38] By early February, its mortars were in Manila supporting cavalrymen from emplacements on city pavements, vacant lots, lawns, golf courses, even tennis courts. From 22 to 25 February elements of Company B fought as infantry in defense of a regimental perimeter within the city.

---

[38] As in the fighting in Europe, the mortar battalions in the Pacific reorganized under the new tables of organization whenever it became convenient.

Certain supported commanders, particularly in the 7th Cavalry Regiment, refused to use chemical mortars for close support missions, claiming that the old M2 sight was inaccurate.[39] But it was with this sight that elements of the 85th massed fire, along with 81-mm. mortars, in the final assault on the Agriculture Building and brought fire to within 200 feet of the mortar observation post. After the cavalry took its objective, a regimental operations officer called the chemical mortar fire "the most accurate fire support we've ever had." Battalion casualties, the highest for a 30-day period of any chemical mortar battalion on Luzon, totaled 7 men killed and 13 wounded.

During the last part of February and before resistance had ended in Manila, XIV Corps gave the 1st Cavalry Division (less one brigade) and the 6th Infantry Division, until recently a part of I Corps, the mission of clearing the Manila watershed and attacking Japanese forces in the Sierra Madre Mountains about ten miles east of the city. These enemy troops, comprising the major enemy concentration in central Luzon, had not taken part in the Manila fighting but had withdrawn to the east with the approach of the American troops. Ensconced in the so-called *Shimbu* Line, Japanese forces put up fanatic resistance in the rugged and rocky foothills of the Sierra Madres.

The 82d and 85th Chemical Mortar Battalions fired in support of these operations. Company A, 85th Battalion, saw a good deal of action with the 7th and 8th Cavalry regiments west of Antipolo. Early in March a squadron commander refused to have one of the mortar platoons engage a target because it was within 500 yards of his troops. Instead, he gave the mission to his 81-mm. mortars, despite the fact that these weapons had a greater dispersion than did the 4.2's. This show of hesitancy regarding mortar support by the 85th Battalion was not the first to come from supported troops. A succession of battalion commanders—there were three incumbents during the first six weeks of 1945—provides another clue to the fact that not all was right with the unit. As of 16 March the firing companies of the 85th reverted to battalion control and underwent an intensive 2-week training period under the new commander, Maj. Maurice G. Green, recently operations officer of the 82d Chemical Mortar Battalion.

The 82d Chemical Mortar Battalion supported the *Shimbu* opera-

[39] Memo, CmlO Sixth Army for ACofS G–3 Sixth Army, 12 Mar 45. S–3 Rpts, 85th Cml Mortar Bn, Sixth Army Rcds, ORB.

tions from 25 February until 30 April. In mid-March the XIV Corps relinquished control of this fighting to XI Corps, and the 82d utilized this transfer of command to reorganize under the latest table of organization. Battalion support in the vicinity of Mount Mataba, one of the bastions of the *Shimbu* Line, resulted in some of the heaviest 4.2-inch mortar fire in the Pacific war. During the 2-week period between 23 March and 5 April the 82d fired nearly 190 missions with an expenditure of over 22,000 rounds. On 6 April two platoons of Company B and one from Company C, in support of an attack by the 63d Infantry, laid a 6,000-yard smoke screen southeast of Mount Mataba and maintained it for eight hours. The smoke masked the advance of the infantry from enemy observation posts on Mount Mataba and a lesser hill which was an immediate objective of the attack. The mortars maintained this screen by firing a total of 16 rounds a minute the first hour and 10 rounds a minute thereafter. Unfortunately, a shortage of ammunition brought a halt to the screen before the troops reached their objective. Three hours later ammunition requested from XI Corps four days earlier arrived at the mortar positions.[40]

On 21 April Company B (less the 3d Platoon), while in support of the 145th Infantry, participated in one of the heaviest preparations fired on Luzon. In order to cover an infantry advance on the slopes of Mount Pacawagan, another of the keys to the *Shimbu* positions, the mortar company fired 2,525 rounds of white phosphorus to set up a 7-hour screen, supplemented by two B-25 aircraft laying a 8,000-yard FS screen. Six days later the crest of Pacawagan fell to troops of the 145th Infantry after a combined weapons preparation and with the aid of a chemical mortar screen.

That the reputation of smoke increased on Luzon is suggested by the following entry in a 6th Infantry Division operational report: "The outstanding use for chemical warfare weapons in the *Shimbu* Line battle was the use of screening smokes. . . ."[41] One of the mortar battalions called attention to the high ratio of white phosphorus used on Luzon,[42] indicative of quite a departure from previous Pacific practice.

---

[40] (1) 2d Ind, CmlO 6th Inf Div to CmlO Sixth Army, 12 Apr 45, on Ltr, CmlO XI Corps to CmlO 6th Div, 8 Apr 45, sub: Smoke Opn. Sixth Army Rcds, 470.6 Smoke Missions. (2) Artillery as well as mortar units had difficulty with ammunition supply.

[41] Digest of Staff Sectional Rpts, 6th Div, Luzon Campaign, 9 Jan–30 Jun 45, p. 126. Opns Rpts, AGO 306 – 0.3 (12490).

[42] 82d Cml Mortar Bn Hist Rpt Luzon Opn, 9 Jan–30 Jun 45, The First 120 Days (hereafter cited as 82d, First 120 Days Luzon), p. 6. CWPN 82 – 0.3 (24515).

Infantry commanders had long been reluctant to request WP fire. Smoke as a means of concealment was often superfluous in the jungle fighting during the early years of the war, and casualties were produced by high explosives. As a consequence, white phosphorus ammunition remained unused while stockpiles of high explosives were bled white.

Actually, white phosphorus ammunition was a versatile munition. In addition to its ability to produce screens and inflict casualties, it served as an incendiary agent. A fourth characteristic, really an extension of its antipersonnel capability, was the tremendous psychological effect it had on the enemy. The main reason for its unpopularity was that infantry commanders were unfamiliar with its many attributes, especially the casualty and incendiary effects.[43]

Several factors contributed to the increased use of smoke shell on Luzon. One of these was the limited supply of high explosive shell which served to call attention to the white phosphorus munition. In February 1945, for example, Col. Richard R. Danek, Chemical Officer, XIV Corps, declared that the supply of chemical mortar ammunition had "reached a critical stage." [44] Several months later Maj. David D. Hulsey, 6th Division chemical officer, stated that during one period in April chemical mortar operations in his sector were "practically nil" because of the "unavailability of 4.2-inch mortar ammunition from XI Corps." [45] Causes for the shortage included limited transportation and deterioration of shell through improper storage, but, more basically, the critical nature of the supply of 4.2-inch mortar ammunition on Luzon resulted from the fact that half of the shells received from the United States were on the list of ammunitions frozen by the War Department because of the possibility of defective fuzes.[46]

Other reasons for the increased use of WP involved matters of terrain and education. In the Philippines, American forces for the first time in the Pacific encountered a battle area of rather extended dimensions and one that featured mountain and hill masses from which the enemy had excellent observation. The Sierra Madres east of Manila and the series

---

[43] 85th Cml Mortar Bn in the M–1 Opns (Luzon) Hist Rpt, 9 Jan–30 Jun 45. CWBN 85 – 0.3.

[44] Memo, Danek for CofS XIV Corps, 25 Feb 45, no sub. XIV Corps File, Rpt, Cml Munitions.

[45] Ltr, CmlO 6th Div to CmlO Sixth Army, 1 May, sub: Cml Warfare Weekly Opns Rtp. 319.1 Sixth Army Rcds, Weekly Activity Rpts, Divs.

[46] (1) Ltr, CG 6th Div to CG Sixth Army through CG XIV Corps, 5 Mar 45, sub: Unsatisfactory Condition of 4.2-inch Cml Mortar Ammunition, and 1st and 2d Inds thereto. XIV Corps File — Rpts, Cml Munitions. (2) Memo, Sixth Army CmlO to Sixth Army G–4, 6 Feb 45. Sixth Army Rcds, 400.34 Equip.

of mountains confronting I Corps in its drive to the northeast were typical of the Luzon terrain. A 6th Division report gave examples of the use of screening smokes: ". . . to deny the enemy observation during infantry attacks, to cover the construction of supply roads, and to screen carrying parties and evacuation of wounded." [47] As for the matter of education, supported commanders, once they had seen the results of WP as an antipersonnel and incendiary agent, were much less loath to call for WP rounds in support of their operations.

Perhaps the best barometer of the reputation of white phosphorus was the official HE–WP ratio for mortar ammunition which fluctuated back and forth between 80–20 and 60–40, in favor of high explosives. In August 1945 General MacArthur's headquarters established the ratio at 60 HE–40 WP, based upon the experience of the major combat commands of the theater.[48]

While XIV Corps landed against light resistance and faced only token enemy forces until the Fort Stotsenburg fighting, I Corps had a tough time almost from the start. The enemy had established strong defenses on I Corps left flank, made more formidable by the rugged mass of hills and mountains. The fact that the Japanese headquarters lay to the rear of these defenses tended to make enemy resistance all the more tenacious. The divisions of I Corps faced not one but a series of difficult missions. Elements were to drive southeast across central Luzon, cover the left flank of the southward advance of XIV Corps, and advance north and northeast in the direction of the towns of Damortis and Rosario and an important road junction just beyond.

An immediate I Corps objective was the enemy position in the Cabaruan Hills, fifteen miles inland from the Lingayen beaches in the sector of the 6th Division. On 22 January Company A, 98th Chemical Mortar Battalion, operating as a unit for the first time on Luzon, supported the 2d Battalion, 20th Infantry, in what was expected to be the culminating effort against Japanese resistance in the Cabaruan Hills.[49] The mortar platoons went into positions about 200 yards from one another in defiladed terrain. Each unit maintained its own observation post on one of the highest hills in the area. These OP's

[47] Digest of Staff Sectional Rpts, 6th Div, Luzon Campaign.

[48] (1) Ltr, Gen Hq USAFPAC to CG's First, Sixth, Eighth, Tenth Armies, *et al.*, 16 Aug 45. Sixth Army Rcds, 471 Ammunition. (2) The ETO arrived at the same percentage although no ratio was definitely prescribed. Rowan comments, 19 Jan 61.

[49] See Smith, *Triumph in the Philippines*, for a description of this action.

were located about 350 yards in front of the mortars and overlooked the enemy positions 600 yards to the front. Wire connected the observation posts with the mortars, although once the platoons moved forward they would have to rely exclusively upon radio communication. At this stage in the fighting the forward observers of all three platoons fired at targets selected by the infantry battalion commander. Ammunition resupply was the province of the regimental supply officer who delivered the shells directly to the platoon positions. When the mortar units displaced forward the regimental supply trucks kept pace.

After laying down a heavy barrage on an area of ten artillery squares, Company A placed white phosphorus on the corners of the enemy position to mark it for aerial bombardment. After the air strike the mortars blanketed the enemy area with WP as the rifle companies of the 2d Battalion, 20th Infantry, moved forward. Companies E and F advanced along opposite sides of a ridge that led into the right flank of the Japanese positions. Company G, located initially in front of the objective, used the smoke to move through a ravine and into the left flank of the enemy-held hill mass. The 1st and 2d Platoons of the mortar company displaced forward in rear of the cannon company; the 3d remained ready to fire on any target of opportunity. The three mortar forward observers as well as the mortar company commander, Capt. G. B. Doolittle, accompanied Company G. During the advance radios served as the only means of communication.

Company G experienced initial success in its flanking maneuver but was suddenly hit on three sides by Japanese fire. At the same time the enemy pinned down Companies E and F. This unexpected opposition came from two sources, from the enemy that survived the preattack bombardments and from those who had slipped into positions under the very smoke that concealed the American advance.

Losing all of its officers, Company G began to scatter without regard for dead, wounded, and equipment. Captain Doolittle of the mortar company managed to halt the withdrawal. He contacted the infantry battalion command post with his radio, the only means of communication left on the hill, and received orders to take charge. The support infantry platoon maneuvered to the left of the enemy's position, relieving pressure on the front. Doolittle called for fire from his three mortar platoons, which by this time had all withdrawn to their original firing positions. White phosphorus mortar rounds not only blinded the

Japanese positions but set fire to brush and grass in which they had taken cover. As enemy opposition ceased, Captain Doolittle organized parties to evacuate the wounded and then led the force in an orderly withdrawal back to the positions from which the attack began. Several days later Cabaruan Hills fell to another infantry battalion.[50]

During the fighting with I Corps the mortars of the 98th Battalion won a fair reputation for their ability to cope with enemy armor. Chemical mortarmen received credit for destroying at least 25 tanks, some of them dug in, and shared credit with the smaller mortars for knocking out 15 or 20 more. On 31 January, for example, after withdrawing from the edge of the town of Muñoz with elements of the 20th Infantry, a mortar platoon forward observer directed fire on two enemy tanks. A direct hit knocked out one of the vehicles and subsequent mortar fire disabled a second. The mortar platoon observer crept up to this tank, jumped upon it, and hurled a grenade inside. As the tank burst into flames, the observer escaped unharmed. Four days later two Japanese tanks raced along a road directly toward a chemical mortar observation post, firing as they came. The observer directed his mortars at the first tank, setting it afire less than fifty yards from his position. The other tank turned and fled, only to be bracketed by mortar rounds. Stalled and with broken tracks, the enemy tank was set aflame by a final mortar round.[51]

Infantry commanders expressed satisfaction with the support given by the 98th. The 6th Division stated its preference for 4.2-inch mortar support against emplaced tanks and field pieces. After the fall of Lupao, a town vigorously defended by the Japanese, the commander of the 35th Infantry declared "the battle would have lasted days longer if the 4.2's had not been available." [52]

During mid-February 1945 I Corps began what proved to be a 4-month drive to the north to rout the enemy from the tenacious posi-

---

[50] (1) Entry No. 1, 20th Inf Unit Journal, 21-22 Jan 45. 306 – INF(20)-0.7 (26300) 16-25 Jan 45. (2) Ltr, CO 98th Cml Mortar Bn to CmlO I Corps, 20 Mar 45, Rpt of Cml Warfare Activities. CWBN 98-0.3 (24423). This source mistakenly dates this action as 23 January 1945 when, in fact, it took place a day earlier. (3) Battle of the Cabaruan Hills, 12-25 Jan 45. CMLHO. (4) Lt. Col. Alexander Batlin, "98th Chemical Mortar Battalion," *Armed Forces Chemical Journal*, vol. VII, No. 2 (October, 1953).

[51] Another technique was the use of the fire of one mortar to drive tanks into preregistered areas, to be neutralized or destroyed by the weapons of the whole platoon.

[52] (1) Ltr, CG 6th Div to Distr, 17 Jul 45, sub: Rpt by Hq 6th Div, p. 32. (2) 98th Cml Mortar Bn, Fifth Month Luzon.

tions of his mountain fastness.[53] In this slow, gruelling campaign the 33d Division advanced toward the port of San Fernando and toward Baguio, summer capital of the Philippines. The 32d Division crept relentlessly along the tortuous Villa Verde Trail toward the heavily fortified Sante Fe–Imugan area, while the 25th Division moved north along Highway 5 from San Jose to Digdig and eventually Sante Fe.

During the second week of February the companies of the 98th Battalion received assignments which were to last almost until the close of the Luzon operation: Company A was attached to the 32d Division, Company B to the 33d, and Company C remained with the 25th. On 21 April Company C, 85th Chemical Mortar Battalion, joined the forces of I Corps, supporting the spectacular drive made by the 37th Division from Sante Fe to Aparri on the northern coast of Luzon.

The 98th Battalion had to contend not only with the enemy but with the terrain and weather. The mountainous region in which the enemy held commanding positions, many of them prepared in advance, gave every advantage to the defenders. These positions, often in defilade, provided ideal targets for the accurate, high angle fire of the 4.2-inch mortars. Forward observation by ground parties, the normal procedure, was hazardous and difficult because of the superiority of Japanese observation posts. Sometimes the mortar platoons overcame this disadvantage by using artillery observers in liaison planes to conduct registration and to fire for effect.[54] During March and early April the rain and muddy ground curtailed mortar shell expenditures by bogging down ammunition resupply and by compelling the constant re-emplacement of the base plates which sank out of sight after one or two rounds.

Nonetheless the weapon proved effective. Company C fired 19,000 rounds (the two other companies fired about the same number) and received credit for sealing about thirty-five caves and killing more than 250 Japanese caught in the open. The unit marked eight targets for air strike with a precision that brought praise both from Fifth Air Force and infantry commanders.

In fighting along the Villa Verde Trail, Company A fired several missions to repel enemy counterattacks, most of them during hours of darkness. Mortarmen at one time manned infantry battalion defense

---

[53] Unless otherwise noted, the account of this part of the campaign has been based upon unit records of the 98th and 85th Chemical Mortar Battalions and on After Action Reports of the 25th, 32d, and 33d Divisions and their components.

[54] 98th Cml Mortar Bn, First 120 Days on Luzon, p. 44.

positions, at the same time maintaining uninterrupted fire support of the front-line companies. Smoke shell was used for screening and casualty effect as well as for burning off occasional grassy slopes, capable of concealing the enemy, which lay in the path of the advancing infantry.

In situations like those found on Luzon, where the weapons companies of the mortar battalions were placed under the operational control of the supported divisions, battalion headquarters played an inconspicuous but important role. In the case of the 98th, for example, the headquarters and headquarters company established a permanent camp in the town of Carmen where the unit could support its weapons companies equally well. Here was the battalion rest area, and here were the battalion personnel, including weapons company clerks, an arrangement which permitted the battalion commander maximum utilization of his administrative personnel. Headquarters controlled the companies by radio and by liaison officers. The Signal Corps Radio 284 served as the basis for this communications network, proving satisfactory at times at distances twice its normal range of thirty miles.[55] Liaison officers made daily visits to each of the weapons companies, contacting as many platoons as time and the situation allowed. During the course of these visits the liaison officers assisted with administrative problems, brought forward maintenance parts and certain supplies from the battalion stock, and exchanged information about the situation as it affected operations. Battalion maintained both a motor pool and radio maintenance facilities which repaired company equipment. Repairs of 85th Battalion equipment involving third and fourth echelon maintenance were turned over to ordnance maintenance organizations because of the lack of appropriate CWS units. Ideally, a chemical service platoon attached to division took care of the maintenance of ammunition at division dumps.

The mortar company commander set up his command post in the vicinity of the division command post or occasionally with the regiment in reserve. The mortar platoons fired for the assault battalion in each of the three regiments. Displacement forward, in ¼-ton trucks and

---

[55] (1) 98th Cml Mortar Bn, Sixth Month Luzon. (2) Batlin, "98th Chemical Mortar Battalion," *Armed Forces Chemical Journal,* vol. VII, No. 2 (October, 1953). (3) The 85th Battalion experienced difficulties with SCR-284 during the hours of darkness when its effective range was reduced to six or seven miles. 85th Cml Mortar Bn in the Luzon Campaign, The First 120 Days (hereafter cited as 85th, First 120 Days Luzon).

trailers, came upon orders of the infantry battalion commander. As in the action described at Cabaruan Hills, the mortar platoons maintained communications with the supported infantry during displacement by SCR-300 radios. Mortar platoons of the 98th Battalion maintained 35 rounds for each gun, while a 2½-ton truck loaded with 300 rounds stood by at the company command post ready to be sent forward whenever the need arose. Location of the firing positions of the mortar platoons varied from unit to unit. In the 98th Battalion, Company A's platoons usually were established within the infantry battalion perimeter, most likely with the support infantry company. Company C, on the other hand, often set up its mortars within the infantry battalion CP perimeter.

One of the difficulties faced by the chemical mortar units on Luzon was an almost constant shortage of manpower. The 98th Chemical Mortar Battalion operated for the six months of the campaign understrength by 5 officers and 130 enlisted men. The 82d Battalion, while possessing a surplus of enlisted men until mid-March, was below strength from that date until the end of the campaign. The 85th Battalion experienced similar troubles.[56] The lack of men was aggravated by a most inadequate number of mortar companies for the simultaneous support of 4 divisions in I Corps, 4 in XIV Corps, and 3 in XI Corps.

Reciprocal familiarity between chemical mortar and combat infantry personnel continued to be less than perfect. It was often a two-edged situation; infantry officers were unacquainted with 4.2-inch mortar potentialities, and chemical personnel, from division chemical officers to those of the mortar company, were unfamiliar with the combat techniques of the infantry. All chance had passed of attaining the ideal solution—joint training for chemical and infantry personnel, or at least familiarization lectures and demonstrations, before attachment in actual combat.[57]

---

[56] (1) 82d, 85th, and 98th Cml Mortar Bns S-3 Rpts, passim. Sixth Army Rcds. (2) 85th, First 120 Days Luzon, p. 11. (3) 98th Cml Mortar Bn, Hist Data Cards.

[57] (1) 82d, First 120 Days Luzon, pp. 13–14. (2) 85th, First 120 Days Luzon, p. 7. (3) 98th, Fifth Month Luzon, pp. 17–19. (4) Personal Ltr, CmlO I Corps to ACCWS for Field Opns, 2 Aug 45.

Central Pacific Area

The Central Pacific Area lacked adequate mortar battalion support throughout the entire war.[58] Despite the efforts of Colonel Unmacht, theater chemical officer, the only mortar unit available prior to May 1944 was the 91st Chemical Company (Motorized) which had been stationed in Hawaii under various designations since 1920. This unit was used in field tests, demonstrations, and joint training exercises, including amphibious assaults with several infantry divisions.

The over-all shortage of chemical mortar battalions and the higher priority of other theaters prevented shipment of these units to the Central Pacific Area until the arrival early in May 1944 of the 88th Chemical Mortar Battalion. Four months later the theater activated the 189th Chemical Mortar Company (Separate). The only other mortar units in CENPAC were the 71st and 72d Chemical Mortar Battalions which did not reach Hawaii until mid-1945, too late to see action before the war ended.[59]

The first chemical mortar action in the Central Pacific took place during the fighting on Kwajalein in the Marshall Islands when the 91st Company commanded by Capt. Joseph E. Atchison fired in support of the 7th Division. During five days in early February 1944 the unit, hampered by an ammunition shortage and severed communications lines, expended about 500 rounds while losing 1 man killed and 14 wounded.[60] The next mortar unit to see action was Company C, 88th Chemical Mortar Battalion, which landed on Saipan in the Marianas with the 27th Infantry Division. Company A of the 88th played a minor role in nearby Guam. In mid-September 1944 Company D of the same battalion fired for the 81st Infantry Division on Angaur and Peleliu in the Palau group. Unlike Companies A and C, rushed to the Marianas within a month after arriving in the theater, Company D received an adequate period of orientation in Hawaii. Offsetting the advantage of thorough and extensive training was a shortage of enlisted men and motor transport. The virtual certainty that mortars and

---

[58] References used in this section consist of: Unit Rcds of the 88th Cml Mortar Bn, 91st Cml Mortar Co (Separate), AAR's of Tenth Army; 96th, 77th, and 7th Divs; 32d and 184th Inf Regts; and the 5th Marine Regt.

[59] AG Hist Data Cards, 91st and 189th Cml Mortar Cos and 88th, 71st, and 72d Cml Mortar Bns.

[60] (1) Ltr, CO 91st Cml Co to CG 7th Div, 18 Feb 44. (2) MPR CWS Ammo Sup, Sec 2F, Feb 44, p. 2a.

ammunition would often have to be man-hauled led to the decision to divide the company into two 5-gun platoons.

Company D landed in the ninth wave on Red Beach, Angaur Island, on 17 September and supported the 322d Infantry in the Solome Lake and Ramanantelo Hill areas. Attached to division artillery, the platoons fired under the direction of artillery air observers. Captured Japanese documents referred to the 4.2-inch as "that high caliber mortar," while supported infantry commanders reported that the weapon caused heavy enemy casualties.

Company D's 1st Platoon moved to Peleliu on 16 October, followed in a week by the 2d Platoon and company headquarters. Attached to the 321st Infantry and later the 323d Infantry Regiments, Company D fired normal night missions of harassment and defense as well as fourteen barrages which ignited napalm from fire bombs dropped by planes among the innumerable enemy caves and trenches.

The final campaign in the Central Pacific—operations in the Ryukyus group—saw the participation of the entire 88th Battalion as well as the 91st Company.[61] In order to gain a limited fleet anchorage and seaplane base before the invasion, the 77th Division, with Company A attached, made an unopposed landing on Kerama Retto. The assault on the main objective, Okinawa, took place on 1 April 1945. Companies B and C of the 88th, attached to the 96th Division, landed about H plus 1 in the ninth and eleventh waves, respectively, in the vicinity of Chatan. Company B, commanded by Capt. Edward L. Lockman, Jr., supported the 383d Infantry moving south along the west coast to the strong enemy defenses on Kakazu Ridge. Company C, under the command of Capt. Rutherford H. Spessard, Jr., supported the 382d Infantry in its advance south to Nishibaru Ridge. The 91st Company, Captain Them commanding, went in on the eighth wave with the 7th Division across Purple and Orange Beaches opposite Kadena Airfield and supported the division advance to the east coast and down to the eastern approaches of the *Shuri* Line. At first, chemical mortar support was not available for the 1st and 6th Marine Divisions.[62]

Chemical mortars on Okinawa, although effective, were used almost entirely for little outside of normal missions fired according to standard methods. The only exceptions occurred when the 91st Company fired

---

[61] For a complete description of the campaign, see Appleman *et al.*, *Okinawa: The Last Battle.*

[62] (1) Tenth Army, Rpt of Opns in the Ryukyus Campaign, Cml Warfare, pp. II–XIII–1–2. (2) 7th Div, Opn Rpt, pp. 1–2. (3) 96th Div, Action Rpt, Ryukyus Campaign, sec. VII, pt. I, p. 3.

a few times under direction of a Navy liaison observer, and when Sound Locator Teams Nos. 3 and 5 were attached to Companies C and D. From 12 April to 8 May these teams directed some firing at point targets but the extreme ranges of these targets limited the use of the mortars. During the first week, at least five Japanese night attacks, supported by tanks and artillery and directed against the 96th Division's perimeter, were repulsed with the help of combined 4.2-inch mortar-artillery fire. In even lighter firing in support of the 7th Division, the mortars laid down small preparations by day and fired to repel Japanese infiltration raids at night. From the second week in April until mid-June, the pattern of chemical mortar support included preparations preceding infantry advance, followed, in many cases, by screens to cover U.S. troops engaged either in consolidating their positions or withdrawing with their casualties under murderous Japanese artillery, mortar, and machine gun fire. The 4.2-inch mortars than engaged in counterbattery and neutralization missions during the remaining daylight hours, followed by night harassing and interdictory fire.

On 21 April a mortarman from the 91st Chemical Mortar Company played a prominent role in repulsing a Japanese attack on the Skyline Ridge positions of the 7th Division. Here is a graphic account of this action:

When, east of the road cut, a man in the stalled third platoon, Company E, was killed, Sgt. Theodore R. MacDonnell, a 91st Chemical Mortar Company observer, was impelled to drastic action. MacDonnell had frequently joined men on the line and shown qualities of a determined infantryman. Now, infuriated, he gathered up a handful of grenades and ran in the face of the machine-gun fire along the slope to a point underneath the spot where he believed the enemy gun to be located, and then started up the 20-foot embankment. When he looked over the crest he failed to spot the gun, but he did see three enemy soldiers and grenaded them. He made two trips to the bottom of the embankment for fresh supplies of grenades, but it was not until his third trip to the crest that he located the machine gun. MacDonnell then slid back to the bottom, grabbed a BAR, and mounted the embankment with it, only to have the weapon jam after the first shot. He skidded to the bottom, seized a carbine, and went back up for the fifth time. On reaching the crest, he stood up and fired point-blank into the machine-gun position, killing the gunner and two covering riflemen. MacDonnell then hurled the machine gun down the slope behind him. A mortar that he found in the position was also sent crashing down the hillside. Sergeant MacDonnell was later awarded the Distinguished Service Cross for his heroism on this occasion.[63]

[63] Appleman et al., Okinawa: The Last Battle, p. 226.

In an average period of seventy days in the line, each mortar company on Okinawa fired approximately 25,000 rounds, a fourth of which was WP shell. Even this rather limited amount of smoke shell appeared excessive to Tenth Army field artillery officers, particularly as in their opinion an "indiscriminate use of smoke, not only by artillery, but by other supporting weapons, obscured both air and ground observation." Most of the Army and Marine divisions participating in the operation commented favorably on the performance of the chemical mortars and their crews. Both the 96th Infantry Division and the 1st Marine Division recommended that a chemical mortar company, and preferably a battalion, be attached regularly to a division. The Tenth Army suggested that each division receive the support of a mortar battalion and that the battalion be employed as a unit only and not fragmented by a series of attachments.[64]

Of the problems encountered by chemical mortar units on Okinawa, shortage of ammunition was unquestionably the most serious. The 88th Battalion took in three units of fire and the 91st Company took in five on the basis of 100 rounds per unit of fire, at the ratio of 70-percent HE and 30-percent WP. After this initial supply was consumed, a shortage, which varied from limited to critical, prevailed for the balance of the operation. On at least four separate occasions, mortar companies had to reduce expenditures or cease firing altogether for periods of from a few days to two weeks. Rain and mud, particularly after 1 May, bogged down ammunition resupply and made it difficult for the chemical mortars, as well as other supporting weapons, to keep up with the infantry. The over-all shortage of chemical mortar shell was partly a result of the higher priority of the European theater. But as in the case on Luzon, 35,000 of the 87,400 rounds of high explosive ammunition received from the zone of interior were in lots suspected of having defective fuzes. Indeed, a muzzle burst was reported by Company B of the 88th on 13 May, the date on which 14 men were listed as wounded in action. The Navy transferred 27,000 rounds of HE shell not em-

[64] (1) 10th Army, Rpt of Opns in the Ryukyus Campaign, ch. X, sec. 3; ch. II, sec. 6. (2) 1st Marine Div, Special Action Rpt, Okinawa Nansei Shoto, ch. X, p. 13. (3) History of Cml Sec AFMIDPAC and Predecessor Comds, 7 Dec 41–2 Sep 45, 4 vols., IV, an. II–i, 22, 33, 49. (4) 383d RCT S–3 Rpts, 10, 29 Apr 45.

ployed in amphibious support operations, but the use of much of this was "restricted to military necessity." The average mortar company expenditures of approximately 335 rounds per day was made possible only by substitution of WP for HE shell, by the above Navy transfers, by dispatch of 50,000 heavy-weight M4 rounds from Hawaii, and by the replacement of all defective fuzes, shipped by high priority air shipment from Hawaii and the United States.[65]

Amphibious Employment of the 4.2-Inch Chemical Mortar

Before the War Department authorized the high explosive mission for the 4.2-inch mortar and before any chemical mortar units reached the theaters of operations, the CWS was developing doctrine for the use of the mortar in assault landings. Beginning in the summer of 1942 this doctrine was developed at the Amphibious Training Center, Camp Edwards, Mass., and continued at Camp Carabelle, Fla. (later Camp Gordon Johnston). Overseas, the U.S. Assault Training Center in England advocated the use of 4.2-inch WP shell for smoke screens for assault landings except in the case of offshore winds, when only high explosives would be used.[66] Elements of the 3d Chemical Mortar Battalion sailed from North Africa for Sicily prepared to support the 3d Division with mortars mounted on six assault craft, a measure made unnecessary with the attainment of tactical surprise.[67]

Despite these preparations in the European theater the amphibious employment of the 4.2-inch mortar occurred only in the Pacific. Colonel Unmacht first suggested the technique to Navy officers in July 1943 at the Makua, Oahu, demonstrations. The Navy liked the idea and played around with it for almost a year. The advantage of the mortar boat plan was that it provided assault troops with heavy effective fire during that period in the landings when they were most vulnerable —the time between the lifting of the naval bombardment and the establishment of supporting weapons on shore.

---

[65] (1) Tenth Army, Rpt of Opns in the Ryukyus Campaign, ch. II, sec. XIII, Chemical Warfare, pp. II–XIII–4, 7. (2) Tenth Army Island Comd, Action Rpt Okinawa, 30 Jun 45, pp. 8–XII–3, 4. (3) History CWS AFMIDPAC, II, an. I–d, 63, 69–71, 82; V, an. II i, 22. (4) Rad CM–IN 535.2, 6 May 45. (5) Rad CM–IN 22045, 23 May 45.

[66] (1) Ltr, Chief Field Serv CWS to CG SOS, 27 May 42, sub: Amph Use of 4.2-inch Cml Mortar. (2) USATC ETO, Conf on Landing Assaults, 24 May–23 Jun 43, 2–c. See addresses by Maj Gen Roberts, Brigadier Wales, and Col Rowan. (3) USATC Tng Memo AMPH–4A CWS, Jan 44.

[67] History of 3d Cml Bn in Campaign of Sicily, pp. 1–2.

In a remarkable case of CWS-Navy co-operation, the kind which typified the activities of Colonel Unmacht on Oahu, there emerged a new type of craft, one armed with 4.2-inch chemical mortars. It was not born without difficulty. The Navy provided three LCT's for the project and later several LCI's. The latter, dubbed LCI(M) (the M for mortar), were to become the standard mortar-landing craft combination.[68]

One of the principal mechanical difficulties in firing the 4.2-inch mortar from the deck of a ship was the development of a suitable mount. The Navy experimented with various devices including one which mounted the mortar solidly in the deck of an LCT. Fourteen rounds fired from the weapon were sufficient to shear the bolts holding the base cap cup to the deck. The mount finally adopted consisted of a wooden box reinforced with steel and filled with a mixture of sand and sawdust. Upon this mixture sat a wooden subbase, the top of which was notched to receive the spades of the base plate. These mounts proved adequate, although excessive firing, such as at Iwo Jima, caused them to break down.

The first attempt to get the mortar boats into action proved abortive. Favorably impressed with these vessels during seven tests again run at Makua in the spring of 1944, the Navy decided to use three of the 4.2-inch-mortar-equipped LCT's in the invasion of Saipan. These plans went awry during the assault rehearsal off Kahoolawe, one of the Hawaiian group. Each of the three LCT's was lashed to the deck of a landing ship tank, for the decision had been made for the smaller vessel to make the long journey to the scene of operations in this piggyback fashion. During an extremely heavy sea two of the LCT's broke their lashings and were washed overboard. The third LCT escaped this fate only to be destroyed at Pearl Harbor when its LST suddenly exploded. Fifty-nine people lost their lives in the resulting holocaust.[69]

Before the end of the Marianas campaign, the Navy revived the mortar boat project. This time the weapons were to be mounted on landing craft, infantry (LCI), four of which were fitted out, each with three 4.2-inch mortars.[70] One weapon was mounted forward in the center of the ship, the others were amidships, one on the port side

[68] Ltr, CCmlO CENPAC to ACCWS for Field Opns, 24 Apr 44, sub: Use of 4.2 Mortars in LCT's.
[69] (1) History, CWS AFMIDPAC, IV, an. II–d, 37–38.   (2) Maj. Carl W. Hoffman, *Saipan: The Beginning of the End* (Washington, 1950), pp. 32–33.
[70] Ltr, CCmlO Central Pacific Area to ACCWS for Field Opns, 24 Jul 44.

FIRING 4.2-INCH CHEMICAL MORTARS FROM THE DECK OF AN LST *in the Pacific.*

and one on the starboard. All fired forward, over the bow. Beneath the mortar mounts the deck was reinforced with steel plating. The two forward troop compartments served as magazines for mortar ammunition, a normal complement being 1,200 rounds. Maj. Leland E. Anderson of the 88th Chemical Mortar Battalion commanded the mortarmen who had come from diverse sources: 4 officers from the 88th, 12 enlisted men from the 91st Chemical Mortar Company, and 4 officers and 88 enlisted men from the 111th Infantry Regiment. Designated as LCI(M) Nos. 739, 740, 741, and 742, the mortar boats were earmarked for the campaign in the Palaus. The four boat crews prepared for the operation by test runs at the Makua site in the Hawaiian Islands and by participation in the invasion rehearsal at Guadalcanal.[71]

[71] (1) Maj Leland E. Anderson, Rpt on Mortar Activity Aboard USS LCI(M)'s 739, 740, 741, 742, 30 Jul–30 Sep 44, dated 10 Oct 44.   (2) History, AFMIDPAC, CWS IV, an II-d, 39, 74–75.

Palau Islands

The first combat employment of chemical mortar boats took place on 15 September 1944 in the Palau Islands.[72] Led by Major Anderson, mortar boats 739, 740, 741, and 742 supported the III Amphibious Corps landings on Peleliu made by the 1st Marine Division. During the initial run on the island LCI(M)'s, moving in at a speed of less than three knots, fired 100 rounds of high explosive ammunition from positions 3,000 to 1,300 yards offshore at the very slow rate of one round per mortar every two minutes. As the mortar boats drew closer, the range of the weapons was decreased by reducing the number of increments.[73] This method of fire was sometimes known as Plan BAKER. Mortar fire covered the northern flank of White Beach for a depth of 200 to 300 yards, with only a few water bursts being observed. These supporting boats lifted their fire as friendly aircraft strafed the beach only to resume it from fixed positions 900 to 1,300 yards offshore. The mortars then placed harassing fire upon the dense woods, areas of defilade, and possible enemy observation posts and installations on the hill to the northwest. Good dispersion resulted from this fire, delivered at ranges varying between 2,100 and 2,610 yards, although the thick foliage and defiladed areas precluded effective observation. The employment of mortar boats from fixed offshore positions was often designated Plan CHARLIE.

A second mission at Peleliu began about an hour after the end of the first run and consisted of the bombardment of the same hill area northwest of the beach area, its rocky top by now a mass of rubble. Firing at ranges of 3,200 yards, each mortar delivered two rounds of high explosive shell a minute from more or less stationary positions 1,800 to 2,100 yards offshore. While winds and currents at Peleliu were not strong enough to cause excessive drift, the little movement which did occur made precise firing difficult. Radar ranges taken by LCI(M) 741, the flagship, as well as visual cross-bearings and fall of shot observations, helped to fix the ship positions and to determine ranges as the vessels drifted or maneuvered. In any event, the resulting dispersion was not detrimental to the general mission of laying down

---

[72] For a complete account of the use of mortar boats in this operation, see Maj. Leland E. Anderson, Employment of LCI (M) in Peleliu and Anguar Operation, Chemical Corps School Monograph, 1949–50 series.

[73] Mortar range is determined by elevation of the barrel and by the addition of increments, small rectangles of powder-impregnated paper, which serve as the propellant charge.

area harassing fire. Enemy mortar fire during the two runs proved ineffective, most rounds falling short.

Firing from a moving boat had little effect upon the accuracy of the mortar. In rough seas lateral, but not vertical, accuracy was impaired. And the latter was the more important factor because of the possibility of hitting friendly troops as they advanced inland.[74]

Two days later, on 17 September, the same four mortar boats supported the 81st Division assault on the island of Angaur, also in the Palaus. Instead of executing Plan BAKER immediately, as had been done at Peleliu, all craft fired on abbreviated Plan CHARLIE—6 to 10 rounds per mortar per minute for 7 minutes from positions 2,400 yards offshore. The group of gunboats then moved toward shore at a speed of four knots. It took 10 minutes to come within 1,000 yards of the beach, during which time each of the mortars fired at the rapid rate of 20 rounds per minute. Excessive noise made the commands of the fire control officer virtually inaudible while smoke did much to hinder observation. Despite these handicaps most of the 2,345 rounds landed in the target area and inflicted extensive damage.

On the following day infantry troops on shore, pinned down by rifles and machine guns, called for supporting fire. There was time for only 2 runs, one of 6 and the other of 8 minutes, at speeds of 4 and 3 knots, respectively. The target area, located on the northwest end of the island, varied in width from 500 to 850 yards and extended from the shore to a depth of 900 yards. At an average firing rate of 5 rounds per mortar per minute, 830 rounds fell in the area. Mine fields prevented the mortar boats from approaching closer than 1,500 yards from shore, but the effectiveness of the mortar barrage was such that 3 minutes after it had been lifted the troops, previously pinned down by enemy fire, encountered no opposition on advancing into the heavy woods.

At the end of the Palau operation CWS officers recommended that mortars on boats making the run toward the shore maintain a constant elevation of 1,000 mils with traverse dependent upon the course of the craft. They also suggested that mortar fire be kept within 400

---

[74] (1) CmlO Central Pacific Base Comd to CmlO USAFICPA, 14 Jul 44, Rpt of Tests on Use of 4.2-inch Mortars in LCT's. (2) Action Rpt Comdr Amphib Group 2—Iwo Jima, pt. IV, Naval Gunfire Support, sec. B, Comments and Recommendations on Fire Support Employ of Gunboat, Mortar, and 5-inch Rocket LCI's. Both in CMLHO.

yards of the assault troops and that mortar ships maintain an offshore range of beween 3,200 and 2,000 yards as a precaution against enemy fire. The latter recommendation was disregarded; subsequently, mortar ships came within 500 yards of the shore. Suggestions about the more effective installation of the mortars on the ships were either not adopted or proved to be without merit.[75]

Leyte Gulf

Two groups of mortar ships supported the landings at Leyte Gulf on 20 October 1944. Each group was composed of four LCI(M)'s, with two LCI(A)'s serving as ammunition ships. Maj. Richmond H. Skinner, CWS, exercised over-all command of mortar firing personnel of the groups. Men from the 98th Infantry Division stationed at Hawaii manned all twenty-four mortars in the two groups and fired in support of the 7th and 96th Divisions under XXIV Corps in the Leyte landings made near Dulag. From the date of departure from Manus Island on 11 October until the objective was reached, these new mortar crews received training in firing methods and commands.

One of the groups (it was known as Group 2) executed Plan BAKER at Orange Beach 2 as mortar boats moved in at a speed of 1½ knots, firing from 2,200 to 400 yards offshore and expending about 480 rounds of HE in 20 minutes. A slow rate of fire of two rounds per gun per minute was maintained while the range was gradually decreased from 2,600 to 740 yards. Twelve hundred yards from the shore enemy mortars or howitzers straddled the mortar boats without causing casualties or damage. The weather was ideal and the sea relatively calm.

After execution of Plan BAKER these mortar boats fired from fixed positions (Plan CHARLIE) on enemy positions in the ravines and on reverse slopes of the Labiranan Head Ravine and Catmon Hill area, silencing the Japanese guns which had been plaguing the troops on the beaches. According to one Navy observer, this mission, completed without observation from computed data and fired at distances from 1,000 to 1,900 yards offshore, proved accurate beyond expectations. Later, Group 2 moved back to the transport area, twelve miles to the

[75] (1) ExecO 88th Cml Mortar Bn, Rpt on Mortar Activity Aboard USS LCI(M) 739, 740, 741, 742, 30 Jul–30 Sep 44, dated 10 Oct 44, pp. 4–6, 15–17, 21–28. (2) Comdr Admin Comd Amphib Forces U.S. Pac Fleet, Plans for Delivery of 4.2" Mortar Fire from LCI(M)'s Equipped With M–1 Modified Cml Mortar Mounts, 11 Jul 45, p. 1. (3) Excerpts from Opns Div, Info Bull, vol. III, No. 7, 13 Dec 44. (4) History, CWS AFMIDPAC, IV, an II–d, 61, 78, 79.

rear, for resupply. It received no further missions that day. Thereafter, until they withdrew on the morning of A plus 5, the mortar
boats of this group used smoke pots to screen the large vessels from
air raids during the hours of both morning and evening twilight.

On the morning of the attack on the Leyte beaches the other group
of mortar boats (known as Group 3) fired on targets south of Yellow
Beach as far as the mouth of the Daguitan River near the town of
Dulag. Spaced from 50 to 75 yards apart the mortar boats began firing
1,500 yards from shore and continued as they slowly moved in to a
position 400 yards from the beaches. This bombardment blanketed an
area 800 yards wide and 900 yards deep. Fifteen minutes after this
beach shelling phase, the mortars began firing on call. Within the next
five hours infantry requests for support resulted in the expenditure of
almost 4,500 rounds. The ships slowly drifted to the left directing
their fire on enemy targets on the south bank of the Daguitan River
and on the approaches of a bridge across that river, an effort which
drove enemy tanks from the road leading to the bridge.

Both mortar boat groups received written commendations from the
leaders of the flotillas which they supported, as well as from the commanders of Amphibious Groups 3 and 6. Admiral Forrest B. Royal,
commander of Group 6, stated: "The performance of LCI's equipped
with 4.2" Army mortars was excellent. The mortar fire was delivered
in a rapid, accurate, and effective manner." Admiral Royal compared
the effectiveness of the mortar ships and the rocket ships.[76] While
praising the "highly successful accomplishments" of both weapons, he
pointed out that the rocket ships were of no further use after their
single crash concentration because they were unable to reload in time
to continue covering the assault waves. On the other hand, the mortars
could fire without letup.[77]

Lingayen Gulf

For a short time after the recall of the mortar boats from the Leyte
fighting, future plans for their use were hazy because of the lack of

[76] 3d Ind, Adm Forrest B. Royal, USN, Comdr Group 6 Amphib Forces U.S. Pac Fleet, to CINCPAC,
21 Nov 44, to Ltr, CO USS LCI 660, 31 Oct 44, sub: USS LCI (M) 660—Action Rpt of Leyete Opn.
Cited in History, CWS AFMIDPAC, IV, an. II–d, 100.

[77] (1) Comdr Amphib Group 6 and Task Unit 79.2, Rpt of Leyte Opn, 4 Nov 44, pp. 5, 7–8. (2)
Ltr, Comdr Task Unit 79.6.21 and Comdr Group 17 to COMINCH, 4 Nov 44, sub: Action Rpt.
(3) Ltr, Comdr LCI (M) Group 18 Temp and Comdr Task Unit 79.7.3 to COMINCH, 23 Oct 44,
sub: Action Rpt, Invasion of Philippines, Island of Leyte. All in CWS 314.7.

information regarding the Luzon operation.[78] Both groups did proceed to New Guinea to pick up men from the 98th Chemical Mortar Battalion, a step made necessary when four landing craft, infantry, which had served as ammunition carriers during the Leyte action, were converted to mortar boats. All mortar craft participated in the mid-December training exercise in Huon Gulf, which simulated the landings that were to take place at Lingayen Gulf, Luzon.

As it turned out, three separate mortar boat groups supported the Sixth Army landings on Luzon. One of these was Task Unit 79.8.1, composed of six LCI(M)'s and commanded by Lt. Comdr. G. W. Hannett and accompanied by Maj. Richmond Skinner. A second group was formed from the converted ammunition carriers, with mortarmen from the 98th Chemical Mortar Battalion. A third group of three LCI(M)'s had its mortars manned by marines, trained by and under the supervision of a detachment from the 98th Chemical Mortar Battalion.[79]

The six mortar boats of Task Unit 79.8.1 supported the XIV Corps landings on the beaches of Lingayen Gulf and then stood ready to furnish fire on call of the 185th Infantry, 40th Division, in its movement inland. The mortar boats were to be ready for any special mission that might arise, as well as to smoke the transport areas during the hours of morning and evening twilight.

The fire plans for support of the assault wave were quite elaborate, including time, range, and rate of fire for the period beginning thirty minutes before the assault until fifteen minutes after the troops had landed. White phosphorus ammunition was put aboard to be used only in case of an onshore wind. General control of the mortar ships was in the hands of the task group and task unit commanders, but individual vessels maintained the responsibility for engaging specific targets. Each mortar ship carried 1,200 rounds of HE, 100 rounds of WP, as well as an ample supply of 20-mm. ammunition. Training of the mortar crews continued even while en route to the objective. Navy men received instruction in the handling of the mortars in the event that casualties would bring a need for extra hands.

S-day for Luzon, 9 January 1945, found climatic conditions favor-

[78] Unless otherwise noted, this account of the Lingayen Gulf operation is based on Hist, CWS AFMIDPAC, vol. IV, an. II–d.

[79] (1) 98th, First 120 Days on Luzon, p. 1   (2) CO USS LCI(M) 359 to COMINCH, 15 Jan 45, Action Rpt, Luzon Opn.

able, with a mild offshore wind and visibility ranging from fifteen to twenty miles. The swell of the sea caused some difficulty with landing operations but did not seriously affect the mortar missions. Shortly after 0600 the six mortar ships broke off from the main body, maneuvering in zigzag fashion through the armada of support ships to their initial positions 2,500 yards from shore. A few minutes later, an enemy suicide bomber swooped down in attack. The Japanese plane itself inflicted no damage, but five men from an LCI(M) received wounds from a 20-mm. shell fired at the enemy by another vessel in the formation. At 0845 the six mortar ships moved into their attack positions; fifteen minutes later they began their scheduled fire.

The LCI(M)'s moved forward, blanketing the beaches to a depth of almost 350 yards with accurate and devastating fire. As the craft approached the shore the number of propellant charges on the mortar shells was progressively decreased. Precise ranges were determined by radar on several of the LCI(M)'s and passed on to the others by prearranged visual signals. The only return fire came from enemy mortars whose shells fell 600 yards offshore. Upon reaching a position 400 yards from shore the mortar boats laid to, but continued their fire on the beaches as the first wave of assault troops passed through. It was now 0934, the time when small arms fire support on the gunboats and mortar ships ceased; naval gunfire had been lifted when the first wave reached a position 800 yards from shore.

The mortar crews continued their support from this close-in position. At one stage a radio message was misinterpreted and four LCI(M)'s ceased fire. Thick smoke precluded visual signals and fire was not resumed until several minutes later, when the noise and smoke had abated. During the initial phase of the assault the mortar unit expended 3,345 rounds of high explosive ammunition. Because of an offshore breeze, only seven rounds of WP were fired, this for ranging in at a position 2,600 yards from shore.

According to plan, the mortar ships ceased fire at 0951 and proceeded obliquely to the port to take up positions some 800 yards offshore where they could fulfill the second part of their mission. Although the mortar boats stood ready to support the 185th Infantry shortly after 1000 on S-day, they received no calls for fire because the infantrymen pushing inland to the Agno River encountered no enemy opposition. The mortar group spent the night of S-day anchored just off the mouth of the river, and next morning placed area fire on enemy troops which, according to the shore fire control party, effectively routed the opposition. Some of the LCI(M)'s replenished their ammunition supply from an LST standing by with a reserve of 4.2-inch shells.

From S plus 1 until S plus 8 the group of mortar ships provided twilight smoke concealment and escort service for the Liberty and Victory ships in the San Fabian transport area, a mission which terminated operations of Task Unit 79.8.1 at Luzon. During this period its mortars fired more than 5,000 rounds of 4.2-inch ammunition; the 20-mm. guns of the unit expended almost 7,700 rounds during antiaircraft operations.

The second group of mortar boats, the four converted from the ammunition detail, supported I Corps landings east of Dagupan. As in the case of Task Unit 79.8.1, these LCI(M)'s provided the ships in its vicinity with the concealment of smoke during the twilight hours so susceptible of enemy air attack. On S plus 3 the group went out of action, its mortar crews returning to their parent unit, the 98th Chemical Mortar Battalion. As far as casualties were concerned this small unit fared rather badly; on S plus 1 an enemy E-boat torpedoed the radar equipped flagship with a loss of 2 officers and 2 enlisted men.[80]

Group 78.1.8, the smallest of the three mortar boat units, also supported the I Corps landings near Dagupan. From positions within 3,000 yards of the beach, each of the group's three mortar boats fired about 100 rounds of high explosives onto a road and railroad track just in from the shore. Advancing to within 1,000 yards of the beach, the mortar boats engaged unspecified targets on both the forward and reverse slopes of the low-lying hills, then retired to await call fire from the 98th Battalion. No enemy fire was received from the beach. On S plus 3 this group shelled a group of the enemy and the railroad station south of Damortis.[81]

Vice Adm. Thomas C. Kinkaid, in command of the Lingayen landings, was especially pleased with the work of the mortar boats, reporting

[80] 98th, First 120 Days on Luzon, pp. 1–2, 4.
[81] CO USS LCI(M) 359 to COMINCH, 15 Jan 45, Action Rpt, Luzon Opn, pp. 1–2.

that they were more effective for beach neutralization than were escort carrier-based planes.[82]

Iwo Jima

The success of the mortar ships in Pacific assault operations prompted the Navy to increase the number of this type of vessel.[83] Some were acquired and equipped in California, others at Pearl Harbor. The men who were to fire the mortars on these boats were exclusively Navy men, trained in Hawaii by a cadre from the 189th Chemical Mortar Company under the direction of Lt. Col. Joseph E. Atchison. Naturally, the Navy crews had much to learn; many had never seen the mortar before. To some this lack of knowledge meant apprehension of the weapon, to others it meant incorrect employment, with damage and danger as a consequence. There were several examples of a second shell being placed in the mortar barrel on top of a misfire and one case where the crew attempted to jam in three rounds. The training in Hawaii, which included two test runs off the coast of Kahoolawe, went a long way in correcting these inadequacies.

On 22 January 1945 the fourteen mortar boats left Pearl Harbor for Iwo Jima where they were joined by the LCI(M)'s which had seen action at Lingayen Gulf. Four CWS officers from the 189th Chemical Mortar Company accompanied the Pearl Harbor contingent, attached for the operation to the mortar group—five units of six ships each.

On the morning of 19 February 1945 the 4th and 5th Marine Divisions landed on the beaches of the island of Iwo Jima in the face of the heaviest enemy beach resistance since Tarawa.[84] The bombardment of the island that preceded the attack was the heaviest of the Pacific war, one that benefited from the experiences of the island assaults that had taken place before. Three of the five mortar units, Numbers 1, 2, and 5, took part in the actual assault phase.

---

[82] (1) Cited in Smith, *Triumph in the Philippines,* ch. IV. (2) In his final report, General Richardson commented on the "devastating mortar fire" which mortar boats placed on the beaches during initial stages of the assault. Final Rpt of CG AFMIDPAC to CofS USA, 15 Mar 46.

[83] Unless otherwise noted, the account of operations at Iwo Jima is based on: (1) CWS TofO Ltr No. 25, 30 May 45, incl 4; (2) Hist, CWS AFMIDPAC, IV, an II–d, 127, V, an III–a, 87; (3) Ltr, Lt Louis L. Mikolajewski, 189th Cml Mortar Co to 14th Cml Warfare Composite Bn, 10 Apr 45, Observations From Aboard LCI(L) Mortar Ships During Invasion of Iwo Jima. All in CMLHO.

[84] For an excellent account of the Iwo Jima operation, see Lt. Col. Whitman S. Bartley, *Iwo Jima: Amphibious Epic* (Washington, 1954).

From H-hour minus 35 until H-hour minus 10 the mortars on these vessels expended 3,240 rounds to bombard specific area targets on the slopes of Mount Suribachi, the 550-foot extinct volcano which dominated the southern end of the island. These mortar groups used a maneuver sometimes described as Plan ABLE. In this plan five LCI(M)'s of a mortar group moved counterclockwise in an elliptical pattern around the sixth vessel, which served as the reference point. Each ship fired only during the period of the run when it was pointed toward the target area. The advantage of this maneuver was the attainment of the high degree of accuracy needed for interdictory fire, accuracy which could not be realized from the decks of sporadically moving ships attempting to maintain a stationary position.

At H-hour Units 2 and 5, proceeding in columns, entered the boat lanes from the west, turned shoreward, formed a line parallel with the sixth wave, and followed it toward the beaches. Reaching a position 2,000 yards from shore, the mortars began firing at a rate of 6 rounds per minute and at a constant range of 3,200 yards. Stopping 1,000 yards from the beaches the mortar ships, now 200 yards apart, maintained fire on a line 1,800 yards inland until H plus 60, when they joined Mortar Support Units 3 and 4 in the rear to repair the damage sustained by the mortar mounts and await further assignment. Group 1, still employing the elliptical maneuver of Plan ABLE, resumed action at H plus 10 with almost four hours of neutralization fire. When this mission terminated Group 1 joined the other units in the rear, thus marking the end of mortar boat support during the assault landings at Iwo Jima.

After this first day the LCI(M)'s, with but few exceptions, fired only night-time missions of harassment and interdiction.[85] The small size of Iwo Jima (its surface area is only 7½ square miles) and its triangular shape made sea support of land operations singularly appropriate. Mortar Units 2 and 5 complied with requests from the forces on land for harassing mortar fire during the first night on shore. Stationed off the eastern and western side of that point of the island tipped by Mount Suribachi, the two mortar units placed fire on the area between the opposing forces to prevent large-scale counterattacks by the enemy. These missions saw the first significant use of white phosphorus shell; as an aid to observation during these hours of dark-

---

[85] *Ibid.*, p. 83n.

ness every fifth round was WP. On subsequent nights mortar units fired similar missions using Plan ABLE and also Plan CHARLIE. Because of heavy counterbattery fire received by the mortar groups they were sometimes directly supported by heavier vessels. The destroyer, USS *Shannon*, for example, covered Mortar Unit 2 as the LCI(M)'s delivered harassing fire on the night of 23 February.

Three mortar boat groups departed on 26 February, and the two that remained reorganized into 5-boat units. Thereafter this sort of support gradually decreased until 3 March, by which time all mortar boats had been recalled. During these last days individual LCI(M)'s provided direct daylight support to shore battalions designated by the Headquarters Landing Force.

Ammunition expenditure of all mortar boats at Iwo Jima came to about 60,000 rounds, of which 20 percent was white phosphorus. The resupply of mortar ammunition from LST to LCI(M) in a fairly rough sea was not always an easy matter. Occasionally the boxes of shell dropped a substantial distance to the deck of the mortar boat, a circumstance which spoke well for the safety feature of the mortar shell fuze. Weapon breakage in this operation caused little alarm although the heavy firing frequently broke down the mortar mounts, taking the weapon out of action for the extent of the mission. Iron straps welded along the sides of the mounts eliminated some of this weakness. Sometimes it was necessary to place bands over the subbase of the mortar to keep it from jumping out of the mount. From all accounts, the mortar crews performed in an exemplary manner; Rear Adm. Harry W. Hill of Amphibious Group 2 termed the successful use of "mortar gunboats" in the early phases of the assault "one of the outstanding features of the operation." [86] According to CWS sources, the Marine Corps expressed its enthusiasm for massed fire from mortar boats during the early days of the landings.[87]

Operations in the Ryukyus

CWS-trained Navy crewmen manned a total of 60 LCI(M)'s which supported Tenth Army in the Ryukyus Campaign. Six days before the main assault of Okinawa, two 6-boat mortar groups supported the diversionary effort against Kerama Retto made by the 77th Infantry

---

[86] Quoted in CWS TofO Ltr 25, p. 16.
[87] History, CWS AFMIDPAC, I, sec. 3, 34.

Division. On 1 April 1945 the XXIV Army Corps and the III Amphibious Corps successfully carried out the main landings on the western coast of Okinawa. Prior to H-hour on that morning seven groups of LCI(M)'s, each comprised of six boats, lined up parallel to the beach behind the assault troops. Each LCI(M) carried 1,000 rounds of HE and 200 rounds of WP. Using Plan BAKER, the 42 boats moved through a calm sea at about one knot, their 126 mortars opening up at a point 1,600 yards from shore at a rate of 10 rounds per gun per minute. Firing over the heads of advancing troops the mortars, in less than an hour, placed about 28,000 rounds on a beach area 1,000 feet deep and 5½ miles wide. The mortar boats themselves received no enemy fire.

Another group of LCI(M)'s supported the 2d Marine Division's L-day feint against the southeast coast of Okinawa. Subsequent 77th Division landings at Ie Shima on 16 April received the support of two groups of mortar boats, while three days later a single group fired for the ruse landing made by the same division in southern Okinawa. From 7 May until 27 June LCI(M)'s, in support of Army and Marine troops, shelled the city of Naha and enemy installations in the vicinity of the capital.[88]

The amphibious use of the 4.2-inch mortar was one of the major contributions of the CWS to the Pacific war. The mortar boat proved extremely effective for close infantry support just before, during, and immediately after amphibious landings. It was then that the assault troops, running the gantlet of enemy fire while attempting to secure a foothold on the beach, benefited from all the support fire that could be provided. The effectiveness of the mortars in this support is best reflected in the steady increase in the number of mortar boats committed to Pacific assault operations. Only four LCI(M)'s saw action in the Palau fighting in September 1944; seven months later a total of sixty supported Tenth Army operations in the Ryukyus.

[88] (1) Tenth Army, Action Rpt Ryukyus, 25 Mar–30 Jun 45, vol. I, pp. 11-V-5, 7-III-2, 7-III-11. (2) Combat Rpt, 1st Lt John R. Ralston, CWS, 189th Cml Mort Co, sub: Use of LCI(M)'s During the Okinawa Campaign, quoted in History, CWS AFMIDPAC, IV, an II-d, 132–35. (3) 77th Inf Div Opns Rpt ICEBERG, Phase I, Ie Shima, 1–27 Apr 45.

CHAPTER XIV

The Flame Thrower in the Pacific:
Guadalcanal to the Marshall Islands

The U.S. Army in World War II used two types of flame throwers, the portable, carried on the soldier's back, and the mechanized, mounted on an armored vehicle, usually a tank. Because flame could penetrate ports and apertures and could be made to turn corners, these special-purpose weapons proved extremely useful in overcoming a determined enemy in strong, stubbornly held defensive positions, invulnerable in most cases to conventional weapons.

The prototype for the portable flame thrower was devised by German engineers sometime between 1900 and 1910. Introduced in World War I against the French at Malencourt, it saw some service on the Western Front where it proved to be a startling, if unreliable, assault weapon. The British and French developed flame throwers of their own by 1916, but the weapon, because of its short range, vulnerability, and lack of tactical doctrine, had limited combat success. It was never used by American troops.[1]

During the interwar period the United States devoted little attention to flame thrower research and development. Miliary men considered it the least valuable incendiary munition and regarded its World War I performance as a total failure, a fact which led the Chief of the Chemical Warfare Service to remark: "In the Chemical Warfare Service it has been the habit for a long while not to mention the flame thrower at all, unless questions were asked about it."[2]

Other nations did not concur in this appraisal. The weapon reappeared in the Abyssinian war of 1935–36, when the Italians employed

---

[1] Capt. Henry Sorenson, "Flame Warfare," *Canadian Army Journal*, vol. 2, Nos. 5 & 6 (August and September, 1948), pp. 31–32.

[2] Fries and West, *Chemical Warfare*, p. 401. Maj. Gen. Amos A. Fries was Chief, CWS, from 1920 to 1929.

the first tank-borne flame thrower. Then in 1937 the Italians demonstrated the use of flame throwers mounted in combat cars and other armored vehicles. The civil war in Spain produced a few German flame tanks. By mid-1940 intelligence reports revealed that the Germans had employed flame throwers in Poland, in their attack on the Belgian fort of Eben Emael, and in their drive across the Low Countries and France.[3] As these reports were scattered, often undocumented, and usually highly colored, doubt remained as to the extent of Axis preparation for the employment of flame throwers. But that such weapons might be useful could no longer be denied by American planners.

In 1940 the United States Army took steps toward the development of a portable flame thrower. On 12 August 1940, the Secretary of War charged the Chief of the Chemical Warfare with the development, manufacture, storage, and issue of the weapon, and during the next year the CWS developed two experimental models.[4] The first, the E1, was quickly discarded; the second, the E1R1, was tested and issued to troops. This model, with slight modifications, was standardized as the M1 portable flame thrower in August 1941. When certain basic deficiencies appeared in this weapon and in the M1A1, an improved version, CWS scientists produced an entirely new flame thrower, the M2-2. This was the group of portable flame weapons used by the U.S. Army in World War II. They were frequently ineffective and faulty, particularly in hands of troops ill trained in matters of operations and tactics. But with the development of a better flame thrower, and with the gradual improvement in tactics and training, this CWS weapon came to play an important part in coping with the unique conditions of the war against Japan.

---

[3] For reports of flame thrower employment from 1935 to 1940, see: (1) Sorenson, "Flame Warfare," *Canadian Army Journal,* vol. 2, Nos. 7 & 8 (October and November, 1948), pp. 18–19; (2) Dept of National Defense, Army (Canada), Cml Warfare Intell Summary, 3 Feb 42, sec. on Germany, pp. F1–F5; (3) British Hist Monograph, Special Weapons and Types of Warfare, pt. III, Flame Warfare Including Incendiaries, p. 110.

[4] (1) Correspondence leading to the portable flame thrower directive is found in CWTC Item 221, 10 Sep 40. (2) For a full discussion of the development and manufacture of the various portable flame thrower models, see Brophy, Miles, and Cochrane, *From Laboratory to Field,* pp. 139–47.

The Portable Flame Thrower in the South Pacific

Guadalcanal

The American portable flame thrower made its first successful combat appearance on 15 January 1943 at Guadalcanal, five months after United States forces began the assault of this South Pacific island. Although the weapon was not available at first, its potentiality against enemy bunkers encountered on the islands—defenses which defied ordinary weapons—soon became apparent. In speaking of the fighting on nearby Tulagi, Maj. Gen. Alexander A. Vandegrift, commanding the 1st Marine Division, stated that flame throwers would have been "practical and effective" against the strong Japanese defenses.[5]

The fortifications encountered on Guadalcanal were typical of those to be found in subsequent fighting in the Pacific. These well camouflaged defenses were made of indigenous material reinforced by whatever metal was available. The compartment of a bunker could be from 4 to 5 feet high, from 6 to 30 feet long, and from 3 to 10 feet wide. Foot-thick coconut logs served as columns and crossbeams, the latter covered by several layers of logs and, later in the war, by quarter-inch sheets of steel. Walls were strengthened by iron or steel rails and sheeting, log pilings, or oil drums filled with sand. The whole elaborate framework was covered with earth and thoroughly camouflaged. Fire trenches, connected by shallow crawl tunnels, usually adjoined the bunker, and entrances were placed in the rear end in positions capable of being covered by other bunkers. Consequently, Japanese bunkers were mutually supporting and practically impervious to the effects of artillery and mortar fire. And they were manned by an enemy who refused to be driven out, but who chose instead to fight until death.[6] There was an obvious and pressing need for a weapon which could reduce such positions instantly and effectively. The flame thrower offered a possible solution to the problem.

Late in 1942 the Americal and the 25th Infantry Divisions and the 2d Marine Division arrived on Guadalcanal to bolster the slackened pace of the American offensive. Each carried a limited number of flame throwers. Beginning in December 1942 a CWS officer conducted

---

[5] Miller, *Guadalcanal: The First Offensive*, pp. 65n, 244, 279n.

[6] (1) *Ibid.*, pp. 243–44. (2) Milner, *Victory in Papua*, pp. 141–43. (3) Ltr, CmlO XIV Corps to CmlO USAFFE, 11 Aug 43, no sub. Sixth Army Cml Sec Rcds, 470.71, Portable Flame Throwers.

on-the-spot training of flame thrower operators, and by mid-January 1943 the troops were ready to give the weapon its initial combat test.[7]

On 15 January 1943 combat engineers of the 8th Marines, 2d Marine Division, attacked enemy defenses surrounding a beach installation. Late in the afternoon they encountered a particularly stubborn Japanese pillbox, and 2 marines equipped with a flame thrower went forward to silence it. Covered by automatic rifles, they crawled to within 25 yards of the position and fired the flame thrower at the bunker. All resistance ceased, and the marines found 5 dead Japanese inside. Although 2 of the enemy had managed to get out, neither had escaped the effects of the flame. One lay 3 feet from the escape hatch, the other had run about 15 feet before collapsing. Encouraged by this result, Marine combat engineers went forward and within 20 minutes wiped out 2 more enemy strongpoints with flame throwers.[8]

The 25th Infantry Division used flame throwers on the same day with far less success. Employed by units of the 35th Infantry, the weapons failed to wipe out enemy pillboxes or to materially aid the assault. Since casualties were high, and malfunctions frequent, the regiment decided not to employ its flame throwers in future engagements.[9] Nevertheless, the weapon was used throughout the mopping-up phase of the campaign by other units and often proved a quick and effective means of reducing difficult enemy positions.

If at the conclusion of the Guadalcanal operation the intrinsic merit of the flame thrower was still in doubt, this combat experience with the weapon did provide answers to several important tactical problems. Units discovered that the flame thrower, because of its limited range and short duration of fire, had to be used in conjunction with other weapons in order to be effective. A trained security detachment armed with rifles, automatic rifles, and smoke grenades was needed to keep the enemy under cover long enough for the flame thrower operator to approach and flame his target. Experience also showed that the engi-

---

[7] Lt Col Leonard L. McKinney, CmlC Hist Study 4, Portable Flame Thrower Opns in World War II, 1949, p. 39.

[8] (1) Lt. Col. Orbie Bostick, "Mercy Killers," Chemical Warfare Bulletin, vol. 30, No. 1 (February–March, 44), 16–17. (2) Miller, Guadalcanal: The first Offensive, p. 279.

[9] (1) Miller, Guadalcanal: The First Offensive, p. 295. (2) Rpt, Opns of the 25th Inf Div on Guadalcanal, 17 Dec 42–5 Feb 43, p. 81. 25th Div 325–11.5.

neers were too busy with other jobs to handle the flame thrower; that the weapon would be better utilized in the hands of the infantry.[10]

To take advantage of these lessons, the division on Guadalcanal, under the direction of the recently activated XIV Corps, set up ambitious training programs. On 27 March 1943 the 25th Division published a training memorandum which withdrew the weapon from the combat engineers and gave it to the ammunition and pioneer platoon of the infantry battalion. The division then organized a series of one-day flame thrower schools to train eight men from each of these platoons to use the weapons.[11] Other units, many of whose chemical and regimental gas officers had themselves been trained by the 25th Division Chemical Section, organized similar training programs. By mid-1943 the general state of flame thrower readiness of Army units on Guadalcanal was relatively good.

New Georgia

Unfortunately, the two divisions on Guadalcanal which had received the least amount of flame thrower training were to employ the weapon on New Georgia. As elements of the 37th and 43d Divisions attacked the western end of the island following their 30 June 1943 landings, they discovered an extensive series of small enemy fortifications similar to those encountered on Guadalcanal. Thoroughly camouflaged, these pillboxes were hard to locate, and once located, even more difficult to neutralize. Since they were organized in depth and mutually supporting, it was almost impossible to approach them from the rear.

On 26 July 1943 three such positions, barely visible in the deep jungle foliage, blocked the advance of the 103d Infantry, 43d Division, with deadly machine gun fire. Capt. James F. Olds, Jr., a XIV Corps CWS staff officer, suggested to the regimental commander the possibility of using flame throwers. The co-ordinated attack which followed began with a 30-minute artillery preparation. As this fire lifted, 6 flame thrower operators from Company C of the 118th Engineer Combat Battalion, supported by infantrymen, crawled toward the bunkers. Reaching a point twenty yards from their target, 2 operators opened fire, crisscrossing their streams of flame to burn off the covering

---

[10] (1) Ltr, McKaig, to Hist Off, 26 Dec 56. Colonel McKaig was 25th Division chemical officer on Guadalcanal. (2) McKinney, Portable Flame Thrower Opns, p. 40.

[11] 25th Inf Div Tng Memo No. 6, 27 Mar 43. Reproduced as App. 1 in McKinney, Portable Flame Thrower Opns, pp. 230–32.

vegetation. The enemy positions for the first time became clearly visible and the 4 other operators discharged their flame directly on target. Resistance ceased in a matter of seconds, and the infantry resumed its advance.[12]

News of this success reached other units and they too began to employ their flame throwers. Two days later, Pvt. Frank Kordeleski of the 145th Infantry, 37th Division, burned out three Japanese pillboxes with a single flame thrower filling. The XIV Corps chemical officer, Col. Robert Gay, reported that during the first six weeks on New Georgia flame throwers had been employed against enemy positions on no fewer than fifty-four occasions.[13]

On New Georgia, as on Guadalcanal, the flame thrower's record was not one of uninterrupted success. Often the inherent weaknesses of the M1's and M1A1's were a source of considerable trouble to the troops who used them. Alike in basic design, these models had two major components, a fuel unit and a gun unit. The fuel unit, which was strapped to the operator's back, consisted of two storage tanks for fuel and one for compressed nitrogen. The nitrogen propelled the fuel from the storage tanks, through the gun unit, onto the target. The gun unit included a fuel tube, a long bent nozzle, a trigger, and a valve to regulate the flow of fuel. The compact electrical system included a battery, spark plug, and a small hydrogen cylinder. When the trigger was pressed, a stream of hydrogen was released, the spark plug ignited the hydrogen, and the resultant flame in turn ignited the fuel as it passed through the gun unit. The complete flame thrower weighed thirty-two pounds empty and seventy pounds filled. Since it held only 5 gallons of fuel, its duration of fire was a mere eight to ten seconds. The M1 had a range of 15 to 20 yards while the M1A1, using fuel thickened with napalm, was capable of firing 40 to 50 yards.[14] The inefficiency of the ignition system was particularly bothersome. Operators found it expedient to carry thermite grenades for emer-

[12] (1) Opn Journal, 118th Engr Bn, 29 Jun–21 Aug 43, dated 20 Sep 43. 118th Engr Bn 20433, 343–43.3. (2) Capt. James F. Olds, Jr., "Flame Throwers Front and Center," *Chemical Warfare Bulletin* vol. 30, No. 3 (June–July, 1944), pp. 5–8. (3) Miller, *CARTWHEEL: The Reduction of Rabaul*, p. 148.

[13] Ltr, CmlO XIV Corps to CmlO USAFFE, 11 Aug 43.

[14] TM 3–375, May 1943, Portable Flame Throwers M1 and M1A1.

gency use, as these grenades when hurled forward on unignited flame thrower fuel would cause instantaneous ignition.[15]

Mechanical failure was not the sole factor contributing to unsatisfactory performance. Of even greater significance was the fact that neither the 37th nor the 43d Infantry Division had been extensively trained in the use of the flame thrower before it was committed on New Georgia. The operators in the 26 July attack, albeit successful, had received but one hour of instruction and this a scant three hours before the assault! Commanders and operators had little understanding of the proper tactical employment of the weapon. Adequate infantry support was not always provided; in some cases not a single rifleman was assigned as protection. Often there was no satisfactory reconnaissance before the mission, and operators who had been ordered to go forward and clean out a lone machine gun emplacement, on reaching a firing position, found several bunkers in front of them. In such situations a single flame thrower was useless. Many company commanders, ignorant of flame thrower tactics, selected untrained men and ordered them to take a flame thrower and "burn out the Japs," a mission which promised little chance of success. Chemical officers reported that the casualty rate among flame thrower operators was directly related to the inadequate infantry support and planning afforded flame thrower missions.[16]

It was apparent that further training of operators and infantry commanders in the tactical uses and limitations of the weapon was essential. Equally obvious was the need for co-ordinated flame thrower teams composed of operators and supporting riflemen.[17]

Bougainville

Though divisions soon began intensified flame thrower training programs designed to overcome the shortcomings revealed on Guadalcanal and New Georgia, few such projects were totally complete by 1 November 1943, the date of the Bougainville landings. But progress

---

[15] (1) Ltr, CmlO XIV Corps to CmlO USAFFE 15 Sep 43, no sub. Sixth Army Cml Sec Rcds, 470.71 Portable Flame Throwers. (2) CmlO 25th Div to CCWS, 25 Apr 43, Rpt of Cml Warfare Activities on Guadalcanal Island. CWS 314.7 Portable Flame Thrower File.

[16] (1) Ltr, CmlO XIV Corps to CmlO USAFFE, 15 Sep 43, no sub. (2) Ltr, ACmlO XIV Corps to Cml XIV Corps, 30 Jul 43, sub: Rpt on Use of Flame Thrower. Sixth Army Rcds, 470.71 Portable Flame Throwers.

[17] CmlO 25th Div to CG 25th Div, 20 Nov 43, Rpt, Flame Thrower Opns During the New Georgia Campaign.

had been made, and when Army and Marine units encountered formidable Japanese defensive installations on Bougainville improvised flame thrower teams generally were available.

On 11 December 1943 the forward advance of the 21st Regiment, 3d Marine Division, was halted by an enemy position on Hill 1000. One of the Marine Corps officers described the obstacle as follows:

The reverse slope position was encountered here, fox-holes at the foot of a knoll with a ten-yard field of fire to the top of the knoll. . . . Interlocking lines of grazing automatic fire were integrated such that approach to the knoll from any direction was cleverly and effectively covered. Little room existed for maneuver on the ridge and due to the height and number of trees 60 and 81 mm. mortars were relatively ineffective. The hill mass likewise constituted a partial mask to the supporting artillery.[18]

The marines hammered at this position for seven days without success. Finally, on 18 December 1943, Hill 1000 was hit by two heavy air strikes. Right after this, six flame throwers, their operators organized in teams, accompanied riflemen in a converging action on the position. The flame throwers supported the infantry advance and aided substantially in destroying enemy positions.[19]

Less successful was the experience during November and December of the 19th Marine Regiment, which found the weapon incapable of neutralizing enemy strongpoints because of its short range. Nevertheless, flame terrified the enemy and on several occasions caused him to flee from his defensive positions.[20]

The 37th Infantry Division found little use for flame throwers during its first two months on Bougainville. The division's 8-man flame thrower squads (one per battalion ammunition and pioneer platoon) suddenly became busy in March.[21] In heavy action on Hill 700 eleven separate flame thrower attacks took place, each resulting in

[18] Lt Col Frank M. Reinecke, USMC, MS, Hellsapoppin Ridge, 8–18 December 1943, The Bougainville Campaign: A Study of Offensive Principles, 1947, p. 10. Marine Corps School, MOS LOG #208-48(c).

[19] (1) Ibid., pp. 17, 19–32. (2) CO 21st Marines to CG 3d Marine Div, 31 Jan 44, Rpt of Opn on Bougainville, in 3d Marine Div Combat Rpt, 1 Nov–28 Dec 43, dated 21 Mar 44. Marine Corps Archives, A5–2.

[20] CO 19th Marine Regt to CG 3d Marine Div, n.d., Rpt of Opns, Nov–Dec 43. 3d Marine Div Combat Rpt, 1 Nov–28 Dec 43, dated 21 Mar 44. Marine Corps Archives, A5–2.

[21] (1) Ltr, CmlO 37th Div to CmlO XIV Corps, 11 Jan 44, sub: Informal Combat Rpt of Lessons Learned in Combined New Georgia & Bougainville Opns. XIV Corps Rpts. (2) Maj Gen Oscar W. Griswold, Bougainville: An Experience in Jungle Warfare, pp. 37–44.

the reduction of a pillbox. In one assault flame thrower teams reduced
two adjacent pillboxes, killing 20 Japanese in one and 25 in the other.[22]

The American Division, also committed on Bougainville, set up an
extensive organization for flame thrower operations. Recalling the
haphazard organization on Guadalcanal, the division decided to build
within each of its regiments a provisional flame thrower platoon. Under
the supervision of the division chemical officer, Maj. Woodson C.
Tucker, the first of these units was formed and assigned to the 132d
Regiment Headquarters Company on 18 February 1944. The platoon
had a 5-man headquarters and six 4-man squads, each allotted two
flame throwers. Similar units were organized within the 182d and
164th Regiments, and all three underwent extensive training to develop
squad and platoon teamwork and to familiarize individuals with all
the weapons of the squad. Exercises stressed co-ordination of rifle
units and flame thrower teams, since tacticians had decided that should
flame thrower targets appear, squads from the platoon working in
conjunction with the infantry units would be detailed to attack them.[23]

Only two of the three provisional flame thrower platoons, those of
the 132d and the 182d Regiments, saw combat action on Bougainville.
Both units took part in the bitter fighting in March 1944 on Hill 260
and during April in the battle of Mavavia in the eastern part of the
island. The provisional flame thrower platoons were highly successful
in each action. In its first commitment in combat on Hill 260 the
132d Regiment's flame unit reduced eight enemy pillboxes in one
hundred seconds of actual firing. The platoon reduced two more on
11 March 1944 while supporting the assault of Company B, 182d
Regiment, on an observation post on the same hill.[24] From 7 to 9 April,
the provisional flame thrower platoon of the 182d Infantry regiment
supported troops of the 93d Division at Mavavia. Assigned primarily

---

[22] XIV Corps Rpt on Lessons Learned in the Bougainville Opns, n.d., pp. 4–5. CWS 314.7
Portable Flame Thrower File.

[23] (1) History, Flame Thrower Platoon of the 132d Inf Regt, Apr 44. CWS 314.7, Portable
Flame Thrower File. (2) CmlO, American Div to ACofS G–3 American Div, 7 Nov 44, Rpt, Flame
Thrower, and Incls. CWS 314.7 Portable Flame Thrower File.

[24] History, Flame Thrower Platoon of the 132d Infantry Regiment, Apr 44. CWS 314.7 Portable
Flame Thrower File. (2) Griswold, Bougainville: An Experience in Jungle Warfare, pp. 96–114.
The Griswold account (pages 119–20) tells of another use of flame in the fierce fighting for Hill 260.
Two Navy men got 200 feet of flexible pipe, connected it to a drum of gasoline, and used oxygen
pressure to pump the liquid into Japanese pillboxes. The gasoline was ignited by white phosphorous
grenades. See also Miller, CARTWHEEL: The Reduction of Rabaul, p. 372. For further attempts
at this type of improvisation, see below, pp. 567–68.

to mopping-up activities, flame thrower operators followed tanks and fired into all pillboxes and suspicious holes. Later in April the platoon supported its parent unit, the 182d Regiment, this time during the fighting in the upper Laruma Valley.[25]

The portable flame thrower's highly impressive record on Bougainville, coupled with its earlier performance on Guadalcanal and New Georgia, clearly demonstrated the value of the weapon in jungle fighting. Despite its shortcomings the flame thrower had made a fairly auspicious beginning. Work remained to be done; as late as April 1944 the XIV Corps recognized that ". . . the tactical capabilities of this weapon have not yet been fully developed." [26] In preparation for the move to the Philippines the XIV Corps and the four Army divisions in the South Pacific (the 25th, 37th, 43d, and American) intensified their training efforts and reorganized their flame thrower teams.[27]

The Southwest Pacific: The First Years

While the portable flame thrower was winning a good name in the South Pacific theater, it was getting a reputation of a wholly different sort in the Southwest Pacific. The origins of its notoriety go back to December 1942 and the Papua Campaign.

Papua

On 6 December Col. Clarence M. Tomlinson, commanding officer of the 126th Infantry, 32d Division, asked the 114th Engineer Combat Battalion for several flame throwers and operators to help overcome enemy machine gun emplacements near the village of Buna. The engineers, equipped with the E1R1 flame thrower, immediately set about testing and servicing these weapons. Although the inspections showed that several of the gas cylinders had developed leaks, some from rust, some from defective material, the flame throwers functioned reasonably well, if at a maximum range of only 20 yards.[28] Five

---

[25] Ltr, CO 182d Inf Regt to CmlO Americal Div, 31 Oct 44, sub: Present Status of the Flame Thrower Platoon. CWS 314.7 Portable Flame Thrower File.

[26] An. No. 3 to XIV Corps Tng Memo No. 8, 29 Apr 44, sub: Tng in the Use of Flame Throwers. Reproduced as app. 3 in McKinney, Portable Flame Thrower Opns, p. 248.

[27] (1) Ibid., pp. 251–52. (2) Incl 2 to 37th Div Tng Memo No. 7, 26 Sep 44, sub: Tng in the Use of Flame Throwers. Reproduced as app. 4 in McKinney, Portable Flame Thrower Opns, pp 253–57.

[28] (1) Ltr, CO 114th Engr Bn to CmlO MAPLE Base (Port Moresby), 19 Dec 42, sub: Malfunctioning of Flame Throwers. CWS SPECVI 470.71/92. (2) Ltr, Col Frank M. Arthur to Hist Off, 3 Mar 59.

operators with two weapons, two refill tanks, and 25 gallons of fuel, reported to the regiment on 7 December, and the next day the regimental operations officer ordered the flame throwers into action.[29] The target was an enemy machine gun bunker ingeniously concealed at the edge of a kunai grass flat. While the flame throwers were being brought forward, M/Sgt. John K. King, of the division chemical section, and one of the company officers, Lieutenant Davidson, performed the necessary reconnaissance. They identified the bunker in the midst of its natural and artificial camouflage and exposed themselves in order to draw fire and pinpoint the location of its ports. A partially demolished breastwork about 35 yards from the bunker furnished cover for anyone approaching the position. It was possible to advance a bit farther toward the bunker in comparative safety through a shallow trench which extended 5 yards out from the breastwork. This would give the operator an attack position only 30 yards from his target.

After the reconnaissance Lieutenant Davidson went forward again, this time accompanied by Cpl. Wilber G. Tirrell, the engineer flame thrower operator. Once more he drew fire from the bunker so that the corporal could see the exact location of the ports.

The plan of operation was practicable and uncomplicated. Corporal Tirrell, his weapon concealed in a burlap sack, was to advance as far as possible in the shallow trench, thirty yards from his objective. As a diversion, three men with automatic weapons were to crawl around on the left flank and fire at the rear of the bunker. Lieutenant Davidson, Sergeant King, and four riflemen were to take positions behind the breastwork, ready to rush the bunker with rifle fire and grenades in the wake of the flame thrower. Corporal Tirrell was to advance at least five yards beyond the end of the trench before releasing the flame and was to keep advancing until the fuel was exhausted.

Before the men took their stations, they checked the flame thrower's ignition system. At the proper moment, the group on the left flank began its diverting fire. The enemy did not answer. Corporal Tirrell moved from his position at the end of the shallow trench and headed toward the bunker. Seven yards beyond the trench he released the initial burst of flame and immediately Lieutenant Davidson and his

---

[29] The following account is based on: Ltr, Actg Div CmlO 32d Div to CG 32d Div, 18 Feb 43, sub: Rpt on the Activities of the 32d Inf Div Cml Sec During the Papuan Campaign. CWS 314.7 Portable Flame Thrower File.

party rushed out from behind the breastwork, only to find themselves in serious trouble. Instead of a powerful burst of flame, the flame thrower emitted a feeble 10-foot squirt, and the Japanese inside the emplacement began pouring machine gun fire into the advancing group. One of the riflemen was hit as soon as he left the cover of the breastwork, Lieutenant Davidson was killed, and the others withdrew. Corporal Tirrell continued to advance, trying vainly to get his weapon to function properly. When he was less than fifteen yards from the bunker he was stunned by a bullet which struck the front of his helmet and he fell to the ground out of sight. During the night he crawled back to safety.[30] Two days later the infantry overcame the position by direct assault.[31]

The cause of the Buna fiasco was never absolutely determined, but its effect was immediate. The infantry's confidence in the flame thrower was shattered. In January 1943 Colonel Copthorne, Chief Chemical Officer, USAFFE, informed General Porter that "the way the flame throwers let the infantry down at a critical point brought them into such ill-repute that I am afraid that they may never want to use them again."[32] In Washington Colonel Benner, chief of the CWS Field Requirements Branch, stated that a weapon such as the flame thrower with its "temperamental nature has no place in modern warfare where ruggedness and reliability are essential."[33]

But if the flame thrower was too temperamental to rely on, it was potentially too useful to abandon. Back on New Guinea, Sergeant King made one last effort to make flame throwers serviceable. New weapons were flown in from Port Moresby, across the mountains, but these, too, were unfit for use. They were checked and serviced and

---

[30] (1) Initial reports of the action listed Corporal Tirrell as having died in the encounter. He actually "played dead" after regaining consciousness and waited until dusk before returning to his position. He did suffer a leg wound inflicted by an enemy rifleman as he escaped, but contrary to early reports he survived and was recommended for citation for his valiant, though unsuccessful efforts. (2) Ltr, Actg Div CmlO 32d Div to CG 32d Div, 18 Feb 43, sub: Rpt on Activities of the 32d Inf Div Cml Sec During the Papuan Campaign. (3) Ltr, CO 114th Engr Bn to CmlO MAPLE Base APO 929, 19 Dec 42, sub: Malfunctioning of Flame Throwers. CWS SPECVI 470.71/92. (4) The account of the Buna flame thrower operation found in Milner, *Victory in Papua*, page 250, based on the earliest reports of the action, gives an incomplete account of the casualties.

[31] On 15 December 1942 a flame thrower was employed against another enemy bunker near Buna. The result was the same as at Buna the week before: the flame thrower "fizzed out and the Japanese shot it up." Milner, *Victory in Papua*, p. 253.

[32] Ltr, CCmlO USAFFE to CCWS, 6 Jan 43, no sub. CWS 319.1/101.

[33] Ltr, Chief Field Rqmts Br to Chief War Plans and Theater Br, 18 Jan 43, sub: Malfunctioning of Flame Throwers. CWS SPCUR 470.71/92.

parts interchanged in an attempt to get at least one weapon that would function properly, but all efforts were unsuccessful.[34]

Matters of Maintenance, Supply, and Training

During the first nine months of 1943 the 10th Chemical Maintenance Company at Brisbane, commanded by Capt. John J. Shaffer, conducted extensive flame thrower tests in order to locate the major sources of trouble, a project which included the thorough overhaul of all flame throwers in the Southwest Pacific Area. The unit discovered that most malfunctions resulted from deteriorated cylinders and batteries which had succumbed to the deleterious temperatures and humidity of the tropics. All flame throwers shipped to the Southwest Pacific or carried as equipment by units arriving in the area were thoroughly tested, repaired, and waterproofed by trained technicians under the direction of Colonel Copthorne and his staff. Though fundamental defects remained, the work of the SWPA Chemical Section went a long way in effectively preventing a repetition of the mishaps suffered on Buna.

Meanwhile, Sixth Army began a comprehensive analysis of the Papua Campaign in an attempt to discover an effective means of reducing Japanese bunkers. The experience of its subordinate units indicated that these fortifications generally could not be destroyed by artillery or mortar fire. Only the foot soldier armed with normal infantry weapons could do the job. Having located a bunker, infantrymen either had to outflank it or to launch repeated frontal assaults until the enemy was overcome. Either tactic normally resulted in heavy casualties.

Although the flame thrower had performed dismally at Buna, Sixth Army had received reports of the successful use of the weapon on Guadalcanal and New Georgia.[35] On the basis of these reports it appeared that a dependable flame thrower could be the answer to the problem of pillbox destruction. By October 1943 the rigorous tests conducted by the 10th Chemical Maintenance Company demonstrated that the flame thrower could be made reliable. Sixth Army therefore decided to include the weapon in its future combat operations and asked that Headquarters, U.S. Army Forces Far East, increase the

---

[34] Ltr, Actg Div CmlO 32d Div to CG 32d Div, 18 Feb 43, sub: Rpt on the Activities of the 32d Inf Div Cml Sec During the Papuan Campaign.

[35] (1) Ltr, CmlO XIV Corps to CmlO USAFFE, 11 Aug 43, no sub. (2) Ltr, CmlO XIV Corps to CmlO USAFFE, 15 Sep 43, no sub. Both in Sixth Army Cml Sec Rcds, 470.71 Flame Thrower.

allotment of flame throwers from twenty-four to sixty per infantry division. This request was approved on 19 October 1943.[36]

Welcome as these decisions were to the CWS, they raised serious problems for chemical officers in the Southwest Pacific. The first difficulty was related to supply. Flame throwers, spare parts, accessory kits, and fuel had become exceedingly scarce at the beginning of 1943. Colonel Morcock, Chemical Officer, USASOS SWPA, had requisitioned 308 M1A1 flame throwers from the United States in March 1943, and had repeated his plea two months later.[37] In July the first shipment of M1A1's arrived to replace obsolete E1R1 and M1 models and by August supplies of M1A1's were sufficient to cover the authorized allowances of Sixth Army units.[38] This balance of supply and demand was upset in October when, as just noted, General MacArthur's headquarters approved Sixth Army's request for the sixty flame thrower allotment for each infantry division. Not until the beginning of 1944 did enough M1A1's again become available to meet increasing combat and training needs. Supplies of spare parts and accessories never did catch up with requirements and both continued in critical demand for the duration of the war.[39]

Two additional factors complicated the supply picture. First, many of the new flame throwers were unusable because of missing or defective parts or because of improper packing or waterproofing.[40] Upon arrival from the United States, these weapons had to be turned over to chemical units for inspection, servicing, and rewaterproofing. Second, it was exceedingly difficult to obtain needed quantities of compressed hydrogen and nitrogen. Because of the shipping shortage, these gases were not sent from the United States and had to be procured at great

[36] Ltr, CG Sixth Army to CG USAFFE, 4 Oct 43, sub: Portable Flame Throwers, and Inds. Sixth Army Rcds, 470.71 Flame Thrower.

[37] Ltr, CmlO USASOS SWPA to SupO Cml Br Overseas Sup Div San Francisco Port of Embarkation, (Oakland, Calif.), 7 Jun 43, sub: Portable Flame Throwers, New M1A1, and Accessories. GSWC 470.7 in CWS SPCVO 470.71 APO 501.

[38] Ltr, CG USAFFE to CG Sixth Army, 21 Aug 43, sub: Flame Throwers, Portable, M1A1, Sixth Army Rcds, 470.71 Flame Throwers.

[39] See above, ch. VI.

[40] (1) Ltr, CG 41st Inf Div to CG USASOS SWPA 27 Oct 43, sub: Condition of Flame Throwers. (2) Ltr, CmlO USASOS SWPA to CmlO's Intermediate and Adv Secs USASOS and CmlO's Bases A, B, D, E, and F, 15 Dec 43, sub: Flame Throwers. Both in Sixth Army Rcds, 470.71 Flame Thrower.

expense and trouble either from naval or air units in the area or from Australian firms.[41]

Even more serious than the problem of supply was that of training. Since the flame thrower was a comparatively new weapon, and until 1943 one largely assigned to the engineers, few of the troops in the Southwest Pacific had been trained to use it. With the allotment in October 1943 of 12 flame throwers to each infantry regiment, it for the first time became necessary to extend flame thrower training to the infantry. The magnitude of the job can be judged by the Sixth Army requirement that each rifle company, cavalry troop, and ammunition and pioneer platoon have at least 4 trained flame thrower operators; this was to be in addition to the 4 trained men for each authorized flame thrower in each engineer company and battalion.[42] Since most commanders wanted to train men in excess of these minimum requirements, the training burden on both the individual unit and the CWS was exceedingly heavy.

Because the dispersal of American units throughout Australia and New Guinea made a single flame thrower training center impracticable, schools were established in several different locations. Flame thrower operators for I Corps' 24th and 41st Infantry Divisions trained at a jungle assault school near Rockhampton, Queensland.[43] The 10th Chemical Maintenance Company held classes for personnel of other units stationed in Australia at the Chemical Warfare Training Center at Brisbane.[44] The Sixth Army Chemical Section provided several traveling teams to teach flame thrower operation to Marine and Army organizations in forward staging areas. These teams, made up of one officer and two enlisted men, conducted a series of three 2-day flame thrower schools for units in New Guinea and the Trobriand Islands.

---

[41] (1) Ltr, 1st Lt Robert P. Rockway to Col Carl L. Marriott, 22 Oct 43, no sub. (2) Memo, CmlO U.S. Adv Base A for CmlO ALAMO Force, 31 Oct 43, no sub. Both in Sixth Army Rcds, 470.71 Flame Thrower.

[42] Sixth Army Tng Memo No. 8, 1 Oct 43, sub: Tng in the Use of Flame Throwers. Sixth Army Cml Sec Rcds, 470.71 Flame Thrower; reprinted as app. 5 in McKinney, Portable Flame Thrower Opns.

[43] Under the leadership of its chemical officer, Colonel Riegelman, I Corps had taken an early lead in the development of flame thrower doctrine and had been the first to issue a training publication on the employment of the weapon in the Southwest Pacific. See: (1) Incl 1 to Ltr, CG I Corps to CG's 24th, 41st (32d Divs, 27 Sep 43, sub: Employ of Flame Throwers, CWS 314.7 Portable Flame Thrower File; (2) I Corps Tng Memo No. 17, 10 Dec 43, sub: Tng in the Use of Flame Throwers, CWS 314.7 File; also reprinted as app. 7 in McKinney, Portable Flame Thrower Opns, pp. 265–67; (3) Riegelman, Caves of Biak, pp. 73–75.

[44] (1) 1st Ind on Ltr, 29 Aug 43, CG USAFFE to CG Sixth Army, 21 Aug 43, sub: Flame Thrower, Portable, M1A1. Sixth Army Rcds, Cml Sec Rcds, 470.71 Flame Thrower. (2) Shaffer Ltr, 19 Sep 56.

Under the leadership of 1st Lt. Robert P. Rockway, the teams had trained 582 flame thrower operators by February 1944.[45]

The flame thrower schools stressed operation, maintenance, and servicing as well as tactics. Based upon past experience, current Sixth Army doctrine prescribed that the flame thrower be included as part of the arms and equipment of an organized assault party rather than be employed as an individual weapon. Sixth Army suggested that an assault party be made up of eighteen men, armed with demolition charges, bangalore torpedoes, rocket launchers, and signal projectors, in addition to regular infantry weapons. These groups were to be trained and readied in order to be immediately available when needed in combat. Three flame thrower teams, each consisting of an operator and assistant operator, were allotted to each assault party.[46]

Improving the flame thrower and training operators to employ it occupied most of 1943. Achievements in both fields were substantial, but since the weapon had not yet performed satisfactorily in the Southwest Pacific, lingering doubts remained as to the ultimate value of such efforts. Flame thrower successes in a variety of operations in the theater between December 1943 and July 1944 helped dispel such doubts.

New Britain and the Admiralties

The first combat use of the flame thrower in the Southwest Pacific after Buna occurred on 15 December 1943 at Pilelo, a tiny island off the coast of New Britain. Troop B of the 112th Cavalry RCT had landed and was moving inland when the leading platoon was halted by fire from two caves. A bazooka quickly silenced one, but the other was so protected by log pilings as to be impervious to both bazooka and machine gun fire. The troop commander then organized an assault party with a flame thrower as its principal weapon. While rifle and automatic weapons fire covered the cave, the flame thrower operator worked his way up and fired his entire charge into the entrance. The rest of the party then rushed the position with hand grenades. When

---

[45] (1) Ltr, CmlO Hq ALAMO Forces to ACofS G–3, Sixth Army, 9 Feb 44, sub: Trained Flame Thrower Pers. (2) Ltr, ACmlO ALAMO Force to CmlO U.S. Forces, Unit 3, 4 Nov 43, sub: Flame Thrower School. (3) For detailed course of instruction at these mobile flame thrower schools, see 114th Engineer Battalion Training Memorandum No. 14, Annex 1, 6 October 1943, Flame Thrower School Schedule. All in Sixth Army Cml Sec Rcds, 353 Flame Thrower Tng.

[46] Sixth Army Tng Memo No. 8, 1 Oct 43, sub: Tng in the Use of Flame Throwers.

the party reached the cave, it found 5 dead and 2 wounded Japanese, all with their clothing ablaze.[47]

Marine units had less success with the flame thrower in the Cape Gloucester section of New Britain. Misfires and mechanical malfunctions were frequent. The M1A1's, despite their waterproofing, became damp and undependable from the incessant rain.[48] The dense foliage and jungle growth on Cape Gloucester normally absorbed the first burst of flame thrower fuel, preventing the flame from reaching its target and further exposing an already vulnerable operator to enemy fire.[49]

Flame throwers made an equally inauspicious beginning in the Admiralties campaign. The 2d Brigade of the 1st Cavalry Division landed on Manus Island on 15 March 1944 with sixteen flame throwers filled and ready for action. Since opposition to the landing was negligible and the first few days produced no suitable flame thrower targets, many units discarded these weapons. But on the fourth day after the landing, advancing troops were harassed by fire from a bunker which had been bypassed by assault troops. It was a perfect target for flame throwers, but none was available. They were found scattered along the route from the beach, and hydrogen and nitrogen cylinders were located near the airstrip, even farther from the front.[50]

The brigade commander, Brig. Gen. Verne D. Mudge, corrected the situation by ordering his chemical officer, Lt. Charles Land, to collect all flame throwers and equipment and take personal charge of flame thrower operations. From then on, the weapons were carried immediately behind the attacking troops. Lieutenant Land accompanied the forward elements, ready to organize and direct flame thrower assault groups against suitable targets. Such targets did not appear until the closing days of the Manus Island operation. It was discovered in

[47] (1) Ltr, CmlO Task Force (93d Cml Composite Co) to CmlO Sixth Army, 30 Dec 43, sub: Official Rpt on Tactical Use of Flame Thrower. Reprinted in CWS 314.7 Observers Rpts (Grothaus-Brady Rpt), SWPA, SOPAC, CENPAC, 29 Mar 44, as an. 4, sec. 5. (2) Miller, CARTWHEEL: The Reduction of Rabaul, p. 285.

[48] (1) Lt. Col. Frank O. Hough, USMCR, and Maj. John A. Crown, USMC, The Campaign on New Britain (Washington, 1952), p. 54. (2) 93d Cml Composite Co, 30 Dec 43, Official Rpt on Tactical Use of Flame Thrower. CWS SPCWS 5205 8-6. 1605/44.

[49] (1) Ltr, Cml Warfare SupO BACKHANDER Force to Cml Warfare IntellO USASOS SWPA, 1 Jan 44, sub: Cml Intell. CWS 314.7 Portable Flame Thrower File. (2) Memo, ACmlO ALAMO Force for G–3, G–4, 16 Feb 44, no sub. Sixth Army Rcds, 333 Inspection Rpts.

[50] Rpt, CmlO 1st Cavalry Div, 3 Jul 44, sub: Use of Flame Throwers in the Admiralty Campaign. CWS 314.7 Portable Flame Thrower File.

mopping up the island that numerous Japanese had quietly remained in their bunkers and allowed the leading elements of the attack to bypass them. Flame thrower teams and demolition squads eliminated these pockets by flaming and blasting every bunker they encountered.[51]

Wakde, Maffin Bay, and Biak

The flame thrower proved its effectiveness anew in May 1944 on Wakde Island, of the Wakde group, off the New Guinea coast. There, after two days of intense fighting, the 163d Infantry, 41st Division, managed to clear out most of the enemy forces. The remaining Japanese took refuge in a network of connecting tunnels and caves in a coral shelf which sloped up sharply from the northeast shore line. Company A of the 27th Engineer Combat Battalion was ordered to clean them out. To do the job the company used dynamite, bazookas, white phosphorus grenades, and flame throwers, but only the flame thrower proved successful against both caves and tunnels. On at least eight separate occasions flame thrower assaults either killed the Japanese defenders outright or drove them from their hiding places into the open, where they became easy targets for riflemen.[52]

Company B of the 27th Engineer Combat Battalion, attached to the 158th Infantry, did equally well with flame throwers in the Maffin Bay area of the New Guinea mainland, across from Wakde Island. On 24 May the engineers, supported by two tanks, destroyed a machine gun emplacement, which had pinned down an infantry company for over three hours.[53] This was the first recorded instance of a co-ordinated tank-flame thrower attack in the Southwest Pacific. A month later, farther to the east at Lone Tree Hill, the pattern was repeated. On 18 June 2d Lt. Theodore Frankel, antitank platoon leader, 1st Infantry, 6th Division, supported by two tanks, knocked out three

[51] (1) *Ibid.* (2) Lt. Col. Kenneth W. Haas, "The Pacific Is Another War," *Chemical Warfare Bulletin*, vol. 30, No. 5 (November–December, 1944), p. 17.

[52] (1) Ltr, CW Tech Intell Team 4 to Chief CmlO USASOS SWPA, 24 Jun 44, sub: Rpt on Use of Cml Warfare Weapons and Munitions. CWS 314.7 Portable Flame Thrower File. (2) McKinney, Portable Flame Thrower Opns, pp. 69–70.

[53] (1) Smith, *Approach to the Philippines*, p. 239. (2) Ltr, Cml Warfare Tech Intell Team 4 to Chief CmlO USASOS SWPA, 24 Jun 44, sub: Rpt on Use of Cml Warfare Weapons and Munitions. CWS 314.7 Portable Flame Thrower File. (3) Ltr, CG Sixth Army to Corps and Divs *et al.*, 6 Sep 44, sub: Cml Warfare Activities During Wakde–Maffin Bay Opns. CWS 314.7 Portable Flame Thrower File.

enemy bunkers with a single flame thrower.[54] Six days later Frankel used the flame thrower in an entirely different kind of attack. The target was an enemy 70-mm. artillery piece emplaced in a cave high on Rocky Point. Frankel organized an assault party consisting of an antitank grenadier, a TNT-armed demolitions man, and several riflemen; he himself carried a flame thrower. The party crawled to a shell hole about twenty yards in front of the cave, from which point Frankel fired several bursts from the weapon. Next the demolition man placed his charge, which knocked out the enemy field piece and buried its crew under the resulting debris. In a 2-day period, Lieutenant Frankel took part in nearly two dozen flame thrower assaults.[55] But the lieutenant's record in this regard was not unique, since engineers of the 6th Engineer Combat Battalion and infantrymen of the 1st and 20th Infantry regiments of the 6th Division carried out scores of successful flame attacks in June 1944, especially in the Lone Tree Hill and Rocky Point sections of the front.[56]

While the battle for Maffin Bay was still in progress, elements of the 41st Infantry Division invaded Biak Island. This island, about 100 miles from New Guinea, was a mass of coral with a veneer of dense jungle vegetation. It abounded with caves ranging in size from shallow cavities just large enough to contain two or three men to networks of caverns capable of accommodating eight or nine hundred. Japanese ingenuity had turned this maze of natural cave and connecting tunnels into an extensive and formidable defensive installation, relatively impervious to the effects of air, naval, and artillery bombardment.[57] The flame thrower played a vital role in the destruction of these powerful defenses. From 27 May to 19 August 1944 it was fired more often than in any other previous campaign in the Southwest Pacific. Fifty-nine flame throwers sprayed 236 gallons of fuel against enemy positions.

[54] (1) Ltr, Task Force CmlO U.S. Forces Unit 1 to CmlO Sixth Army, 21 Jun 44, no sub. Sixth Army Rcds, 470.7 Flame Throwers. (2) Frankel and 2d Lt James J. Harnes, 13 Jul 44, Rpt on Use of Flame Throwers in Maffin Bay Area, Dutch New Guinea. Sixth Army Rcds, 350.05–Wakde.

[55] Frankel and Harnes, Rpt on Use of Flame Throwers in Maffin Bay Area, Dutch New Guinea.

[56] Ltr, CG Sixth Army to Distr, 6 Sep 44, sub: Cml Warfare Activities During the Wakde Island–Maffin Bay Opns. Sixth Army Rcds, 415.3.

[57] (1) Ltr, CG Sixth Army to Distr, 3 Sept 44, sub: Cml Warfare Activities During the Biak Opn. Sixth Army Rcds, 415.3. (2) Riegelman, Caves of Biak, pp. 145–47.

They were used to burn combustible Japanese stores and against a variety of other targets.[58]

Introduction of the Portable Flame Thrower in the Central Pacific Area

Although it was in the South and Southwest Pacific that flame throwers were first employed, it remained for troops in the Central Pacific to demonstrate the full potential of the weapon. This they proceeded to do in a long series of amphibious assaults that, paralleling MacArthur's drive in the Southwest Pacific, carried Army and Marine units from the Gilberts and Marshalls to the very doorstep of Japan. From the start commanders in the Central Pacific, especially Marine leaders, showed an interest in and an enthusiasm for the flame thrower unmatched in other theaters. Forces in the area were also blessed with an adequate and sometimes overabundant supply of the weapon, a relative absence of technical problems that plagued the Southwest Pacific, and sufficient time between engagements to train operators and assault teams. These factors helped to produce the success achieved by the flame thrower in the Central Pacific.

During the last week in July 1943 the Hawaiian Department [59] presented a portable flame thrower demonstration, based on an analysis of operations in the South Pacific, to approximately 1,400 Army, Navy, and Marine officers and enlisted men. The display, demonstrating how Japanese fortified defenses might be attacked and destroyed by assault parties armed with the flame thrower, generated considerable interest.[60]

Later, when plans were being made for the invasion of the Gilbert Islands, the Hawaiian Department chemical office prepared detailed studies of types of Japanese defenses that might be encountered. An examination of these studies convinced planners that the flame thrower would be a desirable weapon in the coming operations; accordingly, the 27th Infantry Division received twenty-four and the 2d Marine Divi-

---

[58] (1) CmlO 41st Inf Div, n.d., Rpt, Cml Phase and Sec Hist Rcd of HORLICKS Opn. CWS 314.7 Portable Flame Thrower File. (2) CmlO 41st Inf Div to CmlO ALAMO Force, 11 Aug 44, Preliminary Tech Rpt—Rpt No. 9. Sixth Army Rcds, 350.05 Biak.

[59] The Hawaiian Department soon became U.S. Army Forces, Central Pacific Area, and later U.S. Army Forces, Pacific Ocean Areas, and U.S. Army Forces, Middle Pacific. Colonel Unmacht served as chemical officer of these headquarters throughout the war.

[60] Memo, Quigley, OACofS G–3 Hawaiian Dept, for Keliher, ACofS G–3, 4 Aug 43, sub: Rpt on Dept Cml Field Exercise. History, CWS AFMIDPAC, vol. II, an. I–c.

MARINES USING CWS FLAME THROWER ON A TARAWA BEACH

sion sixty.[61] Members of the engineer battalion of each division underwent training in flame thrower operations, although even at this time
there was some feeling that it might be wiser to assign the weapons to
infantry rather than to engineer troops.

Portable throwers went into action on 20 November 1943 when the
165th RCT, 27th Division, landed on Makin Atoll and the 2d Marine
Division attacked Betio Island of the Tarawa Atoll. On the former,
enemy opposition was fortunately limited, for flame throwers, drenched
in the landings, failed to function.[62] On Betio marines faced strong
Japanese positions. Here, enemy beach fortifications consisted of numerous concrete, steel, and sand and coconut log pillboxes, plus a number of excellent bombproof shelters. These emplacements were con-

[61] (1) History CWS AFMIDPAC, II, an. II–b, 3–5.   (2) Ltr, Unmacht to Hist Off, 27 Jun 51.
CWS 314.7.
[62] Crowl and Love, *Seizure of the Gilberts and Marshalls*, p. 93.

nected by means of an intricate and highly developed trench and tunnel system.[63]

Flame throwers proved invaluable against these defenses. During the first three days of fighting, the weapon burned out a score of enemy pillboxes, and, surprisingly, permitted marines to take a number of frightened Japanese prisoners. On 22 November a large concrete bomb-proof shelter was assaulted by men of the 2d Battalion, 8th Marines. The marines, using flame throwers, overran the top of the shelter but the Japanese counterattacked within minutes. Flame throwers quickly drove back the enemy and inflicted heavy casualties.[64] As at least two historians of the Pacific fighting have commented: "Perhaps the most valuable weapon on Tarawa proved to be the flame thrower." [65]

Although other units used these weapons with equal effectiveness, there were, unfortunately, far too few flame throwers available. The 1st Battalion, 6th Marines, which had been assigned six flame throwers, used two in close support of tanks and attached the remaining four to the rifle platoon engaged in mopping-up activities. The battalion recommended that it be allotted twelve for future engagements, a desire reflected in the reports of several other units.[66]

As a result of the Gilbert experience, the 7th Infantry Division's allotment of portable flame throwers for the Marshall operations was increased to 192; the 4th Marine Division's to 72.[67] The 7th Division immediately began an intensive training program in these weapons. A squad of combat engineers armed with flame throwers, demolitions, wire cutters, and bangalore torpedoes was assigned to each rifle platoon. Realistic exercises were conducted in assaulting replicas of fortifications likely to be encountered in the Marshalls. The engineers soon learned to move freely under friendly fire and to depend on the infantrymen's

[63] CO 2d Marine Regt to CG 2d Marine Div, 17 Dec 43, Rpt of Opns GALVANIC. Combat Team 2 in 2d Marine Regt, Rpt of Opn—Tarawa, Marine Archives A8–1.

[64] (1) CO 2d Bn 8th Marines 2d Marine Div to CO Combat Team 2, 13 Dec 43, Rpt of Tarawa Opns, 2d Marine Regt—Rpt of Opns Tarawa. Marine Corps Archives A8–1. (2) Stockman, *Battle for Tarawa*, p. 47.

[65] Crowl and Love, *Seizure of the Gilberts and Marshalls*, p. 163.

[66] (1) CO 1st Bn 6th Marines to CO 6th Marine Regt, 3 Dec 43, Special Action Rpt, 6th Marine Regt—Special Action Report—Tarawa. Marine Corps Archives A9–1. (2) CO 8th Marine Regt to CG 2d Mar Div, 1 Dec 43, Special Action Report—Tarawa. Marine Archives A10–1. (3) CO LT 3/2 3d Bn 2d Marine to CG V Amphib Corps, 20 Dec 43, Rpt of Opns GALVANIC. 2d Marine Regt—Rpt of Opns—Tarawa. Marine Archives A8–1.

[67] (1) History, CWS AFMIDPAC, II, an. I-d, 30. (2) CG 4th Marine Div to CG V Amphib Corps, 17 Mar 44, Final Rpt on FLINTLOCK Opn, incl J, p. 17, Final Rpt, Roi. Marine Corps Archives A22–1.

ability to cover them. The latter, in turn, acquired confidence in the engineer's competence in using flame throwers and in placing demolitions rapidly and effectively.[68]

The 4th Marine Division, also readying itself for the Marshall Islands campaign, placed emphasis on assault team training. Equipped with seventy-two portable flame throwers, the division faced the almost impossible task, suggested by higher headquarters, of training two men per infantry platoon,[69] as well as the engineer personnel who normally operated the weapon.[70] The division trained as many individuals as it could, but put its greatest emphasis on organizing assault parties within its combat teams. Typical of these units was the 19-man party organized by the 24th Marines. This team was led by an officer and consisted of a flame thrower group including a flame thrower operator, an assistant operator, and a fuel carrier; a 5-man demolition group; a 3-man bazooka group; and a support group of 7 riflemen and BAR men. Engineer troops comprised the flame thrower and bazooka groups.[71]

The inclusion of a fuel carrier in the assault team was an innovation. Formerly, a flame thrower operator had to leave the forward area and return to a servicing point to refill his weapon. This extra man in the assault team made it possible to insure more rapid weapon refueling. Chemical officers in the Marshalls also adopted the system of supplying additional flame thrower fuel in 5-gallon cans, with an extra pressure cylinder attached, instead of the normal 55-gallon drums, thus expediting the handling of fuel from transports to refilling points and permitting the weapons to be serviced much nearer the front lines.

The actual combat employment of the flame thrower in the Marshall Islands failed to justify fully the extensive preliminary training program. Happily, Japanese defenses on Roi, Namur, Kwajalein, and Eniwetok, pounded by a 3-day preinvasion bombardment, proved less formidable and Japanese resistance less stubborn than had been anticipated. As a consequence, the flame thrower was not needed in the assault phases of the amphibious landings, but was confined to mopping-

[68] (1) Sixth Army Combat Notes No. 2 15 Aug 44, 106–11.6 (7076). (2) Rpt of the 7th Inf Div Participation in FLINTLOCK Opn, 8 Feb 44. 7th Inf Div, 307–0.3 (1037).

[69] V Amphib Corps Tng Memo No. 13–43, 21 Dec 43, Demolition and Flame Thrower Tng. Reprinted as app. 13 in McKinney, Portable Flame Thrower Opns, pp. 284–85.

[70] V Amphib Corps Tng Order No. 17–43, 21 Dec 43, Flame Throwers. Marine Corps School, Log 60–27, reprinted as app. 14 in McKinney, Portable Flame Thrower Opns, pp. 286–92.

[71] CG 4th Marine Div to CG V Amphib Corps, 17 Mar 44, Final Rpt on FLINTLOCK Opn, Incl E, Rpt of Combat Team 24. Marine Corps Archives, A22–1.

up operations and to the elimination of enemy personnel from underground shelters and fortifications.[72] The 4th Marine Division reported the weapon most effective in this work when used in combination with explosives. Flame was hurled at the embrasures and slits of the fortification forcing the occupants to take cover. Next, pole or shaped charges were used to breach the side of the structure, after which grenades, satchel charges, or more flame was used to destroy the occupants.[73]

Because operations in the Marshalls demonstrated that 192 flame throwers were more than an infantry division needed or could adequately handle, Army divisions slated for the Marianas campaign received 141 flame throwers and Marine divisions 81.[74] An analysis of the Marshall campaign also indicated to Army and Marine leaders that trained infantrymen as well as engineer troops were required to operate the flame thrower. This conclusion, similar to that reached independently by commanders in the South and Southwest Pacific, was based on the realization that engineers were normally too busy with other essential duties to devote their full attention to the flame thrower. After the Marshall Islands operation infantrymen became the primary users of the weapon in the Central Pacific.

[72] (1) Rpt, Marshall Islands Japanese Defenses and Battle Damage, prepared by WD Mission for CG CENPAC, 1 Mar 44. 98–USF3–0.3. (2) Maj. Leonard D. Frescoln, "Post-Mortem on the Marshalls," *Chemical Warfare Bulletin*, vol. 30, No. 2 (April–May, 1944), pp. 33–34.

[73] CG 4th Mar Div to CG V Amphib Corps, 17 Mar 44, Final Rpt on FLINTLOCK Opn. Marine Corps Archives A22–1, incl. 1, p. 17.

[74] (1) History CWS AFMIDPAC, II, an. 1–D, 40. (2) CG 3d Marine Div to Comdt of the Marine Corps, 21 Aug 44, Special Action Rpt, FORAGER Opn (Guam), an. B to D–3 Rpt, Marine Corps Archives, A17–1.

CHAPTER XV

The Flame Thrower in the Pacific: Marianas to Okinawa

The Need for a Mechanized Flame Thrower

The stimulus for the development of the mechanized flame thrower, as for the portable, came from the war against Japan where the enemy's excellent defenses and stubborn resistance called attention to the utility of flame. Although the portable flame thrower gradually proved to be an effective weapon against the Japanese, one of its inherent disadvantages, the vulnerability of the operator, suggested the portable's installation in an armored vehicle. It is not to be inferred that CWS engineers in the United States had been unmindful of the possibilities of a mechanized flame thrower; the Chemical Warfare Technical Committee had advocated the development of such a weapon in May 1940. But for various reasons, work on the mechanized models in the zone of interior proceeded slowly and fitfully throughout the entire war.[1]

There were several attempts in the Pacific to mount portable flame throwers in some sort of armored vehicle, a combination made the more appealing by the lack thus far of cannon or other antitank weapons in the enemy bunkers. In the South Pacific Area, for example, the commander of a tank battalion in New Caledonia installed a flame gun in the pistol port of a tank, and a chemical officer on New Georgia modified the flame gun so that it could be fitted into the aperture for the tank's bow machine gun. The 1st Marine Tank Battalion, serving in the Southwest Pacific, mounted several portable flame throwers on its tanks in preparation for the New Britain operation. None of these improvisions could have been called successful. The portable flame thrower was not constructed to withstand the vibrations and jarrings

---

[1] For a discussion of the research and development of mechanized flame throwers, see Brophy, Miles, Cochrane, *From Laboratory to Field.*

of a moving tank, and its fuel capacity was much too limited.[2] Word came from Washingon pointing out the disadvantages of range and fire hazards from such modifications and counseling patience until the arrival of perfected mechanized flame throwers from the zone of interior.[3]

After the bloody battle of Tarawa, which opened Allied offensive operations in the Central Pacific Area, an even greater clamor arose for a mechanized flame weapon. The portable flame thrower had done its part in that battle, but new weapons and techniques were urgently needed to help prevent the repetition of such staggering casualties. In preparation for the Marshall Islands operation scheduled for February 1944 both the 4th Marine Division and the 7th Infantry Division installed M1A1 portable flame throwers, modified by the chemical section of the 7th Division, in light tanks and LVT's, an amphibious tractor. Included in the 7th Division's version were special fuel containers manufactured in Honolulu. But the attempts to waterproof the guns on the LVT's were unsuccessful, and the electrical systems of those flame weapons, drenched on landing, failed completely. The tank-mounted versions, plagued with the basic weaknesses of fragility and low fuel capacity, had but modest success.[4]

The poor results of flame thrower improvisation in the Pacific theaters was no cause for criticism of the responsible chemical officers and tank commanders; the portable flame thrower was basically unsuited for tank adaption. If nothing else, these efforts clearly indicated that improvisation was not the answer and underlined the real need for a mechanized flame thrower in the Pacific fighting.

The Marianas

After the experience at Tarawa, General Richardson, Commanding General, U.S. Army Forces in Central Pacific Area, asked the War Department if mechanized flame throwers were available in the zone of interior. Upon receiving a favorable reply, Richardson requisitioned

---

[2] (1) CWS TofO Ltr No. 6, 8 Oct 43, p. 10. (2) Ltr, CmlO XIV Corps to CCWS, 26 Aug 43, sub: Rpt of Mounting Flame Throwers in Tanks. CWS 314.7 Mechanized Flame Throwers File. (3) Maj John N. Rentz, *Marines in the Central Solomons* (Washington, 1952), p. 156. (4) Ltr, CmlO ALAMO Force to Cml SupO APO 323, 24 Jan 44, no sub. Sixth Army Rcds, 470.71 Flame Throwers.

[3] CWS TofO Ltr No. 16, 12 Jul 44, p. 12.

[4] (1) History, CWS AFMIDPAC, II, an. II-c-1, 2–3; I, sec. 3, pp. 21–22. (2) Crowl and Love, *Seizure of the Gilberts and Marshalls*, p. 233. (3) USAFICPA, Participation in the Kwajalein and Eniwetok Opns, p. 194.

forty auxiliary bow gun flame throwers (E4–5) for use in the Marianas operation.[5] When these failed to arrive, he utilized local resources to fashion substitutes.[6] It was fortunate that this need arose in the Central Pacific, for Hawaii had factories and machine shops and an eager and able chemical officer—Colonel Unmacht, who approached the problem of the mechanized flame thrower with the same efficiency he had shown for the portable.

At this time the marines in the theater were perhaps even more interested in flame weapons than were the Army troops. Late in January 1944 the V Amphibious Corps, preparing for the Marianas, obtained twenty Ronson vehicular flame throwers from Canada. The development work involved in adapting these British-designed weapons for installation in M3A1 light tanks was to fall primarily upon Colonel Unmacht, who utilized CWS, Ordnance Department, Naval, and private facilities for this undertaking. The resulting main armament flame thrower, dubbed Satan, had a range of from 40 to 80 yards, a fuel capacity of 170 gallons, and a duration of fire of 2 minutes, enough, according to Unmacht, to reduce 40 or 50 pillboxes based on 2-second bursts.[7] At a demonstration held for interested officers on 15 April 1944, the marines fully recognized the potential of the mechanized flame thrower. The V Amphibious Corps managed to get ten more Ronson units from Canada, and its commander, Lt. Gen. Holland M. Smith, asked the Army authorities in Hawaii to install the Ronson units in M3A1 light tanks in time for the Marianas operation.[8] Although medium tanks would have had advantages of better protection and more space and mobility, none could be made available in time to meet the required deadline.[9] The Chemical Section, CENPAC, with the co-operation of the 14th Naval District, the V Amphibious Corps, and the Seabees, equipped twenty-four light tanks with the flame

[5] In an auxiliary mechanized flame thrower the flame weapon supplemented the normal armament of the vehicle; in a main armament mechanized flame thrower, as the name implies, the flame thrower was the principal armament.

[6] History, CWS AFMIDPAC, II, an. II–c–1, 70.

[7] (1) History, CWS AFMIDPAC, II, an. II–c–1, ref 14, 4–12. (2) See Brophy, Miles, and Cochrane, *From Laboratory to Field*, for details of the development work in Hawaii. (3) In his brief 8-page final report to the Chief of Staff, U.S. Army, General Richardson paid tribute to this "resourceful and inventive" CWS group which developed a flame-throwing tank that was of "incalculable value." Final Rpt of CG AFMIDPAC to CofS USA, 15 Mar 46.

[8] Memo, CmlO CENPAC for G–3 DCofS and CofS CENPAC, 17 Apr 44, sub: Installation of Ronson Flame Thrower in Light Tank. History, CWS AFMIDPAC, vol. III, ref. 6.

[9] 43d Cml Lab Co, 16 Aug 44, Demonstration of Ronson and Navy Mark I Vehicular Mounted Flame Thrower and Mobile Mechanical Servicing Equip. History, CWS AFMIDPAC, vol. III, ref. 14.

thrower units. As the Satans were being produced Colonel Unmacht conducted a series of 40-hour classes on flame tank operation which were attended by Marine Corps and Army officers and men. By mid-May the weapons were tested, waterproofed, and loaded on ships.

The invasion of the Marianas began early on 15 June 1944 when the V Amphibious Corps, known as the Northern Landing Force and consisting of the 2d and 4th Marine Divisions, invaded Saipan.[10] Each division had 12 Satan tanks. These 12 plus 3 conventional tanks formed a company of three platoons. Each platoon (4 Satans and 1 light tank) was attached to a company of medium tanks—the organic armored support of a marine regiment. Landing on D plus 2 (17 June) the flame tanks saw infrequent use during their first day of battle and then only for the purpose of mopping up. Next day the tanks took part in front-line action and thereafter, as tankers and infantrymen alike quickly learned flame tank techniques, the Satan proved to be an effective weapon.

Targets were varied—pillboxes, brush, canefields, buildings, and caves. Typical action against stiff opposition saw flame tanks neutralizing targets under cover of medium tanks. A tank commander, interviewed shortly after the end of the operation, told of one such action in which the Satan, supported by conventional tanks, came forward to flame a well defended pillbox. As the target started burning, two Japanese sprang out, only to be cut down by rifle fire. Resistance ceased. An examination of the bunker revealed ten other Japanese, grotesquely dead at their firing positions. The tank commander added that the mechanized flame thrower proved to be the only effective weapon against caves.[11]

After the fall of Saipan the 2d and 4th Marine Divisions immediately started preparations for the invasion of Tinian which was to begin on 24 July. In this attack the M3A1 light flame tanks, loaded aboard LCT's and LCM's, followed hard on the heels of the first assault wave. The composition and attachment of flame tank units during the fight-

[10] Admiral Turner's Joint Expeditionary Force was composed of the Northern Landing Force (V Amphibious Corps) scheduled for Saipan and Tinian, the Southern Landing Force (III Amphibious Corps) earmarked for Guam, and a Reserve Force, consisting of the 27th Infantry Division afloat and the 77th Division in Hawaii.

[11] (1) CmlO POA, 21 Aug 44, Rpt, Opns of Armored Flame Throwers by the 4th Marine Div on Saipan and Tinian. History CWS AFMIDPAC, vol. IV, an. II-c-3, ref. 1. (2) Intervs of 4th Marine Div Pers by Tenth Army officers, 4 Sep 44. History CWS MIDPAC, vol. IV, an. II-c-3, refs. 1 and 3.

ing were just as they had been on Saipan.[12] The terrain on Tinian proved much more favorable to tank employment, and this, combined with the recently acquired combat experience, resulted in a profitable use of flame vehicles. The Satans again combined with the medium tanks against the more tenacious points of resistance. They also were successful against caves and when used to burn vegetation concealing enemy positions.[13]

The Southern Landing Force, as the III Amphibious Corps was designated for the Marianas campaign, assaulted Guam on 21 July with the 3d Marine Division, the 1st Provisional Marine Brigade, and the 77th Infantry Division as its principal combat elements. The 3d Tank Battalion, which landed on the first day, had among its armament six M4A2 medium tanks equipped with E4–5 auxiliary bow gun flame throwers. These weapons had arrived from the zone of interior for service tests shortly before the operation began. One of the flame tanks met the enemy at Assan Point on the second day of the battle. Supported by a conventional tank the flame vehicle approached an enemy cave and fired half of its 25-gallon charge into the mouth. Seventeen Japanese soldiers were incinerated. A similar attack near Chonito Cliff resulted in 30 enemy dead. During the next five days the auxiliary flame tanks continued to burn out resistance on Guam.[14]

A few logistical difficulties arose during these flame operations in the Marianas. Planners for the invasion had estimated that the daily expenditure of each flame tank would be one load of fuel; actually, two loads were required. A shortage of napalm meant that most of the flame fuel was either diesel oil mixed with Bunker C fuel obtained from the vessels, or, at times, straight Bunker C. A postcampaign recommendation called for adequate amounts of thickened fuel for future operations to insure a longer, more effective range for the mechanized flame thrower.[15]

Flame tank crews, contrary to some pessimistic predictions, suffered no casualties as a result of actual flame operations, although two men were injured when a vehicle struck an enemy land mine. Fatigue be-

---

[12] Maj. Carl W. Hoffman, USMC, *The Seizure of Tinian* (Washington, 1951), p. 53.

[13] *Ibid.*, pp. 60, 96. (2) Philip A. Crowl, *The Campaign in the Marianas,* UNITED STATES ARMY IN WORLD WAR II (Washington, 1960), p. 298.

[14] Ltr, CO 3d Tank Bn to CG 3d Marine Div, 12 Nov 44, sub: Rpt and Recommendations on Flame Thrower E4–5 in M4A2 Tanks by This Battalion in Guam Opn. CWS 314.7 Mechanized Flame Thrower File.

[15] (1) Hoffman, *Seizure of Tinian*, p. 131.   (2) Interv, 4th Marine Div Pers, 4 Sep 44.

came a problem because of the extremely cramped positions within the light tanks. While the marines were generally impressed by the flame tank performance, they were critical of the range of the flame gun, the limited visibility and light armor of the tanks, the lack of special tools and spare parts, and the manner in which the Ronson was installed in the tank. And experience in the Marianas substantiated the preinvasion opinion that flame throwers should be mounted in medium tanks.[16]

The successful debut of the mechanized flame thrower in the Marianas campaign generally overshadowed the accomplishments of the portable model. The truth was that the two types of flame throwers supplemented one another; the mechanized afforded greater protection to the operator and delivered larger amounts of flame for longer distances, while the portable, capable of quicker and more flexible employment, attacked targets inaccessible to the tank-mounted type. Portable flame throwers saw action on Saipan on D-day before the tanks were landed and proved invaluable during the street fighting in the village of Garapan. Later, these weapons helped overcome stubborn resistance of cave defenses located in Saipan's cliff formations, defenses which the tank-mounted flame throwers could not reach. On Guam the portable flame throwers were committed against the cave defenses of Chonito Cliff within an hour of the actual landings, and they remained busy during the entire three weeks of fighting.[17]

On at least one occasion the two types of flame thrower were employed in the same action. During the battle for Tinian, marines first used the cannon of a medium tank to blast defended caves, then the light flame tanks to spray the openings, and finally assault teams with demolitions and portable flame weapons to actually reduce the positions.[18]

Of the two Army divisions in the operation the 27th continued to assign the weapons to the combat engineers while the 77th gave them to

[16] (1) Interv, 4th Marine Div Pers, 4 Sep 44. (2) CG 4th Marine Div to Comdt Marine Corps, 18 Sep 44, Opn Rpt—Saipan, an. E, p. 11. Marine Corps Archives A14-1 (S&C 48430). (3) Hoffman, *Saipan: The Beginning of the End*, p. 254.

[17] (1) CO 8th Marine Regt to CG 2d Marine Div, 20 Jul 44, Special Action Rpt, FORAGER. Marine Archives A20-1. (2) Crowl, *Campaign in the Marianas*, chs. V, IX. (3) Hoffman, *Saipan: The Beginning of the End*, p. 196. (4) CG 3d Marine Div to Comdt Marine Corps, 21 Aug 44, Special Action Rpt, FORAGER Opn, D-3 Rpt, Narrative of the Campaign.

[18] (1) Lt Col B. A. Hockmuth, USMC, n.d., Rpt, Flame Throwers at Saipan. CWS 314.7. (2) CG 4th Marine Div to CINCPAC and CINCPOA, 25 Sep 44, Opn Rpt—Tinian, an. C, p. 20. Marine Archives, A14-3. (3) Hoffman, *Seizure of Tinian*, p. 96.

the infantry. The marines, prompted by previous experience, assigned the portable flame throwers to the infantry.[19]

Although the portable weapon stood up well under hard usage in the Marianas, weather conditions caused innumerable problems. Many flame throwers were deadlined through battery and spark plug failure and because of inadequate waterproofing. The former difficulty was greatly relieved with the introduction of the new M2–2 flame thrower (flown from the zone of interior) and its improved ignition system.[20] There was a good supply of flame throwers present, but no provision had been made for transporting them or the heavy service equipment needed for their maintenance.[21]

Peleliu

Tarawa had called the Navy's attention to the possible use during the initial stages of an assault landing of a mechanized flame thrower mounted in some sort of landing craft. The National Defense Research Committee provided a speedy solution to this problem. The organization had recently developed the Q model flame thrower for light tanks only to find that vehicle out of favor. It now adapted the Q flame unit to fill the Navy's needs. Newly christened the Navy Mark I, five units of the flame thrower reached Hawaii in April 1944. The Army inherited these units when Navy authorities turned down the model as unsuitable for amphibious operations because of its excessive weight. The 43d Chemical Laboratory also found that this flame unit, with a fuel capacity of 200 gallons, a firing time of 74 seconds, and a maximum range of over 100 yards, was too bulky and heavy for installation in tanks.[22]

Interest in the Mark I flame thrower then arose in another quarter. Early in June 1944 a Navy flame thrower detachment from the United States joined the 1st Marine Division on Guadalcanal which was preparing for the invasion of the Palau Islands. This detachment, con-

---

[19] McKinney, Portable Flame Thrower Opns, pp. 150–54.

[20] The ignition system of the M2–2 consisted of a plastic cylinder with five patches of incendiary material. A trigger on the front handle activated a match-mixture-coated pin which ignited one of the incendiary patches. The entire system was waterproof. The M2–2 weighed seventy pounds when filled and had a capacity of four gallons.

[21] McKinney, Portable Flame Thrower Opns, pp. 150–54.

[22] (1) Memo 2, CmlO CENPAC to TankO G–3 DCofS CENPAC, 6 May 44. (2) 43d Lab Co, 19 May 44, Rpt Demonstration U.S. Navy Flame Thrower Mark I. Both in History, CWS, AFMIDPAC, vol. III, refs. 11, 13.

FLAME THROWER ON AN AMPHIBIOUS TRACTOR BLASTS CAVE *on Peleliu Island.*

sisting of one officer and three enlisted men and attached to the division's amphibian tractor battalion, mounted its three Mark I flame units on LVT(4)'s, the armored amphibian tractor. Tests soon revealed that there were certain drawbacks to this combination. The severe vibrations of the vehicle operating on land shook loose the gunner's protective shield and cracked the porcelain of the spark plugs, failures which were only partially remedied by improvisation and substitution. The naval detachment began to instruct the marines in the operation and maintenance of the flame tractors but, unfortunately, a shortage of napalm prevented adequate training of men and testing of weapons. Three flame units which arrived from Hawaii shortly before embarkation were held in reserve.[23]

[23] (1) Rpt on Activities of the Navy Flame Thrower Detachment in the Palaus Opn, n.d. History, CWS AFMIDPAC, IV, an. II-c-3, 6-7. (2) Maj. Frank O. Hough, USMCR, *The Assault on Peleliu* (Washington, 1950), p. 32.

The island of Peleliu was the principal objective of the 1st Marine Division attack in the Palaus. Each of the three assault regiments was to have a flame tractor in support. Crews of these flame vehicles received briefings on the over-all operation and detailed instructions in their own particular mission. The flame tractor with the 1st Marine Regiment would advance just behind the initial wave of landing craft. Upon reaching the beach it was to fire on targets of opportunity, following the infantry as it pushed inland. Any infantry officer could commandeer the flame tractor if an appropriate target appeared. The flame vehicle with the 5th Regiment would land and advance with the first wave of assault troops, and the 7th Regiment's flame support would accompany a flanking group of landing craft.

The three flame tractors, plus two service tractors carrying an air compressor and extra fuel, were loaded in a landing craft, tank, which in turn made the 2,000-mile journey from Guadalcanal to Peleliu on the deck of a landing ship, tank.

On the day of attack, 15 September 1944, the elaborate plan for using the flame tractors completely broke down. The 1st Marine Regiment was stopped by stiff resistance just beyond the beach, and its flame tractor waited five hours for some kind of order. The flame vehicles with the other regiments were told to stand offshore out of danger. When the three flame tractors eventually landed they stood idle on the beaches, a result no doubt of extreme confusion and the unfamiliarity of the marines with the weapon. Inactivity on the second day was caused by the fact that the air compressor had not yet landed. The flame vehicles saw action on the third day, and from then on their commitment was regular.[24]

The troops used the flame tractor principally to neutralize caves, pillboxes, and dugouts and to burn the cover from the battleground. Japanese, hidden in defiladed positions, were often caught by arching rodlike streams of burning, thickened fuel which hit the reverse slopes. The marines controlled this type of fire by radio from observation posts. In the first phase of the fighting the flame tractors usually worked ahead of the infantry, even ahead of the tanks. As the attack slackened upon reaching the hills, the tanks and infantry provided support for the flame weapons. The latter could have been more effective, particularly from commanding positions on hills and cliffs, but for their

---

[24] Rpt on Activities of the Navy Flame Thrower Detachment in the Palaus Opn.

light armor plate and their lack of all around protection. After the
first few days on Peleliu the employment of the six flame tractors was
steady until about D plus 40 and then sporadic until D plus 75. The
flame weapons attacked about 100 caves and twenty-five pillboxes and
dugouts. They burned off some forty acres of cover, expending fifty
loads of fuel in the process.

The over-all usefulness of this mechanized flame thrower suffered
from the inadequacies of the tractors. Damage to the flame units themselves was negligible and usually repairable within several hours. But
the amphibious tractors could not withstand the rugged terrain and
were constantly out of action with engine troubles, torn tracks, and
broken final drives. The 6 flame throwers were employed for 61 days
(or a total of 366 flame thrower days), and almost one-third of the
time was spent on tractor maintenance. This unfortunate situation
occurred despite the fact that the detachment had a total of 19 tractors
in which to mount the 6 flame units. In addition to these frequent
breakdowns, insufficient training of the crews hampered efficient operations. Gunners sometimes were unable to estimate the range of the
target, and incomplete knowledge of the flame gun prevented the crew
from taking care of small malfunctions in the field. All in all, experience on Peleliu demonstrated that the LVT was not a suitable vehicle for flame throwers; this was the conclusion of the Navy flame
thrower detachment. But despite the failure of the mount, the marines
were impressed by the Navy Mark I flame thrower. In some respects
they considered it superior to the Ronson flame gun used in the Marianas, especially in length of range.[25]

An interesting sidelight to the Peleliu operation was the use of a
high pressure hose to carry flame to targets beyond the range of mechanized flame weapons. During the fighting at Umurbrogol Pocket,
engineers attached a 300-yard hose to a fuel tank and, with pressure
provided by booster pumps, operators sprayed Japanese positions with
flame much as firemen direct water on burning buildings.[26] So impressed was General Richardson with this weapon that he asked Colonel
Unmacht to continue the investigation of its combat potential. In
subsequent tests the chemical section attached a 400-foot length of

---

[25] (1) *Ibid.* (2) Hough, *Assault on Peleliu*, pp. 32, 145, 148, 180–81. (3) Hoffman, *Saipan:
The Beginning of the End*, p. 254. (4) See also Robert Ross Smith, *Approach to the Philippines*,
pp. 539, 545, 563, 571–72.

[26] Hough, *Assault on Peleliu*, p. 175.

standard 1½-inch rubber fire hose to a flame thrower tank and attained a range of 60 yards. Following a demonstration of the device in February 1945 Tenth Army ordered three sets of these hoses, all of which were to see service on Okinawa.[27]

The Philippines

Preparations for the Portable Flame Thrower

In May 1944 Sixth Army's commander, General Krueger, expressed to his staff chemical officer some misgivings about the past performances of the portable flame thrower.[28] As a consequence, a study was made under the aegis of Sixth Army's G–3 to determine what revisions should be made in the Army's official flame thrower doctrine.[29] This study revealed several reasons why the flame thrower had been used with less than maximum effectiveness. Commanders had incomplete understanding of the capabilities and limitations of the weapon; as a result, it was often committed to action without any chance of success or, conversely, was not introduced into situations where it might have been helpful. A corollary to this was the failure of unit commanders to comply with Sixth Army doctrine requiring the employment of portable flame throwers as an integral part of the assault party.[30] A commander, upon brief reconnaissance, would send forward a poorly protected flame thrower on a mission that would have been difficult for a much larger force. Or flame thrower operators would be accompanied by a security detachment which had been hastily formed for the emergency. These improvised groups seldom jelled into the efficient teams envisioned by the writers of Sixth Army's training memo on flame thrower operations.

Commanders had difficulties even when they tried to adhere to the established doctrine. During training, an assault party working as a unit might attain a high standard of proficiency. But in the interval

---

[27] (1) History, AFMIDPAC, II, an I–d, 66; an. II–c–1, 46–48. (2) See below, p. 587.

[28] Ltr, CmlO ALAMO Forces to CmlO I Corps, 17 May 44, no sub. Cited in McKinney, Portable Flame Thrower Opns, p. 91.

[29] This doctrine was expressed in Sixth Army Training Memorandum No. 8, 1 October 1943, sub: Training in the Use of Flame Throwers, reprinted as Appendix 5 in McKinney, Portable Flame Thrower Operations, pages 258–60.

[30] (1) Memo, CmlO ALAMO Force for ACofS G–3 Sixth Army, 8 Jun 44, no sub. Sixth Army 353 Cml Warfare Tng. (2) Memo, CmlO Sixth Army for ACofS G–3 Sixth Army, 21 May 44, no sub. Cml Warfare Sixth Army 353 Flame Thrower Tng.

between the completion of training and the test of battle, the group normally was so broken up by promotions, transfers, and casualties that the maintenance of organizational integrity was impossible. To complicate the situation still more, the flame thrower was officially classified as a secondary weapon. This meant that with the close of the training period flame throwers were returned to unit supply. Thereafter, whenever an attacking force unexpectedly encountered a fortified defensive installation, an assault party could not be sent forward at once. Instead, flame thrower operators first had to go back to the unit supply point to pick up and fill their weapons. Such delays were often costly.[31]

Chemical and other officers concerned with flame thrower operations recognized the inadequacies of Sixth Army flame thrower doctrine, especially as it applied to assault parties. As a remedy they suggested the establishment of permanent units whose principal mission would be attacks on fortifications and to whom the flame thrower would be assigned as a primary weapon. Specifically, some recommended the conversion of chemical processing, 4.2-inch mortar, or antitank units into chemical flame thrower companies or platoons attached to regimental headquarters.[32] Although flame thrower platoons of this type had already been organized with success by regiments of the Americal Division on Bougainville, Sixth Army rejected this idea for its own units. It issued instead, on 22 June 1944, new instructions which emphasized the technical and tactical training of assault teams.[33] Each infantry battalion and cavalry squadron was to form and maintain on a permanent basis at least one assault party, to include a leader, an assistant leader, 4 flame thrower operators, 2 demolitions men, 2 rocket launcher men, 2 BAR operators, and 4 riflemen. Trained to reduce fortified enemy positions, the assault party was to be held in reserve during combat until appropriate targets appeared. Company and battalion commanders and executive officers were expected to familiarize themselves

[31] (1) Ltr, CmlO 1st Cav Div to CmlO ALAMO Force, 6 Dec 43, no sub. Sixth Army, AG 300.6 Misc Memos (1st Cav). (2) Ltr, CG I Corps to CG Sixth Army, 23 Jun 44, sub: Flame Throwers. CWS 314.7 Portable Flame Thrower File. (3) CmlO 41st Div to CmlO ALAMO Force, 30 Jun 44, Preliminary Tech Rpt-Ltr, Rpt 2. Sixth Army 350.05 Biak.

[32] (1) Ltr, CmlO I Corps to CmlO Sixth Army, 13 Jun 44, no sub. CWS 314.7 Portable Flame Thrower File. (2) Ltr, CmlO XIV Corps to CmlO Sixth Army, 9 Jun 44, no sub. Sixth Army Rcds, 353 Flame Thrower Tng. (3) Ltr, CG I Corps to CG Sixth Army, 23 Jun 44, sub: Flame Throwers.

[33] Sixth Army Tng Memo No. 18, 22 Jun 44, no sub. Reprinted as app. 9 in McKinney, Portable Flame Thrower Opns, pp. 273-75.

with the capabilities, limitations, and tactical employment of these assault parties, so that they would be committed with maximum effectiveness.[34]

Having resolved the question of tactical employment, Sixth Army turned to flame thrower servicing problems. It had always been difficult to refill fuel tanks, replace empty gas cylinders, and test and repair flame throwers rapidly and efficiently near the front lines. But as long as demands for the weapon were infrequent, speedy servicing had been a minor consideration. The difficulty reached critical proportions only on Biak, where for the first time flame throwers were in almost daily use.

As an interim measure, Lt. Col. Frank M. Arthur, 41st Division chemical officer, devised a plan for mounting two charging sets, each consisting of two hydrogen and five nitrogen cylinders and a fuel mixing kit, on jeeps and trailers. Teams of technicians from the 94th Chemical Composite Company operated these sets and serviced flame throwers down to the regimental level. Experience proved this system inadequate, since it was at the battalion and the company level that servicing was found to be most desirable.[35]

Although Sixth Army agreed that the assignment of CWS personnel to lower combat units was the most likely solution to the servicing problem, the limited number of chemical troops prevented such dispersal. In planning for the Leyte operation Sixth Army therefore decided that battalion and company personnel would service the flame throwers and perform first echelon maintenance. The task of second and third echelon maintenance and the preparation of proper fuel mixtures was assigned to chemical service platoons attached to corps and divisions. This arrangement was to work even more successfully on Luzon than it did on Leyte, primarily because of the presence on Luzon of a greater number of chemical service platoons.[36]

Employment of the Portable Flame Thrower

The return to the Philippines took place on 20 October with the assault on Leyte by Sixth Army's X and XXIV Corps. The portable

---

[34] *Ibid.*

[35] CmlO 41st Inf Div to CmlO ALAMO Force, 30 Jun 44, Preliminary Tech Rpt-Ltr, Rpt No. 2.

[36] (1) Sixth U.S. Army Rpt of the Luzon Campaign, 9 Jan–30 Jun 45, III, Rpt of the Cml Warfare Officer, 87, 91. (2) CG Sixth Army to Distr, 10 Apr 45, Rpt Cml Warfare Activities During the Leyte Opn.

flame thrower saw action the first day and continued to play a significant role throughout the operation. In all, 229 weapons were on hand and, except for the 11th Airborne, each of the divisions on Leyte used the flame thrower in combat.[37]

The campaign demonstrated the validity of the new Sixth Army policy on tactical doctrine and servicing. Flame thrower operator casualties were light, malfunctions rare, and assault teams successful in the large majority of their missions.[38] Japanese bunker, cave, and dugout defenses on Leyte were elaborate and often ingenious. The success of the flame thrower pointed up the merits of the weapon and the training and skill of the operators.

On 29 October a battalion of the 17th Infantry, 7th Division, encountered the strangest defensive position of the campaign. During the fight for Dagami, Company L came upon a cemetery south of the town which was overgrown with weeds and filled with stone crypts built above the ground. Encountering no resistance the leading elements of the company passed through the graveyard. The support platoon followed. When the platoon was halfway through, a headstone tilted back revealing four Japanese in the grave, armed with rifles and an American BAR. The enemy troops could not be dislodged until a flame thrower came forward and burned them out. The platoon broke up into small details and pushed its way through the rest of the cemetery, eliminating enemy fighters as they were located. Company K, following Company L, also received fire from the stone crypts. It became evident that the enemy had removed the bodies from their tombs, punched holes through the stone, and had thus established a series of small pillboxes. The company commander withdrew to a path in the cemetery and, lining up his men shoulder to shoulder, sent them through the cemetery behind a battery of six flame throwers. This effective, albeit unorthodox, formation burned its way through the macabre defenses, destroying about 30 of the enemy in the process.[39]

Flame thrower assaults by other units on Leyte, though less bizarre, were no less successful. Regiments of the 96th Division, equipped with the new M2-2 flame thrower, found it useful in burning off kunai grass which hid Japanese emplacements. On one occasion a flame

---

[37] CG Sixth Army to Distr, Cml Warfare Activities During the Leyte Opn.

[38] *Ibid.*

[39] (1) 17th Inf, 1 Jan 45, Rpt of KING II Opn. 7th Inf Div 307-Inf (17)-0.3 (15035). (2) Cannon, *Leyte, The Return to the Philippines*, pp. 143–44.

thrower was used at close quarters to repel an enemy attack on American tanks.[40] The division reported that Japanese troops were reluctant to stay in positions attacked by flame throwers and that the weapon was "a very important factor in overcoming the enemy's inherent will to resist." [41]

Reports from the 1st Cavalry Division and the 32d Infantry Division substantiated this estimate of the portable flame thrower. In mid-December an element of the 1st Cavalry Division encountered an enemy emplacement on a narrow ridge in the Mount Minoro sector which commanded the approach along the mountain trail. Repulsed in several frontal attacks cavalrymen, supported by an assault team, circled wide and approached the position from the rear. The flame thrower sprayed the emplacement, and the defenders were cut down by small arms fire as they fled from their position.[42]

On 15 December troops of the 126th Infantry, 32d Division, were halted in the Ormoc corridor by strong resistance from a pillbox and riflemen situated about twenty yards below the crest of a hill. After one attempt to overcome these defenses had failed, the regiment formed an assault party of fifteen riflemen, a bazooka team, and two flame thrower operators. The party crept around the enemy and opened fire simultaneously with grenades, bazookas, and flame throwers. One flame thrower operator directed his fire on the pillbox, while the other sprayed the rifle positions. The attacking riflemen found that the badly burned and demoralized Japanese offered little resistance.[43]

Units on Leyte for the most part adhered closely to Sixth Army flame thrower doctrine. Those who did not soon came to grief. Some unit commanders, for example, continued to use but one flame thrower in an assault party. By thus failing to allow for possible misfires or casualties they endangered the success of their mission. Moreover, despite repeated warnings, weapons were occasionally committed to action without sufficient servicing. The 32d Division, which arrived on Leyte on 14 November 1944, unloaded its flame throwers and sent them directly to the front line without a check. Misfires and malfunctions

---

[40] 382d RCT AAR, 7 Nov 44, KING II (Leyte) Opns. 296–Inf (382)–0.3 (15465).
[41] 96th Div AAR, n.d., KING II, Oct–Dec 44, p. 85. 396–0.3 (11816).
[42] CG X Corps to CG Sixth Army, 13 Jan 45, Rpt of Cml Warfare Activities.
[43] Ltr, CG 32d Div to CG Sixth Army, 27 Feb 45, sub: Cml Warfare Activities in the Leyte Opn. 319.1 Sixth Army Rcds, Leyte.

resulted. Not until the weapons were called back and properly serviced did they function satisfactorily.[44]

The Leyte Campaign was followed in January 1945 by the invasion of Luzon, the largest and most populous island in the Philippines.[45] Although suitable flame thrower targets did not develop during the 9 January landing at Lingayen Gulf, they began to appear a week later in I Corps sectors north and east of the beachhead. Three units of I Corps had particular success with the weapon. On the 26th a company of the 158th RCT, operating in mountainous terrain, encountered a series of long, curved, and defended tunnels which ran about thirty feet into a slope. An assault team moved toward the entrances under cover of smoke from white phosphorus grenades. The flame thrower operator fired a long burst of fuel into the opening of the first tunnel and flushed a number of burning Japanese, who were killed by small arms fire as they fled from the entrance. The other openings were treated in a like manner. Japanese bodies, victims of burns and suffocation, were found along the smouldering corridors in the most remote parts of the tunnels.[46]

Although other units reported similar success with the portable flame thrower, the weapon was not ideally suited for combat in many parts of Luzon. The 43d Division, for example, reported that in the open terrain which featured much of the island, flame thrower operators found their approach much more hazardous than in the undergrowth of the jungle. As a consequence, weapons with longer ranges had to be used in the reduction of enemy fortifications.[47]

The flame thrower proved more effective against urban targets. The bitter battle for Manila marked the first extensive city fighting in the Southwest Pacific, and flame throwers, although untested in this kind of combat, saw much use in the street-to-street struggle. The weapon proved particularly valuable in routing the enemy from the intricate positions of the Intramuros, the old walled city of Manila.[48] The portable flame thrower also played a part in the fighting in the Philippine

[44] (1) *Ibid.* (2) CG X Corps to CG Sixth Army, 13 Jan 45, Rpt of Cml Warfare Activities.

[45] For a general account of the Luzon campaign, see Smith, *Triumph in the Philippines.*

[46] Cml Sec 158th RCT, Cml Intell Rpt, 28 Jan 45. Sixth Army Rcds, Luzon Intell Rpts, 350.05.

[47] 43d Div Hist Rpt, Luzon Campaign, 9 Jan–30 Jun 45, pp. 102–03. 43d Inf Div 343-33.4 (12281).

[48] (1) AAR, Opns of the 37th Inf Div, Luzon, P.I., 1 Nov 44–30 Jun 45. 37th Inf Div 337-3 (22871). (2) AAR, XIV Corps, M-1 Opn (Luzon), pp. 130–32. XIV Corps 214-33.4 (3469). (3) See Smith, *Triumph in the Philippines*, chs. XV, XI.

General Hospital, the Legislative Building, and the General Post Office —fighting which often turned into a series of fierce room-to-room and floor-to-floor battles. American troops blasted holes in walls with explosives and then used flame throwers against the enemy in the next room. The 37th Division reported that it used over three hundred fillings during the Manila operation, or an average of more than four fillings for every flame weapon in the division.[49]

The capture of Manila did not end the fighting on Luzon. There remained the task of clearing out the more remote mountainous regions of the island. In this type of action flame throwers were infrequently used. Units reported that the flame thrower was too heavy, making it difficult for one man to carry for prolonged periods, and, since few extra men were available to haul the weapons, they often were left behind. On several occasions I Corps resorted to Filipino carriers to transport the weapons from the service point to the line of departure, a distance of several thousand yards and at times over steep mountain trails. Under such conditions flame thrower employment was limited to reasonably accessible targets.[50]

The policy of using flame thrower assault parties worked out successfully as long as infantry casualties were low. But when casualty rates mounted and every available man was wanted for the immediate needs of combat, it became impossible to hold these organized teams in permanent reserve. Commanders broke up these groups and sent their personnel to line companies. Missions for which assault parties had been organized fell to the rifle squad or platoon closest to the action.[51]

Sixth Army, disturbed by this situation and desirous of avoiding similar difficulties in its forthcoming campaign on the Japanese mainland, changed its training doctrine somewhat. Representing the accumulated experience of several years of combat, a new directive was issued which differed in only one significant respect from its predecessors—it rejected the concept of "organized assault parties in permanent reserve." Instead, it stipulated that at least three squads from each rifle

---

[49] (1) CG XIV Corps to CG Sixth Army, 1 Jul 45, Rpt, Japanese Defense of Cities as Exemplified by the Battle of Manila, p. 21. Sixth Army G-2 files. (2) AAR, Opns of the 37th Inf Div Luzon, P.I., 1 Nov 44–30 Jun 45.

[50] I Corps, History of the Luzon Campaign, Philippine Islands, 1945, an B-1. I Corps 201-33.4 (21700).

[51] (1) Hist Rpt, 38th Inf Div, Avengers of Bataan, 19 Jan–30 Jun 45, pp. 189–90. 38th Inf Div files 338-33.4 (17806). (2) Hist Rpt, A History of the 63d Inf Opns on Luzon, P.I., 9 Jan–30 Jun 45. 306 Inf (63)-0.3 (26302).

company be trained to use special assault weapons and that four men in each of these squads be flame thrower operators. These trained groups were to operate as normal rifle squads until a situation arose in which they were needed to perform their specialty.[52] This change did not alter the basic concept of using flame throwers solely as component elements of an assault team. What was attempted was a further integration of the flexible assault team within the organizational framework of the normal infantry unit. The war ended before this new system could be tested in combat.

American forces began the Philippine campaign only partially equipped with the new M2–2 flame thrower. As these weapons became available, and as stocks of the M1A1 model were exhausted, the new weapons were issued to combat troops.[53] Supplies of the M2–2 flame thrower never were sufficient to enable the M1A1's to be completely withdrawn from service, but by V–J Day the newer type was in the hands of the majority of units operating in the Philippines.

Those who were obliged to carry the M1A1 had to maintain a vigilant servicing policy, especially during the rainy season, for despite waterproofing the ignition system of the weapon was still unreliable. Those equipped with the M2–2 also had problems. The pressure regulator proved to be entirely unsatisfactory and before the end of the Philippine operations had been replaced by an entirely new type.[54] Flame thrower operators complained that the M2–2 could not maintain pressure long enough, a result of inherent deficiencies in the weapon as well of poor maintenance procedures. Troops who filled the flame thrower forgot that heat was generated when a cylinder was charged and the subsequent cooling-off process could result in a drop of as much as 200 pounds in pressure. Conversely, pressure built up in the fuel tank when the tank was exposed to the direct rays of the sun, blowing out the safety discs in extreme cases.[55]

---

[52] Sixth Army Tng Memo No. 30, 6 Aug 45, reprinted as app. 12 in McKinney, Portable Flame Thrower Opns, pp. 281–83.

[53] (1) Ltr, CG USAFFE to CG's Sixth Army, XIV Corps, and USASOS SWPA, 2 Sep 44, sub: Portable Flame Throwers. (2) Ltr, CG USAFFE to CG's Sixth and Eighth Armies, 21 Sep 44, sub: Flame Throwers. Both in Sixth Army 470.71, Flame Throwers.

[54] Ltr, CmlO Sixth Army to CmlO I Corps et al., 6 Apr 45, sub: Regulators, Pressure Assembly B81–1–778, Grove Type. Sixth Army Rcds, Cml Warfare 470.71.

[55] Ltr, CG Eighth Army to CofS War Dept, 3 Jan 46, sub: Employ of Flame Throwers in the Visaya Campaign, with incls. Eighth Army AG 470.71 (Far East).

The Mechanized Flame Thrower

Not counting a limited use of improvised models, the first employment of the mechanized flame thrower in the Southwest Pacific took place in the Philippines. The XXIV Corps had been slated for the assault on Yap, in the Central Pacific Area, when the Joint Chiefs of Staff canceled the Yap operation and ordered General MacArthur and Admiral Nimitz to invade Leyte on 20 October 1944, two months to the day before the planned date of the operation. The XXIV Corps, which was now to take part in the assault on Leyte, had already embarked for Yap, when this change took place. A terrain study of that island had recommended the utility of the mechanized flame thrower particularly during the assault, and ten Ronson flame throwers, nine on light tanks and one in an amphibious tractor, were in the convoy.[56]

Not only was Leyte's terrain far less suitable for tracked vehicles than that of Yap, but the invasion of Leyte took place during the rainy season, a circumstance which all but immobilized the mechanized vehicles. During the landing one resisting enemy bunker was quickly neutralized by the lone flame tractor, and during the first few days on Leyte the light tank flame throwers burned off the foliage from a number of concealed enemy positions. But the fighting soon reached the mountains, which put the tanks at further disadvantage.[57]

The Luzon fighting saw the arrival of both auxiliary and main armament flame throwers from the zone of interior. The XIV Corps included a tank battalion, equipped with bow gun flame throwers, that was employed in the house-to-house fighting in Manila. In one instance a flame tank neutralized in a few minutes a barricaded building which had defied the infantry for two days. Twenty-five more bow gun flame throwers reached the Sixth Army in mid-April.[58]

On 3 April 1945 the first and only main armament flame throwers from the United States to see action with Army troops overseas arrived on Luzon. These were four NDRC Q model (E7–7) flame throwers mounted in M5A1 light tanks and scheduled for service testing. The flame throwers and a service truck were assigned to the 13th Armored

[56] (1) History, CWS AFMIDPAC, II, an. II–c–1, 21–22. (2) Cannon, *Leyte: The Return to the Philippines*, pp. 8–9.

[57] Tech Intell Rpt 271, 5 Feb 45, p. 2, cited in McKinney, Mechanized Flame Thrower Opns, p. 93.

[58] (1) Rpt of CmlO Sixth Army, Luzon Campaign, 9 Jan–1 Jul 45, pp. 13–15. (2) McKinney, Portable Flame Thrower Opns, p. 24. (3) These bow gun auxiliary flame throwers were of the E4–5 series, standardized as the M3–4–3 in 1945.

Group.[59] By this time the fighting on Luzon had reached its final stages, and the combat activity at Ipo Dam, Balete Pass, Villa Verde Trail, and Baguio took place in mountainous terrain, which made even the maneuvering of light tanks difficult. Moreover, the enemy artillery and mortar fire limited the activity of the thin-skinned M5A1's. In mid-April these main armament tanks were attached to I Corps for 25th Division operations at Balete Pass. Following a demonstration before officers of the division, the tanks, which were assigned to the 27th Regiment, saw action almost at once. The objective was an enemy position located on the reverse slope of a ridge. One of the flame tanks moved along the narrow ridge which provided the only avenue of approach and, when even with the target, turned down the slope and attempted to flame the Japanese. Thwarted by the limited maximum depression of the gun, the tankmen fired two quick bursts and withdrew.[60]

Mechanized flame throwers experienced the usual difficulties of tank-infantry communications. Close contact between the two was particularly important because of the limited visibility in the mountains where infanrymen often had to guide the tank to its objective. A power telephone on the rear deck of the tank was rigged to the turret, allowing the turret operator to communicate with the infantry but only at the cost of cutting off turret traversing power whenever he spoke.[61]

The four main armament flame tanks advanced to the front lines several times during the next twelve days, but remained uncommitted. On 27 April the advance of Company K, 27th Infantry, was stalled for more than twenty-four hours by deadly machine gun and 47-mm. fire from enemy emplacements on the ridge's forward slope and the valley beyond. Thick underbrush, which made friendly grenades ineffective, covered the entire defensive position, while fire from U.S. tanks and artillery was unable to reach the enemy's defiladed position.

In this situation the commanding officer of the flame detachment suggested the use of his tanks. The heavy underbrush made the approach exceedingly difficult and a medium tank and then an armored

---

[59] (1) Ltr, CmlO Hq AFMIDPAC to Chief Info Br OCCWS, 10 Aug 45. (2) Rpt of CmlO Sixth Army, Luzon Campaign, pp. 13–14.

[60] USAFFE Bd Rpt No. 296, 17 May 45, Rpt of Opns of Flame Throwers E7–7 in Light Tanks M5A1. CWS 314.7 Mechanized Flame Thrower File.

[61] (1) Ibid. (2) Rpt of First Combat Mission Fired by E7–7 Flame Gun on M5A1 Light Tank, 16 Apr 45. CWS 314.7 Mechanized Flame Thrower File.

bulldozer were pressed into service to clear a way. Two flame tanks were at the assembly point 200 to 300 yards from the principal target—a pillbox across a ravine at the foot of a large tree. Because of the narrow approach, only one flame tank could advance at a time and, as there was no room for armored support by the medium tanks, two rifle platoons from Company K furnished protection. An infantryman, walking behind the tank, guided it over the crest of the ridge. When the enemy resisted with hand grenades, the bow gunner sprayed the suspected areas with machine gun fire. Approximately fifty yards from the target the tank ran on a log twelve inches in diameter. The driver carefully maneuvered the vehicle until it balanced just forward, thus permitting direct aim down toward the target. The first burst of flame flushed eight Japanese who were killed by supporting infantrymen. Several short bursts, fired across the target, caused the entire area to burn briskly for about five minutes. When the smoke cleared, another dugout became visible and received what was left of the flame fuel. The infantry advanced promptly, and by dusk Company K had taken its objective of Lone Tree Ridge, 200 yards beyond. There were 53 enemy dead in the area, 6 dying in the flame attack and the rest killed by the infantry as they ran from cover. Friendly forces suffered no casualties.[62]

The flame tanks had varying success in the subsequent fighting on Luzon. Sometimes they burned out the enemy; other times they were stymied by their vulnerability to the heavier Japanese weapons. There were few mechanical difficulties and, in spite of heavy rains, no ignition failures. Although infantrymen and tankers were enthusiastic about the flame tanks' ability to rout the enemy from strong positions, these combat tests indicated that the thinly armored light tank was not a satisfactory mount for the flame thrower.[63]

Iwo Jima

The V Amphibious Corps invaded Iwo Jima in February 1945. It was a costly campaign waged against an enemy entrenched in a superlative defensive system. But as one Marine Corps historian has stated:

---

[62] (1) Ltr, CmlO 25th Inf Div to CmlO I Corps, 2 May 45, sub: Rpt on Use of Flame Thrower. CWS 314.7 Mechanized Flame Thrower File. (2) USAFFE Bd Rpt 296, 17 May 45.

[63] (1) USAFFE Bd Rpt 296, 17 May 45. (2) Ltr, CO 13th Armored Co to CG Sixth Army, 31 May 45, sub: Combat Testing of Flame Throwers E7-7 in Light Tanks. Cited in McKinney, Mechanized Flame Thrower Opns, p. 149.

"Never before in the Pacific War had troops engaged in amphibious assault been able to see so clearly the immediate importance of the objective." [64] The tiny island would provide an intermediate base for fighter escorts for the bombers headed toward Japan. It would also be a haven for crippled B–29's unable to make it to airfields in the Marianas.

The preinvasion preparations of the three Marine divisions earmarked for Iwo included work with both the portable and the mechanized flame throwers. For the smaller weapon this preparation consisted mostly of integrating the flame throwers with the assault teams. It was 3d Marine Division policy to have in each of its battalions an assault platoon made up of 6 men from each rifle company and 2 men from the battalion headquarters company. These 20 men, specially trained in the use of flame throwers, rocket launchers, and demolitions, were placed under the immediate control of the battalion commander. The commander in turn could attach the whole platoon, or a part of it, to his assault companies as the situation required. [65] Other Marine divisions devised similar platoons. Regiments of the 4th Marine Division organized 39-man platoons which were attached to each battalion landing team. Squads from these platoons were then assigned to companies for specific missions. [66]

A plentiful supply of M2–2 portable flame throwers made possible these elaborate preparations—the battalion had 27 weapons or 243 for the division. A battalion usually assigned 1 flame thrower to each of its 9 rifle platoons, 9 to the battalion supply section, and the remaining 9 to the regimental service platoon. This arrangement insured the rapid replacement of lost or damaged weapons. It also made possible a reserve flame thrower for every one in use, a justifiable ratio because of the weapon's vulnerability to enemy fire and the fact that it was difficult to service. [67]

The 4th and 5th Marine Divisions each received four Hawaiian-made main armament mechanized flame throwers. The development and procurement of these flame throwers was undertaken by the

[64] Bartley, *Iwo Jima: Amphibious Epic*, p. 23.

[65] 3d Marine Div Tng Order, No. 45–44, 16 Dec 44, Orgn for Employ of Flame Throwers, Rocket Launchers and Demolition in the Inf Bn, reprinted as app. 16 in McKinney, Portable Flame Thrower, pp. 304–06.

[66] CG 4th Marine Div to Comdt Marine Corps, 18 May 45, Opns Rpt, Iwo Jima, an. G (24th RCT). Marine Corps Archives.

[67] *Ibid.*, an. C and an. F (23d RCT).

NEUTRALIZING A CAVE. IWO JIMA

Chemical Section, Pacific Base Command, with help from the Navy, the Marine Corps, other Army elements, and civilians. Briefly, the flame unit, designated the POA CWS H1, consisted of a Ronson flame thrower installed in a salvaged 75-mm. gun tube and mounted in a medium tank. It had a maximum effective range of about 100 yards (with thickened fuel), a capacity of nearly 300 gallons, and a firing time of 150 seconds.[68]

Meanwhile, the Japanese defenders of Iwo Jima had been busy strengthening their defenses. Engineers well versed in fortifications came from Japan to supervise the work. They added a series of trenches and pillboxes to the natural caves which formed the backbone of the island's defenses. Whenever possible these features were integrated

[68] (1) History, CWS AFMIDPAC vol. III, refs. 29, 45–47, and vol. IV, ans. II–c–2 and II–c–3. (2) Ltr Rpt, CO 3d Bn 21st Marines to CO 21st Marines 3d Marine Div, 11 Apr 45, sub: Action Rpt. Marine Corps Archives.

into a single network permitting troops to move from one place to another without exposure. Some of the strongpoints had multiple entrances and apertures which were invulnerable to artillery fire.

The Japanese did their work well. Not only did it take a month to capture this tiny island, but during the course of the operation marines actually saw very few of the enemy. The Japanese commander expressly forbade banzai charges and other mass heroics, ordering his troops to stick to their positions to the last. Moreover, once a position had been silenced, it was by no means safe to assume that it would give no further trouble. The Japanese infiltrated at night, both above and below ground, and re-occupied defenses which previously had been neutralized.[69]

On 19 February 1945 the 4th and 5th Marine Divisions landed on the south coast of Iwo Jima with the 3d Marine Division in reserve. From the beginning, portable flame throwers were a big help in cleaning out caves and pillboxes. A battalion in the 3d Division described the usual employment of the portable weapon. Covered by rifle and BAR fire, the flame operator moved to a firing position on the flank of a target. He then fired across the face of the cave or embrasure, advancing quickly under his own fire until he could shoot directly into the opening. This tactic consistently silenced the position, which was then destroyed by demolition charges.[70]

At the end of the campaign some units commented on the superiority of the M2-2 model over its M1A1 predecessor, particularly in regard to its ignition system. The familiar cry for greater range continued to be heard. As far as maintenance was concerned, experience varied— one battalion reported no difficulty or malfunctions, while others lamented the complete absence of spare parts.[71]

Because enemy emplacements were difficult to approach, flame thrower operator casualties shot upward. The casualty rate on Iwo Jima was probably higher than in any other campaign in the Pacific.

[69] (1) "The Jap Holes In," *Intelligence Bulletin*, III, No. 12 (August, 1945), 60–62. (2) McKinney, Portable Flame Thrower Opns, pp. 159–60.

[70] (1) 1st Bn 21st Marines 3d Marine Div AAR, Iwo Jima, 6 Apr 45. (2) CO 9th Marines to CG 3d Marine Div, AAR, Iwo Jima, 20 Apr 45. (3) Ltr Rpt, CG 4th Marine Div to Comdt Marine Corps, 18 Mar 45, sub: Opns Rpt, Iwo Jima, an. F (23d RCT) and an. G (1st Bn 24th RCT). All in Marine Corps Archives.

[71] Ltr Rpt, CG 4th Marine Div to Comdt Marine Corps, 18 Mar 45, sub: Opns Rpt, Iwo Jima, 19 Feb–16 Mar, an. G (24th RCT), an. H (25th RCT), apps. III, IV. Marine Corps Archives.

One battalion reported 92-percent losses.[72] As a result, there was a scarcity of competent and experienced operators, particularly as the battle
reached its final stages. By way of correction, commanders recommended greater emphasis on flame thrower training and suggested that
all enlisted men be given at least a working knowledge of the weapon.[73]

The eight main armament flame throwers were lightly used during
the first few days of the operation, largely because of the rough terrain.
But within the week the marines became dependent upon flame tank
support and constantly requested its use.[74] Typical tactics were as follows: the Marine infantrymen advanced, drawing fire from enemy
positions; armored dozers then pushed ahead and, protected by tank
and small arms fire, prepared a road to points within range of enemy
positions; flame-throwing tanks moved forward and neutralized the
enemy positions with flame and machine gun fire so that the infantry
could advance; engineers followed closely behind with demolitions
and destroyed the enemy caves and pillboxes to prevent their further
use. This was a slow and laborious process, but any attempt on the
part of the marines to continue the advance before bypassed positions
had been destroyed resulted in heavy casualties, and no real gain could
be made as long as the Japanese could fire on American troops from
the rear.[75]

The northern area of the island was featured by deep gullies, saw-
toothed ridges, sheer cliffs, and eroded, boulder-strewn plateaus, and
here the Japanese holed up for their last desperate stand. A liberal use
of portable and mechanized flame throwers helped to eradicate this
kind of resistance, although the formidable terrain made it hard to get
the flame tanks within effective range of enemy targets. Generally, a
tank dozer nudged out a few yards of roadway and moved aside. The
flame tanks then advanced, sometimes two or three in rapid succession,
and fired while regular tanks stood back and provided cover. This
operation was repeated so often that on some days the 5th Marine Tank

---

[72] Co 2d Bn to CO 21st Marines, 12 Apr 45, Action Rpt, Iwo Jima Opn, 3d Marine Div Rpt, Iwo
Jima, incl D. Marine Corps Archives.
[73] (1) Ibid. (2) CO 21st Marines to CG 3d Marine Div, 10 Apr 45, Action Rpt, Iwo Jima Opn.
Marine Corps Archives.
[74] Armored Force Bd, Rpt of Conf on Mechanized Flame Thrower, E12–7R1, 23 Mar 45. CWS
314.7 Mechanized Flame Thrower File.
[75] (1) 26th RCT 5th Marine Div, AAR, Iwo Jima, an. QUEEN. (2) Bartley, Iwo Jima: Amphibious
Epic, p. 187.

Battalion used between 5,000 and 10,000 gallons of thickened gasoline in its three or four flame tanks. The limited supply of flame tanks and tank dozers was a big handicap. And despite the intricate procedure outlined above the rugged terrain often defied all attempts at penetration.[76]

The fixed assignment of flame tanks to tank companies proved to be impracticable on Iwo. Placed in a battalion pool and stationed at the refueling area, flame tanks were made available by the battalion wherever needed. Tank companies or platoons sent requests through battalion, the infantry companies through liaison personnel. As soon as a flame thrower exhausted its fuel, it returned to the refill station for a new load and possibly a new assignment. In spite of all these measures, troop advances were frequently held up because all flame tanks were engaged elsewhere.[77]

The 4th and 5th Marine Divisions emphasized the greater effectiveness of the main armament type as opposed to the auxiliary flame thrower, of which the 4th Division had twenty-four. These divisions recommended more large capacity flame throwers and their incorporation as organic equipment in all tank battalions.[78] Although the 3d Marine Division entered the Iwo Jima operation without main armament flame throwers, it was later on able to borrow some from the other divisions. In its opinion this type was better against enemy defenses than the auxiliary bow gun flame throwers with their shorter range and limited traverse.[79]

After-action reports for the Iwo Jima operation attested to the value of the flame weapons. Of the two types, the mechanized flame thrower seemed to have come out on top. One battalion commander called it the "best single weapon of the operation."[80] The V Amphibious Corps report referred to the mechanized weapon as the "only effective means"

---

[76] 5th Marne Div, Action Rpt, Iwo Jima, 19 Feb–24 Mar 45, an. LOVE. Marine Corps Archives.

[77] (1) *Ibid.* (2) For a day-by-day log of flame thrower operations on Iwo Jima, see: (1) History, CWS AFMIDPAC, IV, an. II–c–3, 5–32, and McKinney, Mechanized Flame Thrower Opns, app. 4, pp. 286–300.

[78] Comments, 4th Marine Div, Iwo Jima, and 5th Marine Div, Iwo Jima Opns. History CWS AFMIDPAC, IV, an II–c–3, 27–32.

[79] 3d Marine Div, AAR, Iwo Jima. History, CWS AFMIDPAC, vol. IV, an. II–c–3.

[80] CT–28, Action Rpt, Iwo Jima Opn, an. CHARLIE (Opn), see VIII LT–328 Action Rpt, p. 40. Marine Corps Archives.

of reducing many of the concrete pillboxes and blockhouses encountered on the island.[81]

Okinawa

Okinawa was the last battle of the war and one of the hardest. Conducted by Tenth Army on the very doorstep of Japan, it was to involve
more CWS equipment than any other Pacific campaign. Each of the
four Army divisions of XXIV Corps had 141 portable flame throwers;
each of the three Marine divisions of III Amphibious Corps had 243,
the same number as had been taken to Iwo Jima. The 713th Tank
Battalion, converted to a provisional flame thrower unit for the operation, received a complement of 54 POA main armament flame
throwers.[82]

All seven of the divisions to see action on Okinawa were combat
tested and experienced in portable flame thrower operations. Employment of the portable weapon closely paralleled that of earlier actions.
Especially significant was the fighting in the southern portion of the
island where enemy positions most closely resembled those which had
been found on Iwo Jima.[83] Despite these successes the portable flame
thrower was overshadowed on Okinawa by its mechanized counterpart.

The 713th Tank Battalion changed over to a flame battalion in Hawaii, and its own troops had assisted in the installation of the POA
flame throwers in the medium tanks. Tank crews test fired and adjusted their flame weapons, while others of the battalion received instruction in mixing the fuel. A tentative table of organization and
equipment was drawn up to reflect the differences inherent in a flame
tank unit.[84]

In general, each of the three companies of the 713th was attached
to a standard tank battalion in support of a division. In turn, flame
platoons joined tank companies, and sections joined standard platoons.

---

[81] Hq V Amphib Corps Landing Force, Iwo Jima, General Staff Sec Rpt, app. 3, G-3 Rpt, pp.
56-57. Marine Corps Archives.

[82] (1) Ltr, CG Tenth Army to CG USAFPOA, 6 Oct 44, sub: Tank Bn Flame Thrower Primary
Armament, and 1st Ind, n.d. History, CWS AFMIDPAC, vol. III, ref. 51. (2) History CWS
AFMIDPAC, vol. II, an. II-b.

[83] XXIV Corps Action Rpt, Ryukyus, 1 Apr-30 Jun 45, ch. 7, p. 88. XXIV Corps File 224-0.3
(48295).

[84] (1) This TOE is reproduced in History, CWS AFMIDPAC, volume III, Reference 53. (2) For a
popular account of the growing pains of the 713th and its combat experience, see Joseph Morschauser
III, "Blowtorch Battalion," Armor, LXIX, No. 2 (March-April, 1960), pages 30-33.

FLAME-THROWING TANK ATTACKS ENEMY INFANTRYMEN *dug in along an old road on Okinawa.*

A tank platoon, including a section of three flame tanks, was placed in support of an infantry battalion. Flame tank deployment differed within these tank-infantry teams. Sometimes they operated alone with the infantry; sometimes they formed an integral part of the tank platoon; most frequently they waited at forward positions until called upon for particular missions by the tank platoon. When the latter tactic was used the flame tanks, supported by conventional tanks, operated ahead of the infantry until an area had been cleared for the latter's advance. The troops followed closely, protecting the tanks and occupying the ground before the enemy could recover. This support was extended to both Army and Marine divisions.[85]

[85] (1) 713th Tank Bn Armored Flame Thrower (Provisional) AAR Phase I–Nansei Shoto. This 70-page report is reproduced *in toto* in McKinney, Mechanized Flame Thrower Opns, pp. 307–77. (2) Appleman, Burns, Gugeler, and Stevens, *Okinawa, The Last Battle,* p. 456.

Japanese troops defending Okinawa first faced mechanized flame throwers on D plus 18 (19 April 1945), when thirty-one flame tanks expended 3,500 gallons of napalm in the attack on a hill known as Rocky Crags. Conventional tanks led the assault, with flame tanks and infantry from the 7th Infantry Division close behind. The flame throwers continued in support throughout the 6-day battle for the Crags, which extended from the northwest and covered the approaches to Hill 178 and the high ground west to Tanabaru, the division objective.

From 20 to 29 April 1945 other main armament flame throwers, in support of various units of the 7th, 27th, and 96th Infantry Divisions, continued to fire on rocky ridges, fortified caves, dugouts, pillboxes, machine gun nests, and villages. When the Japanese withdrew, they did so in many cases only because of the devastating effect of the flame. American forces appreciated the psychological value of flame; the commanding officer of one tank battalion reported that the infantry in many cases preferred to advance behind a flame tank rather than behind a standard one.[86]

During May the fighting took place along the defensive position in the high ground north of Shuri, the ancient capital of Okinawa. For the first ten days flame tanks supported divisions in the battles for Kochi Ridge, Flattop, Dick Hills, Hill 60, and Nan Hill. Meanwhile, other flame tanks neutralized the network of caves on the reverse slopes of the Maeda escarpment. Still others supported the marines in the savage fire fight for Shuri Heights. The last ten days of May saw torrential rains turn the ground into a quagmire of soft clay that immobilized tanks and other vehicles, while the Japanese *32d Army* executed a successful withdrawal to the high ground on the southern tip of Okinawa. Until the rains came, the flame tanks had used about 75,000 gallons of flame fuel. Only 28 of the 54 original main armaments flame tanks were still in operating condition.

The weather cleared in June and on its ninth day a battle began in which mechanized flame throwers played a significant role. Facing the XXIV Corps on its 6,000-yard front was a strong rocky line running from Yuza-Dake on the west to its eastern anchor, Hill 95. On this end vertical cliffs 250 to 300 feet high rose to a plateau topped by knobs, coral buttresses, and pinnacles. The 7th and 96th Infantry

---

[86] McKinney, Mechanized Flame Thrower Opns, p. 115.

Divisions made little progress in their first attack against the 11,000 troops of the *32d Army* which defended this line.

On 10 June naval gunfire, artillery, and tanks pounded the cliffs, but the 7th Infantry Division advancing upon Hill 95 met accurate machine gun and sniper fire from at least 500 Japanese deployed in depth in that section of the escarpment. Five flame tanks then maneuvered into position and burned off the cover to the approaches to Hill 95. Finally, two skeleton companies of infantry struggled to the top only to be pinned down by enemy fire from farther up the ridge. The commanding officer and two men of Company C, 713th Tank Battalion, scaled the ridge to within thirty yards of the enemy position, pulling a 200-foot fire hose after them. From this point they burned out the defenders who were then slain by the infantry.[87]

The next day the attack was resumed. At one point a section of tanks and flame tanks attacked a 500-yard frontage of the escarpment, driving the Japanese from their position and cutting them down with machine gun fire. Several days later two flame tanks came to the front lines and an extension hose was hauled up a 50-foot high section of the escarpment by means of a rope. The flame, hurled over the far edge, was blown by the wind into the caves on the reverse slope. By moving the hose from one flame tank to another the men destroyed ammunition dumps, fortified positions, and a large number of Japanese troops. That same afternoon five flame throwers lined up at the base of the cliff and fired on caves in its face. The infantry pushed forward slowly and by 1600 hours Hill 95 was wholly in American hands. On the right flank the 17th Infantry advanced with support from flame tanks to capture the village of Azato before nightfall on 13 June 1945 and to tie in with units of the 32d Infantry. Although some mopping up remained to be done, the battle for Hill 95 was over, a typical struggle on Okinawa in which flame tanks helped turn the tide of battle.[88]

Hill 89, the last major strongpoint of southern Okinawa and headquarters of the Japanese *32d Army*, was attacked by the 7th Division on 20 June 1945. Here again was almost unbelievably difficult terrain cut up by natural caves, tunnels, and crevices. For weeks the area had been systematically pounded by naval gunfire, long-range artillery, rockets, and aerial bombing. A number of Japanese surrendered but many others fought to the bitter end.

---

[87] *Ibid.*, p. 119.
[88] History, CWS AFMIDPAC, IV, an. II–c–3, 66–70.

Before the infantry attack the flame thrower and conventional tanks moved out to burn off the remainder of the foliage from Hill 89 and its approaches, which they left an ugly blackened mass of jagged coral. On the second day the flame-throwing tanks advanced in increasing numbers to pour thousands of gallons of burning fuel into caves and crevices. Then the infantry, supported by flame tanks, medium tanks, and artillery, successfully stormed the hill.

Between 22 and 24 June the infantry continued to mop up the top of Hill 89. Flame thrower tanks, used in conjunction with loud-speaker tanks, encouraged soldiers and civilians to surrender. As a team, infantry and flame tanks killed over 100 Japanese and persuaded three times as many to surrender. From the top of the cliff flame tanks repeated the technique of firing toward the sea so that the wind could blow the flaming napalm back into caves too high to be reached from the beach. Concealed ammunition dumps blew up in loud explosions. Load after load of fuel was fired into a huge cavern in which over 1,000 Japanese soldiers were thought to be hiding. Thus the remnants of the Japanese *32d Army* were destroyed, although some mopping up remained in the rest of the island. The battle for Okinawa was over.[89]

During the Ryukyus Campaign the 713th Tank Battalion saw almost continuous action for seventy days and officially received credit for the death of 4,788 Japanese and the capture of 49. At the same time the battalion lost 7 men killed and 110 men wounded, injured, or missing. No one was killed inside a main armament flame tank as a result of enemy action, although 41 tanks were knocked out during the 630 flame tank sorties.[90]

The XXIV Corps reported that the main armament flame tank was one of the most effective weapons used on Okinawa and that the Japanese fear of flame was greatly exploited by the flame tanks. The 7th Infantry Division spoke of the outstanding success of the flame tanks.[91] The periscope mounted flame thrower found little use in the fighting on Okinawa as the large-capacity flame tanks were available.

---

[89] Combat Opns Rpt, Ryukyus Campaign, 32d Inf Regt (7th Inf Div), n.d. Quoted in History, CWS AFMIDPAC, IV, an. II–c–3, 87–91.

[90] 713th Tank Bn Armored Flame Thrower (Provisional) ARR Phase I—Nansei Shoto, 30 Jun 45. CWS 314.7 Mechanized Flame Thrower File.

[91] (1) XXIV Corps AAR, Ryukyus Campaign. History CWS AFMIDPAC, IV, an. II–c–3, 101. (2) 7th Inf Div Opns Rpt, Ryukyus Campaign. Both in History, CWS AFMIDPAC, IV, an. II–c–3, p. 97.

Tank crews developed a fear of the periscope type after the fuel container of one burst and ignited upon being struck by an enemy shell, burning the tank crew to death. This type of auxiliary flame thrower, therefore, was never fully tested in battle.[92] Nor was the bow gun type, with which the III Amphibious Corps was equipped, put to much use, for main armament flame tanks of the 713th Tank Battalion were preferred by Marine as well as Army units.[93]

The 713th Tank Battalion suggested that, instead of having separate armored flame thrower battalions, commanders should replace the light tank company in each standard tank battalion with a flame thrower tank company or else that the latter be added to each battalion. This system, it was thought, would simplify administration and supply, since a flame thrower tank company was normally attached to standard tank battalions for operations. Some general mishandling of the weapon brought forth the recommendation that infantry commanders familiarize themselves with the use and limitations of armored flame throwers and learn how to co-ordinate these weapons with other supporting weapons and infantry.[94]

The Tenth Army and the 713th Tank Battalion agreed that the 75-mm. gun should be retained in flame tanks and mounted coaxially with the flame thrower, but that there should be no reduction in fuel capacity and no decrease in the effectiveness of the flame gun.[95]

Preparations for the Invasion of Japan

During the summer of 1945 United States planners were concerned with the problem of holding down casualties in the invasion of the main Japanese islands. Such battles as Tarawa, Iwo Jima, and Okinawa had illustrated how costly victory in the Pacific could be. The assault on Japan could be expected to exact a heavy toll of American lives unless some means were found for reducing casualties. One of these

---

[92] Ltr, CmlO Tenth Army to CmlO CPBC, 9 Jun 45, sub: Mechanized Flame Throwers. History, CWS, AFMIDPAC, III, ref. 114, 3–4.

[93] Each of the four Army tank battalions had eighteen periscope flame throwers; each Marine tank battalion carried sixteen E4R2–5R1's. Tenth Army Action Rpt, Ryukyus, 26 Mar–30 June 45, p. 4.

[94] 713th Tank Bn Armored Flame Thrower (Provisional) AAR ch. IX, in McKinney, Mechanized Flame Thrower Opns, app. 6, p. 374.

[95] Ltr, CofS Tenth Army to CG POA, 27 May 45, sub: Recommended Changes in Construction of POA CWS-H1 Mechanized Flame Thrower. Tenth Army 400 Cml.

was the full utilization of the main armament mechanized flame thrower.

According to U.S. intelligence reports the terrain of the next objective, the island of Kyushu, was well suited to the type of defense which the Japanese had used so advantageously on Iwo Jima and Okinawa—caves, crevices, fortified reverse slopes, pillboxes, and interlocking fields of fire from mutually supporting positions. Information gleaned from enemy prisoners taken on Okinawa revealed that many positions on Kyushu would be difficult or impossible to reduce with conventional weapons. But flame throwers, particularly mechanized flame throwers, could rout the Japanese from these otherwise impregnable fortifications with a minimum of casualties. Experimental use of extension hoses showed that positions hitherto inaccessible to armor could now be attacked. A large number of flame tanks might burn the Japanese from their well-prepared positions and keep the battle from dragging on interminably.

On 1 July 1945 the Sixth Army, relieved of all combat operations in the Philippines, received directions to prepare four corps, consisting of twelve divisions, and two additional divisions as army troops, for an assault on southern Kyushu on 1 November 1945.

For the Kyushu operation (OLYMPIC) over twice as many main armament flame tanks per division were to be used as had been employed on Okinawa. A tank battalion was to be attached to each assault division and Sixth Army requested sufficient main armament flame throwers to equip one company in each of these battalions.[96] At this time the Sixth Army understood that some 600 main armament flame throwers were being manufactured in the zone of interior, but that only 40 of these would be available in time for OLYMPIC.[97] Therefore, the plan called for the distribution of armored flame throwers in equal lots to each tank battalion as soon as the weapons arrived in the theater. Some 56 additional main armament flame throwers of the POA model were to be obtained from Hawaii.[98] Thus a total of 96 main armament

---

[96] (1) Rpt of Official Travel, Maull to CCWS, 28 Sep 45, sec. III, p. 21. CWS 314.7. (2) Each flame tank company was to have seventeen tanks.

[97] (1) TWX, ASF to CG WESPAC, 10 Jul 45. (2) Ltr, CG USAFPAC to CG Tenth Army, 4 Aug 45, sub: Replacement Tank Mounted Flame Throwers for 713th Tank Bn. Hist CWS AFMIDPAC, vol. III, an. II–c–1, ref. 143. (3) Rpt of Official Travel, Maull to CCWS, 28 Sep 45, sec. III, p. 34. (4) The main armament model from the zone of interior was the E12–7R1.

[98] CM–IN 439, CG Fleet Marine Force Pacific to CINCPOA, 3 Jan 45, and Ltr, CmlO POA to G–3 POA, 4 Jan 45, sub: Flame Thrower Tanks for Fleet Marine Forces. Hist CWS AFMIDPAC, vol. III, an. II–c–1, refs. 94–95.

flame throwers would be used in the initial assault. Since this number was considered insufficient to meet the expected needs for flame, the Sixth Army also decided to equip each medium tank platoon with two auxiliary flame throwers of the bow gun type. The conclusion of hostilities on 15 August 1945 negated the need for these plans.

In the trial of battle the Army and Marine Corps in the Pacific discovered that the value of the flame thrower lay in its ability to reach the enemy in his prepared positions, which were for the most part impervious to conventional weapons. The excessive infantry casualties ordinarily incurred in rooting the Japanese from their defenses were thereby reduced. It appears certain that had the war not come to a sudden close the mechanized flame thrower would have demonstrated its ability to cut these losses to an even greater degree—not to mention the casualties which would be inflicted upon the enemy.

CHAPTER XVI

The Flame Thrower in the War Against Germany

The Portable Flame Thrower in the MTO

Although the combat engineer battalion of each U.S. division invading Northwest Africa carried ashore twenty-four portable flame throwers, American troops did not use the weapon in that campaign. For one thing, no positive need existed for the portable flame thrower in Northwest Africa where much of the fighting was characterized by fast-moving tactics. As the enemy rarely made use of pillboxes or other fixed fortifications and house-to-house combat was negligible, the combat situations in which flame throwers were most valuable did not arise.[1]

Even had conditions been favorable, it is unlikely that flame throwers would have been effectively employed. The campaign took place at a time when the tactical doctrine for the flame thrower was nascent and its supply and maintenance procedures but poorly conceived. If a situation favoring the use of the weapon had suddenly come up, the flame thrower, usually back with the organizational equipment, would not have been readily available.[2]

The inherent technical deficiency of the portable flame thrower itself also stood in the way of effective employment. The models taken to Africa were the E1R1 and the M1, neither of which, it will be recalled, was capable of firing thickened fuel. Not until the spring and early summer of 1943 did the longer ranged M1A1 portable flame thrower become available in the theater as a replacement for the early models.[3] And flame thrower training for the African landings, gen-

---

[1] Ltr, CmlO WTF to CCWS, 21 Dec 42, no sub. CWS 319.1/88.

[2] Ltr, CmlO WTF to CCWS, 2 Dec 42. CWS 320.2/100.

[3] Informal Routing Slip, Maj Perry M. Moore, CWS ExecO NATOUSA, to Engr, G–4 AG, 14 Nov 43, sub: Flame Throwers. 470.71—Apparatus for Using.

erally superficial, was, nonetheless, extensive enough to reveal the deficiencies of the weapon. Although it is difficult to assess the importance of any one of these conditions there can be no doubt about their cumulative effect.[4]

The napalm-firing M1A1 arrived in the theater in time for the preparations which were being conducted for the invasion of Sicily. Although demonstrations revealed a weapon with a range of forty or fifty yards, some Seventh Army units remained unconvinced of any appreciable improvement in the new model. The engineer battalions of two divisions returned their flame throwers to the base depot before embarking for Sicily.[5]

There was only one recorded use of the portable flame thrower by American troops in Sicily. In an action reminiscent of the burning of the Philistine grain fields by Samson, 1st Division engineers burned a Sicilian wheat field in which enemy infantry had taken position.[6] American troops in Sicily soon learned that white phosphorus and high explosives could neutralize the fortifications encountered on the island; flame throwers were not used again throughout the operations.[7] At a 2-day critique after the fighting, division chemical officers expressed doubts about the value of the flame thrower and recommended it be declared an item of Class IV supply, or, in other words, be relegated to the classification of a special-purpose weapon.[8]

Flame thrower training given to Fifth Army units before the Salerno landings consisted of demonstrations and enough technical training to familiarize operators with the weapon. Some units did not even consider it worthwhile to exchange the M1 flame thrower for the newly arrived M1A1, although Salerno-bound engineer battalions did carry their full quota of the weapon.[9] The series of extremely strong German defensive positions across the Italian peninsula aroused enough

---

[4] McKinney, Portable Flame Thrower Opns, p. 181.

[5] (1) Status of Equip Rpt, MTOUSA, 30 Jun 43. (2) McKinney, Portable Flame Thrower Opns, p. 182. (3) 1st Ind, 3 Dec 43, to Ltr, CmlO ETOUSA to CmlO AFHQ, 18 Nov 43, sub: Use of Flame Throwers in Sicilian Campaign. Seventh Army Cml Sec Rcds, 470.71, No. 1, Jan–Feb 45. (4) Status of Class II, IV, and V Supplies, MTOUSA, 31 Jul 43.

[6] CmlO Seventh Army, Rpt of Cml Warfare Opns, Opn HUSKY, n.d. MTOUSA Cml Rcds, 370, Employ, Opns, and Mvmt of Troops, 1942–44.

[7] McKinney, Portable Flame Thrower Opns, p. 183.

[8] Conf of Army, Corps, and Div CmlO's and CO's of all CWS Units in the Seventh Army, 28, 29 Aug 43.

[9] Informal Routing Slip, Cml NATOUSA to Engr G–4, 14 Nov 43, sub: Flame Throwers. MTOUSA Cml Sec Rcds, 470.71—Apparatus for Using.

interest in the portable flame thrower to cause VI Corps in December 1943 to ask the chemical officer of the Fifth Army, for a 2-day school to familiarize troops with the operation and tactical employment of the weapon.[10]

Units engaged in the difficult fighting at Cassino and at Anzio used the weapon with some success against fixed fortifications, particularly when other means had failed to overcome this type of defense.[11] An experience of the 85th division in the Gustav Line helps to illustrate this use. In May 1944 a platoon of Company G, 339th Infantry, had been held up for two days near Tremensuoli by a series of enemy pillboxes which stretched across a dominant ridge two hundred yards away. Finally, Lt. Robert T. Waugh, the platoon leader, secured a portable flame thrower from regimental headquarters. Under the covering fire of small arms and automatic weapons, Sgt. Fred Juliano, an assistant squad leader, crawled with the flame thrower to within fifteen yards of the key pillbox. Three short bursts killed all of its defenders, and the platoon swiftly overcame the other positions with the help of white phosphorus grenades.[12]

The portable flame thrower, for various reasons, saw little use in Italy.[13] To begin with, the reputation of the early models was not such as to commend the weapon to combat commanders, and there had been little experience of any kind in Africa and Sicily to recommend its use in Italy. Moreover, there was hardly any need for the weapon in Italy. The Italian terrain and climate contributed additional problems for the employment of the flame throwers. The rugged mountains encountered throughout most of Italy made it difficult, if not impossible, to man-carry the cumbersome weapon to the front line

---

[10] (1) Daily Journal Fifth Army Cml Sec, 21 Dec 43. (2) Other flame thrower training stemmed from special situations. Before the invasion of southern France, for example, the 36th Division Chemical Section trained over 200 men in portable flame thrower operations. There is no evidence that any of these weapons were used against the enemy, who had put up but token opposition. Ltr, Col Claude J. Merrill, formerly CmlO 36th Div, to Brig Gen James A. Norrell, Chief of Mil History, 5 Jan 61.

[11] A Mil Encyclopedia Based on Opns in the Italian Campaigns, 1943–45 (hereafter cited as A Mil Encyclopedia), prepared by G–3 Sec Hq 15th Army Group, sec. 23, p. 187.

[12] (1) Memo, Lt Col Houston C. Joyner, former CmlO 85th Div, for Hist Off, 2 Aug 48. (2) Sergeant Juliano received the Distinguished Service Cross for his part in the action; Lieutenant Waugh that day began a series of heroic exploits for which he was awarded the Medal of Honor.

[13] (1) Rpt 359, AGF Bd MTOUSA, 27 Mar 45, sub: Current Questions Regarding Inf Opns. Theater Cml Sec Files NATO–MTO, 319.1 AGF Rpts. (2) A Mil Encyclopedia, p. 529. (3) OCCWS, Final Rpt, CWS Spare Parts Team in MTO and ETO, p. 43.

or to keep it apace of the advancing troops once it got there.[14] The cold, wet climate had almost the same deleterious effect as the heat and moisture of the tropics; and, despite numerous reports of misfires, no means was ever devised to waterproof the electrical ignition system as had been done in the Southwest Pacific.[15]

Probably because of the limited opportunity for employing the flame thrower, matters of doctrine and training were somewhat neglected. Although in April 1944 the Fifth Army published a training memorandum [16] which recommended an integrated 8-man team for the deployment of the portable flame thrower (illustrated with examples of successful use on Guadalcanal), there seemed to be as many schemes for employing the weapon as there were divisions. A survey conducted early in 1945 concluded that there was no theater standard for organizing and equipping flame thrower teams.[17]

Assault teams, usually armed with rifles, automatic rifles, bazookas, and antitank grenades, saw a great deal of action against dugouts and fortified houses. Flame throwers were seldom added to this armament because a bazooka shell or antitank grenade fired through a window or door usually sufficed. Pillbox-type fortifications impervious to more conventional weapons, however, were considered appropriate targets for flame throwers.[18]

Closely related to the problem of doctrine was the status of flame thrower training. Despite several 2-day flame thrower schools sponsored by Fifth Army, the lack of adequately trained operators remained a problem throughout the campaign. These shortcomings in doctrine and training occasionally added up to situations wherein untrained operators received poor support from improperly oriented assault teams with the consequent failure of the mission.[19]

---

[14] McKinney, Portable Flame Thrower Opns, pp. 186–87, 190.

[15] (1) *Ibid.*, (2) Fifth Army Cml Sec, Hist Rpt, 1 Mar 45.

[16] Fifth Army Tng Memo No. 8, 5 Apr 44, sub: Technique and Tactical Use of Flame Thrower, reprinted as app. 18, McKinney, Portable Flame Thrower Opns, pp. 312–16.

[17] Rpt 283, AGF BD MTOUSA, 31 Jan 45, sub: CWS. This report and Report 359, cited above, included the policies for flame thrower teams promulgated by IV Corps, the 34th, 88th, and 92d Divisions, and the 1st Armored Division. All differed.

[18] A Mil Encyclopedia, p. 187.

[19] *Ibid.*, pp. 189, 529.

The Portable Flame Thrower in the ETO

Normandy

Pre-Normandy preparations included more effort directed toward the training of flame thrower operators and the preparation of tactical and logistical procedures for the weapon than had been attempted before the invasion of Italy. In October 1943 Headquarters, ETOUSA, published detailed instructions for all units under its control in the tactical use of the portable flame thrower. This training memorandum suggested the assignment of three men—operator, assistant operator, and refill carrier—to each weapon and urged that twice that number be trained. This document stressed the tactical necessity of covering the flame thrower operator with small arms and smoke, but it did not specify the exact composition of the assault party.[20]

As the date of the invasion approached, ETOUSA increased the tempo of its flame thrower preparations. New instructions, in the form of another training memorandum, did little more than reiterate the memo which it superseded.[21] Of more help was the allocation of 150 portable flame throwers to each of the assault divisions of First Army,[22] a number far in excess of the 24 flame throwers which the theater suggested for an infantry division in normal operations.[23]

The assignment of such a large number of flame throwers to the assault regiments naturally increased the problem of training. In general, the status of flame thrower training within the divisions in England was poor. Engineer battalions had received limited doses, but infantry division troops, even of the veteran units, were generally unfamiliar with both the technical and tactical aspects of the weapon. Divisions of the First U.S. Army conducted schools in an effort to correct this deficiency. Third Army units, slated for commitment later than those of First Army, suffered from a lack of flame throwers

---

[20] ETOUSA, Tng Memo No. 33, 6 Oct 43, sub: Portable Flame Thrower, sec. II, reprinted as app. 19 in McKinney, Portable Flame Thrower Opns.

[21] ETOUSA, Tng Memo No. 10, 5 Apr 44, sub: Portable Flame Thrower, sec. I, reprinted as app. 20 in McKinney, Portable Flame Thrower Opns.

[22] FUSA Rpt of Opns, 20 Oct 43–1 Aug 44, bk. VII, p. 190.

[23] (1) Ltr, CmlO SOS ETO to CmlO FUSAG, 5 Jun 44, sub: Flame Throwers. 12th Army Group Rcds, 470.71—Apparatus. (2) The theater made this recommendation after the portable flame thrower became an item of Class IV issue. WD Cir No. 204, 23 May 44. Other support bases of issue were: airborne division, 15; armored division, 18; Ranger battalion, 6; and engineer combat battalion, 24.

(in August 1944 Third Army's supply of the weapon was described as "practically nil"),[24] and a consequent lack of trained operators.[25]

These preparations went for nought; there is no record that the flame thrower was used during the Normandy landings. Many of the weapons were lost in the rough surf, and infantrymen perforce abandoned others in the struggle to get across the beaches in the face of heavy enemy fire. The 14th Chemical Maintenance Company, which landed in Normandy at the end of June, repaired and returned to depot stock over 100 portable flame throwers which it had picked up from salvage piles on the beaches. In any event, German positions encountered on the beachheads usually were not suitable flame thrower targets.[26]

As the initial weeks of the campaign wore on and units moved inland, some flame thrower targets did appear. Cities and towns presented obstacles which occasionally called for flame thrower action, although the 1st and 2d Infantry Divisions reported that the weapon was not particularly useful in ordinary street fighting. The V Corps stated that the limited range of the portable flame thrower restricted its usefulness in fighting in the hedgerows, that ubiquitous feature of the Normandy terrain.[27]

Brittany

The flame thrower was used more in the August and September fighting on the Brittany peninsula, particularly in and around the port of Brest, than at any other time in France. On one occasion the 1st Battalion, 121st Infantry, 8th Division, was held up near Brest by a series of three concrete positions within a two-acre area. Although artillery had failed to reduce the strongpoint, it had left many large shell holes in the vicinity. Using the cover afforded by these craters

[24] Ltr, CG 12th Army Group to CG COMZ ETOUSA, 16 Aug 44, sub: Request for Flame Throwers. 12th Army Group Rcds, 470.71—Apparatus.

[25] (1) McKinney, Portable Flame Thrower Opns, pp. 192–93. (2) Interv, Hist Off with Col W. H. Greene, 12 Jul 48. During World War II Colonel Greene served successively as chemical officer of the 26th Division and the XX Corps.

[26] (1) McKinney, Portable Flame Thrower Opns, pp. 195–96. (2) FUSA Rpt of Opns, 20 Oct 43– 1 Aug 44, bk. VII, p. 197. (3) Informal comments of CWSO 21 Jun 44. CWS 317.4, Portable Flame Thrower.

[27] Observer's Rpt 1, Flame Thrower E4–5, Incl to Ltr, CmlO 12th Army Group to Comdt Cml Warfare School, 14 Nov 44, sub: Flame Thrower Rpts. This report consists of a series of replies by First Army units to a questionnaire on flame thrower operations submitted by Colonel St. John, Chemical Adviser, G–3, SHAEF.

two flame thrower operators, covered by the small arms fire of ten men, were able to crawl within thirty yards of the fortifications. A short burst of flame directed at each pillbox in turn resulted in the hasty surrender of the occupants. The psychological effect of the flame throwers was the determining factor in the success of the operation. Not one enemy soldier had been burned.[28]

A platoon of the 116th Infantry, 29th Division, had a similar experience in the same area. Halted by opposition from a pillbox, the men brought up a portable flame thrower to help cope with the situation. Although the fuel tanks were only partly filled, the operator fired three good bursts into the doorways. The five occupants immediately panicked but were prevented from coming out by the intense heat engulfing the strongpoint. It was a full ten minutes before the fire and heat subsided enough to allow the enemy to emerge, hands in the air. None of them was seriously burned but their nerves were shattered; as the bewildered men passed the flame thrower they shook their heads.[29]

The introduction of the flame thrower did not always spell success. On 27 August 1944, the 38th Infantry, 2d Division, encountered strong enemy positions which dominated an area near Brest. The majority of the strongpoints consisted of heavy reinforced concrete pillboxes, well protected, as German defensive positions usually were, by bands of interlocking fire. The positions seemed impervious to artillery fire. In this extremity three flame thrower teams came forward, each consisting of an operator, assistant operator, and two BAR men. The first team reached its contact point only to have the operator killed and the fuel tanks of the weapon punctured by enemy machine gun fire. The second team reached its firing position but had to withdraw when it found that the weapon's hydrogen line had been torn loose. The third team alone accomplished its mission, eliminating one of the enemy positions.[30]

Lest it be thought that these examples were typical of the fighting in France, the 8th Division action described was one of three times the unit used the flame thrower between 6 June and 25 September 1944

---

[28] Ltr, CG 8th Div to CG VIII Corps, 23 Sep 44, sub: Employ of Vehicular and Portable Flame Throwers. CWS 314.7 Portable Flame Thrower.

[29] Ltr, CmlO 29th Div to CmlO Ninth Army, 21 Oct 44, sub: AAR on Portable Flame Thrower. T–17, B, Portable Flame Thrower (Tactical) 9th Army.

[30] Ltr, CmlO 2d Div to CmlO VIII Corps, 25 Sep 44, sub: Use of Flame Throwers During Brest Campaign. T–17, B, Portable Flame Thrower (Tactical) 9th Army.

and the 2d Division employment was one of two such instances during the entire Brest campaign.[31]

The Siegfried Line

Fast-moving situations did not favor the employment of the flame thrower, and this was the type of operations experienced by the Allied forces once they broke out of Normandy. Matters of logistics, terrain, and stiffening enemy resistance caused this advance to grind to a halt in September 1944. In large part, the stiffening German resistance resulted from the strength of the Siegfried Line, or West Wall, positions which stretched from the southeastern corner of the Netherlands to the Swiss frontier. New techniques and special weapons had to be employed against this maze of dragon tooth obstructions and the intricate complex of concrete and steel and pillbox fortifications. One of these special weapons was the portable flame thrower.

The V Corps, in anticipation of the assault on the Siegfried Line fortifications, investigated the availability of portable flame throwers and found that Army depots had enough to provide each division of the corps with fifty weapons.[32] In XIX Corps, the 30th Division chemical officer secured ninety-nine M1A1 portable flame throwers for the same purpose. He also found that the men who had been trained as operators while the division was still in England were no longer available. Consequently, the division's chemical section and engineer battalion trained enough infantrymen to operate the twenty-five flame throwers allotted to each of the regiments.[33] Some divisions conducted training in assault tactics before moving against the Siegfried Line. This training usually included the employment of the portable flame thrower. Third Army's XX Corps realistically used captured Maginot Line fortifications to work out techniques for overcoming the German defenses.[34]

The actual technique employed to neutralize strongpoints by means of flame throwers varied somewhat among the divisions, but in most cases flame thrower teams went to work after the infantry had ad-

[31] (1) *Ibid.* (2) Ltr, CG 8th Div to CG VIII Corps, 23 Sep 44, sub: Employ of Vehicular and Portable Flame Throwers. CWS 314.7 Portable Flame Thrower.
[32] V Corps AAR Sep 44. 207.03 V Corps.
[33] CmlO 30th Div, 30 Oct 44, Rpt on Use of Flame Throwers on the Siegfried Line. T-17, B, Portable Flame Thrower (Tactical) 9th Army.
[34] Greene Interv, 1 Dec 47.

MEN TRAINING WITH FLAME THROWER *against a captured German pillbox.*

vanced to within about twenty-five yards of its objective. At this point the flame thrower operator, accompanied by men armed with bazookas, white phosphorus grenades, and pole charges, and supported by small arms fire, made the final assault against the fortified position. The flame thrower was capable of penetrating certain embrasures or causing the enemy to close gun ports and other openings, thus allowing the placement of explosives at the vulnerable points of the fortifications.[35]

The 22d Infantry, 4th Division, found an early opportunity to use the flame thrower in operations against West Wall defenses in the area of the Schnee Eifel, just within the German border. During the third week in September, the regiments encountered a series of pillboxes at 100-yard intervals which were either unmanned or had poor

---

[35] (1) Rpt on Breaching of the Siegfried Line, prepared by Engr Sec, XVIII Corps (Airborne), 28 Jan 45, p. 3. Documents of the Siegfried Line, ORB, First Army. (2) Rpt, Lt Thomas W. Leland, CWS, to CmlO First Army, n.d., no sub. Misc Rpts E4–5R1 Flame Thrower, 12th Army Group. This report served as an unofficial manual on flame thrower operations for First Army units.

fields of fire. Flame thrower operators moved to within effective range without too much difficulty. Despite these circumstances, the division reported only one successful flame thrower operation; other attempts failed because of weapon malfunction.[36]

One regiment of the 9th Division reported that flame throwers were of little value against the Siegfried Line positions; and the 30th Division chemical officer stated in November 1944 that he had heard of only one successful use of the flame thrower. The 117th Infantry, 30th Division, reported that the portable weapons were of no value against large bunkers, a judgment affirmed by the engineer battalion of the 9th Division. The engineers of VII Corps stated that although they were equipped with flame throwers and pole charges, these weapons were unnecessary once the neutralizing fire of armored vehicles was brought upon the target. In October 1944 the 1st Division reported that while extra pole charges and flame throwers were kept accessible at all times, the flame thrower was too heavy for use by assault troops.[37]

On the other hand, there were some notable examples of the successful use of portable flame throwers against Siegfried Line fortifications. Despite the adverse comment on the weapon made by the 1st Division, the 26th Infantry reported on 12 October that Company L had "cleaned up" three pillboxes, after they had "worked on them with flame throwers." [38] The same regiment reported further successes with the portable flame thrower in February 1945. On the third of the month the regiment reported that it had "cleaned up a pillbox with flame throwers," flushing out twenty men and three officers in the process. During the next several days the 26th Infantry went on to neutralize a number of additional pillboxes guarding the high ground near Hollerath, Germany, in operations which featured the successful use of portable flame throwers.[39]

[36] (1) Combat Intervs, 4th Inf Div, Schnee Eifel Ridge, 14–20 Sep 44. HRS–CI 33. (2) Charles B. MacDonald describes the Schnee Eifel engagement in *The Siegfried Line Campaign,* UNITED STATES ARMY IN WORLD WAR II (Washington, 1963).

[37] (1) Immediate Rpt 61 (Combat Observations), 12th Army Group, 22 Sep 44. 99/120–0.4, 12th Army Group, Nov 44. (2) Ltr, S–3 2d Bn 117th Inf to ACofS G–2 30th Inf Div, 14 Oct 44, sub: Documentation of Siegfried Line. First Army Rcds, Documents of Siefried Line. (3) Memo, S–3 15th Engr Combat Bn for ACofS G–3 9th Inf Div, 23 Oct 44, sub: Assault Methods Employed by Engrs on Siegfried Line. First Army Rcds, Documents of Siegfried Line. (4) Engr Sec XVIII Corps (Airborne) Rpt on Breaching of the Siegfried Line, 28 Jan 45. (5) 1st Inf Div G–3 Rpt of Opns, 1–31 Oct 44. 301–3 (22345) G–3 Opns Rpt, European Campaign, 1st Inf Div, Oct 44.

[38] 1st Inf Div G–3 Rpt of Opns, 1–31 Oct 44.

[39] 26th Inf AAR, Feb 45. 301–Inf (26)–0.3 Opns Rpt 26th Inf Regt 1st Inf Div (European Campaign).

In a February action in the Seventh Army sector near Bitche, Company B, 399th Infantry, 100th Division, used a flame thrower team as the nucleus of a combination raiding-assault party. This party, led by Lt. Harry G. Flanagan, consisted of the flame thrower operator and assistant, two automatic rifle teams, two men armed with M15 white phosphorus grenades, and riflemen. Its target was a German outpost in a Maginot Line blockhouse. Although enemy sentries detected the approach of the patrol and fired flares in an attempt to pinpoint it, the flame thrower operator, Cpl. Boyd R. Pike, was able to crawl to a position within fifteen yards of the open rear door of the emplacement. From this vantage point Pike fired three bursts at the enemy position, killing a sentry standing in the doorway. Enemy machine guns opened up at once on the patrol. Pike attempted to fire on the source of some of the enemy opposition, the steel turret surmounting the blockhouse, but he ran out of fuel and withdrew. The grenadiers lobbed their white phosphorus grenades against the blockhouse before retiring. On the way back Pike, exhausted by the ordeal, abandoned his flame thrower. All patrol members returned without injury, and even the flame thrower was eventually recovered.[40]

Actually, the number of fortifications against which flame throwers were used was few as compared to the total number assaulted. The incident just cited represented the first use of a portable flame thrower which came to the attention of the chemical officer of Seventh Army. By way of explanation for the limited use of the weapon consider the number of portable flame throwers carried by the units with Seventh Army in February 1945: of the 8 U.S. infantry divisions so assigned, 2 had no flame throwers on hand whatsoever, 1 division had 4, 3 divisions had 6, and 2 others had totals of 12 and 34.[41] It should be remembered that at the beginning of operations the theater had recommended a complement of 24 portable flame throwers.

Evaluation

Portable flame throwers contributed as little to the success of operations in the European theater as they had in the Mediterranean. The weapon was infrequently used, and not always successfully. Some

---

[40] (1) Ltr, CG 100th Div to CG Seventh Army, 14 Feb 45, sub: Use of Flame Thrower With Raiding Party. 470.71-3 AG Rcds, Sixth Army Group. (2) Seventh Army Cml Sec, Hist Rpt, Feb 45. CWS 314.7.

[41] IOM, CmlO to G-4 Seventh Army, 22 Feb 45, sub: M2-2 Portable Flame Throwers.

infantry divisions never used the flame thrower; few considered it valuable. Reasons for this situation, which was in decided contrast to the successful role played by the portable flame thrower in the Pacific campaigns, are not difficult to find.

Foremost was the fact that the fighting in Europe never developed the need for the portable flame thrower, particularly when compared with operations in the Pacific. The latter theaters saw a fanatical enemy determined to resist to the last in defensive positions which were almost impregnable to the normal complement of infantry weapons, even to artillery fire and air action. Moreover, the jungle terrain in which much of the Pacific fighting took place permitted the flame thrower operator to advance to within effective range if he was protected by adequate supporting weapons. The situation was different on the European battlefields. As German defenses featured interlocking bands of fire and long, uninterrupted fields of vision, the utilization of weapons with limited range was difficult. The absence of concealment along the approaches drew attention to the size of the portable flame thrower and particularly to the unique silhouette of an operator with his weapon strapped to his back.[42] The small size of the fuel load was another handicap, particularly when the flame thrower was used against the Siegfried Line fortifications where the enemy might avoid the flame by moving to another room of the emplacement.[43]

The makeup of the German soldier, as contrasted with that of his Axis ally in the Pacific, had an effect upon flame thrower operations. The Japanese infantryman often fought until death, and flame weapons were needed to insure that he was dead. The German soldier, on the other hand, skilled and valorous as he was, surrendered when conditions provided no alternative.[44]

In addition to, and sometimes because of, the factors just related, matters of training, supply, and maintenance conspired against the successful use of the portable flame thrower. Although the assault divisions of the First U.S. Army did receive some training in England

[42] (1) 12th Army Group Immediate Rpt 91 (Combat Observations). 99/12–0.4 Immediate Rpts 12–32, 34–92, 12th Army Group, Jul–Nov 44. (2) 76th Div AAR, 10 Oct 44. (3) Notes of Flame Throwers (Portable), Incl 3 to Rpt on Tour, 26–30 Dec 44 (hereafter cited as Roos Rpt), by 2d Lt Edwin G. Roos, 31 Dec 44. (4) CmlO 30th Div, 30 Oct 44, Rpt on Use of Flame Throwers on the Siegfried Line.

[43] (1) 76th Div AAR, 10 Oct 44. (2) 12th Army Group Immediate Rpt 61 (Combat Observations), 22 Sep 44.

[44] (1) CmlO 30th Inf Div, 30 Oct 44, Rpt on Use of Flame Throwers on the Siegfried Line. (2) Immediate Rpt 91 (Combat Observations). (3) Roos Rpt. (4) 76th Div AAR, 10 Oct 44.

before the Normandy landings, the supply of flame throwers was critical during this period and none was available for other units, the divisions of Third Army, for example. Even when Third Army depots received stocks of portables in anticipation of operations against the Siegfried Line, troops received little training in the weapon.[45] As late as October 1944 some divisions of II Corps had not been furnished with this item, and its low status in Seventh Army units early in 1945, as mentioned above, was not a reflection of extensive use.[46] Seventh Army also reported that use of the weapon was at times limited by the lack of batteries and ignition assemblies; in October 1944 approximately 80 percent of its depot stock of flame throwers was deadlined because of these shortages. In December a shipment of twenty of the M1A1 models included three with defective fuel tanks and others with defective spark generator assemblies.[47] The 5th Division reported the receipt from depots of flame throwers with loose electrical connections and with paint-filled discharge ports.[48]

Commanders and troops in Europe never had the same confidence in the portable flame thrower exhibited by their Pacific counterparts.[49] Infrequent use of the weapon meant not only the neglect of doctrine and training, but that supply and maintenance practices would not be tested and improved. Employment of the weapon often ended disastrously, a circumstance which only added to its shaky reputation. In cases where it might have been effectively used it was sometimes discarded in favor of another weapon.

The Mechanized Flame Thrower

The Requirement for an Auxiliary Model

The role played by the U.S. mechanized flame thrower in the war against Germany was of even less consequence than was that of its portable counterpart. American-made flame throwers were not used at all in the Mediterranean theater. After the Sicily Campaign General

---

[45] (1) Greene Interv, 12 Jul 48. (2) Cole, *Lorraine Campaign*, p. 180n.

[46] Ltr, CmlO III Corp to CmlO Ninth Army, 10 Oct 44, sub: Rpt of Flame Thrower Activities. Ninth Army Cml Sec Files.

[47] Seventh Army Cml Hist Rpt, 1–31 Dec 44.

[48] 7th Engr Combat Bn 5th Div AAR, 21 Oct 44. 305–Engr—0.3 (6618) Master, Jul–Dec 44.

[49] (1) OCCWS Final Rpt, CWS Spare Parts Team in MTO and ETO, pp. 43–44. (2) Conf of Army, Corps, and Div CmlO's and CO's of all CWS units in the Seventh Army, 28 and 29 Aug 43. (3) Cole, *Lorraine Campaign*, p. 180n.

Patton expressed doubt about the tactical value of a mechanized flame thrower. A September 1944 demonstration of two models of the newly developed auxiliary flame thrower for the medium tank elicited no requirement for the weapon. A series of conferences on the mechanized flame thrower led Allied Force Headquarters in December 1944 also to report that no requirement existed for the auxiliary model. One of the major factors in this conclusion was the fact that the Italian terrain was most unfavorable for the use of tanks.[50]

U.S. armored units used the mechanized flame thrower in France and Germany but only in a modest degree. Because the United States had not as yet produced a mechanized flame thrower, American planners for the Normandy invasion turned to the possibility of adapting the British flame thrower unit, then under development, to the U.S. medium tank. The British mounted the flame assembly in the hull of a Churchill Mark VII tank, retaining the 75-mm. gun of the armored vehicle. This flame weapon had a range of something around 120 yards. Called the Crocodile, it featured an armored trailer which held 400 imperial gallons of fuel. In 1943, the Commanding General, ETOUSA, submitted a request for 100 of the British flame throwers for installation in U.S. Sherman tanks. Development and testing of the Sherman-Crocodile proceeded slowly, and the first production model did not appear until March 1944.[51]

In the zone of interior the Armored Force Board had never been enthusiastic about any flame-throwing tank that was a special-purpose weapon, that is, if it had the flame thrower as its main armament, or if it had a distinguishing silhouette. The British Crocodile met the first requirement, but its fuel-carrying trailer certainly made it readily identifiable. In any event, the board urged the Chemical Warfare Service to concentrate its efforts on the auxiliary model, one that maintained the normal armament of the vehicle, which was then under development.[52] The result was an auxiliary flame thrower which was interchangeable with the bow machine gun of either the light or medium tank.

On 9 March 1944 General Eisenhower requested that one of these

---

[50] McKinney, Mechanized Flame Thrower Opns, pp. 30–31.

[51] (1) History of the "Crocodile," 4 Mar 44. ETO Rcds, 470.71—Flame Thrower, ORB. (2) Colonel Magness, project officer of the Sherman-Crocodile flame thrower tank, states that the range was between 175 and 200 yards.

[52] Ltr, Armored Force Bd to CG Armored Comd, 3 Feb 44, no sub. CMLHO.

new bow gun flame throwers be sent to England for testing, inquiring at the same time when 100 more units could be made available. The War Department replied that the ETOUSA could have the single unit by mid-April and 200 flame throwers by 1 June 1944, 100 units for medium tanks, the E4–5, and 100 designed for light tanks, the E5–5.[53] This was heartening news, especially as the requirements of the British Army precluded the delivery of the complete order of Sherman-Crocodiles until sometime in October.[54]

The theater chemical section quickly installed the first auxiliary unit in a medium tank and demonstrated it to interested officers from General Eisenhower's headquarters in late June.[55] In contrast to the long-range Crocodile the auxiliary flame thrower gave a poor performance. Perhaps the strongest point in favor of the American model was its availability. First Army, planning on nine flame throwers per medium tank battalion, asked for 200 auxiliary flame throwers and canceled its requirement for Sherman-Crocodiles.[56] Meanwhile, because of the lack of trained personnel and its somewhat limited mobility, the British Crocodile flame thrower had not lived up to expectations in the first month on the Continent, and General Eisenhower soon canceled the American requirement for the flame tank. The fact that E4–5's were understood to be available and that they had no identifying, mobility-hampering trailer, were doubtless other considerations in the decision.[57]

On 23 August 1944 Lt. Col. G. C. White, OCCWS, conducted a second demonstration of the E4–5 auxiliary flame thrower before high ranking officers of the First and Third Armies. This time the latest model with a capacity of fifty gallons was shown, and the equipment

[53] (1) Rads, CM–IN 7411, 9 Mar 44, and CM–OUT 6014, 15 Mar 44. (2) Memo, CCmlO ETOUSA for CmlO FUSAG, 30 Mar 44, sub: Small Flame Throwers for Installation in Tanks. USFET CWS 470.71—Apparatus for Using Smoke and Gas (1942–44).

[54] (1) Memo, CCmlO ETOUSA for CmlO FUSAG, 30 Mar 44, sub: Small Flame Throwers for Installation in Tanks. (2) Rad, CM–IN 7231, 9 Jun 44. (3) Magness Interv, 5 May 59.

[55] There was no theater interest in the auxiliary unit for the light tank.

[56] Ltr, CG First Army to CG ETOUSA, 11 Jul 44, sub: Tank Mounted Flame Throwers. 470.71—Flame Throwers (1944–45) Hq USFET Armored Sec.

[57] (1) Ltr, CG SHAEF to British Under Secy of State (Dir Special Weapons and Vehicles), 13 Aug 44, sub: Crocodile Flame Throwers. 12th Army Group Rcds, 470.71—Apparatus. (2) Ltr, Cml Adviser G–3 SHAEF to ACCWS for Field Opns, 22 Jul 44, no sub. ETO Personal files, Feb 44–Dec 44. (3) Memo, Cml Adviser G–3 SHAEF for CmlO's in ETO, 16 Sep 44. CWS 314.7 Mechanized Flame Thrower. (4) Ltr, CCmlO ETOUSA to CCWS, 28 Aug 44, sub: Flame Thrower Tank Development. CWO 470.71/303.

BRITISH CROCODILE WITH FUEL TRAILER, *firing at a target 200 yards away during a test in England.*

functioned perfectly at an effective range of fifty yards.[58] The increased capacity came from the addition of a 25-gallon flame fuel tank located over the transmission of the vehicle. The original tank of the same size was situated on the right sponson.[59] The 12th Army Group soon established a requirement for 333 of these auxiliary flame throwers, of which 150 were understood to be immediately available in the zone of interior. First Army, about to assault the Siegfried Line in the vicinity of Aachen, Germany, requested the prompt delivery of the weapons.[60] One hundred and fifty of the E4–5 flame throwers reached the ETO in October 1944 but they were equipped with only one of the two 25-gallon fuel tanks. This caused some concern as the 50-

---

[58] (1) Interv, Hist Off with White. (2) Memo, CmlO 12th Army Group for ACofS G–3 12th Army Group, 25 Aug 44, sub: Flame Thrower Demonstration. 12th Army Group Rcds, 470.71—Apparatus. This was the E4R2–4R3–5R1 model with two 25-gallon fuel containers.

[59] For the history of the development of this and other mechanized flame weapons, see Brophy, Miles, and Cochrane, *From Laboratory to Field.*

[60] (1) Ltr, AG Central Group of Armies to CG COMZ (Forward), 6 Sep 44, sub: Flame Throwers E4–5. AGRO–H, 12th Army Group 470.71—Apparatus. (2) Ltr, Asst AG ETOUSA to CG First Army, 22 Sep 44, sub: Tank Mounted Flame Throwers. AGRO–H, 12th Army Group 470.71—Apparatus.

gallon fuel capacity was a popular feature of the flame throwers. The missing transmission fuel tanks finally arrived in November.[61]

The Main Armament Flame Thrower

If the theater's interest in the auxiliary flame thrower could have been called mild, its concern for the main armament version was almost nonexistent. Army commanders indicated their reluctance to give up standard tanks for main armament flame throwers not only because of the reduced fire power but also because of the additional tanks needed to protect the vulnerable special weapon. And, as General Rowan pointed out, matters were all the worse because tanks and other armored vehicles remained in short supply.

It was not until January 1945 that General Bradley, 12th Army Group commander, requested twelve main armament flame throwers (E12–7R1) for operational testing.[62] The armored forces in the 6th Army Group declined to give up voluntarily any of the regular tanks in order to provide for main armament flame throwers. The Army Group Commander, General Devers, stated that any value gained in the use of the flame thrower would be more than offset by the consequent shortage of regular tanks and personnel.[63]

Word came in late February that ten, not twelve, of General Bradley's flame throwers would be shipped to Europe on the first convoy in May.[64] They were on shipboard ready to sail when the Germans surrendered at Reims on 7 May 1945.

Mechanized Flame Thrower Operations

The American forces did not have mechanized flame throwers when they were first committed to action in France, nor did they have them in any numbers for almost five months after the Normandy landings. This initial lack of experience and training with flame-throwing tanks probably did as much as anything to set the pattern for the insignificant role the weapon was to have in Europe, a role in decided contrast to

---

[61] Rcd of Telephone Conv, Gen Rowan and Col Norman Gillet, 5 Nov 44. CWS 314.7 Mechanized Flame Thrower.

[62] Ltr, CG 12th Army Group to CG ETOUSA, 14 Jan 45, sub: Mechanized Flame Thrower. 12th Army Group Rcds, 470-71—Apparatus.

[63] 1st Ind, 1 Feb 45, to Ltr, CCmlO ETOUSA to Cml Adviser G–3 6th Army Group, 3 Jan 45, no sub. Seventh Army Cml Sec Rcds, 470.71—Flame Thrower Fuels, Jan 43–Feb 45.

[64] Rad, CG COMZ to CG 12th Army Group, 22 Feb 45, sub: Flame Throwers, Mechanized, E12–7R1. 12th Army Group Rcds, 470.71—Apparatus.

that in the British and the Canadian Armies, which used the mechanized flame thrower successfully and on a fairly large scale.[65]

Initially without flame tanks of their own, American forces in France received occasional support of British Crocodile squadrons. In September 1944 Squadron B, 141st Regiment, Royal Armoured Corps, consisting of a headquarters troop and four flame thrower troops, each with three Crocodile flame tanks, reported to Ninth Army's VIII Corps. Three of these flame tanks supported elements of the 29th Division in operations against Fort Montbarey, a key enemy stronghold in Brest. On 14 September these flame tanks participated in the attack on a series of pillboxes near the fort. Although two were knocked out by mines before reaching the objective, the third flamed the pillboxes, which capitulated with a yield of 60 prisoners. Two days later, in the assault on Fort Montbarey itself, Crocodiles fired against the moat and the wall until their fuel was exhausted. Even then the tanks remained in position, their crews throwing white phosphorus hand grenades to cover the final infantry assault. The fort capitulated that evening. Prisoners indicated that the use of flame materially reduced the will to resist.[66]

Favorably impressed by the work of the Crocodiles in the Brest operation, the commanding general of Ninth Army, Lt. Gen. William H. Simpson, on 31 October urged General Bradley to make one squadron available to Ninth Army for the impending operations against the Siegfried Line.[67] At this time the British flame tank squadrons were in great demand by 21 Army Group and Ninth Army received only four Sherman-Crocodile flame throwers, with well-trained crews. These four tanks, issued to a platoon of the 739th Tank Battalion, Special (Mine Exploder), were the only large capacity flame throwers used by American forces in the European Theater of Operations. In support of the 29th Division, which had also worked with flame tanks at Brest, the Sherman-Crocodile platoon crossed the Roer River on 24 February 1945. It then received orders to join in the assault on the citadel at Jülich where enemy small arms fire had impeded the

[65] For a description of British and Canadian flame tank operations, see McKinney, Mechanized Flame Thrower Opns.

[66] (1) Col Claude A. Black, Chief Armored Sec Ninth Army, 20 Sep 44, Rpt on Employ of Churchill "Crocodiles" at Brest, 20 Sep 44.   (2) Roos to CmlO Ninth Army, 31 Dec 44, Rcds Incl 2, Notes on Churchill Flame Thrower Tanks (Crocodiles). Both in CWS 314.7 Mechanized Flame Thrower.

[67] Ltr, CG Ninth Army to CG 12th Army Group, 31 Oct 44, sub: Special Equip (Flame Throwing Tanks). 12th Army Group Rcds, 470.71—Apparatus.

advance for several days. In the plan of attack, the four Crocodiles were to flame the south wall of the sixteenth century citadel from across the moat and fire 75-mm. shells to demolish the gate. Two of the tanks developed trouble before reaching the target, but the remaining two lumbered to within seventy-five yards of the citadel and fired flame over the wall, forcing the defenders underground. Twenty rounds from the 75's sufficed to smash the steel door and permit the tanks to flame the opening. The last German defenders fled just as infantrymen from the 29th Division poured over the moat into the burning citadel.[68]

The only American-made, mechanized flame thrower used by U.S. troops in the European theater was the E4–5, later standardized as the M3–4–3, the auxiliary model which initially had arrived without the transmission fuel tanks. Four of these flame thrower units arrived in the summer of 1944 and saw action with First Army in September. In November, 12th Army Group allotted the 150 E4–5 units on hand as follows: First Army, 75; Third Army, 30; Ninth Army, 45. Third Army had never established a requirement for the flame-throwing tank and held its 30 E4–5 flame throwers in an Army depot.[69]

As a matter of fact, comparatively little use was made of the E4–5 in France and Germany. Unfortunately, the first reported action was a complete failure, a circumstance which may have helped discourage wider use of the weapon. Two medium tanks with E4–5 flame throwers reported to the 741st Tank Battalion, First Army, on 15 September 1944. At the time, both tanks were improperly equipped and one had a defective engine. The 741st Tank Battalion repaired and equipped the vehicles and attached them to Company C. When further trouble developed, one of the tanks was evacuated to an ordnance repair shop. On 18 September, the remaining E4–5 flame tank supported an infantry attack on an enemy pillbox. Because of inadequate pressure the tank had to get within twenty-five yards of the fortification before the flame could reach the embrasure. This action failed to reduce the pillbox, and the infantry did not take the position. In fact, there was doubt whether or not the enemy suffered any casualties from the attack.

[68] Ltr, Adjutant 739th Tank Bn, Special (Mine Exploder) to CmlO Ninth Army, 22 Mar 45, sub: Flame Throwers. ARBN–739–0.1 (7763) History, 739th Tractor Bn, 1 Mar 43—21 Nov 45.
[69] (1) Rad, CG Third Army to CG 12th Army Group, 22 Nov 44, sub: E4–5 Flame Throwers. (2) Memo, Chief Armored Sec 12 Army Group for CWS, G–4, G–3, 12 Oct 44, sub: Flame Throwers E4–5. 12th Army Group Rcds, 470.71—Apparatus.

The tank battalion commander was decidedly unimpressed with the possibilities of the flame tank, although he admitted that the lack of training experience of the crew (it had had one day of preparatory training) might have contributed to the inefficiency of the weapon. Another factor was the distinct, if unwarranted, reluctance of the crews to enter combat with the flame tanks, a reluctance also attributable to a lack of training and indoctrination.[70]

In December, Company B, 709th Tank Battalion, with Ninth Army, attacked hasty entrenchments near the town of Vossenack, Germany. The battalion had received and installed the two flame units just before the action. Unfortunately, there was no time for training the bow gunner-operators; they merely received verbal instructions on how to operate the weapon. The enemy fortifications were in a V-shaped position in a woods near the town. The plan of attack called for clearing the left half of the wedge, followed by a tank and flame tank attack on the right side. The vehicles, with infantrymen clinging to them, approached the objective in a line. As the flame tanks came within range of the positions they opened fire; when the flame fuel was exhausted the infantrymen dismounted and quickly took the positions. Though the operation was a success and the flame tanks achieved the expected result, their performance was nonetheless something less than spectacular. The ignition system worked well, but the range—only twenty yards—was extremely short. The officer in charge blamed this poor performance not so much on the E4–5 as upon the inexperience of the gunners.[71]

Seventh Army issued nine E4–5 flame throwers to the 14th Armored Division but only one had been installed by January 1945. When this flame tank and three standard tanks advanced abreast against a wooded area north of Strasbourg, they encountered an enemy machine gun nest holding up the infantry on the flank. The flame gunner fired his weapon even though the German position was well out of range. The flame traveled only halfway to the position but the defending enemy immediately surrendered. The division promptly installed the eight remaining flame throwers.[72]

---

[70] Combat Observer with V Corps to CG 12th Army Group, 13 Oct 44, Observers Rpt 4. CWS 314.7 Mechanized Flame Thrower.

[71] Roos to CmlO Ninth Army Rpt, Mechanized Flame Thrower Activities (E4R2–5R1). CWS 314.7 Mechanized Flame Thrower.

[72] Ltr, CmlO Seventh Army to Cml Adviser G–3 6th Army Group, 1 Feb 45, sub: Use of E4–5 Flame Thrower. Seventh Army Cml Sec Rcds, 470.71—Flame Thrower, Jan 43—Feb 45.

Another example of the psychological impact of a flame attack took place during the advance of the 743d Tank Battalion from the Roer River to the Rhine. One tank fired several high explosive shells at a German antitank gun, closed in, and poured flame on the position. The defending Germans immediately fled into the shelter of a nearby woods. Flame against troops in the open or in hasty entrenchments usually was extremely successful.[73]

Despite the advantages which resulted from the employment of flame, tank battalions and armored divisions remained unconvinced of the merits of the flame throwing tank. As a consequence, the few examples just cited represent a fairly substantial proportion of the reported flame actions. First Army, realizing that the weapon was seeing little use, acknowledged to its tank battalion commanders the "considerable difficulties . . . encountered with ignition, fuel and first echelon maintenance." Admitting that the shortcomings in the flame thrower had no immediate solution, the Army left the way open for the tank battalion commanders to store the flame throwers. The response to this frankly worded communication was significant. Six tank battalions requested permission to store most of their flame units; only two desired to keep the equipment until a tactical situation afforded the chance of a combat test.[74]

In summary, American forces in Europe used flame-throwing tanks very sparingly. Flame would have been more successful had there been adequate tactical and technical training in the proper use of mechanized flame throwers. Within the tank battalions the constant strain of combat, as contrasted with the intermittent battles in the Pacific, hindered the proper installation of flame-throwing equipment. Units often had to be committed to combat during the period of installation and training, and therefore training in flame thrower maintenance and tactics was often inadequate or entirely lacking. Moreover, the continuing shortage of medium tanks made armored commanders very reluctant to remove tanks from battle for the installation of the flame throwers.

For these reasons, the armored forces made but sporadic gestures at

---

[73] Ltr, CmlO Ninth Army to CmlO 12th Army Group, 30 Apr 45, sub: Mechanized Flame Thrower Activities (E4R2–5R1). CWS 314.7 Mechanized Flame Thrower.

[74] Ltr, First Army Armored Sec to CO Tank Bns, 3 Jan 45, sub: E4–5 Flame Throwers. CWS 314.7 Mechanized Flame Thrower.

establishing a requirement for a mechanized flame thrower, a fact which did little to expedite the development of an acceptable flame unit in the zone of interior. The late arrival of flame units caused little stir among the using forces, and defects of equipment and problems of maintenance did not help the reputation of the weapon. The end result was understandable. Caught in a vicious circle the mechanized flame thrower, much like the portable model, was able to contribute but little support to American forces in Europe.

CHAPTER XVII

Fire From the Air

Aerial incendiaries probably caused as much death and destruction as any other weapon used in World War II. Certainly they were the most important chemical munitions employed, considering their contribution in bringing the war to a successful conclusion. The record of these munitions is all the more remarkable because most of them were investigated, designed, and developed after the United States had entered World War II. Aerial incendiaries, for practical purposes, may be divided into two categories: the incendiary bomb, usually dropped by bomber aircraft on targets far behind enemy lines, and the fire bomb, a type which fighter-bombers used against targets at or near the front. Of the two, the incendiary bomb was by far the most important.[1]

The Incendiary Bomb: The Strategic Weapon

Pre-World War II Developments

The aerial incendiary was used for the first time in World War I. The earliest German incendiaries, dropped on England from zeppelins and airplanes, were shaped like buckets and consisted of a core of thermite wrapped with tarred cotton waste and tarred rope. These crude bombs were unsatisfactory both in incendiary action and ballistic quality. A torpedo-shaped bomb filled with gasoline and paraffin replaced the bucketlike munition, and before the end of the war German scientists had perfected the electron bomb. This 2-pound bomb was composed of a magnesium-thermite filler in a magnesium alloy casing. Though not used in World War I, it is nonetheless im-

---

[1] For details of the research, development, and production of aerial incendiaries, see Brophy, Miles, and Cochrane, *From Laboratory to Field.*

portant as the prototype of a very effective group of World War II incendiaries.[2]

Great Britain's principal incendiary bomb, the Baby Incendiary, weighed but two-fifths of a pound. Filled with a special thermite mixture these small bombs were carried in containers capable of holding either 272 or 144 units. Great Britain used few of its Baby Incendiaries during World War I, although these bombs were in production and were found to be effective.

The United States developed several types of incendiary bombs during World War I. Two bombs, the Mark II and Mark III, were of the intensive type, that is, munitions with a high degree of penetrability and an intensive incendiary action. Both bombs contained a thermite charge which ignited the main incendiary, solidified oil. They differed mainly in size, and hence penetrability; the former weighed approximately forty pounds and the latter about 100. The Mark I, a scatter-type bomb, was intended for use against very inflammable targets. In outward appearance the Mark I resembled the Mark II bomb, but, whereas the latter was filled with solid oil, the Mark I contained a number of waste balls saturated with an inflammable mixture. Two explosive charges ignited these pellets and cast them for a radius of twenty feet.

The United States also developed two incendiary darts, the impetus for which came from the success of the British with their Baby Incendiaries. The first American dart, the Mark I, consisted of an elongated 12-gauge shotgun shell filled with an incendiary material. This munition, which ignited on impact, was designed for use against grain fields and forests. The heavier Mark II dart, composed of a zinc body, a thermite and solid oil filler, and a steel nose, possessed the penetrability needed in a munition to be used against buildings.

Neither the incendiary darts nor the other three American aerial incendiaries saw use in combat. United States air units in France used a French munition, the *Chenard*, reported to be the most efficient of all Allied incendiary bombs.[3]

---

[2] (1) George J. B. Fisher, *Incendiary Warfare* (New York: McGraw-Hill, 1946), pp. 119–21. (2) Memo, Col Zanetti for Maj Gen Claude E. Brigham, n.d., sub: Thermite Incendiary Bombs.

[3] (1) Cml Warfare Monographs, Incendiaries (vol. 43), pts. I, II, June 19. CMLHO. (2) Fries and West, *Chemical Warfare*, pp. 336–47. (3) "Chemical Warfare Service Materials Used by the Air Service," *Chemical Warfare*, VIII, No. 1 (January 15, 1922), 3–4. (4) Aviation Material, Lecture by Gen W. L. Sibert, General Staff College, 11 Mar 20, p. 44.

There was little interest in the United States in an incendiary bomb program during the period between the two World Wars. This neglect resulted largely from an overly optimistic evaluation of the capabilities of high explosive (HE) bombs. In 1934 an Ordnance Department study on the relative effectiveness of incendiary and demolition bombs concluded that "everything that can be accomplished by an incendiary bomb can, in most cases at least, be accomplished as well or better by either a smoke bomb loaded with white phosphorus (WP) or a demolition bomb loaded with a high explosive." [4]

There was one authoritative voice which did call attention to the possibilities of the incendiary bomb. Colonel Zanetti, a CWS Reserve officer on the faculty of Columbia University, insisted several times in the 1930's that the incendiary bomb had a great potential. Colonel Zanetti had worked with these munitions in World War I and had become perhaps the greatest American technical expert in the field. In 1936, when some people were dwelling on the horrors of aerial gas attacks in cities, he graphically pointed out that fire, not gas, was the greatest danger:

> The small size of these [incendiary] bombs may appear almost ridiculous, particularly after considering the tons of gas that are required to produce lethal concentrations; but here comes the essential difference between gas and incendiaries that makes fire far more dangerous to a large city. Gas *dissipates* while fire *propagates*. Each of these small bombs held within itself the devastating possibilities of Mrs. O'Leary's cow. [5]

Moreover, the Army Air Corps was becoming increasingly interested in the potentialities of the incendiary bomb. As early as November 1934 the commandant of the Air Corps Tactical School at Maxwell Field, Ala., recommended to the Chief of Air Corps a project aimed at developing a filling for an incendiary bomb, and one month later he sent the Chief, CWS, the military characteristics for such a munition. By April 1936 the CWS Book of Standards showed a military requirement for an incendiary filling for the 25-pound chemical bomb, and on 30 December 1936 the CWS established a project to find an incen-

---

[4] Memo Study by Maj Hermann H. Zornig, Ord Dept, 17 Jan 34, quoted in Brief Review of Work Done to Date on Incendiaries, by Alton L. Kibler, 10 Apr 34.

[5] J. Enrique Zanetti, "The Forgotten Enemy," *The Independent Journal of Columbia University*, vol. 3, No. 6 (January 10, 1936).

diary bomb filling.[6] Despite these preparations, the eve of the United
States' entry into World War II found it with only one standardized
incendiary bomb, the gasoline filled, 100-pound M47. This situation
existed because of the continuing belief in the superiority of high explosives over incendiaries.[7]

The outbreak of war in Europe called attention as never before to
the possibilities of aerial incendiaries. German planes began to shower
London with magnesium electron bombs and 110-kilo oil bombs, and
the English replied with their 4-pound magnesium munition. The
United States Army could no longer afford to neglect the development
and production of incendiary bombs.[8]

In July 1941 General Porter, Chief, CWS, recalled Colonel Zanetti
to active duty and sent him to London to obtain firsthand information
on the research, development, and production of the British 4-pound
incendiary bomb. Colonel Zanetti returned with formulas for fillings,
blueprints for casings, and procedures for manufacturing, and a period
of extensive work on aerial incendiaries ensued.[9] But there was still a
roadblock to be overcome. Since 1920 the responsibility for incendiary
munitions had been divided between the Ordnance Department and
the Chemical Warfare Service. The former had charge of the procurement of the containers and the storage and issue of the complete incendiary bomb whereas the latter developed the incendiary material
and filled the munition.[10] General Porter strove to consolidate the
incendiary mission under the CWS. His last two assignments, before
he became Chief, CWS, had been with the Army Air Corps so that
he was fully aware not only of the value of aerial incendiaries but also
of the necessity for their undivided control. The argument for a unified
responsibility was especially strong in the case of the magnesium bomb
for the container and incendiary material were one and the same.[11]

[6] CRL Corresp File, Proj A8.5–1, Incendiary, FE (formerly Incendiary Filling for Bombs and
Incendiary, Thermite Type), Nov 32–Jun 38. KCRC.

[7] Rpt of Activities of the Tech Div During World War II, 1 Jan 46, p. 88.

[8] Memo, Chief Plans Div Air Corps for DCofS for Air, 8 Apr 41, sub: Incendiary Aircraft Munitions.

[9] Activities of Tech Div, WWII, pp. 88–90.

[10] WD GO 54, 28 Aug 20.

[11] Notes of Conf in Office of Maj Gen Richard C. Moore, DCofS, 15 Jul 41. TAGO G–4 File 32748.

In September 1941 the CWS received the complete responsibility for the entire incendiary bomb program.[12]

Experiences of the Eighth Air Force

Most new weapons and munitions initially experience difficulty in gaining the confidence of the using arm, and the incendiary bomb proved no exception. Moreover, the early bombs produced by the CWS were far from perfect, an understandable situation when it is realized that most of the work was done in the hurry and bustle after the United States entered World War II. Factors favoring the munition, among which were Germany's success with and Great Britain's respect for aerial incendiaries, did little to lessen the Air Corps' initial apathy, particularly at operational levels.

The British realized the merits of incendiary bombs much sooner than did the United States, for not only had they entered the war earlier but their cities had been targets for bombing raids of the German Luftwaffe. Almost immediately Great Britain established an operational research organization, known as RE/8 (Research and Experiment Station, Section 8), under the Ministry of Home Security. Gathered together there were scientists, statisticians, photo interpreters, and other experts whose duty it was to study the effects of bombing. American personnel, military and civilian, were soon attached to this division whose findings were available to both British and American air commanders.[13]

RE/8 scientists soon found that, in attacks against the industrial cities of Germany, properly employed incendiaries were more efficient

---

[12] As a matter of fact War Department General Order No. 10, 10 September 1941, which provided for this change neglected to transfer the procurement responsibility for "incendiary munitions which are in general consumed in the incendiary process, and substitutes therefor" from Ordnance to the CWS. War Department General Order No. 13, 24 November 1941, corrected this. More on the question of responsibility for incendiaries may be found in Brophy and Fisher, *Organizing for War*, pp. 45–46.

[13] Later, when the utility of RE/8 had been proven, operational research sections were established within the U.S. Army Air Forces. The impetus for this action came in the summer of 1942 when the Joint Chiefs of Staff directed that a study be made of the British experience with operational research activities. General Arnold approved the resultant report and recommended that the commanding generals of the Army Air Forces establish operational research sections within their commands. The Eighth Air Force set up such a section in the VIII Bomber Command in October 1942. (1) Rpt, Lt Bradley Dewey, Jr., to Chief Tech Div CWS, 14 Sep 44. (2) Col John M. Harlan, The Opnl Research Sec at the Eighth AF, 18 Jul 44. Both in CMLHO.

than high explosives.[14] The Royal Air Force in a series of raids against Hamburg in the summer of 1943 went a long way in establishing the validity of this conclusion. Between 24 July and 3 August the RAF, at times supplemented by American bombers, attacked that German city seven times, proving beyond all doubt the destructive power of the incendiary bomb. Almost 1½ million bombs were dropped on Hamburg, the large majority (1 1/3 million) being 4-pound incendiaries.[15] German officials stated that 45,000 people lost their lives, although this number was admittedly inaccurate: "Exact figures could not be obtained out of a layer of human ashes."[16] Of the 122,000 houses standing before the raids, 35,719 were demolished and 4,660 were heavily damaged.[17]

Despite the British success with incendiaries, the Eighth Air Force remained unconvinced of their efficacy. Colonel Kellogg, the first chemical officer of the Eighth Air Force, played an important part in convincing his organization of the usefulness of incendiary bombs. A group of RAF officers who had extensive and successful operational experience with incendiaries vigorously supported his cause. These same RAF officers sparked the organization of an informal American-British discussion group, known as the Zoroastrian Society, which materially aided the Eighth Air Force in defining the nature and characteristics of incendiaries possessing the greatest potential. Meanwhile, both the RAF and the Eighth Air Force carried on an extensive program of munitions trials. As a result of these trials, the U.S. 6-pound incendiary oil bomb, the M69, was rejected and the British 30- and 250-pound incendiaries were accepted as interim weapons pending

[14] Final Rpt on Proj AN–23, Effectiveness of U.S. Incendiary and High-Explosive Bombs, Div 2, NDRC of OSRD, 914 NDRC Rpt A–386 and OSRD Rpt 6445. Air University Lib Maxwell Air Force Base, Ala.

[15] RAF and Eighth AF Statistical Rpt, Bombs Dropped on Hamburg, 24 Jul–3 Aug 43, Incl 1 to Ltr, Armament Officer, U.S. Strategic AF in Europe to Air CmlO AAF, 6 Aug 45, sub: Air Attacks on the City of Hamburg. Tech Lib ACmlC, Md.

[16] Rpt, Hamburg Civil Defense, p. 29., Incl 3 to Ltr cited in n. 15, above.

[17] Rpt of "Fire Storm" Air Raids (Office, Chief of Fire Brigade, Hamburg), pp. 1–3, Incl. 2 to Ltr cited in n. 15, above. (2) The most devastating raid (the night of 27–28 July) produced a fire storm. This phenomenon is born of a great mass of fire combined with little or no surface winds. A huge pillar of heated air and gases rises vertically over the inferno, and cold air rushes in from all sides of the base of the pillar to replace the hot ascending blast. The velocity of these newly created surface winds can tear the clothes from a person's back and uproot trees three feet in diameter. Casualties are great because death comes not only from the flames, but from asphyxiation, the inhalation of the intense heat, and carbon monoxide poisoning. Horatio Bond, "The Fire Attacks German Cities," pp. 84–85, and Anthony J. Mullaney, "German Fire Departments Under Air Attack," p. 100, in *Fire and the Air War* (Boston: National Fire Protection Assn., 1951), edited by Horatio Bond.

the availability of more suitable American bombs and clusters. The most desired U.S. munitions in the early period were the 100-pound cluster of 4-pound magnesium bombs and the 100-pound M47 bomb with an oil and crepe rubber filling. But these desires could not readily be translated into supply since much of the process of development and manufacture had yet to take place in the United States.[18]

The first 100-pound clusters of the M50 bombs arrived in England in 1942. This triumph of adequate supply was short-lived; chemical officers found a great many defective M50's in these early shipments and started a testing program to determine the bad lots. Defective bombs were only part of the problem. The 100-pound incendiary bomb adapter, which clustered the M50's into a convenient package, was operationally unusable because of the danger of released adapter parts striking other planes in the formation or even, in some cases, the tail of the plane that carried it. This was dramatically revealed during the Eighth Air Force's first use of incendiary bombs on 14 May 1943, when falling cluster parts damaged other planes in the formation. Moreover, it was impossible to obtain any degree of accuracy with bombs released from their clusters at such high altitudes. Because of these deficiencies Eighth Air Force suspended the use of the M50 pending receipt of aimable clusters.[19]

Until the adequate clustering device for the M50's appeared, the Eighth Air Force relied to a great degree on the M47. This versatile 100-pound bomb (it actually weighed only sixty-nine pounds) was the sole American aerial incendiary available when the United States entered World War II. In a desperate attempt to provide incendiaries, Colonel Kellogg late in 1942 located a supply of empty M47 bomb casings in Iceland, managed to get them shipped to the United Kingdom, and had 10,000 filled and assembled by air chemical units. At first the M47 contained unthickened gasoline or oil, but later a thickener was added. The outstanding features of the munition were its aimability, penetrability, and its sizable load (forty pounds) of incendiary material. But the M47 also had its problems. While the munition itself was effective, bomb bay suspension arrangements were such that one bomb

---

[18] History, Cml Sec, Eighth AF. (2) Memo, CmlO Eighth AF for CG Eighth AF, 27 Nov 42, sub: Use of Incendiary and HE Bombs. App. G, History, Cml Sec Eighth AF. (3) Interv, Hist Off with Col J. A. Martin, formerly OpnsO Cml Sec Eighth AF, 28 Aug 51. (4) See above, ch. IV, for more logistical details on incendiaries.

[19] (1) History, Cml Sec Eighth AF. (2) History, Cml Warfare Sec 1st Bomb Div. (3) Martin Interv, 28 Aug 51.

occupied a space which could carry a much heavier bomb. By July of 1943 the air chemical sections provided a field expedient to solve this loading difficulty. They paired the bombs by the use of a cable loop-sling. The loop-sling method permitted the suspension of forty-two M47's in a B–17 bomb bay. This was an economical load, and the number of bombs falling together improved the bombing pattern. Furthermore, clustering supplies were readily obtained since the Eighth Air Force prepared slings in the great air repair depot at Burtonwood. Subsequently, Colonel Baum, who succeeded Colonel Kellogg as Eighth Air Force chemical officer in 1943, modified the loop-sling into a short cable toggling device which permitted the suspension of fifty-two bombs in a bomb bay and in effect made an enormous cluster of M47's which was more aimable and made a better bombing pattern.[20]

In the spring of 1943 Eighth Air Force headquarters requested mixed loadings of incendiary and high explosive bombs in a single aircraft on operational missions. The VIII Bomber Command declared this request unfeasible because uneconomical loads would result and because of the danger of mixing the two munitions in the same aircraft. The chemical officers agreed with the bomber command on mixed loadings but renewed their proposals of incendiary loads in view of the new development with respect to the M47. During the summer, Colonel Kellogg persuaded Col. Curtis E. LeMay to authorize M47 incendiary loadings for missions against industrial targets in occupied France. These missions conclusively demonstrated the effectiveness of incendiary bombing in general and the M47 incendiary in particular. Although a lack of fuzes caused the suspension of the employment of M47's for a month during this critical period, the Eighth Air Force was now firmly committed to the use of incendiaries, and the outstanding success of the first major incendiary raid in October, against a factory at Heddernheim, Germany, reinforced that decision. The Eighth Air Force analysis of the Heddernheim mission indicated that the incendiaries were far more effective, weight for weight, than high explosives.[21] For the next three months, the M47 was the favored incendiary, and keeping a supply on hand became a major problem as all

[20] (1) *Ibid.* (2) Ltr, Lt Col Robert N. Isbell, ExecO Cml Sec USSTAF, to Air CmlO AAF WD, 15 Sep 44, sub: Correction to the Rpt of the AAF Bd, Proj (M–5) 261. Eighth AF 519.225.

[21] (1) Ltr, CG Eighth AF to CG VIII Bomb Comd, 10 Mar 43, sub: Use of Incendiary Bombs, and 1st Ind, CG VIII Bomb Comd to CG Eighth AF, n.d. Eighth AF 471.6 in Eighth AF 519.225–4. (2) History, Cml Sec Eighth AF. (3) Martin Interv, 28 Aug 51.

incendiary expenditures mounted from 408.2 tons in September 1943, to 1,292.6 tons in October, 2,382.9 tons in November, and 4,189.6 tons, 40 percent of the total bomb load, in December.[22]

The M17 500-pound cluster for the M50 bomb was first put into operational use in January 1944. This aimable cluster eliminated most of the difficulties inherent in those clusters which were quick opening and made the M50 one of the most effective incendiary bombs of World War II.[23] An M50 (technically the AN–M50A1 and later the AN–M50A2) was a 4-pound bomb based on the plans brought back from England by Colonel Zanetti. Consisting of a core of thermate and a casing of magnesium alloy, the M50 had a high degree of penetrability and an intensive burning action. These qualities made it particularly suitable for use against construction in Germany, 95 percent of which consisted of brick and stone.[24] Because of this construction, fire divisions (that area which will be burned out by an unchecked fire) could be not only buildings but their individual rooms. The M50 had to have great penetrating power in order to pierce the heavy roofs, and the fact that it was small meant that a bomber, in seeking out the numerous fire divisions, could carry many more than if the bomb were larger.

In direct contrast with the M50 was America's largest incendiary bomb, the 500-pound M76, popularly known as the Block Burner. The M76 resulted from an Army Air Forces request for a large, highly aimable incendiary bomb for use against industrial targets. It contained incendiary gel (PT) which, upon the detonation of an explosive charge, was scattered in large gobs over a 100-foot radius. The M76 was used against Berlin on 6 March 1944 with moderate success, enough at least to warrant a request from the Eighth Air Force to the zone of interior for a priority shipment of these heavy incendiaries. Subsequent operations, however, proved that the efficiency of the bomb did not warrant its employment. Because of its size, there were relatively few targets against which it could be used. Moreover, there was a low percentage of incendiary fuel as contrasted with the total weight of the bomb. By September, because no future operational use of the M76

[22] Statistical Summary of Eighth AF Opns, European Theater, 17 Aug 42–8 May 45.

[23] Cml Warfare Sec Eighth AF, Jan 44–Jul 45.

[24] (1) Memo,, C. W. Tyson, 28 Nov 41, sub: Info Gained from Messrs H. F. Allen and H. Austin on Building Construction Abroad. CRL Corres File Proj A8.6–1—Incendiaries, Solid Oil, FY 1942. KCRC. (2) Thermate was a mixture of 80 percent thermite and 20 percent of the Ordnance Department's M8 flare mixture.

LOADING 500-POUND CLUSTERS OF MAGNESIUM BOMBS INTO A B-24 *of the Eighth Air Force, somewhere in England.*

was anticipated, the stations of the Eighth Air Force had returned most of their M76 bombs to Air Forces depots.[25]

All together the Eighth Air Force dropped 97,046 tons of incendiary bombs on German targets compared with 569,751 tons of high explosives and 20,352 tons of fragmentation bombs. The large majority of the incendiaries were M50's, in M17 clusters, and M47's.[26] Taken as a reflection of the role of the incendiary bomb in the Eighth Air Force's campaigns against Germany, this figure is little more than modest. The RAF expended many more aerial incendiaries than did the American air unit. To explain this, the essential difference between the two air forces must be borne in mind. The RAF was devoted to a policy of night, area raids against the cities of Germany. The Eighth Air Force,

[25] Cml Warfare Sec Eighth AF, Jan 44–Jul 45.
[26] Statistical Summary of Eighth AF Opns, European Theater 17 Aug 42–8 May 45.

on the other hand, confident in its bomb sight and in the protection derived from fighter escort and formation flying, pursued a policy of daylight raids against specific industrial targets. Urban areas were more susceptible to incendiary bombs than were the individual plants and factories. And while the Eighth Air Force only gradually realized that incendiaries had a part in industrial bombing, the RAF quickly saw the efficacy of the incendiary against larger area urban targets. The Eighth Air Force's use of aerial incendiaries was effective, but not spectacular, and most of the damage to German cities resulted from RAF operations. This relative lack of success cannot be construed as a criticism of the American air unit, whose mission was different from that of the RAF.

The Incendiary Bombing of Japan

The war in the Pacific was marked by the most spectacular and effective use of the aerial incendiary bomb. After March 1945, General LeMay's all-out incendiary attacks against the vulnerable Japanese cities brought to a culmination the recognition which the incendiary bomb had gradually been winning throughout the war. It was air power which played a very important part in Japan's decision to capitulate, and it was the incendiary bomb which helped to make air power such a decisive force.

The use of aerial incendiaries against Japan varied considerably from that against Germany and German occupied Europe. For one thing, air fields for the bombardment of Japanese cities were not immediately available as in the case of the Eighth Air Force, which had English bases well within range of German cities. It was not until the Mariana Islands, located some 1,500 miles south of Tokyo, had been taken that American bombers found themselves within bombing range of the Japanese capital and the other important cities on the island of Honshu. Up till that time, the targets throughout the island chains on the road back, and even in Japanese-held China, were not particularly appropriate for incendiary bombing missions.

Another great difference between the air war against Japan and that against Germany was the extreme vulnerability of the Japanese cities to fire. Although fire destruction could be and was wrought on many German cities, they were less likely targets for the incendiary bomb than those of Japan. Ninety-five percent of German construction, as noted earlier, was brick and stone, and the roofing material, a very vital consideration in starting fires, usually consisted of tile or slate. In contrast, 80 percent of the construction in Japan made use of wood and paper. There was a nucleus of modern fireproofed buildings in the business areas of most Japanese cities, but, generally speaking, the structures of urban areas were made of very inflammable materials. These areas were so compact, so devoid of fire barriers, that an uncontrolled fire could spread very quickly.

The Twentieth Air Force supervised the incendiary blow against Japan. This unusual organization was activated in Washington on 4 April 1944, with General Henry H. Arnold, Commanding General, AAF, as its commander or "executive agent." The Joint Chiefs of Staff were to make all major decisions about the deployment, missions, and target objectives of the Twentieth Air Force. Its weapon was the very long range bomber, the B–29, and its two principal subordinate units (the actual operating units) were the XX and XXI Bomber Commands.[27]

Oddly, the XX Bomber Command saw the light of day and in fact delivered its first bombs against Japanese targets before the activation of the Twentieth Air Force. The first major contingent of the command left the United States on 5 January 1944 and arrived at New Delhi, India, eight days later. Permanent bases for the XX Bomber Command were in India and the advanced bases were located in the vicinity of Chengtu, in western China. Plagued by logistical difficulties and hindered by the fact that the advanced bases were within range of only the cities of Kyushu, among the Japanese targets, the operations of the command were not particularly effective. In fact, it was soon realized that these missions would be little more than "shakedown" training preparatory to the time that B–29 bases could be constructed in the Mariana Islands.

The summer of 1944 saw the American conquest of the greater part of the Marianas, including the islands of Saipan, Guam, and Tinian. This meant that B–29 bases could be located within range of the important cities of Honshu. Even as the three islands were being mopped up, the XXI Bomber Command began constructing airfields for its

---

[27] Craven and Cate, eds., *The Pacific: Matterhorn to Nagasaki*, pp. 38–39. Unless otherwise noted, the background material concerning the Twentieth Air Force is based on this excellent volume.

five wings. The first strategic mission was flown from Saipan on 24 November 1944.

From November 1944 until the early days of the following March, the XXI Bomber Command used conventional strategic bombing tactics against the cities of Japan. In Europe the Eighth Air Force had developed the concept of precision bombing and to some it seemed to be the solution for the air war against Japan. With a large percentage of the bomb load consisting of high explosives, planes flew high altitude daylight missions against individual industrial targets. For example, on 14 January 1945 B–29's dropped ninety-four tons of HE on the Mitsubishi Aircraft Plant in Nagoya with only fair results. That this industrial target was attacked seven more times in a period of several months is some indication of the comparative ineffectiveness of these raids.[28] European experience was being translated to Pacific use, and not too successfully.

Precision bombing was *not* the solution for Japanese targets. The physical construction of Japan's industrial and urban areas was much more combustible than that of Germany. Japanese cities frequently experienced peacetime conflagrations; German cities did not. Industry and labor in Japan were far more concentrated than in Germany. Moreover, area incendiary attacks against Japan would give its "household" industries, upon whose products the larger plants depended, a tremendous setback.[29]

In December 1944 General Arnold's headquarters, aware of the vulnerability to fire of Japanese cities, requested that the XXI Bomber Command mount a full-scale incendiary attack against Nagoya. Brig. Gen. Haywood S. Hansell, commanding general of the air unit and a firm believer in daylight, precision bombing, protested but nevertheless ordered incendiary missions against that city, the first being directed against the Mitsubishi Aircraft Engine Works. Encountering bad weather, the force of forty-eight planes bombed the target using radar and inflicted little damage. Early in January 1945, fifty-seven B–29's, with an incendiary-fragmentation bomb load, struck urban Nagoya, but smoke from the fires made observation and hence evaluation of the results impossible. For the Japanese, probably the most unfortunate

---

[28] Col Theodore P. Gahan, The Status of Incendiaries in the Army Air Forces (Thesis prepared at the Air Command and Staff School, Air University, Maxwell Field, Ala.), May 1947, pp. 6–7.

[29] "Fire Blitz," *Impact* (August, 1945), p. 14.

effect of this rather mediocre mission was the development of an overly optimistic opinion of their inefficient fire-fighting system.[30]

General LeMay replaced General Hansell on 20 January 1945. At first this move brought little change in the tactics and results of the missions of the XXI Bomber Command. Some success resulted from the high altitude precision bombardment of particular Japanese industries, but this success fell far below the expectations almost everyone had for the VLR bomber, the B–29. In an effort to achieve better results, General LeMay made radical changes in his bombing techniques. First, he planned to send his planes not against individual plants and factories, but against Japan's combustible cities, filled with home industries as well as with various military installations. Although this plan was itself a departure from the established routine, the courage LeMay needed in making his decision came not from changing targets but from his faith in new methods by which the targets would be attacked. The innovations in tactics all were based on the idea of dropping the most damaging payload on the crowded, inflammable enemy cities.

The planes were to attack at altitudes of from 6,000 to 7,000 feet instead of the usual 20,000 and 30,000, a change partly prompted by the weather encountered over the island of Honshu. At the higher altitude strong winds buffeted the aircraft causing not only an unduly large consumption of gasoline but inflicting punishment on men and planes as well. Moreover, cloud formations over Honshu prevented the visual bombardment of targets on all but a very few occasions. In another change, the planes were to make individual runs against the target instead of attacking in formation. Formation flying was the established practice of the Eighth Air Force, and it provided an all-around defense against attacks by enemy fighter planes. But it also involved rendezvous points for the planes and hence a greater consumption of gasoline. In still another innovation. LeMay ordered the B–29's to attack under the cover of darkness, a tactic expected to achieve surprise and take advantage of the enemy's weak defensive weapons, night fighters and radar gun-laying devices. Finally, the aircraft were to be stripped of all armament. The savings in weight resulting from the absence of armament and the lesser demands for gasoline meant that a

[30] Craven and Cate, eds., *The Pacific: Matterhorn to Nagasaki,* pp. 563-65.

greater amount of payload could be carried. And this payload was to consist exclusively of incendiary bombs.[31]

The XXI Bomber Command first used these tactics on its historic mission No. 40 flown against Tokyo on the night of 9–10 March 1945. The planes carried two types of incendiary bombs, the M47A2 and the M69.[32] The Pathfinder units, one squadron of each of the three participating wings, carried the M47's which served not only as aiming points but which also started appliance fires—those fires large enough to be controlled only by special fire-fighting apparatus. The M69's used by the rest of the force started a multitude of small fires that soon joined to form large ones.[33] The M47 had been used extensively in Europe, but the M69, because of its poor penetrating power, had proved unsuitable for German targets. This very characteristic made it particularly appropriate for use against the flimsy construction of Japanese buildings.

The ingenious M69, unlike most other American incendiaries, was not based on a European prototype but was strictly an American development. The over-all weight of this hexagonal shaped, light-cased munition was six pounds; its incendiary filling, napalm, weighed three pounds. The bomb, having a terminal velocity of 225 feet per second, was stabilized in flight by cloth streamers rather than by fins. A delay fuze, activated by the impact, ignited an ejection charge which expelled the incendiary material through the tail of the bomb. Thus when the bomb came to rest it functioned like a small mortar; when flat on the floor it could eject flaming napalm as far as 100 feet until it struck an object in its path.[34]

The first B–29's left Guam at 1735 on 9 March, and by 2020 the entire attacking force was airborne. Although the planes encountered some bad weather on the way to Tokyo, they identified the coast initial point and target without difficulty. The first bombs landed on Tokyo at 0015 on the following morning. It took but thirty minutes for the

[31] (1) "The B–29ers," *Impact* (September–October 1945), pp. 78–79. (2) Twentieth AF, Special Rpt on the Incendiary Attacks Against Japanese Urban Industrial Areas (hereafter cited as Twentieth AF Special Rpt on Incendiary Attacks) n.d., pp. 5–6.

[32] The M47 bombs were toggled together, six to a 500-pound bomb station by the T19 cluster adapter, developed by the Chemical Section of the XXI Bomber Command. Twentieth AF Special Rpt on Incendiary Attacks, p. 6.

[33] (1) Twentieth AF Special Rpt on Incendiary Attacks, p. 6. (2) USSBS, Effects of Incendiary Bomb Attacks on Japan, Apr 47, p. 117.

[34] NDRC (Div 11), 3 Oct 45, Comparative Effectiveness of Small Incendiary Bombs on Industrial Targets, pp. 9–10.

TOKYO, AFTER THE INCENDIARY BOMBING OF 9–10 MARCH, 1945

development of fires of conflagration size, and by that time the situation was so far out of hand that efforts to combat the flames were fruitless. The multitude of bombs (1,665 tons were dropped on Tokyo), the combustible nature of the structures, and the high winds all contributed to the creation of the inferno.

Some people were able to escape through the wide fire lanes, but many others were encircled by the flames and died of suffocation and burns. Those who fled to the canals faced death in the scalding water or were crushed by the terrified mob which crowded in on top of them. This raid alone caused the death of an estimated 83,793 people and almost 41,000 more received injuries. Over one million people lost their homes.

The fire destroyed 15.8 square miles in the center of Tokyo. All buildings in the area were entirely destroyed or seriously damaged. Although some of the modern, fire-resistant structures were not totally destroyed, the majority of even this type was left as sagging skeletons. Glass, steel bars, and concrete melted in the intense heat; wooden buildings went up in flames before the fire front had reached them. Such was the havoc wrought by the first of the "blitz" raids against the cities of Japan.

The results achieved by the XXI Bomber Command left no doubt as to the validity of the revolutionary tactics of General LeMay. Tokyo had been surprised by both the low altitude and the magnitude of the attack. The command suffered but moderate losses; 14 of the 279 planes over Tokyo failed to return. These losses came not from enemy fighter opposition, which failed to damage a single B–29, but from flak. The combination of bombs used was excellent.

Following the Tokyo raid at about 2-day intervals, Nagoya, Osaka, Kobe, and again Nagoya received the terrible punishment of incendiary bombing. Throughout the rest of the Pacific war a total of sixty-nine Japanese cities were subjected to these "blitz" attacks.[35]

The Fire Bomb: The Tactical Weapon

Incendiary munitions were useful in tactical air missions—those flown in the combat zone for the purpose of influencing the local tactical situation. Enemy strongholds, motorized vehicles, troop concentrations, and military stores were targets particularly vulnerable to fire. Sometimes tactical aircraft used M47 and M50 bombs against these targets, and occasionally they dropped an M76, but another type of incendiary munition, the fire bomb (often called the napalm or blaze bomb), proved most effective against tactical targets.

Employment in Europe

A fire bomb was simply a large capacity container filled in the field with napalm gel.[36] It began as a field improvisation. Fighter planes carried jettisonable fuel tanks for long missions, and it became customary for the pilots, on the trip homeward, to drop these tanks on targets

---

[35] (1) Twentieth AF Special Rpt on Incendiary Attacks, pp. 6–9. (2) USSBS, Effects of Incendiary Bomb Attacks on Japan, pp. 94, 97, 102. (3) USSBS, Final Rpt Covering Air-Raid Protection and Allied Subjects in Japan, Feb 47, p. 70 (4) "B-29ers" and "The Z-29 Payoff," *Impact* (September–October, 1945), pp. 78, 79, 85.

[36] Fire bombs were of a variety of sizes, depending upon the kind of containers on hand. The bombs which saw the most use were of 165-, 75-, 100-, 108-, and 110-gallon capacity.

ATTACHING AN EMPTY 108-GALLON FIRE BOMB TANK TO THE FUSELAGE *of a P-47.*

of opportunity, igniting the gasoline with tracer ammunition. It was only a small step to provide these tanks with igniters more convenient and reliable than tracer ammunition. The CWS devised an igniter from an all-ways fuze and a shortened section of a 2-pound magnesium bomb which was clamped on the side of the gasoline tank. It was soon realized that thickened fuel would provide a more satisfactory fire than ordinary gasoline, so air and chemical officers in Europe began thickening gasoline in spare tanks with oil, or rosin oil and lime, or when they were available, with the approved thickeners, British perspex and American napalm. Because the thickened fuel required a better igniter, chemical officers adapted the white phosphorus grenade for the purpose. One of the most favorable features of the bomb was the ease with which it could be constructed from materials which were relatively abundant, since the spare tanks, often made of process paper, were stocked in quantity. The ratio of filling to the over-all weight of the munition was high. The extreme accuracy with which the fire bomb could be placed on small targets was another major advantage, although this precision was possible only when the bombs were released from a low altitude, something pilots under heavy antiaircraft attack could not always do.[37] An example of the effectiveness of the fire bomb against point targets took place on 25 August 1964 when sixteen fighter planes, carrying twenty-four 165-gallon napalm bombs and eight 500-pound HE bombs, attacked the headquarters of Generalfeldmarschall Guenther von Kluge, German Army Group commander, at Verzy, France. Twenty-two of the napalm tanks made direct hits on the buildings comprising the headquarters; eight houses were completely destroyed.[38]

Although men were more vulnerable than material to the fire bomb, motorized vehicles, marshaling yards, warehouses, and other combustible buildings made excellent napalm bomb targets. Fighter planes carrying this munition flew frequent missions against the Germans while the latter were attempting to escape encirclement at Falaise. During this period twelve P–38 fighters, each carrying two 165-gallon fire bombs, attacked a concentration of enemy trucks and armor, destroying or damaging an estimated thirty or forty vehicles. At the time of the Ardennes counteroffensive American planes used fire bombs effectively against German motor transportation and armored concentrations in the wooded sections of the area. When fighter planes dropped seventy-two fire bombs on the marshaling yards at St. Quentin, France, 400 of the 500 railway cars in the yards were destroyed.[39]

The munition was sometimes used in conjunction with artillery or high explosive bombs in attacks against fortified towns or strongpoints consisting of open emplacements and earth and log fortifications. In one approved sequence, these positions first were subjected to artillery fire or high explosive bombing. Then planes dropped fire bombs on the rubble forcing the enemy into the open. Just before the infantry assault, the artillery placed its fire on the exposed enemy troops.[40] The fire bomb, however, had little or no effect against heavy fortifications such as the pillboxes of the Siegfried Line. And, reports to the contrary,

[37] (1) Broughton Weekly News Letter No. 26A, 7 Dec 44, and No. 40A, 12 Apr 45. (2) Msg MF 01268, CG USSTAF to CG Eighth AF, 11 Oct 44. Eighth AF 519.225.1. (2) Craven and Cate, eds., *Europe: TORCH to POINTBLANK*, pp. 654–55.
[38] (1) Cml Warfare Munitions Used by Ninth Air Force, Incl 3, CWS TofO Ltr No. 26, 30 Jun 45. (2) Fire Bomb Opns, Incl 5, CWS TofO Ltr No. 19, 3 Nov 44.
[39] (1) Cml Warfare Munitions Used by Ninth Air Force, Incl 3, CWS TofC Ltr No. 26, 30 Jun 45. (2) Ninth AF, Use and Effectiveness of Napalm Fire Bombs, 9 Feb 45, Incl 4, CWS TofO Ltr No. 23, 3 Apr 44. (3) Broughton Weekly News Ltr No. 26A, 7 Dec 44.
[40] (1) Ninth AF, Use and Effectiveness of Napalm Fire Bombs, 9 Feb 45, Incl 4, CWS TofO Ltr No. 23, 3 Apr 44. (2) CWS TofO Ltr No. 28, 31 Aug 45, p. 20.

the Operational Research Section of the IX Bomber Command found that the fire bomb was not instrumental in the surrender of the fortress of St. Malo on the French coast.[41]

Use in the Pacific

In the war against Japan, the fire bomb saw use from the mainland of Asia to the many small islands of the Pacific. As in Europe, the munition gave best results when used to produce casualties. Some observers in the Pacific went as far as to say that matériel destruction should be but a secondary mission for the fire bomb and then only if the target were highly combustible. Apart from its casualty potential the fire bomb had definite psychological effect on enemy troops; ground commanders agreed that enemy morale suffered an obvious decrease after a fire bomb attack. The Japanese on Tinian, after experiencing several fire bomb attacks, broke from their positions upon the approach of fighter planes with belly tanks and ran in a direction that was at right angles to the flight of the planes. But whether used against troops or other targets, fire bombs to be effective had to be dropped in adequate numbers. Prisoners of war stated that widely dispersed fire bomb hits had little or no effect on the morale of a unit.[42]

When used against emplacements the fire bomb performed the additional service of burning off the dense foliage and camouflage which so often surrounded Japanese positions. The Commanding General, 81st Infantry Division, stated, "Napalm bombing serves as an excellent means of uncovering hostile strong points in jungle and cave warfare. Unless the enemy is prepared to meet it by special provisions in his caves, this fire will drive him into the open where he can be reached with HE shells."[43]

Used in collaboration with regular incendiary and HE bombs, the napalm bomb burned cities and towns in Burma and China whose wooden buildings housed supplies for Japanese operations. For example, the Fourteenth Air Force struck Paoching with M50 and M69 incendiary bombs and demolition and napalm bombs. In this particular

[41] (1) Broughton Weekly News Ltr No. 26A, 7 Dec 44; No. 15, 16 Sep 44. (2) Craven and Cate state that although the fire bomb strike at St. Malo was "spectacular, and much photographed," the napalm "though burning out one surface shelter, produced little effect on the garrison." Craven and Cate, eds., Europe: ARGUMENT to V–E Day, p. 262.

[42] Fire Bomb Opns, Incl 5, CWS TofO Ltr No. 19, 3 Nov 44.

[43] Quoted in Use of Napalm (Fire) Bombs in the Palaus Opn, Incl 5, CWS TofO Ltr No. 23, 3 Apr 45.

case the results (the destruction of 20 percent of the city) were substandard because of the mud and brick walls of the buildings and because many of the bombs fell on previously burned areas. In Burma, fire bombs alone received credit for the evacuation of one Japanese-held city.[44]

During the Luzon campaign American air units dropped on the enemy a total of 1,054,200 gallons of napalm-thickened gasoline, of which an estimated 989,000 gallons were effectively placed on targets. The failures were the result of defective igniters and of faulty release mechanisms. While on certain missions there may have been an unusually high percentage of duds (these, likely as not, were ignited by strafing), in the over-all picture the fire bomb performed efficiently.[45]

The most effective use of the fire bomb took place during the fight for Ipo Dam, north of the city of Manila.[46] After the fall of the Philippine capital the Japanese forces withdrew to this area and augmented the natural defensive features of the terrain with a network of trenches and fortified caves. The low supply of water in Manila made the recapture of the dam imperative, and fighter-bombers of the Fifth Air Force supported troops of XI Corps as they attacked to take this important facility. During the initial stage of the operation (3–5 May 1945), 238 planes dropped demolition and fire bombs on the outlying defenses of the dam with good results. The final all-out effort to seize the dam took place on 17 May. On the day before, fighter planes again struck the Ipo defenses, this time with 50,000 gallons of napalm. On the day of the attack 240 fighter-bombers dropped 62,500 gallons of napalm. A Fifth Air Force report described the technique:

Five enemy strong points were selected as target areas, each one consisting of about 3,000,000 square yards. Obviously, in a target of this size, the term saturation bombing is used in a tactical rather than physical sense, meaning that sufficient bomb coverage was provided to negate enemy opposition. To administer the blanket of fire treat-

---

[44] (1) Incendiary and Fire Bomb Attack on Paoching, China, CWS TofO Ltr No. 26, 30 Jan 45, p. 11. (2) CWS Munitions Used Operationally by First Tactical Air Force, CWS TofO Ltr No. 25, 30 May 45, p. 17.

[45] (1) Rpt, CmlO Sixth Army, Luzon Campaign (9 Jan–1 Jul 45), pp. 15–16. (2) An. to Cml Opns and Tech Per Rpt 8, CmlO I Corps, 21 Jun 45, sub: Rpt of Napalm Bombings. (3) An. I to Cml Opns and Tech Per Rpt No. 7, CmlO I Corps, 13 Jun 45, sub: Rpt on Napalm Bombings. All in CMLHO.

[46] (1) Craven and Cate, eds., *The Pacific: Matterhorn to Nagasaki*, p. 436. (2) Smith, *Triumph in the Philippines*, ch. XXI.

ment, 200 to 250 5th AF fighters came in low, wave after wave, four to eight abreast, with air and ground controllers giving target information and regulating traffic. At first, the closely spaced fighters found that smoke from preceding waves obscured the target. The problem was overcome by directing the bombing runs downwind, with each successive wave dropping its bombs on the near side of the bursts from the wave which preceded it. The fighter bombers followed each other at 10- to 15-second intervals. A-20's then came in, showering the area with parafrags and winding up with a thorough strafing.[47]

Positions in the area which had withstood infantry attacks for almost a week, were taken after only feeble resistance and minimum casualties. Whether these results were entirely due to the use of napalm is not certain. One chemical officer, for example, viewing one of the attacks from the air, concluded that its effect was little more than harassing. But most observers were inclined to place greater emphasis on the effectiveness of the fire bomb, and General Krueger, Sixth Army commander, went so far as to say that these attacks "made possible the early capture of the vital Ipo Dam." [48]

All together during World War II the American Army Air Force dropped about 37,000 CWS fire bombs (14,000 tons) on German and Japanese targets. Two-thirds of the bombs and an even higher percentage of the tonnage were used in the Pacific war. No matter where the fire bombs were used reaction to their method of employment seemed to be the same. To insure the best results they had to be dropped in adequate numbers and from altitudes ranging from 50 to 100 feet; the efficiency of a napalm strike was increased when co-ordinated with HE bombs, artillery fire, or strafing; the most effective targets for the munition were enemy strongholds and troop concentrations, extremely inflammable material, and motorized vehicles.[49]

[47] Quoted in "Napalm—Fire Bombs Turn Trick Against Holed-Up Nips in Luzon," *Impact* (August, 1945), pp. 48–53.

[48] (1) *Ibid.* (2) Memo, CmlO, I Corps for CofS I Corps, 18 May 45, no sub. Sixth Army File, 471.6. (3) After the war, General Yamashito, Japanese commander on Luzon, stated that napalm had little effect against the rain-soaked terrain of the island. Quoted in Craven and Cate, eds., *The Pacific: From Matterhorn to Nagasaki*, p. 443.

[49] (1) CWS Munitions Used Operationally by First Tactical Air Force, CWS TofO Ltr No. 25, 30 May 45, p. 18. (2) Ninth AF, Use and Effectiveness of Napalm Fire Bomb, 3 Apr 45, Incl 4, CWS TofO Ltr 23. (3) Broughton Weekly News Ltr No. 40A, 12 Apr 45.

CHAPTER XVIII

CWS Overseas—An Evaluation

The CWS had much to learn in World War II. The service entered the war as the custodian of one of the most awesome weapons to come out of World War I. Even while experiencing the diplomatic, political, and military antipathy to gas that was manifest during the years between the wars, many CWS officers, military analysts, and strategists (and many pacifists) believed that gas and air power would rule the next global conflict. When war broke out in Europe gas was not used in spite of the fact that England must have presented a tempting target. This state of affairs affected the CWS in the United States in two ways: the service had to adjust to the idea of preparing for a gas war which might never be fought and for a nongas war which involved missions hitherto either secondary or nonexistent.

The problems of a nongas war, such as was fought in World War II, centered about use of smoke, flame, and incendiaries, natural appendages to the mission of a technical service which dealt largely with the products of the science of chemistry.

The CWS did in fact prepare for both kinds of war. Its staff officers and combat and service units performed usefully, even while fulfilling their insurance roles. To do this, to achieve the goal of effective participation in the war effort, involved ingenuity, resourcefulness, and adaptability of the highest order.

Attendant upon both of these differing objectives was the matter of meeting demands for a rapid expansion, for the activation of new organizations and units, and for the mass production and distribution of new weapons and materials. The CWS, like other elements of the Armed Forces, received resources of men and money undreamed of in the difficult years through which it had just passed. In 1940 the CWS had an active strength of 93 officers and 1,035 enlisted men; in 1943 these figures were 8,103 and 61,688. Within the space of these three years the civilian rolls increased twentyfold. Appropriations for 1940 were just over two million dollars; two years later they exceeded one billion. This transition from famine to feast was not an easy one to make. The development and efficient management of programs to provide for the greatly expanded mission of the CWS involved many problems, not the least of which, according to General Porter, was the effective use of all the money allotted to the service. It was necessary to balance funds against priority schedules and limited allocations of men, materials, storage space, and transportation.

The CWS branches established by the Army in each of the overseas areas of war operations also dealt with problems of priorities and allocations. But the CWS overseas, perhaps even more than the CWS at home, felt the full impact of preparing for a kind of war which was not being fought while contributing significantly to the war which was being fought.

Administration and Manpower

Among other things the CWS in World War II had to learn about the character, structure, and channels of overseas organizations. In spite of between-the-wars planning and training, the CWS on the eve of conflict was essentially as unprepared to form its overseas branches as it was for waging gas warfare. Part of this difficulty was the lack of manpower—there were not enough senior officers even to form the nuclei of several theater of operations staff sections. So it was that Colonel Copthorne went to SWPA without the support of even one other Regular officer. Only two other Regulars supported Colonel Unmacht in the Hawaiian Department. The European theater was deprived of all but three of its senior CWS officers to make their experience available for the North African forces. While nearly all of the leading CWS officers in the United States and overseas—Porter, Waitt, Rowan, Copthorne, and Shadle—highly praised the energy, resourcefulness, and intelligence of Reserve and temporary officers, most of these emergency officers, during the critical phase of the formulation of overseas organizations, were inexperienced and they lacked a knowledge of current policies and plans. It is a tribute to the Reserve and temporary officers that they learned so quickly and performed so well.

A part of CWS unpreparedness to establish overseas branches stemmed from the changes imposed upon the Army by global warfare. It became impossible to have the direct communication with the

OCCWS which many officers had expected. It became necessary to deal with the Allies, to act within the framework of international policy. Although acting within this framework, most overseas chemical officers, with the notable exception of Shadle, found themselves set apart from the Allied agencies, operating even below the joint Army-Navy-Army Air Forces level, at the level of the Army supply services. Even in Shadle's case, his presence in an Allied headquarters isolated him to some extent from the field agencies and to a greater extent from the War Department. Furthermore, there was the necessary but nevertheless restrictive requirement for OCCWS to deal formally with its overseas branches through ASF and OPD.

The lack of administrative preparedness was also due in part to the fact that the CWS did not "fit" into the organizational patterns of World War II. The service was in the anomalous position of being both a supply and technical service; an organization which furnished staff advice, conceivably even in tactical and strategic fields; a service legally responsible for firing-line units; and a service equipped to do research in the field. Most of the other technical services had a similar range of responsibilities, but none was spread so thin, none had combat units primarily equipped with their own weapons; moreover, all other services had supply and service support as a primary mission. World War II organizational doctrine tended to categorize activities into those of "service" or those of "combat." The CWS overseas never succeeded in persuading some field commanders that its activities and units, even front-line smoke generator units, were not in the supply and service category.

In the face of such determined categorization, most CWS overseas branches worked outside or on the fringes of the official organization. The CWS in each area or theater became highly individualistic. In the European theater Rowan used his personal persuasion with command and staff elements and his close personal ties with other CWS officers to maintain a unity of service and accomplish his mission. He and his subordinates, insofar as they were able, operated their own administrative system, their own intelligence activity, their own technical and liaison organization, and their own supply service. Such independence was possible only because the European theater and theater Communications Zone headquarters permitted and even encouraged it. The

ASF inspectors did not approve of this independence, but without it the CWS ETO could not have accomplished its missions.

The CWS administrative effort overseas most nearly like that in the European theater was in the Central Pacific Area. There Colonel Unmacht vigorously asserted CWS independence with the active concurrence and support of first the senior Army headquarters and later the combined and joint Pacific Ocean Areas headquarters. Unmacht was the only overseas chief chemical officer who also commanded CWS troops other than the theater or area laboratory company. Unmacht was also the only overseas chief chemical officer who was specifically designated to co-ordinate and compile a joint Army, Army Air Forces, and Navy gas warfare plan although Rowan, as Porter's representative, and Copthorne, on temporary duty in GHQ SWPA, participated in both combined and joint planning while Shadle, as a staff officer in a combined headquarters, had advisory functions in the joint and combined field. Unmacht and his subordinates certainly maintained a very close connection between research and development and the firing line even to the extent of carrying on research, development, and manufacture in the theater of operations.

Colonel Copthorne in SWPA likewise saw that new developments reached combat chemical officers, but he did so in a different manner from that of either Rowan or Unmacht. Copthorne and his CWS colleagues had far fewer resources than did the CWS branches in Europe or the Central Pacific; they did not have as close a relationship with the combined and joint headquarters; and they had to contend with the considerable problems of enormous distances and a tropical environment. Copthorne could not, therefore, unify his service and assert its independence in the same way that Rowan and Unmacht did, but he could co-ordinate his services by providing the mechanisms for understanding and common effort among field and rear area chemical officers. These mechanisms were area and even theaterwide conferences, the creation of a centralized area training facility, the provision of centralized technical intelligence activities, and a continued emphasis on the problems of chemical warfare in the tropics. Copthorne and the field chemical officers in SWPA operated in greater isolation from the CWS in the United States and even from their colleagues in their own area than did other chemical officers overseas. Their solutions to problems, except for the determination of tropical gas warfare doctrine in which they co-operated with the CWS in the United States, were ordinarily their own. Consequently, field army, corps, and division chemical officers in SWPA acted as independently as did their colleagues anywhere else in the world, and, with one exception, they operated through a wider range of chemical responsibilities. This is not to say that they did more and better work than their colleagues elsewhere, but that they did have a more varied experience in the chemical field.

The only elements having just as great a variety of chemical experience were to be found in the field armies in North Africa, Sicily, and Italy. Since Shadle preferred to emphasize his own staff role and to give field elements their head, Colonels Barker and Guild in Fifth Army and Colonel Humphreville in Seventh Army found themselves, again by their own preference, operating a CWS of their own. Barker and Coblentz, in a unique partnership, carried on development and manufacture and operated their own supply system. As a result, there was less co-ordination and unity in the CWS in the North African and Mediterranean theater than elsewhere in the world, but again the required job was done. The much lesser threat of gas warfare in the Mediterranean area made it particularly appropriate to accomplish the CWS administrative task differently there.

In summary of the worldwide CWS administrative experience, it can be said that every overseas branch of the CWS surveyed found some means of creating a service that accorded with the concepts held by Fries and Porter. The lot of the chemical technician in what was supposed to be a technician's war was not an easy one, but the chemical technician managed to do what he was called on to do by dint of much improvisation and ingenuity.

Logistics

In logistics, as in administration, the CWS branches overseas dealt with the two problems of gas warfare supply and nongas warfare supply. Also as in administration, each CWS overseas branch created its own supply system according to geographical environment and according to the kind of combat forces to be supported in its area. In the European theater, where the build-up of forces and materials went on for nearly two years before the attack, there was time to develop for chemical supply a system of centralized CWS control over a decentralized operation.

The sophisticated CWS ETO credit system of distribution, while by no means original with the CWS, was admirably suited to a small service handling only a small number of fast-moving items. Since a combat commander using this system could ask for materials credited to his organization when and where convenient, the system gave the combat commander control over the forward movement of supplies. The big stumbling block was in having supplies ready for call. The CWS ETO distribution system, through no basic fault of the system itself, tended to break down when supplies were unavailable or when depots and dumps could not be organized and stocked as desired. When strains were put on the system, General Rowan and all of his subordinates, often acting informally, jumped in to make the system function by obtaining and moving supplies. Aided by such application of energy at all levels, the CWS ETO supply system for the most part did manage to carry on. Supply failures or near failures arose in connection with mortar shells, incendiary bombs, and spare parts, but in each case the trouble was that materials were unavailable in the United States. And in each case of failure or near failure the CWS ETO was able to make adjustments which at least eased matters.

CWS ETO supply problems were slightly easier to handle because that theater had the most men and facilities. Distances were shorter and transportation, while nearly always in critical demand, was more plentiful than elsewhere in the world. North Africa was quite another story in this respect. Distances were great and existing road and rail nets were few and poor. These natural drawbacks, the inexperience of the Army in global supply at this early stage, and enemy submarine and air warfare helped shape the CWS NATOUSA supply system. The independence and isolation of CWS elements in the theater also had an effect. Base sections and combat organization chemical officers created their own supply system which eventually became the "impetus from the front" system. What materials Colonels Barker and Coblentz could not get from the theater SOS or from the United States, they manufactured or reclaimed. When necessary the combat organization chemical officers reinforced their requests for materials through command channels. General Shadle meanwhile handled the "impetus from the rear" supply system and did his part in fighting the battles of overages and shortages. Both CWS NATOUSA–MTOUSA supply systems worked, but only because the chemical officers made them work against considerable odds.

CWS SWPA officers were able to make their supply system work in the face of even greater odds. Enormous distances, chronic shortages of transportation and communications facilities, and the almost un-believable deterioration of materials in the tropical environment plagued them from the time combat began. For at least the first half of the war they could rely on the economy of neither the United States nor Australia to furnish enough materials in usable condition. They were hampered by low priorities and force-level allocations which did not permit building up area reserves. Again, improvisation and ingenuity provided the answers. Again, items were built, reclaimed, and rebuilt through area efforts. In SWPA the area SOS and even GHQ stepped in to provide procedures for forward organization and trans-portation. Eventually, as more ships and more equipment became avail-able all over the globe, the United States provided ships block-loaded for balanced resupply of combat forces. Area supply problems, while still difficult, became a simple matter of computing necessary block loads, of receiving, handling, and maintaining the materials in these loads.

The War Department policy restricting the build-up of area reserves threatened to become a CWS problem in POA just as in SWPA, but shortages did not become critical because anticipated demands were larger than actual demands and because Hawaiian Department resources were large enough to allow for improvisations and substitutions. In POA combat supply, transport space allocation and loading were care-fully controlled by the area joint headquarters. The POA CWS soon learned to work within the joint system, and the result, admittedly under relatively ideal circumstances, was the smoothest CWS supply operation of World War II.

Excepting the supply of toxics, which was a preparedness matter, the CWS managed to accomplish its major logistics mission. The overseas branches displayed enough ingenuity to prevent any of the supply shortages, except for spare parts, from becoming more than temporarily critical. Yet, there is little doubt that more supplies would have been used had the CWS been able to furnish them sooner and in greater quantities. For example, no area anywhere in the world was ever pro-vided with enough chemical mortar shells. More mortars could have been employed in most cases. Demands for white phosphorus grenades were frequently not met, and probably many more power-driven decontaminating apparatus could have been used for carrying water, providing showers, and the like. POA experience indicates that a flame-throwing tank could have been extensively employed if it had been possible to provide an adequate model at an early date.

Many more CWS service units could also have been employed. The CWS overseas could have used more maintenance units in the field, and experience demonstrates that chemical laboratories could easily have become general-purpose overseas research and development agencies. More decontaminating units could have been used in general services work, and more processing companies could have been doing laundry and dry cleaning.

The use of CWS units and materials in secondary missions raised the question of whether it was indeed a CWS function to furnish equipment and units for these missions and whether it would have been practical and reasonable to provide them had they been available. World War II experience does not give definite answers to these questions or to the corollary and perhaps overriding question of whether the CWS should have had any logistics functions overseas. All the other technical services were larger and all had established logistics procedures. The Quartermaster Corps handled impregnated clothing and protective covers: why should it not handle all protective items? Quartemaster provided bath and laundry units: why should it not provide all such services? Ordnance stored and issued vast quantities of ammunition including, in some areas, chemical toxics: why should that service not handle all ammunition items? The Corps of Engineers provided and employed heavy equipment, like the chemical decontaminating apparatus and commercial gases: why should it not provide all such equipment and the attendant services?

The tentative answer, based on World War II experience is, as Fries found in World War I, that these services were already overburdened with their responsibilities and were unable or unwilling to handle the detailed problems connected with chemical supply and service. The antigas impregnation of clothing is a highly technical and even hazardous process. The Quartermaster Corps in all areas was willing to work out a co-operative arrangement with the CWS for handling protective clothing, but it was unwilling to undertake the impregnating task. Since the CWS had the impregnating units, it would have been grossly wasteful not to use them, in the absence of gas warfare, to help Quartermaster with its laundry and dry cleaning. It would likewise have been wasteful not to use the decontaminating units and apparatus, which the other services would have been hard pressed to employ in event of gas warfare, in any way possible to improve the comfort or well-being of troops in the field. Ammunition supply was a thorny problem which at least some CWS officers felt should have been handled by Ordnance, particularly since the CWS frequently found gas warfare preparedness and planning a full time mission, and some chemical officers did persuade their Ordnance colleagues to handle it. In most cases, however, Ordnance had enough to do in supplying the artillery and the infantry without also handling a relatively few grenades and smoke and mortar shells. The chemical items also posed technical problems. Potentially explosive smoke pots could not be safely stored with other ordnance items, and leaking toxic munitions required expert attention. In the European theater, in SWPA, and in the Mediterranean area, these technical problems led Ordnance to turn over much of its toxic storage responsibility to CWS. In POA the toxic storage mission was officially transferred to CWS. In sum, the answer to the question of functions and responsibilities seemed to be that, since the CWS had to be overseas to guide preparations for gas warfare, there was no reason why it should not perform related secondary tasks, particularly when training and equipment permitted CWS units to accomplish certain of these tasks more expeditiously than units of its sister services.

The Weapons

The development of the large area smoke mission during World War II can be traced with greater precision than can that of most munitions. The need for concealment of extensive targets in rear areas arose in World War I with the introduction of bomber aircraft. In the period between the wars Chemical Warfare Service attempts to develop a way to conceal vulnerable rear area targets were made meaningful by the growing increase in the range of airplanes and by the development of the air arm of the Navy. But the CWS was generally unsuccessful in these attempts—means were not on hand for the production of smoke in needed amounts. And covering a target with too little smoke did nothing more, of course, than attract an enemy bombardier's attention.

Early in 1942 the CWS produced smoke apparatus which met the necessary requirements, the M1 mechanical generator which created an artificial fog not by combustion but by the condensation of water and oil. Its principal drawback was its 3,000-pound weight and its awkward size. The small, compact M2 model, which appeared in 1944, overcame both of these handicaps.

Smoke generator companies first saw overseas action in Northwest Africa, providing screens for the ports through which flowed the men and material for the fight against Rommel's and other German forces. In this capacity, there still prevailed the basic mission of the large area screen—concealment of rear area targets from observation. The smoke installation at Naples, the largest of the war, also concealed a vital harbor from the bombers of the Luftwaffe. But at about this point in the conflict the smoke units were given a new mission, which, by the end of the war, was to assume paramount importance. There were two reasons for this change in emphasis. As the war progressed the Allies gradually won control of the air, a circumstance which diminished the need for rear area concealment. At the same time American troops were fighting up the boot of Italy, always, it seemed, in the face of superior German observation. As a consequence, smoke units freed from rear area duty were shifted to the forward zones.

An effective employment of this kind of smoke screen in Italy was somewhat hampered by bulk and weight of the M1 generator. Smoke troops in France and Germany were spared this difficulty for they had the compact M2 generator in time to use it in support of the crossings of the many rivers which lay between the Americans and eventual victory.

This is not to imply that the transition from rear area to forward area operation was easy and uncomplicated. There were lessons to be learned by both the supporting and the supported units and tactics and techniques had to be developed for the rather radical change of arenas. Not the least challenge was the need for smoke troops, whose duties changed almost overnight from rear support to action in the foremost areas of the combat zone, to adapt themselves to their new role.

The 4.2-inch mortar brought the World War II infantryman into closer contact with the CWS than did perhaps anything else. The splendid reputation of this weapon depended on a mission change dictated by uncertainty over the possibility of gas warfare. Originally designed to fire toxic chemicals and smokes, the mortar would have been rather expensive insurance in a gasless war. The logical step, of course, was the addition of the high explosive mission. Chemical mortar battalions thereby filled a dual capacity: they stood ready in the event of the introduction of gas warfare by the enemy, and they supported infantry units with smoke and high explosive. Although the gas warfare readiness of the mortar units never received the test of battle, there can be no doubt about the successful accomplishment of the second mission. Few in number and greatly overworked, the chemical mortar battalions served as the infantry commander's hip pocket artillery, capable of placing accurate and heavy fire upon targets within a range of 4,000–5,000 yards. The limited number of units (as late as December 1944 there were only four with the 12th Army Group), meant that they continued in the line while a succession of supported units was relieved. Infantry divisions would come and go but the mortar units seemed part of the terrain.

The CWS in World War II had mixed success with flame throwers, the portable as well as the mechanized. With regard to the mechanized model there was some indecision on the part of the using arm as to the characteristics, indeed as to the very necessity, for such a specialized vehicle. Moreover, in no other field of CWS endeavor was there so little liaison between the users in the field and the developers in the zone of interior. Because of this lack of liaison and because of available facilities and vigorous CWS people in Hawaii, the mechanized flame thrower support in at least one Pacific area came principally from local sources, not from the United States. And this support resulted in the most effective combat employment of the mechanized flame thrower in the war.

The war against Japan also saw the most effective use of the portable flame thrower. Reasons for the usefulness of flame weapons in the Pacific are not hard to find. American forces found themselves confronted by a stubborn enemy who was taught to believe that death for the Emperor was something worthy of aspiration. This kind of enemy ensconced in skillfully constructed fortifications would not be routed by artillery and mortar fire. Quite often the flame thrower, capable of delivering a lethal stream of fire through narrow apertures, was the only effective weapon for use against these formidable defenses. It must also be remembered that much of the fighting in the early days of the Pacific war took place in jungle terrain, and the resulting concealment enabled the operator to carry his bulky, easily recognized portable flame thrower much closer to the enemy without being observed. Credit must be given to CWS staff officers and service troops who, by the formulation of tactical doctrine and by the application of maintenance procedures, were instrumental in making the portable model the effective munition it was.

The war against Germany was a different story, for neither the mechanized nor the portable flame throwers contributed much to that phase of the conflict. European battlefields and German defenses were often typified by excellent fields of fire which boded ill for the relatively short range of both types of flame weapon. In Europe, unlike in the Pacific, no situation ever arose wherein the flame weapon provided a vital key in overcoming the enemy. Consequently, there was no impetus for overcoming the weapon's initial drawbacks—short range, lack of tactical doctrine, problems of maintenance, and the lack of knowledge on the part of the using arms.

The incendiary bomb had the distinction of being one of the most effective munitions employed strategically by United States forces in World War II. Ranging from a compact 4-pound, metallic model to an oil-filled 500-pounder, these bombs, developed and procured by the CWS and employed by the Army Air Forces, wrought almost unparalleled destruction. The fire bomb, the tactical corollary of the incendiary, proved effective when dropped by fighter-bomber aircraft on a variety of targets in the forward areas.

The Army Air Forces expended nearly a quarter-million incendiary and fire bombs on German and Japanese targets. The accounts of the devastation resulting from incendiary missions leave no doubt as to the important part played by these munitions in achieving Allied victory. Because of a long-standing faith in high explosives and because of defects in some of the early bombs, the Air Forces was slow to accept the new munition. Indeed, it was not until the last six months of the war that the aerial incendiary really came into its own. Back of this record were two important factors. First, the stress of war eliminated certain peacetime lethargies and led to the development

of some good, even ingenious, incendiary bombs. And second, coura-
geous operational leadership, exemplified by the role of General LeMay,
proved beyond all doubt the importance of the aerial incendiary.

To attempt to select the most important reason for Japan's capitu-
lation is to tread uncertain ground. Many factors were involved, the
atomic explosions over Hiroshima and Nagasaki being by far the most
spectacular. Yet, the testimony of Japanese leaders and the mute
evidence of her burned-out cities certainly point to the incendiary
campaign of the XXI Bomber Command as an important element in
the defeat of Japan.

Readiness for Gas Warfare

There is no easy measurement for CWS overseas accomplishments
in gas warfare preparedness since plans, men, and materials were not
put to the test. It is possible to assess the factors upon which chemical
officers during World War II believed preparedness depended. The
first of these factors was an administrative and organizational pattern
which would have permitted chemical officers to function in all their
areas of interest from tactical and strategic advice to decontamination
service in the field.

Administratively and organizationally the CWS was only partially
prepared for gas warfare. In Europe, while the chief chemical officer
held a staff position under the theater commander, he did not have
a position in the supreme tactical and strategic headquarters, SHAEF.
Colonel St. John's presence in SHAEF would have helped so far as
the function of providing advice is concerned, but his lack of a direct
and formal channel to the chief chemical officer might have proved a
handicap. The informal relationship which existed between Rowan
and the air chemical officers and between Rowan and the United States
Navy officers with interests in the chemical field would probably have
served as a basis for co-operative effort among the U.S. forces.

General Shadle, from his position in the combined headquarters,
AFHQ, would have been able to co-ordinate both Allied and American
gas warfare activities in the Mediterranean area. Colonel Copthorne
in SWPA would undoubtedly have had a tough problem in making the
necessary expansion into USAFFE and GHQ since he lacked the
required staff and since his relationships with the Allies and even

the Army Air Forces and the U.S. Navy were informal and tenuous at the best.

Colonel Unmacht, enjoying the confidence and support of his Army commander, and from 1943 as official co-ordinator of POA chemical planning for all forces, would have been in as good a position as Shadle's. Unmacht's drawback would have been his lack of staff officers.

In all areas, army group, army, corps, and division, chemical officers would in most cases have been ready for the administrative load of gas warfare. Only the advent of such warfare could have tested Rowan's contention that the secondary and unrelated tasks performed in the absence of gas warfare would in most instances lessen the readiness and effectiveness of the chemical staff officers. It would probably have been necessary to augment chemical sections at all levels, but it seems likely that officers and men of other arms and services could have been diverted from tasks of lower priority in the case of gas warfare. Below the division level the inauguration of gas warfare would likely have resulted in a wild scramble to select, train, and retrain unit gas officers and unit gas noncommissioned officers, but, in view of the fact that nearly every soldier received some gas warfare training, the roster should soon have been filled. More chemical mortar battalions and chemical service units would certainly have been required, but, assuming a high priority for gas warfare activities and the availability of equipment, other units could have been converted, possibly in a matter of days, probably in a matter of weeks. Areas having a lesser variety of units and a smaller total strength would have been hard put to find units for conversion since the advent of gas warfare would probably have intensified rather than lessened other forms of combat.

The second factor regarded by chemical officers as basic in gas warfare preparedness—training—was from the CWS point of view the least difficult preparedness activity to handle. The theater school in Europe, the area CWS school in SWPA, the army schools in the Mediterranean area, and Unmacht's series of courses in POA provided chemical training for thousands of soldiers. Most of these trainees would have required refresher courses were it not for the fact that, as a senior technical services officer told a chemical officer in Europe, soldiers learn fast and remember well when their lives depend on learning. These area schools and combat and service organization schools could have been quickly expanded with a minimum of effort, because most CWS officers and men, at least in the combat organization chemical sections, had some experience in conducting chemical training. Since few chemical officers ever believed they had been allotted enough training time, most had prepared short courses which they were ready to present in almost any location on almost no notice.

The third factor in preparedness—intelligence—was one which presented many difficulties. There had been no active Army intelligence agency in the United States before World War II. The Office of the Assistant Chief, WDGS, G–2, was so restricted that it could not even begin to meet the demands for all sorts of technical intelligence until late in the war. By that time the technical services had trained and sent out their own teams or had, like Colonel Copthorne, activated teams overseas. These teams and combat chemical officers did an outstanding job of collecting enemy equipment, and the various theater and area laboratories produced complete analyses. The indications were that the enemy, both Germans and Japanese, were defensively well prepared. Direct evidence of German or Japanese intentions on use of gas was lacking.

While technical intelligence was well done, it was not enough. Only the British and the U.S. Office of Strategic Services were able to gather more direct information. Their reports were useful but fragmentary, incomplete, and misleading. There were rumors of a new German gas, but neither British or Americans even guessed at the composition, toxicity, and possible means of employment of the German organophosphate compounds, the so-called G or nerve agents, until some toxic munitions were captured at the close of the war. The intelligence agencies reported stocks of German toxics in France before the invasion, but none were found until Allied troops reached the German homeland. In sum, the enemy never discovered Allied intentions and the Allies never discovered enemy intentions. It was cold comfort to CWS officers to know at the end of the war that enemy intelligence was no better than American.

Planning was the fourth factor bearing on gas warfare preparedness. The early theater gas warfare plans, required by the War Department in December 1942, were poor because not enough was then known about the character of World War II fighting to make adequate plans, and because materials and chemical units had not yet been provided in sufficient quantity to form a basis for planning. In the next two years the plans became detailed and specific, and in most areas they originated in or were approved by the highest Allied headquarters. Plans were therefore comprehensive. These theater plans almost never reached or were known to chemical officers in the field. It is consequently not possible to judge whether field chemical officers believed the plans could be carried out in event of gas warfare. Since some plans, like those in POA, actually identified target areas and since the logistics and operational requirements were carefully checked by overseas staffs and OCCWS, it seems probable that plans were both realistic and feasible. But, however good the plans were, they were only as good as the supply of gas munitions for retaliation.

Supply was the fifth and probably most important factor in gas warfare preparedness. After the first year of the war the supply of gas masks was ample in all areas of the world. That supply improved further with the provision of the new lightweight mask late in 1943 and early in 1944. The CWS produced enough protective clothing in the United States or overseas to furnish reasonable protection by late 1943. Protective clothing resupply, especially in SWPA, could have been delivered by air only through high priority, but such priority could probably have been obtained. Even had delivery been slow in coming, all units could have reimpregnated their own clothing in the field in an emergency. Collective protection and decontamination would probably have been inadequate according to World War II standards, but some CWS officers, including General Porter, maintained that the standard was unrealistically high. In the opinion of these officers, it would have been necessary to bypass areas heavily contaminated with persistent gases in any case, so that the need for decontamination would be confined to strategic roads, airfields, and supply points.

The supply of toxic agents overseas admittedly amounted only to token quantities. At the time of President Roosevelt's 1942 pronouncement, his threatened swift retaliation for enemy initiation of gas warfare would have been impossible. The fourteen days of aerial toxic munitions in Europe after the fall of 1943 represented a substantial first-strike capability, but for resupply, air delivery on high priority would have been necessary. By the time of the Rapido and Winter Line operations in Italy early in 1944, the U.S. forces possessed enough toxic munitions to lay alternate bands of persistent and nonpersistent gases most of the way across the Italian peninsula. Again, resupply would have been by air. In the Pacific areas first-strike capabilities were even lower—with toxic munitions supplies in POA equal to an attack on an area the size of Iwo Jima and in SWPA to but five days' operation. Porter and Waitt, along with USCWS officers, were confident that these token amounts would have served for initial retaliation and that aircraft and fast ships could have created a resupply pipeline. Under their plan, stocks in the United States would have sustained the overseas offensive until new stocks could have been built up. They calculated that U.S. enemies would not have been able to initiate gas warfare on all fronts at the same time, and that gas warfare initiated in the Pacific could have been confined to a small area for a considerable period.

Why Gas Was Not Used

Why was gas not used in World War II? To pin down all the reasons is difficult if not impossible. Some of the factors were not constant; they underwent alterations as the war progressed and situations changed. Different factors affected different nations.

The principal factor deterring the United States from initiating gas warfare was clearly national policy. Although the United States was not a party to any international agreement outlawing gas warfare, its policy throughout World War II was set in precise terms. Twice during the early years of the conflict President Roosevelt categorically stated that the United States would use gas only in retaliation against an enemy nation using it. This statement by the President and Commander in Chief became the official United States position throughout the war. The United States policy on gas was, in fact, largely determined by the deep feeling of its President about that particular kind of warfare.[1]

But other elements enter the picture. Notwithstanding the tremendous influence of President Roosevelt and his predominant place in policy and decision making, military leaders would have presented arguments in rebuttal had they entertained any deep-seated doubt as to the wisdom of the Presidential point of view. But, with the excep-

---

[1] Roosevelt, in vetoing a 1937 bill aimed at changing the name of the Chemical Warfare Service to Chemical Corps, wrote: "It has been and is the policy of this government to do everything in its power to outlaw the use of chemicals in warfare. Such use is inhuman and contrary to what modern civilization should stand for. . . ." See Brophy and Fisher, *Organizing for War*, pp. 21–22.

tion of minor stirrings near the end of the war, gas warfare had no advocates in high places.

Military reluctance began with the experience of the AEF in World War I. Despite the excellent leadership of General Fries, it would appear that many of the higher unit staffs and commanders placed little reliance on the gas arm, in sharp contrast to their German, British, and French counterparts. Incidents demonstrating the reluctance of some unit commanders to employ gas for fear of retaliation and the possible injury to friendly troops have already been related. A survey of the records of First Army indicate that a real understanding of the use of gas, particularly persistent, did not occur until late in the war. For example, the initial First Army field order for the St. Mihiel operation included no gas plan whatsoever. And although First Army used gas effectively in the Meuse-Argonne fighting, there is nothing in the records to indicate that its corps and divisions were aware of an over-all plan.[2]

It will be remembered that in the fight for a permanent CWS, General Fries found support in Congress, industry, and civil servants— not in the Army. Generals Pershing and March both opposed the creation of a chemical service. There is no evidence to suggest that top commanders ever acquired much faith in gas warfare. In fact, it is hard to believe that the War Department in the period between the wars would have reduced CWS activities to those of a primarily defensive nature had it had faith in gas warfare.

Another factor to be considered in reviewing American gas warfare policy is the part played by public opinion. There can be no doubt that gas warfare emerged from World War I with the reputation of a horror weapon even when field experience did not substantiate this view. Although reasons for this reputation are varied, one source of opprobrium could very well have been the Allied propaganda program waged against the German introduction of large-scale gas warfare. The pros and cons on gas were also debated at the time of the two international conventions of the 1920's which considered its status in the realm of international law. While that status was not officially determined as far as the United States was concerned, the deliberations

---

[2] Rexmond C. Cochrane, The 78th Div at the Kriemhilde Stellung, Oct 18, Study 2, U.S. Army CmlC Hist Studies, Gas Warfare in World War I, Jul 57, pp. 76–78. Cochrane states that no Army, corps, or division record examined makes mention of the most important Army gas decision—the use of mustard on the flanks and drive through the center.

within these conventions could hardly have been without influence in a world turning toward pacifism. Little evidence has yet been produced to show that public opinion actually was a positive force contrary to gas warfare, but the important thing is that public opinion was believed to be contrary to gas warfare. President Roosevelt, usually an astute judge of the public temper and a leader of public opinion, certainly encountered no widespread opposition to his pronouncements on gas warfare.

Whatever the reasons, American military leaders paid little attention to gas in World War II. In the early years of the war, it would have been an unwise risk because the enemy had been on a wartime footing much longer and had a trump card in air superiority. Besides, two decades of neglect could not be undone overnight, and the American wherewithal for offensive gas warfare was slim, indeed. Later, when the tide turned in favor of the Allies, it seemed unnecessary to introduce gas. The war was being won without it. The greatest pause for reflection on the employment of gas took place after the series of costly American victories in the war against Japan. Use of gas was contemplated to overcome stubborn Japanese defenses and thus reduce American assault casualties, but the war ended before any positive action arose.[3]

The British gas policy during the war was based on the same principle as that of the United States—retaliation. In the early days of the conflict, the lack of an offensive capability and the predominance of the Luftwaffe (and consequent vulnerability of British cities) permitted no alternative to this policy. Britain would have been unlikely to change her policy as long as German air attacks continued on England. These attacks were followed, after the Luftwaffe became ineffective, by German missile bombardment nearly to the end of 1944. By this time the Allies had long been on the offensive. Apparently many British military leaders shared the idea common among the belligerents that gas was a weapon to be used only in defensive or static operations. Even had commanders welcomed the employment of gas in the assault, its use would have brought further strains upon the overburdened British economy. While gas defensive preparations improved in the United Kingdom throughout the war and while she maintained a small retaliatory capacity to complement that of the

---

[3] See Brophy and Fisher, *Organizing for War*, pp. 86–88.

United States, all-out gas warfare would have required significantly increased effort. Furthermore, the British, who had ratified the Geneva Protocol and had reaffirmed this stand in 1939, felt that international agreement prohibited their initiation of gas warfare.

Although Germany had no policy prohibiting the employment of gas warfare during World War II, there was a strong trend of official opinion against German initiation of gas warfare. This trend was based on several constant factors and a series of factors which arose from appraisals of Germany's situation during various periods of the war.

The constant factors were: (1) Hitler had a personal antipathy to gas warfare; (2) the military High Command and the field commanders devoted their attention to strategy, tactics, and weapons which excluded gas warfare; (3) the High Command believed that international public opinion would be outraged should Germany become a gas warfare aggressor in contravention of international agreements. Given the Axis record, it is doubtful that the public opinion factor would have had much weight in a decision not to wage gas warfare had the military situation been favorable to its use.

At no time during World War II, in the opinion of the German military leaders, was the situation favorable for the initiation of gas warfare. In the early period of the war when both ground and aerial blitzkrieg tactics were so successful, gas warfare either would have hampered the German advance or would have posed technical and logistical problems which Germany was not then prepared to face. Later, when Germany was forced into the defensive, the use of gas would have been decidedly to Germany's advantage, especially in the defense of the continental coast. But by this time (1944–45) the Allies had air superiority, and German leaders feared decisive retaliation in kind against the German homeland. The Germans estimated correctly, as a captured German general told General Shadle, that Allied, and particularly American, defensive equipment was far superior to the German (Germany had no large stock of protective clothing, for example). The Germans apparently overestimated Allied offensive capabilities, and they apparently believed that the Allies, like themselves, had discovered new gases. In both stages of the conflict, logistics played an important part in the German decision not to wage gas warfare. Early in the war, Germany had neither gases nor gas troops in any appreciable quantities. Later in the war, the toxic stockpile was adequate for defensive action, but the transportation and communications systems were strained to the point of collapse, and on some occasions did break down. Also, it was questionable whether overburdened German industry could manufacture gases rapidly enough and in sufficient quantity to sustain gas warfare both offensively and defensively on all fronts.

As in the case of Germany, the reasons for the failure of Japan to initiate gas warfare in World War II are varied and complex. There was no moral compunction on the part of the Japanese for not using gas; they had used it in isolated cases against the Chinese. Early in the war, forging ahead against little resistance, the Japanese had no reason to use gas. When the Japanese began to experience reverses, they did so in areas which could well have called for gas warfare; mustard gas would have been appropriate for use by troops retreating through a jungle terrain. But by this time the Japanese faced enormous shipping problems. A logistical system which failed to provide food for Japanese troops in New Guinea could hardly have supported gas warfare. Later, the predominance of American air power must have been another factor in Japan's decision not to resort to gas. Japanese civilians were ill prepared to defend themselves against gas attacks, and B–29's on the Marianas were within easy range of the homeland. Although early in the conflict the Japanese had the resources and facilities for producing war gases, these diminished as the years wore on. After the war U.S. investigators found that the Japanese were poorly prepared for modern large-scale chemical warfare, offensive or defensive. Rather limited amounts of war gases were on hand.

Had Allied intelligence been able to divine the intentions of the Germans and Japanese, a large portion of Allied preparations for gas warfare might have been abandoned. On the other hand, if the Allies had been any less prepared than they were, the Germans might have used—and General Bradley felt that this would have been decisive—a light sprinkling of persistent gas on OMAHA Beach. Although lacking sustained offensive capability, the Japanese could have put an equally decisive sprinkling of mustard on the approaches to Buna and Gona or on the Lingayen beaches. If the Japanese had not believed their homeland vulnerable to gas, they might have launched a kamikaze gas attack on the storm-battered U.S. Navy force off Okinawa. It is therefore probable that United States gas warfare preparedness in World War II was worth the effort. Certainly the nongas warfare efforts of the CWS justified the activities of the service. The incendiary bomb was the mainstay of the aerial assault on the Japanese homeland. In acknowledgment of its contribution, the chemical mortar became an infantry weapon following the war. Artificial smoke often proved a great boon in Korea, and the Marine Corps entered the Korean battles with World War II CWS flame tanks assembled in Hawaii. General Porter sums up the World War II CWS experience by saying that the CWS maintained a strong service which contributed to the war effort everywhere—from the laboratory to the fighting line. The "Chemicals in Combat" did their job so well that in 1946 the service was redesignated the United States Army Chemical Corps and fully accepted by the Military Establishment.

Bibliographical Note

Despite a measure of War Department standardization during World War II, little consistency was found in the zone of interior or theater of operations records relating to the Chemical Warfare Service in World War II. Sources of great importance for one overseas area would prove useless or nonexistent for another. Consequently, while administration and organization records proved most fruitful, portions of this work depend heavily on historical reports, monographs, studies, secondary works, and interviews.

The following is a listing of the archives with an indication of the collections used:

Military Branch, Federal Records Center, General Services Administration, Region No. 3, Alexandria, Virginia—Files of the Office, Chief of the Chemical Warfare Service. These files are cited by using the prefix CWS in the file number. CWS 314.7 and CWS 319.1, properly a part of this collection, are temporarily in the custody of the Office of the Historian, U.S. Army Edgewood Arsenal (formerly U.S. Army Chemical Corps Historical Office), and will be transferred to official archives.

Office of Military Archives, National Archives and Records Service—Files of Operations Division and G–4 Division, WDGS; files of Army Service Forces; overseas unit and organization historical files. File number citations for WDGS records are prefixed by the abbreviated designation of the specific staff division; those for Army Service Forces by the letters, SOS or ASF. Although the War Department Adjutant General's Office was a part of the ASF organization, references to the files for that office are cited with the prefix AG. Overseas unit and organization historical files are not arranged by the normal Army decimal file system, but are cited by the abbreviated unit or organization designation.

Kansas City Records Center—Unit and organization administrative, decimal files. These records are identified in citations by abbreviated unit or organization designation and the decimal file number. They can be distinguished from unit and organization historical files in Office of Military Archives, National Archives, by the presence of the decimal file number. Several forays were made into the Kansas City collection; the most notable find there were the records of the Chemical Section, Headquarters, North African–Mediterranean Theater of Operations.

Archives of the Air University—Army Air Forces unit and organization records, including administrative, decimal files, and draft histories. Citation is in the same form as those for ground, service, and headquarters organizations and units.

The Marine Corps Archives—Marine Corps unit and organization reports. Citation is in same form as Air Forces and ground units and organizations.

A number of monographs, studies, technical reports, draft histories, and published histories proved to be invaluable for background material, for basic information, and for clues to the location of archival sources. Some of these monographs and studies were prepared by the U.S. Army Chemical Corps Historical Office and are now available in the Office, Chief of Military History. Among these, particular note should be made of the World War II series, especially Dr. Paul W. Pritchard's Smoke Generator Operations in Mediterranean and European Theaters of Operations (Study No. 1); History of German Chemical Warfare in World War II, Part I, Military Aspects, by Generalleutnant Herman Ochsner (Study No. 2); and Lt. Col. Leonard L. McKinney's two studies, Portable Flame Thrower Operations in World War II (Study No. 4) and Mechanized Flame Thrower Operations in World War II (Study No. 5). Particularly useful among the draft or partially completed Chemical Corps studies are: Paul W. Pritchard, Ben R. Baldwin, and Alfred J. Bingham, Readiness for Gas Warfare in Theaters of Operations, and Ben R. Baldwin, Operational History of the Chemical Battalions and the 4.2-inch Mortar in World War II, Parts I and II, the Sicilian and Italian campaigns. Rexmond C. Cochrane's series of monographs on gas warfare in World War I were also used.

The Office, Chief of Military History, provided several other groups of studies and histories. The Army Service Forces monographs on logistical problems were of great assistance as was the History of Allied Force Headquarters. The histories and after action reports of a number of organizations and units from army groups to chemical mortar battalions and even service units were extensively used. In the group was also the Logistical History of the North African Theater of Operations–Mediterranean Theater of Operations. The unpublished group included draft histories of communications zone, base section, and base organization, especially for the North African–Mediterranean theater and the Southwest Pacific area. The prize of the unpublished group, from the CWS point of view, is the History of the Chemical Section, U.S. Army Forces Middle Pacific and Predecessor Commands. This history provides considerably more information on that area than does any other source, and, except for gaps in treating preparedness, it is amazingly comprehensive.

The CWS technical reports, along with many evaluations of munitions and plans, both for the United States and its Allies, were deposited in the Technical Library, Army Chemical Center, Md., and have been identified and described in *From Laboratory to Field*.[1] The best World War I source, pending the preparation of an official volume on gas warfare in World War I, is the draft History of the Chemical Warfare Service, American Expeditionary Forces. Copies of this study are available in the Technical Library and in the Office of the Historian, U.S. Army Edgewood Arsenal. Finally, as regards monographs and studies, special note should be made of the excellent Marine Corps series on operations in the Pacific. Also worthy of special note is the *American Forces in Action* series, which has been useful although documented and more complete accounts have in most instances appeared in the series UNITED STATES ARMY IN WORLD WAR II. The volumes published in this series have proved invaluable, and the following have been particularly important:

Roy E. Appleman, James M. Burns, Russell A. Gugelar, and John Stevens, *Okinawa: The Last Battle* (Washington, 1948).

Martin Blumenson, *Breakout and Pursuit* (Washington, 1961).

Joseph Bykofsky and Harold Larson, *The Transportation Corps: Operations Overseas* (Washington, 1957).

Ray S. Cline, *Washington Command Post: The Operations Division* (Washington, 1951).

Philip A. Crowl, *Campaign in the Marianas* (Washington, 1960).

—— and Edmund G. Love, *Seizure of the Gilberts and Marshalls* (Washington, 1955).

[1] Brophy, Miles, Cochrane, *From Laboratory to Field*, pp. 455–58.

Gordon A. Harrison, *Cross-Channel Attack* (Washington, 1951).

George F. Howe, *Northwest Africa: Seizing the Initiative in the West* (Washington, 1957).

Richard M. Leighton and Robert W. Coakley, *Global Logistics and Strategy, 1940–1943* (Washington, 1955).

Charles B. MacDonald, *The Siegfried Line Campaign* (Washington, 1963).

Maurice Matloff and Edwin M. Snell, *Strategic Planning for Coalition Warfare, 1942–1943* (Washington, 1953).

Maurice Matloff, *Strategic Planning for Coalition Warfare, 1943–1944* (Washington, 1959).

John Miller, jr., *CARTWHEEL: The Reduction of Rabaul* (Washington, 1959).

———, *Guadalcanal: The First Offensive* (Washington, 1949).

John D. Millett, *The Organization and Role of the Army Service Forces* (Washington, 1954).

Samuel Milner, *Victory in Papua* (Washington, 1957).

Louis Morton, *The Fall of the Philippines* (Washington, 1953).

Forrest C. Pogue, *The Supreme Command* (Washington, 1954).

Roland G. Ruppenthal, *Logistical Support of the Armies, Volume I* (Washington, 1953).

———, *Logistical Support of the Armies, Volume II* (Washington, 1959).

Robert Ross Smith, *The Approach to the Philippines* (Washington, 1953).

———, *Triumph in the Philippines* (Washington, 1963).

Alvin P. Stauffer, *The Quartermaster Corps: Operations in the War Against Japan* (Washington, 1956).

In addition to these published works, the authors also consulted Robert W. Coakley and Richard M. Leighton, Global Logistics and Strategy, 1944–1945, a volume in preparation for the series UNITED STATES ARMY IN WORLD WAR II.

Other secondary works consulted were:

Horatio Bond, ed., *Fire and the Air War* (Boston: National Fire Protection Assn., 1951).

General Omar N. Bradley, *A Soldier's Story* (New York: Henry Holt and Company, Inc., 1951).

Wesley Frank Craven and James L. Cate, eds., "The Army Air Forces in World War II," especially vol. II, *Europe: TORCH to POINTBLANK, August 1942 to December 1943* (Chicago: University of Chicago Press, 1949); vol. III, *Europe: ARGUMENT to V–E Day, January 1944 to May 1945* (Chicago: University of Chicago Press, 1951); vol. V, *The Pacific: MATTERHORN to Nagasaki, June 1944 to August 1945* (Chicago: University of Chicago Press, 1953).

General Walter Krueger, *From Down Under to Nippon* (Washington: Combat Forces Press, 1953).

Harold Riegelman, *Caves of Biak* (New York: Dial, 1955).

C. H. Foulkes, *"Gas!" The Story of the Special Brigade* (Edinburgh and London: W. Blackwood & Sons, 1934).

Amos A. Fries and Clarence J. West, *Chemical Warfare* (New York: McGraw-Hill, 1921).

Rudolph Hanslian *et al.*, *Der Chemische Krieg* (3d ed., Berlin: Mittler, 1939).

Victor Lefebure, *The Riddle of the Rhine* (New York: The Chemical Foundation, 1923).

Alden H. Waitt, *Gas Warfare* (New York: Duell, Sloan and Pearce, 1942).

Henri le Wita, *Autour de la Guerre Chimique* (Paris: Tallandier, 1928).

The authors, with the assistance of other members of the U.S. Army Chemical Corps Historical Office staff, interviewed or corresponded with as many overseas CWS officers as could be contacted. While the quality of these interviews varied greatly from individual to individual, most were very helpful. Those which have been cited, and many others used to provide general background material, are presently filed in the Office of the Historian, U.S. Army Edgewood Arsenal. Copies will be included in the permanent historical files when those files are transferred to official archives.

List of Abbreviations

AA	Antiaircraft
AAR	After action report
ACCWS	Assistant Chief, Chemical War Service
ACmlC	Army Chemical Center
ACofS	Assistant Chief of Staff
ADSEC	Advance Section, Communications Zone
ADSOS	Advance Services of Supply
Adv	Advance
AEAF	Allied Expeditionary Air Forces
AEF	American Expeditionary Forces
AF	Air Force
AFHQ	Allied Force Headquarters
AFMIDPAC	U.S. Army Forces, Middle Pacific
AFPAC	U.S. Army Forces, Pacific
AFSC	Air Force Service Command
AG	Adjutant General
AGF	Army Ground Forces
AGWAR	Adjutant General, War Department
Amphib	Amphibian; amphibious
AO	Air officer
ASC	Air Support Command
ASF	Army Service Forces
ASP	Ammunition supply point
BADA	Base Air Depot Area
BAR	Browning automatic rifle
Bomb	Bombardment
BW	Biological warfare
ca.	circa
CCWS	Chief, Chemical Warfare Service
CENPAC	Central Pacific Area
CG	Commanding general
CinC	Commander in Chief
CINCPAC	Commander in Chief, Pacific Fleet
CINCSWPA	Commander in Chief, Southwest Pacific Area
CCmlO	Chief chemical officer
CM–IN	Classified message, incoming
Cml	Chemical

CmlC	Chemical Corps
CMLHO	Chemical Corps Historical Office
CmlO	Chemical officer
CM–OUT	Classified message, outgoing
CPBS	Central Pacific Base Command
CO	Commanding officer
Co	Company
CofOrd	Chief of Ordnance
CofS	Chief of Staff
CofT	Chief of Transportation
Comdr	Commander
COMINCH	Commander in Chief, U.S. Fleet
COMZ	Communications Zone
CONAD	Continental Advance Section
Contl	Control
Corresp	Correspondence
COSSAC	Chief of Staff to the Supreme Allied Commander
CP	Command post
CPBC	Central Pacific Base Command
CTF	Center Task Force
CWS	Chemical Warfare Service
CWSO	Chemical Warfare Service Officer
CWTC	Chemical Warfare Technical Committee
DA	Department of the Army
DANC	Decontaminating agent, noncorrosive
DCCWS	Deputy Chief, Chemical Warfare Service
DF	Disposition form
Dir	Director
Dist	District
Distr	Distribution
EBS	Eastern Base Section
EEIST	Enemy equipment intelligence service team
ETO	European Theater of Operations
ETOUSA	European Theater of Operations, U.S. Army
ExO	Executive officer
FEC	French Expeditionary Corps
FECOMZ	Forward Echelon, Communications Zone
FETU	Far Eastern Technical Unit
FM	Field manual
FS	CWS symbol for a solution of sulphur trioxide in chlorosulfonic acid, a smoke mixture
FUSA	First U.S. Army

FUSAG	First U.S. Army Group
G–1	Personnel section of divisional or higher staff
G–2	Intelligence section of divisional or higher staff
G–3	Operations section of divisional or higher staff
G–4	Supply section of divisional or higher staff
GHQ	General Headquarters
GO	General Orders
Gp	Group
HC	Symbol for hexachlorethane, a smoke mixture
HE	High explosive
Hist	Historical
Hq	Headquarters
Incl	Inclosure
Ind	Indorsement
Instr	Instruction
Intell	Intelligence
Interv	Interview
IOM	Interoffice memo
Lab	Laboratory
LCI	Landing craft, infantry
LCI(A)	Landing craft, infantry (ammunition)
LCM	Landing craft, mechanized
LCT	Landing craft, tank
LCVP	Landing craft, vehicle and personnel
Lib	Library
LST	Landing ship, tank
LVT	Landing vehicle, tracked
LVT(4)	Landing vehicle, tracked, unarmored
Maint	Maintenance
MBS	Mediterranean Base Section
Mil	Military
Min	Minutes
MPR	Monthly progress report
MSR	Material status report
MTOUSA	Mediterranean Theater of Operations, U.S. Army
NATO	North African Theater of Operations
NATOUSA	North African Theater of Operations, U.S. Army
NCO	Noncommissioned officer
NDRC	Nation Defense Research Committee
NYPE	New York Port of Embarkation
OCCWS	Office of the Chief of the Chemical Warfare Service
OCS	Officer candidate school

Off	Office
OP	Observation post
OPD	Operations Division
Opn	Operation
Ord	Ordnance
Orgn	Organization
OSRD	Office of Scientific Research and Development
PBS	Peninsular Base Section
PCD	Panama Canal Department
Per	Periodic
Pers	Personal; Personnel
Phila	Philadelphia
POA	Pacific Ocean Areas
POW	Prisoner of war
PROCO	Projects for continental operation
Proj	Project
PT	Patrol boat, motor torpedo boat
RAF	Royal Air Force
Rcd	Record
RCT	Regimental combat team
Rpt	Report
Rqmts	Requirements
S–3	Operations officer or section of regimental or lower staff
Sec	Section
Serv	Service
SG	Smoke generator
SHAEF	Supreme Headquarters, Allied Expeditionary Forces
SOLOC	Southern Line of Communications
SOPAC	South Pacific Area
SPBC	South Pacific Base Command
SPOBS	Special Observer Group
SOS	Services of Supply
Sup	Supply
SWPA	Southwest Pacific Area
T/A	Table of allowances
TAG	The Adjutant General
TBA	Table of basic allowances
TDMR	Technical Division Memo Report
Tech	Technical
TF	Task Force
TM	Technical manual
Tng	Training

TOE	Table of organization and equipment
TofO	Theater of Operations
TUSA	Third U.S. Army
UGNCO	Unit gas noncommissioned officer
UGO	Unit gas officer
USAFBI	U.S. Army Forces in the British Isles
USAFFE	U.S. Army Forces in the Far East
USAFIA	U.S. Army Forces in Australia
USAFICPA	U.S. Army Forces, Central Pacific Area
USAFISPA	U.S. Army Forces in the South Pacific Area
USAFMIDPAC	U.S. Army Forces, Middle Pacific
USAFPOA	U.S. Army Forces, Pacific Ocean Areas
USAR	U.S. Army Reserve
USATC	U.S. Assault Training Center
USASOS	U.S. Army Services of Supply
USCWC	U.S. Chemical Warfare Committee
USFET	U.S. Forces in the European Theater
USSBS	U.S. Strategic Bombing Survey
USSTAF	U.S. Strategic Air Forces
VLR	Very long range
WD	War Department
WDGS	War Department General Staff
WP	White phosphorus
WPD	War Plans Division
WTF	Western Task Force
ZI	Zone of interior

Code Names

ALAMO Force   Code for U.S. Sixth Army while operating as a special ground task force headquarters directly under GHQ SWPA.

ANVIL   Early plan for invasion of southern France.

AVALANCHE   Invasion of Italy at Salerno.

BACKHANDER   Task force for operations on Cape Gloucester, New Britain.

BLACKSTONE   Unit of Western Task Force which landed at Safi, French Morocco.

BOLERO   Build-up of U.S. forces and supplies in United Kingdom for cross-Channel attack.

COBRA   U.S. First Army operation designated to penetrate the German defenses west of St. Lô and secure Coutances, France.

DRAGOON   The plan for the Allied invasion of southern France, code name that replaced ANVIL.

FLINTLOCK   The Marshall Islands operations.

FORAGER   Operations for the capture of the Mariana Islands.

HORLICKS   Allied operation against Biak Island, 27 May–30 August 1944.

HURRICANE   Assault force for Biak, New Guinea.

HUSKY   Allied invasion of Sicily, July 1943.

ICEBERG   Invasion of the Ryukyu Islands.

MAPLE Base   Port Moresby.

OLYMPIC   Plan for March 1946 invasion of Kyushu, Japan.

OMAHA   Normandy beach assaulted by troops of U.S. V Corps, 6 June 1944.

OVERLORD   Allied cross-Channel invasion of northwest Europe, June 1944.

PERSECUTION   Assault force for Aitape operations, New Guinea.

PLUM   Code name for the Philippines.

QUEEN   12th Army Group operation on Roer Plain between Wurm and Roer Rivers.

RAINBOW   Various plans prepared between 1939 and 1941 to meet Axis aggression involving more than one enemy.

RAINCOAT   Assault on Camino hill mass, Italy.

RECKLESS   Assault force for Hollandia operation.

ROUNDUP   The name by which plans for cross-Channel invasion were known until the summer of 1943.

SHINGLE   Amphibious operation at Anzio, Italy.

TORCH   The Allied invasion operation in North Africa, November 1942.

TRADEWIND   Task force for Morotai.

UTAH   The Normandy beach assaulted by the U.S. VII Corps on 6
                  June 1944.

UNITED STATES ARMY IN WORLD WAR II

The multivolume series, UNITED STATES ARMY IN WORLD WAR II, consists of a number of subseries which are planned as follows: The War Department, The Army Air Forces, The Army Ground Forces, The Army Service Forces, The Western Hemisphere, The War in the Pacific, The Mediterranean Theater of Operations, The European Theater of Operations, The Middle East Theater, The China–Burma–India Theater, The Technical Services, Special Studies, and Pictorial Record.

The following volumes have been published or are in press:*

The War Department

Chief of Staff:Prewar Plans and Preparations
Washington Command Post: The Operations Division
Strategic Planning for Coalition Warfare: 1941–1942
Strategic Planning for Coalition Warfare: 1943–1944
Global Logistics and Strategy: 1940–1943
The Army and Economic Mobilization
The Army and Industrial Manpower

The Army Ground Forces

The Organization of Ground Combat Troops
The Procurement and Training of Ground Combat Troops

The Army Service Forces

The Organization and Role of the Army Service Forces

The Western Hemisphere

The Framework of Hemisphere Defense
Guarding the United States and Its Outposts

The War in the Pacific

The Fall of the Philippines
Guadalcanal: The First Offensive
Victory in Papua
CARTWHEEL: The Reduction of Rabaul
Seizure of the Gilberts and Marshalls
Campaign in the Marianas
The Approach to the Philippines

*The volumes on the Army Air Forces, published by the University of Chicago Press, are not included in this list.

Index